BELIEF, KNOWLEDGE, AND TRUTH
Readings in the Theory of Knowledge

❖

BELIEF, KNOWLEDGE, and TRUTH

❖

Readings in the Theory of Knowledge

❖

Edited by

Robert R. Ammerman

University of Wisconsin

and

Marcus G. Singer

University of Wisconsin

CHARLES SCRIBNER'S SONS
New York

To
Albert, Arthur, and Julius

PREFACE

The original, and perhaps still the literal, meaning of "anthology" is a collection of flowers of literature, that is, beautiful passages, especially verse. It is not in this sense that the present collection is an anthology, but anthology nonetheless it is. The selections included may not be flowers of literature, but they are representative and vital contributions to that catch-all area of philosophy that has come to be known as theory of knowledge—even though it deals with many topics besides knowledge—or epistemology. ("Epistemics" is a better word, but the world is not yet ready for it.)

At the time this book was conceived, in 1961, there were no rival collections available. Its unusually long gestation period, during which it evolved from a book that was intended to have a use at all levels of advancement and also serve as a source book in the subject, to the present somewhat less ambitious collection, has also seen the publication of several other garlands of epistemology. Although it is tempting to play the comparing and evaluating game, it is not always appropriate; we trust that the appearance of this collection will enrich the opportunities open to students of philosophy.

The writings herein included are invitations to participate in philosophizing. They differ in level of difficulty and interest, and not all, it must be admitted, are written with the greatest elegance. But philosophy is not poetry, even though it can still be read with and for pleasure. Francis Turner Palgrave, in the Preface to *The Golden Treasury*, speaks of "the Wisdom which comes through Pleasure." It may be that that is the only sort of wisdom worth having. At any rate, it is possible to attain it from at least some of the writings herein included.

The Wisdom which comes through Pleasure, however, is a by-product, and not an aim of the present collection. The point of an anthology of philosophical writings is the advancement of philosophy itself. And, at least in epistemology, most philosophers have not been poets, but "prose writers, hoping to be understood." [1] An anthology of philosophical writings helps advance philosophy itself by bringing together in one place a number of diverse and conflicting considerations which it is essential to keep in mind and effectively balance if one is going to achieve any adequate understanding of a problem or any idea of its resolution. Let us take seriously, even though it is possible to disagree with it as well, the idea of Arthur Lovejoy that philosophy is

[1] John Maynard Keynes, A *Treatise on Probability* (London: Macmillan and Co., Limited, 1921), p. vi.

essentially a collective and cooperative business. . . . Given a sufficiently well defined problem, philosophy can really get forward with it only by bringing together in their logical interconnection all the considerations which have occurred . . . to acute and philosophically initiated minds as significantly pertinent to that problem. These considerations will always be numerous, they will always, during the progress of any philosophical inquiry, be conflicting, and they must be contributed by many minds of diverse types and different training and preconceptions. But no typical and, so to say, normal consideration can with safety be left unconsidered, if the philosopher's distinctive but difficult duty of logical circumspection is to be observed, and if the joint inquiry is to be brought to a critically reasoned and convincing result. . . .[2]

Lovejoy goes on to say that "the true procedure of philosophy as a science —as distinct from the philosophic idiosyncrasies of individuals—is . . . that of a Platonic dialogue on a grand scale. . . ."

It was partly with this idea in mind that the selections presented here were chosen for inclusion. A necessary limitation was provided by our idea, itself a subject for strangely furious controversy, of what the subject consists in. But within this limitation we were guided by certain criteria for inclusion. A selection had to be interesting or stimulating to undergraduates, or else it had to be of such transcendent importance in the history of the subject that it would be an absurdity to exclude it. Contrary to an idea we had at the outset, it turned out that not many works met this last condition. One example is Aristotle on Truth (selection 42). Selections which in our judgment met the former condition are the little known ones by Arthur Kenyon Rogers (6 and 53). It is perhaps arguable just how the selections by F. H. Bradley (12 and 45) fit into this scheme.

This then is the theory on which this book is constructed. Palgrave says of his "little Collection" that it differs "from others in the attempt made to include in it all the best . . . and none beside the best," an aim reflected in his title.[3] We have made no such attempt, and make no such claim. There are other collections available which provide quite different selections (we have listed these in the Bibliography), and no doubt others on the way (we have not listed these). But that a selection is likely to be

[2] Arthur O. Lovejoy, *The Revolt Against Dualism* (La Salle, Illinois: The Open Court Publishing Company, 1930), p. ix.

[3] Francis Turner Palgrave, *The Golden Treasury of the Best Songs and Lyrical Poems in the English Language* (1861), Preface (London: Oxford University Press, World's Classic Series, 1914, p. ix; previous quotation was from p. xii). The greater part of "The Very Idea" by Lloyd Frankenberg, in his *Invitation to Poetry* (Garden City, New York: Doubleday & Company, Inc., 1956), pp. 27–32, provides an excellent discussion of the very idea of an anthology.

interesting and intelligible to undergraduates with no special preparation in the subject, or likely to stimulate thought and discussion, or else of such importance for thinking on these matters that it would be unreasonable for it not to be included—these are at least workable criteria; and even so, it was necessary to leave out a great many items we had originally hoped to include.

Since we did not attempt to compile a source book in the history of epistemology, no effort was made to include writings by famous and widely discussed philosophers, just to have our book include a collection of famous names. Somewhat regretably, therefore, nothing is included by Plato, Descartes, Hobbes, Berkeley, Moore, or Broad. Nor have we included any representatives of such philosophical schools or revolutionary movements as Dialectical Materialism, Thomism, Hinduism, Buddhism, Existentialism, or earlier (static) or current (dynamic) Phenomenology. Such an attempt to cover the subject would only cover it over. Nonetheless, there is more than the usual variety of viewpoints represented herein, and no one philosophical school is granted a monopoly.

As in our previous collection,[4] no introductory and teaching apparatus has been included. We preferred to use the room at our disposal for selections from other writers, and have thought it best neither to start nor to finish by telling the reader what epistemology is all about. The reader who is puzzled by this question can get some idea of what epistemology is about (but not all about) from the table of contents—and better yet, by reading further.

Something, however, should be said to explain the absence of any selections on Memory. This resulted from lack of space, and also from our conviction, arrived at after much deliberation, that the problems of memory are not absolutely fundamental or vital in the theory of knowledge. Some useful writings on the problems of memory are listed in a special section in the bibliography. And since we could not include as many selections on the problems connected with perception as we had hoped to, a special section in the bibliography is given to this topic. Space limitations also account for the absence of any selections on science, "the scientific method," reasoning, or evidence. We arrived at the view that an adequate representation here would require a separate volume—and some good collections in the philosophy of science are available.

Most of the selections used have been included complete, without excisions (with the exception of occasional footnotes). Some have been internally edited, and some—a very few—consist only of excerpts. This has been done where in our judgment such editing would help meet the

4 *Introductory Readings in Philosophy* (New York: Charles Scribner's Sons, 1962).

purposes we have had in mind and help a selection fit the criteria we have specified. It was important that a selection be intelligible as it stands, that knowledge of some special vocabulary or some previous controversy not be necessary to understand it, and such considerations led to these decisions. Selections that have been edited in this way are always clearly specified in the editorial footnotes; omissions are indicated by the usual ellipses, and editorial additions by the usual brackets.

We wish to acknowledge a debt of gratitude to the late James Pratt for making a number of suggestions and comments that have helped us in seeing our way; to Fred Dretske for his suggestions, which we actually adopted; to Julius Weinberg, for bibliographical and translational assistance; to Trudy Smith for useful help in compiling the bibliography; and to Diane Fischer for invaluable help with the bibliography, in putting the book together, in collecting information (if not knowledge), and in correcting the proofs.

After the proofs comes knowledge. And after a number of years, perhaps, comes the sort of knowledge not much discussed elsewhere in this volume, nor indeed in the usual treatises on epistemology, which is referred to in the following passage:

> What a man knows at fifty that he did not know at twenty is, for the most part, incommunicable. The laws, the aphorisms, the generalizations, the universal truths, the parables and the old saws —all of the observations about life which can be communicated handily in ready, verbal packages—are as well known to a man at twenty who has been attentive as to a man at fifty. He has been told them all, he has read them all, and he has probably repeated them all before he graduates from college; but he has not lived them all.
>
> What he knows at fifty that he did not know at twenty boils down to something like this: The knowledge he has acquired with age is not the knowledge of formulas, or forms of words, but of people, places, actions—a knowledge not gained by words but by touch, sight, sound, victories, failures, sleeplessness, devotion, love—the human experiences and emotions of this earth and of oneself and other men; and perhaps, too, a little faith, and a little reverence for things you cannot see.[5]

R. R. A.
M. G. S.

Madison, Wisconsin
December 18, 1968

[5] Adlai E. Stevenson, *What I Think* (New York: Harper & Brothers, 1956), p. 174. (Compare with selection 24.)

TABLE OF CONTENTS

BELIEF, KNOWLEDGE, AND TRUTH
Readings in the Theory of Knowledge

PART I

BELIEF

BELIEF

David Hume (1711–1776)

The idea of an object is an essential part of the belief of it, but not the whole. We conceive many things, which we do not believe. In order then to discover more fully the nature of belief, or the qualities of those ideas we assent to, let us weigh the following considerations.

'Tis evident, that all reasonings from causes or effects terminate in conclusions, concerning matter of fact; that is, concerning the existence of objects or of their qualities. 'Tis also evident, that the idea of existence is nothing different from the idea of any object, and that when after the simple conception of anything we wou'd conceive it as existent, we in reality make no addition to or alteration on our first idea. Thus when we affirm, that God is existent, we simply form the idea of such a being, as he is represented to us; nor is the existence, which we attribute to him, conceiv'd by a particular idea, which we join to the idea of his other qualities, and can again separate and distinguish from them. But I go farther; and not content with asserting, that the conception of the existence of any object is no addition to the simple conception of it, I likewise maintain, that the belief of the existence joins no new ideas to those, which compose the idea of the object. When I think of God, when I think of him as existent, and when I believe him to be existent, my idea of him neither increases nor diminishes. But as 'tis certain there is a great difference betwixt the simple conception of the existence of an object, and the belief of it, and as this difference lies not in the parts or composition of the idea, which we conceive; it follows, that it must lie in the *manner*, in which we conceive it.

Suppose a person present with me, who advances propositions, to which I do not assent, *that* Caesar *dy'd in his bed, that silver is more fusible than lead, or mercury heavier than gold*; 'tis evident, that notwithstanding my incredulity, I clearly understand his meaning, and form all the same ideas, which he forms. My imagination is endow'd with the same

From A *Treatise of Human Nature* (1739), part III, sect. 7 of Bk. I. The title of this selection has been supplied by the editors who have omitted the footnote from the original and added a paragraph from the appendix.

powers as his; nor is it possible for him to conceive any idea, which I cannot conceive; nor conjoin any, which I cannot conjoin. I therefore ask, Wherein consists the difference betwixt believing and disbelieving any proposition? The answer is easy with regard to propositions, that are prov'd by intuition or demonstration. In that case, the person, who assents, not only conceives the ideas according to the proposition, but is necessarily determin'd to conceive them in that particular manner, either immediately or by the interposition of other ideas. Whatever is absurd is unintelligible; nor is it possible for the imagination to conceive anything contrary to a demonstration. But as in reasonings from causation, and concerning matters of fact, this absolute necessity cannot take place, and the imagination is free to conceive both sides of the question, I still ask, *Wherein consists the difference betwixt incredulity and belief?* since in both cases the conception of the idea is equally possible and requisite.

'Twill not be a satisfactory answer to say, that a person, who does not assent to a proposition you advance; after having conceiv'd the object in the same manner with you; immediately conceives it in a different manner, and has different ideas of it. This answer is unsatisfactory; not because it contains any falsehood, but because it discovers not all the truth. 'Tis confest, that in all cases, wherein we dissent from any person, we conceive both sides of the question; but as we can believe only one, it evidently follows, that the belief must make some difference betwixt that conception to which we assent, and that from which we dissent. We may mingle, and unite, and separate, and confound, and vary our ideas in a hundred different ways; but 'till there appears some principle, which fixes one of these different situations, we have in reality no opinion: And this principle, as it plainly makes no addition to our precedent ideas, can only change the *manner* of our conceiving them.

All the perceptions of the mind are of two kinds, *viz.* impressions and ideas, which differ from each other only in their different degrees of force and vivacity. Our ideas are copy'd from our impressions, and represent them in all their parts. When you wou'd any way vary the idea of a particular object, you can only increase or diminish its force and vivacity. If you make any other change on it, it represents a different object or impression. The case is the same as in colors. A particular shade of any color may acquire a new degree of liveliness or brightness without any other variation. But when you produce any other variation, 'tis no longer the same shade or color. So that as belief does nothing but vary the manner, in which we conceive any object, it can only bestow on our ideas an additional force and vivacity. An opinion, therefore, or belief may be most accurately defined, A LIVELY IDEA RELATED TO OR ASSOCIATED WITH A PRESENT IMPRESSION.

Here are the heads of those arguments, which lead us to this conclusion. When we infer the existence of an object from that of others, some object must always be present either to the memory or senses, in order to be the foundation of our reasoning; since the mind cannot run up with its inferences *in infinitum*. Reason can never satisfy us that the existence of any one object does ever imply that of another; so that when we pass from the impression of one to the idea or belief of another, we are not determin'd by reason, but by custom or a principle of association. But belief is somewhat more than a simple idea. 'Tis a particular manner of forming an idea: And as the same idea can only be vary'd by a variation of its degrees of force and vivacity; it follows upon the whole, that belief is a lively idea produc'd by a relation to a present impression, according to the foregoing definition.[1]

This operation of the mind, which forms the belief of any matter of fact, seems hitherto to have been one of the greatest mysteries of philosophy; tho' no one has so much as suspected, that there was any difficulty in explaining it. For my part I must own, that I find a considerable difficulty in the case; and that even when I think I understand the subject perfectly, I am at a loss for terms to express my meaning. I conclude, by an induction which seems to me very evident, that an opinion or belief is nothing but an idea, that is different from a fiction, not in the nature, or the order of its parts, but in the *manner* of its being conceiv'd. But when I wou'd explain this *manner*, I scarce find any word that fully answers the case, but am oblig'd to have recourse to everyone's feeling, in order to give him a perfect notion of this operation of the mind. An idea assented to *feels* different from a fictitious idea, that the fancy alone presents to us: And this different feeling I endeavor to explain by calling it a superior *force*, or *vivacity*, or *solidity*, or *firmness*, or *steadiness*. This variety of terms, which may seem so unphilosophical, is intended only to express that act of the mind, which renders realities more present to us than fictions, causes them to weigh more in the thought, and gives them a superior influence on the passions and imagination. Provided we agree about the thing, 'tis needless to dispute about the terms. The imagination has the command over all its ideas, and can join, and mix, and vary them in all the ways possible. It may conceive objects with all the circumstances of place and time. It may set them, in a manner, before our eyes in their true colors, just as they might have existed. But as it is impossible, that that faculty can ever, of itself, reach belief, 'tis evident, that belief consists not in the nature and order of our ideas, but in the manner of their conception, and in their feeling to the mind. I confess, that 'tis impossible to explain

[1] [The following paragraph was added by Hume in the appendix—ed. note.]

perfectly this feeling or manner of conception. We may make use of words, that express something near it. But its true and proper name is *belief*, which is a term that every one sufficiently understands in common life. And in philosophy we can go no farther, than assert, that it is something *felt* by the mind, which distinguishes the ideas of the judgment from the fictions of the imagination. It gives them more force and influence; makes them appear of greater importance; infixes them in the mind; and renders them the governing principles of all our actions.

This definition will also be found to be entirely conformable to every one's feeling and experience. Nothing is more evident, than that those ideas, to which we assent, are more strong, firm and vivid, than the loose reveries of a castlebuilder. If one person sits down to read a book as a romance, and another as a true history, they plainly receive the same ideas, and in the same order; nor does the incredulity of the one, and the belief of the other hinder them from putting the very same sense upon their author. His words produce the same ideas in both; tho' his testimony has not the same influence on them. The latter has a more lively conception of all the incidents. He enters deeper into the concerns of the persons: represents to himself their actions, and characters, and friendships, and enmities: He even goes so far as to form a notion of their features, and air, and person. While the former, who gives no credit to the testimony of the author, has a more faint and languid conception of all these particulars; and except on account of the style and ingenuity of the composition, can receive little entertainment from it.

❖ 2 ❖

BELIEF AND DOUBT
Richard Whately (1787–1863)

It is most important to keep in mind the self-evident, but often-forgotten maxim that *Disbelief is Belief*; only, they have reference to *opposite*

From *Elements of Rhetoric* (London: John W. Parker and Son, 7th ed., 1857), part I, chapter ii, section 5, pp. 51–2. The title of this selection has been supplied by the editors.

conclusions. E.g., To disbelieve the real existence of the city of Troy, is to believe that it was feigned: and *which* conclusion implies the greater credulity, is the question to be decided. To some it may appear more, to others, less, probable, that a Greek poet should have celebrated (with whatever exaggerations) some of the feats of arms in which his countrymen had actually been engaged, than that he should have passed by all these, and resorted to such as were wholly imaginary.

So also, though the terms "infidel" and "*un*believer" are commonly applied to one who rejects Christianity, it is plain that to *dis*believe its divine origin, is to believe its human origin: and *which* belief requires the more credulous mind, is the very question at issue.

The proper opposite to Belief is either conscious *Ignorance,* or *Doubt.* And even Doubt may sometimes amount to a kind of Belief; since deliberate and confirmed Doubt, on a question that one has attended to, implies a "verdict of *not proven*";—a *belief that there is not sufficient evidence* to determine either one way or the other. And, in some cases this conclusion would be accounted a mark of excessive credulity. A man who should doubt whether there is such a city as Rome, would imply his belief in (what most would account a moral impossibility) the *possibility* of such multitudes of independent witnesses having concurred in a fabrication.

It is worth remarking, that many persons are of such a disposition as to be nearly incapable of *remaining* in doubt on any point that is not wholly uninteresting to them. They speedily make up their minds on each question, and come to *some* conclusion, whether there are any good grounds for it or not. And judging—as men are apt to do in all matters—of others, from themselves, they usually discredit the most solemn assurances of anyone who professes to be in a state of doubt on some question; taking for granted that if you do not adopt their opinion, you must be of the opposite.

Others again there are, who are capable of remaining in doubt as long as the reasons on each side seem exactly *balanced;* but not otherwise. Such a person, as soon as he perceives any—the smallest—preponderance of probability on one side of a question, can no more refrain from deciding immediately, and with full conviction, on that side, than he could continue to stand, after having lost his equilibrium, in a slanting position, like the famous tower at Pisa. And he will accordingly be disposed to consider an acknowledgment that there are somewhat the stronger reasons on one side, as equivalent to a confident decision.

The tendency to such an error is the greater, from the circumstance that there are so many cases, in practice, wherein it is essentially necessary to come to a *practical* decision, even where there are no sufficient grounds for feeling *fully convinced* that it is the right one. A traveller may be in doubt, and may have no means of deciding with just confidence, which of two roads he ought to take; while yet he must, at a venture, take one of them. And the like happens in numberless transactions of ordinary life, in which we are obliged practically to make up our minds at once to take one course or another, even where there are no sufficient grounds for a full conviction of the understanding.

The infirmities above-mentioned are those of *ordinary* minds. A smaller number of persons, among whom however are to be found a larger proportion of the intelligent, are prone to the opposite extreme; that of not deciding, as long as there are reasons to be found on both sides, even though there may be a clear and strong preponderance on the one, and even though the case may be such as to call for a practical decision. As the one description of men rush hastily to a conclusion, and trouble themselves little about premises, so, the other carefully examine premises, and care too little for conclusions. The one decide without inquiring, the other inquire without deciding.

❖   3   ❖

DOUBT, BELIEF, AND INQUIRY
Charles Sanders Peirce (1839–1914)

. . . We generally know when we wish to ask a question and when we wish to pronounce a judgment, for there is a dissimilarity between the sensation of doubting and that of believing.

But this is not all which distinguishes doubt from belief. There is a practical difference. Our beliefs guide our desires and shape our actions. The Assassins, or followers of the Old Man of the Mountain, used to rush into death at his least command, because they believed that obedience to him would insure everlasting felicity. Had they doubted this, they would not have acted as they did. So it is with every belief, according to its degree. The feeling of believing is a more or less sure indication of there

From "The Fixation of Belief," sections 3 and 4, *Popular Science Monthly*, 1877. The title of this selection has been supplied by the editors.

being established in our nature some habit which will determine our actions. Doubt never has such an effect.

Nor must we overlook a third point of difference. Doubt is an uneasy and dissatisfied state from which we struggle to free ourselves and pass into the state of belief; while the latter is a calm and satisfactory state which we do not wish to avoid, or to change to a belief in anything else.[1] On the contrary, we cling tenaciously, not merely to believing, but to believing just what we do believe.

Thus, both doubt and belief have positive effects upon us, though very different ones. Belief does not make us act at once, but puts us into such a condition that we shall behave in a certain way, when the occasion arises. Doubt has not the least effect of this sort, but stimulates us to action until it is destroyed. This reminds us of the irritation of a nerve and the reflex action produced thereby; while for the analogue of belief, in the nervous system, we must look to what are called nervous associations—for example, to that habit of the nerves in consequence of which the smell of a peach will make the mouth water.

The irritation of doubt causes a struggle to attain a state of belief. I shall term this struggle *inquiry*, though it must be admitted that this is sometimes not a very apt designation.

The irritation of doubt is the only immediate motive for the struggle to attain belief. It is certainly best for us that our beliefs should be such as may truly guide our actions so as to satisfy our desires; and this reflection will make us reject any belief which does not seem to have been so formed as to insure this result. But it will only do so by creating a doubt in the place of that belief. With the doubt, therefore, the struggle begins, and with the cessation of doubt it ends. Hence, the sole object of inquiry is the settlement of opinion. We may fancy that this is not enough for us, and that we seek not merely an opinion, but a true opinion. But put this fancy to the test, and it proves groundless; for as soon as a firm belief is reached we are entirely satisfied, whether the belief be false or true. And it is clear that nothing out of the sphere of our knowledge can be our object, for nothing which does not affect the mind can be a motive for a mental effort. The most that can be maintained is, that we seek for a belief that we shall *think* to be true. But we think each one of our beliefs to be true, and, indeed, it is mere tautology to say so.

That the settlement of opinion is the sole end of inquiry is a very important proposition. It sweeps away, at once, various vague and erroneous conceptions of proof. A few of these may be noticed here.

[1] I am not speaking of secondary effects occasionally produced by the interference of other impulses.

1. Some philosophers have imagined that to start an inquiry it was only necessary to utter or question or set it down on paper, and have even recommended us to begin our studies with questioning everything! But the mere putting of a proposition into the interrogative form does not stimulate the mind to any struggle after belief. There must be a real and living doubt, and without all this discussion is idle.

2. It is a very common idea that a demonstration must rest on some ultimate and absolutely indubitable propositions. These, according to one school, are first principles of a general nature; according to another, are first sensations. But, in point of fact, an inquiry, to have that completely satisfactory result called demonstration, has only to start with propositions perfectly free from all actual doubt. If the premises are not in fact doubted at all, they cannot be more satisfactory than they are.

3. Some people seem to love to argue a point after all the world is fully convinced of it. But no further advance can be made. When doubt ceases, mental action on the subject comes to an end; and, if it did go on, it would be without a purpose. . . .

❖ **4** ❖

KNOWING AND BELIEVING

H. A. Prichard (1871–1947)

. . . . 1. We must first recognize the fundamental nature of the difference between knowing and believing.

2. We must recognize that whenever we know something we either do, or at least can, by reflecting, directly know that we are knowing it, and that whenever we believe something, we similarly either do or can directly know that we are believing it and not knowing it.

As regards (1), that there is such a fundamental difference is not something which everyone will readily admit, and some will go on to the

From H. A. Prichard, *Knowledge and Perception*, 1950, pp. 86–89, reprinted by permission of the Clarendon Press, Oxford. The present selection is from a set of lectures on the theory of knowledge, delivered at Oxford in the years 1927–1932. The title of this selection has been supplied by the editors.

end denying it. Nevertheless, I am confident that at least the more you consider the matter the more difficult you will find it to deny the existence of the difference.

For the sake of brevity and clearness I propose to try to state dogmatically the nature of the difference, and in doing so, I shall for the most part only be trying to state Cook Wilson's view.[1] In saying that I am going to speak dogmatically I mean two things. I mean first that I am not going to offer reasons for what I am going to assert. These for the most part would from the nature of the case have to take the form of trying to meet objections; and this I propose to try to do later. I mean secondly that the statements are meant to express what I know to be *knowledge* on my part and not *opinion*, and so what is beyond controversy.

But if "controversial" stands for any doctrine which has been disputed, then my statements will express a doctrine which is controversial, and controversial in the highest degree. Thus any of you who have had the benefit of knowing or hearing Professor J. A. Smith or Professor Joachim will realize that they would deny the truth of every statement I am going to make. But, of course, it does not follow from the mere fact that a statement is controversial in this sense that it does not express knowledge on the part of the individual who states it, and that therefore, since everything is controversial in this sense, it is useless for you to try to attain knowledge about anything.

1. Knowing is absolutely different from what is called indifferently believing or being convinced or being persuaded or having an opinion or thinking, in the sense in which we oppose thinking to knowing, as when we say "I think so but am not sure." Knowing is not something which differs from being convinced by a difference of degree of something such as feeling of confidence, as being more convinced differs from being less convinced, or as a fast movement differs from a slow movement. Knowing and believing differ in kind as do desiring and feeling, or as do a red color and a blue color. Their difference in kind is not that of species and genus, like that of a red color and a color. To know is not to have a belief of a special kind, differing from beliefs of other kinds; and no improvement in a belief and no increase in the feeling of conviction which it implies will convert it into knowledge. Nor is their difference that of being two species of a common genus. It is not that there is a general kind of activity, for which the name would have to be thinking, which admits of two kinds, the better of which is knowing and the worse believing, nor is knowing something called thinking at its best, thinking not at its best being believing. Their relatedness consists rather in the facts (*a*) that believing presupposes knowing,

[1] Cook Wilson, *Statement and Inference*, part I, chap. 11; part II, chaps. 1, 2, 3.

though, of course, knowing something other than what we believe, and
(b) that believing is a stage we sometimes reach in the endeavor to attain
knowledge.

To convince ourselves of the difference between knowing and believing we need only notice that on the one hand we should only say that we
know something when we are certain of it, and conversely, and that in the
end we have to allow that the meaning of the terms is identical; whereas,
on the other hand, when we believe something we are uncertain of it.

Further there are certain things about knowing and believing which it
is essential to recognize, i.e. know, when we are considering Descartes.

(a) Though obviously knowledge is not false, and though obviously,
when we know, we are not mistaken, knowledge is not *true*. It is neither
true nor false, just as a color is neither heavy nor light. On the other hand,
beliefs are either true or false.

(b) Though some beliefs are true and others are false, there is no special kind of belief distinguished from others by some special characteristic
such as that of being a condition of perceiving something clearly and distinctly, which, as being the kind it is, is necessarily true. Or, to put this
otherwise, there is no such thing as a kind of opinion called true opinion—
as Plato often implies that there is. In fact there is no sort of condition of
mind of which it can truly be said that it is necessarily true; what seems
nearest to this is the condition of knowing, which is necessarily not false,
but yet is not true. And it may be noticed here that it is a tribute to Plato's
philosophical insight, that though he considered there was a kind of
opinion called true opinion, a kind which if it existed would be necessarily
true, in the *Theaetetus*, where he tries to answer the question "What is
knowledge?" he will have nothing to do with the view that it is true opinion.

2. Consider the second condition, which I said must be satisfied before we can get the matter straight. We must recognize that when we
know something we either do, or by reflecting can, know that our condition is one of knowing that thing, while when we believe something, we
either do or can know that our condition is one of believing and not of
knowing: so that we cannot mistake belief for knowledge or vice versa.

Consider instances: When knowing, for example, that the noise we
are hearing is loud, we do or can know that we are knowing this and so
cannot be mistaken, and when believing that the noise is due to a car we
know or can know that we are believing and not knowing this. The knowledge, however, is in both cases direct; we do not know, for example, that
our state is one of knowing that the noise we hear is loud indirectly, i.e. by
knowing that it has some character, other than that of knowing, which we

know any state must have if it is to be one of knowing—such as that of being an act of clear and distinct perceiving; we know directly that it is of the sort which knowing is; and so, too, with our knowledge that our state is one of believing.

Further, it should be noticed that in knowing that some state in which we are is one of knowing or of believing, as the case may be, we are necessarily knowing the sort of thing which knowing is and the sort of thing which believing is, even though it is impossible for us or anyone else to define either, i.e. to state its nature in terms of the nature of something else. This is obvious, because even in knowing in a given case that my condition is one of believing and not of knowing, I must be knowing the sort of thing that knowing is, since otherwise I should not know that my condition is not one of knowing, just as in knowing that some line is not straight, I must—as Plato saw—be knowing what straightness is. . . .

✧ 5 ✧

KNOWLEDGE AND BELIEF

Norman Malcolm (1911–   )

"We must recognize that when we know something we either do, or by reflecting, can know that our condition is one of knowing that thing, while when we believe something, we either do or can know that our condition is one of believing and not of knowing: so that we cannot mistake belief for knowledge or vice versa." [1]

This remark is worthy of investigation. Can I discover *in myself* whether I know something or merely believe it?

Let us begin by studying the ordinary usage of "know" and "believe." Suppose, for example, that several of us intend to go for a walk and that you propose that we walk in Cascadilla Gorge. I protest that I should like

From Norman Malcolm, *Knowledge and Certainty:* Essays and Lectures © 1963. Reprinted by permission of Prentice-Hall, Inc., Englewood Cliffs, N.J. This paper originally appeared in *Mind*, 1952, and appears here in revised form.
[1] H. A. Prichard, *Knowledge and Perception* (Oxford: The Clarendon Press, 1950), p. 88 [p. 12 this volume].

to walk beside a flowing stream and that at this season the gorge is probably dry. Consider the following cases:

(1) You say "I believe that it won't be dry although I have no particular reason for thinking so." If we went to the gorge and found a flowing
stream we should not say that you *knew* that there would be water but that
you thought so and were right.

(2) You say "I believe that it won't be dry because it rained only
three days ago and usually water flows in the gorge for at least that long
after a rain." If we found water we should be inclined to say that you knew
that there would be water. It would be quite natural for you to say "I knew
that it wouldn't be dry"; and we should tolerate your remark. This case
differs from the previous one in that here you had a *reason*.

(3) You say "I know that it won't be dry" and give the same reason
as in (2). If we found water we should have very little hesitation in saying
that you knew. Not only had you a reason, but you *said* "I know" instead
of "I believe." It may seem to us that the latter should not make a difference—but it does.

(4) You say "I know that it won't be dry" and give a stronger reason,
e.g., "I saw a lot of water flowing in the gorge when I passed it this morning." If we went and found water, there would be no hesitation at all in
saying that you knew. If, for example, we later met someone who said
"Weren't you surprised to see water in the gorge this afternoon?" you
would reply "No, I *knew* that there would be water; I had been there earlier in the day." We should have no objection to this statement.

(5) Everything happens as in (4), except that upon going to the
gorge we find it to be dry. We should not say that you knew, but that you
believed that there would be water. And this is true even though you declared that you knew, and even though your evidence was the same as it
was in case (4) in which you did know.

I wish to make some comments on the usage of "know," "knew," "believe," and "believed," as illustrated in the preceding cases:

(*a*) Whether we should say that you knew, depends in part on
whether you had grounds for your assertion and on the strength of those
grounds. There would certainly be less hesitation to say that you knew in
case (4) than in case (3), and this can be due only to the difference in the
strength of the grounds.

(*b*) Whether we should say that you knew, depends in part on how
confident you were. In case (2), if you had said "It rained only three days
ago and usually water flows in the gorge for at least that long after a rain;
but, of course, I don't feel absolutely sure that there will be water," then
we should *not* have said that you knew that there would be water. If you

lack confidence that p is true then others do not say that you know that p is true, even though *they* know that p is true. Being confident is a necessary condition for knowing.

(*c*) Prichard says that if we reflect we cannot mistake belief for knowledge. In case (4) you knew that there would be water, and in case (5) you merely believed it. Was there any way that you could have discovered by reflection, in case (5), that you did not know? It would have been useless to have reconsidered your grounds for saying that there would be water, because in case (4), where you *did* know, your grounds were identical. They could be at fault in (5) only if they were at fault in (4), and they were not at fault in (4). Cases (4) and (5) differ in only one respect —namely, that in one case you did subsequently find water and in the other you did not. Prichard says that we can determine by reflection whether we know something or merely believe it. But where, in these cases, is the material that reflection would strike upon? There is none.

There is only one way that Prichard could defend his position. He would have to say that in case (4) you did *not* know that there would be water. And it is obvious that he would have said this. But this is false. It is an enormously common usage of language to say, in commenting upon just such an incident as (4), "He knew that the gorge would be dry because he had seen water flowing there that morning." It is a usage that all of us are familiar with. We so employ "know" and "knew" every day of our lives. We do not think of our usage as being loose or incorrect—and it is not. As philosophers we may be surprised to observe that it *can* be that the knowledge that p is true should differ from the belief that p is true *only* in the respect that in one case p is true and in the other false. But that is the fact.

There is an argument that one is inclined to use as a proof that you did not know that there would be water. The argument is the following: It could have turned out that you found no water; if it had so turned out you would have been mistaken in saying that you would find water; therefore you could have been mistaken; but if you could have been mistaken then you did not know.

Now it certainly *could* have turned out that the gorge was quite dry when you went there, even though you saw lots of water flowing through it only a few hours before. This does not show, however, that you did not know that there would be water. What it shows is that *although you knew you could have been mistaken*.[2] This would seem to be a contradictory re-

---

[2] [Some readers seem to have thought that I was denying here that "I knew that p" entails "that p." That was not my intention, and my words do not have that implication. If I had said *"although you knew you were mistaken,"* I should have denied the

sult; but it is not. It seems so because our minds are fixed upon another usage of "know" and "knew"; one in which "It could have turned out that I was mistaken," implies "I did not know."

When is "know" used in this sense? I believe that Prichard uses it in this sense when he says that when we go through the proof of the proposition that the angles of a triangle are equal to two right angles we *know* that the proposition is true (p. 89). He says that if we put to ourselves the question: Is our condition one of knowing this, or is it only one of being convinced of it? then "We can only answer 'Whatever may be our state on other occasions, here we are knowing this.' And this statement is an expression of our *knowing* that we are knowing; for we do not *believe* that we are knowing this, we know that we are" (p. 89). He goes on to say that if someone were to object that we might be making a mistake "because for all we know we can later on discover some fact which is incompatible with a triangle's having angles that are equal to two right angles, we can answer that we *know* that there can be no such fact, for in knowing that a triangle must have such angles we also know that nothing can exist which is incompatible with this fact" (p. 90).

It is easy to imagine a non-philosophical context in which it would have been natural for Prichard to have said "I know that the angles of a triangle are equal to two right angles." Suppose that a young man just beginning the study of geometry was in doubt as to whether that proposition is true, and had even constructed an ingenious argument that appeared to prove it false. Suppose that Prichard was unable to find any error in the argument. He might have said to the young man: "There must be an error in it. I know that the angles of a triangle are equal to two right angles."

When Prichard says that "nothing can exist which is incompatible with" the truth of that proposition, is he prophesying that no one will ever have the ingenuity to construct a flawless-looking argument against it? I believe not. When Prichard says that "we" *know* (and implies that *he* knows) that the proposition is true and *know* that nothing can exist that is incompatible with its being true, he is not making any *prediction* as to what the future will bring in the way of arguments or measurements. On the contrary, he is asserting that *nothing* that the future might bring could ever count as evidence against the proposition. He is implying that he would not *call* anything "evidence" against it. He is using "know" in what I shall call its "strong" sense. "Know" is used in this sense when a

---

above entailment and, also, I should have misused "knew." The difference between the strong and weak senses of "know" (and "knew") is not that this entailment holds for the strong but not for the weak sense. It holds for both. If it is false that *p*, then one does not (and did not) know that *p*.]

person's statement "I know that p is true" implies that the person who makes the statement would look upon nothing whatever as evidence that p is false.

It must not be assumed that whenever "know" is used in connection with mathematical propositions it is used in the strong sense. A great many people have *heard* of various theorems of geometry, e.g., the Pythagorean. These theorems are a part of "common knowledge." If a schoolboy doing his geometry assignment felt a doubt about the Pythagorean theorem, and said to an adult "Are you *sure* that it is true?" the latter might reply "Yes, I know that it is." He might make this reply even though he could not give proof of it and even though he had never gone through a proof of it. If subsequently he was presented with a "demonstration" that the theorem is false, or if various persons reputed to have a knowledge of geometry soberly assured him that it is false, he might be filled with doubt or even be convinced that he was mistaken. When he said "Yes, I know that it is true," he did not pledge himself to hold to the theorem through thick and thin. He did not absolutely exclude the possibility that something could prove it to be false. I shall say that he used "know" in the "weak" sense.

Consider another example from mathematics of the difference between the strong and weak senses of "know." I have just now rapidly calculated that 92 times 16 is 1472. If I had done this in the commerce of daily life where a practical problem was at stake, and if someone had asked "Are you sure that $92 \times 16 = 1472$?" I might have answered "I *know* that it is; I have just now calculated it." But also I might have answered "I know that it is; but I will calculate it again to *make sure*." And here my language points to a distinction. I say that I *know* that $92 \times 16 = 1472$. Yet I am willing to *confirm* it—that is, there is something that I should *call* "making sure"; and, likewise, there is something that I should *call* "finding out that it is false." If I were to do this calculation again and obtain the result that $92 \times 16 = 1372$, and if I were to carefully check this latter calculation without finding any error, I should be disposed to say that I was previously mistaken when I declared that $92 \times 16 = 1472$. Thus when I say that I know that $92 \times 16 = 1472$, I allow for the possibility of a *refutation*; and so I am using "know" in its weak sense.

Now consider propositions like $2 + 2 = 4$ and $7 + 5 = 12$. It is hard to think of circumstances in which it would be natural for me to say that I know that $2 + 2 = 4$, because no one ever questions it. Let us try to suppose, however, that someone whose intelligence I respect argues that certain developments in arithmetic have shown that $2 + 2$ does not equal 4. He writes out a proof of this in which I can find no flaw. Suppose that his demeanor showed me that he was in earnest. Suppose that several persons of normal intelligence became persuaded that his proof was correct and that $2 + 2$ does not equal 4. What would be my reaction? I should say "I can't see what is wrong with your proof; but it *is* wrong, because I *know* that $2 + 2 = 4$." Here I should be using "know" in its strong sense. I should not admit that any argument or any future development in mathematics could show that it is false that $2 + 2 = 4$.

The propositions $2 + 2 = 4$ and $92 \times 16 = 1472$ do not have the same status. There *can* be a demonstration that $2 + 2 = 4$. But a demonstration would be for me (and for any average person) only a curious exercise, a sort of *game*. We have no serious interest in proving that proposition.[3] It does not *need* a proof. It stands without one, and would not fall if a proof went against it. The case is different with the proposition that $92 \times 16 = 1472$. We take an interest in the demonstration (calculation) because that proposition *depends* upon its demonstration. A calculation may lead me to reject it as false. But $2 + 2 = 4$ does *not* depend on its demonstration. It does not depend on anything! And in the calculation that proves that $92 \times 16 = 1472$, there are steps that do not depend on any calculation (e.g., $2 \times 6 = 12$; $5 + 2 = 7$; $5 + 9 = 14$).

There is a correspondence between this dualism in the logical status of mathematical propositions and the two senses of "know." When I use "know" in the weak sense I am prepared to let an investigation (demonstration, calculation) determine whether the something that I claim to know is true or false. When I use "know" in the strong sense I am not prepared to look upon anything as an *investigation*; I do not concede that anything whatsoever could prove me mistaken; I do not regard the matter as open to any *question*; I do not admit that my proposition could turn out to be false, that any future investigation *could* refute it or cast doubt on it.[4]

We have been considering the strong sense of "know" in its application to mathematical propositions. Does it have application anywhere in

[3] Some logicians and philosophers have taken an interest in proving that $2 + 2 = 4$ (e.g., Leibniz, *New Essays on the Understanding*, Bk. IV, ch. 7, sec. 10; Frege, *The Foundations of Arithmetic*, sec. 6). They have wished to show that it can be deduced from certain premises, and to determine what premises and rules of inference are required in the deduction. Their interest has not been in the *outcome* of the deduction.
[4] Compare these remarks about the strong sense of "know" with some of Locke's statements about "intuitive knowledge": ". . . in this the mind is at no pains of proving or examining. . . ." "This part of knowledge . . . leaves no room for hesitation, doubt, or examination. . . ."
"It is on this intuition that depends all the certainty and evidence of all our knowledge; which certainly every one finds to be so great, that he cannot imagine, and therefore not require a greater. . . ." Locke, *Essay*, Bk. IV, ch. 2, sec. 1.

the realm of *empirical* propositions—for example, to propositions that assert or imply that certain physical things exist? Descartes said that we have a "moral assurance" of the truth of some of the latter propositions but that we lack a "metaphysical certainty." [5] Locke said that the perception of the existence of physical things is not "so certain as our intuitive knowledge, or the deductions of our reason" although "it is an assurance that deserves the name of knowledge." [6] Some philosophers have held that when we make judgments of perception such as that there are peonies in the garden, cows in the field, or dishes in the cupboard, we are "taking for granted" that the peonies, cows, and dishes exist, but not knowing it in the "strict" sense. Others have held that all empirical propositions, including judgments of perception, are merely hypotheses.[7] The thought behind this exaggerated mode of expression is that any empirical proposition whatever *could* be refuted by future experience—that is, it *could* turn out to be false. Are these philosophers right?

Consider the following propositions:

(i) The sun is about ninety million miles from the earth.
(ii) There is a heart in my body.
(iii) Here is an ink-bottle.

In various circumstances I should be willing to assert of each of these propositions that I know it to be true. Yet they differ strikingly. This I see when, with each, I try to imagine the possibility that it is false.

(i) If in ordinary conversation someone said to me "The sun is about twenty million miles from the earth, isn't it?" I should reply "No, it is about ninety million miles from us." If he said "I think that you are confusing the sun with Polaris," I should reply, "I *know* that ninety million miles is roughly the sun's distance from the earth." I might invite him to verify the figure in an encyclopedia. A third person who overheard our conversation could quite correctly report that I knew the distance to the sun, whereas the other man did not. But this knowledge of mine is little better than hearsay. I have seen that figure mentioned in a few books. I know nothing about the observations and calculations that led astronomers to accept it. If tomorrow a group of eminent astronomers announced that a great error had been made and that the correct figure is twenty million

---

[5] Descartes, *Discourse on the Method*, part IV.
[6] Locke, *Essay*, Book IV, ch. 11, sec. 3.
[7] E.g., ". . . no proposition, other than a tautology, can possibly be anything more than a probable hypothesis." A. J. Ayer, *Language, Truth and Logic*, second ed. (New York: Dover Publications, Inc., 1951), p. 38.

miles, I should not insist that they were wrong. It would surprise me that such an enormous mistake could have been made. But I should no longer be willing to say that I *know* that ninety million is the correct figure. Although I should *now* claim that I know the distance to be about ninety million miles, it is easy for me to envisage the possibility that some future investigation will prove this to be false.

(ii) Suppose that after a routine medical examination the excited doctor reports to me that the X-ray photographs show that I have no heart. I should tell him to get a new machine. I should be inclined to say that the fact that I have a heart is one of the few things that I can count on as absolutely certain. I can feel it beat. I know it's there. Furthermore, how could my blood circulate if I didn't have one? Suppose that later on I suffer a chest injury and undergo a surgical operation. Afterwards the astonished surgeons solemnly declare that they searched my chest cavity and found no heart, and that they made incisions and looked about in other likely places but found it not. They are convinced that I am without a heart. They are unable to understand how circulation can occur or what accounts for the thumping in my chest. But they are in agreement and obviously sincere, and they have clear photographs of my interior spaces. What would be my attitude? Would it be to insist that they were all mistaken? I think not. I believe that I should eventually accept their testimony and the evidence of the photographs. I should consider to be false what I now regard as an absolute certainty.

(iii) Suppose that as I write this paper someone in the next room were to call out to me "I can't find an ink-bottle; is there one in the house?" I should reply "Here is an ink-bottle." If he said in a doubtful tone "Are you sure? I looked there before," I should reply "Yes, I know there is; come and get it."

Now could it turn out to be false that there is an ink-bottle directly in front of me on this desk? Many philosophers have thought so. They would say that many things could happen of such a nature that if they did happen it would be proved that I am deceived. I agree that many extraordinary things could happen, in the sense that there is no logical absurdity in the supposition. It could happen that when I next reach for this ink-bottle my hand should seem to pass *through* it and I should not feel the contact of any object. It could happen that in the next moment the ink-bottle will suddenly vanish from sight; or that I should find myself under a tree in the garden with no ink-bottle about; or that one or more persons should enter this room and declare with apparent sincerity that they see no ink-bottle on this desk; or that a photograph taken now of the top of the desk should clearly show all of the objects on it except the ink-bottle. Having admitted that these things *could happen*,[8] am I compelled to admit that if they did happen then it would be proved that there is no ink-bottle here *now?* Not at all! I could say that when my hand seemed to pass through the ink-bottle I should *then* be suffering from hallucination; that if the ink-bottle suddenly vanished it would have miraculously ceased to exist; that the other persons were conspiring to drive me mad, or were themselves victims of remarkable concurrent hallucinations; that the camera possessed some strange flaw or that there was trickery in developing the negative. I admit that in the next moment I could find myself under a tree or in the bathtub. But this is not to admit that it could be revealed in the next moment that I am now dreaming. For what I admit is that I might be instantaneously transported to the garden, but not that in the next moment I might *wake up* in the garden. There is nothing that could happen to me in the next moment that I should call "waking up"; and therefore nothing that could happen to me in the next moment would be accepted by me now as proof that I now dream.

Not only do I not *have* to admit that those extraordinary occurrences would be evidence that there is no ink-bottle here; the fact is that I *do not* admit it. There is nothing whatever that could happen in the next moment or the next year that would by me be called *evidence* that there is not an ink-bottle here now. No future experience or investigation could prove to me that I am mistaken. Therefore, if I were to say "I know that there is an ink-bottle here," I should be using "know" in the strong sense.

It will appear to some that I have adopted an *unreasonable* attitude toward that statement. There is, however, nothing unreasonable about it. It seems so because one thinks that the statement that here is an ink-bottle *must* have the same status as the statements that the sun is ninety million miles away and that I have a heart and that there will be water in the gorge this afternoon. But this is a *prejudice.*

In saying that I should regard nothing as evidence that there is no ink-bottle here now, I am not *predicting* what I should do if various astonishing things happened. If other members of my family entered this room and, while looking at the top of this desk, declared with apparent sincerity that

---

8 [My viewpoint is somewhat different here from what it is in "The Verification Argument." There I am concerned with bringing out the different ways in which such a remark as "these things *could* happen" can be taken. I wish to show, furthermore, that from none of the senses in which the remark is *true* does it follow that it is *not certain* that the things in question will *not* happen. Finally, I hold there, that it is perfectly certain that they will not happen. Here, I am not disagreeing with any of those points, but I am adding the further point that my admission that, in some sense, the things *could happen*, does not require me to admit that *if* they were to happen, that would be evidence that there is no ink-bottle here now.]

they see no ink-bottle, I might fall into a swoon or become mad. I *might* even come to believe that there is not and has not been an ink-bottle here. I cannot foretell with certainty how I should react. But if it is *not* a prediction, what is the meaning of my assertion that I should regard nothing as evidence that there is no ink-bottle here?

That assertion describes my *present* attitude towards the statement that here is an ink-bottle. It does not prophesy what my attitude *would* be if various things happened. My present attitude toward that statement is radically different from my present attitude toward those other statements (e.g., that I have a heart).[9] I do *now* admit that certain future occurrences would disprove the latter. Whereas no imaginable future occurrence would be considered by me *now* as proving that there is not an ink-bottle here.

These remarks are not meant to be autobiographical. They are meant to throw light on the common concepts of evidence, proof, and disproof. Every one of us upon innumerable occasions of daily life takes this same attitude towards various statements about physical things, e.g., that here is a torn page, that this dish is broken, that the thermometer reads 70, that no rug is on the floor. Furthermore, the concepts of proof, disproof, doubt, and conjecture *require* us to take this attitude. In order for it to be possible that any statements about physical things should *turn out to be false* it is necessary that some statements about physical things *cannot* turn out to be false.

This will be made clear if we ask ourselves the question, When do we *say* that something turned out to be false? When do we use those words? Someone asks you for a dollar. You say "There is one in this drawer." You open the drawer and look, but it is perfectly empty. Your statement turned out to be false. This can be said because you *discovered* an empty drawer. It could not be said if it were only probable that the drawer is empty or were still open to question. Would it make sense to say "I had better make sure that it is empty; perhaps there is a dollar in it after all?" Sometimes; but not always. Not if the drawer lies open before your eyes. That remark is the prelude to a search. What search can there be when the emptiness of the drawer confronts you? In certain circumstances there is nothing that you would call "making sure" that the drawer is empty; and likewise nothing that you would call "its turning out to be false" that the

---

[9] [The word "attitude" is not very satisfactory, but I cannot think of another noun that would do the trick. By "my attitude" I mean, here, *what I should say and think* if various things were to happen. By "my *present* attitude" I mean what I should say and think now, when I imagine those things as happening, in contrast with what I should say and think at some future time if those things actually did happen at that time. It is this distinction that shows that my description of "my present attitude" is not a *prophecy*.]

drawer is empty. You *made* sure that the drawer is empty. One statement about physical things *turned out to be false* only because you *made sure* of another statement about physical things. The two concepts cannot exist apart. Therefore it is impossible that *every* statement about physical things *could* turn out to be false.

In a certain important respect some a priori statements and some empirical statements possess the same logical character. The statements that $5 \times 5 = 25$ and that here is an ink-bottle, both lie beyond the reach of doubt. On both, my judgment and reasoning *rests*. If you could somehow undermine my confidence in either, you would not teach me *caution*. You would fill my mind with chaos! I could not even make *conjectures* if you took away those fixed points of certainty; just as a man cannot *try* to climb whose body has no support. A conjecture implies an understanding of what certainty would be. If it is not a certainty that $5 \times 5 = 25$ and that here is an ink-bottle, then I do not understand what it is. You cannot make me doubt either of these statements or treat them as hypotheses. You cannot persuade me that future experience could refute them. With both of them it is perfectly unintelligible to me to speak of a "possibility" that they are false. This is to say that I know both of them to be true, in the strong sense of "know." And I am inclined to think that the strong sense of "know" is what various philosophers have had in mind when they have spoken of "perfect," "metaphysical," or "strict certainty." [10]

It will be thought that I have confused a statement about my "sensations," or my "sense-data," or about the way something *looks* or *appears* to me, with a statement about physical things. It will be thought that the things that I have said about the statement "Here is an ink-bottle" could be true only if that statement is interpreted to mean something like "There appears to me to be an ink-bottle here," i.e., interpreted so as not to assert or imply that any physical thing exists. I wish to make it clear that my statement "Here is an ink-bottle" is *not* to be interpreted in that way. It would be utterly fantastic for me in my present circumstances to say "There appears to me to be an ink-bottle here."

If someone were to call me on the telephone and say that he urgently needed an ink-bottle I should invite him to come here and get this one. If

---

[10] Descartes, for example, apparently took as his criterion for something's being "entirely certain" that he could not *imagine* in it the least ground of doubt: ". . . je pensai qu'il fallait . . . que je retasse comme absolument faux tout ce en quoi je pourrais imaginer le moindre doute, afin de voir s'il ne me resterait point après cela quelque chose en ma créance qui fut entièrement indubitable" (*Discourse*, Part IV). And Locke (as previously noted) said of "intuitive knowledge" that one *cannot imagine* a greater certainty, and that it "leaves no room for hesitation, doubt, or examination." *Essay*, Bk. IV, ch. 2, sec. 1.

he said that it was extremely urgent that he should obtain one immediately and that he could not afford to waste time going to a place where there might not be one, I should tell him that it is an absolute certainty that there is one here, that nothing could be more certain, that it is something I absolutely guarantee. But if my statement "There is an ink-bottle here" were a statement about my "sensations" or "sense-data," or if it meant that there *appears* to me to be an ink-bottle here or that something here looks to me like an ink-bottle, and if that is all that I meant by it—then I should react quite differently to his urgent request. I should say that there is probably an ink-bottle here but that I could not *guarantee* it, and that if he needs one very desperately and at once then he had better look elsewhere. In short, I wish to make it clear that my statement "Here is an ink-bottle" is strictly about physical things and not about "sensations," "sense-data," or "appearances." [11]

Let us go back to Prichard's remark that we can determine by reflection whether we know something or merely believe it. Prichard would think that "knowledge in the weak sense" is mere belief and not knowledge. This is wrong. But if we let ourselves speak this way, we can then see some justification for Prichard's remark. For then he would be asserting, among other things, that we can determine by reflection whether we know something in the strong sense or in the weak sense. This is not literally true; however, there is this truth in it—that reflection can make us realize that we are *using* "I know it" in the strong (or weak) sense in a particular case. Prichard says that reflection can show us that "our condition is one of knowing" a certain thing, or instead that "our condition is one of believing and not of knowing" that thing. I do not understand what could be meant here by "our condition." The way I should put it is that reflection on *what we should think* if certain things were to happen may make us realize that we should (or should not) call those things "proof" or "evidence" that what we claim to know is not so. I have tried to show that the distinction between strong and weak knowledge does not run parallel to the distinction between a priori and empirical knowledge but cuts across it, i.e., these two kinds of knowledge may be distinguished *within* a priori knowledge and *within* empirical knowledge.

Reflection can make me realize that I am using "know" in the strong

---

[11] [The remainder of the essay is newly written. The original conclusion was wrongly stated. The reader is referred to the following exchange between Richard Taylor and myself, in respect to the original paper: Taylor, "A Note on Knowledge and Belief," *Analysis*, XIII, June 1953; Malcolm, "On Knowledge and Belief," *Analysis*, XIV, March 1954; Taylor, "Rejoinder to Mr. Malcolm," *ibid.*]

sense; but can reflection show me that I *know* something in the strong sense (or in the weak)? It is not easy to state the logical facts here. On the one hand, if I make an assertion of the form "I know that *p*" it does not follow that *p*, whether or not I am using "know" in the strong sense. If I have said to someone outside my room "Of course, I know that Freddie is in here," and I am speaking in the strong sense, it does not *follow* that Freddie is where I claim he is. This logical fact would not be altered even if I *realized* that I was using "know" in the strong sense. My reflection on what I should say if . . . , cannot show me that I *know* something. From the fact that I should not call anything "evidence" that Freddie is not here, it does not follow that he *is* here; therefore, it does not follow that I *know* he is here.

On the other hand, in an actual case of my using "know" in the strong sense, I cannot envisage a possibility that what I say to be true should turn out to be not true. If I were speaking of *another person's* assertion about something, I *could* think both that he is using "know" in the strong sense and that nonetheless what he claims he knows to be so might turn out to be not so. But *in my own case* I cannot have this conjunction of thoughts, and this is a logical and not a psychological fact. When *I* say that I know something to be so, using "know" in the strong sense, it is unintelligible *to me* (although perhaps not to others) to suppose that anything could prove that it is not so and, therefore, that I do not know it.[12]

[12] This is the best summary I can give of what is wrong and right in Prichard's claim that one can determine by reflection whether one knows something or merely believes it. A good part of the ideas in this essay were provoked by conversations with Wittgenstein. A brief and rough account of those talks is to be found in *Ludwig Wittgenstein: A Memoir* (New York: Oxford University Press, 1958), pp. 87–92. Jaakko Hintikka provides an acute treatment of the topic of "knowing that one knows," with special reference to Prichard's claim. See his *Knowledge and Belief* (Ithaca: Cornell University Press, 1962), ch. 5.

THE NATURE OF BELIEF

Arthur Kenyon Rogers (1868–1936)

I have so far been using the term belief without any attempt to define its nature very strictly; and while this may seem a dangerous method in philosophy, it is one that in the present instance can scarcely be avoided altogether. No one can advance a single step in inquiry of any sort without exercising the right to believe, and without presupposing therefore that he is well enough acquainted with the experience of believing to recognize its presence, whatever his success or failure in setting forth explicitly his meaning. Even in case it were to prove impossible therefore to analyze the concept further, I should still claim the right to use it, especially since I find everyone about me using it without hesitation. As a matter of fact the term is one of which it is exceptionally hard to give a satisfactory account; but the task nevertheless is one that ought not to be entirely evaded.

It is probably safe to assume, to begin with, that the content of belief can always be put in a certain form—I believe *that* something is so and so. This may prove misleading, however, unless we notice that such a form of statement covers two possibilities that do not on the surface seem identical. It suggests in the first instance that the object of belief is a *relationship* that holds between two terms—that green is other than pink, or that the Romans conquered Gaul. But we also may, if we choose, change the form of the assertion on occasion, and may say that we believe *in* something which is not a relationship or a "fact," but a "thing." I believe, for example, in this pen which I now hold in my hand. It is true that I am equally able to put the content of this last belief in the form of a relational proposition, and to say *that* I believe the pen is real, or has existence. But unless we presuppose that "existence" is itself nothing but a logical term or concept on a par with any other, this still leaves in some degree "belief in" distinguishable from "belief that." And it may first be asked, accordingly, whether it is a belief in "realities," or a belief in relational connections, that throws most light on the essential nature of believing.

The second alternative is the one that probably would receive the approval of most philosophers. There are two reasons however, of a general sort, which lead me to think that this is open to objection. In the first place, it proceeds on an assumption which, though it is very widely held, appears to be out of harmony with certain generally accepted facts. One would seldom suspect, from a reading of the major part of even recent philosophical literature, that belief is concerned essentially with anything except an intellectual analysis of content. For the empiricists, this content is sensational. For the opponents of empiricism it is logical or dialectical. But in both cases alike belief has no intimate and necessary relation to the practical life, and the needs of the animal organism. It is the presumption of the objective sciences, however, that man is first of all an animal. And if this is so, the beginnings of belief will most naturally be looked for in connection, not with a disinterested analysis of psychological or of logical data out of which objects are later and in a secondary way built up, but with the recognized presence of actual things and forces on the use or avoidance of which survival is dependent. The presumption is therefore in so far not in favor of the second thesis.

There is another point against it also. It may seem an over-refinement of language to say that I *perceive* that two parallel lines never meet, instead of *believing* it. But in the field of ultimate analysis no distinction is too small to be safely overlooked. And, properly interpreted, the distinction appears to be a valid and useful one, as the discussion of certainty has already shown. Most people would admit that in the case of *certain* knowledge it sounds, on close inspection, a little strange to say that we *believe* it. We *know* it, or see that indubitably it is so; belief suggests an element of doubt which here is lacking. This carries a suggestion therefore, at any rate, that it is not to the perception of relationships that the term is most directly relevant. Meanwhile there is no doubt another sense in which the statement that parallel lines never meet does represent a belief—when we are thinking, not of the immediate perception of a relationship, but of the projection of this relationship into the world as an ideal to which objects are going to live up. Here indeed we have the element of faith which makes the term belief appropriate. But also we have passed from the field of pure logical apprehension, to that reference to existents which is involved in the alternative conception.

It is this alternative, therefore, which I shall take as a more promising starting point; and I shall proceed to inquire what account, if any, can be given of the act of believing regarded as an essential requirement of survival. Along the lines of the English tradition in philosophy, there are two chief suggestions that will furnish a possible line of attack. There is, to begin with, what tends to be the answer of the associationist philosophy— that belief is reducible to an expectation of the future appearance of some familiar mental content. Taken as it stands, however, this is an evasion of the issue. It might perhaps account for *what* we believe. But it is not obviously an answer to the question, In what does believing as an experience itself consist? At best it reduces belief to *expectation;* and only by ruling out arbitrarily a considerable portion of the commonly recognized content of belief can this identification be maintained. And even if we were to regard it as the only form that belief takes, the essential point that makes it a belief would still remain unaccounted for in the analysis. All that association by itself supplies is the *fact that* one content follows another into consciousness, plus the possible memory of this same connection in the past; and neither singly nor in combination do these amount to an expectant belief. Instead of finding an explanation of belief in expectation, expectation itself must wait upon a theory of belief for its understanding.

The second suggestion toward a theory of belief is a more distinctive and promising one. Made in the first instance by Professor Bain, less as itself a sufficient account of the matter than as an element in a considerably more complicated theory, it attracted general attention, only to be repudiated later on by its author. It has however repeatedly been revived by subsequent thinkers, though usually without much attempt to meet the specific difficulties involved. Here the essence of belief is found in a "preparedness to act." This has at least the very considerable merit that it abandons a purely intellectualistic explanation, and brings belief into connection with the active life process. On the other hand, in the form in which Bain left it, there is an apparent lack of identity between the theoretical analysis and the testimony of concrete experience. However close the connection with action may be—and it seems difficult to escape a feeling that some connection exists—the mere sense of active movement, or of a readiness to act, *is* not all we mean by having a belief; we have only to compare the two things to see plainly that they are not the same. Belief unquestionably has an intellectual content which the mere feeling of movement does not supply.

It is not however impossible, it might be urged, to remedy this lack, and to import an intellectual content also into the same general situation which a "preparedness to act" implies. The defect of the alternative to which Bain himself was led—the reduction of belief to the expectation of an associated experience to come—has already been set forth. But if we were to substitute instead the recognition, not necessarily a very explicit recognition, of an *end* that is being served, or of an object felt to be related to a teleological process, we should be in some sense in connection again with the "activity" aspect which Bain tried to introduce. It might accordingly be suggested, as a possible hypothesis, that belief consists, not in movement itself, but in the intellectual recognition of the teleological situation which organic movement implies—a recognition of the presence of objective conditions, namely, such as bear a causal relationship to the expression of impulse or desire. To "believe in" a perceived object would be, then, to realize this relation of the object to the active attitude which the body assumes with reference to it.

I am disposed to regard such a thesis as to a certain extent on the right track. But as it stands it suffers from a fatal defect. In saying that I recognize an object as a condition of organic activity, I am already implying that this object is an object of belief. That is to say, the content to which belief has been reduced is still no more than intellectual content, unless it be recognized not only as figuring in the logical description of a purposive situation—if this were all, I could not even have the thought of such a situation without also believing in it—but as a *reality*, an actually existing circumstance which conduct has to take into account. The moment I begin talking of "reality," however, I presuppose already the presence of belief. There must be some further account therefore of the difference between a condition of action which is merely possible or thinkable, and one that also is conceived as actual.

But while bare action on the one side, and the intellectual recognition of objective conditions of action on the other, are neither of them sufficient to describe belief, it is not impossible that if we take the two together they may prove more adequate. Action, overt or incipient, is not believing. The thought of a means to or a condition of action is not believing, since it may remain a *mere* thought. But it seems open to conjecture that the sense of difference which we feel between such a mere thought or fancy, and the belief in a real object, may have its source in the actual release of energy which marks the beginning of action. Here we are no longer attempting to reduce belief to movement pure and simple. We do not have belief unless there is also the intellectual recognition of something that stands in relation to the process of active life. And the final touch which converts this into belief is itself also a conscious feeling. But the source of such a feeling may nevertheless be the presence of an incipient release in the direction of attainment, through the removal of organic checks to action.

An examination of the belief situation gives, I think, some plausibility to this hypothesis. As we descend in the scale of life, the release of action in the presence of the object tends to be immediate and instinctive, and the intellectual content only of the vaguest sort; here it would generally be agreed that belief is hardly a proper name to apply. As a distinctive experience, belief arises only after a period of doubt and hesitation has given rise to some recognition of the conditions to be met, and has made us acquainted with the difference between action arrested and action released. Its emergence into consciousness is at least coincident, therefore, with the removal of checks upon freely moving action; and it seems the most natural thing to find a causal relation here as well. This would mean in the first place that the source of belief is subconscious and organic—a thesis which experience will verify. We do not choose to believe; we find ourselves believing. And it seems a fair description of the fact to say that we find ourselves feeling free to pass on now to the attainment of ends which have temporarily been held up. I say that we feel free to pass on, for, in the second place, it is in this sense of there being no hindrance in our path, rather than in the actual pursuit of active ends, that belief consists; it is a conscious and intellectual rather than a conative sort of experience, and belongs to the stage when we are contemplating rather than doing. I do not feel quite certain about the natural description of our state of mind where conduct is actually moving forward. I imagine it would often be truer here to say that belief is implied, rather than that it actually is present. But since overt action may be accompanied also by a continued intellectual recognition of its conditions, the matter is not one of great theoretical importance, and we might expect to find the situation descriptively uncertain.

In what has just been said, I am not intending to deny that there may be cases of belief which are not preceded by an actual period of initial doubt. The essential point is not that in every belief action must first be restrained by indecision, but that belief belongs to an intellectual stage which is not itself overt action, but a state of readiness to act, with the attending sense of an open path ahead. And while genetically this implies experiences of doubt and hesitation which have taught us the advantages of going slow and looking before we leap, in the human animal as he now is constituted the intellectual life has to a considerable extent severed its original close connection with experimental action, and numerous beliefs come to us from our nurture and surroundings which we never stop to question. Closer inspection however furnishes ground for thinking that facts of this sort are themselves favorable on the whole to the thesis that belief as a conscious experience normally implies preceding doubt and inhibition. For it is notorious that when a so-called belief comes too easily, we often are mistaken about its genuineness. It holds the mind only because we have had no occasion to put it into practice; and when we are really called to act upon it, its hollowness and insincerity are at once exposed.

❖ 7 ❖

KNOWLEDGE, OPINION, CONVICTION, AND BELIEF
John Cook Wilson (1849–1915)

. . . 1. Consider knowledge and opinion. We easily see that opinion involves knowledge; but we also see that the opinion itself must not be confounded with that knowledge. It is characteristic of the cases where we form an opinion that we notice a certain quality in the evidence, in virtue of which we say the evidence known to us is stronger for one alternative than for the other. We know, that is, that certain facts are in favor of A's being B, but either that they do not prove it or that there are facts against, though not decisively against, A's being B. But this estimate is not the opinion. We are affected by it so as to form the opinion, yet the opinion is neither the knowing which constitutes the estimate nor any kind of knowledge. It is a peculiar thing—the result of the estimate—and we call it by a peculiar name, opinion. For it, taken in its strict and proper sense, we can use no term that belongs to knowing. For the opinion that A is B is founded on evidence we know to be insufficient, whereas it is of the very nature of knowledge not to make its statements at all on grounds recognized to be insufficient, nor to come to any decision except that the grounds are insufficient; for it is here that in the knowing activity we stop. In knowing, we can have nothing to do with the so-called "greater strength" of the evidence on which the opinion is grounded; simply because we know that this "greater strength" of evidence of A's being B is compatible with A's not being B after all. Beyond then the bare abstrac-

Secs. 49–53, part II, chapter 3 of *Statement and Inference* (1926), Vol. I, by John Cook Wilson, pp. 99–109. Reprinted by permission of the Clarendon Press, Oxford. The title of this selection has been supplied by the editors.

tion of conscious activity, there is no general character or quality of which
the essential natures of both knowledge and opinion are differentiations, or
of which we could say in ordinary language that each was a kind. One need
hardly add that there is no verbal form corresponding to any such fiction as
a mental activity manifested in a common mental attitude to the object
about which we know or about which we have an opinion. Moreover it is
vain to seek such a common quality in belief, on the ground that the man
who knows that A is B and the man who has that opinion both believe
that A *is* B. Belief is not knowledge and the man who knows does not
believe at all what he knows; he knows it. We might as well say at once
that knowledge is a kind of opinion as that it is a kind of belief.

2. We have spoken of opinion such as is consciously formed and recognized as an opinion and not as knowledge by the person who forms it;
and, however determined we may be in such a case to act as if the opinion
were knowledge, our expression of it shows that we do not confound it
with knowledge, and hence follows what has been said about the distinction of judgment which is decision from opinion. There is here a certain
simulation of an act of judging which, however, ought not to mislead us.
For, though I am not sure that A is B (and therefore, though inclined to it
as probable, I have not *decided*), I may decide to *act* as if A were B. I may
have to make up my mind between two alternative courses of action and,
knowing neither, I may choose all A is B as the more probable and the one
therefore that I shall act upon (although probability is not the sole ground
of such decision). There is then a mental decision, which may be said to
be in favor of all A is B, a practical decision, getting it is true greater definiteness by the fact that we act upon it, but not the judgment (or decision) *that* A *is* B.

However, we find in ordinary language another term, belief, akin to
opinion, yet distinguished from it, so that sometimes a man would actually
prefer the term belief to opinion. When this is done it would be felt that
the uncertainty which seems to be associated with opinion has caused us to
avoid that word. This again implies some (say) "superior" certainty about
belief. This fact we cannot afford to neglect. Such distinctions in language
are never unimportant. In the first place we observe that the tendency
would be to use the term "superior" certainty and to avoid "absolute" certainty; and then we at once reflect that in certainty there are no degrees
and that certainty therefore is not the right word. Yet we feel that there *is*
something, when we compare belief and opinion, which does somehow
vary in degree and we naturally ask what this is. In the case of a given belief, for example, that A is B, as long as we hesitate to call it knowledge, or
at least betray ourselves by using the word belief and avoiding the word

knowledge, we cannot really have decided that A is B unless, on reflection, we can say we *know* A is B. That is why judgment does not seem a proper designation for this attitude of ours. There is a clear decision in our resolution to "act on our belief," i.e., to behave as if A were B, taking some practical resolution in consequence. But this decision in the case of belief is not the whole matter, for such a decision may also be made in the case of an opinion. Again, in a practical decision there are no degrees. We decide to act on a belief or we do not. Nevertheless, comparing the practical decisions with one another, we observe a difference. In the case of a given opinion, we should risk treating it as if true for certain purposes; for others we should not, because the consequences would be too serious for us if we were wrong. In general, on a belief we risk more than on an opinion. Thus, though there are no degrees in decision, we observe a difference of degree in the importance of the decisions; but what is behind that? Now it may truly be said that the more evidence there is in favor of A's being B, the more we incline to risk on it. But this is not yet the complete account. In a given case (not in all cases) of belief, we should have a real judgment, a true intellectual decision, that there was so much evidence for A's being B; also, a real decision, but a practical one, to behave as if it were true in a certain practical issue; yet we refrain from certain other practical decisions which we should certainly make if we *knew* that A was B.

Now, this obviously cannot be explained by saying that the evidence is enough to justify us in the one case in taking A is B as true, but not in another case and in other circumstances. The evidence is the same both times and cannot change its strength in consequence of the difference between the practical issues. As evidence, if it justifies taking the thing to be true once, it justifies it always. We cannot really account for the facts unless we take note of that subjective feeling, already indicated by the word inclination, in what has been said of opinion. Corresponding to these different degrees of practical importance in our decisions in the case of different opinions and beliefs, there is a varying degree of feeling of confidence. This is *sui generis*; and we have really been getting at the recognition of its true positive nature by distinguishing it from that with which it might be confounded. Such confidence is not an attitude that we take toward knowledge. It is a matter of knowledge that the angles at the base of an isosceles triangle are equal. We constantly apply it in practice, yet we should never say that one who did so acted with "great confidence in the truth" of this proposition. To a high degree of such confidence, where it naturally exists, is attached the word belief, and language here, as not infrequently, is true to distinctions which have value in our consciousness. It is not opinion, it is not knowledge, it is not properly even judgment.

To sum up then, we have a true judgment or intellectual decision that there is evidence in favor of A being B. We have further a certain degree of the feeling of confidence (an ultimate and irreducible feeling) about A's being B, depending upon our estimate of the evidence and *frequently influenced by our wishes or fears.* In consequence of this, we risk a decision, not intellectual, but practical, by resolving to act in a certain case as if A were B.

3. Two remarks may here be made, one on the nature of this practical decision, the other on the inclination, or feeling of confidence, which accompanies opinion and belief.

The decision in question is always practical, a decision of the will; but it by no means follows that it has no theoretical application. In the case of a scientific investigation it frequently happens that the investigator has to choose between two opinions, to choose which of them he shall treat as if it were true, so as to embody it in his theory and make deductions from it, there being sufficient evidence for neither. The decision then, though practical, is made in the interests of a theory and the consequences of it may be purely theoretical.

The feeling of confidence which accompanies opinion and belief depends partly, at least, on what we call "the strength of the evidence," and is stronger if the evidence seems stronger. This idea of strength involves an illusion. It is only of evidence which is *not* sufficient that we use the word "strong" at all. In knowing, we can have nothing to do with the so-called *greater strength* of the evidence in question. The reason is we know that this strongest evidence in favor of an hypothesis, provided we can call it only strongest, is compatible with the falsity of the hypothesis, and so our confidence may be futile. However strong evidence may be, it is not anything which can influence reality; yet, in this feeling of *increased confidence* with increased strength of evidence, we are *unconsciously treating it as if it could.* The strength of evidence is merely something for us; indeed we never speak of the strength of evidence except where we suppose that it doesn't prove what is stated, that is when the evidence is *not* sufficient. The increase in it is only an increase in our knowledge, yet we tend to confuse this advance of ours, our greater hold on the facts as we may call it, with some objective force gaining a greater hold on the objective facts. We know, that is, that the existence of the facts which constitute the evidence is not something physically stronger which overpowers the set of facts constituting the weaker evidence on the other side, and so necessitating A's being B; yet, in opinion and belief, we at least *behave* as if this were so and that, although the strongest cases of circumstantial evidence get refuted by the facts. The illusion is almost irresistible and is the rule, not the exception, with the student of physical science and in any department where probable reasoning is found. This fallacy is often illustrated in the treatment of probability by its mathematical measure, and in argument from statistics.

The illusion is reflected in language and subserved thereby. Thus we say A is *probably* B, where the adverb which refers solely to our subjective inclination is made to qualify grammatically the verb of objective existence. In any case language does not clearly and transparently show the real truth of the matter or the fallacy would not be so universal.

4. By contrast with opinion and belief, both of which contain an element which is not clear thinking, we have hitherto confined the word judgment to true judgments.

This however is not usual, and the fact that false judgments are supposed to be possible leads to a further consideration about erroneous states of consciousness, the existence of which has to some extent been implied already.

The judgment that all A is B is a decision on evidence that A is B, and we must return to the nature of this decision. If we know that the evidence is insufficient, we cannot possibly decide or judge that A is B. What we really decide and judge about is the character of the evidence. Though we cannot decide on insufficient evidence, we may form an opinion, and this remains true so long as we have any doubt whatever about the sufficiency of the evidence. Whether, therefore, or not every judgment is a decision on sufficient evidence—and no evidence is sufficient which does not absolutely prove, whether in other words every judgment is necessarily true or not; this, at least, is clear that, in judgment proper, if a man "judges" A is B, he is himself sure that the evidence is sufficient.

But now, this being so, is it possible that in judgment proper the man who is sure that the evidence is conclusive should be mistaken? If so, we should have two kinds of judgment, the common element being that, in both, the person who judges A is B is sure that the evidence proves that A is B. In the case, then, of one sort of judgment, the man is right and his judgment would be an apprehension; in the other case he would be wrong and his judgment would not be an apprehension. This distinction is natural and accords with ordinary usage, and what we have said of opinion goes so far to confirm it. For, though we may say the opinion that A is B is an untrue opinion when A is not B, it is not accurate to say that the man who forms this untrue opinion is deceived or mistaken, since by hypothesis, in consciously forming an opinion, he does not judge that A is B. He is quite aware that the evidence does not prove A is B, however much it may incline him to suppose that A is B and to act on that assumption. It follows that what we suppose to be deception, and mistake proper, has not been provided for under opinion. So now if we assume, in the case of judgment, that, should the evidence be insufficient, a man must know it is so, and therefore decides only on sufficient evidence, there would be no place in judgment either for what seems to us mistake proper. There would then be no place for error proper, unless judgment could be false.

Nevertheless, this distinction of judgment into true and false is not so easy as it looks, and is indeed fraught with difficulties.

It is essential to suppose in false judgment, as above conceived, that the man should be sure that the evidence in favor of A is B is conclusive, for, if he were not sure, he would be aware that he was only forming an opinion. Suppose it possible that there should be such a mistake about evidence; what would be the ordinary way of describing the man's frame of mind? Probably, if people were thrown back on the ordinary categories, as they couldn't say it was knowledge they would call it opinion. But this is an entirely incorrect use of the word opinion, for it is certainly not opinion to the man, who does not regard himself as merely forming an opinion. We may say it has no more value than opinion, but it is wrong to say that it is an opinion of the man's. For opinion implies consciousness of the insufficiency of the evidence, whereas it is just the characteristic of the case before us that the man is sure the evidence *is* sufficient. It is only a form of this to say the man does not know but thinks that he knows. But again, in any distinction that can be made between thinking and knowing, this is not true of the man's own frame of mind. He certainly does not say to himself "I think I know," for that must mean he knows he does not know.

Since however the man in question doesn't know and is unaware that he doesn't know and further behaves as if he did know, we doubtless incline to say of him that he thinks or supposes or believes that he knows A is B. But now we have seen that the man's attitude of mind to his own process of decision is not *thinking* in any sense in which we oppose thinking to knowing. The fact is that, if we look first at what is decided, the man doesn't know that A is B, for *ex hypothesi* A is not B, nor does he "think" that A is B in the sense of forming an opinion, nor does he suppose that A is B, nor does he believe, strictly, that A is B. The man who decides that evidence proves that A is B doesn't himself "suppose" A is B—the word is quite alien to the attitude—and just the same is true of belief. Secondly, if we look at his attitude to his own mental process, not only does he not "think," "suppose," or "believe" that A is B, but also he does not think, suppose, or believe that he knows A is B; for these phrases are self-contradictory. To his consciousness, then, from neither point of view, can we apply these words "apprehension," "opinion," "supposition," or "belief."

Now this should cause us hesitation; though, perhaps, we may incline to think that the result is only that these categories—opinion, supposition, belief, and apprehension—do not apply to the man's consciousness and that it is both right and sufficient to say that he not only judges or decides on incomplete evidence, but decides that the incomplete evidence is proof; in fact to say that this is simply the nature of false judgment.

We find ourselves, however, faced by a new and serious difficulty. The man who makes the supposed kind of mistake decides that the evidence proves; and so he is in exactly the same frame of mind as when he decides that the evidence proves and it really does prove. His conviction would be of just the same kind to himself in both cases; both when he doesn't know and where his conclusion is true (which we might at first be inclined to call knowledge). If this were not so, the man would at once become aware of the difference, see that he had not found the evidence conclusive, and would then either form an opinion or look again at the evidence. His conviction then being of the same kind to himself when his conclusion was right and when it was wrong, he would be unable to distinguish the one mental state from the other; the confident state when right and the equally confident state when wrong. We might put this by saying that he has no criterion of truth or knowing. That however would be misleading because it would imply the fallacy that there could be a general criterion of knowledge by which we should know what was knowing and what was not.

Alternatively we might say that the man doesn't know whether he is knowing or not. However, the phrase "know that we know" may again mislead, because it rather tends to imply that we could conduct a process, for instance proving that A is B, and then decide otherwise that it was a knowing process. But the decision itself would be a knowing process and so we should get into an unending series of knowings. Moreover if we could so decide, in a new attitude of thought, about the given process, we should not decide that A is B until this second process and this second decision, namely the decision that the process of arriving at "A is B" was a knowing process, had taken place.

But in the first process, just because it is a knowing process (by hypothesis), we have already decided that A is B; indeed, it is by this process alone that we can so decide and not by any decision about the process itself. The consciousness that the knowing process is a knowing process must be contained within the knowing process itself.

A correct way to put the case before us seems to be that the two processes, the two states of mind in which the man conducts his arguments, the correct and the erroneous one, are quite indistinguishable to the man himself. But if this is so, as the man does not know in the erroneous state of mind, neither can he know in the other state.

The conclusion of the process is true in the latter case, but that does not make the supposed decision or judgment into knowledge. Thus, if the given case of false judgment were really possible, we should never be sure that any demonstration was true and therefore there would be no such thing as demonstrative knowledge.

5. The result then appears to be this. Judgment being decision on evidence after deliberation, there seem to be two alternatives. First, either it is seen that the evidence is insufficient and then it is not decided or judged that A is B, and so at most there results the opinion that A is B, not the judgment that A is B, and the man is not deceived even if the opinion is untrue, inasmuch as he knows that it is not a certainty. Or else, it is not seen that the evidence is insufficient and the man decides on evidence which does not prove. In this case he is entirely mistaken, and this would be false judgment. But this assumption of false judgment leads to the impossibility of any demonstrative reasoning, that is, of any reasoning which would be knowledge in any proper sense.

Hence we are led to a second alternative, that in what concerns reasoning the only kind of mistake is the mistaken opinion, which is not mistaken reasoning, and that in reasoning itself there can be no mistake. This is the same as saying that there is no such thing as false judgment. But this seems to leave no place for the most important kind of error: for it seems obvious that a man may be wholly mistaken and, the evidence being insufficient, may say, if asked, that he knows A is B, and has not merely an opinion that A is B. Thus he at least appears to judge and decide that A is B on insufficient evidence.

The objections to both alternatives seem valid. On the hypothesis that there can be false judgment we could never be sure that any "demonstration" was knowledge. Yet we are sure there is such, and so somehow false judgment is not possible. On the other hand, there are cases of deception, in the full sense, and error is not confined to false opinion (in the proper sense of opinion). We conclude, therefore, that the analysis is imperfect, that there is real error other than false opinion, and that it does not lie in false judgment, taking judgment in its strict and proper sense.

The complete answer must be deferred to the discussion of inference; but the distinction on which the solution turns will be made clear by a discussion of states of consciousness which simulate judgment and which cannot be described in terms either of judgment, belief, or opinion.

THE ETHICS OF BELIEF

William Kingdon Clifford (1845–1879)

A shipowner was about to send to sea an emigrant ship. He knew that she was old, and not over-well built at the first; that she had seen many seas and climes, and often had needed repairs. Doubts had been suggested to him that possibly she was not seaworthy. These doubts preyed upon his mind and made him unhappy; he thought that perhaps he ought to have her thoroughly overhauled and refitted, even though this should put him to great expense. Before the ship sailed, however, he succeeded in overcoming these melancholy reflections. He said to himself that she had gone safely through so many voyages and weathered so many storms that it was idle to suppose she would not come safely home from this trip also. He would put his trust in Providence, which could hardly fail to protect all these unhappy families that were leaving their fatherland to seek for better times elsewhere. He would dismiss from his mind all ungenerous suspicions about the honesty of builders and contractors. In such ways he acquired a sincere and comfortable conviction that his vessel was thoroughly safe and seaworthy; he watched her departure with a light heart, and benevolent wishes for the success of the exiles in their strange new home that was to be; and he got his insurance money when she went down in midocean and told no tales.

What shall we say of him? Surely this, that he was verily guilty of the death of those men. It is admitted that he did sincerely believe in the soundness of his ship; but the sincerity of his conviction can in no wise help him, because *he had no right to believe on such evidence as was before him.* He had acquired his belief not by honestly earning it in patient investigation, but by stifling his doubts. And although in the end he may have felt so sure about it that he could not think otherwise, yet inasmuch

The first part of a three-part essay which appeared originally in the *Contemporary Review,* January 1877, and was reprinted in Clifford's posthumous *Lectures and Essays,* 1879.

as he had knowingly and willingly worked himself into that frame of mind, he must be held responsible for it.

Let us alter the case a little, and suppose that the ship was not unsound after all; that she made her voyage safely, and many others after it. Will that diminish the guilt of her owner? Not one jot. When an action is once done, it is right or wrong forever; no accidental failure of its good or evil fruits can possibly alter that. The man would not have been innocent, he would only have been not found out. The question of right or wrong has to do with the origin of his belief, not the matter of it; not what it was, but how he got it; not whether it turned out to be true or false, but whether he had a right to believe on such evidence as was before him.

There was once an island in which some of the inhabitants professed a religion teaching neither the doctrine of original sin nor that of eternal punishment. A suspicion got abroad that the professors of this religion had made use of unfair means to get their doctrines taught to children. They were accused of wresting the laws of their country in such a way as to remove children from the care of their natural and legal guardians; and even of stealing them away and keeping them concealed from their friends and relations. A certain number of men formed themselves into a society for the purpose of agitating the public about this matter. They published grave accusations against individual citizens of the highest position and character, and did all in their power to injure those citizens in the exercise of their professions. So great was the noise they made, that a Commission was appointed to investigate the facts; but after the Commission had carefully inquired into all the evidence that could be got, it appeared that the accused were innocent. Not only had they been accused on insufficient evidence, but the evidence of their innocence was such as the agitators might easily have obtained, if they had attempted a fair inquiry. After these disclosures the inhabitants of that country looked upon the members of the agitating society, not only as persons whose judgment was to be distrusted, but also as no longer to be counted honorable men. For although they had sincerely and conscientiously believed in the charges they had made, yet *they had no right to believe on such evidence as was before them.* Their sincere convictions, instead of being honestly earned by patient inquiring, were stolen by listening to the voice of prejudice and passion.

Let us vary this case also, and suppose, other things remaining as before, that a still more accurate investigation proved the accused to have been really guilty. Would this make any difference in the guilt of the accusers? Clearly not; the question is not whether their belief was true or false, but whether they entertained it on wrong grounds. They would no doubt say, "Now you see that we were right after all; next time perhaps you will believe us." And they might be believed, but they would not thereby become honorable men. They would not be innocent, they would only be not found out. Every one of them, if he chose to examine himself *in foro conscientiae*, would know that he had acquired and nourished a belief, when he had no right to believe on such evidence as was before him; and therein he would know that he had done a wrong thing.

It may be said, however, that in both of these supposed cases it is not the belief which is judged to be wrong, but the action following upon it. The shipowner might say, "I am perfectly certain that my ship is sound, but still I feel it my duty to have her examined, before trusting the lives of so many people to her." And it might be said to the agitator, "However convinced you were of the justice of your cause and the truth of your convictions, you ought not to have made a public attack upon any man's character until you had examined the evidence on both sides with the utmost patience and care."

In the first place, let us admit that, so far as it goes, this view of the case is right and necessary; right, because even when a man's belief is so fixed that he cannot think otherwise, he still has a choice in regard to the action suggested by it, and so cannot escape the duty of investigating on the ground of the strength of his convictions; and necessary, because those who are not yet capable of controlling their feelings and thoughts must have a plain rule dealing with overt acts.

But this being premised as necessary, it becomes clear that it is not sufficient, and that our previous judgment is required to supplement it. For it is not possible so to sever the belief from the action it suggests as to condemn the one without condemning the other. No man holding a strong belief on one side of a question, or even wishing to hold a belief on one side, can investigate it with such fairness and completeness as if he were really in doubt and unbiassed; so that the existence of a belief not founded on fair inquiry unfits a man for the performance of this necessary duty.

Nor is that truly a belief at all which has not some influence upon the actions of him who holds it. He who truly believes that which prompts him to an action has looked upon the action to lust after it, he has committed it already in his heart. If a belief is not realized immediately in open deeds, it is stored up for the guidance of the future. It goes to make a part of that aggregate of beliefs which is the link between sensation and action at every moment of all our lives, and which is so organized and compacted together that no part of it can be isolated from the rest, but every new addition modifies the structure of the whole. No real belief, however trifling and fragmentary it may seem, is ever truly insignificant; it prepares us to receive more of its like, confirms those which resembled it before, and weakens others; and so gradually it lays a stealthy train in our inmost thoughts, which may some day explode into overt action, and leave its stamp upon our character forever.

And no one man's belief is in any case a private matter which concerns himself alone. Our lives are guided by that general conception of the course of things which has been created by society for social purposes. Our words, our phrases, our forms and processes and modes of thought, are common property, fashioned and perfected from age to age; an heirloom which every succeeding generation inherits as a precious deposit and a sacred trust to be handed on to the next one, not unchanged but enlarged and purified, with some clear marks of its proper handiwork. Into this, for good or ill, is woven every belief of every man who has speech of his fellows. An awful privilege, and an awful responsibility, that we should help to create the world in which posterity will live.

In the two supposed cases which have been considered, it has been judged wrong to believe on insufficient evidence, or to nourish belief by suppressing doubts and avoiding investigation. The reason of this judgment is not far to seek: it is that in both these cases the belief held by one man was of great importance to other men. But for as much as no belief held by one man, however seemingly trivial the belief, and however obscure the believer, is ever actually insignificant or without its effect on the fate of mankind, we have no choice but to extend our judgment to all cases of belief whatever. Belief, that sacred faculty which prompts the decisions of our will, and knits into harmonious working all the compacted energies of our being, is ours not for ourselves, but for humanity. It is rightly used on truths which have been established by long experience and waiting toil, and which have stood in the fierce light of free and fearless questioning. Then it helps to bind men together, and to strengthen and direct their common action. It is desecrated when given to unproved and unquestioned statements, for the solace and private pleasure of the believer; to add a tinsel splendor to the plain straight road of our life and display a bright mirage beyond it; or even to drown the common sorrows of our kind by a self-deception which allows them not only to cast down, but also to degrade us. Whoso would deserve well of his fellows in this matter will guard the purity of his belief with a very fanaticism of jealous care, lest at any time it should rest on an unworthy object, and catch a stain which can never be wiped away.

It is not only the leader of men, statesman, philosopher, or poet, that owes this bounden duty to mankind. Every rustic who delivers in the village alehouse his slow, infrequent sentences, may help to kill or keep alive the fatal superstitions which clog his race. Every hard-worked wife of an artisan may transmit to her children beliefs which shall knit society together, or rend it in pieces. No simplicity of mind, no obscurity of station, can escape the universal duty of questioning all that we believe.

It is true that this duty is a hard one, and the doubt which comes out of it is often a very bitter thing. It leaves us bare and powerless where we thought that we were safe and strong. To know all about anything is to know how to deal with it under all circumstances. We feel much happier and more secure when we think we know precisely what to do, no matter what happens, than when we have lost our way and do not know where to turn. And if we have supposed ourselves to know all about anything, and to be capable of doing what is fit in regard to it, we naturally do not like to find that we are really ignorant and powerless, that we have to begin again at the beginning, and try to learn what the thing is and how it is to be dealt with—if indeed anything can be learned about it. It is the sense of power attached to a sense of knowledge that makes men desirous of believing, and afraid of doubting.

This sense of power is the highest and best of pleasures when the belief on which it is founded is a true belief, and has been fairly earned by investigation. For then we may justly feel that it is common property, and holds good for others as well as for ourselves. Then we may be glad, not that I have learned secrets by which I am safer and stronger, but that we men have got mastery over more of the world; and we shall be strong, not for ourselves, but in the name of Man and in his strength. But if the belief has been accepted on insufficient evidence, the pleasure is a stolen one. Not only does it deceive ourselves by giving us a sense of power which we do not really possess, but it is sinful, because it is stolen in defiance of our duty to mankind. That duty is to guard ourselves from such beliefs as from a pestilence, which may shortly master our own body and then spread to the rest of the town. What would be thought of one who, for the sake of a sweet fruit, should deliberately run the risk of bringing a plague upon his family and his neighbors?

And, as in other such cases, it is not the risk only which has to be considered; for a bad action is always bad at the time when it is done, no matter what happens afterwards. Every time we let ourselves believe for unworthy reasons, we weaken our powers of self-control, of doubting, of judicially and fairly weighing evidence. We all suffer severely enough from the maintenance and support of false beliefs and the fatally wrong actions which they lead to, and the evil born when one such belief is entertained is great and wide. But a greater and wider evil arises when the credulous character is maintained and supported, when a habit of believing for unworthy reasons is fostered and made permanent. If I steal money from any person, there may be no harm done by the mere transfer of possession; he may not feel the loss, or it may prevent him from using the money badly. But I cannot help doing this great wrong towards Man, that I make myself dishonest. What hurts society is not that it should lose its property, but that it should become a den of thieves; for then it must cease to be society. This is why we ought not to do evil that good may come; for at any rate this great evil has come, that we have done evil and are made wicked thereby. In like manner, if I let myself believe anything on insufficient evidence, there may be no great harm done by the mere belief; it may be true after all, or I may never have occasion to exhibit it in outward acts. But I cannot help doing this great wrong toward Man, that I make myself credulous. The danger to society is not merely that it should believe wrong things, though that is great enough; but that it should become credulous, and lose the habit of testing things and inquiring into them; for then it must sink back into savagery.

The harm which is done by credulity in a man is not confined to the fostering of a credulous character in others, and consequent support of false beliefs. Habitual want of care about what I believe leads to habitual want of care in others about the truth of what is told to me. Men speak the truth to one another when each reveres the truth in his own mind and in the other's mind; but how shall my friend revere the truth in my mind when I myself am careless about it, when I believe things because I want to believe them, and because they are comforting and pleasant? Will he not learn to cry, "Peace," to me, when there is no peace? By such a course I shall surround myself with a thick atmosphere of falsehood and fraud, and in that I must live. It may matter little to me, in my cloud-castle of sweet illusions and darling lies; but it matters much to Man that I have made my neighbors ready to deceive. The credulous man is father to the liar and the cheat; he lives in the bosom of this his family, and it is no marvel if he should become even as they are. So closely are our duties knit together, that whoso shall keep the whole law, and yet offend in one point, he is guilty of all.

To sum up: it is wrong always, everywhere, and for anyone, to believe anything upon insufficient evidence.

If a man, holding a belief which he was taught in childhood or persuaded of afterwards, keeps down and pushes away any doubts which arise about it in his mind, purposely avoids the reading of books and the company of men that call in question or discuss it, and regards as impious those questions which cannot easily be asked without disturbing it—the life of that man is one long sin against mankind.

If this judgment seems harsh when applied to those simple souls who have never known better, who have been brought up from the cradle with a horror of doubt, and taught that their eternal welfare depends on what they believe, then it leads to the very serious question, Who hath made Israel to sin? . . .

Inquiry into the evidence of a doctrine is not to be made once for all, and then taken as finally settled. It is never lawful to stifle a doubt; for either it can be honestly answered by means of the inquiry already made, or else it proves that the inquiry was not complete.

"But," says one, "I am a busy man; I have no time for the long course of study which would be necessary to make me in any degree a competent judge of certain questions, or even able to understand the nature of the arguments." Then he should have no time to believe. . . .

❖ 9 ❖

THE WILL TO BELIEVE

William James (1842–1910)

1. . . . Let us give the name of *hypothesis* to anything that may be proposed to our belief; and just as the electricians speak of live and dead wires, let us speak of any hypothesis as either *live* or *dead*. A live hypothesis is one which appeals as a real possibility to him to whom it is proposed. If I ask you to believe in the Mahdi, the notion makes no electric connection with your nature—it refuses to scintillate with any credibility at all. As a hypothesis it is completely dead. To an Arab, however (even if he be not one of the Mahdi's followers), the hypothesis is among the mind's possibilities: it is alive. This shows that deadness and liveness in a hypothesis are not intrinsic properties, but relations to the individual thinker. They are measured by his willingness to act. The maximum of liveness in an hypothesis means willingness to act irrevocably. Practically, that means belief; but there is some believing tendency wherever there is willingness to act at all.

Next, let us call the decision between two hypotheses an *option*. Options may be of several kinds. They may be—first, *living* or *dead*; secondly,

From *The Will to Believe and Other Essays* (1897).

forced or *avoidable*; thirdly, *momentous* or *trivial*; and for our purposes we may call an option a *genuine* option when it is of the forced, living, and momentous kind.

(1) A living option is one in which both hypotheses are live ones. If I say to you: "Be a theosophist or be a Mohammedan," it is probably a dead option, because for you neither hypothesis is likely to be alive. But if I say: "Be an agnostic or be a Christian," it is otherwise: trained as you are, each hypothesis makes some appeal, however small, to your belief.

(2) Next, if I say to you: "Choose between going out with your umbrella or without it," I do not offer you a genuine option, for it is not forced. You can easily avoid it by not going out at all. Similarly, if I say, "Either love me or hate me," "Either call my theory true or call it false," your option is avoidable. You may remain indifferent to me, neither loving nor hating, and you may decline to offer any judgment as to my theory. But if I say, "Either accept this truth or go without it," I put on you a forced option, for there is no standing place outside of the alternative. Every dilemma based on a complete logical disjunction, with no possibility of not choosing, is an option of this forced kind.

(3) Finally, if I were Dr. Nansen and proposed to you to join my North Pole expedition, your option would be momentous; for this would probably be your only similar opportunity, and your choice now would either exclude you from the North Pole sort of immortality altogether or put at least the chance of it into your hands. He who refuses to embrace a unique opportunity loses the prize as surely as if he tried and failed. *Per contra*, the option is trivial when the opportunity is not unique, when the stake is insignificant, or when the decision is reversible if it later prove unwise. Such trivial options abound in the scientific life. A chemist finds a hypothesis live enough to spend a year in its verification: he believes in it to that extent. But if his experiments prove inconclusive either way, he is quit for his loss of time, no vital harm being done. It will facilitate our discussion if we keep all these distinctions in mind. . . .

2. . . . The thesis I defend is . . . this: *Our passional nature not only lawfully may, but must, decide an option between propositions, whenever it is a genuine option that cannot by its nature be decided on intellectual grounds; for to say, under such circumstances, "Do not decide, but leave the question open," is itself a passional decision—just like deciding yes or no—and is attended with the same risk of losing the truth.* . . .

3. . . . Wherever the option between losing truth and gaining it is not momentous, we can throw the chance of *gaining truth* away, and at any rate save ourselves from any chance of *believing falsehood*, by not making up our minds at all till objective evidence has come. In scientific ques-

tions, this is almost always the case; and even in human affairs in general, the need of acting is seldom so urgent that a false belief to act on is better than no belief at all. Law courts, indeed, have to decide on the best evidence attainable for the moment, because a judge's duty is to make law as well as to ascertain it, and (as a learned judge once said to me) few cases are worth spending much time over: the great thing is to have them decided on *any* acceptable principle, and got out of the way. But in our dealings with objective nature we obviously are recorders, not makers, of the truth; and decisions for the mere sake of deciding promptly and getting on to the next business would be wholly out of place. Throughout the breadth of physical nature facts are what they are quite independently of us, and seldom is there any such hurry about them that the risks of being duped by believing a premature theory need be faced. The questions here are always trivial options, the hypotheses are hardly living (at any rate not living for us spectators), the choice between believing truth or falsehood is seldom forced. The attitude of skeptical balance is therefore the absolutely wise one if we would escape mistakes. What difference, indeed, does it make to most of us whether we have or have not a theory of Röntgen rays, whether we believe or not in mind-stuff, or have a conviction about the causality of conscious states? It makes no difference. Such options are not forced on us. On every account it is better not to make them, but still keep weighing reasons *pro et contra* with an indifferent hand.

I speak, of course, here of the purely judging mind. For purposes of discovery such indifference is to be less highly recommended, and science would be far less advanced than she is if the passionate desires of individuals to get their own faiths confirmed had been kept out of the game. . . . On the other hand, if you want an absolute duffer in an investigation, you must, after all, take the man who has no interest whatever in its results: he is the warranted incapable, the positive fool. The most useful investigator, because the most sensitive observer, is always he whose eager interest in one side of the question is balanced by an equally keen nervousness lest he become deceived. Science has organized this nervousness into a regular *technique*, her so-called method of verification; and she has fallen so deeply in love with the method that one may even say she has ceased to care for truth by itself at all. It is only truth as technically verified that interests her. The truth of truths might come in merely affirmative form, and she would decline to touch it. Such truth as that, she might repeat with Clifford, would be stolen in defiance of her duty to mankind. Human passions, however, are stronger than technical rules. "*Le coeur a ses raisons*," as Pascal says, "*que la raison ne connait pas*"; and however indifferent to all but the bare rules of the game the umpire, the abstract intellect, may be, the concrete players who furnish him the materials to judge of are usually, each one of them, in love with some pet "live hypothesis" of his own. Let us agree, however, that wherever there is no forced option, the dispassionately judicial intellect with no pet hypothesis, saving us, as it does, from dupery at any rate, ought to be our ideal.

The question next arises: Are there not somewhere forced options in our speculative questions, and can we (as men who may be interested at least as much in positively gaining truth as in merely escaping dupery) always wait with impunity till the coercive evidence shall have arrived? It seems *a priori* improbable that the truth should be so nicely adjusted to our needs and powers as that. In the great boarding-house of nature, the cakes and the butter and the syrup seldom come out so even and leave the plates so clean. Indeed, we should view them with scientific suspicion if they did.

4. *Moral questions* immediately present themselves as questions whose solution cannot wait for sensible proof. A moral question is a question not of what sensibly exists, but of what is good, or would be good if it did exist. Science can tell us what exists; but to compare the *worths*, both of what exists and of what does not exist, we must consult not science, but what Pascal calls our heart. Science herself consults her heart when she lays it down that the infinite ascertainment of fact and correction of false belief are the supreme goods for man. Challenge the statement, and science can only repeat it oracularly, or else prove it by showing that such ascertainment and correction bring men all sorts of other goods which man's heart in turn declares. The question of having moral beliefs at all or not having them is decided by our will. Are our moral preferences true or false, or are they only odd biological phenomena, making things good or bad for *us*, but in themselves indifferent? How can your pure intellect decide? If your heart does not *want* a world of moral reality, your head will assuredly never make you believe in one. Mephistophelian skepticism, indeed, will satisfy the head's play-instincts much better than any rigorous idealism can. Some men (even at the student age) are so naturally cool-hearted that the moralistic hypothesis never has for them any pungent life, and in their supercilious presence the hot young moralist always feels strangely ill at ease. The appearance of knowingness is on their side, of *naivete* and gullibility on his. Yet, in the articulate heart of him, he clings to it that he is not a dupe, and that there is a realm in which (as Emerson says) all their wit and intellectual superiority is no better than the cunning of a fox. Moral skepticism can no more be refuted or proved by logic than intellectual skepticism can. When we stick to it that there *is* truth (be it of either kind), we do so with our whole nature, and resolve to stand or fall by the results. The skep-

tic with his whole nature adopts the doubting attitude; but which of us is the wiser, Omniscience only knows.

Turn now from these wide questions of good to a certain class of questions of fact, questions concerning personal relations, states of mind between one man and another. *Do you like me or not?*—for example. Whether you do or not depends, in countless instances, on whether I meet you halfway, am willing to assume that you must like me, and show you trust and expectation. The previous faith on my part in your liking's existence is in such cases what makes your liking come. But if I stand aloof, and refuse to budge an inch until I have objective evidence . . . ten to one your liking never comes. How many women's hearts are vanquished by the mere sanguine insistence of some man that they *must* love him! He will not consent to the hypothesis that they cannot. The desire for a certain kind of truth here brings about that special truth's existence; and so it is in innumerable cases of other sorts. Who gains promotions, boons, appointments, but the man in whose life they are seen to play the part of live hypotheses, who discounts them, sacrifices other things for their sake before they have come, and takes risks for them in advance? His faith acts on the powers above him as a claim, and creates its own verification.

A social organism of any sort whatever, large or small, is what it is because each member proceeds to his own duty with a trust that the other members will simultaneously do theirs. Wherever a desired result is achieved by the cooperation of many independent persons, its existence as a fact is a pure consequence of the precursive faith in one another of those immediately concerned. A government, an army, a commercial system, a ship, a college, an athletic team, all exist on this condition, without which not only is nothing achieved, but nothing is even attempted. A whole train of passengers (individually brave enough) will be looted by a few highwaymen, simply because the latter can count on one another, while each passenger fears that if he makes a movement of resistance, he will be shot before any one else backs him up. If we believed that the whole car-full would rise at once with us, we should each severally rise, and train-robbing would never even be attempted. There are, then, cases where a fact cannot come at all unless a preliminary faith exists in its coming. *And where faith in a fact can help create the fact,* that would be an insane logic which should say that faith running ahead of scientific evidence is the "lowest kind of immorality" into which a thinking being can fall. Yet such is the logic by which our scientific absolutists pretend to regulate our lives!

5. In truths dependent on our personal action, then, faith based on desire is certainly a lawful and possibly an indispensable thing.

But now, it will be said, these are all childish human cases, and have nothing to do with great cosmical matters, like the question of religious faith. Let us then pass on to that. Religions differ so much in their accidents that in discussing the religious question we must make it very generic and broad. What then do we now mean by the religious hypothesis? Science says things are; morality says some things are better than other things; and religion says essentially two things.

First, she says that the best things are the more eternal things, the overlapping things, the things in the universe that throw the last stone, so to speak, and say the final word. "Perfection is eternal"—this phrase of Charles Secretan seems a good way of putting this first affirmation of religion, an affirmation which obviously cannot yet be verified scientifically at all.

The second affirmation of religion is that we are better off even now if we believe her first affirmation to be true.

Now, let us consider what the logical elements of this situation are *in case the religious hypothesis in both its branches be really true.* (Of course, we must admit that possibility at the outset. If we are to discuss the question at all, it must involve a living option. If for any of you religion be a hypothesis that cannot, by any living possibility, be true, then you need go no farther. I speak to the "saving remnant" alone.) So proceeding, we see, first, that religion offers itself as a *momentous* option. We are supposed to gain, even now, by our belief, and to lose by our non-belief, a certain vital good. Secondly, religion is a *forced* option, so far as that good goes. We cannot escape the issue by remaining skeptical and waiting for more light, because, although we do avoid error in that way *if religion be untrue,* we lose the good, *if it be true,* just as certainly as if we positively chose to disbelieve. It is as if a man should hesitate indefinitely to ask a certain woman to marry him because he was not perfectly sure that she would prove an angel after he brought her home. Would he not cut himself off from that particular angel-possibility as decisively as if he went and married someone else? Skepticism, then, is not avoidance of option; it is option of a certain particular kind of risk. *Better risk loss of truth than chance of error*—that is your faith-vetoer's exact position. He is actively playing his stake as much as the believer is; he is backing the field against the religious hypothesis, just as the believer is backing the religious hypothesis against the field. To preach skepticism to us as a duty until "sufficient evidence" for religion be found, is tantamount therefore to telling us, when in presence of the religious hypothesis, that to yield to our fear of its being error is wiser and better than to yield to our hope that it may be true. It is not intellect against all passions, then; it is only intellect with one passion laying down its law. And by what, forsooth, is the supreme wisdom of this passion warranted? Dupery for dupery, what proof is there that dupery through hope is so much worse than dupery through fear? I, for one, can see no proof; and I simply refuse obedience to the scientist's command to imitate his kind of option, in a case where my own stake is important enough to give me the right to choose my own form of risk. If religion be true and the evidence for it be still insufficient, I do not wish, by putting your extinguisher upon my nature (which feels to me as if it had after all some business in this matter), to forfeit my sole chance in life of getting upon the winning side—that chance depending, of course, on my willingness to run the risk of acting as if my passional need of taking the world religiously might be prophetic and right.

All this is on the supposition that it really may be prophetic and right, and that, even to us who are discussing the matter, religion is a live hypothesis which may be true. Now, to most of us religion comes in a still further way that makes a veto on our active faith even more illogical. The more perfect and more eternal aspect of the universe is represented in our religions as having personal form. The universe is no longer a mere *It* to us, but a *Thou*, if we are religious; and any relation that may be possible from person to person might be possible here. For instance, although in one sense we are passive portions of the universe, in another we show a curious autonomy, as if we were small active centers on our own account. We feel, too, as if the appeal of religion to us were made to our own active goodwill, as if evidence might be forever withheld from us unless we met the hypothesis halfway. To take a trivial illustration: just as a man who in a company of gentlemen made no advances, asked a warrant for every concession, and believed no one's word without proof, would cut himself off by such churlishness from all the social rewards that a more trusting spirit would earn—so here, one who should shut himself up in snarling logicality and try to make the gods extort his recognition willy-nilly, or not get it at all, might cut himself off forever from his only opportunity of making the gods' acquaintance. This feeling, forced on us we know not whence, that by obstinately believing that there are gods (although not to do so would be so easy both for our logic and our life) we are doing the universe the deepest service we can, seems part of the living essence of the religious hypothesis. If the hypothesis *were* true in all its parts, including this one, then pure intellectualism, with its veto on our making willing advances, would be an absurdity; and some participation of our sympathetic nature would be logically required. I, therefore, for one, cannot see my way to accepting the agnostic rules for truth-seeking, or wilfully agree to keep my willing nature out of the game. I cannot do so for this plain reason, that *a rule of thinking which would absolutely prevent me from acknowledging certain kinds of truth if those kinds of truth were really there, would be an irrational rule.* That for me is the long and short of the formal logic of the situation, no matter what the kinds of truth might materially be.

I confess I do not see how this logic can be escaped. But sad experience makes me fear that some of you may still shrink from radically saying with me, *in abstracto*, that we have the right to believe at our own risk any hypothesis that is live enough to tempt our will. I suspect, however, that if this is so, it is because you have got away from the abstract logical point of view altogether, and are thinking (perhaps without realizing it) of some particular religious hypothesis which for you is dead. The freedom to "believe what we will" you apply to the case of some patent superstition; and the faith you think of is the faith defined by the schoolboy when he said, "Faith is when you believe something that you know ain't true." I can only repeat that this is misapprehension. *In concreto*, the freedom to believe can only cover living options which the intellect of the individual cannot by itself resolve; and living options never seem absurdities to him who has them to consider. When I look at the religious question as it really puts itself to concrete men, and when I think of all the possibilities which both practically and theoretically it involves, then this command that we shall put a stopper on our heart, instincts, and courage, and *wait*—acting of course meanwhile more or less as if religion were *not* true—till doomsday, or till such time as our intellect and senses working together may have raked in evidence enough—this command, I say, seems to me the queerest idol ever manufactured in the philosophic cave. Were we scholastic absolutists, there might be more excuse. If we had infallible intellect with its objective certitudes, we might feel ourselves disloyal to such a perfect organ of knowledge in not trusting to it exclusively, in not waiting for its releasing word. But if we are empiricists, if we believe that no bell in us tolls to let us know for certain when truth is in our grasp, then it seems a piece of idle fantasticality to preach so solemnly our duty of waiting for the bell. Indeed we *may* wait if we will—I hope you do not think that I am denying that—but if we do so, we do so at our peril as much as if we believed. In either case we *act*, taking our life in our hands. No one of us ought to issue vetoes to the other, nor should we bandy words of abuse. We ought, on the contrary, delicately and profoundly to respect one another's mental freedom: then only shall we bring about the intellectual republic; then only shall we have that spirit of inner tolerance without which all our outer tolerance is soulless, and which is empiricism's glory; then only shall we live and let live, in speculative as well as in practical things. . . .

FAITH, BELIEF, AND ACTION

William James (1842–1910)

. . . There is one element of our active nature which . . . philosophers as a rule have with great insincerity tried to huddle out of sight in their pretension to found systems of absolute certainty. I mean the element of faith. Faith means belief in something concerning which doubt is still theoretically possible; and as the test of belief is willingness to act, one may say that faith is the readiness to act in a cause the prosperous issue of which is not certified to us in advance. It is in fact the same moral quality which we call courage in practical affairs. . . .

The necessity of faith as an ingredient in our mental attitude is strongly insisted on by the scientific philosophers of the present day; but by a singularly arbitrary caprice they say that it is only legitimate when used in the interests of one particular proposition—the proposition, namely that the course of nature is uniform. That nature will follow tomorrow the same laws that she follows today is, they all admit, a truth which no man can *know*; but in the interests of cognition as well as of action we must postulate or assume it. . . .

With regard to all other possible truths, however, a number of our most influential contemporaries think that an attitude of faith is not only illogical but shameful. Faith in a religious dogma for which there is no outward proof, but which we are tempted to postulate for our emotional interests, just as we postulate the uniformity of nature for our intellectual interests, is branded by Professor Huxley as "the lowest depth of immorality." Citations of this kind from leaders of the modern *Aufklärung* might be multiplied almost indefinitely. Take Professor Clifford's article on the "Ethics of Belief." He calls it "guilt" and "sin" to believe even the truth without "scientific evidence." But what is the use of being a genius, unless *with the same scientific evidence* as other men, one can reach more truth

Excerpted from "The Sentiment of Rationality," in *The Will to Believe* (1897). The title of this selection has been supplied by the editors.

than they? Why does Clifford fearlessly proclaim his belief in the conscious-automaton theory, although the "proofs" before him are the same which make Mr. Lewes reject it? . . . Simply because, like every human being of the slightest mental originality, he is peculiarly sensitive to evidence that bears in some one direction. It is utterly hopeless to try to exorcise such sensitiveness by calling it the disturbing subjective factor, and branding it as the root of all evil. . . . Pretend what we may, the whole man within us is at work when we form our philosophical opinions. Intellect, will, taste, and passion cooperate just as they do in practical affairs; and lucky it is if the passion be not something as petty as a love of personal conquest over the philosopher across the way. The absurd abstraction of an intellect verbally formulating all its evidence and carefully estimating the probability thereof by a vulgar fraction by the size of whose denominator and numerator alone it is swayed, is ideally as inept as it is actually impossible. It is almost incredible that men who are themselves working philosophers should pretend that any philosophy can be, or ever has been, constructed without the help of personal preference, belief, or divination. . . .

If I am born with such a superior general reaction to evidence that I can guess right and act accordingly, and gain all that comes of right action, while my less gifted neighbor (paralyzed by his scruples and waiting for more evidence which he dares not anticipate, much as he longs to) still stands shivering on the brink, by what law shall I be forbidden to reap the advantages of my superior native sensitiveness? Of course I yield to my belief in such a case as this or distrust it, alike at my peril, just as I do in any of the great practical decisions of life. If my inborn faculties are good, I am a prophet; if poor, I am a failure: nature spews me out of her mouth, and there is an end to me. In the total game of life we stake our persons all the while; and if in its theoretic part our persons will help us to a conclusion, surely we should also stake them here, however inarticulate they may be.

But in being myself so very articulate in proving what to all readers with a sense for reality will seem a platitude, am I not wasting words? We cannot live or think at all without some degree of faith. Faith is synonymous with working hypothesis. The only difference is that while some hypotheses can be refuted in five minutes, others may defy ages. A chemist who conjectures that a certain wallpaper contains arsenic, and has faith enough to lead him to take the trouble to put some of it into a hydrogen bottle, finds out by the results of his action whether he was right or wrong. But theories like that of Darwin, or that of the kinetic constitution of matter, may exhaust the labors of generations in their corroboration, each tester of their truth proceeding in this simple way—that he acts as if it were true, and expects the result to disappoint him if his assumption is false. The longer disappointment is delayed, the stronger grows his faith in his theory. . . .

Now, I wish to show what to my knowledge has never been clearly pointed out, that belief (as measured by action) not only does and must continually outstrip scientific evidence, but that there is a certain class of truths of whose reality belief is a factor as well as a confessor; and that as regards this class of truths faith is not only licit and pertinent, but essential and indispensable. The truths cannot become true till our faith has made them so.

Suppose, for example, that I am climbing in the Alps, and have had the ill-luck to work myself into a position from which the only escape is by a terrible leap. Being without similar experience, I have no evidence of my ability to perform it successfully; but hope and confidence in myself make me sure I shall not miss my aim, and nerve my feet to execute what without those subjective emotions would perhaps have been impossible. But suppose that, on the contrary, the emotions of fear and mistrust preponderate; or suppose that, having just read the *Ethics of Belief*, I feel it would be sinful to act upon an assumption unverified by previous experience—why, then I shall hesitate so long that at last, exhausted and trembling, and launching myself in a moment of despair, I miss my foothold and roll into the abyss. In this case (and it is one of an immense class) the part of wisdom clearly is to believe what one desires; for the belief is one of the indispensable preliminary conditions of the realization of its object. *There are then cases where faith creates its own verification.* Believe, and you shall be right, for you shall save yourself; doubt, and you shall again be right, for you shall perish. The only difference is that to believe is greatly to your advantage.

The future movements of the stars or the facts of past history are determined now once for all, whether I like them or not. They are given irrespective of my wishes, and in all that concerns truths like these subjective preference should have no part; it can only obscure the judgment. But in every fact into which there enters an element of personal contribution on my part, as soon as this personal contribution demands a certain degree of subjective energy which, in its turn, calls for a certain amount of faith in the result—so that, after all, the future fact is conditioned by my present faith in it—how trebly asinine would it be for me to deny myself the use of the subjective method, the method of belief based on desire! . . .

The highest good can be achieved only by our getting our proper life; and that can come about only by help of a moral energy born of the faith that in some way or other we shall succeed in getting it if we try pertinaciously enough. This world *is* good, we must say, since it is what we make it—and we shall make it good. How can we exclude from the cognition of a truth a faith which is involved in the creation of the truth? . . . All depends on the character of the personal contribution. . . . Wherever the facts to be formulated contain such a contribution, we may logically, legitimately, and inexpugnably believe what we desire. The belief creates its verification. The thought becomes literally father to the fact, as the wish was father to the thought. . . .

The essential thing to notice is that our active preference is a legitimate part of the game—that it is our plain business as men to try one of the keys, and the one in which we most confide. If then the proof exist not till I have acted, and I must needs in acting run the risk of being wrong, how can the popular science professors be right in objurgating in me as infamous a "credulity" which the strict logic of the situation requires? If this really be a moral universe; if by my acts I be a factor of its destinies; if to believe where I may doubt be itself a moral act analogous to voting for a side not yet sure to win—by what right shall they close in upon me and steadily negate the deepest conceivable function of my being by their preposterous command that I shall stir neither hand nor foot, but remain balancing myself in eternal and insoluble doubt? Why, doubt itself is a decision of the widest practical reach, if only because we may miss by doubting what goods we might be gaining by espousing the winning side. But more than that! It is often practically impossible to distinguish doubt from dogmatic negation. If I refuse to stop a murder because I am in doubt whether it be not justifiable homicide, I am virtually abetting the crime. If I refuse to bale out a boat because I am in doubt whether my efforts will keep her afloat, I am really helping to sink her. If in the mountain precipice I doubt my right to risk a leap, I actively connive at my destruction. He who commands himself not to be credulous of God, of duty, of freedom, of immortality, may again and again be indistinguishable from him who dogmatically denies them. Skepticism in moral matters is an active ally of immorality. Who is not for is against. The universe will have no neutrals in these questions. In theory as in practice, dodge or hedge, or talk as we like about a wise skepticism, we are really doing volunteer military service for one side or the other. . . .

BELIEF AND WILL

H. H. Price (1899–   )

There are various familiar expressions which suggest that believing has some characteristics in common with action. This has led certain philosophers to maintain that belief is something voluntary, and they have spoken of "the will to believe." Indeed, we all agree with these philosophers up to a point. We all agree that there is such a thing as "wishful thinking"; and the sort of thinking here referred to is believing, or at any rate half-believing. Again, when we are confronted by some doubtful and complex question, one person may sum up his conclusion about it by saying "I believe that p" and another may say "I prefer to believe that q." In such a case we should all admit that a man can properly be said to choose which of several alternative answers he will believe.

Some philosophers, however, have gone farther. They have not only maintained that believing, or some believing, is voluntary. They have also maintained that belief is at least sometimes a matter of moral obligation; that there are circumstances in which a man *ought* to believe a proposition p or disbelieve a proposition q. Here they are not using the word "ought" in what might be called its intellectually-normative sense, a mild and harmless sense which would worry nobody. They do not just mean that it would be reasonable for Mr. A to believe the proposition p, given the evidence which he has. They mean that he is morally obliged to believe it, that he will be morally blameworthy if he fails to believe it, and still more so if he disbelieves it. As we shall see later, they even think that in some circumstances a man is morally obliged to believe a proposition p even though the evidence which he has may be unfavorable to it; or that he is morally obliged to go on believing it as firmly as before, even when the evidence for the proposition is weakened, or the evidence against it is strengthened, as a

From *Belief and Will*, Aristotelian Society, Supplementary Volume XXVIII (1954), pp. 1–26. Reprinted by courtesy of the author and of the Editor of The Aristotelian Society. Copyright 1954 *The Aristotelian Society*.

result of some new piece of information he has acquired. These doctrines about a duty to believe are strange and even alarming. But there are certain common ways of speaking and thinking about belief which lead very naturally in that direction. Perhaps it may be of some interest to consider them and to ask what their implications are. As I have said, they are ways of speaking and thinking which suggest that believing has something in common with action.

Let us begin with the word "cannot." As there are things we cannot do, there are also propositions which we cannot believe. "I just cannot believe that." "Nothing would induce me to believe it." Sometimes this inability is attributed to another person, not to ourselves. "The story is true, but naturally *he* cannot believe it." And sometimes we say this kind of thing without specifying any particular believer. There are propositions which no one can believe. They are just unbelievable. Thus it is just unbelievable that at 11 p.m. on January 1st the temperature on the roof of the Air Ministry in London was 85 deg. Fahrenheit.

The interesting thing about this inability or incapacity to believe is that we regard it as the upper limit of a scale of increasing difficulty in believing. It may be easy, or quite easy, to believe such and such a proposition; or it may be rather difficult to believe, or very difficult; or it may be almost impossible to believe; or finally, quite impossible. These phrases about degrees of difficulty are sometimes used quite generally, without reference to a particular believer. It is not very easy, or it is rather difficult, to believe that there are Abominable Snowmen in the Himalayas. But sometimes a man says of himself "It is difficult for *me* to believe that." And sometimes he says it of another specified person or class of persons. It is very difficult for an Englishman to believe that the Dutch contributed a good deal to the defeat of the Spanish Armada in 1588, and perhaps it is not very easy for a Dutchman to believe that the English did. It is difficult for the Senior Tutor of St. Benedict's College to believe that the college hockey team will be defeated in tomorrow's hockey match, though perhaps he can just bring himself to believe it.

We may next notice that there are several different sorts of situation in which the phrase "cannot believe" is used. When it is said that such and such a thing cannot be done or cannot happen, it is always appropriate to ask "Why?" Statements of impossibility are elliptical. When we say that something is impossible (cannot be done, cannot happen) we mean that there is something else, not at the moment specified, which prevents it or precludes it. And it is always appropriate to ask what this preventing factor is.

Now sometimes what prevents a man from believing a proposition p, what *makes* him unable to believe it, is just the fact that he is taking a reasonable attitude to this proposition. There are two ways in which this may happen, corresponding to the two criteria which we use for deciding whether a belief is reasonable, the consistency criterion on the one hand, and the evidential criterion on the other. If it is reasonable for me to believe p, then p must be consistent with all the other propositions I believe. And further, the evidence which I have must be on balance favorable to p.

Let us first consider the consistency criterion. Obviously, that fact that p is inconsistent with some other proposition q which I believe is not by itself a sufficient ground to justify me in saying "I cannot believe p." It will only justify me in saying "I cannot *both* believe p *and* believe q." It might be, then, that the reasonable course is to reject q and accept p, or again to suspend judgment about both.

But what if the proposition p is *internally* inconsistent? Surely in this case, at any rate, the consistency criterion will be enough by itself to justify me in saying "I cannot believe that"? Suppose a fisherman tells me that he caught a warm-blooded fish in the River Cherwell today. Surely I am justified in saying "I simply cannot believe it"?

Nevertheless, it is logically possible that the man did catch a creature which looked like a fish, lived in water, had scales and fins, and yet was warm-blooded; and that the only way he could think of for describing it was this *paradoxical*, i.e., logically-inconsistent, expression "a warm-blooded fish." He would have been wiser, perhaps to make the inconsistency perfectly plain and obvious. He should have followed the example of Professor Wisdom's man who was asked whether it was raining and replied "It is and it isn't." He should have said "What I caught was a fish and yet it was not." But then, surely, I should have been all the more justified in saying "I cannot believe it"? Well, if the inconsistency of his statement was my sole justification for saying so, my inability to believe him would no doubt have been reasonable, but it would also have been imperceptive. I should be showing an insensitiveness to the limitations and imperfections of language.

What I ought to say is "What do you mean?" or "How do you mean?" Perhaps he will then explain that the creature had some or many of the characteristics of a fish, but was also warm-blooded. When he has given his explanation I shall still say "I cannot believe your story," and my inability to believe it will still be reasonable. But the grounds of this reasonableness are now quite different from what they were at first. There is no longer any inconsistency in his story, now that he has explained what he meant. It is logically possible that there should be a creature which is in many ways like a trout and yet is warm-blooded. If I *now* say "I cannot believe that," I say so not on logical grounds, but on evidential ones. It is now the evidential criterion of reasonableness, and not the consistency criterion, which justifies my inability to believe. It is empirically improbable, very improbable indeed, that there should be such a creature as he describes. All the knowledge I have about living creatures, and all the testimony I have been able to get from zoological experts, is evidence against the man's story.

I would suggest, then, that when the proposition we are considering is about matters of fact (i.e., is not a proposition of logic or of pure mathematics) the evidential criterion of reasonableness, and not the consistency criterion, is much the more important of the two. If we cannot believe the proposition, our inability to believe it must be justified in the end on *evidential* grounds.

Nevertheless, when reasonable people are unable to believe a proposition, because of the very strong evidence they have against it, the proposition may happen to be true all the same. Similarly when they say, and say reasonably, that they have *difficulty* in believing a proposition (because of the strong, though not overwhelmingly strong, evidence which they have against it) the proposition may happen to be true. Here I cannot forbear to mention the duck-billed platypus. A creature which lays eggs, has a duck-like beak, and fur, and four webbed feet—how *could* there be such an animal? When the creature was first reported, it was very reasonable for people to say "We just cannot believe this story." Moreover, it was especially reasonable for experts to say it. All the then available zoological evidence made it very improbable that such a beast should exist. What one is reasonably incapable of believing may nevertheless be true. There is therefore a sense in which it may be right, sometimes—reasonable or "right and proper"—to disbelieve a proposition which is in fact true; and equally, of course, to believe a proposition which is in fact false.

There is indeed a connection between believing reasonably and believing truly. (I shall have more to say about it later.) If there were not, there would not be much point in being reasonable about one's beliefs or one's disbeliefs. If you believe reasonably, your beliefs as a whole are likely, in the long run, to be more often true than false. But obviously this does not entail that if you believe reasonably *all* your beliefs will be true. And similarly, if or so far as you are reasonable in your believing, the propositions you are *unable* to believe are likely to be on the whole and in the long run false rather than true. But this again does not entail that *all* the propositions which you are reasonably incapacitated from believing are false. In

one's inability to believe, as in one's believing, one may on occasion be reasonable but mistaken. Similarly, in both cases alike, one may be unreasonable but correct. What makes me unable to believe a proposition p may be
pure prejudice or stupidity or sheer cussedness; but p may be false for all
that. What makes it easy for me to believe another proposition q may be
something equally unreasonable; nevertheless, q may happen to be true.

It was worthwhile to explain that inability to believe something *can* be perfectly reasonable, just because it is so very often unreasonable or at any rate
non-reasonable. When a man says "I cannot believe p," "nothing would
induce me to believe it," what prevents him from believing it, very often, is
not that he has strong evidence against the proposition, nor yet the fact
that he has detected an internal inconsistency in it, but just some emotion
or desire which he has. He cannot believe the proposition because he so
much *wants* it to be false, or because the situation would be so upsetting or
shocking or terrifying if the proposition were true. He just cannot believe
that the train will arrive late, because he will get into so much trouble if it
does. Some people cannot believe that the works of John Bunyan have any
merit at all, because he came from Bedford and they have such an intense
dislike for that town and everything to do with it. This same dislike makes
them unable, or hardly able, to believe that the road which passes through
Bedford is the shortest route from Oxford to Cambridge. A more serious
sort of example, which I shall discuss later, is one in which much stronger
emotions are involved—stronger in the sense both of being more intense
and of being more deeply rooted, as it were, in our emotional life. Newman says somewhere that a man cannot believe that his most intimate
friend is false to him. Again, in time of war a fervent patriot cannot believe
that his country was the aggressor, and up to the last moment he cannot
believe that it is going to be defeated.

I am not sure, however, whether this "cannot" is always a pure and
simple inability—i.e., whether it always means that it just is not in the person's power to believe the proposition. What makes me doubt this is the
fact that in such circumstances we sometimes say not just "I cannot believe
it" but "I cannot and will not believe it" ("I can't believe it, and what is
more, I won't").

This conjunctive statement or conjunctive expression of attitude is
rather puzzling. At first sight there even seems to be a logical inconsistency
in it. Surely if it makes sense to say "I will not believe it" (i.e., "I have
resolved not to") then it must be true that I *can* believe it—the very thing
which the first part of my utterance denies. If I resolve not to do X, or
refuse to do it, surely X must be something which I am able to do. If a

man says "I won't get up" surely he is thereby admitting that he is able to get up. He has the power to get up, but he refuses to exercise it. You can only refuse to exercise a power if you do actually have it, or at least assume that you have.

But when a man says "I can't and won't believe this," perhaps "I can't" means something like "I cannot afford to," rather than "I am unable to" or "am incapable of." If one cannot afford to do something, or cannot afford to allow it to happen, it is of course in one's power to do it or to allow it to happen. And so it makes perfectly good sense to add "and what is more I *will not* do it" or "I *will not* allow it to happen."

Now "cannot" *is* sometimes an abbreviation for "cannot afford to." I cannot go out for a long walk in the country today. I haven't got the time, because I must finish writing a lecture. By saying "I cannot" I do not mean at all that it is not in my power to go. It certainly is. I could perfectly well get into my car the next minute and drive out to the Chiltern Hills and spend the whole day in the woods looking for woodcocks. And just because it *is* in my power to go, it would make sense to add "I will not go," i.e., "I have resolved not to."

Similarly, there are propositions which a man cannot afford to believe, and therefore will not believe. He is not likely to say himself that he cannot afford to believe a proposition p, though other people may say this in talking about him. What he says, probably, is just "I cannot believe it," which might mean, and more usually would mean, just that he is unable to believe it, incapable of believing it. Perhaps by using the word "cannot" in this ambiguous way, without further explanation, he may conceal from himself the difference which there is between "not being able to afford to" and simply not having it in one's power. But if he adds "and what is more, I *won't* believe it," he gives himself away. He would be wiser to say just "I can't believe it," and stop at that.

Why is it that a man cannot afford to believe a proposition p? There are several possible answers. The most obvious answer, and no doubt often the true one, is just from an emotional point of view he cannot afford it. His existing emotional attitudes and desires commit him, so to speak, to some other proposition q; and he is aware that if p were true, q would be false, or its probability would be greatly decreased. For example, q might be the proposition that Mr. A, a politician whom he greatly admires, is a thoroughly honest and highly intelligent man. When he is told, even by an informant whom he admits to be generally reliable, or reads, even in the columns of *The Times* newspaper, that Mr. A has said or done something very dishonest or very stupid, he cannot afford to believe it and he *will* not believe it.

Sometimes what he is emotionally committed to is not just one proposition, but a highly organized system of propositions, a theory or doctrine of some kind, for instance the Marxist interpretation of history. And then he cannot afford to believe any proposition which would falsify or weaken that system. For example, he cannot afford to believe that many of the people who went on Crusades in the Middle Ages were moved by motives of simple Christian piety. He cannot afford to believe this proposition, and he refuses to believe it.

But when someone cannot afford to believe a proposition p, his motives may be more respectable than these. Misguidedly or not, he may think it is his *duty* to believe a proposition q, which would be rendered false or less probable if p were true. Again, he may think it his duty to go on believing q as firmly as he did before, in spite of the adverse evidence which has just been brought to his notice. Then, taking the moral attitude he does, he cannot *morally* afford to believe the proposition p. When he says "I cannot believe p" (adding, perhaps, "and I won't believe it") this is rather like saying that one *cannot* go to London today, because one has promised to have tea with one's next door neighbor this afternoon, or to take one's Australian cousin round the colleges of Oxford. This moral justification which one gives for saying one cannot go may of course be fictitious. But the fiction only works because such moral justifications for the "cannot" are often perfectly genuine.

I shall have more to say later about the conception of a duty to believe. The point at present is merely to elucidate the sense of "cannot believe" in which it means "cannot afford to." It is possible that someone cannot afford this on moral grounds, i.e., because of the (second-order) belief which he has that there are certain propositions which he is morally obliged to believe, and not merely because of his emotional commitments.

Finally, there is still another sort of inability to believe which does not fall under any of the heads so far mentioned. Here, it is not that one has strong evidence to the contrary (*rational* inability to believe) nor yet that one cannot afford to believe the proposition, either because of emotional commitments or on moral grounds. What the "cannot believe" indicates may be just intellectual inertia. The man is simply unable to make the intellectual readjustments which would be required if he did accept the proposition. He would have to reconsider many of his present beliefs if he did, modifying some of them and abandoning others. Perhaps he would be willing to make these changes if he could. But the task is too much for him. He just lacks the necessary intellectual power, the mental flexibility which would be needed.

We may now consider some implications of this whole group of phrases, of which "cannot believe" is one. Others are "can believe," "easy to believe," "difficult to believe," "almost impossible to believe"; and also "will not believe" and "quite willing to believe." Taken together, these phrases suggest that belief is, normally, something voluntary; that we can decide voluntarily what to believe and what not to believe.

"Cannot believe," taken by itself, might of course appear to suggest the contrary. But as we have seen, the "cannot" often means "cannot afford to," and this has the implication that it *is* in one's power to believe the proposition if one chooses. Only, as it happens, one makes the opposite choice, because of the emotionally disagreeable results of believing, or sometimes because one would have a feeling of moral guilt if one did believe the proposition. It is true that there are cases where "cannot believe" does just mean literally what it says, namely that it just is not in the man's power to believe the proposition. But it looks as if these cases were regarded as exceptional; as if the normal and ordinary state of things were that we *can* believe whatever we choose to believe. This suggestion that belief is normally something voluntary is strengthened when we recall what was said earlier. Inability to believe seems to be regarded as the upper limit of a scale of increasing difficulty. The word "difficult," in its various degrees, is only applicable to things which are in our power. It *is* in our power to achieve them, though only with an effort—small, great, or very great, as the case may be. And finally, the suggestion that belief is normally something voluntary is strengthened still further when we consider such expressions as "I *won't* believe that," "I just *refuse* to believe it."

Accordingly, it is not at all surprising to find that some people use moral obligation words in connection with believing, as I have already remarked. If or to the extent that believing is something under our voluntary control, it does at any rate make sense to say that X ought, is morally bound, to believe a proposition p, and ought not to believe q or has no moral right to believe it; though there might still, of course, be exceptional cases where he could not help believing q or could not help withholding belief from p. (Cf. "He could not help breaking his promise, because the train was an hour late.")

The consequences of this doctrine that there is sometimes a moral obligation to believe are of course pretty horrifying. The religious wars of the 16th and 17th centuries were based on just such a theory. High-principled persecutors, religious or political (and some persecutors *are* high-principled) would justify their actions by saying that X is morally bound to believe a proposition p; and if he does not believe it, or even believes its contradictory not-p, this "misbelief" of his can only be due to

moral wickedness, or badness of will. It is in the man's power to believe p
if he chooses, and he has a moral obligation to believe it. He prefers not to
do his duty. Surely he deserves to be punished for this moral delinquency;
and the more important the proposition is which he refuses to believe, the
more drastic the punishment should be.

But though the doctrine does have these terrifying implications, it
might of course be true for all that. Moreover, someone might argue, I
suppose, that although there is a *prima facie* duty to punish misbelievers,
or suppress them by force, there is a conflicting *prima facie* duty which always, in practice, outweighs it; namely, the duty to preserve peace both
within our own community, and between one community and another.

There is no doubt that some people do use moral obligation words in
connection with beliefs. They say that X *ought* to believe a proposition p;
and not just in the intellectually-normative sense of the word "ought,"
meaning that if he were to believe p, he would be believing reasonably, but
in the moral sense of "ought." They really do think that X has a moral
duty to believe p, or to go on believing it when he is inclined to give up
his belief. What has led them to such an extraordinary opinion? Let us
consider some examples.

You may remember the story about the Dean of a certain college in-
terviewing an undergraduate who had climbed into the college at 2 a.m.
that morning. The undergraduate gave some very unconvincing explanation; he had not realized that his watch was 2½ hours slow. The Dean replied "Of course I am bound to believe you; and now I am going to fine
you £5." But when the Dean said "I am bound (morally obliged) to believe you," with the implication that he had actually carried out this moral
duty of believing, it would seem that his remark was highly elliptical. He
meant "I am morally obliged to *say the words* 'I believe you,' and I hereby
do say them"; or again, "I am morally obliged *not* to use words expressive
of doubt or disbelief about your story, and I hereby refrain from using
them." A solicitor might say the same sort of thing to a client whom he
has undertaken to defend. "Of course I am bound to believe what you tell
me." He may say this, although he has the gravest doubts of his client's
veracity. The moral duty which he acknowledges and carries out is just the
duty to say the words "I believe you" or to refrain from saying words which
would express disbelief or doubt.

It may be true, sometimes, that one really does have a moral duty to
utter words expressive of belief, or to refrain from uttering words expressive
of doubt. It may also sometimes be our duty to *act as if* we believed a
proposition, or to act in other ways as if we believed it, for uttering words
to someone is itself a kind of action. I find a rather disreputable looking

individual wandering about the garden by night. He says he was looking for the back door because he wanted to ask the way to the London road. I take him to the front gate and show him which way he should go, though all the time I strongly suspect that his intention was to burgle the house.

But though we may sometimes have a moral obligation to express belief or to act as if we believed—things which certainly are under our voluntary control—it will not of course follow from this that we ever have a moral obligation to *believe* (or not to believe, as the case may be). And it will not follow that believing itself is under our voluntary control, merely because the outward signs of it are.

Let us now consider a more plausible example, where it does look as if belief itself, not merely the outward signs of it, might be a matter of moral obligation. I am thinking of a situation which quite often occurs in Victorian novels, and I suppose it must have occurred quite often in real life at that time, though it is not so common in our present degenerate period. It would seem that 19th century ladies acknowledged a moral obligation to believe that their husbands or fiancés were impeccably virtuous. When testimony, even quite strong testimony, was put before them to the contrary, they thought it their moral duty to persist in their belief all the same; to *go on* believing, as firmly as before, that their husbands or fiancés were impeccably virtuous, in spite of this adverse evidence. And it would seem that many of them succeeded in carrying out this duty, amidst universal applause. They might perhaps have some inclination to consider the adverse evidence on its merits. But this inclination must be resisted and overcome. Granted that one has a moral duty to believe p, one has a consequent duty to disbelieve q where the truth of q, if it were true, would be evidence against the truth of p; and not only where q, if true, would be *conclusive* evidence against the proposition which it is one's duty to believe, but also when it would be strong or fairly strong evidence against, even though not conclusive.

Sometimes, it would seem, this duty of believing (and of not believing) was supposed to extend still further. It was held that there was a moral obligation to believe that all the members of one's family were persons of the highest excellence, or at least of great excellence; and an obligation to go on believing this, come what may; and a consequent obligation to *dis*believe evidence to the contrary—always, or at least nearly always, for just occasionally the adverse evidence might be so overwhelming that it would be beyond the power of even the most high-principled person to resist it.

What are we to make of this doctrine? I suspect that it is still quite widely held, though not perhaps in quite such an uncompromising form, and nowadays it is not so often stated explicitly. It looks rather like saying that in some cases one has a moral obligation to be prejudiced or biassed, and a moral obligation to persist in one's prejudice even when one is inclined to adopt a more reasonable and "objective" attitude. We should all agree that such a persistence in one's prejudice might sometimes be excusable, and indeed that it might be a psychological consequence of something highly admirable, namely an affectionate disposition. But can we really suppose that there is ever a moral duty to be prejudiced, and to persist in one's prejudice when one is confronted with strong evidence against the proposition one believes? That, surely, is what the doctrine comes to. It says that you have a duty to believe a proposition p, and a consequent duty to go on believing p as firmly as before, even when you are presented with strong evidence to the contrary; and from this, in turn, it follows that you have a duty to reject or disbelieve the adverse evidence. When presented with this adverse evidence, you may no doubt have an inclination to give up believing p, or at any rate to believe it with less confidence than you did before. But in these special cases (the doctrine says) you have a moral duty to resist such inclinations; and you *can* resist them, if you try hard enough.

We must now consider a question which is sure to have occurred to you already. *Can* one really make oneself believe something, or make oneself go on believing it, just by an effort of will—by a great effort in this case, where the adverse evidence is strong, and by a smaller effort in others? Indeed, are our beliefs really under our voluntary control at all? Hume, you will remember, thought it quite obvious that they are not. It seemed to him evident that it is *not* in our power to believe whatever we please.[1]

It is true that we do sometimes use volitional words in describing the acquisition of beliefs ("I decided that p," "I made up my mind that p"). But we must not allow ourselves to be confused by the fact that something rather like preferring or choosing does quite often occur as a stage in the process by which a belief is formed, especially when we acquire our belief in a reasonable manner, after careful consideration of the evidence *pro* and *con*. Believing a proposition is, I think, a disposition and not an occurrence or "mental act," though the disposition is not necessarily a very long-lived one and may only last a few seconds. (For a few seconds I believed that the sound was made by an airplane. Then I ceased to believe this, and believed instead that the sound came from a racing motor car with a defective silencer.) But although believing p is a disposition, and not an occurrence, there is a characteristic sort of mental occurrence which we may

1 *Treatise*. Appendix. Everyman edition, Vol. 2, pp. 313–314.

sometimes notice when we are in process of *acquiring* such a disposition. I am going to call this occurrence "assenting" to the proposition. Similarly, when once a belief-disposition has established itself, one of the many different ways in which it may manifest itself thereafter is by subsequent acts of assenting or assent-occurrences. Now when our belief is a reasonable one, this assenting, and especially the initial assent, has a *preferential* character. For some time we were in a state of indecision, sitting on the fence as it were. We considered various alternative propositions p, q, and r, together with the evidence for and against each of them. But finally, as a result of this weighing of evidence, we prefer or "plump for" p, because this is the alternative which our evidence, taken as a whole, appears to us to favor. We no longer sit on the fence as we were doing before, but come down on one side. We decide for p in *preference* to q and r.

Now because of this preferential element in it, assent may look rather like voluntary choice. But the appearance is deceptive. It is not a free choice at all, but a forced one. If you are in a reasonable frame of mind (as we are assuming that you are in this case) you cannot help preferring the proposition which the evidence favors, much as you may wish you could. I mean, you cannot help preferring the proposition which *your* evidence favors, the evidence *you* are at the moment attending to, though the evidence which other people have may of course be different. It is no good refusing to assent to p in such circumstances, though of course you may *say* to other people, or even to yourself, "I refuse to assent to it." It just is not in your power to avoid assenting to the proposition which the evidence (your evidence) favors, or to assent instead to some other proposition when the evidence (your evidence) is manifestly unfavorable to it.

Thus we come back to the question raised before. Can one make oneself believe something, or make oneself go on believing it, just by an effort of will? How would one set about performing this duty—if it is indeed a duty? It seems to me pretty clear that one cannot do it directly, by just making a voluntary effort here and now. Nevertheless, there is some sense in the expressions "I won't believe q," "I will believe p," or "I will go on believing p as before, in spite of all." Indirectly, though not directly, and over a period of time, though not instantaneously, one *can* voluntarily control one's beliefs—at any rate up to a point. If so, it does at any rate make sense (whether or not it is true) to suggest that there are some propositions which we have a moral duty to believe and others which we have a moral duty to disbelieve.

Beliefs can be gradually cultivated, though they cannot be instantaneously produced, or abolished, at will. They can also be preserved when one is in danger of losing them. Doubts or inclinations to disbelief, occasioned by adverse evidence, cannot be abolished instantaneously by a mere *fiat* of will here and now. But we have it in our power to weaken our doubts little by little, until at last they fade away and are felt no longer. This is a thing one can do (usually) if one tries hard enough and long enough, and thereby one can voluntarily restore or revive a belief which one was in danger of losing. So again it does make sense, whether or not it is true, to say that one sometimes has a moral duty to take steps to preserve one's belief in spite of strong adverse evidence. The prerequisite that "ought implies can" is after all fulfilled. And when someone who intends to carry out this duty says "I *will* go on believing p," "I *refuse* to give up believing it," he should be understood to mean that he has resolved to take these steps, and to persist in his gradual belief-restoring procedure until the cure is complete. We must now consider how he is to set about it.

The crucial point here is that the direction of our attention is to a large extent in our own power. One can voluntarily avert one's attention from the adverse evidence; one can refuse to consider it whenever it comes into one's mind. Or if this is too difficult at first (it becomes easier in time) one can at least weaken the effect of the adverse evidence by directing one's attention to the general truth that testimony is often erroneous, or to the possibility that there may be some alternative explanation of the events reported. Again, one can fix one's attention upon the evidence which favors the proposition one wants to believe or to go on believing, as well as averting one's attention from the adverse evidence. There is almost sure to be some favorable evidence, and there may well be a good deal. Make the most of it. Dwell on it in thought as much as you can.

By such systematic and voluntary direction of the attention, continued over a sufficiently long period, one may manage, in time, to do what is demanded. By degrees, though not immediately, one will probably get back into the state where one again believes the proposition p without any doubts or qualms. "I must be loyal to X not only in my actions but in my inmost thoughts." That is the obligation which these Victorian ladies were supposed to undertake.[2] "Being loyal to him in one's inmost thoughts" consisted, I suggest, in a habit of directing one's attention appropriately, by attending carefully and repeatedly to all the evidence which is creditable to X, and averting one's attention from all the evidence which is discreditable to him. By such methods one gets back into the state where the *only* evidence before one's mind is favorable to the proposition one wishes to be-

2 If I recollect rightly, it is formulated in this way by one of Trollope's heroines.

lieve. When that state is reached, and so long as it is maintained, there is
no difficulty in believing the proposition as firmly as one did before, when
the adverse evidence had not yet come to one's notice.

This, I suspect, is what these Victorian ladies did, and were so highly
approved of for doing. This was how they managed to carry out the rather
difficult duty, which public opinion imposed on them, of believing—or
continuing to believe—in spite of adverse evidence. Of course, if the adverse evidence was *very* strong, the voluntary effort required for directing
one's attention continually in the appropriate manner might be very great.
But then the moral approval one received for fulfilling one's duty was correspondingly higher.

I said just now that by this voluntary and systematic direction of attention they got themselves into a state where the only evidence *before
their minds* was favorable to the proposition which they "ought" to believe. What their unconscious or subconscious state of mind might be, is
another question. One might suspect, perhaps, that the memory of the adverse evidence, which they so carefully and diligently dismissed from consciousness, was not got rid of altogether; that it was still retained unconsciously (all the more so because strong emotions were attached to it) and
still had its effect upon them. If you could have examined their dreams, or
their slips of the tongue or the pen, or other things they said and did when
they were "off their guard," you might have found that Mrs. X's unconscious beliefs about Mr. X were rather different from her conscious ones,
and even opposed to them.

There is, however, another method of voluntarily cultivating beliefs,
and perhaps these Victorian ladies practiced it too. Probably it has had its
practitioners in all ages, since the dawn of human history. This method is
not concerned with the evidence for or against the proposition one wishes
to believe or go on believing. And if it is effective it gets one into a state
where one no longer bothers about evidence at all.

Here again the essential point is the voluntary direction of attention.
But now we just fix our attention on the proposition itself. We dwell on it
in thought, and bring it before our mind repeatedly. We also consider repeatedly the consequences which the proposition entails, and the further
consequences which it makes probable. This may be summed up by saying
that one fixes one's attention repeatedly on what it would be like if the
proposition were true. If one is good at imaging, one may also find it
helpful to *image* in as much detail as possible the kind of situation there
would be if the proposition were true. Images, for some people at least,
have a more powerful emotional effect than words have. So if we can succeed in "cashing" the proposition with images, emotional attitudes will

tend to be aroused with regard to it. Thereby we shall come to take the proposition more seriously. By cashing it with images, we shall come to "realize what it means" in a way we did not before. It will cease to be a mere verbal formula, as perhaps it was at first, or was in danger of becoming. This is one of the points which Newman is making when he distinguishes between "Real Assent" and "Notional Assent," if I understand him rightly.[3]

This procedure of dwelling upon the proposition in thought may be supplemented by Behavioristic methods. Whenever an opportunity arises, you make a point of acting as if the proposition were true, and you get yourself into the habit of acting in that manner. You even go out of your way to *make* opportunities of acting as if the proposition were true. For example, you go out of your way to be seen in X's company when you could easily have avoided it. You go out of your way to attend minor meetings of the Party, though you would have got into no trouble if you had stayed at home. By this procedure you commit yourself, as it were, to the proposition which you wish to believe. Pascal recommends somewhere that if a man's religious faith is weak, he should "Use holy water and order masses to be said."

By such methods—by dwelling upon a proposition continually and repeatedly, by considering again and again what it would be like if it were true and imagining in detail what it would be like (if you can), by acting as if the proposition were true on all occasions to which its truth or falsity is relevant, and by increasing the number of these occasions whenever possible—by such means you will gradually get into a state of believing the proposition. You will wake up one fine day and find that you do believe it. Or if you believed it already, by these methods you will get into a state where you believe it almost unshakeably; a state in which you no longer have to bother about adverse evidence, or indeed about favorable evidence either. You may still be perfectly ready to discuss the evidence, adverse as well as favorable, showing due respect to those who disagree with you. You may even write whole books on the subject. But all this will be done with a certain inner reservation, as it were. The discussion of the evidence will not make any real difference to you. Your belief will still remain as it was, whichever way the discussion goes. Of course, the state you have got into is one of non-reasonable belief, just because it is independent of the evidence (which will not necessarily prevent the proposition believed from being true). But the point at present is that it *is* a state of belief, and of very firm belief too; and that it is brought into existence by your own voluntary

---

[3] *Grammar of Assent*, ch. 4. The word "real," I think, is used by this classically-minded writer, in its Latin sense of "thingish" (cf. the legal phrase "Real Property").

efforts, or *mutatis mutandis* restored by your own voluntary efforts when you were in danger of losing it. Everyone admits, of course, that such a state can be produced in us *in*voluntarily, by what is called "Social Conditioning" (the process which Hume in the *Treatise* calls "education"). But it was worthwhile to point out that it can be produced voluntarily too, though only with considerable effort and trouble, continued over a long period of time.

I conclude from these considerations that when William James talked about "the will to believe," there was after all some sense in what he said, though the name is not a very good one, and the process should rather be described as the voluntary cultivation of belief. It would seem too that there is some sense in saying "I *won't* believe q," "I *will* believe p" or "I *will* go on believing it, in spite of everything." Moreover, when we say "it is difficult or very difficult for me (or for X) to believe this," "it is easy, or quite easy, for me to believe that" these words really do sometimes have the literal and volitional sense which they have in other contexts. It is true that these volitional words—"won't," "will," "difficult," "easy"—have no application to a momentary act of assent. The most one can voluntarily do there is to say the words "I assent to p" or otherwise behave as if one were assenting to it, for instance by signing one's name on the dotted line at the foot of the page. But these volitional words do apply to beliefs, in the sense in which a belief is a persistent state or disposition. This state can be acquired or abolished, strengthened or weakened, by a longish course of voluntary effort, though not by a mere momentary *fiat* of will here and now. Moreover, it is conceivable that when someone says "I cannot possibly bring myself to believe p," he is mistaken. Perhaps he could and would acquire this belief if he tried hard enough and long enough, and used the psychological techniques (directing attention etc.) which I have described. Similarly, a man may be mistaken when he says "I cannot go on believing p as I did." Perhaps he could and would restore his belief by means of these methods, if he tried hard enough and long enough. Of course, when he says he cannot bring himself to believe the proposition p, or to go on believing it as he used to, he may be saying that the evidence which he has, or the new evidence he has just acquired, makes it unreasonable for him to believe the proposition. If so, he will no doubt refuse to use the belief-inducing techniques which I have described. But this refusal is a voluntary choice too. He resolves to go on being reasonable, to continue to regulate his beliefs in accordance with the strength of the evidence available to him.

But what about the doctrine that there is sometimes a *moral obligation* to believe things? If what I have said is correct, and there is such a thing as "voluntary belief," in the sense I have explained, it is not just absurd to maintain that there are some propositions which it is our moral duty to believe; as it would be, if Hume had been right in thinking that belief is wholly involuntary. It is true that this duty, if it is one, should rather be described as a duty to direct our attention in certain ways and to continue doing so, a process which may be expected to *result* in belief, or in the restoration of a belief we might otherwise have lost. But to say "X has a duty to believe p" (or to go on believing it) would be a natural enough abbreviation for "he has a duty to take steps which will result in his believing p" (or in his continuing to believe it).

Nevertheless, the doctrine that there is sometimes a moral obligation to believe may still be false, even though it is not absurd. Even though it is often in our power to cultivate beliefs by a course of voluntary effort, it does not follow from this that we ever have a moral obligation to make such efforts. Even in the sphere of outward conduct there are surely many actions which are morally indifferent. They are neither actions which we are morally bound to do, nor actions which we are morally bound to refrain from. And the voluntary cultivation of beliefs, or the voluntary strengthening of beliefs we already have, might likewise be morally indifferent activities. If they are, it is something to be thankful for. We have already noticed the horrifying consequences which follow from the doctrine that there is a moral obligation to believe.

But surely it *is* sometimes a man's duty to direct his attention in this way rather than that, and to continue doing so? Of course it may be. It is the professional duty of a plumber's apprentice, at least in his working hours, to direct his thoughts to the properties of lead, and to do so repeatedly, until these properties are thoroughly familiar to him. It is the professional duty of a classical schoolmaster to consider intently and frequently the anomalous behavior of certain Greek and Latin verbs. Again, if you have promised to give a message to someone by word of mouth, it may be your duty to go over the contents of the message on the way, and to do so several times, so that you will not have forgotten it by the time you arrive. Moreover, if, or to the extent that, the direction of our thoughts in this way rather than that has an effect on other people for good or harm, in a telepathic manner, to that extent the notion of moral obligation applies to it.

But in so far as the direction of our attention is relevant to the formation of beliefs or to the strengthening or weakening of beliefs which we already have, I think we should be very reluctant to admit that the notion of moral obligation applies to it. My grounds for saying so are themselves in part moral or quasi-moral ones. It seems to me that we are all far too much addicted to blaming people as it is. If we are to be allowed, or even encouraged, to blame them for the way they direct their thoughts, as well as for their actions, there will be a perfect orgy of moral indignation and condemnation, and charity will almost disappear from the world.

Let us consider the example of the Victorian ladies which I discussed before. Surely it is clear that they did *not* have a duty to cultivate these beliefs about the virtues of their husbands or fiancés. They did *not* have a duty to suppress their doubts on the matter by systematically averting their attention from the adverse evidence. To do so may well have been excusable, but surely it was not morally obligatory. Still less did they have a duty to adopt the second procedure I mentioned, by which one gets oneself into a state of believing which is indifferent to evidence altogether—a non-rational state of unquestioning and undoubting acceptance.

One might even be inclined to say that they had a duty to do precisely the opposite, a duty to consider the evidence both *pro* and *con*, with the result that they would give up their beliefs (or hold them with less confidence, as the case may be) if the adverse evidence was strong enough. And *a fortiori*, one might be inclined to say, they not only had no duty to adopt, but actually had a duty to avoid, the second procedure, which results in a non-rational state of undoubting acceptance, a state in which one is indifferent to evidence altogether. In short, we might be inclined to say that there is a moral duty to be *reasonable* in one's believing, or as reasonable as one can; a duty to consider impartially all the evidence one can lay hands upon, regardless of one's likes or dislikes, and to believe in accordance with the evidence. It would follow from this that we might often have a duty to revise or abandon one of our beliefs when new evidence was brought to our notice; and also, I suppose, that we have a duty to suspend judgment when the evidence is evenly balanced, or too slight in quantity to justify a reasonable belief either way.

But if we do say these things, I think we go too far the other way; too far in the opposite direction from those moralists by whom these Victorian ladies were victimized. I think we are confusing the moral "ought" with the prudential "ought."

Reasonable belief, and therefore the impartial consideration of evidence, *is* something which is to one's long-term advantage, however distressing it may sometimes be in the short run. If we say that a man *ought* to believe only that proposition which the evidence favors, that he *ought* to consider the evidence impartially, this is like saying that a man with a decayed tooth ought to go to the dentist; it is to his long-term advantage to go, though it is unpleasant or inconvenient at the moment. Or again, it is like saying that Smith ought to get up at 7:30 tomorrow morning, because he will miss his train if he does not get up by then. (We may suppose that he is going on a holiday, and missing his train will harm nobody but himself.)

Or perhaps one should put it this way, as I think Professor Braithwaite would: what is for our long-term advantage, though often unpleasant in the short run, is the *general policy* of forming one's beliefs in accordance with the balance of the evidence. Why is this policy to be recommended on prudential grounds? Because it is for our advantage that the propositions we believe should be true, or that as many of them as possible should be true. This is obviously advantageous on practical grounds. True beliefs are better guides to action than false ones. But I think we also have some desire for truth for its own sake. Even when it makes no practical difference, we prefer to believe truly rather than falsely. We only need beliefs at all as a substitute for knowledge where knowledge is not available, or not at present available. (This still remains so even if you think that knowledge is just a special sort of belief; only you will then say that beliefs which do not qualify as knowledge are a substitute for those which do.) False beliefs are poor substitutes for knowledge, though it must be admitted that sometimes we cannot acquire true ones without holding false ones first, and then testing them and finding them to be false.

Now by adopting the policy of forming our beliefs reasonably, the policy of believing in accordance with the evidence and revising or abandoning our beliefs, in the light of new evidence, we do not of course ensure that *all* the propositions we believe will be true, or even that any of them will be *certainly* true. But when we reflect on the meaning of the word "evidence," we see that the policy of believing in accordance with the evidence is the only one which will ensure that the propositions we believe are more *likely* to be true than false. For when we say that such and such facts or experiences are evidence for a proposition p, we just mean that they make it likely in some degree to be true. And so in preferring a proposition for which the evidence is stronger to a proposition for which the evidence is weaker, we are *ipso facto* preferring the one which is more likely to be true. The statement that one is more likely to believe truly if one believes reasonably (that is, in accordance with the evidence) is an analytic statement which follows from the meanings of the expressions "evidence for" and "likely to be true."

Thus, if it is to our long-term advantage to believe truly rather than falsely, it is also to our long-term advantage to adopt and to stick to the policy of believing reasonably. I conclude, then, that there are very good grounds for applying the *prudential* "ought" to the process of forming beliefs, though there are no good grounds for applying the *moral* "ought" to it.

Thus, if I am right, it is misleading to speak of the "Ethics of Belief." But there *is* such a thing as the Economics of Belief, if one may use the word "Economics" in a wide and old-fashioned sense to mean "the theory of prudence," the theory of those activities, both mental and physical, which conduce to our long-term advantage.

❖ 12 ❖

FAITH [1]

F. H. Bradley (1846–1924)

The object of these pages is to inquire as to the meaning of faith. They will be concerned, not merely with religious faith, but with faith in general. I will endeavor first to fix loosely and within limits the sense of the term, and will go on next to state and to explain a narrower view which has much to recommend it. I shall have, however, to point out, thirdly, that this view is not in accordance with all the facts. Unless, that is, we take it as a definition more or less arbitrary, it requires modification. From this I shall proceed to adduce by way of illustration a number of instances, and will finally ask how philosophy and faith are connected. I may, however, add that for myself the inquiry as to the meaning of our term possesses no great importance. As long, that is, as some definite sense is attached to the word, I do not for myself much care how it is defined.

From *Essays on Truth and Reality*, ch. 2, by F. H. Bradley (1914). Reprinted by permission of the Clarendon Press, Oxford.
[1] This chapter appeared first in the *Philosophical Review* of March 1911. It was written, so far as I remember, some four years previously. The reader will notice that the scope of the inquiry is limited. Faith is treated here merely from what may be called the formal side. The aim has been simply to define faith so as to enable one to ask, in any particular case, Is this faith or not? What may be called the material aspect of faith—the question as to what truths of various kinds can, and how far they should, come by way of faith—has been throughout ignored.

I. It is obvious that faith is in some way opposed to knowledge proper, but it is obvious also that faith implies some kind of believing and knowing. If you descend, that is, below a certain intellectual level, the word "faith" becomes inapplicable. It is therefore not knowledge but knowledge of a certain kind which is excluded by faith, or which, to speak more accurately, falls outside of that which constitutes faith's essence. Mere feeling (I do not ask here if this is to be called knowledge) is certainly not faith. I do not deny that a man may have faith in that which he feels, but in any case his faith must go beyond mere feeling. And the same thing must be said once more of sensible perception. You cannot have faith in what you see, so long as you have nothing but seeing. And again everything that can be called intellectual perception must, as such, be external to faith. The mere apprehension of a principle or of a logical sequence is certainly not that which, taken by itself, we should call faith. And we may go on generally in the same sense to exclude all knowledge so far as that is grounded in ideas or is verified in facts.

On the one side, the object of faith must be ideal. To believe in a person, for instance, is, however vaguely, to believe something about him. In order to have faith I must, that is, entertain an idea. On the other side, not every such entertainment is faith. For faith is limited to that ideal region where, apart from faith, doubt is possible. Its positive essence lies in the overcoming or prevention of doubt, actual or possible, as to an idea. And the doubt further, as we have seen, must be excluded in a way which cannot in the ordinary sense be called logical. The nonlogical overcoming from within of doubt as to an idea, or the similar prevention of such doubt, appears, so far, to be the general essence of faith.

II. I will now proceed to state a meaning in which faith may be more narrowly understood. We have here a view which, except as an arbitrary definition, will not cover all the facts, but which nevertheless is instructive and in great part tenable. There are two questions which are naturally asked as to the nature of faith. How in particular is faith able to prevent or to overcome doubt, and what is the result of faith's presence? I have spoken of these two questions as two, because in the end, as I think, they must be divided. But for the view which I am about to state briefly, no such division exists.

Faith according to this view will exist so far as an idea is a principle of action, whether theoretical or practical.[2] The doubt is not first removed or

---

[2] The reader is not to identify this view with what is called Pragmatism. Pragmatism, as I understand it, is merely a one-sided perversion of the more complete view. Its essence consists in the attempt to subordinate every aspect of mind to what it calls prac-

prevented before we act, but by and in the process of our acting. And our
state in thus acting remains faith so long as and so far as the idea is not
verified. Thus, to take theory first, an attempt to reconstruct the world
ideally might, and, we may even add, must begin in faith, but the process
ceases to depend on faith so far as it visibly succeeds. And, if our theory
ever became intelligible throughout, faith would have ceased wholly to
exist in it, since no further doubt as to that theory's beginning or end
would be possible. On the other hand, apart from such complete verification, faith must always remain, since your doubt, actual or possible, is
removed only because, and so far as, you resolve to act in a certain manner.
What overcomes your doubt, therefore, is in the end action and not vision.
And on the practical side the same account holds good. For practical success tends to banish doubt as to those ideas on which we act, and therefore, so far as it goes, tends to remove the condition of faith. But because
neither in theory nor in practice is a complete success attainable throughout and in detail, we are left, so far as this aspect goes, still dependent on
faith.

Even on such a view, the reader will have noticed, faith is not essentially practical, if that word is taken (as above) in its more ordinary sense.
On the other hand, all faith both in its origin and its result will (upon this
view) be active. Doubt, that is, will be overcome always by that which I
may be said to do,—to do, if not in practice, at least theoretically. My contemplation even may be called active, and must everywhere, so far as doubt
is removed by action, imply faith. So that, if we like to use "practical" in
the widest sense as equivalent to "active," faith (on this view) will be essentially practical. But the view, however much truth it contains, cannot in
my opinion be defended. It does not throughout answer to the facts. Even
in the widest sense of practice I cannot find that faith is always practical in
its origin or even always in its issue.

(a) The origin of faith, it seems to me clear, may be what we call
emotional; and, even perhaps apart from emotion, faith can arise through
what may be termed a non-active suggestion. The reason why I have come
to believe in an idea must in some cases be said to be aesthetic, and in
others sympathetic and social; or again it may be found in the magnetic
force of a commanding personality. To maintain that in every one of such
cases I believe because of something that I do, and that faith arises
through action, would surely be contrary to fact. And the objection that in
such cases there is no possibility of doubt, and that there is therefore no

---

tice, the meaning of practice not having been first ascertained. But, in reprinting the
above, I should like to qualify the statement as to the "essence" by the proviso "if it has
any essence."

faith, seems once more untenable. To me it seems clear that I may believe in ideas the opposite of which I am able to conceive, and that my possible doubt is overcome by an influence which is not properly intellectual, and yet which certainly does not consist in action. And I do not see how to deny that such a process is faith. If and so far as I go on to act, the action, I agree, will and must affect the source from which it arises. But we have here a subsequent reaction, and to conclude from this to the nature of the first origin seems illogical.

(b) Hence, even in the widest sense of the term, the origin of faith is certainly not in all cases practical. And it may be doubted whether even the result can in all cases be called action. For example (to take first action which is practical in the narrower sense) I may believe that tonight it will rain because some one in whose opinion I trust tells me so. And this belief may, so far as I see, in no way influence what I call my conduct. And to urge that under other conditions that influence *would be* there, and that therefore it *is* there, to myself seems not permissible. Hence the issue of faith need not always be called practical, if that term is to keep its ordinary meaning.

And even if we extend that meaning so as to embrace every kind of mental action, a difficulty may still remain. If I believe upon faith that tonight it will rain, my conduct, we saw, may remain uninfluenced. A difference of some kind will, however, have been made in what in the widest sense I may call my mental furniture. And, since I always in some way am acting theoretically, the difference made by any belief, however seemingly irrelevant, in my mental furniture, must affect every subsequent theoretical action, and therefore may be said to consist in activity. So far as I really and actually believe that tonight it will rain, so far any judgment of mine with regard to anything in the universe will be affected, and the result of my faith will thus be action. To this extreme contention I may naturally object that, whether I believe that it will or will not rain, may make apparently no visible difference. Still I may be asked, in reply, why and how the idea of rain is kept before me at all unless it is connected with some subsequent mental action? We should thus be brought to the question, whether, and if so in what sense, I have faith so long as I do not exercise it, and so long as there is no actual idea before my mind.

I do not wish to discuss this here, but must insist on the conclusion that the first origin of my belief must in some cases be passive. Again, as to the result, it is questionable how far in some cases we can speak of any actual result at all. We may infer a result on general grounds, but there may be nothing that we can verify in detail. And, further, an action resulting from faith need not be practical. We must therefore conclude that certainly faith does not in all cases arise from action, and that, whether it issues necessarily, in act, even a theoretical act, seems highly doubtful.

If we pass from faith in general to religious faith, this conclusion must be altered. Religious faith consists, I should say, in the identification of my will with a certain object. It essentially is practical and must necessarily be exercised in conduct. I do not contend that in its origin all religious faith must be practical. On the contrary, it may be generated, I believe, in a variety of manners. But, except so far as the accepted idea is carried out practically, the belief (we should perhaps most of us agree) is not properly religious. And of course the practical exercise of a belief must react on its origin. But, unless we wish to lay down a definition which is more or less arbitrary, I do not see that we are justified in arguing from the nature of religious faith to that of faith in general. For reasons that have been given I could not agree that everywhere faith involves the identification of my will with an idea.

III. It may perhaps help the reader to judge as to the truth of the doctrine we have laid down, if I go on to offer some applications in detail. And a certain amount of repetition may perhaps be excused. It is not, for instance, faith where I draw deductions from a principle accepted on faith. So far as the sequence is visible, faith so far is absent. Further, an unverifiable assumption as to detail—an assumption made because a principle demands it—seems hardly to be faith, unless so far as the principle itself is taken on faith. Wherever a principle is seen and grasped apart from faith, my confident acting on this principle should not be called faith. And from the other side, where through weakness of will I fail to act on my knowledge, we must not everywhere identify this defect with want of faith. In the first place, the knowledge itself may or may not rest on faith, and again, the knowledge itself may still be faith even if it apparently is followed by no action. It is only, we saw, in the case of religious faith that this must be denied. The apparent fact of my failure to act upon knowledge will always, I presume, create difficulty, since the detail in each instance may vary and is hard to observe correctly. In some cases my failure may have its origin in doubt, in doubt, that is, not with regard to the principle but as to the detail of its application here and now. And, so far as the right ideas would be secured and the contrary ideas banished by knowledge or faith, my want of action may be attributed to a defect in faith or knowledge. But there are other cases where such an account of the matter seems not to answer to the facts.[3] To pass to another point, when we hear that

[3] I have discussed this difficult question in an article in *Mind*, N.S., No. 43.

"the infant, who has found the way to the mother's breast for food, and to her side for warmth, has made progress in the power of faith," [4] we are at once struck by the inappropriateness of the phrase. The action in such a case need not arise from any kind of belief and idea. And in the second place, where there is an idea from which the action proceeds, the conditions may exclude the possibility of faith. Where an idea, suggested by perception or otherwise, cannot be doubted, faith is obviously inapplicable. Faith, in the proper sense, cannot begin until the child is capable of entertaining a contrary idea.

At the risk of wearying the reader I will add some further illustration. When serving on a jury a man may come to a decision in various ways. If he accepts and rejects testimony, and in the end judges according to probability and by what he knows of the world, the process so far is not faith. If he is influenced by another man simply because he infers that the other man knows better, faith once more is absent. If he is influenced by the other man otherwise, let us say morally and emotionally, and in consequence follows the other man with belief, this is certainly faith. But we cannot call the same thing faith where, and so far as, the belief is absent. The influence of another person on my conduct tends, we may say, normally to influence my belief, but this consequence may be absent, and, if so, we cannot speak of faith proper. Finally, if our juryman cannot decide rationally, and if he says, "Since I must decide in some way, I will take the plaintiff as being in the right," that again certainly is not faith. The man's doubt here is not overcome, nor is there any principle, rational or otherwise, which he accepts as the ground of his particular decision.

IV. I will end by asking whether and, if so, in what sense faith is implied in philosophy. The question how far in philosophy we can be said to go to work with our whole nature, and not merely with our intellect, need not here be discussed. But, to pass this by, philosophy, I should say, in a sense must depend upon faith. For we do not rest simply on a datum, on a given fact or a given axiom. On the contrary, we may be said to depend on a principle of action. We seek, that is, a certain kind of satisfaction, and we proceed accordingly. In and for philosophy (I do not ask if this holds also in the separate sciences) truth in the end is true because I have a certain want and because I act in a certain manner. The criterion may be said in the last resort to involve my act and choice. And thus in the end truth is not true because it is simply seen or follows logically from what is seen. Further, philosophy in my judgment cannot verify its principle in detail

4 Bain, *Emotions*, Ed. III, p. 506.

and throughout. If it could do this, faith would be removed, and, so far as it does this, faith ceases. But, so far as philosophy is condemned to act on an unverified principle, it continues still to rest upon faith.

You may indeed object that here there can be no faith since here doubts are impossible, but this objection, I think, will hardly stand. The doubts may be said to be impossible only because of our principle of action. And, if it were not for our faith, we have perhaps a right to say that the other ideas, now meaningless, might at least in some irrational sense be entertained. But how we are to decide on this point, and whether we are to assert or to deny that philosophy in the end rests on faith, is to my mind of no great consequence.

❖ 13 ❖

SUPERSTITION AND FAITH

C. J. Ducasse (1881–   )

. . . The two terms, superstition and faith, are commonly used rather loosely and variously. Hence no definition of them that is precise is likely to fit all current instances of their application. The definitions offered here, however, which specify with some exactness the sense in which they are intended to be used in these pages, also attempt to respect the ordinary usage of the terms so far as it is firm.

It is sometimes said that superstitions are things some other person believes, but which one's self disbelieves. Evidently, however, this is not what anyone means to assert about a given belief when he declares it to be a superstition. He means not only that he disbelieves the proposition which the other person believes, but also that that proposition is false. Indeed, even this is not enough to define superstition, since belief of something false is also what we have in instances of simple error—i.e., of error not superstitious. The additional characteristics which differentiate superstition from mere error seem to be (a) that in superstition the false proposition concerned is believed *gratuitously*, that is, without any evidence

From C. J. Ducasse, A *Philosophical Scrutiny of Religion*, pp. 72–75. Copyright © 1953 by the Ronald Press Company, New York.

which would prove, or, so far as it happened to go, would make probable, that the proposition is true; and (b) that in superstition the existence and operation of some supernatural agency is assumed. That superstition is also something more or less pernicious follows, of course, from its character as error, since an erroneous belief tends to cause behavior of kinds inappropriate to the true facts.

Error not superstitious, on the other hand, is belief based on evidence, but on items of evidence which happen to be misleading because, although by themselves they make probable that the proposition concerned is true, nevertheless additional evidence exists which is not considered, but which is sufficient to prove the proposition false.

By superstition, then, we shall mean gratuitous belief of a false or probably false proposition that presupposes the existence and operation of some supernatural agency. This seems to be what we mean if we call superstitious, for example, the belief held by some at one time that the world would end in the year A.D. 1000. As the centuries elapsed since that date have proved, it was false that the world would end at that time, and belief that it would do so was superstitious because held despite the lack of any evidence to support it, and because God's supernatural agency was supposed involved.

Of course, that "superstition" means gratuitous belief of a false or probably false proposition presupposing something supernatural does not entail that anything a given person declares to be a superstition really is one, for those who hold the belief which he declares superstitious may hold it because of some item of evidence they have that points to its being true; and the person in view may not know that this evidence exists and is what determines their belief. Or he may be mistaken in thinking that the proposition they believe is false; or in thinking that the agency they assume is a supernatural one. Yet, as the example given above shows, some beliefs really are superstitions and really are known to be so; for there are propositions which imply supernatural agency and which some persons believe without evidence, and which can definitely be proved to be false.

With regard to faith, there appear to be one general and one more specific sense in which the term is used in discussions of religion. The general sense is belief, perhaps based on some evidence, but very firm, or at least more firm, or/and of more extensive content, than the evidence possessed by the believer rationally warrants. It is difficult to see why faith, as consisting simply in this, should be regarded as a virtue. Examples of belief which, in most or perhaps in all persons having it, would be faith in the sense just described would be conviction that there is for human beings a life after death; or conviction that each man has lived on earth one or more times before his present life; or conviction that the Bible is the word of a divine being, or more specifically of a divine being such as monotheism describes; or conviction that such a being exists; etc.

The more specific sense, which "faith" seems to have in cases where it would be a virtue, would be illustrated by the statement, for example, that faith can "move mountains"; or when one speaks of "faith" healings; or of the value of faith in God. "Faith" then apparently means not only (*a*) very firm belief, either unsupported or insufficiently supported by evidence; but in addition either (*b*) that the content of the belief tends to be made true by the very act of believing it firmly; or (*c*) that the content of the belief is of such a nature that firm belief of it tends to have certain valuable results. An example illustrating this second case would be provided by belief that a powerful and loving God exists, who has us in his keeping. There is no doubt that, irrespective of whether it is true or false that such a God exists, firm belief that he does exist is capable of generating in the believer a precious feeling of security.

On the other hand, an example illustrating the case (*b*) would be that if a person is faced with a task he has never before attempted and which he has no evidence he can perform, and yet he firmly believes that he can do it, this very belief is a factor which makes success more likely than doubt of his ability would have done; i.e., that belief tends to make it true that he can do the task. Again, in the instance of faith healings, what is today known of the somatic effects of various mental states shows that firm faith that a certain bodily change will occur can sometimes contribute to bring it about. And of course it is not positively known that the effects of such faith can be only on the body of the person who has the faith. Instances are from time to time alleged to have occurred and to have been carefully verified, where the faith of a parent resulted in the healing of an infant too young to have any faith or to understand what was being attempted. In such instances, the healing is usually ascribed to divine intervention, but if the healing really occurred and really was not due to ordinary physiological processes, it would be simpler to suppose that the parent's faith operated somehow directly on the infant's body, than to suppose that it operated first on a divine being, who was thereby moved then to heal the infant. We do not understand any better what the specific *modus operandi* of the healing is if we ascribe it to a divine being, than we do if we ascribe it directly to the faith of the parents; and *entia non sunt multiplicanda praeter necessitatem.*

AUTHORITY

Morris R. Cohen (1880–1947)

The prestige of authority, it is generally recognized, rests most firmly in custom. By increasing the means of travel and communication, and thus making it possible for us to visualize ways other than those under which we have grown up, the Industrial Revolution has been one of the most potent forces in undermining the prestige of the customary. By showing the people of Europe that they could take things into their own hands and change the traditional form of government, laws, and even the system of weights and measures, the French Revolution made the path of the questioning and revolutionary spirit more easy. But it also frightened those impressed with the fact that the basis of civilized society rests on habitual obedience and deference to organized authority. From the latter point of view, modern history is a fall from a social order in which every one knows his place and its duties to a bewildering chaos of conflicting claims without any authoritative guidance. The claims of authority have, therefore, been usually pressed or repelled with more poignancy than philosophic detachment.

In discussing the principle of authority we should distinguish between the necessities of conduct and those of purely theoretic decisions. This distinction is frowned upon in an age which so glorifies practical conduct as to regard purely theoretic contemplation either as impossible or as a sinful waste of human energy. Nevertheless, the distinction is quite clear and important. In matters of conduct, we are frequently compelled to decide at once between exclusive alternatives. We must, for instance, either get married or not, go to church or stay out, accept a given position or else refuse it. In theoretic issues, however, we may avoid either alternative by suspending judgment, e.g., when we realize the inadequacy of our information or evidence. It is true, of course, that most people, after having made a deci-

From *Reason and Nature* (1931), Book I, chapter two, section 1, pp. 23–33. Reprinted by permission of the Free Press, copyright © 1931 by Morris R. Cohen, renewed 1959 by Lenora Cohen Rosenfield.

sion, do not like to entertain any doubts as to the adequacy of its theoreti justification. But by no canon of intellectual integrity can dislike of doubt constitute a proof of the truths assumed.

In practice, then, it is often much more important to come to a decision one way or another than to wait for adequate reasons on which to base a right decision. Often, indeed, such waiting is a sheer impossibility. Hence mankind frequently finds it necessary to settle doubts by means that have nothing to do with reason. Among such means are the throwing of a coin or of dice (of which the Urim and Thumim may have been an example) the flight of birds, the character of the entrails in the sacrifice, or the rav ings of the smoke-intoxicated priestess of Dodona. Note that not only minor questions, but important ones like war, have been decided that way The desire to find justifying reasons for adhering to decisions once made may promote the belief that these non-rational ways of terminating issue are controlled by supernatural powers on whom it is safer to rely. But in most cases, the given practice is much older than the various explanation offered for it, and its function in eliminating doubt and bringing about de cision is undoubtedly the primary fact. Modern anthropology is making u realize the superficial character of the old rationalism which regarded the claims of all magicians or prophets to supernatural power or inspiration as premeditated fraud. In primitive communities magical power and the sovereignty which goes with it, are often literally thrust on certain individuals who generally share the prevalent ideas and illusions. We thrust sovereignty on others because most of us are unhappy under the great burden of having to make decisions. We can see this in our own day in the way in which the sovereignty of final or authoritative decision has been imposed in many fields upon our newspapers. Worried by doubts as to the correct dress for her boy of ten at an afternoon party, the anxious mother writes to the newspaper. Wishing to be certain as to what is the proper judgment to be passed on a play or concert, we hasten to consult the next morning's newspaper. The latter thus becomes an authority on dress, on the pronunciation and use of words, on the proper conduct for young women engaged or in love, etc.

Political authority or sovereignty has its basis in just this need to have practical controversies settled. When we are parties to a suit, we are anxious that the issue be settled justly, i.e., in our favor. But there is a general interest on the part of all members of the community in having controversies settled one way or another. Otherwise we fall into a state of perpetual war or anarchy. So important is this, especially to people depending on routine work like agriculture or industry, that mankind has borne the most outrageous tyranny on the part of semi-insane despots, rather than by revolt break the habit of obedience and face the dangers of anarchy before the rebel leader effectively asserts his own tyranny. It was not an Oriental, but the most influential of Occidental philosophers, Aristotle, who argued that even an admittedly bad law ought not to be replaced by a reasonably better one, because changing the law diminishes a prestige which is most effectively based on habitual obedience.

English and American communities are apt to flatter themselves on having eliminated tyranny or despotism by the rational devices of parliamentary or constitutional government. The men of the eighteenth century believed it possible to have a government by laws and not by men. (Some lawyers believe this today, perhaps because they do most of the governing.) It is, doubtless, possible by political devices to minimize certain of the grosser forms of tyranny; and a certain amount of discussion of a more or less rational character may profitably be introduced into the shaping of our laws. But so long as men fall short of perfect knowledge and good will, they will have to obey laws which they find oppressive and unjust—laws made, administered, and interpreted, not by an abstract reason in heaven, nor by a mythical will of all the people, but by ordinary human beings with all their human limitations upon them. If every individual refused to obey any law that seemed to him immoral, the advantages of a state of law over anarchy would be lost. This is not to deny that tyranny may go to such excesses as to make the temporary anarchy of revolution preferable. But in the ordinary course of human affairs such occasions must be regarded as exceptional or relatively infrequent. Actually, therefore, though some forms of government may in the long run work more reasonably or more agreeably to the will of its citizens, the principle of authority means that the good citizen will submit to what is in fact the arbitrary will or unwise opinion of some boss, legislator, administrator, or judge. Lawyers and sentimentalists may try to hide this unpleasant fact by such fictions as "the law is nothing but reason, the will of the people, etc." But wilfully to confuse such fictions with the actual facts is to corrupt reason at its source.

The practical necessity for authority does not mean that only an absolute monarchy or a hereditary nobility can guarantee a regime of law and order. Experience has amply shown that a titular absolute king may in fact be helpless in the hands of irresponsible courtiers, and that hereditary nobilities may be unruly as well as selfish—just as democracies may in fact be ruled by natural leaders or well-organized cliques. In practice authoritarians are people who are so afraid of the perils of change that they blind themselves to the absurdities and iniquities of the established order, while reformers and revolutionists are so impressed with the existing evils that they give little heed to the even greater evils which their proposals may generate. The true rationality or wisdom of any course of conduct obviously depends upon a true estimate of all its consequences, and such estimate is avoided both by those who will not hear of any change and by those who think that *any* change is necessarily good (because they identify change with life).

In thus recognizing the unavoidable character of authority in communal life, must our reason also abdicate and declare that whatever we must submit to is also right? That is exactly the position of those who, like Mr. Balfour, argue that since our individual reason is highly fallible, the need of order and morality demands the submission of reason itself to authority—defined as a "group of non-rational causes, moral, social, and educational—which produces its results by psychic processes other than reasoning." [1] Authorities, however, differ and in the end they cannot support themselves without reason.

In the history of the reaction against the rationalism of the Enlightenment, we find three main sources of authority to which individual reason is asked to submit. These are: (a) the church, (b) tradition, and (c) the opinions of our superiors or "betters."

(A) THE CHURCH

It would obviously take us far afield to examine all the arguments of those who have urged that our fallible individual reason must submit to the infallible authority of the church. But there is a serious difficulty common to all of them, to wit, the great multiplicity of churches, each claiming to be the one instituted by divine authority for the whole of mankind. In ancient days it was possible for men like Dante to view the Roman Catholic Church as the church of all mankind, and to regard all those outside of it as misled by "schismatics" like Mohammed. When, however, Christianity is the religion of a minor part of the human race, divided into so many sects and shades of opinion that it is difficult to say what it is that is common to all of them, and when, moreover, the authority of all supernaturalism is challenged by an increasing number of educated people, surely the old argument from catholicity, that the teachings of the church have been recognized always and everywhere, has lost its force. De Maistre, the most clear-headed of modern apologists, argues that the Pope must be infallible because practical affairs demand some one supreme arbiter. But he dashes his head in vain against the existence of Protestant countries like England, Prussia, and the United States. Any attempt to prove that the authority of the Roman Church is superior to that, for instance, of the Anglican

[1] Balfour, *Foundations of Belief*, p. 219 [this volume p. 107, below].

Church must involve reference to the facts of history. These are at best matters of probability; and it is hardly possible to support a claim to infallibility on the basis of historic probabilities.

There is a popular tendency nowadays for those who think militaristic imperialism to be the logical outcome of the Sermon on the Mount, to justify Christianity on the ground that it has produced the most powerful civilization. But apart from the question how far modern Western civilization is due to Christianity, the historic fact quite clearly indicates that it is only in the last three centuries that some of the Christian nations have outstripped all the non-Christian ones in material power. In the course of the last thirteen centuries whole peoples in Asia, Europe, and Africa have been converted from Christianity to Islam, while very few have followed the opposite path. This, of course, is not to the rationalist an argument for Mohammedanism. But it certainly disarms the old argument that the spread of Christianity is itself a miracle testifying to the truth of Christian teachings.

The old rationalistic idea of finding the core of truth in that which is common to all the different religions is now generally abandoned. It is inconsistent with the authoritarian claims of every church to be in exclusive possession of the supreme wisdom. But the view of Santayana, that the diverse conflicting religions differ only as do different languages, involves the even more thoroughgoing abandonment by every church of all claim to the possession of distinctive truth. Such thoroughgoing skepticism may fit in with the complacent orthodoxy and extreme worldliness of the Lord Chancellor who told a delegation of dissenters, "Get your damned church established and I will believe in it." It may even fit in with the popular prejudice that every one ought to adhere to the religion of his fathers. But in the end no church can hope to attract thinking people or keep them unless it makes an effort to substantiate some claims to truth in the court of reason.

(B) TRADITION

The second form of the appeal to authority against individual reason is the appeal to traditional belief. This may already be seen in Burke's *Reflections on the French Revolution*. In the political life of England and America, Burke has remained the patron saint of all those who would like to see people act on settled beliefs rather than waste time reasoning as to what *is* the right. What is the use of reasoning at all if it leads not to fixed conclusions? Despite the dubious character of his historical contentions and predictions, Burke's great appeal from the reason of individual philosophers to the cumulative wisdom of the ages has become one of the persistent notes of our intellectual life. An extreme and therefore instructive form of it is seen when pious American lawyers like Judge McClain argue against *any* constitutional change on the ground that the constitution embodies the cumulative wisdom of two thousand years of Anglo-Saxon experience—and who will dare to put his private individual reason against that?

It is, of course, easy enough to meet this with the reply that our ancestors were only human and hence subject to error; and that a good deal of what they have left us, e.g., in medicine, is cumulative foolishness. Moreover, the wisdom in our heritage is largely the result of the ideas of individuals who were innovators in their day, so that the elimination of individual reason would mean the death rather than the growth of vital tradition.

But though the extreme form of the argument for tradition can be shown to be untenable, its essence is not thereby eliminated. The essence of the argument for tradition and authority is the actual inability of any single individual thoroughly to apply the process of reasoning and verification to all the propositions that solicit his attention. To doubt *all* things in the Cartesian fashion until they can be demonstrated is impossible practically and theoretically. It is impossible practically, as Descartes himself admitted, because we cannot postpone the business of living until we have reasoned out everything; and it is impossible theoretically because there cannot be any significant doubt except on the basis of some knowledge. To doubt any proposition, to question whether it is true, involves not only a knowledge of its meaning, but also some knowledge of what conditions are necessary to remove our doubt. Actually all of us do and must begin with a body of traditional or generally accepted beliefs. For it does not and cannot occur to us to doubt any one proposition unless we see some conflict between it and some other of our accepted beliefs. But when such conflict is perceived within the body of tradition, the appeal to reason has already manifested itself. It may well be contended that many errors are eliminated by the attrition of time, so that any belief long held by a large group of people has a fair presumption in its favor. Unfortunately, however, errors also strike deep roots. Legends grow and abuses become so well established by tradition that it becomes hopeless to try to eradicate them. The history of long-persistent human error certainly looms large in any fair survey of our past. We may argue that what has stood the test of ages of experience cannot be altogether wrong. But it is also true that what has found favor with large multitudes, though sound in the main, can hardly contain a very high accuracy or discrimination between truth and error.

(C) EXPERT OPINION

Unless we are to fly in the face of all human experience we must admit that some people are, by aptitude, educatioh, or experience, wiser or better informed than others.

It thus seems unpardonable stupidity to rely on our own frail reason, when we can avail ourselves of the judgment of those better qualified. Unfortunately, however, it is not a simple matter to find out who is actually best qualified to decide a given issue. Since the practical disappearance of the doctrine that kings, because of their divine appointment, can do no wrong and are always entitled to unquestioning obedience, there remains only one class of divinely appointed ex-officio superiors, viz. parents. That the conduct of children should conform to the wishes of their parents in matters affecting the life of the family is highly desirable and unavoidable. Parents not only have the power of enforcing obedience, but, all other things being equal, have more experience and therefore generally sounder judgment. Yet nothing but mischief results when respect for parents is conceived as incompatible with questioning the infallibility of their judgment. The necessity of practical obedience does not justify closing the minds of children to free intellectual inquiry when the latter is in the least possible. An emphatically anti-rational phase of parental authority appears when parents assume the right to dictate to colleges what religious, political, or economic doctrines are too dangerous to put before their sons and daughters supposed to be engaged in finding the truth about these subjects. Parents have no right to prevent children from learning more than they know themselves, or to shut the gates of reason.

The difficulty of finding who in any realm *are* our superiors is brought out most clearly by examining that Utopia of shallow "scientific" reformers, viz. government by experts. A priori, Plato's arguments for government by the competent (as against election of officers by lot or ballot) seem unanswerable. But ecclesiastical, as well as political, history shows that government by experts or bureaucracy, from China to Germany and the medieval church, is no more safe against error and abuse than any other human arrangement. Rigorous training and *esprit de corps* may prevent certain abuses. But they breed a narrow class-pride and a subordination of the general interest to the routine of administration, if not to the material interests of the governing group. Against Plato's arguments it is well to remember that the method of electing officials by lot worked so satisfactorily among the Greeks that they regarded it as essential to free democratic government and never gave it up except when compelled by external force such as that of the Macedonians. It was, indeed, great practical wisdom to adapt the duties of office to the competence of possible officials rather than plan for offices that require unattainable ideal governors. The old doctrine that though people cannot govern they can choose the proper governors, finds serious difficulty when we reflect how little opportunity there is to examine with real care the precise qualifications of the candidates or their actual achievements in office.

Nor is the choice of experts by their own associates free from the limitations of human ignorance. The old homely adage: "Get a reputation as an early riser and you can sleep all day," is true in law, medicine, and other professions. Few experts have extensive opportunity of checking up the work of every other expert; and a great deal of professional prestige is based on meretricious grounds. Reputations may be based on previous achievements which happen to have hit a shining mark by an unusually favorable turn of wind. Even in science the best work is sometimes done by unknown young men who, by the time their work becomes known and appreciated, have passed the zenith of their natural abilities.

In passing judgment on the work of scientific experts we must discriminate between data, or matters of fact, and logic, or methods of reasoning. Confronted by what seems an error of reasoning on the part of a great master such as Laplace or Maxwell, an ordinary man may well doubt whether it is not his own judgment that is at fault. But the masters *have* committed errors which lesser men have been able to discover. Certainly no scientist can openly abandon his reason and assert that a demonstrable error ceases to be one when uttered by a great master.

When we come to matters of fact, the reasonable deference to those in a better position to know is, of course, greater. This is seen best in the case of history. Here absolute proof is unattainable, and in the weighing of probabilities there is involved an element of trust in certain witnesses. If any one refuses to trust Herodotus and doubts the occurrence of the Battle of Thermopylae, we can only bring in certain corroborative witnesses. But the credibility of these witnesses also involves an element of trust. When the amount of corroborative testimony is as great as it is for the existence of George Washington or Napoleon, one who persists in his doubts and attributes the consensus of our witnesses to conspiracy or common delusion is just as unreasonable as one who should refuse to plant potatoes for fear that they might be transformed into tigers and devour his whole family. Yet, though the refusal of all trust in the testimony of others lands us in a state perilously near the insane, the careful or scientific historian is precisely the one who critically scrutinizes the witnesses on whom he must rely. He must closely question what qualified them to report the given facts and what possible motives may have led them to emphasize one phase of what happened rather than another. In history as in a court of law, therefore, the element of trust in the testimony of others has to submit to a process of weighing credibility by reference to the probabilities of human experience. These probabilities are ultimately subject to the laws of mathematics applied to such experience as every individual may in a greater or smaller measure verify for himself. For this reason large experience is a necessary qualification for the historian. But pure reason, in the form of logic, is indispensable not only in determining the weight of the various probabilities, but also in opening the historian's mind to the various possibilities to which habit blinds us.

Similar considerations hold in respect of the experimental scientist. The laboratory worker cannot go very far if he discards all the observations of others. Not only must he practically rely on the authority of the general conclusions and the observation of others, but he cannot begin his work without differentiating and attaching greater authority to some part of the tradition of science than to some other part. Suppose, for instance, that he wishes to verify the fact of the pressure of light, which is generally accepted on the authority of the mathematics of Maxwell, and the experiments of Lebedev, Nichols, and Hull. If he wishes to test this, he will have to rely on the general laws of optics and mechanics assumed in the very use of his instruments of observation. Yet no single proposition of science is authoritative in the sense that we have no right to question it on the basis of our individual reason. Nineteenth-century mathematics and physics have progressed by leaps and bounds through questioning long-established results glorified with the names of Euclid, Newton, and others.

To be sure, the vast majority of people who are untrained can accept the results of science only on authority. But there is obviously an important difference between an establishment that is open and invites every one to come, study its methods, and suggest improvement, and one that regards the questioning of its credentials as due to wickedness of heart, such as Newman attributed to those who questioned the infallibility of the Bible.

These elementary considerations show how shallow is the reasoning of those who think we can ever dispense with *all* authority and tradition. Yet rationalism obviously remains justified. Reason must determine the proper use of authority. The fact that we cannot possibly doubt *all* things at once does not privilege *any one* proposition to put itself above all question. The position of reason is analogous to that of the executive head of a great enterprise. He cannot possibly examine the work of all his subordinates, yet he can hold every one accountable. The mere fact that every one is likely to be called to account produces a situation markedly different from what would result if some were put above accountability. An even more apt analogy has been drawn between the principle of authority and the credit which makes modern currency systems possible. Rational science treats its credit notes as always redeemable on demand, while non-rational authoritarianism regards the demand for the redemption of its paper as a disloyal lack of faith.

❖ 15 ❖

AUTHORITY AND REASON

Arthur James Balfour (1848–1930)

I

. . . It would be, perhaps, an exaggeration to assert that the theory of authority has been for three centuries the main battlefield whereon have met the opposing forces of new thoughts and old. But if so, it is only because, at this point at least, victory is commonly supposed long ago to have declared itself decisively in favor of the new. The very statement that the rival and opponent of authority is reason seems to most persons equivalent to a declaration that the latter must be in the right, and the former in the wrong; while popular discussion and speculation have driven deep the general opinion that authority serves no other purpose in the economy of Nature than to supply a refuge for all that is most bigoted and absurd.

The current theory by which these views are supported appears to be something of this kind. Everyone has a "right" to adopt any opinions he pleases. It is his "duty," before exercising this "right," critically to sift the reasons by which such opinions may be supported, and so to adjust the degree of his convictions that they shall accurately correspond with the evidences adduced in their favor. Authority, therefore, has no place among the legitimate causes of belief. If it appears among them, it is as an intruder, to be jealously hunted down and mercilessly expelled. Reason, and reason only, can be safely permitted to mold the convictions of man-

From *The Foundations of Belief* (London: Longmans, Green & Co. Ltd., 1895, 8th ed. 1902), part III, chapter 2.

kind. By its inward counsels alone should beings who boast that they are rational submit to be controlled.

Sentiments like these are among the commonplaces of political and social philosophy. Yet, looked at scientifically, they seem to me to be, not merely erroneous, but absurd. Suppose for a moment a community of which each member should deliberately set himself to the task of throwing off so far as possible all prejudices due to education; where each should consider it his duty critically to examine the grounds whereon rest every positive enactment and every moral precept which he has been accustomed to obey; to dissect all the great loyalties which make social life possible, and all the minor conventions which help to make it easy; and to weigh out with scrupulous precision the exact degree of assent which in each particular case the results of this process might seem to justify. To say that such a community, if it acted upon the opinions thus arrived at, would stand but a poor chance in the struggle for existence is to say far too little. It could never even begin to be; and if by a miracle it was created, it would without doubt immediately resolve itself into its constituent elements.

For consider by way of illustration the case of Morality. If the right and the duty of private judgment be universal, it must be both the privilege and the business of every man to subject the maxims of current morality to a critical examination; and unless the examination is to be a farce, every man should bring to it a mind as little warped as possible by habit and education, or the unconscious bias of foregone conclusions. Picture, then, the condition of a society in which the successive generations would thus in turn devote their energies to an impartial criticism of the "traditional" view. What qualifications, natural or acquired, for such a task we are to attribute to the members of this emancipated community I know not. But let us put them at the highest. Let us suppose that every man and woman, or rather every boy and girl (for ought Reason to be ousted from her rights in persons under twenty-one years of age?), is endowed with the aptitude and training required to deal with problems like these. Arm them with the most recent methods of criticism, and set them down to the task of estimating with open minds the claims which charity, temperance and honesty, murder, theft and adultery respectively have upon the approval or disapproval of mankind. What the result of such an experiment would be, what wild chaos of opinions would result from this fiat of the Uncreating Word, I know not. But it might well happen that even before our youthful critics got so far as a rearrangement of the Ten Commandments, they might find themselves entangled in the preliminary question whether judgments conveying moral approbation and disapprobation were of a kind which reasonable beings should be asked to entertain at all; whether "right" and "wrong" were words representing anything more permanent and important than certain likes and dislikes which happen to be rather widely disseminated, and more or less arbitrarily associated with social and legal sanctions. I conceive it to be highly probable that the conclusions at which on this point they would arrive would be of a purely negative character. The ethical systems competing for acceptance would by their very numbers and variety suggest suspicions as to their character and origin. Here, would our students explain, is a clear presumption to be found on the very face of these moralizings that they were contrived, not in the interests of truth, but in the interests of traditional dogma. How else explain the fact, that while there is no great difference of opinion as to what things are right or wrong, there is no semblance of agreement as to why they are right or why they are wrong. All authorities concur, for instance, in holding that it is wrong to commit murder. But one philosopher tells us that it is wrong because it is inconsistent with the happiness of mankind, and that to do anything inconsistent with the happiness of mankind is wrong. Another tells us that it is contrary to the dictates of conscience, and that everything which is contrary to the dictates of conscience is wrong. A third tells us that it is against the commandments of God, and that everything which is against the commandments of God is wrong. A fourth tells me that it leads to the gallows, and that, inasmuch as being hanged involves a sensible diminution of personal happiness, creatures who, like man, are by nature incapable of doing otherwise than seek to increase the sum of their personal pleasures and diminish the sum of their personal pains cannot, if they really comprehend the situation, do anything which may bring their existence to so distressing a termination.

Now whence, it would be asked, this curious mixture of agreement and disagreement? How account for the strange variety exhibited in the premises of these various systems, and the not less strange uniformity exhibited in their conclusions? Why does not as great a divergence manifest itself in the results arrived at as we undoubtedly find in the methods employed? How comes it that all these explorers reach the same goal when their points of departure are so widely dispersed? Plainly but one plausible method of solving the difficulty exists. The conclusions were in every case determined before the argument began, the goal was in every case settled before the travelers set out. There is here no surrender of belief to the inward guidance of unfettered reason. Rather is reason coerced to a fore-ordained issue by the external operation of prejudice and education, or by the rougher machinery of social ostracism and legal penalty. The framers of ethical systems are either philosophers who are unable to free themselves from the unfelt bondage of customary opinion, or advocates who find it safer to exercise their liberty of speculation in respect to premises about which nobody cares, than in respect to conclusions which might bring them into conflict with the police.

So might we imagine the members of our emancipated community discussing the principles on which morality is founded. But, in truth, it were a vain task to work out in further detail the results of an experiment which, human nature being what it is, can never be seriously attempted. That it can never be seriously attempted is not, be it observed, because it is of so dangerous a character that the community in its wisdom would refuse to embark upon it. This would be a frail protection indeed. Not the danger of the adventure, but its impossibility, is our security. To reject all convictions which are not the products of free speculative investigation is, fortunately, an exercise of which humanity is in the strictest sense incapable. Some societies and some individuals may show more inclination to indulge in it than others. But in no condition of society and in no individual will the inclination be more than very partially satisfied. Always and everywhere our Imaginary Observer, contemplating from some external coign of vantage the course of human history, would note the immense, the inevitable, and on the whole the beneficent, part which Authority plays in the production of belief.

II

This truth finds expression, and at first sight we might feel inclined to say recognition also, in such familiar commonplaces as that every man is the "product of the society in which he lives," and that "it is vain to expect him to rise much above the level of his age." But aphorisms like these, however useful as aids to a correct historical perspective, do not, as ordinarily employed, show any real apprehension of the verity on which I desire to insist. They belong to a theory which regards these social influences as clogs and hindrances, hampering the free movements of those who might under happier circumstances have struggled successfully towards the truth; or as perturbing forces which drive mankind from the even orbit marked out for it by reason. Reason, according to this view, is a kind of Ormuzd[1] doing constant battle against the Ahriman of tradition and authority. Its gradual triumph over the opposing powers of darkness is what we mean by Progress. Everything which shall hasten the hour of that triumph is a gain; and if by some magic stroke we could extirpate, as it were in a moment, every cause of belief which was not also a reason, we should, it appears, be

1 [Zoroastrian spirit of good. Ahriman is the spirit of evil—ed. note.]

the fortunate authors of a reform in the moral world only to be paralleled by the abolition of pain and disease in the physical. I have already indicated some of the grounds which induce me to form a very different estimate of the part which reason plays in human affairs. Our ancestors, whose errors we palliate on account of their environment with a feeling of satisfaction, due partly to our keen appreciation of our own happier position and greater breadth of view, were not to be pitied because they reasoned little and believed much; nor should we necessarily have any particular cause for self-gratulation if it were true that we reasoned more and, it may be, believed less. Not thus has the world been fashioned. But, nevertheless, this identification of reason with all that is good among the causes of belief, and authority with all that is bad, is a delusion so gross and yet so prevalent that a moment's examination into the exaggerations and confusions which lie at the root of it may not be thrown away.

The first of these confusions may be dismissed almost in a sentence. It arises out of the tacit assumption that reason means *right* reason. Such an assumption, it need hardly be said, begs half the point at issue. Reason, for purposes of this discussion, can no more be made to mean right reason than authority can be made to mean legitimate authority. True, we might accept the first of these definitions, and yet deny that all right belief was the fruit of reason. But we could hardly deny the converse proposition, that reason thus defined must always issue in right belief. Nor need we be concerned to deny a statement at once so obvious and so barren.

The source of error which has next to be noted presents points of much greater interest. Though it be true, as I am contending, that the importance of reason among the causes which produce and maintain the beliefs, customs, and ideals which form the groundwork of life has been much exaggerated, there can yet be no doubt that reason is, or appears to be, the cause over which we have the most direct control, or rather the one which we most readily identify with our own free and personal action. We are acted on by authority. It molds our ways of thought in spite of ourselves, and usually unknown to ourselves. But when we reason we are the authors of the effect produced. We have ourselves set the machine in motion. For its proper working we are ourselves immediately responsible; so that it is both natural and desirable that we should concentrate our attention on this particular class of causes, even though we should thus be led unduly to magnify their importance in the general scheme of things.

I have somewhere seen it stated that the steam engine in its primitive form required a boy to work the valve by which steam was admitted to the cylinder. It was his business at the proper period of each stroke to perform this necessary operation by pulling a string; and though the same object has long since been attained by mechanical methods far simpler and more trustworthy, yet I have little doubt that until the advent of that revolutionary youth who so tied the string to one of the moving parts of the engine that his personal supervision was no longer necessary, the boy in office greatly magnified his functions, and regarded himself with pardonable pride as the most important, because the only rational, link in the chain of causes and effects by which the energy developed in the furnace was ultimately converted into the motion of the fly-wheel. So do we stand as reasoning beings in the presence of the complex processes, physiological and psychical, out of which are manufactured the convictions necessary to the conduct of life. To the results attained by their cooperation reason makes its slender contribution; but in order that it may do so effectively, it is beneficently decreed that, pending the evolution of some better device, reason should appear to the reasoner the most admirable and important contrivance in the whole mechanism.

The manner in which attention and interest are thus unduly directed towards the operations, vital and social, which are under our direct control, rather than those which we are unable to modify, or can only modify by a very indirect and circuitous procedure, may be illustrated by countless examples. Take one from physiology. Of all the complex causes which cooperate for the healthy nourishment of the body, no doubt the conscious choice of the most wholesome rather than the less wholesome forms of ordinary food is far from being the least important. Yet, as it is within our immediate competence, we attend to it, moralize about it, and generally make much of it. But no man can by taking thought directly regulate his digestive secretions. We never, therefore, think of them at all until they go wrong, and then, unfortunately, to very little purpose. So it is with the body politic. A certain proportion (probably a small one) of the changes and adaptations required by altered surroundings can only be effected through the solvent action of criticism and discussion. How such discussion shall be conducted, what are the arguments on either side, how a decision shall be arrived at, and how it shall be carried out, are matters which we seem able to regulate by conscious effort and the deliberate adaptation of means to ends. We therefore unduly magnify the part they play in the furtherance of our interests. We perceive that they supply business to the practical politician, raw material to the political theorist; and we forget amid the buzzing of debate the multitude of incomparably more important processes, by whose undesigned cooperation alone the life and growth of the State are rendered possible.

III

There is, however, a third source of illusion, respecting the importance of reason in the actual conduct of human affairs, which well deserves the attentive study of those who, like our Imaginary Observer, are interested in the purely external and scientific investigation of the causes which produce belief. I have already in this chapter made reference to the "spirit of the age" as one form in which authority most potently manifests itself; and undoubtedly it is so. Dogmatic education in early years may do much. The immediate pressure of domestic, social, scientific, ecclesiastical surroundings in the direction of specific beliefs may do even more. But the power of authority is never more subtle and effective than when it produces a psychological "atmosphere" or "climate" favorable to the life of certain modes of belief, unfavorable, and even fatal, to the life of others. Such "climates" may be widely diffused, or the reverse. Their range may cover a generation, an epoch, a whole civilization, or it may be narrowed down to a sect, a family, even an individual. And as they may vary infinitely in respect to the extent of their influence, so also they may vary in respect to its intensity and quality. But whatever be their limits and whatever their character, their importance to the conduct of life, social and individual, cannot easily be overstated.

Consider, for instance, their effect on great classes of belief with which reasoning, were it only on account of their mass, is quite incompetent to deal. If all credible propositions, all propositions which somebody at some time had been able to believe, were only to be rejected after their claims had been impartially tested by a strictly logical investigation, the intellectual machine would be over-burdened, and its movements hopelessly choked by mere excess of material. Even such products as it could turn out would, as I conjecture (for the experiment has never been tried), prove but a motley collection, so diverse in design, so incongruous and ill-assorted, that they could scarcely contribute the fitting furniture of a well-ordered mind. What actually happens in the vast majority of cases is something very different. To begin with, external circumstances, mere conditions of time and place, limit the number of opinions about which anything is known, and on which, therefore, it is (so to speak) materially possible that reason can be called upon to pronounce a judgment. But there are internal limitations not less universal and not less necessary. Few indeed are the beliefs, even among those which come under his observation, which any individual for a moment thinks himself called upon seriously to consider with a view to their possible adoption. The residue he summarily disposes of, rejects without a hearing, or, rather, treats as if they had not even that *prima facie* claim to be adjudicated on which formal rejection seems to imply.

Now, can this process be described as a rational one? That it is not the immediate result of reasoning is, I think, evident enough. All would admit, for example, that when the mind is closed against the reception of any truth by "bigotry" or "inveterate prejudice," the effectual cause of the victory of error is not so much bad reasoning as something which, in its essential nature, is not reasoning at all. But there is really no ground for drawing a distinction as regards their mode of operation between the "psychological climates" which we happen to like and those of which we happen to disapprove. However various their character, all, I take it, work out their results very much in the same kind of way. For good or for evil, in ancient times and in modern, among savage folk and among civilized, it is ever by an identic process that they have sifted and selected the candidates for credence, on which reason has been afterwards called upon to pass judgment; and that process is one with which ratiocination has little or nothing directly to do.

But though these "psychological climates" do not work through reasoning, may they not themselves, in many cases, be the products of reasoning? May they not, therefore, be causes of belief which belong, though it be only at the second remove, to the domain of reason rather than to that of authority? To the first of these questions the answer must doubtless be in the affirmative. Reasoning has unquestionably a great deal to do with the production of psychological climates. As "climates" are among the causes which produce beliefs, so are beliefs among the causes which produce "climates," and all reasoning, therefore, which culminates in belief may be, and indeed must be, at least indirectly concerned in the effects which belief develops. But are these results rational? Do they follow, I mean, on reason *qua* reason; or are they, like a schoolboy's tears over a proposition of Euclid, consequences of reasoning, but not conclusions from it?

. . . I [have] considered Rationalism, not as a psychological climate, a well-characterized mood of mind, but as an explicit principle of judgment, in which the rationalizing temper may for purposes of argument find definite expression. To Rationalism in the first of these senses—to Rationalism, in other words, considered as a form of Authority—I now revert; taking it as an incident specially suited to our purpose, not only because its meaning is well understood, but because it is found at our own level of intellectual development, and we can therefore study its origin and character with a kind of insight quite impossible when we are dealing with the "climates" which govern in so singular a fashion the beliefs of primitive races. These, too, may be, and I suppose are, to some extent, the products of reasoning. But the reasoning appears to us as arbitrary as the resulting "climates" are repugnant; and though we can note and classify the facts, we can hardly comprehend them with sympathetic understanding.

With Rationalism it is different. How the discoveries of science, the growth of criticism, and the diffusion of learning should have fostered the rationalizing temper seems intelligible to all, because all, in their different degrees, have been subject to these very influences. Not everyone is a rationalist; but everyone, educated or uneducated, is prepared to reject without further examination certain kinds of statement which, before the rationalizing era set in, would have been accepted without difficulty by the wisest among mankind.

Now this modern mood, whether in its qualified or unqualified (i.e., naturalistic) form, is plainly no mere product of non-rational conditions, as the enumeration I have just given of its most conspicuous causes is sufficient to prove. Natural science and historical criticism have not been built up without a vast expenditure of reasoning, and (though for present purposes this is immaterial) very good reasoning, too. But are we on that account to say that the results of the rationalizing temper are the work of reason? Surely not. The rationalist rejects miracles; and if you force him to a discussion, he may no doubt produce from the ample stores of past controversy plenty of argument in support of his belief. But do not therefore assume that his belief is the result of his argument. The odds are strongly in favor of argument and belief having both grown up under the fostering influence of his "psychological climate." For observe that precisely in the way in which he rejects miracles he also rejects witchcraft. Here there has been no controversy worth mentioning. The general belief in witchcraft has died a natural death, and it has not been worth anybody's while to devise arguments against it. Perhaps there are none. But, whether there be or not, no logical axe was required to cut down a plant which had not the least chance of flourishing in a mental atmosphere so rigorous and uncongenial as that of rationalism; and accordingly no logical axe has been provided.

The belief in mesmerism, however, supplies in some ways a more instructive case than the belief either in miracles or witchcraft. Like these, it found in rationalism a hostile influence. But, unlike these, it could call in almost at will the assistance of what would now be regarded as ocular demonstration. For two generations, however, this was found insufficient. For two generations the rationalistic bias proved sufficiently strong to pervert the judgment of the most distinguished observers, and to incapacitate them from accepting what under more favorable circumstances they would have called the "plain evidence of their senses." So that we are here presented with the curious spectacle of an intellectual mood or temper, whose origin was largely due to the growth of the experimental sciences, making it impossible for those affected to draw the simplest inference, even from the most conclusive experiments.

This is an interesting case of the conflict between authority and reason, because it illustrates the general truth for which I have been contending, with an emphasis that would be impossible if we took as our example some worn-out vesture of thought, threadbare from use, and strange to eyes accustomed to newer fashions. Rationalism, in its turn, may be predestined to suffer a like decay; but in the meanwhile it forcibly exemplifies the part played by authority in the formation of beliefs. If rationalism be regarded as a non-rational effect of reason and a non-rational cause of belief, the same admission will readily be made about all other intellectual climates; and that rationalism should be so regarded is now, I trust, plain to the reader. The only results which reason can claim as hers by an exclusive title are of the nature of logical conclusions; and rationalism, in the sense in which I am now using the word, is not a logical conclusion, but an intellectual temper. The only instruments which reason, as such, can employ are arguments; and rationalism is not an argument, but an impulse towards belief, or disbelief. So that, though rationalism, like other "psychological climates," is doubtless due, among other causes, to reason, it is not on that account a rational product; and though in its turn it produces beliefs, it is not on that account a rational cause.

From the preceding considerations it may, I think, be fairly concluded, firstly, that reason is not necessarily, nor perhaps usually, dominant among the immediate causes which produce a particular "psychological climate." Secondly, that the efficiency of such a "climate" in promoting or destroying beliefs is quite independent of the degree to which reason has contributed to its production; and, thirdly, that however much the existence of the "climate" may be due to reason, its action on beliefs, be it favorable or hostile, is in its essential nature wholly non-rational.

IV

The most important source of error on this subject remains, however, to be dealt with; and it arises directly out of that jurisdiction which in matters of belief we can hardly do otherwise than recognize as belonging to Reason by a natural and indefeasible title. No one finds (if my observations in this matter are correct) any serious difficulty in attributing the origin of other people's beliefs, especially if he disagree with them, to causes which are not reasons. That interior assent should be produced in countless cases by custom, education, public opinion, the contagious convictions of countrymen, family, party, or Church, seems natural, and even obvious. That but a small number, at least of the most important and fundamental beliefs, are held by persons who could give reasons for them, and that of this small number only an inconsiderable fraction are held in consequence of the reasons by which they are nominally supported, may perhaps be admitted with no very great difficulty. But it is harder to recognize that this law is not merely, on the whole, beneficial, but that without it the business of the world could not possibly be carried on; nor do we allow, without reluctance and a sense of shortcoming, that in our own persons we supply illustrations of its operation quite as striking as any presented to us by the rest of the world.

Now this reluctance is not the result of vanity, nor of any fancied immunity from weaknesses common to the rest of mankind. It is, rather, a direct consequence of the view we find ourselves compelled to take of the essential character of reason and of our relations to it. Looked at from the outside, as one among the complex conditions which produce belief, reason appears relatively insignificant and ineffectual; not only appears so, but *must* be so, if human society is to be made possible. Looked at from the inside, it claims by an inalienable title to be supreme. Measured by its results it may be little; measured by its rights it is everything. There is no problem it may not investigate, no belief which it may not assail, no principle which it may not test. It cannot, even by its own voluntary act, deprive itself of universal jurisdiction, as, according to a once fashionable theory, primitive man, on entering the social state, contracted himself out of his natural rights and liberties. On the contrary, though its claims may be ignored, they cannot be repudiated; and even those who shrink from the criticism of dogma as a sin, would probably admit that they do so because it is an act forbidden by those they are bound to obey; do so, that is to say, nominally at least, for a reason which, at any moment, if it should think fit, reason itself may reverse.

Why, under these circumstances, we are moved to regard ourselves as free intelligences, forming our opinions solely in obedience to reason; why we come to regard reason itself, not only as the sole legitimate source of belief—which, perhaps, it may be—but the sole source of legitimate beliefs —which it assuredly is not, must now, I hope, be tolerably obvious, and needs not to be further emphasized. It is more instructive for our present purpose to consider for a moment certain consequences of this antinomy between the equities of Reason and the expediencies of Authority which rise into prominence whenever, under the changing conditions of society, the forces of the latter are being diverted into new and unaccustomed channels.

It is true, no doubt, that the full extent and difficulty of the problems involved have not commonly been realized by the advocates either of authority or reason, though each has usually had a sufficient sense of the strength of the other's position to induce him to borrow from it, even at the cost of some little inconsistency. The supporter of authority, for instance, may point out some of the more obvious evils by which any decrease in its influence is usually accompanied: the comminution of sects, the divisions of opinion, the weakened powers of cooperation, the increase of strife, the waste of power. Yet, so far as I am aware, no nation, party, or Church has ever courted controversial disaster by admitting that, if its claims were impartially tried at the bar of Reason, the verdict would go against it. In the same way, those who have most clamorously upheld the prerogatives of individual reason have always been forced to recognize by their practice, if not by their theory, that the right of every man to judge on every question for himself is like the right of every man who possesses a balance at his bankers to require its immediate payment in sovereigns. The right may be undoubted; but it can only be safely enjoyed on condition that too many persons do not take it into their heads to exercise it together. Perhaps, however, the most striking evidence, both of the powers of authority and the rights of reason, may be found in the fact already alluded to, that beliefs which are really the offspring of the first, when challenged, invariably claim to trace their descent from the second, although this improvised pedigree may be as imaginary as if it were the work of a college of heralds. To be sure, when this contrivance has served its purpose it is usually laid silently aside, while the belief it was intended to support remains quietly in possession, until, in the course of time, some other, and perhaps not less illusory, title has to be devised to rebut the pleas of a new claimant.

If the reader desires an illustration of this procedure, here is one taken at random from English political history. Among the results of the movement which culminated in the Great Rebellion was of necessity a marked diminution in the universality and efficacy of that mixture of feelings and beliefs which constitutes loyalty to national government. Now loyalty, in some shape or other, is necessary for the stability of any form of polity. It is one of the most valuable products of authority, and, whether in any particular case conformable to reason or not, is essentially unreasoning. Its theoretical basis therefore excites but little interest, and is of very subordinate importance so long as it controls the hearts of men with undisputed sway. But as soon as its supremacy is challenged, men begin to cast about anxiously for reasons why it should continue to be obeyed.

Thus, to those who lived through the troubles which preceded and accompanied the Great Rebellion, it became suddenly apparent that it was above all things necessary to bolster up by argument the creed which authority has been found temporarily insufficient to sustain; and of the arguments thus called into existence two, both of extraordinary absurdity, have become historically famous—that contained in Hobbes's "Leviathan," and that taught for a period with much vigor by the Anglican clergy under the name of Divine right. These theories may have done their work; in any case they had their day. It was discovered that, as is the way of abstract arguments dragged in to meet a concrete difficulty, they led logically to a great many conclusions much less convenient than the one in whose defense they had been originally invoked. The crisis which called them forth passed gradually away. They were repugnant to the taste of a different age, "Leviathan" and "passive obedience" were handed over to the judgment of the historian.

This is an example of how an ancient principle, broadly based though it be on the needs and feelings of human nature, may be thought now and again to require external support to enable it to meet some special stress of circumstances. But often the stress is found to be brief; a few internal alterations meet all the necessities of the case; to a new generation the added buttresses seem useless and unsightly. They are soon demolished, to make way in due time, no doubt, for others as temporary as themselves. Nothing so quickly waxes old as apologetics, unless, perhaps, it be criticism.

A precisely analogous process commonly goes on in the case of new principles struggling into recognition. As those of older growth are driven by the instincts of self-preservation to call reasoning to their assistance, so these claim the aid of the same ally for purposes of attack and aggression; and the incongruity between the causes by which beliefs are sustained, and the official reasons by which they are from time to time justified, is usually as glaring in the case of the last novelty in doctrine as in that of some long descended and venerable prejudice. Witness the ostentatious futility of the theories—"rights of man," and so forth—by the aid of which the modern democratic movement was nursed through its infant maladies.

Now these things are true, not alone in politics, but in every field of human activity where authority and reason cooperate to serve the needs of mankind at large. And thus may we account for the singular fact that in many cases conclusions are more permanent than premises, and that the successive growths of apologetic and critical literature do often not more seriously affect the enduring outline of the beliefs by which they are occasioned than the successive forests of beech and fir determine the shape of the everlasting hills from which they spring.

V

Here, perhaps, I might fitly conclude this portion of my task, were it not that one particular mode in which Authority endeavors to call in reasoning to its assistance is so important in itself, and has led to so much confusion both of thought and of language, that a few paragraphs devoted to its consideration may help the reader to a clearer understanding of the general subject. Authority, as I have been using the term, is in all cases contrasted with Reason, and stands for that group of non-rational causes, moral, social, and educational, which produces its results by psychic processes other than reasoning. But there is a simple operation, a mere turn of phrase, by which many of these non-rational causes can, so to speak, be converted into reasons without seeming at first sight thereby to change their function as channels of Authority; and so convenient is this method of bringing these two sources of conviction on to the same plane, so perfectly does it minister to our instinctive desire to produce a reason for every challenged belief, that it is constantly resorted to (without apparently any clear idea of its real import), both by those who regard themselves as upholders and those who regard themselves as opponents of Authority in matters of opinion. To say that I believe a statement because I have been taught it, or because my father believed it before me, or because everybody in the village believes it, is to announce what everyday experience informs us is a quite adequate *cause* of belief—it is not, however, *per se*, to give a *reason* for belief at all. But such statements can be turned at once into reasons by no process more elaborate than that of explicitly recognizing that my teachers, my family, or my neighbors, are truthful persons, happy in the possession of adequate means of information—propositions which in their turn, of course, require argumentative support. Such a procedure may, I need hardly say, be quite legitimate; and reasons of this kind are probably the principal ground on which in mature life we accept the great mass of our subordinate scientific and historical convictions. I believe, for instance, that the moon falls in toward the earth with the exact velocity required by the force of gravitation, for no other reason than that I believe in the competence and trustworthiness of the persons who have made the necessary calculations. In this case the reason for my belief and the immediate cause of it are identical; the cause, indeed, is a cause only in virtue of its being first a reason. But in the former case this is not so. *Mere* early training, paternal authority, or public opinion, were causes of belief before they were reasons; they continued to act as non-rational causes after they became reasons; and it is not improbable that to the very end they contributed less to the resultant conviction in their capacity as reasons than they did in their capacity as non-rational causes.

Now the temptation thus to convert causes into reasons seems under certain circumstances to be almost irresistible, even when it is illegitimate. Authority, as such, is from the nature of the case dumb in the presence of argument. It is only by reasoning that reasoning can be answered. It can be, and has often been, thrust silently aside by that instinctive feeling of repulsion which we call prejudice when we happen to disagree with it. But it can only be replied to by its own kind. And so it comes about that whenever any system of belief is seriously questioned, a method of defence which is almost certain to find favor is to select one of the causes by which the belief has been produced, and forthwith to erect it into a reason why the system should continue to be accepted. Authority, as I have been using the term, is thus converted into "an authority," or into "authorities." It ceases to be the opposite or correlative of reason. It can no longer be contrasted with reason. It becomes a species of reason, and as a species of reason it must be judged.

So judged, it appears to me that two things pertinent to the present discussion may be said of it. In the first place, it is evidently an argument of immense utility and of very wide application. As I have just noted, it is the proximate reason for an enormous proportion of our beliefs as to matters of fact, past and present, and for that very large body of scientific knowledge which even experts in science can have no opportunity of personally verifying. But, in the second place, it seems not less clear that the argument from "an authority" or "authorities" is almost always useless as a *foundation* for a system of belief. The deep-lying principles which alone deserve this name may be, and frequently are, the product of authority. But the attempt to ground them dialectically upon *an* authority can scarcely be attempted, except at the risk of logical disaster.

Take as an example the general system of our beliefs about the material universe. The greater number of these are, as we have seen, quite legitimately based upon the argument from "authorities"; not so those few which lie at the root of the system. These also are largely due to Authority. But they cannot be rationally derived from "authorities"; though the attempt so to derive them is almost certain to be made. The "universal experience," or the "general consent of mankind," will be adduced as an authoritative sanction of certain fundamental presuppositions of physical science; and of these, at least, it will be said, *securus judicat orbis terrarum*.[2] But a very little consideration is sufficient to show that this procedure is illegitimate, and that, as I have pointed out, we can neither know that the verdict of mankind has been given, nor, if it has, that anything can properly be inferred from it, unless we first assume the truth of the very principles which that verdict was invoked to establish. . . .

VI

Enough has now, perhaps, been said to indicate the relative positions of Reason and Authority in the production of belief. To Reason is largely due the growth of new and the sifting of old knowledge; the ordering, and in part the discovery, of that vast body of systematized conclusions which constitute so large a portion of scientific, philosophical, ethical, political, and theological learning. To Reason we are in some measure beholden, though not, perhaps, so much as we suppose, for hourly aid in managing so much of the trifling portion of our personal affairs entrusted to our care by Nature as we do not happen to have already surrendered to the control of habit. By Reason also is directed, or misdirected, the public policy of communities within the narrow limits of deviation permitted by accepted custom and tradition. Of its immense indirect consequences, of the part it has played in the evolution of human affairs by the disintegration of ancient creeds, by the alteration of the external conditions of human life, by the production of new moods of thought, or, as I have termed them, psychological climates, we can in this connection say nothing. For these are no rational effects of reason; the causal nexus by which they are bound to reason has no logical aspect; and if reason produces them, as in part it certainly does, it is in a manner indistinguishable from that in which similar consequences are blindly produced by the distribution of continent and ocean, the varying fertility of different regions, and the other material surroundings by which the destinies of the race are modified.

When we turn, however, from the conscious work of Reason to that which is unconsciously performed for us by Authority, a very different spectacle arrests our attention. The effects of the first, prominent as they are through the dignity of their origin, are trifling compared with the all-pervading influences which flow from the second. At every moment of our lives, as individuals, as members of a family, of a party, of a nation, of a

2 [The one who has confidence in himself judges in the world's affairs—ed. note.]

Church, of a universal brotherhood, the silent, continuous, unnoticed influence of Authority molds our feelings, our aspirations, and, what we are more immediately concerned with, our beliefs. It is from Authority that Reason itself draws its most important premises. It is in unloosing or directing the forces of Authority that its most important conclusions find their principal function. And even in those cases where we may most truly say that our beliefs are the rational product of strictly intellectual processes, we have, in all probability, only got to trace back the thread of our inferences to its beginnings in order to perceive that it finally loses itself in some general principle which, describe it as we may, is in fact due to no more defensible origin than the influence of Authority.

Nor is the comparative pettiness of the *rôle* thus played by reasoning in human affairs a matter for regret. Not merely because we are ignorant of the data required for the solution, even of very simple problems in organic and social life, are we called on to acquiesce in an arrangement which, to be sure, we have no power to disturb; nor yet because these data, did we possess them, are too complex to be dealt with by any rational calculus we possess or are ever likely to acquire; but because, in addition to these difficulties, reasoning is a force most apt to divide and disintegrate; and though division and disintegration may often be the necessary preliminaries of social development, still more necessary are the forces which bind and stiffen, without which there would be no society to develop.

It is true, no doubt, that we can, without any great expenditure of research, accumulate instances in which Authority has perpetuated error and retarded progress; for, unluckily, none of the influences, Reason least of all, by which the history of the race has been molded have been productive of unmixed good. The springs at which we quench our thirst are always turbid. Yet, if we are to judge with equity between these rival claimants, we must not forget that it is Authority rather than Reason to which, in the main, we owe, not religion only, but ethics and politics; that it is Authority which supplies us with essential elements in the premises of science; that it is Authority rather than Reason which lays deep the foundations of social life; that it is Authority rather than Reason which cements its superstructure. And though it may seem to savor of paradox, it is yet no exaggeration to say, that if we would find the quality in which we most notably excel the brute creation, we should look for it, not so much in our faculty of convincing and being convinced by the exercise of reasoning, as in our capacity for influencing and being influenced through the action of Authority.

NOTE

Much criticism has been directed against the use to which the word "Authority" has been put in this chapter. And there can be no doubt that a terminology which draws so sharp a distinction between phrases so nearly identical as "authority" and "an authority" must be open to objection.

Yet it still seems to me difficult to find a more suitable expression. There is no word in the English language which describes what I want to describe, and yet describes nothing else. Every alternative term seems at least as much open to misconception as the one I have employed, and I do not observe that those who have most severely criticized it, have suggested an unobjectionable substitute. Professor Pringle Pattison (Seth) in a most interesting and sympathetic review of this work [3] goes the length of saying that my use of the word is a "complete departure from ordinary usage." [4] But I can hardly think that this is so. However else the word may be employed in common parlance, it is surely often employed exactly as it is in this chapter—namely, to describe those causes of belief which are not reasons and yet are due to the influence of mind on mind. Parental influence is typical of the species: and it would certainly be in conformity with accepted usage to describe this as "Authority." A child does not accept its mother's teaching because it regards its mother as "an authority" whom it is reasonable to believe. The process is one of non-rational (not *irrational*) causation. Again I do not think it would be regarded as forced to talk of the "authority of public opinion" or the "authority of custom" exactly with the meaning which such expression would bear in the preceding chapter. "He submitted to the *authority* of a stronger will." "He never asked on what basis the claims of his Church rested; he simply bowed, as from his childhood he had always bowed, to her unchallenged *authority*." "No doubts were ever entertained, no inconvenient questions were ever asked, about the propriety of a practice which was enforced by the *authority* of unbroken custom." I think it will be admitted that in all these examples the word "authority" is used in the sense I have attributed to it, that this sense is a natural sense, and that no other single word could advantageously be substituted for it. If so, the reasons for its employment seem not inadequate.

I feel on even stronger ground in replying to the criticisms passed on

[3] Since republished in *Man's Place in the Cosmos*.
[4] *Op. cit.* p. 265.

my use here of the word "reason." Professor Pattison, though he does not like it, admits that it is in accordance with the practice of the older English thinkers. I submit that it is also in accordance with the usage prevalent in ordinary discourse. But I go further and say that I am employing the word in the sense in which it is always employed when "reason" is contrasted with "authority." If a man boasts that all his opinions have been arrived at by "following reason," he is referring not to the Universal Reason or Logos, but to his own faculty of discursive reason: and what he wishes the world to understand is that his beliefs are based on reasoning, not on authority or prejudice. Now this is the very individual whom I had in my mind when writing this chapter: and if I had been debarred from using the words "reason" and "reasoning" in their ordinary everyday meaning, I really do not see in what language I could have addressed myself to him at all.

❖ 16 ❖

INTUITION

Morris R. Cohen (1880–1947)

Let us begin by noting that though there has always been some conflict between pious or mystic theology and rationalistic philosophy, there had not been, previous to the eighteenth century, any marked conflict between intuitionism and rationalism. The reason for this is obvious if we remember that in the classical or Aristotelian-scholastic doctrine intuitive reason served all the functions now claimed for anti-rational intuition. Just as discursive reason established the necessary truth of propositions by deriving them from axioms according to the rules of logic, so intuitive reason enabled us to see these axioms as true or self-evident in themselves. But the spread of modern science and the development of radical changes in modern life brought to light a critical difference between these two kinds of

From *Reason and Nature* (1931), Book I, chapter two, section 3, pp. 46–54. Used by permission of the Free Press, copyright © 1931 by Morris R. Cohen, renewed 1959 by Lenora Cohen Rosenfield.

reason. For while the question of the correctness of mathematical proof occasions relatively little difference of opinion, the rational self-evidence of various axiomatic principles is a matter of most divergent and seemingly irreconcilable opinions. This certainly seems to be the case in subjects like rational theology, ethics, aesthetics, and other branches of philosophy. Canvass the opinion of people as to what they consider inherently reasonable, axiomatic, or self-evident, and you will find that in an overwhelming proportion of cases, this quality is attributed to the familiar or to what happens in fact to have been unquestioned. The questioning of that which we have been accustomed to accept and on which we have habitually relied is profoundly disturbing. Hence we naturally resist the questioner's challenge and we hold to our primary beliefs with increased vehemence. This is plainly seen when naïve people are confronted with the demand to show the evidence for the views that they regard as certain. They answer, generally, with some emphatic: It is so; I know it is so; I am sure it is so; or: How could it be otherwise? In a homogeneous community, the challenge of the doubter or skeptic may thus be crushed by the common feeling of certainty on the part of all the respectable. But in a period of rapidly developing science in which all sorts of preconceived opinions turn out to be false, doubt cannot be so readily eliminated. Moreover, in a heterogeneous community or in a time of struggle for power between different groups, questioning the first principles of our opponents is greatly admired and encouraged. In any case modern mathematics and physics have found the systematic questioning of self-evident axioms a fruitful source of new insight.

All this makes it now difficult to hold the old doctrine of an intuitive reason as an immediate revelation of the material propositions that are infallibly true in themselves. But to be certain of our cherished views—whatever they happen to be—and to hold them as inherently superior to the views of others, is a primitive vital desideratum; and if this primitive certainty is not called intuitive reason or the faculty of innate or a priori ideas, it is called by some other name such as common sense, intuition, instinct, faith, or something else.

(A) INTUITION AND COMMON SENSE

These terms were adopted by Reid and his followers when Hume ventured to challenge the older rationalistic doctrine of causality and the theologic structure which rested on it. Reid, undoubtedly, made some telling points in regard to realism and the impossibility of doubting the existence of all objective order. But despite his tremendous influence in France and Italy as well as in America, his method proved utterly barren. His followers simply elevated every challenged traditional belief into a fundamental intuition of the mind.

In exact science this method has been discredited, since all sorts of propositions formerly held as indubitably self-evident are now known to be false. But in the less rigorous realms of philosophy where we lack direct experimental checks on most of our statements, this elevation of the plausible into the axiomatic still prevails. Particularly true is this in the realm of legal philosophy and ethics where the doctrine of conscience still represents the old intuitionism.

It used to be a prevailing belief that a code of all the laws that should govern human conduct could be readily deduced from a few simple principles similar to Euclid's axioms. These principles were supposed to have been inscribed by Nature in the heart or conscience of every human individual. American courts still sometimes argue: "*We need no elaborate arguments. We need only consult conscience or the eternal principles of right and wrong, etc., to see that. . . .*" But the history of laws and the fate of codes have disillusioned us somewhat in this respect. With increased study of history, even American lawyers are beginning to question whether the maxims of our bills of rights are such eternal principles.

Conscience is still generally viewed as a private oracle which gives immediate answers to all our moral questions. Note, however, that though its dictates are often regarded as final and superior to all other authority, few ever draw the anarchic implications of this. We seldom excuse an atrocious act on the ground that the conscience of the perpetrator may be different from ours. If told that the Thug or Assassin acts according to his conscience we are likely to remark: So much the worse for his conscience. Indeed, a study of actual moral judgments in any community leaves little doubt that the dictates of conscience coincide, in the main, with the canons of generally accepted respectability. Direct teaching in childhood, natural imitation, and the general pressure of prevailing attitudes make us grow up with the habit of judging every one by the prevailing standard of respectability. As this habit is naturally carried over and applied to our own acts, we have the phenomenon of conscience.

This view of conscience as having its roots in tradition and habit does not deny individual variations of insight into moral problems. Nor does it deny the importance of maintaining our convictions where they happen to differ from those that at a given time dominate our community. The point is rather that so long as conscience is viewed as immediate and infallible, neither the social-authoritarian nor the individualistic-anarchic view of it will help us to deal with the actual mass of taboo, superstition, and moral confusion which characterize the prevailing moral judgments of any human community at any time. In the light of the actual variability of moral judgment in different groups and the ease with which the sense of right is molded by custom, training, and our own interests, we cannot regard the appeal to prevailing intuitions of right and wrong as absolutely decisive. If it is urged that there can be no moral judgment at all unless there is at its basis an intuitive sense or apprehension of right and wrong, we can only reply that such a sense, like the sense of physical reality, is necessary but insufficient for theoretical or practical purposes. It must submit to rational criticism in which the claim of every intuition is balanced by those of conflicting ones. The duty to follow our conscience is conditioned upon making it as enlightened as possible. In practice, limited time and limited energy may compel us to stop ethical inquiry at some arbitrary point. It then becomes necessary for us to abide by the best principles that we can reach in our limited deliberation. But to stop the questioning of conscience by maintaining that its dictates are absolute and self-evident can only result in hideous moral confusion.

(B) THE ILLATIVE SENSE AND INTUITIVE ASSENT

A somewhat neglected variant of intuitionism is the doctrine of the illative sense as developed by Cardinal Newman in his *Grammar of Assent*. It would be difficult to find anywhere else such skillful or felicitous illustrations of the difference between reasoning as described in formal treatises on logic and the ways in which active minds actually jump at fruitful inferences. Napoleon perceiving at once the proper moment to make a charge, the skillful diagnostician seeing in a flash what is behind a complicated disease, the quick perception of the proper thing to say and to do which we call tact, and a host of similar examples, all seem to illustrate the intuitive rather than the formal-logical character of effective or creative thinking. But all this is futile as an attack on logic or as a substitute for it. It would be relevant if logic were a description of the way we actually think, instead of a method of determining the correctness or incorrectness of inferences. A Napoleon, an expert diagnostician, and a person of remarkable tact, can and do make mistakes in their rapid inferences; and when any one of these is challenged, it is surely no adequate reply to say: I have an intuition, or my illative sense tells me.

It has been contended by De Maistre, James and other apologists for religion that no one ever changes his belief in God or immortality as a result of arguments. This may sound plausible but it is hard to see evidence for its truth. The effect of arguments is seldom appreciated immediately. We are frequently influenced by arguments which we stoutly resisted on previous occasions when others urged them upon us. It is to fly in the face of history to assert that the arguments of philosophers and theologians like Kant or Schleiermacher have had no effect whatsoever on the course of religious opinions. In any case the claim that certain convictions rest on the assent of the whole personality and not on intellectual argument is not an argument in their favor but often a euphemistic way of admitting that they rest on no evidence. In a world where we often have to stake our life on uncertainties, one may legitimately prefer to take his chance on an attractive prejudice, on an agreeable "hunch" or intuition, rather than on a process of reasoning from evidence which may not be free of error. But such an attitude certainly does not further knowledge; and by no stretch of the imagination can it guarantee superior attainment of truth.

(C) INTUITIONISM AND ONTOLOGISM

Can the difficulties of intuitionism be averted by assuming one rather than many self-evident intuitions? This was attempted by the Italian philosopher Rosmini, who made the intuition of *being* the basis of his system.[1] Assuredly nothing can be more certain than that there is being, and that all logical thought operates only by assuming it as the matrix wherein all rational relations or distinctions subsist. But the outer fate of the Rosminian philosophy provides a clue to its inner deficiencies. Its critics like Mamiani and Gioberti had no difficulty in showing that from the intuition of mere being—actual or possible—nothing of any specific importance could be inferred. On the other hand, to the extent that the primary intuition included the being of God as its object, it inevitably led to elements of pantheism which the Catholic Church was quick to detect and to condemn—and, I venture to add, rightly so. For no genuine religion is possible for the great mass of humanity except as it stimulates and is in turn fed by the sense of transcendence, of something greater than our petty selves and beyond that which we can grasp immediately. To be sure, the Church has kept great mystics like St. Bernard. But it regards the mystic vision as a supernatural gift rather than a primitive possession. The practical import of this distinction is enormous since on it depends the continued necessity of Church discipline as a perpetual check on the vagaries of mystic visions.

[1] See Rosmini, *Origin of Ideas*; T. Davidson, *Rosmini's Philosophical System*; L. Ferri, *La Philosophie Italienne.*

(D) INTUITION, LIFE, AND INSTINCT

Few habits are so characteristically modern as the vague use of the term *life* as honorific rather than descriptive. That the nature of life (like that of other realities) has not yet been completely grasped by human intelligence is an old and tragic truth. But that by merely living we have a source of knowledge different from and higher than that attained by rational science, is a rather new doctrine. It seems to be intimately connected with the current use of the word *life* as a glorification of our impulses no matter how pathologic or pathogenic. But the very difficulties of the latter cause every vigorous people to develop rational restraints. Otherwise life is degraded and brutally impoverished if not utterly destroyed. So in theoretic matters the first deliverances of the experience we call living are so full of illusion and contradiction that vigorous mentality seeks rational science as a deliverance (in part at least) from mortal error.

The assertion that by intelligence we know only phenomena while in mere living we know the absolute reality of things receives a certain plausibility from the widespread popular faith in introspection as the supreme and even primary form of knowledge. I take it, however, that the development of modern empirical psychology has brought ample evidence for the view that introspection is at least as full of difficulty and subject to error as any other form of observation. It certainly requires scientific training and much reflection to make its results reliable.

Life, as we know it introspectively, seems to present a greater continuity and interpenetration of parts than does the physical world. This gives a prima facie plausibility to Bergson's polemic against mechanistic explanations of life such as are offered by dogmatic positivists. Despite, however, the multitude of references to biologic literature, Bergson is hardly fortunate in his empirical illustrations.

Nor need we take seriously Bergson's central argument that because intelligence is developed in the process of evolution for practical purposes, it cannot know life. The premise of this argument—in which Bergson follows positivists like Spencer and Mach—is dubious and his conclusion is a *non sequitur*, if not in contradiction with his own premises.

It is vain to argue as to what purpose nature or evolution had in producing intelligence, or whether it had any purpose. We can tell the power of intelligence only by its actual operation before us. From the latter point of view there is little reason for doubting that intelligence plays a minor role as a biologic function—unintelligent species multiply and fill the earth —but in the field of natural science intelligence is the most powerful instrument for the discovery of *truth* that man has as yet developed. The reliability of any other method of reaching truth pales into insignificance compared to it. The very *utility* of science indeed depends on its truth. Bergson's argument from evolution assumes in fact the truth of scientific biology with its categories of organism, variation in time, environmental factors, etc. His premise thus assumes that by rational biologic science we do to some extent know the processes of life. From such an assumption no reputable logic can conclude that therefore the intellect cannot know the process of life.

Those who prefer to base philosophy on suggestive metaphors distrust and profess to be unconvinced by logical arguments; but you cannot both distrust logic and claim logical cogency for your own (fallacious) arguments.

In general, we may say that intelligence is the rational organization or distillation of the experience of living. Mere life apart from intelligent thought is dumb and blind. Unless intelligence illumines the meaning of our vital activity we can make no significant assertion about it nor draw any conclusion from it. That is why intuitionism has proved sterile not only in physics and ethics but also in the philosophy of art. For the essence of art is in articulate and coherent expression; and no philosophy which stresses formless feeling can throw light on the problem of artistic creation or its intelligent appreciation.

It ought in fairness to be added that by the intuition of life Bergson frequently means something similar to Spinoza's *intuitio*, to wit: a completion rather than a rejection of reason. But there can be no doubt that Bergson also draws an absolute separation and opposition between intuition and intelligence. The former is identical with instinct and extolled over the latter as the organic over the mechanical. His followers have certainly stressed this phase of his thought.

Like intuitive self-evidence or the illative sense, the expression "instinctive knowledge" is a popular device to protect favorite convictions from the necessity of rationally justifying themselves. Indeed "instinctive knowledge" seems to be but our old friend Innate Ideas in a rather thin biologic disguise. The biologic affiliation of the term *instinct* facilitates the suggestion of intimacy with life, and makes more plausible the denial that rational intelligence can know life. In the end, however, scientific biology while dealing with a subject-matter that is more complicated than inorganic physics pursues methods which are but the extension of the rational methods of physics.

Unlike most current writers Bergson uses the word instinct in a fairly definite sense. It denotes biologic acts that are congenital, attached to defi-

nite organic structures, and unmodifiable, at least during the life of the individual. With this conception of instinct we cannot speak of instinctive
knowledge without stretching the term *knowledge* in a way to debase our
intellectual currency. Thus Bergson speaks of the knowledge that the new-
born babe has of its mother's breast. If this be knowledge, why not also call
the sleeper's reflex withdrawal of a tickled limb an instance of knowledge?
But is digestion or the growing of teeth and hair knowledge? There is no
reason for asserting that every biologic act originates in a conscious purpose. Detailed empirical evidence is necessary to justify such a sweeping
generalization; and in any case, such a generalization should not be smug-
gled in by simply stretching the term *knowledge*. . . .

❖ 17 ❖

OPINING, KNOWING, AND BELIEVING

Immanuel Kant (1724–1804)

The holding of a thing to be true is an occurrence in our understanding
which, though it may rest on objective grounds, also requires subjective
causes in the mind of the individual who makes the judgment. If the judgment is valid for everyone, provided only he is in possession of reason, its
ground is objectively sufficient, and the holding of it to be true is entitled
conviction. If it has its ground only in the special character of the subject,
it is entitled *persuasion*.

Persuasion is a mere illusion, because the ground of the judgment,
which lies solely in the subject, is regarded as objective. Such a judgment
has only private validity, and the holding of it to be true does not allow of
being communicated. But truth depends upon agreement with the object,
and in respect of it the judgments of each and every understanding must
therefore be in agreement with each other. . . . The criterion whereby we
decide whether our holding a thing to be true is conviction or mere persua-

From *Critique of Pure Reason* (1st ed., 1781; 2nd ed., 1787), part II, chapter ii,
section 3. Translated by Norman Kemp Smith (1929). Translation used by permission of
Macmillan & Co. Ltd., London; St. Martin's Press, Inc., New York; and The Macmillan Company of Canada, Limited.

sion is therefore external, namely, the possibility of communicating it and of finding it to be valid for all human reason. For there is then at least a presumption that the ground of the agreement of all judgments with each other, notwithstanding the differing characters of individuals, rests upon the common ground, namely, upon the object, and that it is for this reason that they are all in agreement with the object—the truth of the judgment being thereby proved.

So long, therefore, as the subject views the judgment merely as an appearance of his mind, persuasion cannot be subjectively distinguished from conviction. The experiment, however, whereby we test upon the understanding of others whether those grounds of the judgment which are valid for us have the same effect on the reason of others as on our own, is a means, although only a subjective means, not indeed of producing conviction, but of detecting any merely private validity in the judgment, that is, anything in it which is mere persuasion.

If, in addition, we can specify the subjective *causes* of the judgment, which we have taken as being its objective *grounds*, and can thus explain the deceptive judgment as an event in our mind, and can do so without having to take account of the character of the object, we expose the illusion and are no longer deceived by it, although always still in some degree liable to come under its influence, insofar as the subjective cause of the illusion is inherent in our nature.

I cannot *assert* anything, that is, declare it to be a judgment necessarily valid for everyone, save as it gives rise to conviction. Persuasion I can hold to on my own account, if it so pleases me, but I cannot, and ought not, to profess to impose it as binding on anyone but myself.

The holding of a thing to be true, or the subjective validity of the judgment, in its relation to conviction (which is at the same time objectively valid), has the following three degrees: *opining, believing,* and *knowing. Opining* is such holding of a judgment as is consciously insufficient, not only objectively, but also subjectively. If our holding of the judgment be only subjectively sufficient, and is at the same time taken as being objectively insufficient, we have what is termed *believing.* Lastly, when the holding of a thing to be true is sufficient both subjectively and objectively, it is *knowledge.* The subjective sufficiency is termed *conviction* (for myself), the objective sufficiency is termed *certainty* (for everyone). There is no call for me to spend further time on the explanation of such easily understood terms.

I must never presume to *opine,* without *knowing at least something* by means of which the judgment, in itself merely problematic, secures connection with truth, a connection which, although not complete, is yet more than arbitrary fiction. Moreover, the law of such a connection must be certain. For if, in respect of this law also, I have nothing but opinion, it is all merely a play of the imagination, without the least relation to truth. Again, *opining* is not in any way permissible in judging by means of pure reason. For since such judging is not based on grounds of experience, but being in every case necessary has all to be arrived at *a priori*, the principle of the connection requires universality and necessity, and therefore complete certainty; otherwise we should have no guidance as to truth. Hence it is absurd to have an opinion in pure mathematics; either we must know, or we must abstain from all acts of judgment. It is so likewise in the case of the principles of morality, since we must not venture upon an action on the mere opinion that it is *allowed*, but must know it to be so.

In the transcendental employment of reason, on the other hand, while opining is doubtless too weak a term to be applicable, the term knowing is too strong. In the merely speculative sphere we cannot therefore make any judgments whatsoever. For the subjective grounds upon which we may hold something to be true, such as those which are able to produce belief, are not permissible in speculative questions, inasmuch as they do not hold independently of all empirical support, and do not allow of being communicated in equal measure to others.

But it is only from a *practical point of view* that the theoretically insufficient holding of a thing to be true can be termed believing. This practical point of view is either in reference to *skill* or in reference to *morality*, the former being concerned with optional and contingent ends, the latter with ends that are absolutely necessary.

Once an end is accepted, the conditions of its attainment are hypothetically necessary. This necessity is subjectively, but still only comparatively, sufficient, if I know of no other conditions under which the end can be attained. On the other hand, it is sufficient, absolutely and for everyone, if I know with certainty that no one can have knowledge of any other conditions which lead to the proposed end. In the former case my assumption and the holding of certain conditions to be true is a merely contingent belief; in the latter case it is a necessary belief. The physician must do something for a patient in danger, but does not know the nature of his illness. He observes the symptoms, and if he can find no more likely alternative, judges it to be a case of phthisis. Now even in his own estimation his belief is contingent only; another observer might perhaps come to a sounder conclusion. Such contingent belief, which yet forms the ground for the actual employment of means to certain actions, I entitle *pragmatic belief*.

The usual test, whether that which someone asserts is merely his persuasion—or at least his subjective conviction, that is, his firm belief—is *betting*. It often happens that someone propounds his views with such positive and uncompromising assurance that he seems to have entirely set aside all thought of possible error. A bet disconcerts him. Sometimes it turns out that he has a conviction which can be estimated at a value of one ducat, but not of ten. For he is very willing to venture one ducat, but when it is a question of ten he becomes aware, as he had not previously been, that it may very well be that he is in error. If, in a given case, we represent ourselves as staking the happiness of our whole life, the triumphant tone of our judgment is greatly abated; we become extremely diffident, and discover for the first time that our belief does not reach so far. Thus pragmatic belief always exists in some specific degree, which, according to differences in the interests at stake, may be large or may be small.

But in many cases, when we are dealing with an object about which nothing can be done by us, and in regard to which our judgment is therefore purely theoretical, we can conceive and picture to ourselves an attitude for which we regard ourselves as having sufficient grounds, while yet there is no existing means of arriving at certainty in the matter. Thus even in purely theoretical judgments there is an *analogon of practical* judgments, to the mental entertaining of which the term *"belief"* is appropriate, and which we may entitle *doctrinal belief*. I should be ready to stake my all on the contention—were it possible by means of any experience to settle the question—that at least one of the planets which we see is inhabited. Hence I say that it is not merely opinion, but a strong belief, on the correctness of which I should be prepared to run great risks, that other worlds are inhabited.

Now we must admit that the doctrine of the existence of God belongs to doctrinal belief. For as regards theoretical knowledge of the world, I can *cite* nothing which necessarily presupposes this thought as the condition of my explanations of the appearances exhibited by the world, but rather am bound so to employ my reason as if everything were mere nature. Purposive unity is, however, so important a condition of the application of reason to nature that I cannot ignore it, especially as experience supplies me so richly with examples of it. But I know no other condition under which this unity can supply me with guidance in the investigation of nature, save only the postulate that a supreme intelligence has ordered all things in accordance with the wisest ends. Consequently, as a condition of what is indeed a contingent, but still not unimportant purpose, namely, to have guidance in the investigation of nature, we must postulate a wise Author of the world. Moreover, the outcome of my attempts [in explanation of nature] so frequently confirms the usefulness of this postulate, while nothing decisive can be cited against it, that I am saying much too little if I proceed to declare that I hold it merely as an opinion. Even in this theoretical relation it can be said that I firmly believe in God. This belief is not, therefore, strictly speaking, practical; it must be entitled a doctrinal belief, to which the *theology* of nature (physico-theology) must always necessarily give rise. In view of the magnificent equipment of our human nature, and the shortness of life so ill-suited to the full exercise of our powers, we can find in this same divine wisdom a no less sufficient ground for a doctrinal belief in the future life of the human soul.

In such cases the expression of belief is, from the *objective* point of view, an expression of modesty, and yet at the same time, from the *subjective* point of view, an expression of the firmness of our confidence. Were I even to go the length of describing the merely theoretical holding of the belief as a hypothesis which I am justified in assuming, I should thereby be pledging myself to have a more adequate concept of the character of a cause of the world and of the character of another world than I am really in a position to supply. For if I assume anything, even merely as an hypothesis, I must at least know so much of its properties that I require to assume, *not its concept*, but *only its existence*. The term "belief" refers only to the guidance which an idea gives me, and to its subjective influence in that furthering of the activities of my reason which confirms me in the idea, and which yet does so without my being in a position to give a speculative account of it.

But the merely doctrinal belief is somewhat lacking in stability; we often lose hold of it, owing to the speculative difficulties which we encounter, although in the end we always inevitably return to it.

It is quite otherwise with *moral belief*. For here it is absolutely necessary that something must happen, namely, that I must in all points conform to the moral law. The end is here irrefragably established, and according to such insight as I can have, there is only one possible condition under which this end can connect with all other ends, and thereby have practical validity, namely, that there be a God and a future world. I also know with complete certainty that no one can be acquainted with any other conditions which lead to the same unity of ends under the moral law. Since, therefore, the moral precept is at the same time my maxim (reason prescribing that it should be so), I inevitably believe in the existence of God and in a future life, and I am certain that nothing can shake this belief, since my moral principles would thereby be themselves overthrown, and I cannot disclaim them without becoming abhorrent in my own eyes.

Thus even after reason has failed in all its ambitious attempts to pass beyond the limits of all experience, there is still enough left to satisfy us, so far as our practical standpoint is concerned. No one, indeed, will be able to boast that he *knows* that there is a God, and a future life; if he knows this, he is the very man for whom I have long [and vainly] sought. All knowledge, if it concerns an object of mere reason, can be communicated; and I might therefore hope that under his instruction my own knowledge would be extended in this wonderful fashion. No, my conviction is not *logical*, but *moral* certainty; and since it rests on subjective grounds (of the moral sentiment), I must not even say, "It *is* morally certain that there is a God, etc," but "*I am* morally certain, etc." In other words, belief in a God and in another world is so interwoven with my moral sentiment that as there is little danger of my losing the latter, there is equally little cause for fear that the former can ever be taken from me.

The only point that may seem questionable is the basing of this rational belief on the assumption of moral sentiments. If we leave these aside, and take a man who is completely indifferent with regard to moral laws, the question propounded by reason then becomes merely a problem for speculation, and can, indeed, be supported by strong grounds of analogy, but not by such as must compel the most stubborn skepticism to give way.[1] But in these questions no man is free from all interest. For although, through lack of good sentiments, he may be cut off from moral interest, still even in this case enough remains to make him *fear* the existence of a God and a future life. Nothing more is required for this than that he at least cannot pretend that there is any *certainty* that there is *no* such being and *no* such life. Since that would have to be proved by mere reason, and therefore apodeictically, he would have to prove the impossibility of both, which assuredly no one can reasonably undertake to do. This may therefore serve as *negative* belief, which may not, indeed, give rise to morality and good sentiments, but may still give rise to an analogon of these, namely, a powerful check upon the outbreak of evil sentiments.

But, it will be said, is this all that pure reason achieves in opening up prospects beyond the limits of experience? Nothing more than two articles of belief? Surely the common understanding could have achieved as much, without appealing to philosophers for counsel in the matter.

I shall not here dwell upon the service which philosophy has done to

[1] The human mind (as, I likewise believe, must necessarily be the case with every rational being) takes a natural interest in morality, although this interest is not undivided and practically preponderant. If we confirm and increase this interest, we shall find reason very teachable and in itself more enlightened as regards the uniting of the speculative with the practical interest. But if we do not take care that we first make men good, at least in some measure good, we shall never make honest believers of them.

human reason through the laborious efforts of its criticism, granting even that in the end it should turn out to be merely negative. . . . But I may at once reply: Do you really require that a mode of knowledge which concerns all men should transcend the common understanding, and should only be revealed to you by philosophers? Precisely what you find fault with is the best confirmation of the correctness of the above assertions. For we have thereby revealed to us, what could not at the start have been foreseen, namely, that in matters which concern all men without distinction nature is not guilty of any partial distribution of her gifts, and that in regard to the essential ends of human nature the highest philosophy cannot advance further than is possible under the guidance which nature has bestowed even upon the most ordinary understanding.

❖ 18 ❖

CONCERNING OPINION

John Laird (1887–1946)

1. GENERAL

According to Cardinal Newman, Catholics speak of theological opinion, not as of something necessarily doubtful, but in contrast, firstly, to anything known for certain; and, secondly, to the vital and essential assurance that is implied in the faith a Christian must live by.[1] Opinion, in this sense, is something not necessary to believe, although perhaps overwhelmingly probable, according to Catholic premises; and, at the same time, something which, being but probable, cannot be fully evidenced knowledge. On the other hand, many opinions do not even approach cogitative conviction and assurance. They are qualified and provisional decisions upon evidence known to be insufficient, where there should be no question

From *Knowledge, Belief and Opinion* by John Laird (Book II, chapter vi, pp. 167–81). Copyright, 1930, The Century Co. Copyright renewed, 1958, by John Laird. Reprinted by permission of Appleton-Century-Crofts, Educational Division of Meredith Corporation.

[1] *Grammar of Assent*, p. 57.

of a categorical Yes or No. And logically-minded persons recognize the fact perfectly well.

Semilogical and illogical persons, it is true, are frequently inclined to forget that their opinions are *only* opinions. It is the easiest thing in the world to jump to an unqualified assent, where there is no logical title to do more than incline toward provisional assent upon a favorable balance of probability, relative to decidedly insufficient evidence. In this respect, all of us, unless we are on our guard for special reasons, are frequently only semilogical. And obstinate men very often are quite illogical in this matter. "I am of opinion that the works of Burns is of an immoral tendency," Sir J. M. Barrie's Bowie Haggart said; "I have not read them myself, but such is my opinion."

The upper limit of opinion, in this sense, is belief (or something very near it), although it is never knowledge. The lower limit, on the other hand, would seem to be simply what is not beyond all conjecture or supposal. True, an opinion is an opinion based, even at the lowest level, upon a survey of conjectures, but some opinions are such that only one conjecture is before the opiner's mind, so that the survey is of this one conjecture only. The limiting case of the opinable, therefore, seems to be just the limiting case of potential surmise that is conceivably plausible.

It is possible, of course, to attempt to restrict "opinion" to a narrower connotation. Thus Cardinal Newman also held that opinion came midway between what he called profession and credence (which came below it), on the one hand, and what he called presumption and speculation (which came above it), on the other hand.[2]

Newman's criterion in this instance was logical. Profession he defined as a "notional" assent that had no personal intellectual effort behind it. To follow the fashions of the day in wine, or dress, or literature; to call oneself a Whig or a Tory because of the family tradition—in a word, to give lip-service to catchwords and allegiance to the unexamined—is what "profession" means. It is unworthy of the name of opinion. Credence, again (he maintained) is the same thing a little improved when judged by the standards of logic, but not, according to Newman, sufficiently improved to be, properly speaking, an opinion. What we pick up from newspapers in the way of information of an incapsulated, journalistic sort, or what reverberates as an echo from our travels is to be accounted mere credence. It is a gentleman's information, as opposed to a professional man's, the "ungrudging prompt assent" of a mind that may be polished and tolerably acute, but that has no particular reason for *thinking* about the matter. It is the kind of belief, according to Newman, that has never been subjected to

2 *Grammar of Assent*, pp. 40 ff.

ıny shock or strain, although it might very well be capable of surviving such ın ordeal if the ordeal came.

By "opinion," in contrast to "profession" or "credence," Newman meant neither more nor less than strict logical probability. "I shall here use the word," he said, "to denote an assent, but an assent to a proposition, not as true, but as probably true, that is, to the probability of that which the proposition enunciates; and as that probability may vary in strength without limits, so may the cogency and moment of the opinion." [3]

Above opinion, Newman placed presumption and speculation on the ground that these latter came nearer to (or might actually reach) cogitative certainty, although not deductive knowledge. By presumption he meant the assent to first principles (i.e., to fundamental principles regarded as inevitable and as true although not necessarily as self-evident). And by speculation he meant cogitative insight, quoting in corroboration of his terms the Shakespearean statement, "Thou hast no speculation in those eyes."

On the whole, since "probability" precisely defines what Newman here called "opinion," it seems unnecessary and inexpedient to have a second technical term for the same thing, unless usage plainly constrains us to have one. And commonly we do not thus restrict the term "opinion." When we speak of a "climate of opinion" (the phrase, I think, was Buckle's), we certainly include profession and credence in the "climate," and mean only to indicate that there is logical uncertainty in the air, whether or not the majority of the people who breathe it are, for the time being, convinced. When we speak of our own opinions, we may normally refer to those surmises concerning which we have tried to do a little original thinking, but may also refer to personal credence that we admit we have not attempted to examine. When we speak of political opinions, we think of views that are not shared by all members of the community, although many who hold such opinions do so with strong conviction. We use the word because we know that persons legally sound in mind and in many instances not less capable than we ourselves are of coming to a decision upon evidence, nevertheless decide differently from the way in which we ourselves decide, or, it may be, decline to decide.

From the logical standpoint, we do mean to imply, in all such cases, that we are dealing, not with certainties, but with plausibilities. On the other hand, we do not deny individual psychological assurance or conviction, and we do not mean to say anything at all about the extent to which those who opine have even an inkling of the logical status of their opinions. Our point is that such conclusions *are* matter of opinion whether

[3] *Ibid.*, p. 51.

those who hold the opinion are, or are not, aware of this logical circumstance.

Again, we *want* the word opinion to be as broad as is reasonably possible, but we tend to restrict the range of "probability" to something that is measurable according to an intelligible scale of equiprobability. This tendency to restrict probability to measurable probability is perhaps a mistake, but there are advantages in possessing a term that indicates only what inclines us to assent (but does not logically necessitate assent) whether or not this inclination is too indeterminate to be measured. And this, I think, is precisely the sense in which we commonly, and correctly, speak of "opinion."

2. WHAT IS MEANT BY A "COMPETENT" OPINION

In general, we distinguish between a "competent" or a "sensible" opinion and an opinion that is not to be described in any such terms; and as we all know, a competent opinion is often very hard to come by. Is it possible, then, to indicate with some precision what is meant by a competent opinion? The attempt is worth the making, because no other opinions are worth the having.

Negatively, we may affirm with some confidence that a mere opinion cannot be competent where knowledge or definitive proof is available. There might be relatively skillful guessing in such instances, but knowledge decrees a better way. A bridge player, for example, who guesses that the seven of trumps in his hand is higher than the last remaining trump in his adversary's hand, is not, properly speaking, a competent player although he need not be frankly incompetent. He ought to have counted all the trumps and to have noted all their denominations. If he had done so, he would *know*.

At the other end of the scale, we should say, with somewhat diminished confidence, that, where the evidence is *very* insufficient, a competent person would decline to give, and a very competent person would decline to form, any opinion whatsoever. This view appears to contradict much that is frequently stated *ex cathedra* by writers on the theory of mathematical probability, but the contradiction need not be more than apparent. Mathematicians measure a "probability" relative to the least scrap of evidence, and hesitate (if, like Mr. Keynes [4] and Mr. von Kries, they hesitate at all) only if they have strong grounds for suspecting that some few of these scraps of evidence are too indeterminate to yield a basis for any measurement. In general, however, the obstacle that prevents a "competent"

[4] *A Treatise on Probability*, pp. 42 ff.

person from expressing any opinion at all is his knowledge of the extreme inadequacy of the relevant information he possesses. Relative to his evidence he might give an opinion, but he is too prudent to do so. He does not expect to have exhaustive evidence, but he prefers to have an appreciable, perhaps a very appreciable, *weight* [5] of evidence before he ventures to pronounce an opinion.

In addition to the above, the chief point that arises concerns the relations between a competent expert opinion and the competence of a layman's opinion in matters partly of expertise. This problem bristles with difficulties. In professional circles, a competent opinion, especially if challenged in the law courts, means little more than an opinion that a duly qualified person might give, without revealing gross negligence, and without making the sort of mistake that no one except an ignoramus could possibly perpetrate. In this sense, the standard of "competence" is very low indeed; and for the purposes of this discussion it seems preferable to indicate a higher standard of "competence" in opinion. We might say, perhaps, that an "expert" opinion is one that a proficient, or even an eminent, member of some given profession might give without making an obvious slip, and which, although it might be mistaken, showed the influence of a master hand to some appreciable extent even in the mode of its error.

Are we, then, to say that no one except an expert is entitled to form an opinion at all in matters that require technical experience, and that common sense opinions are to be accepted, either with or without a pinch of salt, only in the instances in which any one man's views, given reasonable care and attention, are just as good as another's? Are the experts, in all other instances, the sole depositaries of such logic as is to be had?

Such a view would seem unreasonable. In the first place, it is easier to criticize with effect than to construct with effect, and therefore, in subjects not excessively technical (and in some parts even of highly technical subjects) a layman may be entirely competent to form an adverse or a favorable opinion about expert evidence, although he might be quite incapable of taking the lead in such matters. He might similarly (sometimes at least) be capable of acting as an umpire between divergent experts, as judges in the courts frequently are, although not, of course, always. Again, experts may have the defects of their expert qualities. They may be over-subtle. They may be too eager to obtain a "system," and insufficiently aware that what is sketchy or lath-and-plaster in the system ought to be more solid. They may also have an axe to grind.

Laymen do not have all these defects in quite the same way. They are under- rather than over-subtle. They have reverence only for well-estab-

5 Cf. Keynes, *op. cit.*, e.g., p. 312.

lished "systems," and the axes they have to grind are, in general, different axes. It does not follow, of course, that these opposite defects cancel one another. To pit under-subtlety against over-subtlety is a dangerous and a stupid way of attempting to reach the truth; and the standing problems of trial by jury, or of the practice of appointing Royal Commissions that contain only a few "experts," must remain standing problems. There is no doubt that an ordinary jury is not competent to form a sound opinion (in many cases) without proper direction from the judge, and also no doubt that the judge may misdirect or the jury grievously misapprehend their directions. On the other hand, there are grave dangers in officialdom and in professionalism, and there are certain reasonable objections to be taken to the extent to which matters of literary criticism, philosophy, economics, and political or natural science are in the hands of "academic" people. Hence the theory of Royal Commissions, according to which (on the whole and in most instances) experts have to explain and to defend their opinions in such a way as to persuade a majority of persons well versed in public affairs but not specially trained on the severely technical issues. (The experts, however, have a good deal to say, in private, about the other members.)

In various ways, therefore, although not in all particulars, a layman's opinion, or a general practitioner's, may be worth considering by a specialist, and a specialist's (perhaps) by a super-specialist. If it were not so, where is the principle to stop? No one can be a super-specialist in everything pertaining to his job, to say nothing of everything else, and we pity the patient who has to be examined by a dozen super-specialists. His ailments, however, may be numerous and complicated.

Opinions of some weight, therefore, may be pretty widely diffused. But how widely?

3. THE LIMITS OF CONJECTURE

A celebrated passage in the concluding chapter of Sir Thomas Browne's *Hydriotaphia* runs as follows:

"What Song the *Syrens* sang, or what name *Achilles* assumed when he hid himself among women, though puzzling questions are not beyond all conjecture. What time the persons of these Ossuaries entred the famous Nations of the dead, and slept with Princes and Counsellors, might admit a wide solution. But who were the proprietaries of these bones, or what bodies these ashes made up, were a question above Antiquarism. . . . There is no antidote against the *Opium* of time, which temporally considereth all things. . . . But the antiquity of oblivion blindly scattereth her poppy, and deals with the memory of men without distinction to merit of perpetuity."

This, in sum, is our question. What is beyond all conjecture, and does not admit even of the widest solution, cannot be matter of serious opinion. Where there are no data, or data so slender as to be completely worthless, there can not be an opinion that earns its name.

I think we may say, firstly, that whatever is meaningless cannot be either supposed or conjectured. Here, however, explanations are clearly required. For, as recent philosophical literature has shown, the meaning of "meaning" is not at all self-evident.

In the first place, "meaning" may be simple indication, as pointing with the finger, or some other such gesture. "I mean that" or "Keep off the grass. This means *you*" are illustrations. Private individuals are aware that they are pointing out something in particular and not something else; and in various ways we believe ourselves capable of inducing other people to refer to what we refer to. The first meaning of "meaning," therefore, is simple indication; and anything may be meant in this sense that may be pointed to.

In the second place, "meaning" may refer to the way in which, as we say, one thing indicates another, or suggests it. In a certain sense, this interpretation of meaning includes gestures. For these are events that signify other events. The same is true of the abbreviated gestures in conventionalized gesture language, in spoken language, in hieroglyphics, in mathematical symbols.

Most of these are arbitrary signs in which the symbol suggests what is symbolized through a conventional association. There might, however, be "natural" signs, as Reid suggested when he set about to improve Berkeley's theory whereby a divine (but essentially arbitrary) language made the evidence of sight suggest the evidence of touch to all men at all times. Again, most of the above signs are *substitute* signs, where the sign *stands for*, or does duty for, the thing signified, a point that does not hold of the first sense of "meaning," viz. simple indication.

The clearest and most important instance of this second kind is the connotative indication of logic, where one term means-what-is-meant-by, or indicates-what-is-indicated-by, some other term. This also is a phenomenon of suggestion. Anything that indicates or suggests anything else must do so *to a mind*. Without a mind, things might be connected but could never be suggestive. On the other hand, the suggestion may be due to a logical or to a factual connection, and need not be arbitrary or the product of mere (or alogical) association.

When we say that an opinion must at least have some meaning, we refer, in general, to this second sense of "meaning," and this second sense of "meaning" may be so very wide, or, again, so very conventional and so very personal and subjective, that it may be doubted whether this restriction of opinion to what has "meaning" is actually an effective restriction. To say that an opinion must be somehow suggestible to some one is not to say very much. Even dreams would be included in this category.

Attempting, therefore, to amend a statement that is far too wide, we might say that an opinion must seem to have logical or evidential meaning. It must be a possible interpretation of the kind of suggestion that is, or seems to be, relevant logical evidence. To that extent opinion cannot be wholly uncritical.

This amended description carries us a certain way, but not very far. What may *seem* to be relevant or logical to a savage, to a child, or to a peasant is a wide and curious collection, much of which would be summarily dismissed as "meaningless" by warier and more sophisticated persons. And the more sophisticated part of the world's population lives itself in a brittle shelter. For there are few who would have the effrontery to affirm that many, at least, of their best attested opinions might not prove, in the end, to be logically indefensible, or to have mistaken a spurious for a genuine analogy. What is consistent with itself and with the evidence, and what does not seem to be inconsistent with itself and with the evidence, are obviously very different indeed. Yet actual opinions are of the latter, not merely of the former, class.

Even where inconsistency is admitted and recognized in any opinion, the reality of the opinion is not always questioned. "I see that the thing can't be quite what I say it is, but you know what I mean" is a common form of statement and is not necessarily indefensible.

Again, where inconsistency arises, the state of affairs may be highly complicated. We have to consider (1) the parts and (2) the specific manner of their alleged conjunction. Even in the case of some plain absurdity like a round square, the parts, viz. "round" and "square," have meaning in the sense both that they can be indicated and that they can be defined. What is absurd is their conjunction in such a way that whatever has all the properties of the first has also all the properties of the second. Where the manner of the specific conjunction is less brutally obvious, impossible inconsistencies may easily escape notice, and in that case there may be genuine, although not defensible, opinion. It is always possible, moreover, that some analogous but slightly different conjunction may avoid inconsistency. If we suspect that this is possible, we adhere to our opinions, while admitting that they may need some revision in what we airily call matters of detail.

A point historically momentous in this connection concerns the logical status of the mysteries of the Christian religion. I may illustrate, once again, by referring to a contention of Cardinal Newman's concerning the Holy Trinity.

What Newman argued in substance was that the "Tres et unus" of Augustine, which gives the substance of the Athanasian Creed, is only an intellectual or theological mystery. Regarded as a "lex orandi et credendi" or, in other words, as a part of the believer's faith and vital participation or communion with deity, it is not a mystery at all. The various parts of this doctrine of the godhead (Newman enumerated nine of them in all) [6] are all laid hold on by every genuine believer. Each is a part of his Christian life, and as a simple believer he is neither asked nor expected to combine every feature in his life intellectually into a coherent pattern. There is, therefore, no mystery at all at the level of faith, and of good works, and of prayer, just as there is no mystery in a man's living his own existence. If a man creates a mystery about his life when he tries to form a philosophical theory about living, so much the worse for his intellectual capacities. Similarly, if he cannot understand how deity can be three and also one (Newman did not try to say, as some have said, that God was numerically one and non-numerically three), the fault should be assumed to lie in the man's intellectual or theological capacity. "We know one truth about Him and another truth,—but we cannot image both of them together; we cannot bring them before us by one act of the mind; we drop the one while we turn to take up the other. None of them is fully dwelt on and enjoyed, when they are viewed in combination." [7]

In this argument several different strands should be disentangled.

(1) If the mystery be simply that no theologian has hitherto succeeded in stating all the vital truths that describe man's communion with God in a fully comprehensible fashion, it is not even an intellectual *mystery*, although it remains an intellectual, or theological, *problem*.

(2) If what is meant is that certain theologians (and particularly the framers of the great creeds) have succeeded in describing the principal attributes of deity in a consistent, although in a very abstract, fashion, but that most humble folk cannot understand the theological solution, and cannot even keep nine propositions in their minds at once, there might be mystery for the laity, but there would not be mystery for the better theologians. But

(3) If what is meant is that certain of these theological propositions clearly contradict one another, and that each several proposition indis-

[6] *Grammar of Assent*, pp. 131 ff.
[7] *Ibid.*, p. 127.

putably describes, without the possibility of mistake, a necessary aspect of religious experience, then there is something more than mystery. There is utter impossibility; and it should be doubted whether any one either believed or opined what he clearly perceived to involve such a contradiction.

It seems unnecessary to proceed further with the consideration of this particular boundary of the territory of the opinable—the boundary, namely, that results from the requisite that what is opined must not be meaningless. What sometimes purports to be an alternative expression of the same view, however (although it may be substantially different), requires separate consideration. I mean the view that every opinion must at least be "conceivable."

The difficulty in this view is that the word "conceivable" suffers from a very mischievous ambiguity. It may mean "logically thinkable," and in that sense there is no difference whatever between "being conceivable" and "having an authentic meaning." The word, however, may also mean "imaginable in a pictorial way" (whether fanciful or otherwise), and this alternative and different meaning of "conceivable" should not be held to be a necessary prerequisite of a serious, or indeed of any, opinion.

In the first place, it need not be true that whatever is thinkable is imaginable in a pictorial way. Consider, for example, the statements, "A point has position but no magnitude" or "*Mere* position in time or space is causally irrelevant in Nature." These statements, whether or not they are true, are at least thinkable, but they are not pictorially imaginable. The first is intelligible, say, if, following Eudoxus, we think of the logical meaning of the intersection of the boundaries of two surfaces in the same plane; and it is separately intelligible although not separately imaginable. The second, similarly, is an affair of conception, not an affair of possible imagery. *Mere* position is unimaginable, but is thinkable if anything in these subjects is thinkable. (I am speaking, be it noted, not of mere position in "absolute space" or in "absolute time," but of the intelligible, yet unimaginable, meaning of position as such.)

A second, and more difficult, question is whether that which is pictorially imaginable is *therefore* thinkable, and consequently something that might be accepted, at least in the provisional way of opinion.

If our conclusions . . . were not mistaken, much that is imaginable is not a possible decision on evidence. For fancies are imaginable; and, in so far as the conceivable includes the fancied, it is not true that everything fancied is either believed or opined to be possible. It is possible *as a fancy* but need not be considered possible as an object of perception or as a thinkable member of the executive order of the world. The mere fact that in a daydream we might fancy ourselves Kings of Afghanistan, renouncing

European ways, is not a proof that we could ever be definitely and seriously of this opinion and yet retain our sanity.

Opinion, in short, is a narrower conception than imagination in one way, although in another way there is more logic in it (that is to say, more in the way of evidence) than in pictorial imagination. We might say, indeed, that opinions cannot be utterly incredible, at any rate to the opiner, although many fancies may be utterly incredible, even to the fancier. This is not to say that opinion and belief are ultimately the same. It is only to say that an opinion must be a possible candidate for belief. And the mere absence of incredibility is not a sufficient ground for believing, or a usual cause of belief.

4. THE LIMITS OF CREDULITY

Are there, then, any limits to human credulity, or to possible human opinion, other than the proviso that anything believed or opined must have some apparent meaning in the opiner's mind, and that it is not confessed to be frankly fanciful?

There is at least the appearance of prudence in answering this question in the negative. How can we set limits to what *somebody* has opined?

Consider, for example, witchcraft, demonology, and the other superstitions which human beings have not only opined but have believed in the mass for many centuries. Consider "magic, astrology, sorcery, divination, omens, the raising of spirits, auguries, auspices, necromancy, cabalism, oracles, the interpretation of dreams, pythonesses, sibyls, manes, lares, talismans, the presence of demons in flesh and blood, incubi, succubi, familiar lemures, vampirism, possession, lycanthropy, spirits, ghosts, specters, phantoms, lutins, sylphides, fairies, goblins, the evil eye, enchantments, etc." [8] Consider old wives' tales concerning, in the language of the poet Burns, "devils, ghosts, fairies, brownies, witches, warlocks, spunkies, kelpies, elf-candles, dead-lights, wraiths, apparitions, cantraips, giants, enchanted towers, dragons and other trumpery." Consider the alleged miracles of the early Christian saints and fathers, how St. Hilarion sprinkled the horses of the Christian Italicus with holy water, thereby enabling Italicus to win a chariot race against the pagan duumvir of Gaza, and all the "other trumpery" of this grotesque legend. Consider what St. Augustine regarded as evidence of fact, how he declared that the salamander lives in fire, that the hardest diamonds may be cut by the help of goats' blood, that the flesh of peacocks is incorruptible, how he related that seventy miracles had been wrought by the body of St. Stephen within two years in his own diocese of

8 *Boismont on Hallucinations,* Translation by Hulme, pp. 280 ff.

Hippo, and how he had knowledge of five authentic cases of the restoration of the dead to life.[9]

In the face of these considerations is it possible to allege that there is any limit to human credulity, even among the greatest of mankind?

In the main, these catalogues of signs and wonders refer to an order of belief and of opinion that has ceased to be held by most persons educated in the European tradition at the present day, although not by the majority of the world's inhabitants even now. To pile illustration upon illustration, therefore, should not be more impressive than to proffer a necessarily abbreviated catalogue of the wonders of modern science. In the days before the reign of experimental science, men's beliefs and opinions were not so much pre-logical as pre-experimental, and they had time in which to elaborate their pre-experimental views. We are critical to the extent, and in the way, in which we have been taught to be critical; and so were they. What they accepted on the authority of a saint, a herbalist, or a medicine-man is not in itself more incredible than what we accept on the evidence of a doctor, a psychologist, a physicist, or an astronomer, and it may not be less conformable to the accepted standards of the day. We shall be fortunate indeed if future ages do not have a good deal to say about *our* credulousness; and although future ages, let us hope, will be unable to deny that our prepossession in favor of natural science is much better grounded than the prepossessions of medicine-men, it is not unlikely that our tendency to shut our minds to everything that does not profess to have received experimental proof will call for, and receive, the severest animadversions.

Writing in the middle of last century, Mill pointed out that "the facts of travelling seventy miles an hour, painless surgical operations, and conversing by instantaneous signals between London and New York, held a high place, not many years ago, among reputed impossibilities." [10] The list today might be greatly extended; indeed the reputed impossibilities seem to be dwindling every day. This, indeed, is no evidence that the older magics will return. Old women will not learn the more easily to ride upon broomsticks, because the wealthier among them can now be transported by airplane at a moderate fee. If the dreams of the alchemists come true, these dreams will not be fulfilled according to the ancient prescriptions of alchemy. Certain ancient superstitions may be revived—and withdrawn from the category of superstition. But more is to be hoped from the enlargement of our outlook than from any reversion to ancient and discarded methods.

To say that anything is utterly incredible is to say that it is met, and that it ought to be met, by a shut mind; and it is rash, to say the least,

[9] Cf. Lecky, *The Rise and Influence of Rationalism in Europe*, p. 163.
[10] *System of Logic*, Book III, Ch. 25, note.

to boast that there are limits to open-mindedness other than the limits of demonstrable impossibility. To insist upon proper caution is quite another thing. An open mind need not be a careless mind, and it is possible to be hospitable without accepting all one's acquaintances as lifelong companions. The range of what is not beyond all conjecture and admits of a wide solution should be as extensive as the canons of proof permit.

PART II

KNOWLEDGE

KNOWLEDGE

John Locke (1632–1704)

I. OF KNOWLEDGE IN GENERAL

Since the mind, in all its thoughts and reasonings, hath no other immediate object but its own ideas, which it alone does or can contemplate, it is evident that our knowledge is only conversant about them.

Knowledge then seems to me to be nothing but the perception of the connection and agreement, or disagreement and repugnancy, of any of our ideas. In this alone it consists. Where this perception is, there is knowledge; and where it is not, there, though we may fancy, guess, or believe, yet we always come short of knowledge. For, when we know that white is not black, what do we else but perceive that these two ideas do not agree? When we possess ourselves with the utmost security of the demonstration that the three angles of a triangle are equal to two right ones, what do we more but perceive, that equality to two right ones does necessarily agree to, and is inseparable from, the three angles of a triangle?

But, to understand a little more distinctly, wherein this agreement or disagreement consists, I think we may reduce it all to these four sorts: (1.) Identity, or diversity. (2.) Relation. (3.) Coexistence, or necessary connection. (4.) Real existence.

First, As to the first sort of agreement or disagreement, viz., identity or diversity. It is the first act of the mind, when it has any sentiments or ideas at all, to perceive its ideas, and, so far as it perceives them, to know each what it is, and thereby also to perceive their difference, and that one is not another. This is so absolutely necessary, that without it there could be no knowledge, no reasoning, no imagination, no distinct thoughts at all. By this the mind clearly and infallibly perceives each idea to agree with itself, and to be what it is; and all distinct ideas to disagree, i.e., the one not to be the other: and this it does without pains, labor, or deduction, but at first view,

From An Essay Concerning Human Understanding, Book IV, chapters 1 and 2 (1690), the fourth edition (1700). The title of this selection has been supplied by the editors.

by its natural power of perception and distinction. And though men of art have reduced this into those general rules, "What is, is"; and, "It is impossible for the same thing to be and not to be," for ready application in all cases wherein there may be occasion to reflect on it; yet it is certain that the first exercise of this faculty is about particular ideas. A man infallibly knows, as soon as ever he has them in his mind, that the ideas he calls "white" and "round" are the very ideas they are, and that they are not other ideas which he calls "red" or "square." Nor can any maxim or proposition in the world make him know it clearer or surer than he did before, and without any such general rule. This, then, is the first agreement or disagreement which the mind perceives in its ideas, which it always perceives at first sight; and if there ever happen any doubt about it, it will always be found to be about the names, and not the ideas themselves, whose identity and diversity will always be perceived as soon and as clearly as the ideas themselves are, nor can it possibly be otherwise.

Secondly, The next sort of agreement or disagreement the mind perceives in any of its ideas may, I think, be called "relative," and is nothing but the perception of the relation between any two ideas, of what kind soever, whether substances, modes, or any other. For, since all distinct ideas must eternally be known not to be the same, and so be universally and constantly denied one of another: there could be no room for any positive knowledge at all, if we could not perceive any relation between our ideas, and find out the agreement or disagreement they have one with another, in several ways the mind takes of comparing them.

Thirdly, The third sort of agreement or disagreement to be found in our ideas, which the perception of the mind is employed about, is coexistence, or non-coexistence in the same subject; and this belongs particularly to substances. Thus when we pronounce concerning "gold" that it is fixed, our knowledge of this truth amounts to no more but this, that fixedness, or a power to remain in the fire unconsumed, is an idea that always accompanies and is joined with that particular sort of yellowness, weight, fusibility, malleableness and solubility in *aqua regia*, which make our complex idea, signified by the word "gold."

Fourthly, The fourth and last sort is that of actual real existence agreeing to any idea. Within these four sorts of agreement or disagreement is, I suppose, contained all the knowledge we have or are capable of; for, all the inquiries that we can make concerning any of our ideas, all that we know or can affirm concerning any of them, is, that it is or is not the same with some other; that it does or does not always coexist with some other idea in the same subject; that it has this or that relation to some other idea; or that it has a real existence without the mind. Thus, "Blue is not yellow," is of identity. "Two triangles upon equal bases between two parallels are equal," is of relation. "Iron is susceptible of magnetical impressions," is of coexistence. "God is," is of real existence. Though identity and coexistence are truly nothing but relations, yet they are so peculiar ways of agreement or disagreement of our ideas, that they deserve well to be considered as distinct heads, and not under relation in general; since they are so different grounds of affirmation and negation, as will easily appear to anyone who will but reflect on what is said in several places of this Essay. I should now proceed to examine the several degrees of our knowledge, but that it is necessary first to consider the different acceptations of the word "knowledge."

There are several ways wherein the mind is possessed of truth, each of which is called "knowledge."

First, There is "actual knowledge," which is the present view the mind has of the agreement or disagreement of any of its ideas, or of the relation they have one to another.

Secondly, A man is said to know any proposition which having been once laid before his thoughts, he evidently perceived the agreement or disagreement of the ideas whereof it consists; and so lodged it in his memory, that whenever that proposition comes again to be reflected on, he, without doubt or hesitation, embraces the right side, assents to and is certain of the truth of it. This, I think, one may call "habitual knowledge"; and thus a man may be said to know all those truths which are lodged in his memory by a foregoing clear and full perception, whereof the mind is assured past doubt as often as it has occasion to reflect on them. For, our finite understandings being able to think clearly and distinctly but on one thing at once, if men had no knowledge of any more than what they actually thought on, they would all be very ignorant; and he that knew most would know but one truth, that being all he was able to think on at one time.

Of habitual knowledge there are also, vulgarly speaking, two degrees:—

First, The one is of such truths laid up in the memory as, whenever they occur to the mind, it actually perceives the relation is between those ideas. And this is in all those truths whereof we have an intuitive knowledge, where the ideas themselves, by an immediate view, discover their agreement or disagreement one with another.

Secondly, The other is of such truths, whereof the mind having been convinced, it retains the memory of the conviction without the proofs. Thus a man that remembers certainly that he once perceived the demonstration that the three angles of a triangle are equal to two right ones, is certain that he knows it, because he cannot doubt of the truth of it. In his adherence to a truth where the demonstration by which it was at first known is forgot, though a man may be thought rather to believe his memory than really to know, and this way of entertaining a truth seemed formerly to me like something between opinion and knowledge, a sort of assurance which exceeds bare belief, for that relies on the testimony of another; yet, upon a due examination, I find it comes not short of perfect certainty, and is, in effect, true knowledge. That which is apt to mislead our first thoughts into a mistake in this matter is, that the agreement or disagreement of the ideas in this case is not perceived, as it was at first, by an actual view of all the intermediate ideas whereby the agreement or disagreement of those in the proposition was at first perceived; but by other intermediate ideas, that show the agreement or disagreement of the ideas contained in the proposition whose certainty we remember. For example: in this proposition, that "the three angles of a triangle are equal to two right ones," one who has seen and clearly perceived the demonstration of this truth, knows it to be true, when that demonstration has gone out of his mind, so that at present it is not actually in view, and possibly cannot be recollected: but he knows it in a different way from what he did before. The agreement of the two ideas joined in that proposition is perceived; but it is by the intervention of other ideas than those which at first produced that perception. He remembers, i.e., he knows (for remembrance is but the reviving of some past knowledge) that he was once certain of the truth of this proposition, that "the three angles of a triangle are equal to two right ones." The immutability of the same relations between the same immutable things is now the idea that shows him, that if the three angles of a triangle were once equal to two right ones, they will always be equal to two right ones. And hence he comes to be certain, that what was once true in the case is always true; what ideas once agreed will always agree: and, consequently, what he once knew to be true he will always know to be true, as long as he can remember that he once knew it. Upon this ground it is that particular demonstrations in mathematics afford general knowledge. If, then, the perception that the same ideas will eternally have the same habitudes and relations be not a sufficient ground of knowledge, there could be no knowledge of general propositions in mathematics; for no mathematical demonstration would be any other than particular: and when a man had demonstrated any proposition concerning one triangle or circle, his knowledge would not reach beyond that particular diagram. If he would extend it farther, he must renew his demonstration in another instance, before he could know it to be true in another like triangle, and so on; by which means one could never come to the knowledge of any general propositions. Nobody, I think, can deny that Mr. Newton certainly knows any proposition that he now at any time reads in his book to be true, though he has not in actual view that admirable chain of intermediate ideas whereby he at first discovered it to be true. Such a memory as that, able to retain such a train of particulars, may be well thought beyond the reach of human faculties: when the very discovery, perception, and laying together that wonderful connection of ideas is found to surpass most readers' comprehension. But yet it is evident the author himself knows the proposition to be true, remembering he once saw the connection of those ideas, as certainly as he knows such a man wounded another, remembering that he saw him run him through. But because the memory is not always so clear as actual perception, and does in all men more or less decay in length of time, this amongst other differences, is one which shows that demonstrative knowledge is much more imperfect than intuitive, as we shall see in the following chapter.

II. OF THE DEGREES OF OUR KNOWLEDGE

All our knowledge consisting, as I have said, in the view the mind has of its own ideas, which is the utmost light and greatest certainty we, with our faculties and in our way of knowledge, are capable of, it may not be amiss to consider a little the degrees of its evidence. The different clearness of our knowledge seems to me to lie in the different way of perception the mind has of the agreement or disagreement of any of its ideas. For if we will reflect on our own ways of thinking, we shall find that sometimes the mind perceives the agreement or disagreement of two ideas immediately by themselves, without the intervention of any other: and this, I think, we may call "intuitive knowledge." For in this the mind is at no pains of proving or examining, but perceives the truth, as the eye doth light, only by being directed towards it. Thus the mind perceives that white is not black, that a circle is not a triangle, that three are more than two, and equal to one and two. Such kind of truths the mind perceives at the first sight of the ideas together, by bare intuition, without the intervention of any other idea; and this kind of knowledge is the clearest and most certain that human frailty is capable of. This part of knowledge is irresistible, and, like bright sunshine, forces itself immediately to be perceived as soon as ever the mind turns its view that way; and leaves no room for hesitation, doubt, or examination, but the mind is presently filled with the clear light of it. It is on this intuition that depends all the certainty and evidence of all our knowledge, which certainly every one finds to be so great that he cannot imagine, and therefore not require, a greater: for a man cannot conceive himself capable of a greater certainty, than to know that any idea in his mind is such as he perceives it to be; and that two ideas, wherein he perceives a difference, are different, and not precisely the same. He that demands a greater certainty than this demands he knows not what, and shows only that he has a mind to be a skeptic without being able to be so. Certainty depends so wholly on this intuition, that in the next degree of knowledge, which I call "demonstrative," this intuition is necessary in all the connections of the intermediate ideas, without which we cannot attain knowledge and certainty.

The next degree of knowledge is, where the mind perceives the agreement or disagreement of any ideas, but not immediately. Though wherever the mind perceives the agreement or disagreement of any of its ideas, there be certain knowledge; yet it does not always happen that the mind sees that agreement or disagreement which there is between them, even where it is discoverable; and in that case remains in ignorance, and at most gets no farther than a probable conjecture. The reason why the mind cannot always perceive presently the agreement or disagreement of two ideas, is, because those ideas concerning whose agreement or disagreement the inquiry is made, cannot by the mind be so put together as to show it. In this case then, when the mind cannot so bring its ideas together as, by their immediate comparison and, as it were, juxtaposition or application one to another, to perceive their agreement or disagreement, it is fain, by the intervention of other ideas (one or more, as it happens), to discover the agreement or disagreement which it searches; and this is that which we call "reasoning." Thus the mind, being willing to know the agreement or disagreement in bigness between the three angles of a triangle and two right ones, cannot, by an immediate view and comparing them, do it: because the three angles of a triangle cannot be brought at once, and be compared with any one or two angles; and so of this the mind has no immediate, no intuitive knowledge. In this case the mind is fain to find out some other angles, to which the three angles of a triangle have an equality; and finding those equal to two right ones, comes to know their equality to two right ones.

Those intervening ideas which serve to show the agreement of any two others, are called "proofs"; and where the agreement or disagreement is by this means plainly and clearly perceived, it is called "demonstration," it being shown to the understanding, and the mind made to see that it is so. A quickness in the mind to find out these intermediate ideas (that shall discover the agreement or disagreement of any other), and to apply them right, is, I suppose, that which is called "sagacity."

This knowledge by intervening proofs, though it be certain, yet the evidence of it is not altogether so clear and bright, nor the assent so ready, as in intuitive knowledge. For though in demonstration the mind does at last perceive the agreement or disagreement of the ideas it considers, yet it is not without pains and attention: there must be more than one transient view to find it. A steady application and pursuit is required to this discovery: and there must be a progression by steps and degrees before the mind can in this way arrive at certainty, and come to perceive the agreement or repugnancy between two ideas that need proofs and the use of reason to show it.

Another difference between intuitive and demonstrative knowledge, is, that though in the latter all doubt be removed, when by the intervention of the intermediate ideas the agreement or disagreement is perceived: yet before the demonstration there was a doubt; which in intuitive knowledge cannot happen to the mind that has its faculty of perception left to a degree capable of distinct ideas, no more than it can be a doubt to the eye (that can distinctly see white and black), whether this ink and this paper be all of a color. If there be sight in the eyes, it will at first glimpse, without hesitation, perceive the words printed on this paper, different from the color of the paper: and so, if the mind have the faculty of distinct perception, it will perceive the agreement or disagreement of those ideas that produce intuitive knowledge. If the eyes have lost the faculty of seeing, or the mind of perceiving, we in vain inquire after the quickness of sight in one, or clearness of perception in the other.

It is true, the perception produced by demonstration is also very clear; yet it is often with a great abatement of that evident luster and full assurance that always accompany that which I call "intuitive"; like a face reflected by several mirrors one to another, where, as long as it retains the similitude and agreement with the object, it produces a knowledge; but it is still in every successive reflection with a lessening of that perfect clearness and distinctness which is in the first, till at last, after many removes, it has a great mixture of dimness, and is not at first sight so knowable, especially to weak eyes. Thus it is with knowledge made out by a long train of proofs.

Now, in every step reason makes in demonstrative knowledge, there is an intuitive knowledge of that agreement or disagreement it seeks with the next intermediate idea, which it uses as a proof: for if it were not so, that yet would need a proof; since without the perception of such agreement or disagreement there is no knowledge produced. If it be perceived by itself, it is intuitive knowledge: if it cannot be perceived by itself, there is need of some intervening idea, as a common measure, to show their agreement or disagreement. By which it is plain, that every step in reasoning that produces knowledge has intuitive certainty; which when the mind perceives, there is no more required but to remember it, to make the agreement or disagreement of the ideas, concerning which we inquire, visible and certain. So that to make anything a demonstration, it is necessary to perceive the immediate agreement of the intervening ideas, whereby the agreement or disagreement of the two ideas under examination (whereof the one is always the first, and the other the last in the account) is found. This intuitive perception of the agreement or disagreement of the intermediate ideas, in each step and progression of the demonstration, must also be carried exactly in the mind, and a man must be sure that no part is left out: which, because in long deductions, and the use of many proofs, the memory does not always so readily and exactly retain; therefore it comes to pass, that this is more imperfect than intuitive knowledge, and men embrace often falsehood for demonstrations.

The necessity of this intuitive knowledge, in each step of scientifical or demonstrative reasoning, gave occasion, I imagine, to that mistaken axiom, that all reasoning was *ex prœcognitis et prœconcessis*; which, how far it is mistaken, I shall have occasion to show more at large where I come to consider propositions, and particularly those propositions which are called "maxims"; and to show that it is by a mistake that they are supposed to be the foundations of all our knowledge and reasonings.

It has been generally taken for granted, that mathematics alone are capable of demonstrative certainty: but to have such an agreement or disagreement as may intuitively be perceived being, as I imagine, not the privilege of the ideas of number, extension, and figure alone, it may possibly be the want of due method and application in us, and not of sufficient evidence in things, that demonstration has been thought to have so little to do in other parts of knowledge, and been scarce so much as aimed at by any but mathematicians. For, whatever ideas we have wherein the mind can perceive the immediate agreement or disagreement that is between them, there the mind is capable of intuitive knowledge; and where it can perceive the agreement or disagreement of any two ideas, by an intuitive perception of the agreement or disagreement they have with any intermediate ideas, there the mind is capable of demonstration, which is not limited to ideas of extension, figure, number, and their modes.

The reason why it has been generally sought for and supposed to be only in those, I imagine, has been not only the general usefulness of those sciences, but because, in comparing their equality or excess, the modes of numbers have every the least difference very clear and perceivable: and though in extension every the least excess is not so perceptible, yet the mind has found out ways to examine and discover demonstratively the just equality of two angles, or extensions, or figures; and both these, i.e., numbers and figures, can be set down by visible and lasting marks, wherein the ideas under consideration are perfectly determined; which for the most part they are not, where they are marked only by names and words.

But in other simple ideas, whose modes and differences are made and counted by degrees, and not quantity, we have not so nice and accurate a distinction of their differences as to perceive or find ways to measure their just equality or the least differences. For, those other simple ideas being appearances or sensations produced in us by the size, figure, number, and motion of minute corpuscles singly insensible, their different degrees also depend upon the variation of some or all of those causes; which, since it cannot be observed by us in particles of matter whereof each is too subtile to be perceived, it is impossible for us to have any exact measures of the different degrees of these simple ideas. For, supposing the sensation or idea we name "whiteness," be produced in us by a certain number of globules, which, having a verticity about their own centers, strike upon the *retina* of the eye with a certain degree of rotation, as well as progressive swiftness; it will hence easily follow, that the more the superficial parts of any body are so ordered as to reflect the greater number of globules of light, and to give them that proper rotation which is fit to produce this sensation of white in us, the more white will that body appear that from an equal space sends to the *retina* the greater number of such corpuscles with that peculiar sort of motion. I do not say, that the nature of light consists in very small round globules, nor of whiteness in such a texture of parts as gives a certain rotation to those globules when it reflects them; for I am not now treating physically of light or colors: but this, I think, I may say, that I cannot (and I would be glad anyone would make intelligible that he did) conceive how bodies without us can any ways affect our senses, but by the immediate contact of the sensible bodies themselves, as in tasting and feeling, or the impulse of some insensible particles coming from them, as in seeing, hearing, and smelling; by the different impulse of which parts, caused by their different size, figure, and motion, the variety of sensations is produced in us.

Whether then they be globules or no; or whether they have a verticity about their own centers that produces the idea of whiteness in us; this is certain, that the more particles of light are reflected from a body, fitted to give them that peculiar motion which produces the sensation of whiteness in us, and possibly, too, the quicker that peculiar motion is, the whiter does the body appear from which the greater number are reflected, as is evident in the same piece of paper put in the sunbeams, in the shade, and in a dark hole; in each of which it will produce in us the idea of whiteness in far different degrees.

Not knowing therefore what number of particles, nor what motion of them, is fit to produce any precise degree of whiteness, we cannot demonstrate the certain equality of any two degrees of whiteness; because we have no certain standard to measure them by, nor means to distinguish every the least real difference; the only help we have being from our senses, which in this point fail us. But where the difference is so great as to produce in the mind clearly distinct ideas, whose differences can be perfectly retained, there these ideas of colors, as we see in different kinds, as blue and red, are as capable of demonstration as ideas of number and extension. What I have here said of whiteness and colors, I think, holds true in all secondary qualities and their modes.

These two, viz., intuition and demonstration, are the degrees of our knowledge; whatever comes short of one of these, with what assurance soever embraced, is but faith or opinion, but not knowledge, at least in all general truths. There is, indeed, another perception of the mind employed about the particular existence of finite beings without us; which, going beyond bare probability, and yet not reaching perfectly to either of the foregoing degrees of certainty, passes under the name of "knowledge." There can be nothing more certain, than that the idea we receive from an external object is in our minds; this is intuitive knowledge. But whether there be anything more than barely that idea in our minds, whether we can thence certainly infer the existence of anything without us which corresponds to that idea, is that whereof some men think there may be a question made; because men may have such ideas in their minds when no such thing exists, no such object affects their senses. But yet here, I think, we are provided with an evidence that puts us past doubting; for I ask anyone, whether he be not invincibly conscious to himself of a different perception when he looks on the sun by day, and thinks on it by night; when he actually tastes wormwood, or smells a rose, or only thinks on that savor or odor? We as plainly find the difference there is between any idea revived in our minds by our own memory, and actually coming into our minds by our senses, as we do between any two distinct ideas. If any one say, "A dream may do the same thing, and all these ideas may be produced in us without any external objects"; he may please to dream that I make him this answer: (1.) That it is no great matter whether I remove his scruple or no: where all is but dream, reasoning and arguments are of no use, truth and knowledge nothing. (2.) That I believe he will allow a very manifest difference between dreaming of being in the fire, and being actually in it. But yet if he be resolved to appear so skeptical as to maintain, that what I call "being actually in the fire" is nothing but a dream; and that we cannot thereby certainly know that any such thing as fire actually exists without us; I answer, that we certainly finding that pleasure or pain follows upon the application of certain objects to us, whose existence we perceive, or dream that we perceive, by own senses: this certainty is as great as our happiness or misery, beyond which we have no concernment to know or to be. So that, I think, we may add to the two former sorts of knowledge this also, of the existence of particular external objects by that perception and consciousness we have of the actual entrance of ideas from them, and allow these three degrees of knowledge, viz., intuitive, demonstrative, and sensitive: in each of which there are different degrees and ways of evidence and certainty.

But since our knowledge is founded on and employed about our ideas only, will it not follow from thence that it is conformable to our ideas; and that where our ideas are clear and distinct, or obscure and confused, our knowledge will be so too? To which I answer, No; for our knowledge consisting in the perception of the agreement or disagreement of any two ideas, its clearness or obscurity consists in the clearness or obscurity of that perception, and not in the clearness or obscurity of the ideas themselves; v.g., a man that has as clear ideas of the angles of a triangle, and of equality to two right ones, as any mathematician in the world, may yet have but a very obscure perception of their agreement, and so have but a very obscure knowledge of it. But ideas which by reason of their obscurity or otherwise are confused, cannot produce any clear or distinct knowledge; because as far as any ideas are confused, so far the mind cannot perceive clearly whether they agree or disagree. Or, to express the same thing in a way less apt to be misunderstood, he that hath not determined the ideas to the words he uses cannot make propositions of them, of whose truth he can be certain.

KNOWLEDGE BY ACQUAINTANCE
AND KNOWLEDGE BY DESCRIPTION
Bertrand Russell (1872–   )

The object of the following paper is to consider what it is that we know in cases where we know propositions about "the so-and-so" without knowing who or what the so-and-so is. For example, I know that the candidate who gets most votes will be elected, though I do not know who is the candidate who will get most votes. The problem I wish to consider is: What do we know in these cases, where the subject is merely described? I have considered this problem elsewhere [1] from a purely logical point of view; but in what follows I wish to consider the question in relation to theory of knowledge as well as in relation to logic, and in view of the above-mentioned logical discussions, I shall in this paper make the logical portion as brief as possible.

In order to make clear the antithesis between "acquaintance" and "description," I shall first of all try to explain what I mean by "acquaintance." I say that I am *acquainted* with an object when I have a direct cognitive relation to that object, i.e., when I am directly aware of the object itself. When I speak of a cognitive relation here, I do not mean the sort of relation which constitutes judgment, but the sort which constitutes presentation. In fact, I think the relation of subject and object which I call acquaintance is simply the converse of the relation of object and subject which constitutes presentation. That is, to say that S has acquaintance with O is essentially the same thing as to say that O is presented to S. But the associations and natural extensions of the word *acquaintance* are different from those of the word *presentation*. To begin with, as in most cognitive words, it is natural to say that I am acquainted with an object even at mo-

From *Mysticism and Logic* (1917) by Bertrand Russell. Reprinted by permission of George Allen & Unwin Ltd., London. This essay originally appeared in the *Proceedings of the Aristotelian Society*, 1910–11.
[1] See references later.

ments when it is not actually before my mind, provided it has been before my mind, and will be again whenever occasion arises. This is the same sense in which I am said to know that $2 + 2 = 4$ even when I am thinking of something else. In the second place, the word *acquaintance* is designed to emphasize, more than the word *presentation*, the relational character of the fact with which we are concerned. There is, to my mind, a danger that, in speaking of presentation, we may so emphasize the object as to lose sight of the subject. The result of this is either to lead to the view that there is no subject, whence we arrive at materialism; or to lead to the view that what is presented is part of the subject, whence we arrive at idealism, and should arrive at solipsism but for the most desperate contortions. Now I wish to preserve the dualism of subject and object in my terminology, because this dualism seems to me a fundamental fact concerning cognition. Hence I prefer the word *acquaintance*, because it emphasizes the need of a subject which is acquainted.

When we ask what are the kinds of objects with which we are acquainted, the first and most obvious example is *sense-data*. When I see a color or hear a noise, I have direct acquaintance with the color or the noise. The sense-datum with which I am acquainted in these cases is generally, if not always, complex. This is particularly obvious in the case of sight. I do not mean, of course, merely that the supposed physical object is complex, but that the direct sensible object is complex and contains parts with spatial relations. Whether it is possible to be aware of a complex without being aware of its constituents is not an easy question, but on the whole it would seem that there is no reason why it should not be possible. This question arises in an acute form in connection with self-consciousness, which we must now briefly consider.

In introspection, we seem to be immediately aware of varying complexes, consisting of objects in various cognitive and conative relations to ourselves. When I see the sun, it often happens that I am aware of my seeing the sun, in addition to being aware of the sun; and when I desire food, it often happens that I am aware of my desire for food. But it is hard to discover any state of mind in which I am aware of myself alone, as opposed to a complex of which I am a constituent. The question of the nature of self-consciousness is too large, and too slightly connected with our subject, to be argued at length here. It is difficult, but probably not impossible, to account for plain facts if we assume that we do not have acquaintance with ourselves. It is plain that we are not only *acquainted* with the complex "Self-acquainted-with-A," but we also *know* the proposition "I am acquainted with A." Now here the complex has been analyzed, and if "I" does not stand for something which is a direct object of acquaintance, we shall have to suppose that "I" is something known by description. If we wished to maintain the view that there is no acquaintance with Self, we might argue as follows: We are acquainted with *acquaintance*, and we know that it is a relation. Also we are acquainted with a complex in which we perceive that acquaintance is the relating relation. Hence we know that this complex must have a constituent which is that which is acquainted, i.e., must have a subject-term as well as an object-term. This subject-term we define as "I." Thus "I" means "the subject-term in awarenesses of which *I* am aware." But as a definition this cannot be regarded as a happy effort. It would seem necessary, therefore, either to suppose that I am acquainted with myself, and that "I," therefore, requires no definition, being merely the proper name of a certain object, or to find some other analysis of self-consciousness. Thus self-consciousness cannot be regarded as throwing light on the question whether we can know a complex without knowing its constituents. This question, however, is not important for our present purposes, and I shall therefore not discuss it further.

The awarenesses we have considered so far have all been awarenesses of particular existents, and might all in a large sense be called sense-data. For, from the point of view of theory of knowledge, introspective knowledge is exactly on a level with knowledge derived from sight or hearing. But, in addition to awareness of the above kind of objects, which may be called awareness of *particulars*, we have also (though not quite in the same sense) what may be called awareness of *universals*. Awareness of universals is called *conceiving*, and a universal of which we are aware is called a *concept*. Not only are we aware of particular yellows, but if we have seen a sufficient number of yellows and have sufficient intelligence, we are aware of the universal *yellow*; this universal is the subject in such judgments as "yellow differs from blue" or "yellow resembles blue less than green does." And the universal yellow is the predicate in such judgments as "this is yellow," where "this" is a particular sense-datum. And universal relations, too, are objects of awarenesses; up and down, before and after, resemblance, desire, awareness itself, and so on, would seem to be all of them objects of which we can be aware.

In regard to relations, it might be urged that we are never aware of the universal relation itself, but only of complexes in which it is a constituent. For example, it may be said that we do not know directly such a relation as *before*, though we understand such a proposition as "this is before that," and may be directly aware of such a complex as "this being before that." This view, however, is difficult to reconcile with the fact that we often know propositions in which the relation is the subject, or in which the relata are not definite given objects, but "anything." For example, we know that if one thing is before another, and the other before a third, then the first is before the third; and here the things concerned are not definite things, but "anything." It is hard to see how we could know such a fact about "before" unless we were acquainted with "before," and not merely with actual particular cases of one given object being before another given object. And more directly: A judgment such as "this is before that," where this judgment is derived from awareness of a complex, constitutes an analysis, and we should not understand the analysis if we were not acquainted with the meaning of the terms employed. Thus we must suppose that we are acquainted with the meaning of "before," and not merely with instances of it.

There are thus at least two sorts of objects of which we are aware, namely, particulars and universals. Among particulars I include all existents, and all complexes of which one or more constituents are existents, such as this-before-that, this-above-that, the-yellowness-of-this. Among universals I include all objects of which no particular is a constituent. Thus the disjunction "universal-particular" includes all objects. We might also call it the disjunction "abstract-concrete." It is not quite parallel with the opposition "concept-percept," because things remembered or imagined belong with particulars, but can hardly be called percepts. (On the other hand, universals with which we are acquainted may be identified with concepts.)

It will be seen that among the objects with which we are acquainted are not included physical objects (as opposed to sense-data), nor other people's minds. These things are known to us by what I call "knowledge by description," which we must now consider.

By a "description" I mean any phrase of the form "a so-and-so" or "the so-and-so." A phrase of the form "a so-and-so" I shall call an "ambiguous" description; a phrase of the form "the so-and-so" (in the singular) I shall call a "definite" description. Thus "a man" is an ambiguous description, and "the man with the iron mask" is a definite description. There are various problems connected with ambiguous descriptions, but I pass them by, since they do not directly concern the matter I wish to discuss. What I wish to discuss is the nature of our knowledge concerning objects in cases where we know that there is an object answering to a definite description, though we are not *acquainted* with any such object. This is a matter which is concerned exclusively with *definite* descriptions. I shall, therefore, in the sequel, speak simply of "descriptions" when I mean "definite descriptions." Thus a description will mean any phrase of the form "the so-and-so" in the singular.

I shall say that an object is "known by description" when we know that it is *"the so-and-so,"* i.e., when we know that there is one object, and no more, having a certain property; and it will generally be implied that we do not have knowledge of the same object by acquaintance. We know that the man with the iron mask existed, and many propositions are known about him; but we do not know who he was. We know that the candidate who gets most votes will be elected, and in this case we are very likely also acquainted (in the only sense in which one can be acquainted with some one else) with the man who is, in fact, the candidate who will get most votes, but we do not know which of the candidates he is, i.e., we do not know any proposition of the form "A is the candidate who will get most votes" where A is one of the candidates by name. We shall say that we have *"merely* descriptive knowledge" of the so-and-so when, although we know that the so-and-so exists, and although we may possibly be acquainted with the object which is, in fact, the so-and-so, yet we do not know any proposition *"a* is the so-and-so," where *a* is something with which we are acquainted.

When we say "the so-and-so exists," we mean that there is just one object which is the so-and-so. The proposition *"a* is the so-and-so" means that *a* has the property so-and-so, and nothing else has. "Sir Joseph Larmor is the Unionist candidate" means "Sir Joseph Larmor is a Unionist candidate, and no one else is." "The Unionist candidate exists" means "some one is a Unionist candidate, and no one else is." Thus, when we are acquainted with an object which we know to be the so-and-so, we know that the so-and-so exists, but we may know that the so-and-so exists when we are not acquainted with any object which we know to be the so-and-so, and even when we are not acquainted with any object which, in fact, is the so-and-so.

Common words, even proper names, are usually really descriptions. That is to say, the thought in the mind of a person using a proper name correctly can generally only be expressed explicitly if we replace the proper name by a description. Moreover, the description required to express the thought will vary for different people, or for the same person at different times. The only thing constant (so long as the name is rightly used) is the object to which the name applies. But so long as this remains constant, the particular description involved usually makes no difference to the truth or falsehood of the proposition in which the name appears.

Let us take some illustrations. Suppose some statement is made about Bismarck. Assuming that there is such a thing as direct acquaintance with oneself, Bismarck himself might have used his name directly to designate the particular person with whom he was acquainted. In this case, if he made a judgment about himself, he himself might be a constituent of the judgment. Here the proper name has the direct use which it always wishes to have, as simply standing for a certain object, and not for a description of the object. But if a person who knew Bismarck made a judgment about him, the case is different. What this person was acquainted with were certain sense-data which he connected (rightly, we will suppose) with Bismarck's body. His body as a physical object, and still more his mind, were only known as the body and the mind connected with these sense-data. That is, they were known by description. It is, of course, very much a matter of chance which characteristics of a man's appearance will come into a friend's mind when he thinks of him; thus the description actually in the friend's mind is accidental. The essential point is that he knows that the various descriptions all apply to the same entity, in spite of not being acquainted with the entity in question.

When we, who did not know Bismarck, make a judgment about him, the description in our minds will probably be some more or less vague mass of historical knowledge—far more, in most cases, than is required to identify him. But, for the sake of illustration, let us assume that we think of him as "the first Chancellor of the German Empire." Here all the words are abstract except "German." The word "German" will again have different meanings for different people. To some it will recall travels in Germany, to some the look of Germany on the map, and so on. But if we are to obtain a description which we know to be applicable, we shall be compelled, at some point, to bring in a reference to a particular with which we are acquainted. Such reference is involved in any mention of past, present, and future (as opposed to definite dates), or of here and there, or of what others have told us. Thus it would seem that, in some way or other, a description known to be applicable to a particular must involve some reference to a particular with which we are acquainted, if our knowledge about the thing described is not to be merely what follows logically from the description. For example, "the most long-lived of men" is a description which must apply to some man, but we can make no judgments concerning this man which involve knowledge about him beyond what the description gives. If, however, we say, "the first Chancellor of the German Empire was an astute diplomatist," we can only be assured of the truth of our judgment in virtue of something with which we are acquainted—usually a testimony heard or read. Considered psychologically, apart from the information we convey to others, apart from the fact about the actual Bismarck, which gives importance to our judgment, the thought we really have contains the one or more particulars involved, and otherwise consists wholly of concepts. All names of places—London, England, Europe, the earth, the Solar System—similarly involve, when used, descriptions which start from some one or more particulars with which we are acquainted. I suspect that even the Universe, as considered by metaphysics, involves such a connection with particulars. In logic, on the contrary, where we are concerned not merely with what does exist, but with whatever might or could exist or be, no reference to actual particulars is involved.

It would seem that, when we make a statement about something only known by description, we often *intend* to make our statement, not in the form involving the description, but about the actual thing described. That is to say, when we say anything about Bismarck, we should like, if we could, to make the judgment which Bismarck alone can make, namely, the judgment of which he himself is a constituent. In this we are necessarily defeated, since the actual Bismarck is unknown to us. But we know that there is an object B called Bismarck, and that B was an astute diplomatist. We can thus *describe* the proposition we should like to affirm, namely, "B was an astute diplomatist," where B is the object which was Bismarck. What enables us to communicate in spite of the varying descriptions we employ is that we know there is a true proposition concerning the actual Bismarck, and that, however we may vary the description (so long as the description is correct), the proposition described is still the same. This proposition, which is described and is known to be true, is what interests us; but we are not acquainted with the proposition itself, and do not know *it*, though we know it is true.

It will be seen that there are various stages in the removal from acquaintance with particulars: there is Bismarck to people who knew him, Bismarck to those who only know of him through history, the man with the iron mask, the longest-lived of men. These are progressively further removed from acquaintance with particulars, and there is a similar hierarchy in the region of universals. Many universals, like many particulars, are only known to us by description. But here, as in the case of particulars, knowledge concerning what is known by description is ultimately reducible to knowledge concerning what is known by acquaintance.

The fundamental epistemological principle in the analysis of propositions containing descriptions is this: *Every proposition which we can understand must be composed wholly of constituents with which we are acquainted.* From what has been said already, it will be plain why I advocate this principle, and how I propose to meet the case of propositions which at first sight contravene it. Let us begin with the reasons for supposing the principle true.

The chief reason for supposing the principle true is that it seems scarcely possible to believe that we can make a judgment or entertain a supposition without knowing what it is that we are judging or supposing about. If we make a judgment about (say) Julius Caesar, it is plain that the actual person who was Julius Caesar is not a constituent of the judgment. But before going further, it may be well to explain what I mean when I say that this or that is a constituent of a judgment, or of a proposition which we understand. To begin with judgments: a judgment, as an occurrence, I take to be a relation of a mind to several entities, namely, the entities which compose what is judged. If, e.g., I judge that A loves B, the judgment as an event consists in the existence, at a certain moment, of a specific four-term relation, called *judging*, between me and A and love and B. That is to say, at the time when I judge, there is a certain complex whose terms are myself and A and love and B, and whose relating relation is *judging*. My reasons for this view have been set forth elsewhere,[2] and I shall not repeat them here. Assuming this view of judgment, the constituents of the judgment are simply the constituents of the complex which is the judgment. Thus, in the above case, the constituents are myself and A and love and B and judging. But myself and judging are constituents shared by all my judgments; thus the *distinctive* constituents of the particular judgment in question are A and love and B. Coming now to what is meant by "understanding a proposition," I should say that there is another relation possible between me and A and love and B, which is called my *supposing* that A loves B.[3] When we can *suppose* that A loves B, we "understand the proposition" *A loves B*. Thus we often understand a proposition in cases where we have not enough knowledge to make a judgment. Supposing, like judging, is a many-term relation, of which a mind is one term. The other terms of the relation are called the constituents of the proposition supposed. Thus the principle which I enunciated may be restated as follows: *Whenever a relation of supposing or judging occurs, the terms to which the supposing or judging mind is related by the relation of supposing or judging must be terms with which the mind in question is acquainted.* This is merely to say that we cannot make a judgment or a supposition without knowing what it is that we are making our judgment or supposition about. It seems to me that the truth of this principle is evident as soon as the principle is understood; I shall, therefore, in what follows,

---

[2] *Philosophical Essays*, "The Nature of Truth." I have been persuaded by Mr. Wittgenstein that this theory is somewhat unduly simple, but the modification which I believe it to require does not affect the above argument [1917].

[3] Cf. Meinong, *Ueber Annahmen*, *passim*. I formerly supposed, contrary to Meinong's view, that the relationship of supposing might be merely that of presentation. In this view I now think I was mistaken, and Meinong is right. But my present view depends upon the theory that both in judgment and in assumption there is no single Objective, but the several constituents of the judgment or assumption are in a many-term relation to the mind.

assume the principle, and use it as a guide in analyzing judgments that contain descriptions.

Returning now to Julius Caesar, I assume that it will be admitted that he himself is not a constituent of any judgment which I can make. But at this point it is necessary to examine the view that judgments are composed of something called "ideas," and that it is the "idea" of Julius Caesar that is a constituent of my judgment. I believe the plausibility of this view rests upon a failure to form a right theory of descriptions. We may mean by my "idea" of Julius Caesar the things that I know about him, e.g., that he conquered Gaul, was assassinated on the Ides of March, and is a plague to schoolboys. Now I am admitting, and indeed contending, that in order to discover what is actually in my mind when I judge about Julius Caesar, we must substitute for the proper name a description made up of some of the things I know about him. (A description which will often serve to express my thought is "the man whose name was *Julius Caesar*." For whatever else I may have forgotten about him, it is plain that when I mention him I have not forgotten that that was his name.) But although I think the theory that judgments consist of ideas may have been suggested in some such way, yet I think the theory itself is fundamentally mistaken. The view seems to be that there is some mental existent which may be called the "idea" of something outside the mind of the person who has the idea, and that, since judgment is a mental event, its constituents must be constituents of the mind of the person judging. But in this view ideas become a veil between us and outside things—we never really, in knowledge, attain to the things we are supposed to be knowing about, but only to the ideas of those things. The relation of mind, idea, and object, on this view, is utterly obscure, and, so far as I can see, nothing discoverable by inspection warrants the intrusion of the idea between the mind and the object. I suspect that the view is fostered by the dislike of relations, and that it is felt the mind could not know objects unless there were something "in" the mind which could be called the state of knowing the object. Such a view, however, leads at once to a vicious endless regress, since the relation of idea to object will have to be explained by supposing that the idea itself has an idea of the object, and so on *ad infinitum*. I therefore see no reason to believe that, when we are acquainted with an object, there is in us something which can be called the "idea" of the object. On the contrary, I hold that acquaintance is wholly a relation, not demanding any such constituent of the mind as is supposed by advocates of "ideas." This is, of course, a large question, and one which would take us far from our subject if it were adequately discussed. I therefore content myself with the above indications, and with the corollary that, in judging, the actual objects concerning which we judge, rather than any supposed purely mental entities, are constituents of the complex which is the judgment.

When, therefore, I say that we must substitute for "Julius Caesar" some description of Julius Caesar, in order to discover the meaning of a judgment nominally about him, I am not saying that we must substitute an idea. Suppose our description is "the man whose name was *Julius Caesar*." Let our judgment be "Julius Caesar was assassinated." Then it becomes, "the man whose name was *Julius Caesar* was assassinated." Here *Julius Caesar* is a noise or shape with which we are acquainted, and all the other constituents of the judgment (neglecting the tense in "was") are *concepts* with which we are acquainted. Thus our judgment is wholly reduced to constituents with which we are acquainted, but Julius Caesar himself has ceased to be a constituent of our judgment. This, however, requires a proviso, to be further explained shortly, namely, that "the man whose name was *Julius Caesar*" must not, as a whole, be a constituent of our judgment, that is to say, this phrase must not, as a whole, have a meaning which enters into the judgment. Any right analysis of the judgment, therefore, must break up this phrase, and not treat it as a subordinate complex which is part of the judgment. The judgment "the man whose name was *Julius Caesar* was assassinated" may be interpreted as meaning "one and only one man was called *Julius Caesar*, and that one was assassinated." Here it is plain that there is no constituent corresponding to the phrase "the man whose name was *Julius Caesar*." Thus there is no reason to regard this phrase as expressing a constituent of the judgment, and we have seen that this phrase must be broken up if we are to be acquainted with all the constituents of the judgment. This conclusion, which we have reached from considerations concerned with the theory of knowledge, is also forced upon us by logical considerations, which must now be briefly reviewed.

It is common to distinguish two aspects, *meaning* and *denotation*, in such phrases as "the author of Waverley." The meaning will be a certain complex, consisting (at least) of authorship and Waverley with some relation; the denotation will be Scott. Similarly "featherless bipeds" will have a complex meaning, containing as constituents the presence of two feet and the absence of feathers, while its denotation will be the class of men. Thus when we say "Scott is the author of Waverley" or "men are the same as featherless bipeds," we are asserting an identity of denotation, and this assertion is worth making because of the diversity of meaning.[4] I believe that

---

4 This view has been recently advocated by Miss E. E. C. Jones. "A New Law of Thought and its Implications," *Mind*, January, 1911.

the duality of meaning and denotation, though capable of a true interpretation, is misleading if taken as fundamental. The denotation, I believe, is not a constituent of the proposition, except in the case of proper names, i.e., of words which do not assign a property to an object, but merely and solely name it. And I should hold further that, in this sense, there are only two words which are strictly proper names of particulars, namely, "I" and "this." [5]

One reason for not believing the denotation to be a constituent of the proposition is that we may know the proposition even when we are not acquainted with the denotation. The proposition "the author of Waverley is a novelist" was known to people who did not know that "the author of Waverley" denoted Scott. This reason has been already sufficiently emphasized.

A second reason is that propositions concerning "the so-and-so" are possible even when "the so-and-so" has no denotation. Take, e.g., "the golden mountain does not exist" or "the round square is self-contradictory." If we are to preserve the duality of meaning and denotation, we have to say, with Meinong, that there are such objects as the golden mountain and the round square, although these objects do not have being. We even have to admit that the existent round square is existent, but does not exist.[6] Meinong does not regard this as a contradiction, but I fail to see that it is not one. Indeed, it seems to me evident that the judgment "there is no such object as the round square" does not presuppose that there is such an object. If this is admitted, however, we are led to the conclusion that, by parity of form, no judgment concerning "the so-and-so" actually involves the so-and-so as a constituent.

Miss Jones [7] contends that there is no difficulty in admitting contradictory predicates concerning such an object as "the present King of France," on the ground that this object is in itself contradictory. Now it might, of course, be argued that this object, unlike the round square, is not self-contradictory, but merely non-existent. This, however, would not go to the root of the matter. The real objection to such an argument is that the law of contradiction ought not to be stated in the traditional form "A is not both B and not B," but in the form "no proposition is both true and false." The traditional form only applies to certain propositions, namely, to those which attribute a predicate to a subject. When the law is stated of propositions, instead of being stated concerning subjects and predicates, it

[5] I should now exclude "I" from proper names in the strict sense, and retain only "this" [1917].
[6] Meinong, *Ueber Annahmen*, 2nd ed., Leipzig, 1910, p. 141.
[7] *Mind*, July, 1910, p. 380.

is at once evident that propositions about the present King of France or the round square can form no exception, but are just as incapable of being both true and false as other propositions.

Miss Jones [8] argues that "Scott is the author of Waverley" asserts identity of denotation between *Scott* and *the author of Waverley*. But there is some difficulty in choosing among alternative meanings of this contention. In the first place, it should be observed that *the author of Waverley* is not a *mere* name, like *Scott*. *Scott* is merely a noise or shape conventionally used to designate a certain person; it gives us no information about that person, and has nothing that can be called meaning as opposed to denotation. (I neglect the fact, considered above, that even proper names, as a rule, really stand for descriptions.) But *the author of Waverley* is not merely conventionally a name for Scott; the element of mere convention belongs here to the separate words, *the* and *author* and *of* and *Waverley*. Given what these words stand for, *the author of Waverley* is no longer arbitrary. When it is said that Scott is the author of Waverley, we are not stating that these are two *names* for one man, as we should be if we said "Scott is Sir Walter." A man's name is what he is called, but however much Scott had been called the author of Waverley, that would not have made him be the author; it was necessary for him actually to write Waverley, which was a fact having nothing to do with names.

If, then, we are asserting identity of denotation, we must not mean by *denotation* the mere relation of a name to the thing named. In fact, it would be nearer to the truth to say that the *meaning* of "Scott" is the *denotation* of "the author of Waverley." The relation of "Scott" to Scott is that "Scott" means Scott, just as the relation of "author" to the concept which is so called is that "author" means this concept. Thus if we distinguish meaning and denotation in "the author of Waverley," we shall have to say that "Scott" has meaning but not denotation. Also when we say "Scott is the author of Waverley," the *meaning* of "the author of Waverley" is relevant to our assertion. For if the denotation alone were relevant, any other phrase with the same denotation would give the same proposition. Thus "Scott is the author of Marmion" would be the same proposition as "Scott is the author of Waverley." But this is plainly not the case, since from the first we learn that Scott wrote Marmion and from the second we learn that he wrote Waverley, but the first tells us nothing about Waverley and the second nothing about Marmion. Hence the meaning of "the author of Waverley," as opposed to the denotation, is certainly relevant to "Scott is the author of Waverley."

We have thus agreed that "the author of Waverley" is not a mere

[8] *Mind*, July, 1910, p. 379.

name, and that its meaning is relevant in propositions in which it occurs. Thus if we are to say, as Miss Jones does, that "Scott is the author of Waverley" asserts an identity of denotation, we must regard the denotation of "the author of Waverley" as the denotation of what is *meant* by "the author of Waverley." Let us call the meaning of "the author of Waverley" M. Thus M is what "the author of Waverley" means. Then we are to suppose that "Scott is the author of Waverley" means "Scott is the denotation of M." But here we are explaining our proposition by another of the same form, and thus we have made no progress toward a real explanation. "The denotation of M," like "the author of Waverley" has both meaning and denotation, on the theory we are examining. If we call its meaning M', our proposition becomes "Scott is the denotation of M'." But this leads at once to an endless regress. Thus the attempt to regard our proposition as asserting identity of denotation breaks down, and it becomes imperative to find some other analysis. When this analysis has been completed, we shall be able to reinterpret the phrase "identity of denotation," which remains obscure so long as it is taken as fundamental.

The first point to observe is that, in any proposition about "the author of Waverley," provided Scott is not explicitly mentioned, the denotation itself, i.e., Scott, does not occur, but only the concept of denotation, which will be represented by a variable. Suppose we say "the author of Waverley was the author of Marmion," we are certainly not saying that both were Scott—we may have forgotten that there was such a person as Scott. We are saying that there is some man who was the author of Waverley and the author of Marmion. That is to say, there is someone who wrote Waverley and Marmion, and no one else wrote them. Thus the identity is that of a variable, i.e., of an indefinite subject, "someone." This is why we can understand propositions about "the author of Waverley," without knowing who he was. When we say "the author of Waverley was a poet," we mean "one and only one man wrote Waverley, and he was a poet"; when we say "the author of Waverley was Scott" we mean "one and only one man wrote Waverley, and he was Scott." Here the identity is between a variable, i.e., an indeterminate subject ("he"), and Scott; "the author of Waverley" has been analyzed away, and no longer appears as a constituent of the proposition.[9]

The reason why it is imperative to analyze away the phrase "the author of Waverley" may be stated as follows. It is plain that when we say "the author of Waverley is the author of Marmion," the *is* expresses iden-

[9] The theory which I am advocating is set forth fully, with the logical grounds in its favor, in *Principia Mathematica*, Vol. I, Introduction, chap. III; also, less fully, in *Mind*, October, 1905.

tity. We have seen also that the common *denotation*, namely Scott, is not a constituent of this proposition, while the *meanings* (if any) of "the author of Waverley" and "the author of Marmion" are not identical. We have seen also that, in any sense in which the meaning of a word is a constituent of a proposition in whose verbal expression the word occurs, "Scott" means the actual man Scott, in the same sense (so far as concerns our present discussion) in which "author" means a certain universal. Thus, if "the author of Waverley" were a subordinate complex in the above proposition, its *meaning* would have to be what was said to be identical with the *meaning* of "the author of Marmion." This is plainly not the case; and the only escape is to say that "the author of Waverley" does not, by itself, have a meaning, though phrases of which it is part do have a meaning. That is, in a right analysis of the above proposition, "the author of Waverley" must disappear. This is effected when the above proposition is analyzed as meaning: "Some one wrote Waverley and no one else did, and that some one also wrote Marmion and no one else did." This may be more simply expressed by saying that the propositional function "*x* wrote Waverley and Marmion, and no one else did" is capable of truth, i.e., some value of *x* makes it true, but no other value does. Thus the true subject of our judgment is a propositional function, i.e. a complex containing an undetermined constituent, and becoming a proposition as soon as this constituent is determined.

We may now define the denotation of a phrase. If we know that the proposition "*a* is the so-and-so" is true, i.e., that *a* is so-and-so and nothing else is, we call *a* the denotation of the phrase "the so-and-so." A very great many of the propositions we naturally make about "the so-and-so" will remain true or remain false if we substitute *a* for "the so-and-so," where *a* is the denotation of "the so-and-so." Such propositions will also remain true or remain false if we substitute for "the so-and-so" any other phrase having the same denotation. Hence, as practical men, we become interested in the denotation more than in the description, since the denotation decides as to the truth or falsehood of so many statements in which the description occurs. Moreover, as we saw earlier in considering the relations of description and acquaintance, we often wish to reach the denotation, and are only hindered by lack of acquaintance: in such cases the description is merely the means we employ to get as near as possible to the denotation. Hence it naturally comes to be supposed that the denotation is part of the proposition in which the description occurs. But we have seen, both on logical and on epistemological grounds, that this is an error. The actual object (if any) which is the denotation is not (unless it is explicitly mentioned) a constituent of propositions in which descriptions occur; and this is the reason why, in order to understand such propositions, we need acquaintance with the constituents of the description, but do not need acquaintance with its denotation. The first result of analysis, when applied to propositions whose grammatical subject is "the so-and-so," is to substitute a variable as subject, i.e. we obtain a proposition of the form: "There is *something* which alone is so-and-so, and that *something* is such-and-such." The further analysis of propositions concerning "the so-and-so" is thus merged in the problem of the nature of the variable, i.e., of the meanings of *some, any,* and *all.* This is a difficult problem, concerning which I do not intend to say anything at present.

To sum up our whole discussion: We began by distinguishing two sorts of knowledge of objects, namely, knowledge by *acquaintance* and knowledge by *description.* Of these it is only the former that brings the object itself before the mind. We have acquaintance with sense-data, with many universals, and possibly with ourselves, but not with physical objects or other minds. We have *descriptive* knowledge of an object when we know that it is *the* object having some property or properties with which we are acquainted; that is to say, when we know that the property or properties in question belong to one object and no more, we are said to have knowledge of that one object by description, whether or not we are acquainted with the object. Our knowledge of physical objects and of other minds is only knowledge by description, the descriptions involved being usually such as involve sense-data. All propositions intelligible to us, whether or not they primarily concern things only known to us by description, are composed wholly of constituents with which we are acquainted, for a constituent with which we are not acquainted is unintelligible to us. A judgment, we found, is not composed of mental constituents called "ideas," but consists of an occurrence whose constituents are a mind [10] and certain objects, particulars or universals. (One at least must be a universal.) When a judgment is rightly analyzed, the objects which are constituents of it must all be objects with which the mind which is a constituent of it is acquainted. This conclusion forces us to analyze descriptive phrases occurring in propositions, and to say that the objects denoted by such phrases are not constituents of judgments in which such phrases occur (unless these objects are explicitly mentioned). This leads us to the view (recommended also on purely logical grounds) that when we say "the author of Marmion was the author of Waverley," Scott himself is not a constituent of our judgment, and that the judgment cannot be explained by saying that it affirms identity of denotation with diversity of meaning. It also,

[10] I use this phrase merely to denote the something psychological which enters into judgment, without intending to prejudice the question as to what this something is.

plainly, does not assert identity of meaning. Such judgments, therefore, can only be analyzed by breaking up the descriptive phrases, introducing a variable, and making propositional functions the ultimate subjects. In fact, "the so-and-so is such-and-such" will mean that "x is so-and-so and nothing else is, and x is such-and-such" is capable of truth. The analysis of such judgments involves many fresh problems, but the discussion of these problems is not undertaken in the present paper.

❖   21   ❖

KNOWING HOW AND KNOWING THAT
Gilbert Ryle (1900–   )

Preamble

In this paper, I try to exhibit part of the logical behavior of the several concepts of intelligence, as these occur when we characterize either practical or theoretical activities as clever, wise, prudent, skillful, etc.

The prevailing doctrine (deriving perhaps from Plato's account of the tripartite soul) holds: (1) that Intelligence is a special faculty, the exercises of which are those specific internal acts which are called acts of thinking, namely, the operations of considering propositions; (2) that practical activities merit their titles "intelligent," "clever," and the rest only because they are accompanied by some such internal acts of considering propositions (and particularly "regulative" propositions). That is to say, doing things is never itself an exercise of intelligence, but is, at best, a process introduced and somehow steered by some ulterior act of theorizing. (It is also assumed that theorizing is not a sort of doing, as if "internal doing" contained some contradiction.)

To explain how thinking affects the course of practice, one or more go-between faculties are postulated which are, by definition, incapable of con-

The Presidential Address to the Aristotelian Society, November 5, 1945. Reprinted from the *Proceedings of the Aristotelian Society*, Vol. 46 (1945–46), pp. 1–16, by courtesy of the author and of the Editor of the Aristotelian Society. Copyright 1946 The Aristotelian Society.

sidering regulative propositions, yet are, by definition, competent correctly to execute them.

In opposition to this doctrine, I try to show that intelligence is directly exercised as well in some practical performances as in some theoretical performances and that an intelligent performance need incorporate no "shadow-act" of contemplating regulative propositions.

Hence there is no gap between intelligence and practice corresponding to the familiar gap between theory and practice. There is no need, therefore, to postulate any Janus-headed go-between faculty, which shall be both amenable to theory and influential over practice.

That thinking-operations can themselves be stupidly or intelligently performed is a notorious truth which by itself upsets the assumed equation of "exercising intelligence" with "thinking." Else "stupid thinking" would be a self-contradictory expression and "intelligent thinking" would be a tautology. It also helps to upset the assumed type-difference between thinking and doing, since only subjects belonging to the same type can share predicates. But thinking and doing do share lots of predicates, such as "clever," "stupid," "careful," "strenuous," "attentive," etc.

To bring out these points I rely largely on variations of one argument. I argue that the prevailing doctrine leads to vicious regresses, and these in two directions. (1) If the intelligence exhibited in any act, practical or theoretical, is to be credited to the occurrence of some ulterior act of intelligently considering regulative propositions, no intelligent act, practical or theoretical, could ever begin. If no one possessed any money, no one could get any money on loan. This is the turn of the argument that I chiefly use. (2) If a deed, to be intelligent, has to be guided by the consideration of a regulative proposition, the gap between that consideration and the practical application of the regulation has to be bridged by some go-between process which cannot by the presupposed definition itself be an exercise of intelligence and cannot, by definition, be the resultant deed. This go-between application-process has somehow to marry observance of a contemplated maxim with the enforcement of behavior. So it has to unite in itself the allegedly incompatible properties of being kith to theory and kin to practice, else it could not be the applying of the one in the other. For, unlike theory, it must be able to influence action, and, unlike impulses, it must be amenable to regulative propositions. Consistency requires, therefore, that this schizophrenic broker must again be subdivided into one bit which contemplates but does not execute, one which executes but does not contemplate and a third which reconciles these irreconcilables. And so on forever.

(Some philosophers postulate a special class of acts, known as "volitions," to perform this desperate task. Others postulate some special impulses which can both motivate action and lend docile ears to regulative propositions.) In fact, of course, whatever "applying" may be, it *is* a proper exercise of intelligence and it is *not* a process of considering propositions.

Regresses of this pattern show, I suggest, not only that the prevailing doctrine is mistaken in equating exercises of intelligence with acts of theorizing, but also what sort of a mistake it is. It is that radical sort of mistake which can be labelled a "type-mistake." I shall here content myself with stating summarily what this mistake is. I do not develop this logicians' moral in the remainder of this paper.

Adverbs expressing intelligence-concepts (such as "shrewdly," "wittily," "methodically," "scrupulously," etc.) have hitherto been construed in the wrong logical type or category, namely, as signalizing the occurrence of special internal acts of that proprietary brand which we call "thought" or "theory."

But in fact they signalize not that a performance incorporates extra acts, whether of this brand or of any other brand, but that the performance itself possesses a certain style, method or *modus operandi*. Intelligently to do something (whether internally or externally) is not to do two things, one "in our heads" and the other perhaps in the outside world; it is to do one thing in a certain manner. It is somewhat like dancing gracefully, which differs from St. Vitus' dance, not by its incorporation of any extra motions (internal or external) but by the way in which the motions are executed. There need be no more moves in a job efficiently performed than in one inefficiently performed, though it is patent that they are performed in very different ways. Nor need a tidy room contain an extra article of furniture to be the *real* nominee of the adjective "tidy."

Phrases such as "technical skill," "scrupulous conduct" and even "practical reason" denote capacities to execute not tandem operations but single operations with special procedures.

This is why ordinary language does not provide specific verbs corresponding to our specific intelligence-adverbs and adjectives.

(This is not quite true of the adverb "voluntarily," since here philosophers have coined the specific verb "to will." But this verb has no ingenious employment. If it was ever employed, it would be a proper question to ask, "When we will, do we always, sometimes or ever will voluntarily?" Attempts to answer this question would quickly get the verb relegated to its proper place, on the shelf tenanted by "phlogiston.")

To put it in Aristotelian terms, intelligence-concepts belong to the category not of ποιεῖν [1] or of πάσχειν [2] but of πῶς.[3] This is why we, like Aristotle, squirm when we hear intelligence-criteria addressed as "Values" or "The Good." For these locutions and associated courtesies suggest that they are superior but occult substances, which is an even worse type-mistake than treating them as superior but occult activities or occurrences.

Philosophers have not done justice to the distinction which is quite familiar to all of us between knowing that something is the case and knowing how to do things. In their theories of knowledge they concentrate on the discovery of truths or facts, and they either ignore the discovery of ways and methods of doing things or else they try to reduce it to the discovery of facts. They assume that intelligence equates with the contemplation of propositions and is exhausted in this contemplation.

I want to turn the tables and to prove that knowledge-how cannot be defined in terms of knowledge-that and further, that knowledge-how is a concept logically prior to the concept of knowledge-that. I hope to show that a number of notorious cruces and paradoxes remain insoluble if knowing-that is taken as the ideal model of all operations of intelligence. They are resolved if we see that a man's intelligence or stupidity is as directly exhibited in some of his doings as it is in some of his thinking.

Consider, first, our use of the various intelligence-predicates, namely, "wise," "logical," "sensible," "prudent," "cunning," "skillful," "scrupulous," "tasteful," "witty," etc., with their converses "unwise," "illogical," "silly," "stupid," "dull," "unscrupulous," "without taste," "humorless," etc. What facts or what sorts of facts are known to the sensible which are not known to the silly? For example, what truths does the clever chessplayer know which would be news to his stupid opponent? Obviously there is no truth or set of truths of which we could say "If only the stupid player had been informed of them, he would be a clever player," or "When once he had been apprised of these truths he would play well." We can imagine a clever player generously imparting to his stupid opponent so many rules, tactical maxims, "wrinkles," etc., that he could think of no more to tell him; his opponent might accept and memorize all of them, and be able and ready to recite them correctly on demand. Yet he might still play chess stupidly, that is, be unable intelligently to apply the maxims, etc.

The intellectualist (as I shall call him) might defend his case by objecting that the stupid player did not "really" or "fully" know these truths.

[1] [Action—ed. note.]
[2] [Passion—ed. note.]
[3] [How, in what manner—ed. note.]

He had them by heart; but this was perhaps just a set of verbal habits, like the school-boy's rote-knowledge of the multiplication table. If he seriously and attentively considered these truths he would then be or become a clever player. Or, to modify the suggestion to avert an obvious rejoinder, if he seriously and attentively considered these truths not just while in bed or while in church but while playing chess, and especially if he considered the maxim relevant to a tactical predicament at the moment when he was involved in that predicament, then he would make the intelligent move. But, unfortunately, if he was stupid (*a*) he would be unlikely to tell himself the appropriate maxim at the moment when it was needed and (*b*) even if by luck this maxim did occur to him at the moment when it was needed, he might be too stupid to follow it. For he might not see that it was the appropriate maxim or if he did, he might not see how to apply it. In other words it requires intelligence not only to discover truths, but also to apply them, and knowing how to apply truths cannot, without setting up an infinite process, be reduced to knowledge of some extra bridge-truths. The application of maxims, etc., is certainly not any mere contemplation of them. Equally certainly it can be intelligently or stupidly done. (This is the point where Aristotle's attempted solution of Socrates' puzzle broke down. "How can the back-slider know moral and prudential maxims and still fail to behave properly?" This is only a special case of the general problem. "How can a man be as well-informed as you please and still be a fool?" "Why is a fool not necessarily an ignoramus?")

To switch over to a different example. A pupil fails to follow an argument. He understands the premises and he understands the conclusion. But he fails to see that the conclusion follows from the premises. The teacher thinks him rather dull but tries to help. So he tells him that there is an ulterior proposition which he has not considered, namely, that *if these premises are true, the conclusion is true*. The pupil understands this and dutifully recites it alongside the premises, and still fails to see that the conclusion follows from the premises even when accompanied by the assertion that these premises entail this conclusion. So a second hypothetical proposition is added to his store; namely, that the conclusion is true if the premises are true as well as the first hypothetical proposition that if the premises are true the conclusion is true. And still the pupil fails to see. And so on forever. He accepts rules in theory but this does not *force* him to apply them in practice. He considers reasons, but he fails to reason. (This is Lewis Carroll's puzzle in "What the Tortoise said to Achilles." I have met no successful attempt to solve it.)

What has gone wrong? Just this, that knowing how to reason was assumed to be analyzable into the knowledge or supposal of some propositions, namely, (1) the special premises, (2) the conclusion, plus (3) some extra propositions about the implication of the conclusion by the premises, etc., etc., *ad infinitum*.

"Well but surely the intelligent reasoner *is* knowing rules of inference whenever he reasons intelligently." Yes, of course he is, but knowing such a rule is not a case of knowing an extra fact or truth; it is knowing how to move from acknowledging some facts to acknowledging others. Knowing a rule of inference is not possessing a bit of extra information but being able to perform an intelligent operation. Knowing a rule is knowing how. It is realized in performances which conform to the rule, not in theoretical citations of it.

It is, of course, true that when people can reason intelligently, logicians can then extract the nerve of a range of similar inferences and exhibit this nerve in a logicians' formula. And they can teach it in lessons to novices who first learn the formula by heart and later find out how to detect the presence of a common nerve in a variety of formally similar but materially different arguments. But arguing intelligently did not before Aristotle and does not after Aristotle require the separate acknowledgement of the truth or "validity" of the formula. "God hath not . . . left it to Aristotle to make (men) rational." Principles of inference are not extra premises and knowing these principles exhibits itself not in the recitation of formulae but in the execution of valid inferences and in the avoidance, detection and correction of fallacies, etc. The dull reasoner is not ignorant; he is inefficient. A silly pupil may know by heart a great number of logicians' formulae without being good at arguing. The sharp pupil may argue well who has never heard of formal logic.

There is a not unfashionable shuffle which tries to circumvent these considerations by saying that the intelligent reasoner who has not been taught logic knows the logicians' formulae "implicitly" but not "explicitly"; or that the ordinary virtuous person has "implicit" but not "explicit" knowledge of the rules of right conduct; the skillful but untheoretical chessplayer "implicitly" acknowledges a lot of strategic and tactical maxims, though he never formulates them and might not recognize them if they were imparted to him by some Clausewitz of the game. This shuffle assumes that knowledge-how must be reducible to knowledge-that, while conceding that no operations of acknowledging-that need be actually found occurring. It fails to explain how, even if such acknowledgements did occur, their maker might still be a fool in his performance.

All this intellectualist legend must be rejected, not merely because it tells psychological myths but because the myths are not of the right type to account for the facts which they are invented to explain. However many strata of knowledge-that are postulated, the same crux always recurs that a fool might have all that knowledge without knowing how to perform, and a sensible or cunning person might know how to perform who had not been introduced to those postulated facts; that is, there still remains the same gulf, as wide as ever, between having the postulated knowledge of those facts and knowing how to use or apply it; between acknowledging principles in thought and intelligently applying them in action.

I must now try to speak more positively about what it is like to know-how. (*a*) When a person knows how to do things of a certain sort (e.g., make good jokes, conduct battles or behave at funerals), his knowledge is actualized or exercised in what he does. It is not exercised (save *per accidens*) in the propounding of propositions or in saying "Yes" to those propounded by others. His intelligence is exhibited by deeds, not by internal or external dicta. A good experimentalist exercises his skill not in reciting maxims of technology but in making experiments. It is a ruinous but popular mistake to suppose that intelligence operates only in the production and manipulation of propositions, i.e., that only in ratiocinating are we rational. (*b*) When a person knows how to do things of a certain sort (e.g., cook omelettes, design dresses or persuade juries), his performance is in some way governed by principles, rules, canons, standards or criteria. (For most purposes it does not matter which we say.) It is always possible in principle, if not in practice, to explain why he tends to succeed, that is, to state the reasons for his actions. It is tautology to say that there is a method in his cleverness. But his observance of rules, principles, etc., must, if it is there at all, be realized in his performance of his tasks. It need not (though it can) be also advertised in an extra performance of paying some internal or external lip-service to those rules or principles. He *must* work judiciously; he *may* also propound judgments. For propounding judgments is just another special activity, which can itself be judiciously or injudiciously performed. Judging (or propositional thinking) is one (but only one) way of exercising judiciousness or betraying silliness; it has its own rules, principles and criteria, but again the intelligent application of these does not prerequire yet another lower stratum of judgments on how to think correctly.

In short the propositional acknowledgement of rules, reasons or principles is not the parent of the intelligent application of them; it is a stepchild of that application.

In some ways the observance of rules and the using of criteria resemble the employment of spectacles. We look through them but not at them.

And as a person who looks much at his spectacles betrays that he has difficulties in looking through them, so people who appeal much to principles
show that they do not know how to act.

There is a point to be expounded here. I have been arguing in effect
that ratiocination is not the general condition of rational behavior but only
one species of it. Yet the traditional associations of the word "rational" are
such that it is commonly assumed that behavior can only be rational if the
overt actions taken are escorted by internal operations of considering and
acknowledging the reasons for taking them, i.e., if we preach to ourselves
before we practice. "How else" (it would be urged) "could principles,
rules, reasons, criteria, etc., govern performances, unless the agent thought
of them while or before acting?" People equate rational behavior with premeditated or reasoned behavior, i.e., behavior in which the agent internally
persuades himself by arguments to do what he does. Among the premises
of these postulated internal arguments will be the formulae expressing the
principles, rules, criteria or reasons which govern the resultant intelligent
actions. This whole story now seems to me false in fact and refutable in
logic. We do not find in fact that we persuade ourselves by arguments to
make or appreciate jokes. What sorts of arguments should we use? Yet it
certainly requires intelligence or rationality to make and see jokes. But
worse than this, when we do, as often happens, go through the process of
persuading ourselves to do things, this process is itself one which can be
intelligently or stupidly executed. So, if the assumption were correct, it
would be necessary for us to start one stage further back and to persuade
ourselves with second-order arguments to employ first-order persuasions of
a cogent and not of a silly type. And so on *ad infinitum*. The assumption,
that is, credits the rationality of any given performance to the rational execution of some anterior performance, which would in its turn require
exactly the same treatment. So no rational performance could ever be
begun. Aristotle's Practical Syllogism fails to explain intelligent conduct,
since its explanation is circular. For the postulated syllogizing would itself
need to be intelligently conducted.

What has happened once again is that intellectualists have tried to explain prudence, say, or skill by reference to a piece of acknowledging-that,
leaving unexplained the fact that this internal operation would itself have
to be cannily executed. They have tried to explain, e.g., practical flair by
reference to an intellectual process which, unfortunately for their theory,
again requires flair.

We should, before leaving this side of the matter, notice one variant
of the doctrine that knowing-how is reducible to a set of knowings-that. It

could be argued that as knowing-how always involves the knowing of a rule (in some broad sense of "rule"), this could be equated with the knowing not of *any* sort of truth, but of the truth of a general hypothetical of the pattern "whenever so and so, then such and such." For much, though not all, intelligent behavior does consist in taking the steps likely to lead to desired results. The knowledge involved might therefore be knowing that when actions of a certain sort are taken in certain situations, results of a certain sort tend to occur.

The answer to this is two-fold: (i) a man might accept any set of such hypothetical propositions and still not know how to cook or drive a car. He might even know them well enough to be a good teacher and still be stupid in his own performances. Conversely a girl might be a clever cook who had never considered any such general hypothetical propositions. If she had the knack or flair, she could do without news of the inductive generalization.

(ii) The suggested general hypotheticals are inductive generalizations. But making sound, as distinct from rash inductions is itself an intelligent performance. Knowing how to make inductions cannot await news of this higher-order induction, that when people assemble certain quantities of evidence in certain ways and produce conclusions of certain sorts, those conclusions tend to be true. Else induction could never begin; nor could the suggested higher-order induction have any data.

There is another difficulty. Sometimes we do go through the internal operation of persuading ourselves to do things, just as we often go through the external operation of persuading other people to do things. Let us suppose that the persuasion is cogent, i.e., that the recipient is convinced by it. What happens then? Does he necessarily do what he has been persuaded to do? Does he necessarily practice what he preaches? Notoriously not. I frequently persuade myself to smoke less, filling and lighting my pipe at the very moment when I am saying "yes" to the conclusion of the argument. Like Medea, I listen and am convinced, but I do not obey. You say "Ah, but you weren't 'really' or 'effectively' convinced. You said 'yes' in some theoretical or academic way, but you were not wise enough to say 'yes' in the practical way of putting your pipe back in your pocket." Certainly. This proves that unwisdom in conduct cannot be defined in terms of the omission of any ratiocinations and consequently that wisdom in conduct cannot be defined solely in terms of the performance of any ratiocinations. The intelligent application in practice of principles, reasons, standards, etc., is not a legatee of the consideration of them in theory; it can and normally does occur without any such consideration. Indeed we could not consider principles of method in theory unless we or others al-

ready intelligently applied them in practice. Acknowledging the maxims of
a practice presupposes knowing how to perform it. Rules, like birds, must
live before they can be stuffed.

(c) We certainly can, in respect of many practices, like fishing, cooking and reasoning, extract principles from their applications by people who
know how to fish, cook and reason. Hence Izaak Walton, Mrs. Beeton and
Aristotle. But when we try to express these principles we find that they
cannot easily be put in the indicative mood. They fall automatically into
the imperative mood. Hence comes the awkwardness for the intellectualist
theories of stating what are the truths or facts which we acknowledge when
we acknowledge a rule or maxim. We cannot call an imperative a truth or
falsehood. The Moral Law refuses to behave like a fact. You cannot affirm
or deny Mrs. Beeton's recipes. So, in the hope of having it both ways, they
tend to speak guardedly of the "validity" rather than the "truth" of such
regulative propositions, an idiom which itself betrays qualms about the reduction of knowing-how to knowing-that.

What is the use of such formulae if the acknowledgement of them is
not a condition of knowing how to act but a derivative product of theorizing about the nerves of such knowledge? The answer is simple. They are
useful pedagogically, namely, in lessons to those who are still learning how
to act. They belong to manuals for novices. They are not quasi-premises in
the postulated self-persuasions of those who know how to act; for no such
self-persuasions occur. They are imperative because they are disciplinary,
because they are in the idiom of the mentor. They are banisters for tod-
dlers, i.e., they belong to the methodology and not to the methods of intelligent practices. What logicians have long half-realized about the *venue*
and functions of their rule-formulae has yet to be learned by moral philosophers about their imperatives and ought-statements. When they have
learned this they will cease to ask such questions as whether conscience is
an intuitive or discursive faculty. For knowing how to behave is not a sort
of knowing-that, so it is neither an intuitive nor a discursive sort of
knowing-that. The question itself is as nonsensical as would be the corresponding question about the sense of humor or the ability to infer. Other
bogus ethico-epistemological questions also vanish, like the question
whether imperatives or ought-statements are synthetic or analytic, *à priori*
or *à posteriori* truths. How should we deal with such questions if posed
about Mrs. Beeton's recipes?

Another ethical muddle is also cleared up. Philosophers sometimes say
that conscience issues imperatives or dictates. Now "conscience" is an old-
fashioned faculty-word, but if the assertion means that the conscientious
man exercises his conscientiousness by issuing propositions or prescrip-

tions, then this is false. Knowing how to behave is exhibited by correct behavior, just as knowing how to cook is exhibited by palatable dishes. True, the conscientious man may be asked to instruct other agents how to behave, and then he will, if he knows how, publish maxims or specific prescriptions exemplifying maxims. But a man might know how to behave without knowing how to give good advice.

Sometimes a man might give good advice who did not know how to behave. Knowing how to advise about behavior is not the same thing as knowing how to behave. It requires at least three extra techniques: ability to abstract, ability to express and ability to impress. In another class of cases, a generally conscientious man might, in certain interference-conditions, not know how to behave, but be puzzled and worried about his line of action. He might then remind himself of maxims or prescriptions, i.e., he might resume, for the moment, the adolescent's task of learning how to behave. He would be issuing imperatives or ought-propositions to himself, but he would be doing so just because he did not know how to behave. He would be patching up a gap in his knowledge-how. And he might be bad at self-counsel without being a bad man. He might have a correct "hunch" that his self-suasions were invalid, though he could detect no fallacy in them. There would be a circle in the attempted description of conscience as a faculty which issues imperatives; for an imperative is a formula which gives a description or partial definition of what is known when some one knows how to behave. You couldn't define a good chef as one who cites Mrs. Beeton's recipes, for these recipes describe how good chefs cook, and anyhow the excellence of a chef is not in his citing but in his cooking. Similarly skill at arguing is not a readiness to quote Aristotle but the ability to argue validly, and it is just this ability some of the principles applied in which were extracted by Aristotle. Moral imperatives and ought-statements have no place in the lives of saints or complete sinners. For saints are not still learning how to behave and complete sinners have not yet begun to learn. So neither experiences scruples. Neither considers maxims.

Logical rules, tactical maxims and technical canons are in the same way helpful only to the half-trained. When a person knows how to do things of a certain sort, we call him "acute," "shrewd," "scrupulous," "ingenious," "discerning," "inventive," "an expert cook," "a good general," or "a good examiner," etc. In doing so we are describing a part of his character, or crediting him with a certain dispositional excellence. Correspondingly when we describe some particular action as clever, witty or wise, we are imputing to the agent the appropriate dispositional excellence. The way in which rules, standards, techniques, criteria, etc., govern his particular performances is one with the way in which his dispositional excellences are actualized in those performances. It is second nature in him to behave thus and the rules, etc., are the living nerves of that second nature. To be acute and consistent in reasoning is certainly to apply rules of inference to the propositions considered. But the reasoner does not have both to consider propositions and to cast sidelong glances at a formula; he just considers the propositions efficiently. The rules are the rails of his thinking, not extra termini of it. The good chess player observes rules and tactical principles, but he does not think of them; he just plays according to them. We observe rules of grammar, style and etiquette in the same way. Socrates was puzzled why the knowledge which constitutes human excellence cannot be imparted. We can now reply. Learning-how differs from learning-that. We can be instructed in truths, we can only be disciplined in methods. Appropriate exercises (corrected by criticisms and inspired by examples and precepts) can inculcate second natures. But knowledge-how cannot be built up by accumulation of pieces of knowledge-that.

An explanatory word is necessary here. "Discipline" covers two widely disparate processes, namely, habituation and education, or drill and training. A circus-seal can be drilled or "conditioned" into the performance of complicated tricks, much as the recruit is drilled to march and slope arms. Drill results in the production of automatisms, i.e., performances which can be done perfectly without exercising intelligence. This is habituation, the formation of blind habits. But education or training produces not blind habits but intelligent powers. In inculcating a skill I am not training a pupil to do something blindly but to do something intelligently. Drill dispenses with intelligence, training enlarges it. (It is a pity that Aristotle's sensible account of the formation of wise characters has been vitiated by the translator's rendering of ἐθισμός as "habituation." Aristotle was talking about how people learn to behave wisely, not how they are drilled into acting mechanically.) When the recruit reaches the stage of learning to shoot and read maps he is not drilled, but taught. He is taught to perform in the right way, i.e., to shoot and to use maps with "his head." Unlike the ₂seal he becomes a judge of his own performance—he learns what mistakes are and how to avoid or correct them. He learns how to teach himself and so to better his instructions. He acquires not a habit but a skill (though naturally skills contain habits). (Neglect of this distinction between conditioning and training is what vitiates Hume's account of Induction.) The fact that mathematics, philosophy, tactics, scientific method and literary style cannot be imparted but only inculcated reveals that these too are not bodies of information but branches of knowledge-how. They are not sciences but (in the old sense) disciplines. The experts in them cannot tell us what they know, they can only show what they know by operating with cleverness, skill, elegance or taste. The advance of knowledge does not consist only in the accumulation of discovered truths, but also and chiefly in the cumulative mastery of methods.

One last point. I have, I hope, proved that knowing-how is not reducible to any sandwich of knowings-that, and that our intelligence-predicates are definable in terms of knowing-how. I now want to prove that knowing-that presupposes knowing-how

(1) To know a truth, I must have discovered or established it. But discovering and establishing are intelligent operations, requiring rules of method, checks, tests, criteria, etc. A scientist or a historian is primarily a man who knows how to decide certain sorts of questions. Only secondarily is he a man who has discovered a lot of facts, i.e., has achieved successes in his application of these rules, etc. (though of course he only learns how to discover through exercises in discovery. He does not begin by perfecting his method and only later go on to have successes in applying it.) A scientist, that is, is primarily a knower-how and only secondarily a knower-that. He couldn't discover any particular truths unless he knew how to discover. He could know how to discover, without making this or that particular discovery.

(2) But when I have found out something, even then irrespective of the intelligence exercised in finding it out, I can't be said to have knowledge of the fact unless I can intelligently exploit it. I mean this. I might once have satisfied myself of something, say the distance between Oxford and Henley; and I might have enshrined this in a list of road distances, such that I could on demand reel off the whole list, as I can reel off the multiplication table. So in this sense I have not forgotten what I once found out. But if, when told that Nettlebed is so far out from Henley, I cannot tell you how far Nettlebed is from Oxford, or if, when shown a local map, I can see that Oxford to Banbury is about as far as Oxford to Henley but still cannot tell you how far Oxford is from Banbury or criticize false estimates given by others, you would say that I don't know the distance any longer, i.e., that I have forgotten or that I have stowed it away in a corner where it is not available.

Effective possession of a piece of knowledge-that involves knowing how to use that knowledge, when required, for the solution of other theoretical or practical problems. There is a distinction between the museum-possession and the workshop-possession of knowledge. A silly person can be stocked with information, yet never know how to answer particular questions.

The uneducated public erroneously equates education with the imparting of knowledge-that. Philosophers have not hitherto made it very clear what its error is. I hope I have provided part of the correction.

❖ 22 ❖

IF I KNOW I CAN'T BE WRONG

J. L. Austin (1911–1960)

One final point about "How do you know?," the challenge to the user of the expression "I know," requires still to be brought out by consideration of the saying that "If you know you can't be wrong." Surely, if what has so far been said is correct, then we are often right to say we *know* even in cases where we turn out subsequently to have been mistaken—and indeed we seem always, or practically always, liable to be mistaken.

Now, we are perfectly, and should be candidly, aware of this liability, which does not, however, transpire to be so very onerous in practice. The human intellect and senses are, indeed, *inherently* fallible and delusive, but not by any means *inveterately* so. Machines are inherently liable to break down, but good machines don't (often). It is futile to embark on a "theory of knowledge" which denies this liability: such theories constantly end up by admitting the liability after all, and denying the existence of "knowledge."

"When you know you can't be wrong" is perfectly good sense. You are prohibited from saying "I know it is so, but I may be wrong," just as you are prohibited from saying "I promise I will, but I may fail." If you are aware you may be mistaken, you oughtn't to say you know, just as, if you are aware you may break your word, you have no business to promise. But of course, being aware that you may be mistaken doesn't mean merely being aware that you are a fallible human being: it means that you have some concrete reason to suppose that you may be mistaken in this case. Just as "but I may fail" doesn't mean merely "but I am a weak human

From "Other Minds" in Aristotelian Society, Supplementary Volume XX (1946), pp. 169–175; reprinted in J. L. Austin's *Philosophical Papers* (1961), pp. 65–71. Reprinted by courtesy of the Editor of the Aristotelian Society. Copyright 1946 The Aristotelian Society.

being" (in which case it would be no more exciting than adding "D.V."):
it means that there is some concrete reason for me to suppose that I shall
break my word. It is naturally *always* possible ("humanly" possible) that I
may be mistaken or may break my word, but that by itself is no bar against
using the expressions "I know" and "I promise" as we do in fact use them.

At the risk (long since incurred) of being tedious, the parallel between saying "I know" and saying "I promise" may be elaborated.[1]

When I say "S is P," I imply at least that I believe it, and, if I have
been strictly brought up, that I am (quite) sure of it: when I say "I shall
do A," I imply at least that I hope to do it, and, if I have been strictly
brought up that I (fully) intend to. If I only believe that S is P, I can add
"But of course I may (very well) be wrong": if I only hope to do A, I can
add "But of course I may (very well) not." When I only believe or only
hope, it is recognized that further evidence or further circumstances are
liable to make me change my mind. If I say "S is P" when I don't even
believe it, I am lying: if I say it when I believe it but am not sure of it, I
may be misleading but I am not exactly lying. If I say "I shall do A" when
I have not even any hope, not the slightest intention, of doing it, then I
am deliberately deceiving: if I say it when I do not fully intend to, I am
misleading but I am not deliberately deceiving in the same way.

But now, when I say "I promise," a new plunge is taken: I have not
merely announced my intention, but, by using this formula (performing
this ritual), I have bound myself to others, and staked my reputation, in a
new way. Similarly, saying "I know" is taking a new plunge. But it is *not*
saying "I have performed a specially striking feat of cognition, superior, in
the same scale as believing and being sure, even to being merely quite
sure": for there *is* nothing in that scale superior to being quite sure. Just as
promising is not something superior, in the same scale as hoping and intending, even to merely fully intending: for there *is* nothing in that scale
superior to fully intending. When I say "I know," I *give others my word*: I
give others my authority for saying that "S is P."

When I have said only that I am sure, and prove to have been mistaken, I am not liable to be rounded on by others in the same way as when

---

[1] It is the use of the expressions "I know" and "I promise" (first person singular,
present indicative tense) alone that is being considered. "If I knew, I can't have been
wrong" or "If she knows she can't be wrong" are not worrying in the way that "If I
('you') know I ('you') can't be wrong" is worrying. Or again, "I promise" is quite
different from "he promises": if I say "I promise," I don't say I *say* I promise, I
promise, just as if he says he promises, he doesn't say he says he promises, he promises:
whereas if I say "he promises," I do (only) say he *says* he promises—in the other
"sense" of "promise," the "sense" in which *I* say *I* promise, only *he* can say he promises.
I *describe* his promising, but I *do* my own promising and he must do *his* own.

I have said "I know." I am sure *for my part*, you can take it or leave it: accept it if you think I'm an acute and careful person, that's your responsibility. But I don't know "for my part," and when I say "I know" I don't mean you can take it or leave it (though of course you *can* take it or leave it). In the same way, when I say I fully intend to, I do so for my part, and, according as you think highly or poorly of my resolution and chances, you will elect to act on it or not to act on it: but if I say I promise, you are *entitled* to act on it, whether or not you choose to do so. If I have said I know or I promise, you insult me in a special way by refusing to accept it. We all *feel* the very great difference between saying even "I'm *absolutely* sure" and saying "I know": it is like the difference between saying even "I firmly and irrevocably intend" and "I promise." If someone has promised me to do A, then I am entitled to rely on it, and can myself make promises on the strength of it: and so, where someone has said to me "I know," I am entitled to say *I* know too, at second hand. The right to say "I know" is transmissible, in the sort of way that other authority is transmissible. Hence, if I say it lightly, I may be *responsible* for getting *you* into trouble.

If you say you *know* something, the most immediate challenge takes the form of asking "Are you in a position to know?": that is, you must undertake to show, not merely that you are sure of it, but that it is within your cognizance. There is a similar form of challenge in the case of promising: fully intending is not enough—you must also undertake to show that "you are in a position to promise," that is that it is within your power. Over these points in the two cases parallel series of doubts are apt to infect philosophers, on the ground that I cannot foresee the future. Some begin to hold that I should never, or practically never, say I know anything— perhaps only what I am sensing at this moment: others, that I should never, or practically never, say I promise—perhaps only what is actually within my power at this moment. In both cases there is an obsession: if I know I *can't be wrong*, so I can't have the right to say I know, and if I promise I *can't fail*, so I can't have the right to say I promise. And in both cases this obsession fastens on my inability to make *predictions* as the root of the matter, meaning by predictions claims to know the future. But this is doubly mistaken in both cases. As has been seen, we may be perfectly justified in saying we know or we promise, in spite of the fact that things "may" turn out badly, and it's a more or less serious matter for us if they do. And further, it is overlooked that the conditions which must be satisfied if I am to show that a thing is within my cognizance or within my power are conditions, not about the future, but about *the present and the past*: it is not demanded that I do more than *believe* about the future.[2]

[2] If "Figs never grow on thistles" is taken to mean "None ever have and none ever

We feel, however, an objection to saying that "I know" performs the same sort of function in talking as "I promise." It is this. Supposing that things turn out badly, then we say, on the one hand "You're proved wrong, so you *didn't* know," but on the other hand "You've failed to perform, although you *did* promise." I believe that this contrast is more apparent than real. The sense in which you "did promise" is that you did *say* you promised (did say "I promise"): and you did *say* you knew. That is the gravamen of the charge against you when you let us down, after we have taken your word. But it may well transpire that you never fully intended to do it, or that you had concrete reason to suppose that you wouldn't be able to do it (it might even be manifestly impossible), and in another "sense" of promise you *can't* then have promised to do it, so that you *didn't* promise.

Consider the use of other phrases analogous to "I know" and "I promise." Suppose, instead of "I know," I had said "I swear": in that case, upon the opposite appearing, we should say, exactly as in the promising case, "You *did* swear, but you were wrong." Suppose again that, instead of "I promise," I had said "I guarantee" (e.g., to protect you from attack): in that case, upon my letting you down, you can say, exactly as in the knowing case "You *said* you guaranteed it, but you *didn't* guarantee it." [3] Can the situation perhaps be summed up as follows? In these "ritual" cases, the approved case is one where *in the appropriate circumstances*, I say a certain formula: e.g., "I do" when standing, unmarried or a widower, beside woman, unmarried or a widow and not within the prohibited degrees of relationship, before a clergyman, registrar, etc., or "I give" when it is mine to give, etc., or "I order" when I have the authority to, etc. But now, if the situation transpires to have been in some way not orthodox (I was already married: it wasn't mine to give: I had no authority to order), then we tend to be rather hesitant about how to put it, as heaven was when the saint blessed the penguins. We call the man a bigamist, but his second marriage was not a marriage, is null and void (a useful formula in many cases for avoiding saying either "he did" or "he didn't"): he did "order" me to do it, but, having no authority over me, he *couldn't* "order" me: he did warn me it was going to charge, but it wasn't or anyway I knew much

---

will," then it is implied that I *know* that none ever have, but only that I *believe* that none ever will.

[3] "Swear" "guarantee" "give my word" "promise," all these and similar words cover cases both of "knowing" and of "promising," thus suggesting the two are analogous. Of course they differ subtly from each other: for example, *know* and *promise* are in a certain sense "unlimited" expressions, while when I swear I swear *upon* something, and when I guarantee I guarantee that, upon some adverse and more or less to be expected circumstance arising, I will take *some more or less definite action* to nullify it.

more about it than he did, so in a way he couldn't warn me, didn't warn me.[4] We hesitate between "He didn't order me," "He had no right to order me," "He oughtn't to have said he ordered me," just as we do between "You didn't know," "You can't have known," "You had no right to say you knew" (these perhaps having slightly different nuances, according to what precisely it is that has gone wrong). But the essential factors are (a) You said you knew: you said you promised (b) You were mistaken: you didn't perform. The hesitancy concerns only the precise way in which we are to round on the original "I know" or "I promise."

To suppose that "I know" is a descriptive phrase, is only one example of the *descriptive fallacy,* so common in philosophy. Even if some language is now purely descriptive, language was not in origin so, and much of it is still not so. Utterance of obvious ritual phrases, in the appropriate circumstances, is not *describing* the action we are doing, but *doing* it ("I do"): in other cases it functions, like tone and expression, or again like punctuation and mood, as an intimation that we are employing language in some special way ("I warn," "I ask," "I define"). Such phrases cannot, strictly, *be* lies, though they can "imply" lies, as "I promise" implies that I fully intend, which may be untrue. . . .

❖ 23 ❖

KNOWING

A. D. Woozley (1912–   )

1. DIFFERENCES BETWEEN KNOWING AND BEING SURE

That, however they may be related, knowing and being sure are different, can be shown by two quite simple considerations. First, one can be sure and be wrong, but one cannot know and be wrong. From the fact that you

---

Sections 8 and 9 of Chapter 8 (pp. 187–91) of A. D. Woozley's *Theory of Knowledge* (1949). Used here by permission of the author and of the Hutchinson Publishing Group Ltd. The title of this selection has been supplied by the editors.
4 "You can't warn someone of something that isn't going to happen" parallels "You can't know what isn't true."

are sure that it is raining it does not follow that it is raining, but from the fact that you know that it is raining it does follow that it is raining. It does not, of course, follow from the fact that you *say* that you know it is raining; for you may say you know and be wrong about that, for you do not know. If a man says he is sure it is raining (and if we do not suppose that he is lying) and we discover that it is, in fact, not raining, we say that he was sure but he was wrong. But if he said not that he was sure but that he knew that it was raining, and we discovered that it was not raining, then we should say that he *thought* he knew but he was wrong. In the first case, we do not say, "He *thought* he was sure, but he was not sure" [1] (to be contrasted with the fact that we do say, "He *thought* he knew, but he did not know"); and in the second case we do not say, "He knew, but he was wrong" (to be contrasted with the fact that we do say, "He was sure, but he was wrong").

A second difference between knowing and being sure is that to say, "I know that . . ." offers a guarantee in a way in which to say, "I am sure that . . ." does not. Suppose at a party you ask me who is the man talking to our hostess and I reply that it is Dr. Brown, and suppose that in response to further inquiries from you (for you do not know Dr. Brown, but have long been anxious to meet him), I insist that I know it is Dr. Brown. If, on the strength of that, you introduce yourself to him and find that he is not Dr. Brown at all, you would then round on me for unreliability in a way in which you might be less inclined to round on me if I had only said that I was sure that the man was Dr. Brown. Saying that I know both pledges myself in a way that saying I am sure does not, and also emphasizes that what I say that I know is a hard, impersonal fact which is quite independent of me. Saying that I am sure does not offer the same 100 per cent guarantee, and does not insist on the dissociation of the fact from myself.[2] Again, one is ready to qualify sureness ("I'm pretty sure . . . not quite sure . . . almost sure," etc.) in a way in which one is not prepared to qualify knowledge.[3]

[1] We do sometimes say that a man thought he was sure, but he was not sure, but not on the ground that what he was sure of turned out to be false; what he thought he was sure of might indeed even turn out to be true. E.g., a man might say that he was sure that he could perform a certain trick, and yet by the way he tackled the trick show that he was not sure, even though he succeeded in doing it.
[2] This certifying or guaranteeing character of "I know that . . ." is clearly brought out in a discussion by J. L. Austin in *Supplementary Proceedings of the Aristotelian Society*, Vol. XX, pp. 170–4 [this volume pp. 180–84].
[3] The qualification "I almost know . . ." is used, in a way that does not correspond to almost being sure, where the knowledge is knowledge how. An actor may almost know his part, or a small boy his nine times table, in the sense that they can almost recite them without mistakes.

Nevertheless, being sure is necessary to knowledge, for it would not be sense to say, "I know that it is raining, but I am not quite sure of it." We may, therefore, say so far that knowing involves:

(i) that what is known is true;

(ii) that the person knowing is sure that it is true.

However, although these are necessary conditions, they are not yet sufficient, for it would not be difficult to think of situations in which both conditions were fulfilled and yet one could not truly be said to know. For instance, Professor Hubble may be sure that the universe is expanding at a speed higher than that of any normal explosion, and he may be right, but he does not know that the universe is expanding at that speed; for the data which he has observed, namely, the shift towards red of the light of remote nebulae, are consistent with alternative hypotheses to his own. Or a pessimist may be sure that it will rain tonight because he is giving a large fireworks party, and he may turn out to be right, for it does rain tonight, but he would hardly be said to have known that it would rain. On reading a newspaper report of the prosecution's case in a murder trial I may be sure that the defendant will be found guilty, and I may be right (for he is subsequently found guilty), but I certainly do not know that he will be found guilty; for that I should at least require to have heard or to have read a fair summary of the case for the defense quite apart from questions about the impartiality or the sound judgment of the jury.

2. CONDITIONS OF KNOWLEDGE

If p is the proposition in question, then a man does not know p, even although he is sure of p, and although p is true, in any of the following conditions:

(a) he has no evidence for p;

(b) he is wrong about the evidence;

(c) he is wrong about the relation of the evidence to p.

The pessimist who claims to know that his fireworks party will be spoiled by rain does not know, because he has no evidence for saying that it will be so spoiled; he comes under condition (a). Conditions (b) and (c) concern mistakes about evidence, but mistakes of different kinds. Mistakes under (b) consist of being misinformed about the data which one is using as evidence, e.g., as the sky grows darker, taking it to be due to the piling up of rain clouds, when it is, in fact, due to clouds of smoke from oil storage tanks on fire; I might under that misapprehension unjustifiably predict that rain would spoil my fireworks party tonight. The astronomer would be making a similar mistake if he supposed that the light from the distant nebulae showed a red shift, when actually it did not; and the newspaper reader would be making a similar mistake if he supposed, on reading the heading, "Queen Elizabeth Held Up By Breakdown," that the liner had been delayed, when in fact the train in which the Queen of England was travelling had been held up by a breakdown farther along the line. The astronomer could not, in such circumstances, know that the universe was expanding at the speed of an explosion (even although he was right, and it was); and the newspaper reader could not know that the liner would dock at Southampton behind schedule (even although he was right, and it would).

Mistakes under (c) are probably more common. Here one is wrong not about the evidence itself, but about its function *as* evidence, about its relation to the conclusion, either because it is not evidence for the conclusion, or because, although it is evidence for the conclusion, it is not sufficient.

An instance of the first would be an accusation of forgery built up on a hasty comparison of two signatures and the supposition that they were written by the same man, when a more careful scrutiny would have shown that they were not. An instance of the second (more common than the first) would be a charge of murder depending on the presence of the defendant's fingerprints on the door handle of the room in which the body was found; the fingerprints are certainly some evidence, but far from sufficient, for several other people might have had occasion to visit the room at about the time of the murder, each with as good a motive for committing the murder as the defendant had; and in order to point suspicion towards the defendant (who certainly did visit the room) the others might have been careful to wear gloves or not to touch the door handle. In each of these two cases the charges might be correct, for the defendants did commit respectively the forgery and the murder, but in neither case could it be known from the facts mentioned above as evidence that the defendants were guilty.

To know, then, a man must

(a) have evidence;

(b) be right about the evidence; and

(c) be right about the relation of the evidence to the conclusion. He must also be sure that he is right under (b) and (c). It is not necessary to knowing p that the man should go through a long and explicit process of self-questioning under (*b*) and (*c*). A man's claim to know that Gandhi is dead is legitimate if he *can* now prove it; it is not necessary that he should just *have* proved it.

❖   24   ❖

KNOWLEDGE OF THE WORLD

T. H. White (1906–1964)

. . . There is a thing called knowledge of the world, which people do not have until they are middle-aged. It is something which cannot be taught to younger people, because it is not logical and does not obey laws which are constant. It has no rules. Only, in the long years which bring women to the middle of life, a sense of balance develops. You can't teach a baby to walk by explaining the matter to her logically—she has to learn the strange poise of walking by experience. In some way like that, you cannot teach a young woman to have knowledge of the world. She has to be left to the experience of the years. And then, when she is beginning to hate her used body, she suddenly finds that she can do it. She can go on living—not by principle, not by deduction, not by knowledge of good and evil, but simply by a peculiar and shifting sense of balance which defies each of these things often. She no longer hopes to live by seeking the truth—if women ever do hope this—but continues henceforth under the guidance of a seventh sense. Balance was the sixth sense, which she won when she first learned to walk, and now she has the seventh one—knowledge of the world.

The slow discovery of the seventh sense, by which both men and women contrive to ride the waves of a world in which there is war, adultery, compromise, fear, stultification and hypocrisy—this discovery is not a matter for triumph. The baby, perhaps, cries out triumphantly: I have balance! But the seventh sense is recognized without a cry. We only carry on with our famous knowledge of the world, riding the queer waves in a habitual, petrifying way, because we have reached a stage of deadlock in which we can think of nothing else to do.

And at this stage we begin to forget that there ever was a time when we lacked the seventh sense. We begin to forget, as we go stolidly balancing along, that there could have been a time when we were young bodies flaming with the impetus of life. It is hardly consoling to remember such a feeling, and so it deadens in our minds.

But there was a time when each of us stood naked before the world, confronting life as a serious problem with which we were intimately and passionately concerned. There was a time when it was of vital interest to us to find out whether there was a God or not. Obviously the existence or otherwise of a future life must be of the very first importance to somebody who is going to live her present one, because her manner of living it must hinge on the problem. There was a time when Free Love versus Catholic Morality was a question of as much importance to our hot bodies as if a pistol had been clapped to our heads.

Further back, there were times when we wondered with all our souls what the world was, what love was, what we were ourselves.

All these problems and feelings fade away when we get the seventh sense. Middle-aged people can balance between believing in God and breaking all the commandments, without difficulty. The seventh sense, indeed, slowly kills all the other ones, so that at last there is no trouble about the commandments. We cannot see any more, or feel, or hear about them. The bodies which we loved, the truths which we sought, the Gods whom we questioned: we are deaf and blind to them now, safely and automatically balancing along toward the inevitable grave, under the protection of our last sense. "Thank God for the aged," sings the poet:

> Thank God for the aged
> And for age itself, and illness and the grave.
> When we are old and ill, and particularly in the coffin,
> It is no trouble to behave. . . .

OF SKEPTICISM WITH REGARD TO REASON

David Hume (1711–1776)

In all demonstrative sciences the rules are certain and infallible; but when we apply them, our fallible and uncertain faculties are very apt to depart from them, and fall into error. We must, therefore, in every reasoning form a new judgment, as a check or control on our first judgment or belief; and must enlarge our view to comprehend a kind of history of all the instances, wherein our understanding has deceiv'd us, compar'd with those, wherein its testimony was just and true. Our reason must be consider'd as a kind of cause, of which truth is the natural effect; but such-a-one as by the irruption of other causes, and by the inconstancy of our mental powers, may frequently be prevented. By this means all knowledge degenerates into probability; and this probability is greater or less, according to our experience of the veracity or deceitfulness of our understanding, and according to the simplicity or intricacy of the question.

There is no Algebraist nor Mathematician so expert in his science, as to place entire confidence in any truth immediately upon his discovery of it, or regard it as anything, but a mere probability. Every time he runs over his proofs, his confidence increases; but still more by the approbation of his friends; and is rais'd to its utmost perfection by the universal assent and applauses of the learned world. Now 'tis evident, that this gradual increase of assurance is nothing but the addition of new probabilities, and is deriv'd from the constant union of causes and effects, according to past experience and observation.

In accompts of any length or importance, Merchants seldom trust to the infallible certainty of numbers for their security; but by the artificial structure of the accompts, produce a probability beyond what is deriv'd from the skill and experience of the acomptant. For that is plainly of itself some degree of probability; tho' uncertain and variable, according to the degrees of his experience and length of the accompt. Now as none will

From *A Treatise of Human Nature* (1739), Book I, part iv, section 1.

maintain, that our assurance in a long numeration exceeds probability, I may safely affirm, that there scarce is any proposition concerning numbers, of which we can have a fuller security. For 'tis easily possible, by gradually diminishing the numbers to reduce the longest series of addition to the most simple question, which can be form'd, to an addition of two single numbers; and upon this supposition we shall find it impracticable to show the precise limits of knowledge and of probability, or discover that particular number, at which the one ends and the other begins. But knowledge and probability are of such contrary and disagreeing natures, that they cannot well run insensibly into each other, and that because they will not divide, but must be either entirely present, or entirely absent. Besides, if any single addition were certain, every one wou'd be so, and consequently the whole or total sum; unless the whole can be different from all its parts. I had almost said, that this was certain; but I reflect, that it must reduce *itself*, as well as every other reasoning, and from knowledge degenerate into probability.

Since therefore all knowledge resolves itself into probability, and becomes at last of the same nature with that evidence, which we employ in common life, we must now examine this latter species of reasoning, and see on what foundation it stands.

In every judgment, which we can form concerning probability, as well as concerning knowledge, we ought always to correct the first judgment, deriv'd from the nature of the object, by another judgment, deriv'd from the nature of the understanding. 'Tis certain a man of solid sense and long experience ought to have, and usually has, a greater assurance in his opinions, than one that is foolish and ignorant, and that our sentiments have different degrees of authority, even with ourselves, in proportion to the degrees of our reason and experience. In the man of the best sense and longest experience, this authority is never entire; since even such-a-one must be conscious of many errors in the past, and must still dread the like for the future. Here then arises a new species of probability to correct and regulate the first, and fix its just standard and proportion. As demonstration is subject to the control of probability, so is probability liable to a new correction by a reflex act of the mind, wherein the nature of our understanding, and our reasoning from the first probability become our objects.

Having thus found in every probability, beside the original uncertainty inherent in the subject, a new uncertainty deriv'd from the weakness of that faculty, which judges, and having adjusted these two together, we are oblig'd by our reason to add a new doubt deriv'd from the possibility of error in the estimation we make of the truth and fidelity of our faculties. This is a doubt, which immediately occurs to us, and of which, if we wou'd closely pursue our reason, we cannot avoid giving a decision. But this decision, tho' it shou'd be favorable to our preceeding judgment, being founded only on probability, must weaken still further our first evidence, and must itself be weaken'd by a fourth doubt of the same kind, and so on *in infinitum*; till at last there remain nothing of the original probability, however great we may suppose it to have been, and however small the diminution by every new uncertainty. No finite object can subsist under a decrease repeated *in infinitum*; and even the vastest quantity, which can enter into human imagination, must in this manner be reduc'd to nothing. Let our first belief be never so strong, it must infallibly perish by passing thro' so many new examinations, of which each diminishes somewhat of its force and vigor. When I reflect on the natural fallibility of my judgment, I have less confidence in my opinions, than when I only consider the objects concerning which I reason; and when I proceed still farther, to turn the scrutiny against every successive estimation I make of my faculties, all the rules of logic require a continual diminution, and at last a total extinction of belief and evidence.

Shou'd it here be ask'd me, whether I sincerely assent to this argument, which I seem to take such pains to inculcate, and whether I be really one of those skeptics, who hold that all is uncertain, and that our judgment is not in *any*thing possest of *any* measures of truth and falshood; I shou'd reply, that this question is entirely superfluous, and that neither I, nor any other person was ever sincerely and constantly of that opinion. Nature, by an absolute and uncontrolable necessity has determin'd us to judge as well as to breathe and feel; nor can we any more forbear viewing certain objects in a stronger and fuller light, upon account of their customary connection with a present impression, than we can hinder ourselves from thinking as long as we are awake, or seeing the surrounding bodies, when we turn our eyes towards them in broad sunshine. Whoever has taken the pains to refute the cavils of this *total* skepticism, has really disputed without an antagonist, and endeavor'd by arguments to establish a faculty, which nature has antecedently implanted in the mind, and render'd unavoidable.

My intention then in displaying so carefully the arguments of that fantastic sect, is only to make the reader sensible of the truth of my hypothesis, *that all our reasonings concerning causes and effects are deriv'd from nothing but custom; and that belief is more properly an act of the sensitive, than of the cogitative part of our natures.* I have here prov'd, that the very same principles, which make us form a decision upon any subject, and correct that decision by the consideration of our genius and capacity, and of the situation of our mind, when we examin'd that subject; I say, I have prov'd, that these same principles, when carry'd farther, and apply'd to every new reflex judgment, must, by continually diminishing the original evidence, at last reduce it to nothing, and utterly subvert all belief and opinion. If belief, therefore, were a simple act of the thought, without any peculiar manner of conception, or the addition of a force and vivacity, it must infallibly destroy itself, and in every case terminate in a total suspense of judgment. But as experience will sufficiently convince any one, who thinks it worthwhile to try, that tho' he can find no error in the foregoing arguments, yet he still continues to believe, and think, and reason as usual, he may safely conclude, that his reasoning and belief is some sensation or peculiar manner of conception, which 'tis impossible for mere ideas and reflections to destroy.

But here, perhaps, it may be demanded, how it happens, even upon my hypothesis, that these arguments above-explain'd produce not a total suspense of judgment, and after what manner the mind ever retains a degree of assurance in any subject? For as these new probabilities, which by their repetition perpetually diminish the original evidence, are founded on the very same principles, whether of thought or sensation, as the primary judgment, it may seem unavoidable, that in either case they must equally subvert it, and by the opposition, either of contrary thoughts or sensations, reduce the mind to a total uncertainty. I suppose, there is some question propos'd to me, and that after revolving over the impressions of my memory and senses, and carrying my thoughts from them to such objects, as are commonly conjoin'd with them, I feel a stronger and more forcible conception on the one side, than on the other. This strong conception forms my first decision. I suppose, that afterwards I examine my judgment itself, and observing from experience, that 'tis sometimes just and sometimes erroneous, I consider it as regulated by contrary principles or causes, of which some lead to truth, and some to error; and in ballancing these contrary causes, I diminish by a new probability the assurance of my first decision. This new probability is liable to the same diminution as the foregoing, and so on, *in infinitum*. 'Tis therefore demanded, *how it happens, that even after all we retain a degree of belief, which is sufficient for our purpose, either in philosophy or common life.*

I answer, that after the first and second decision; as the action of the mind becomes forc'd and unnatural, and the ideas faint and obscure; tho' the principles of judgment, and the ballancing of opposite causes be the same as at the very beginning; yet their influence on the imagination, and the vigor they add to, or diminish from the thought, is by no means equal. Where the mind reaches not its objects with easiness and facility, the same principles have not the same effect as in a more natural conception of the ideas; nor does the imagination feel a sensation, which holds any proportion with that which arises from its common judgments and opinions. The attention is on the stretch: The posture of the mind is uneasy; and the spirits being diverted from their natural course, are not govern'd in their movements by the same laws, at least not to the same degree, as when they flow in their usual channel.

If we desire similar instances, 'twill not be very difficult to find them. The present subject of metaphysics will supply us abundantly. The same argument, which wou'd have been esteem'd convincing in a reasoning concerning history or politics, has little or no influence in these abstruser subjects, even tho' it be perfectly comprehended; and that because there is requir'd a study and an effort of thought, in order to its being comprehended: And this effort of thought disturbs the operation of our sentiments, on which the belief depends. The case is the same in other subjects. The straining of the imagination always hinders the regular flowing of the passions and sentiments. A tragic poet, that wou'd represent his heroes as very ingenious and witty in their misfortunes, wou'd never touch the passions. As the emotions of the soul prevent any subtile reasoning and reflection, so these latter actions of the mind are equally prejudicial to the former. The mind, as well as the body, seems to be endow'd with a certain precise degree of force and activity, which it never employs in one action, but at the expense of all the rest. This is more evidently true, where the actions are of quite different natures; since in that case the force of the mind is not only diverted, but even the disposition chang'd, so as to render us incapable of a sudden transition from one action to the other, and still more of performing both at once. No wonder, then, the conviction, which arises from a subtile reasoning, diminishes in proportion to the efforts, which the imagination makes to enter into the reasoning, and to conceive it in all its parts. Belief, being a lively conception, can never be entire, where it is not founded on something natural and easy.

This I take to be the true state of the question, and cannot approve of that expeditious way, which some take with the skeptics, to reject at once all their arguments without inquiry or examination. If the skeptical reasonings be strong, say they, 'tis a proof, that reason may have some force and authority: if weak, they can never be sufficient to invalidate all the conclusions of our understanding. This argument is not just; because the skeptical reasonings, were it possible for them to exist, and were they not destroy'd by their subtility, wou'd be successively both strong and weak, according to the successive dispositions of the mind. Reason first appears in possession of the throne, prescribing laws, and imposing maxims, with an absolute sway and authority. Her enemy, therefore, is oblig'd to take shelter under her protection, and by making use of rational arguments to prove the fallaciousness and imbecility of reason, produces, in a manner, a patent under her hand and seal. This patent has at first an authority, proportion'd to the present and immediate authority of reason, from which it is deriv'd. But as it is suppos'd to be contradictory to reason, it gradually diminishes the force of that governing power, and its own at the same time; till at last they both vanish away into nothing, by a regular and just diminution. The skeptical and dogmatical reasons are of the same kind, tho' contrary in their operation and tendency; so that where the latter is strong, it has an enemy of equal force in the former to encounter; and as their forces were at first equal, they still continue so, as long as either of them subsists; nor does one of them lose any force in the contest, without taking as much from its antagonist. 'Tis happy, therefore, that nature breaks the force of all skeptical arguments in time, and keeps them from having any considerable influence on the understanding. Were we to trust entirely to their self-destruction, that can never take place, 'till they have first subverted all conviction, and have totally destroy'd human reason.

❖   26   ❖

OF MR. HUME'S SKEPTICISM
WITH REGARD TO REASON

Thomas Reid (1710–1796)

In the *Treatise of Human Nature*, Bk. I. Part IV. § 1, the author undertakes to prove two points: *First,* That all that is called human knowledge (meaning demonstrative knowledge) is only probability; and *secondly,* That this probability, when duly examined evanishes by degrees, and leaves at last no evidence at all: so that, in the issue, there is no ground to believe any one proposition rather than its contrary; and "all those are certainly fools who reason or believe anything."

According to this account, reason, that boasted prerogative of man,

From *Essays on the Intellectual Powers of Man* (1785), Essay VII, chapter 4.

and the light of his mind, is an *ignis fatuus* [1] which misleads the wandering travellers and leaves him at last in absolute darkness.

How unhappy is the condition of man, born under a necessity of believing contradictions and of trusting to a guide who confesses himself to be a false one!

It is some comfort that this doctrine can never be seriously adopted by any man in his senses. And after this author had shown that "all the rules of logic require a total extinction of all belief and evidence," he himself, and all men that are not insane, must have believed many things, and yielded assent to the evidence which he had extinguished.

This indeed he is so candid as to acknowledge. "He finds himself absolutely and necessarily determined to live and talk and act like other people in the common affairs of life. And since reason is incapable of dispelling these clouds, most fortunately it happens that nature herself suffices to that purpose, and cures him of this philosophical melancholy and delirium."

This was surely a very kind and friendly interposition of nature, for the effects of this philosophical delirium, if carried into life, must have been very melancholy.

It may, however, not be improper to inquire whether, as the author thinks, it was produced by a just application of the rules of logic or, as others may be apt to think, by the misapplication and abuse of them.

First, Because we are fallible, the author infers that all knowledge degenerates into probability.

That man, and probably every created being, is fallible; and that a fallible being cannot have that perfect comprehension and assurance of truth which an infallible being has—I think ought to be granted. It becomes a fallible being to be modest, open to new light, and sensible that, by some false bias or by rash judging, he may be misled. If this be called a degree of skepticism, I cannot help approving of it, being persuaded that the man who makes the best use he can of the faculties which God has given him, without thinking them more perfect than they really are, may have all the belief that is necessary in the conduct of life, and all that is necessary to his acceptance with his Maker.

It is granted, then, that human judgments ought always to be formed with a humble sense of our fallibility in judging.

This is all that can be inferred by the rules of logic from our being fallible. And if this be all that is meant by our knowledge degenerating into probability, I know no person of a different opinion.

But it may be observed that the author here uses the word probability

[1] [A delusive principal—ed. note.]

in a sense for which I know no authority but his own. Philosophers under-stand probability as opposed to demonstration, the vulgar as opposed to certainty; but this author understands it as opposed to infallibility, which no man claims.

One who believes himself to be fallible may still hold it to be certain that two and two make four, and that two contradictory propositions cannot both be true. He may believe some things to be probable only, and other things to be demonstrable, without making any pretense to infalli-bility.

If we use words in their proper meaning, it is impossible that demon-stration should degenerate into probability from the imperfection of our faculties. Our judgment cannot change the nature of the things about which we judge. What is really demonstration will still be so, whatever judgment we form concerning it. It may likewise be observed that, when we mistake that for demonstration which really is not, the consequence of this mistake is not that demonstration degenerates into probability, but that what we took to be demonstration is no proof at all; for one false step in a demonstration destroys the whole, but cannot turn it into another kind of proof.

Upon the whole, then, this first conclusion of our author, That the fallibility of human judgment turns all knowledge into probability, if un-derstood literally, is absurd; but if it be only a figure of speech, and means no more but that in all our judgments we ought to be sensible of our fallibility, and ought to hold our opinions with that modesty that becomes fallible creatures—which I take to be what the author meant—this I think nobody denies, nor was it necessary to enter into a laborious proof of it.

One is never in greater danger of transgressing against the rules of logic than in attempting to prove what needs no proof. Of this we have an instance in this very case, for the author begins his proof that all human judgments are fallible with affirming that some are infallible.

"In all demonstrative sciences," says he, "the rules are certain and infallible; but when we apply them, our fallible and uncertain faculties are very apt to depart from them, and fall into error."

He had forgot, surely, that the rules of demonstrative sciences are discovered by our fallible and uncertain faculties, and have no authority but that of human judgment. If they be infallible, some human judgments are infallible; and there are many in various branches of human knowledge which have as good a claim to infallibility as the rules of the demonstrative sciences.

We have reason here to find fault with our author for not being skeptical enough, as well as for a mistake in reasoning, when he claims infallibility to certain decisions of the human faculties in order to prove that all their decisions are fallible.

The *second* point which he attempts to prove is, That this probability, when duly examined, suffers a continual diminution and at last a total extinction.

I examine the proof of a theorem of Euclid. It appears to me to be strict demonstration. But I may have overlooked some fallacy, therefore I examine it again and again, but can find no flaw in it. I find all that have examined it agree with me. I have now that evidence of the truth of the proposition which I and all men call demonstration, and that belief of it which we call certainty.

Here my skeptical friend interposes and assures me that the rules of logic reduce this demonstration to no evidence at all. I am willing to hear what step in it he thinks fallacious, and why. He makes no objection to any part of the demonstration, but pleads my fallibility in judging. I have made the proper allowance for this already, by being open to conviction. But, says he, there are two uncertainties, the first inherent in the subject, which I have already shown to have only probable evidence; the second arising from the weakness of the faculty that judges. I answer, it is the weakness of the faculty only that reduces this demonstration to what you call probability. You must not therefore make it a second uncertainty, for it is the same with the first. To take credit twice in an account for the same article is not agreeable to the rules of logic. Hitherto, therefore, there is but one uncertainty—to wit, my fallibility in judging.

But, says my friend, you are obliged by reason to add a new uncertainty, derived from the possibility of error in the estimation you make of the truth and fidelity of your faculties. I answer—

This estimation is ambiguously expressed; it may either mean an estimation of my liableness to err by the misapplication and abuse of my faculties, or it may mean an estimation of my liableness to err by conceiving my faculties to be true and faithful, while they may be false and fallacious in themselves, even when applied in the best manner. I shall consider this estimation in each of these senses.

If the first be the estimation meant, it is true that reason directs us, as fallible creatures to carry along with us in all our judgment a sense of our fallibility. It is true also that we are in greater danger of erring in some cases and less in others, and that this danger of erring may, according to the circumstances of the case, admit of an estimation which we ought likewise to carry along with us in every judgment we form.

When a demonstration is short and plain; when the point to be proved does not touch our interest or our passions; when the faculty of judging, in such cases, has acquired strength by much exercise—there is less danger of erring; when the contrary circumstances take place, there is more.

In the present case every circumstance is favorable to the judgment I have formed. There cannot be less danger of erring in any case, excepting perhaps when I judge of a self-evident axiom.

The Skeptic further urges that this decision, though favorable to my first judgment, being founded only on probability, must still weaken the evidence of that judgment.

Here I cannot help being of a quite contrary opinion; nor can I imagine how an ingenious author could impose upon himself so grossly, for surely he did not intend to impose upon his reader.

After repeated examination of a proposition of Euclid, I judge it to be strictly demonstrated; this is my first judgment. But as I am liable to err from various causes, I consider how far I may have been misled by any of these causes in this judgment. My decision upon this second point is favorable to my first judgment, and therefore, as I apprehend, must strengthen it. To say that this decision, because it is only probable, must weaken the first evidence seems to me contrary to all rules of logic and to common sense.

The first judgment may be compared to the testimony of a credible witness; the second, after a scrutiny into the character of the witness, wipes off every objection that can be made to it, and therefore surely must confirm and not weaken his testimony.

But let us suppose that in another case I examine my first judgment upon some point, and find that it was attended with unfavorable circumstance, what, in reason, and according to the rules of logic, ought to be the effect of this discovery?

The effect surely will be, and ought to be, to make me less confident in my first judgment, until I examine the point anew in more favorable circumstances. If it be a matter of importance, I return to weigh the evidence of my first judgment. If it was precipitate before, it must now be deliberate in every point. If at first I was in passion, I must now be cool. If I had an interest in the decision, I must place the interest on the other side.

It is evident that this review of the subject may confirm my first judgment notwithstanding the suspicious circumstances that attended it. Though the judge was biassed or corrupted, it does not follow that the sentence was unjust. The rectitude of the decision does not depend upon the character of the judge but upon the nature of the case. From that only it must be determined whether the decision be just. The circumstances that rendered it suspicious are mere presumptions which have no force against direct evidence.

Thus, I have considered the effect of this estimation of our liableness to err in our first judgment, and have allowed to it all the effect that reason and the rules of logic permit. In the case I first supposed, and in every case where we can discover no cause of error, it affords a presumption in favor of the first judgment. In other cases it may afford a presumption against it. But the rules of logic require that we should not judge by presumption where we have direct evidence. The effect of an unfavorable presumption should only be, to make us examine the evidence with the greater care.

The skeptic urges, in the last place, that this estimation must be subjected to another estimation, that to another, and so on *in infinitum*; and as every new estimation takes away from the evidence of the first judgment, it must at last be totally annihilated.

I answer, *first,* It has been shown above that the first estimation, supposing it unfavorable, can only afford a presumption against the first judgment; the second, upon the same supposition, will be only the presumption of a presumption; and the third, the presumption that there is a presumption of a presumption. This infinite series of presumptions resembles an infinite series of quantities, decreasing in geometrical proportion, which amounts only to a finite sum.

Secondly, I have shown that the estimation of our first judgment may strengthen it; and the same thing may be said of all the subsequent estimations. It would, therefore, be as reasonable to conclude that the first judgment will be brought to infallible certainty when this series of estimations is wholly in its favor, as that its evidence will be brought to nothing by such a series supposed to be wholly unfavorable to it. But in reality one serious and cool re-examination of the evidence by which our first judgment is supported, has, and in reason ought to have, more force to strengthen or weaken it than an infinite series of such estimations as our author requires.

Thirdly, I know no reason nor rule in logic that requires that such a series of estimations should follow every particular judgment.

A wise man who has practised reasoning knows that he is fallible and carries this conviction along with him in every judgment he forms. He knows likewise that he is more liable to err in some cases than in others. He has a scale in his mind by which he estimates his liableness to err, and by this he regulates the degree of his assent in his first judgment upon any point.

The author's reasoning supposes that a man, when he forms his first judgment, conceives himself to be infallible; that by a second and subsequent judgment he discovers that he is not infallible; and that by a third judgment, subsequent to the second, he estimates his liableness to err in such a case as the present.

If the man proceed in this order, I grant that his second judgment will with good reason bring down the first from supposed infallibility to fallibility, and that his third judgment will in some degree either strengthen or weaken the first, as it is corrected by the second.

But every man of understanding proceeds in a contrary order. When about to judge in any particular point, he knows already that he is not infallible. He knows what are the cases in which he is most or least liable to err. The conviction of these things is always present to his mind, and influences the degree of his assent in his first judgment, as far as to him appears reasonable.

If he should afterwards find reason to suspect his first judgment, and desires to have all the satisfaction his faculties can give, reason will direct him not to form such a series of estimations upon estimations, as this author requires, but to examine the evidence of his first judgment carefully and coolly; and this review may very reasonably, according to its result, either strengthen or weaken, or totally overturn his first judgment.

This infinite series of estimations, therefore, is not the method that reason directs, in order to form our judgment in any case. It is introduced without necessity, without any use but to puzzle the understanding, and to make us think that to judge, even in the simplest and plainest cases, is a matter of insurmountable difficulty and endless labor; just as the ancient Skeptic, to make a journey of two thousand paces appear endless, divided it into an infinite number of stages.

But we observed that the estimation which our author requires may admit of another meaning which indeed is more agreeable to the expression, but inconsistent with what he advanced before.

By the possibility of error in the estimation of the truth and fidelity of our faculties may be meant that we may err by esteeming our faculties true and faithful while they may be false and fallacious, even when used according to the rules of reason and logic.

If this be meant, I answer, *first*, That the truth and fidelity of our faculty of judging is, and must be, taken for granted in every judgment and in every estimation.

If the skeptic can seriously doubt of the truth and fidelity of his faculty of judging when properly used, and suspend his judgment upon that point till he finds proof his skepticism admits of no cure by reasoning, and he must even continue in it until he have new faculties given him which shall have authority to sit in judgment upon the old. Nor is there any need of an endless succession of doubts upon this subject, for the first puts an end to all judgment and reasoning and to the possibility of conviction by that means. The skeptic has here got possession of a stronghold which is impregnable to reasoning, and we must leave him in possession of it till nature, by other means, makes him give it up.

Secondly, I observe that this ground of skepticism from the supposed infidelity of our faculties contradicts what the author before advanced in this very argument—to wit, that "the rules of the demonstrative sciences are certain and infallible, and that truth is the natural effect of reason, and that error arises from the irruption of other causes."

But perhaps he made these concessions unwarily. He is therefore at liberty to retract them, and to rest his skepticism upon this sole foundation, That no reasoning can prove the truth and fidelity of our faculties. Here he stands upon firm ground, for it is evident that every argument offered to prove the truth and fidelity of our faculties takes for granted the thing in question, and is therefore that kind of sophism which logicians call *petitio principii.*[2]

All we would ask of this kind of skeptic is that he would be uniform and consistent, and that his practice in life do not belie his profession of skepticism with regard to the fidelity of his faculties; for the want of faith, as well as faith itself, is best shown by works. If a skeptic avoid the fire as much as those who believe it dangerous to go into it, we can hardly avoid thinking his skepticism to be feigned, and not real.

Upon the whole, I see only two conclusions that can be fairly drawn from this profound and intricate reasoning against reason. The first is, That we are fallible in all our judgments and in all our reasonings. The second, That the truth and fidelity of our faculties can never be proved by reasoning, and therefore our belief of it cannot be founded on reasoning. If the last be what the author calls his hypothesis, I subscribe to it, and think it not an hypothesis but a manifest truth; though I conceive it to be very improperly expressed, by saying that belief is more properly an act of the sensitive than of the cogitative part of our nature.

2 [Begging the question—ed. note.]

THE GIVEN

H. H. Price (1899–   )

Every man entertains a great number of beliefs concerning material things, e.g., that there is a square-topped table in this room, that the earth is a spheroid, that water is composed of hydrogen and oxygen. It is plain that all these beliefs are based on sight and on touch (from which organic sensation cannot be separated): based upon them in the sense that if we had not had certain particular experiences of seeing and touching, it would be neither *possible* nor *reasonable* to entertain these beliefs. Beliefs about imperceptibles such as molecules or electrons or X-rays are no exception to this. Only they are based not directly on sight and touch, but indirectly. Their direct basis consists of certain others beliefs concerning scientific instruments, photographic plates, and the like. Thus over and above any intrinsic uncertainty that they themselves may have, whatever uncertainty attaches to these more basic beliefs is communicated to them. It follows that in any attempt either to analyze or to justify our beliefs concerning material things, the primary task is to consider beliefs concerning perceptible or "macroscopic" objects such as chairs and tables, cats and rocks. It follows, too, that no theory concerning "microscopic" objects can possibly be used to throw doubt upon our beliefs concerning chairs or cats or rocks, so long as these are based directly on sight and touch. Empirical Science can never be more trustworthy than perception, upon which it is based; and it can hardly fail to be *less* so, since among its non-perceptual premises there can hardly fail to be some which are neither self-evident nor demonstrable. Thus the not uncommon view that the world which we perceive is an illusion and only the "scientific" world of protons and electrons is real, is based upon a gross fallacy, and would destroy the very premises upon which Science itself depends.

My aim . . . is to examine those experiences in the way of seeing and

From *Perception* (1932; 2nd ed., 1950), chapter I, pp. 1–20. Used by permission of Associated Book Publishers Ltd., London.

touching upon which our beliefs concerning material things are based, and
to inquire in what way and to what extent they justify these beliefs. Other
modes of sense-experience, e.g., hearing and smelling, will be dealt with
only incidentally. For it is plain that they are only auxiliary. If we possessed
them, but did not possess either sight or touch, we should have no beliefs
about the material world at all, and should lack even the very conception of
it. Possessing sight or touch or both, we can use experiences of these other
senses as signs of obtainable but not at the moment actual experiences of
seeing or touching, and thereby gain indirectly information which these
inferior senses in themselves provide no hint of.

It may appear to some people that Science, particularly Physiology,
can answer these questions for us. But it should already be clear that this is
a mistake. Thus if it be said that when a man sees something, e.g., a
tomato, light rays emanating from the object impinge upon his retina and
this stimulates the optic nerve, which in turn causes a change in the optic
centers in his brain, which causes a change in his mind: there are two
comments to be made. 1. No doubt this is in fact a perfectly true account,
but what are our *grounds* for believing it? Obviously they are derived from
observation, and mainly if not entirely from visual observation. Thus the
Physiologist has not explained in the least how visual observation justifies a
man in holding a certain belief about a tomato, e.g., that it is spherical. All
he has done is to put forward certain *other* beliefs concerning a retina and
a brain. Those other beliefs have themselves to be justified in exactly the
same way as the first belief, and we are as far as ever from knowing what
way that is. Instead of answering our question, we have found another
instance of it. Nor is this result surprising. Since the premises of Physiology
are among the propositions into whose validity we are inquiring, it is hardly
likely that its conclusions will assist us. 2. In any case, Science only professes to tell us what are the *causes* of seeing and touching. But we want to
know what seeing and touching themselves *are*. This question lies outside
the sphere of Science altogether.

Thus there is no short cut to our goal. We must simply examine
seeing and touching for ourselves and do the best we can. What, then, is it
to see or to touch something? Let us confine ourselves to sight for the
moment and return to the instance of the tomato.

When I see a tomato there is much that I can doubt. I can doubt
whether it is a tomato that I am seeing, and not a cleverly painted piece of
wax. I can doubt whether there is any material thing there at all. Perhaps
what I took for a tomato was really a reflection; perhaps I am even the
victim of some hallucination. One thing however I cannot doubt: that
there exists a red patch of a round and somewhat bulgy shape, standing out

from a background of other color-patches, and having a certain visual depth, and that this whole field of color is directly present to my consciousness. What the red patch is, whether a substance, or a state of a substance, or an event, whether it is physical or psychical or neither, are questions that we may doubt about. But that something is red and round then and there [1] I cannot doubt. Whether the something persists even for a moment before and after it is present to my consciousness, whether other minds can be conscious of it as well as I, may be doubted. But that it now *exists*, and that I am conscious of it—by me at least who am conscious of it this cannot possibly be doubted. And when I say that it is "directly" present to my consciousness, I mean that my consciousness of it is not reached by inference, nor by any other intellectual process (such as abstraction or intuitive induction), nor by any passage from sign to significate. There obviously must be some sort or sorts of presence to consciousness which can be called "direct" in this sense, else we should have an infinite regress. Analogously, when I am in the situations called "touching something," "hearing it," "smelling it," etc., in each case there is something which at that moment indubitably exists—a pressure (or prement patch), a noise, a smell; and that something is directly present to my consciousness.

This peculiar and ultimate manner of being present to consciousness is called *being given*, and that which is thus present is called a *datum*. The corresponding mental attitude is called *acquaintance, intuitive apprehension*, or sometimes *having*. Data of this special sort are called *sense-data*. And the acquaintance with them is conveniently called *sensing*; though sometimes I think, this word is used in another sense. It is supposed by some writers that sense-data are mental events, and these writers appear to think that the word "sensing," if used at all, ought to mean the coming-into-being of sense-data, not the intuitive apprehension of them. (For their coming-into-being will then be a mental process.) This seems to be a very inconvenient usage. We need some word for the intuitive apprehension of sense-data. We cannot say "perceiving" (for that, as we shall see, has at least two other meanings already). And "sensing" is the obvious word to use. At any rate in this book we shall always use it in this sense. When we have occasion to speak of the process which is the coming-into-being of a sense-datum we shall call it *sense-datum-genesis*.

It is true that the term "given" or "datum" is sometimes used in a wider and looser sense to mean "that, the inspection of which provides a premise for inference." Thus the data of the historian are the statements which he finds in documents and inscriptions: the data of the general are

---

[1] "There" means "In spatial relations to other color-patches present to my consciousness at the same time."

the facts reported by his aircraft and his intelligence service: the data of the detective are the known circumstances and known results of the crime; and so on. But it is obvious that these are only data relatively and for the purpose of answering a certain question. They are really themselves the results of inference, often of a very complicated kind. We may call them data *secundum quid*. But eventually we must get back to something which is a datum *simpliciter*, which is not the result of any previous intellectual process. It is with data *simpliciter*, or rather with one species of them, that we are concerned.

How do sense-data differ from other data, e.g., from those of memory or introspection? We might be tempted to say, in the manner in which they come to be given, viz. as a result of the stimulation of a sense-organ. This will not do. For first, the sense-organs are themselves material things, and it seems quite likely that the term "material thing" cannot be defined except by reference to sense-data; and if so we should have a vicious circle. And secondly, even though we doubted the existence of all material things, including our own body and its organs, it would still be perfectly obvious that sense-data differ from other sorts of data. The only describable differentia that they seem to have is this, that they lead us to conceive of and believe in the existence of certain material things, whether there are in fact any such things or not. (Visual and tactual sense-data do this directly, the others indirectly, as explained above.) But it seems plain that there is also another characteristic common and peculiar to them, which may be called "sensuousness." This is obvious on inspection, but it cannot be described.

Does sensing differ from other forms of intuitive apprehension? Or is there only one sort of intuitive apprehension, and does the difference between (say) sensing, remembering and the contemplation of mental images lie only in the nature of the apprehensa? The question is difficult, nor does it seem very important. Perhaps we may say that there are two sorts of intuitive apprehension, one directed upon *facts*, e.g., the fact that I am puzzled or was puzzled, or again the fact that $2 + 2 = 4$, or that courage is good: another directed upon *particular existents*, e.g., this color-patch or this noise or that visual image, or again upon this feeling of disgust and that act of wondering. The first is apprehension *that*, the second is apprehension *of*. The term *acquaintance* is properly reserved for the second, and we shall so use it in future.

Are there several different sorts of acquaintance, e.g., sensing, self-consciousness, and contemplation of mental images? I cannot see that there are. The difference seems to be wholly on the side of the data. If so, *a fortiori* there are not different kinds of sensing. Visual sensing will simply be the acquaintance with color-patches, auditory sensing the acquaintance with sounds, and so on; the acquaintance being the same in each case. No doubt there will be different kinds of *sense-datum-genesis*, just as there are different kinds of sense-data. And if any one likes to use the term "visual sensing" [2] to mean the genesis of color-patches and "auditory sensing" to mean the genesis of noises, he may; and of·course he is then entitled to say that there *are* different kinds of sensing. But this has not the slightest tendency to show that there are different kinds of sensing in *our* sense of the word (which is also the usual one).

If the term sense-datum is taken in the strictly limited meaning that we have given it, I do not see how anyone can doubt that there are sense-data. Yet it is certain that many philosophers do profess to doubt this and even to deny it. Indeed the sense-datum has come in for a good many hard words. It has been compared to the Wild Goose which we vainly chase: or again it is the Will o' the Wisp which lures the Realist further and further from Reality. According to an eminent Idealist philosopher,[3] our modern interest in the sense-datum is just one more manifestation (among so many others) of the degeneracy of an age which prefers the childish, the easy, and the barbarous to the laborious achievement of Intelligence and Civilization. Or again—a charge hardly compatible with this—it is derided as the invention of sophisticated philosophers, as no datum at all. Nor are our opponents content with brilliant metaphors. They have plausible arguments to put forward, and these we must try to answer. It is obvious that we cannot do more than this. It is impossible from the nature of the case to *prove* that there are sense-data or data of any other sort. The utmost we can do is to remove misunderstandings which prevent people from searching for them and from acknowledging them when found. After that, we can only appeal to every man's own consciousness.

The doctrine that there are no sense-data may take two forms, a wider and a narrower, which are not always clearly separated.

1. It is said that the very notion of givenness is an absurd and self-contradictory notion, that from the nature of the case nothing can ever be given at all. This is the most radical criticism that we have to meet. It may be called the A *priori* Thesis.

2. There is also what may be called the Empirical Thesis. This does not say that there is an absurdity in the very notion of givenness. It only

---

[2] The substitution of "seeing" for visual sensing, "hearing" for auditory sensing, etc., would make confusion even worse confounded. For in the ordinary sense of the word *see*, what I see is not a color-patch, but a material thing, e.g., a table or a tomato. Likewise *hear*, *smell*, etc., are in ordinary usage ambiguous. I hear the train, or I hear a noise. I smell the rose, or I smell a smell.

[3] Professor H. J. Paton, *The Idea of the Self*; University of California Publications in Philosophy, Vol. 8, pp. 76–7.

says that we can never in fact find anything which is given. And it concludes that either there is no Given at all, or if there is any, it is found only in the experience of new-born children, idiots, and people falling into or just coming out of fainting fits: in which case (it is urged) the Given is clearly of no importance to the philosopher, for it is quite beyond the reach of investigation, and therefore cannot be appealed to as evidence for anything.

Either of these theses if established would be very damaging. The A *priori* Thesis is the most radical, but also the easier to answer. The Empirical Thesis is the really difficult one to meet, and we shall have to make some concessions to it. Nevertheless, the arguments by which it is ordinarily supported are open to very grave objections.

The "A priori" Thesis. The main argument in favor of this may be summed up as follows:

It is impossible to apprehend something without apprehending some at least of its qualities and relations. In the language of Cambridge logicians, what we apprehend is always a *fact*—something of the form "that A is B" or "the B-ness of A." You cannot apprehend just A. For instance, you cannot apprehend a round red patch without apprehending that it is red and round and has certain spatial relations. But if we apprehend that it has these qualities and relations, we are not passively "receiving" or (as it were) swallowing; we are actively thinking—judging or classifying—and it is impossible to do less than this.

To this I answer, it is very likely true, but it is irrelevant. The argument only proves that nothing stands *merely* in the relation of givenness to the mind, without also standing in other relations: i.e., that what is given is always also "thought about" in some sense or other of that ambiguous phrase. But this does not have the slightest tendency to prove that *nothing is given at all.* The fact that A and B are constantly conjoined, or even necessarily connected, does not have the slightest tendency to prove that A does not exist.[4] How could it, since it itself presupposes the existence of A? That arguments of this sort should be so frequently used, and should be thought so conclusive, is one of the curiosities of philosophical controversy.

Secondly, we may attack the enemy on his own ground and ask him how we can think without having something to think about. This *subject* or *subject-matter* about which we think must be somehow brought before

---

[4] A stands here for "Givenness" and B for "thought-of-ness." The argument is the one commonly used against what is called *vicious abstraction*. Sometimes the conclusion is not that A does not exist but that A is identical with B: but here again it is presupposed in the premises that they are different—else how could they be necessarily connected?

the mind, if we are to think about it, and it cannot always be brought there by previous thinking, or we should have an infinite regress. This means that something must be *given*. And sensing is one of the ways (I do not say the only one) in which subject-matters for thought are given to us. No doubt it is important to insist that this intuitive "receiving" of a datum is never more than an element in our total state of mind.[5] But still it *is* an element, and an essential one.

The Empirical Thesis. This maintains that it is in fact impossible to discover any data. For if we try to point to an instance, it is said, we shall have to confess that the so-called datum is not really given at all, but is the product of interpretation.

This doctrine is put forward both in the interests of Subjective Idealism, which holds that each mind lives in a private world of its own, and in the interests of that Objective or Rationalistic Idealism which holds that the world is entirely constructed by "Thought," or by "Mind" with a capital M. But it may be suspected that sometimes the one party uses arguments which are only appropriate to the other.

We must begin by protesting with Professor G. E. Moore against the word "interpretation," which is used to cover several quite different processes and is at best only a metaphor. For instance, it may mean either *association of ideas*, or some form of *thinking*. We shall begin with the first.

Effects of Association. We can easily find cases where the Given seems to have been contaminated, as it were, by the effects of association. Thus it would be said that Visual Depth beyond a pretty short range is plainly not given, but is due to the revival, by association, of the traces of past kinaesthetic and tactual experience. Or again a distant snowy peak looks cold, but is it not obvious that its coldness cannot be given? The sounds of a foreign language, say Italian, sound quite different when I have learned to speak the language myself. They then fall apart, as it were, into words and word-groups, which they never did before. (At first I heard just one continuous sound.) This is due to the traces of the kinaesthetic experiences experienced in speaking the language oneself, and further to one's newly-acquired knowledge of what the words mean—for this knowledge too has left its "traces." But neither the kinaestheta nor the meanings can be *heard*. Both are "read into" what we hear. Proof-reading and Psychic Blindness also provide instances. But here the effect of the traces is negative instead of positive. Instead of seeing what is not there, we fail to see what is there.

Objections to the Argument. Let us first take the argument on its own

[5] Cf. Discussion of Perceptual Acceptance, below, ch. VI.

ground, without criticizing its premises. We must then answer that no doubt the facts are as stated, but they do not prove what is wanted. Indeed, if anything, they prove the very opposite, viz., that there *are* data and that we know what they are.

1. If nothing whatever is given to me when I look at the mountain or hear the sounds, the phrase "due to association" loses all sense. Association is a relation, and if we speak of it, we imply that there are at least two terms to be associated: what is associated must be associated *with something*. When the mountain looks cold to me, the presence of the coldness to my mind is due to association. But with what is the coldness associated? Obviously with the color and shape. These then *are* given: *their* presence cannot be explained by association, for they are what the associated qualities join on to. And if, preferring another metaphor, you say that what I see is "contaminated by" the traces of past experiences, or "overlaid with" them: I answer, that where there is contamination there must be something which is contaminated, and where there is overlaying there must be something which is overlaid.

2. Is it not dangerous to specify *what* characteristics are due to association? We are told "What you see looks cold, distant and solid; and obviously coldness, distance and solidity cannot be given to sight." But how does the critic know that they are not given to sight? The only answer must be: "Because color and two-dimensional shape are the only qualities that *are* given to sight." But in that case there is after all a datum of sight, and the critic knows what it is.

3. Is it not dangerous to give a name to the associations, to speak of them, for instance, as *tactual* associations, *kinaesthetic* associations and the like? For this presupposes that the associated characteristics, though not given now, have been given in the past. For instance, if you say that the apparent coldness and solidity of the seen mountain-peak are due to tactual associations, and therefore are not given to sight at this moment, you admit that they have been given to touch in the past. Otherwise what is the sense of using the word "tactual"? And even if, more wary, you merely say that the presence of these qualities is due just to the traces of past experience, we must press you to specify what kind of past experience. And you will be obliged to say, past *sense*-experience, and so you will have admitted that these qualities have been given in the past. Thus in order to prove that A *is* not given, one has to assume that B *has been* given.

So far we have been attacking the critics of the Given upon their own ground. And that ground is this. They begin by assuming that there is a distinction between "the real given" or the given-as-it-is-in-itself on the one hand, and "what the given seems to be" on the other. And they then argue that we cannot know what this given-as-it-is-in-itself is. That the argument when we pursue it into detail is incoherent, and proves the very opposite of what it is supposed to prove, we have seen. We must now attack the initial assumption and point out:

4. That the distinction between the Given as it really is and what the Given seems to be [6] is altogether untenable. I scarcely know how to prove this. Is it not just obvious that if something seems to be given, it is given? For in the sphere of the given (as in that of pleasure and pain) what seems, is. Indeed we might go farther. We might say that the notion of seeming has no *application* to the given: and that, by the very definitions of "seeming" and of "given." When A seems to be B, this really means that some mind unreflectively believes A to be B, or as we say "takes" it to be B. Now if so, there must be some *evidence* upon which this taking is (however hastily and unreflectively) based. Thus if it seems to me to be raining, the evidence is that I hear a pitter-patter sound. This does not *seem* to be a pitter-patter sound; it *is* one. And only because there *is* this sound can it seem to have a certain cause, viz., rain falling on the roof. And though the rain which there seems to be may not after all exist (for it may have been a shower of gravel or peas) the sound nonetheless exists, and does have a pitter-patter character. In short, the Given is by definition that which by being itself actual and intuitively apprehended, makes it possible for something else to seem to exist or to have a certain quality. Of course certain characteristics may be given which some philosopher thinks *ought not* to be given, e.g., solidity. So much the worse for him, that is all. He must have held a false theory of what is "giveable." If something is given, it is given, and we must just make the best of it. In a matter of this kind we cannot and will not accept the dictation of theorists.

To clinch my point, I will try to show how these errors may have arisen. They arise, I think, from a confusion between two standpoints or modes of investigation, (a) the physiological and (b) the immanent or phenomenological. The physiologist finds that many of the characteristics of the visual field are not due to the electromagnetic stimulus which affects the retina; or even that none of its characteristics are entirely due to this. He therefore concludes that those characteristics are not given. But we must point out that he is using the term "given" in an utterly different sense from ours, a *causal* sense: he is using it to mean "due to a physical stimulus external to the organism"—or he may even be meaning that this stimulus *is* what is given.

[6] In his *Philosophical Studies*, pp. 243–7, Professor G. E. Moore has suggested that sense-data may seem to be what they are not. But he admits that this suggestion may be "sheer nonsense." (We shall have to refer to it again in another connection.)

But our standpoint is quite a different one. We are asking what is *given to consciousness*, or presented to the mind. We are not inquiring into the causes which may have led to its being given. Further (as has been shown already), our standpoint is the more fundamental one. For the physiologist's only evidence for believing that there is an organism, and physical stimuli affecting it, is derived from observation: that is, from the presentation to him—to him, not to his organism—of data in *our* sense of the word.

To sum up this rather intricate discussion:

1. It is true that what is given now to a certain mind depends to a surprisingly large extent upon what has been given to that mind in the past. But this, so far from disproving the existence either of present or of past data, asserts the existence of both, and enables us to describe their nature in a way we could not do before.

2. It is true that the facts concerning association adduced by our critics do make the causal explanation of the datum more complicated than one might expect. But to say that they prove that there are no data is to deny the very fact of association itself, which presupposes the existence of past data. And to say that the causal explanation of something is complicated is to assert, not to deny, the existence of the something to be explained.

3. The facts adduced do not hinder but help the Realist, that is, the man who wishes to use his data to gain knowledge or true belief about a Real which exists whether known and believed about or not. For the datum, it turns out, gives information not only about the present or the immediate past, but also—*via* earlier data—about the remote past. And the past is as much a part of the real word as the present, and quite as interesting. Moreover, the datum, we have found, gives information not merely about the non-mental, but also about the mind to which it is presented (e.g., a psychoanalyst can argue from the peculiarities of a man's data, say the hallucinations from which he suffers, to the existence of such and such a suppressed complex in the man's mind). Why should it be supposed that this would upset the Realist? The mind is just as much a part of the Real, and just as fit an object for inquiry, as any mountaintop or teacup. And if we can collect information about it from the given, so much the better for us. We ought to be glad that the given is so full of a number of things, and accept the gift in the spirit in which it is offered.

So much for the first sense of the word "interpretation." There are however two others which we must consider. And first, interpretation may mean *thinking* of some kind or other. To interpret something may mean to apprehend (immediately or inferentially), or again to believe or opine or conjecture, that it has a certain characteristic. Thus if on hearing a certain noise we infer that it is the signal for dinner, we should be said to be interpreting what we hear. And even if one merely judges that it is a loud shrill sound, even this would be called interpretation by the philosophers with whom we are now concerned.

I do not wish to maintain that the line between this intellectual sense of the word "interpretation," and the associative sense of it which we discussed first, is altogether easy to draw. For it seems likely that association is on the one side more intellectual, on the other more plastic, and so to say less "wooden" and external, than the traditional account of it would suggest. But that is a matter which we are not obliged for our present purposes to discuss. It is sufficient to point out that by interpretation people sometimes mean an "unconscious" process, whose existence and nature can only be inferred from its results, and this is what we have already discussed under the name of association; whereas sometimes they mean an actually experienced activity, whose existence does not need to be inferred, because we are immediately aware of it in self-consciousness. It is this latter process which I have called the intellectual or "thinking" sort of interpretation; and this is what we must now discuss.

The argument which we have to meet is as follows: Even if there be something which is given it is quite impossible for us to know it.[7] For if we attempt to describe any so-called datum, e.g., this view which I now see, the very act of describing alters it.[8] What we have at the end of the process is not the datum but a set of propositions, and the only relic of the datum is the term "this" which stands as their subject. Thus every attempt to describe the given is bound to fail. But if we cannot describe it, i.e., say what characters it has, we obviously do not know it. It is just the hypothetical and inaccessible somewhat which was present before the process of describing began. And this applies even to the very simplest and naïvest act of describing e.g., this is red, this is hard.

This argument, especially when adorned with a multitude of learned illustrations and expounded at many pages' length, is apt to seem very formidable. But we must point out that it rests on the assumption that *if I know or believe that something has a certain nature, it follows that it cannot possibly have the nature that I know or believe it to have*: i.e., that from the fact that I know or believe that A is B, it follows that A cannot really be B. This assumption when openly and unmetaphorically

[7] On this view the distinction between knowledge by acquaintance and knowledge about does not arise. Indeed the whole contention is that there *is* no acquaintance.
[8] The view that the describing alters not it but the *givenness* of it will be dealt with below, p. 17 [p. 217 this volume].

stated is so extraordinary that it is difficult at first sight to understand how anyone can accept it. But I think that on further reflection we can find certain facts, and certain confused conceptions of these facts, which do tend to make it plausible.

1. In the first place, the describing of something is an *active* process, something that we *do*. It is no wonder that Idealist philosophers speak in this connection of "the work" of thought, for in any cases but the simplest, the describing of what we see or hear is exceedingly difficult. An indefinitely large amount of extraneous knowledge may be involved in it. The greatest concentration of attention, the most happy and illuminating facility in recalling appropriate parallels, may well be necessary. Anyone can, indeed, grasp that this is a black cross on a white ground; but it needs a Conrad to describe the data presented to the voyager in the China seas, and all the labors of all the great painters scarcely suffice to enable us to comprehend the pattern of the prospect which we can see from our own front doors.

In face of such efforts as these, it may be asked, what becomes of our Given? Can it really be the same at the end of this work as it was at the beginning? To say that it is completely unaffected is surely to say that the *work* has had no result. Nor can we draw a line anywhere between the simple statement "This is a black cross on a white ground" and the elaborate, subtle, tortuous passage (perhaps pages long) of the novelist or the traveller. If the second transforms the datum into something which is not a datum at all, so must the first. The datum-as-it-is-in-itself will be the unknowable limit of the series, which we approach more closely as our description becomes simpler and simpler, but never actually reach.—Or will it even be that? For at which end of the series do we come nearest to the datum as it really is? Does a bovine *naïveté* really bring us nearer to it than subtilty and sophistication?—especially when we remember that *naïveté* itself is often a most laborious achievement, which only the most sophisticated can attain to. It seems impossible to say. In short, the pursuit of the datum in itself seems to be a perfect wild-goose chase. We do not even know where we are to look for it, or when in our blundering attempts we are beginning (as children say) to get "warm."

To all this kind of argumentation we must firmly answer, that it rests upon too narrow a notion of activity. Describing is a form of thinking, and thinking is an activity, often a very difficult one indeed. But it does not follow that it *alters* the thing about which we think. Practical activity does alter the thing upon which we act. For instance, the activity of walking alters the position and state of the walker's body: and the activity of beating someone alters the man who is beaten. But intellectual activity does not alter that upon which it is directed. If it alters anything, it alters only one's own mind, causing it to pass (say) from a state of uncertainty to a state of certainty, or from confusion to clarity.[9] Indeed that is the obvious difference between intellectual and practical activity. But though obvious, it is concealed from people for the following reasons. First, intellectual activity, though it does not itself alter the object, may lead to practical activity which does. If I had not understood that this was a wasp, I should not have hit it. Again, intellectual activity is, as it were, included in practical activity as an essential element. We "control" our action by recognition of the circumstances, by the thought of a plan or principle which we are seeking to realize in or by the action, and by the apprehension of certain alternative ways of realizing it. There is no such thing as unintelligent action. *Das Thun ist auch Denken.* Further, even in the most purely theoretical activity we must attend, and attending seems to be kind of willing. But these facts, though important, do not have the faintest tendency to show that intellectual activity and practical activity are identical, or even alike. As we have seen before, from the fact that A and B are connected, however intimately, we cannot infer that A is identical with B, still less that A does not exist.

So much for the first confusion which leads philosophers to think that if I know or believe that A is B, it follows that A cannot really be B.

2. The second confusion arises from the use of such words as *analysis.* When we describe something, it is natural to say that we are analyzing it or "breaking it up." And the next step is, to assimilate this intellectual analysis to chemical analysis or anatomical dissection. It is held that just as dissection destroys a living organism, so intellectual analysis destroys that which is analyzed, and substitutes something else in its place: "we murder to dissect." For instance, it substitutes for an organic whole a set of parts externally related by a mere "and" relation, or replaces a concrete individual by a set of universals or concepts. And accordingly since all thought may be regarded as analysis, we are forbidden to think, or warned that the thinkable is very far from being the real.

But is this metaphor to impose on us forever? Is it not plain that intellectual analysis is utterly different from dissection? In intellectual analysis, I do not *do* anything to the object before me. I *find* relations within it. I *discover* that it possesses various characteristics—say redness and roundness—and I apprehend certain differences between those characteristics. But those relations and characteristics were there before I discovered them. The only change that has occurred is a change in myself. I

[9] I understand that some of the schoolmen said that in the activity of thinking the intellect *perfects itself.*

was ignorant, and now I know. Nor does the fact that in order to find them I must often *compare* the present given with other data given in the past at all affect the matter. Comparison does not alter the things compared. It is merely the *detection of a likeness*. The likeness may be what is called far-fetched—in the descriptive writing of Conrad (for instance) it often is. But it is there all the same: and when we call it far-fetched, we only mean that most of us would not have succeeded in discovering it.

Before leaving this part of the subject, we may observe that all this applies to "synthesis" also. What is called "synthesis" or sometimes "construction" by philosophers is not really a putting together of entities originally separated: it is the detection or discovery of an objective complex which has been there all along. The discovery is metaphorically called a synthesis, because it comes about in and by means of an active process of comparison.

3. The third confusion in the minds of those who hold that thought destroys or transforms the given which is thought about has to do with *attention*. Mr. Bradley somewhere asks "Does attention change its object?" Like another famous doubter, he does not stay for an answer. But I think he means to suggest that attention does alter its object. And I think that many of the critics of the Given have tacitly adopted the suggestion, though without putting the issue in this plain way. It is thought that as we attend to something, this something becomes more and more "clear," and at the same time more and more complex. It starts by being a mere "something or other" and it ends by being (say) a Gothic pinnacle, or a group of oak trees arranged in a quincunx.

This, I suppose, is the doctrine. Yet when plainly stated it is so extraordinary that it is hard to see how anyone can have the audacity to hold it. To alter something is to cause a change in it. But the kind of change which is supposed to occur in the object of attention is altogether fantastic. In a genuine change the object passes from the possession of one determinate character to the possession of another at the same level of determinateness. Thus if it changes shape it may pass from circular to elliptical: if color, from peacock green to turquoise blue. But the change which attention is supposed to cause is not of this sort at all. It is a passage *from the possession of a generic character to the possession of a specific one*, and from that to the possession of one still more specific: or again it is a passage from possession of an indeterminate character to the possession of more and more determinate ones. Thus in regard to shape, the thing (as I attend to it) will first have just shape in general, then rectilinear shape in general, then it will become triangular, and lastly perhaps it will be an equilateral triangle. In regard to color, it will first have coloredness in general, then it will be green, then bluish green, and finally peacock green.

Now is it not plain as day that this is not change at all? Change is the passage from one characteristic to another characteristic of *equal determinateness*. But this so-called change is in another dimension altogether: it is from the less determinate to the more determinate. Is it not obvious that the change—the growing determinateness—is simply in our mode of apprehension and not in the thing apprehended? It is we who apprehend more and more determinately the always fully determinate character which the thing all along possessed.

Further, the doctrine involves another absurdity: that of supposing that an entity can exist with only generic or indeterminate qualities, e.g., that a color-patch can exist which is just colored and is neither red nor green, blue nor yellow. Such would be the fate of all those unfortunate entities which do not happen to get attended to.

So much for the confusions which lead philosophers to think that the attempt to know anything about the Given must alter it, and to conclude that if anything is given at all, it is unknowable. We have tried to show that the intellectual activities of describing, comparing, etc., do not alter that which is "analyzed" or described, but merely reveal its nature and its relation to other things in the world.

It may however be suggested that though that which is given is not altered by the attempt to know about it, yet its *givenness* is destroyed by that attempt; so that although a certain red patch after being described is the same entity as it was before, yet it is not the same datum—for it is no longer a datum at all, but has become an "intellectum" instead. Thus any alleged knowledge about data would really be a knowledge about ex-data; and we could still say that the datum *qua datum* is unknowable—unknowable in the sense in which a bachelor is incapable of being a husband.

It is plain that this supposed alteration is different from the former one, which we have already dismissed. The alteration of A is one thing, the alteration of A's relation to the mind is another.

Now we must admit that if a datum A is reflected upon and described, it is no longer *merely* a datum. For the sake of argument we will even go further, and allow that everything which can be said to be given to a mind is also "judged about" by that mind, i.e., recognized to have certain qualities and relations, at any rate certain very general ones. But from the fact that something is no longer (and perhaps never was) a datum merely, we cannot conclude that it is not a datum at all. Again from the fact that we recognize (and describe) something as red and round, we can conclude that we are not *merely* acquainted with it: but that we are *not* acquainted with it—this by no means follows. Indeed it is difficult, to say the least, to understand how we could describe color-patches or noises or tactual pressures, unless they were somehow there before us to be described, or in general how we could recognize anything as so-and-so unless we were acquainted with it. Certainly the fact that we can describe and recognize it will never prove that we are *not* acquainted with it! We must conclude then that the given is still given, however much we know about it. Knowledge-about is the usual, perhaps the inevitable, companion of acquaintance, but it is not its executioner.

We may sum up this discussion as follows. When I am in the situation which is described as seeing something, touching something, hearing something, etc., it is certain in each case that a color-patch, or a pressure, or a noise exists at that moment and that I am acquainted with this color-patch, pressure or noise. Such entities are called sense-data, and the acquaintance with them is conveniently called sensing; but it differs from other instances of acquaintance only in its object, not in its nature, and it has no species. The usual arguments against the reality and against the knowability of sense-data break down on examination. They only prove at most that there is no sense-datum which is not the object of other sorts of consciousness besides sensing, and that the causes of most sense-data are more complicated than might have been expected: and in these conclusions there is nothing to disturb us.

In conclusion we may point out that the admission that there are sense-data is not a very large one; it commits us to very little. It may be worthwhile to mention explicitly a number of things which we are *not* committed to.

1. We are not committed to the view that sense-data *persist* [10] through the intervals when they are not being sensed. We have only to admit that they *exist* at the times when they are being sensed.

2. We are not committed to the view that several minds can be acquainted with the *same* sense-datum. We have only to admit that every mind is acquainted with *some* sense-data from time to time.

3. We are not committed to any view about what is called "the status" of sense-data in the Universe, either as regards the *category* they

[10] Or more strictly, that there are persistent *sensibilia* which become sense-data temporarily when they are sensed. Cf. Mr. Bertrand Russell's *Mysticism and Logic*, p. 148.

fall under, or as regards their relations with other types of existent entities. They may be events, or substances, or states of substances. They may be physical; i.e., they may be parts of or events in material objects such as chairs and tables or (in another theory) brains. They may be mental, as Berkeley and many others have held. They may be neither mental nor physical.

4. We are not committed to any view about their *origin*. They may originate as a result of processes in material objects, or of mental processes, or of both. Or again, it may be that the boot is on the other leg: it may be that they are the ultimate constituents of the Universe, and material things (perhaps minds as well) may be just collections of them; in which case they "just are," and have no origin and no explanation, since everything else is explained by reference to them.

Thus the term sense-datum is meant to be a *neutral* term. The use of it does not imply the acceptance of any particular theory. The term is meant to stand for something whose existence is indubitable (however fleeting), something from which all theories of perception ought to start, however much they may diverge later.

And I think that all past theories have in fact started with sense-data. The Ancients and the Schoolmen called them *sensible species*. Locke and Berkeley called them *ideas of sensation*, Hume *impressions*, Kant *Vorstellungen*. In the nineteenth century they were usually known as sensations, and people spoke of visual and auditory sensations when they meant color-patches and noises; while many contemporary writers, following Dr. C. D. Broad, have preferred to call them *sensa*.

All these terms have the defect of begging questions. If we speak of *sensible species* we assume that sense-data are physical, a sort of effluences flying off the external objects into our sense-organs. If we use terms like *idea, impression,* and *sensation* we commit ourselves to the view that sense-data are mental events. *Sensum* is very much the best. But it is generally used to mean a "third kind" of entity, neither mental nor physical. And although we are not at present in a position to assert that sense-data are physical or that they are mental, neither are we in a position to deny either of these alternatives. (Thus "sense-data are sensa" is not a tautology, but a synthetic proposition.)

An incidental virtue of the term *sense-datum* is that it enables us to give a brief and intelligible account of the traditional theories concerning perception and the external world, and so to make use of the work of our predecessors without wasting time in tedious historico-lexicographical investigations.

PHENOMENALISM

A. J. Ayer (1910–)

I shall be concerned in this paper with phenomenalism as a theory of perception. In the form in which it is usually held nowadays, it is the theory that physical objects are logical constructions out of sense-data. Assuming that we understand what is meant by a physical object, in the sense in which chairs and tables and match boxes are physical objects, we are left with the questions: What is a logical construction? and What are sense-data? At the risk of repeating an excessively familiar story, I shall begin with the sense-data.

I believe that the word "sense-datum" was first used as a technical term in philosophy by Bertrand Russell: and he defined sense-data as objects of acquaintance. But this definition leaves us none the wiser unless we know what is meant in this context by "acquaintance." In the ordinary way, we talk of being acquainted with persons, or with places, or even with facts: but this does not give us a sufficient indication of what it is to be acquainted with a sense-datum. When someone tells me that he is glad to make my acquaintance, no doubt he is also making the acquaintance of sense-data, in some sense, but the sense in which he is supposed to be acquainted with them is not the same as that in which he is acquainted with me. But in what sense, then, is he acquainted with them? Some technical sense, presumably. But, if so, it needs to be explained: and until it has been explained the term "sense-datum" has not been satisfactorily defined. Neither do we escape this difficulty by defining sense-data as the objects of "sensing" or "direct apprehension" or "direct awareness," as various philosophers have proposed. For these also are technical terms, and there is no familiar usage of them by reference to which their meaning in this context is to be understood.

From *Aristotelian Society Proceedings*, Vol. 47, 1946–47, pp. 163–196. Reprinted by courtesy of the author and of the Editor of the Aristotelian Society. Copyright 1947 The Aristotelian Society.

This may seem a trivial point, but I think that it is worth making because I suspect that behind these definitions lurks the suggestion that sense-data are objects of knowledge. That is, I suspect that such artificial expressions as "direct apprehension" or "direct awareness," or even the more natural "acquaintance," as they are used in this context, are euphemisms for the word "knowledge," which is itself too sacred, or too dangerous, to pronounce. But if sense-data are to be defined as objects of knowledge then I do not think that there are sense-data, because I do not think that there are objects of knowledge. And by this I do not mean that it is just not the case that we know any objects, though we might have known some if we had been luckier or cleverer. Nor, like some philosophers, am I using the word "knowledge" so strictly that everything that is ordinarily taken for knowledge turns out really not to be so. What I mean is that there cannot be objects of knowledge, because to speak of knowing objects, in the sense here intended, is to commit a type fallacy. Admittedly, the word "know" is often used as a transitive verb. I may say, for example, that I know a person if I have been in his company, and we recognize each other when we meet: or, in a slightly different sense, I may say that I know him if by being in his company I have learned how he is likely to behave. Again, I may say that I know a place if I have been there; or perhaps it may be required that I should have been there sufficiently often to be able to find my way about it, or for the various parts of it to be familiar to me. And many other examples could be given, in which the criteria for the proper use of "know" as a transitive verb would be found to cover a fairly extensive range. But it is not this sort of thing that philosophers have in mind when they say, or imply, that there are objects of knowledge. The sense of "know" with which they are concerned is the sense in which we speak of knowing that something or other is the case. And in this sense it is meaningless to speak of knowing objects. Failure to realize this has contributed, I think, to a famous piece of philosophical mythology, the act-object analysis of sensation. For once it is assumed that having a sensation involves knowing an object, then it may seem reasonable to apply to this case the principle that what is known must be independent of the knowing of it: and so we come to the fashionable refutations of Berkeley which consist in distinguishing the act of awareness, as a mental entity, from the object, not necessarily mental, which is the accusative of the act. But what are these acts of awareness supposed to be? No doubt sentences of the form "A is aware of X," or "A is conscious of X" are often given a meaning which is such that the propositions which they then express are found to be true: but it does not follow from this that the expressions "being aware of" or "being conscious of" are names for anything. And, indeed, not only do I not find any referents for such names when I analyze my sensations empirically, but I do not know what they are supposed to stand for. I do not know what it would be like to come upon an act of awareness. Consequently, if sense-data were defined as the objects of such acts, I should remain unconvinced that there were sense-data.

Professor Price, who has made himself the guardian of sense-data—he is not their parent but it is he who had chiefly interested himself in their welfare: it is to him more than anyone that they owe their present position of honor in the philosophical world—has another method of defining them. He says that when I look at a physical object, for instance a tomato, there is much that I can doubt. I can doubt whether it is not a reflection, or a cleverly painted piece of wax, or even a complete hallucination. But, he goes on to argue, there remains something that I cannot doubt. I cannot doubt that "there exists a red patch of a round and somewhat bulgy shape, standing out from a background of other color-patches, and having a certain visual depth, and that this whole field of color is directly present to my consciousness." And it is this object whose existence I cannot doubt that he proposes to call a sense-datum. But why can I not doubt it? What prevents me? It is not a question of my psychology. It is not just that I cannot now bring myself to doubt the existence of this bulgy patch, because that leaves open the possibility that I might. If I schooled myself in doubting, I might achieve it. But clearly this is not what Price means. He wants to say that the existence of what he calls the sense-datum is objectively beyond doubt: so that if anyone managed to deny it, he would necessarily be wrong. Thus, there is a sense in which, having accepted the premises of a valid deductive argument, I cannot doubt the conclusion, though there is also a sense in which I can doubt it, since I may not be sure that I have drawn the inference correctly. Similarly, I may be unsure of the truth of an analytic proposition, but there is also a sense in which it may be said that I cannot doubt it, if it is necessarily true. It is not in this sense, however, that I cannot doubt the existence of the bulgy patch. For it would not be self-contradictory to say that no such object existed. But perhaps what is meant when it is said that I cannot doubt the existence of the patch is that it does not make sense to say "I doubt if this patch exists." It may be suggested that the reason why I cannot doubt it is that one cannot properly speak of doubting in such a case. But the trouble with this is that there is a perfectly good sense of the word "exist" in which it does make sense to say that I doubt if this bulgy patch exists. If I were not sure whether the appearance of the patch in question was not a constituent of a dream, it would be entirely proper to describe my situation by saying that I doubted whether the patch existed. Accordingly, one has to go on to explain that the sense of "exist" in which it is meaningless to say "I doubt if this patch exists" is the special sense that is appropriate to sense-data and not to physical objects. And thus we are once more brought back in a circle.

All the same, it is not very hard to see what Price and the other philosophers who talk about sense-data are getting at. For suppose that I am having an experience which it would be natural for me to describe by saying that I was holding a match-box in my hand and looking at it. In that case, assuming the experience to be veridical, there is a familiar sense of the words "see" and "touch" in which what I am now seeing and touching is simply "this match-box." And there is also a familiar sense of the words "see" and "touch" in which what I am now seeing and touching is not the whole match-box but only a part of its surface. Now, in both these senses, if it should happen that the match-box does not exist, if I am dreaming or having an illusion, then either I am seeing something, or a part of something, other than a match-box, something that I mistake for a match-box, or, in the case of a total hallucination, I am not seeing or touching anything. But it is also possible to use the words "see" and "touch" in such a way that even if I am dreaming or having a complete hallucination, so that there is no physical object there, it can still be said that there is some object that I am seeing or touching, and further, that this object really has the characteristics that the physical object, which I mistakenly think that I am seeing or touching, in the other senses of the words "see" and "touch," appears to me to have. And what I am seeing in *this* sense may perhaps be a certain patch of color, "standing out from a background of other color patches and having a certain visual depth," though I am inclined on psychological grounds to doubt whether this would be an accurate description of any normal visual experience. Let us then call the whole of what everyone sees in this sense at any given moment, his "visual sense-field." Then a visual sense-datum may be defined as anything that is the constituent of a visual sense-field. And, in general, a sense-datum may be defined as anything that is the constituent of a sense-field.

At this point it may be objected that I have not got away from the act-object analysis of sensation. For I have explained the use of the word "sense-datum" in terms of a special use of words like "touch" and "see" and these are transitive verbs. But the answer is that there is no need to assume that such words as "seeing" and "touching," in this usage, are names for mental acts. If the word "sensing" be used to designate the experience of which seeing, touching, and the rest, in this usage, are the various modes, then to say of something that it is sensed need be taken to imply no more than that it is sensibly present, or, in other words, that it appears: and to specify that it is seen or touched is merely to indicate what manner of appearance is in question. We might therefore say that to be seen is to appear visually, that to be touched is to appear tactually, and so on, though we should still have to distinguish different senses of "appear" as correlates of the different senses of "touch" and "see." Thus what we obtain by introducing the term "sense-datum" is a means of referring to appearances without prejudging the questions what it is, if anything, that they are appearances *of*, and what it is, if anything, that they appear *to*. And here it may be advisable to make the familiar point that the use of this term "sense-datum" is not intended to carry any factual implications about the character of these appearances. It is not designed, for example, to beg the question in favor of an atomic as opposed to a *gestalt* theory of sensation. Thus, when philosophers like Professor Stout make it an objection to "the sense-datum theory," and so to phenomenalism, that what is sensibly "given" is something more substantial than a mere sense-datum, their argument is beside the mark. It is an empirical question whether the contents, say, of a visual-field are more accurately to be described as patches of color or colored "objects." But even if it is described, on empirical grounds that what is seen is, in some sense, a colored "object," it will still be a sense-datum, according to our usage.

Now if the word "sense-datum" is understood in this way, then if it is ever true that a physical object is being perceived, it must also be true that some sense-datum is being sensed. If, for example, it is a fact that I am seeing a match-box, in the appropriate sense of the word "see," then it *follows* that, in the appropriately different sense of the word "see," I am seeing some sense-datum. But the converse does not hold. I believe that I am now perceiving a match-box and this belief is directly based on the evidence of my senses. But from the fact that I am sensing the sense-data that I am now sensing it does not *follow* that I am perceiving a match-box. For if we disregard all the other evidence available to me, including the evidence of my memories, my having the sense-experience that I am now having is compatible with there being no such match-box there; it is compatible with my being the victim of an illusion. Thus, when I say, truly as it happens, that I am now perceiving a match-box, part of what I am saying is that I am sensing sense-data of a certain kind; but only part. I am saying that and something more. But what more? That is our problem. And the phenomenalists' answer to it is that the more that I am saying is that further sense-data of the appropriate sort would, in the appropriate conditions, be obtainable.

If this answer is correct, then it seems to follow that the statement that I am perceiving this match-box, or whatever other physical object may be taken as an example, must be equivalent to some set of statements about sense-data. And since to say that I am perceiving a match-box entails saying that the match-box exists, the statement that this match-box exists must also, in that case, be equivalent to some set of statements about sense-data. And to say, as phenomenalists do, that physical objects are logical constructions out of sense-data is merely another way of expressing this. It does not mean that physical objects are literally composed of sense-data, or that physical objects are fictions and only sense-data real. It means simply that statements about physical objects are somehow reducible to statements about sense-data, or, as it is sometimes put, that to say anything about a physical object is to say something, though not necessarily the same thing, about sense-data. This, then, is the claim that we have to discuss.

II.

The first point to be made is that if we confine ourselves to actual sense-data, this claim can evidently not be upheld. For to revert to our example, this match-box is not continuously perceived either by me or by anybody else. And yet at times when no one is perceiving it, that is, when there are no sense-data that are directly relevant to its existence, the match-box may still exist. In other words, it is not self-contradictory, though it may in certain cases be false, to say both that a given physical object exists in a certain place, and throughout a certain period of time, and that during that period of time no one was sensing any such sense-data as would constitute direct evidence for the existence of the physical object in question. Consequently, if the sense-datum language is to do the work that phenomenalists require of it, it must permit us to refer to possible sense-data. And what this means is that some at least of the statements about sense-data that are supposed to yield the equivalence of statements about physical objects will have to be hypothetical. They will have to state not that any sense-data have occurred, are occurring, or will occur, but that in certain specifiable conditions certain sense-data would occur. The difficulty, as we shall see, is to specify the conditions.

Now it would seem that the best way for a phenomenalist to prove his case would be to set about giving us some examples. We should expect him to take a statement like "there is a flowerpot on the window sill," and give us its equivalent in terms of sense-data. But this is something that no phenomenalist has ever yet done, or even, to my knowledge, seriously tried to do. We are told that statements about physical objects must be translatable into statements about sense-data, but we do not get any translations. The most we get are more or less vague descriptions of the sort of way such translations might run. We are given recipes for making translations; but they seem to be recipes that no one can ever put into use. One reason for this, of course, is the poverty of our sensory language. The vocabulary that we have for describing colors, shapes, and the rest is not sufficient for our purpose: so that we are constantly reduced to saying things like "the sort of sense-data that you get when you look at a match-box" or "the sort of sense-data that you get when you hear a telephone ring," where the reference to the physical object is needed to identify the sense-data in question. But I suppose that a suitable vocabulary could be invented, if some ingenious person thought that it was worth his trouble: so that if this were all that stood in the phenomenalist's way he might be entitled to hold that his program could be carried out, "at least in principle." But there are more serious difficulties.

One that is often brought forward is that no statement about a physical object can be conclusively verified; on the ground that, however much favorable evidence there may be for it, it is always conceivable that further evidence will show it to have been false all along. And from this premiss it is correctly deduced that no statement about a physical object can be equivalent to any finite set of statements about sense-data. For each of the statements about sense-data will be a description of a single piece of evidence in favor of the statement about the physical object; and if the evidence is to be sufficient the number of these descriptions must be infinite. I used to accept this argument but now I am inclined to reject it. The assumption is that if, for example, I am looking at my telephone and suddenly see it change into what appears to be a flowerpot, or vanish altogether, or what you will, that proves that it never was a telephone. To put the case more precisely, suppose that a series of visual and tactual sense-data were succeeded "in the same place," which here may be taken to mean "in similar spatial relations to similar sense-data," by sense-data characteristic of the appearance of a flowerpot, or that, while the surrounding conditions appear to remain unchanged, there cease to be any sense-data characteristic of the appearance of a physical object in the "place" where the sense-data characteristic of the appearance of a telephone previously were, that proves that I must have been mistaken in taking these sense-data to be the appearances of a real telephone. But does it? The only way of deciding what it proves is to consider what one would say in such a case, that is, how one would describe such a situation. What I should, in fact, say would be that my present experience was hallucinatory: that the illusion lay not in the long series of my past "perceptions" of a telephone, but in my present "perception" of a flowerpot. But suppose that I applied the usual tests for hallucinations, and that they were negative. Suppose that the object that I seemed to be perceiving felt as well as looked like a flowerpot, and that it went on looking and feeling like a flowerpot, and that when I asked other people about it they said that they perceived a flowerpot, too. In that case I should probably give up the idea that I was having a hallucination, though it may be remarked that if the evidence that previously led me to believe that I was perceiving a telephone was not conclusive, then the evidence that I was not subsequently having a halluci-nation with regard to the flowerpot would not be conclusive either. If no evidence is conclusive all the competing hypotheses remain open. But suppose that the evidence is such that I do in fact rule out the hypothesis that my "perception" of the flowerpot is a sustained illusion. I *might* then say that I had been deceived all the time about the telephone. I might even start to distrust my memory, and wonder whether it had not always been the case that I perceived a flowerpot, though here the testimony of others would be a check. But what I think I *should* say is: "It *was* a telephone and all of a sudden it changed into a flowerpot." I should think this odd, certainly. I should probably write to the newspapers about it. And then if the ensuing correspondence showed me that other people had had similar experiences, I should begin to feel more comfortable. "It has to be admitted," I should say, "that physical objects do sometimes undergo these abrupt changes. I wonder what the scientific explanation is."

No doubt this example sounds excessively fanciful, but not long ago I did have a fountain pen that suddenly vanished. At one moment I was looking at it, touching it, writing with it, and the next moment it had disappeared. I could not find it any more and never have found it to this day. Of course, I do not really believe that it vanished. "Pens do not just vanish," I say, in default of stronger evidence that they do. But still less do I believe that it never was a pen. I do not say: "The run of favorable evidence has come to an end as I was always warned that it might. My belief that it really was a pen that I was perceiving implied that the run of favorable evidence would continue indefinitely. Consequently my belief was false." What I say is: "There must be some explanation. Perhaps I turned my back on it for an instant, though I do not remember doing so, and somebody crept in and took it. Or, more probably, it dropped some-where and I have not searched for it hard enough." And from this I conclude that when I said, as I often have in the past, like other philoso-phers, that however strongly one's sense-data may support the hypothesis that one is perceiving a physical object of a certain sort, further experience may show one to have been mistaken, I was not serious. For when a situation arose which, on the face of it, supported this view, I did not interpret it in that way at all. I did not even seriously consider the possibility that what I had for so long been taking to be a pen never really had been a pen. Neither do I think that I am peculiar in this respect. I think that the explanation that it never really was a pen is one that, in the circumstances, nobody would consider seriously.

What bearing has this upon the phenomenalist's claim? As I said before, no single sense-experience, taken by itself, ever proves that a physical object exists. From the bare fact that I am sensing *these* visual sense-data it does not follow that this is a match-box. Nevertheless the occurrence of these visual sense-data, taken in conjunction with what I remember, fully justifies the statement that this is a match-box, and would justify it, I should now maintain, even if the "match-box" were to vanish the next instant. By itself the occurrence of just these sense-data would not be sufficient, but in conjunction with previous experience it is. This previous experience may consist of previous perceptions of the physical object in question, that is, previous sensings of the appropriate sense-data, but it need not. In certain circumstances I might be fully justified in believing in the existence of a physical object that I had never before perceived: and in such cases the strength of the evidence would lie in the general character of my previous experience. For my belief that *this* is a physical object, and a physical object of a certain sort, is not based solely on the occurrence of sense-data which are manifestations of *this*: it is derived also from a more general belief that I live in a world of physical objects of which things that look like this are specimens: and this belief is supported by a mass of past experiences. So much so that if this assumption were to break down altogether, if, from this moment on, sense-data were to arrange themselves, as Price once suggested they might, in an eurythmic rather than a thing-like order, I should not say: "I was wrong all the time: there never were any physical objects." I should say: "The world has changed: there used to be physical objects, but now there are none any more."

Does it follow then that at any rate some statements about a physical object can be translated into statements about sense-data, namely into those statements which describe the sense-data, past and present, the occurrence of which fully justifies us, on the occasions when we are so justified, in asserting that the physical object exists? Not necessarily. For in that case the truth of the statements referring to sense-data would be both a necessary and a sufficient condition of the truth of the statement about the physical object. And while I have argued that in certain cases it may be sufficient, I have not shown, nor do I think that it can be shown, that it is also necessary. No doubt the truth of some statement or other about sense-data is always a necessary condition of the truth of any statement which implies the existence of a physical object: but I do not think that it is ever possible to discover a finite set of statements about sense-data of which it can truly be said in a particular case that precisely these are necessary. In other words, though you may be able to discover sets of sufficient conditions, you cannot list them exhaustively. You cannot say, for example, exactly how much experience, nor exactly what type of experience, a child must have had in order to be fully justified, on the evidence available to him, in saying: "This is a ball." In a concrete case you can safely allow that he has sufficient evidence. But you cannot rightly say that it is necessary, because there will always be an indefinite number of other sensory experiences that would have done just as well. Thus, it makes no difference whether his general belief in the existence of physical objects is derived from the sense-data he has obtained when playing with rattles or when playing with teddy-bears: it makes no difference whether he punches a ball or strokes it, whether the angle from which he sees it makes it appear round to him or oval, whether the light is such that it seems to him to be red or orange. The sense-data that are sufficient, in conjunction with his previous experience, to establish the existence of the ball must all fall within a certain range: a sense-datum characteristic of the appearance of an alarm-clock would not fit the case: but the number of possible sense-data that fall within that range is indefinite, while the previous sensory experiences that may go to make the present evidence sufficient not only are indefinite in number, but themselves fall within a range that is extremely wide: And this is one reason why it is impossible to translate a statement about a physical object into any finite set of statements about sense-data. It is not, as has sometimes been suggested, that the physical object is eternally on probation, so that to try to establish its existence by sense-perception is like trying to fill a bottomless well. The reason is that all statements about physical objects are indefinite. The well can be filled, but there are an infinite number of ways of filling it. Consequently, the comparatively definite statements that one makes about sense-data, to the effect that such and such sense-data are being or have been obtained, or that in such and such conditions such and such sense-data would be obtained, cannot be exact translations of the indefinite statements that one makes about physical objects. And by this I mean not, of course, that a statement about a physical object is necessarily indefinite at its own level, but that it is necessarily indefinite at the level of sense-data.

III.

If this be admitted, what becomes of the phenomenalist's case? What is there left for him to claim? It has been suggested that he should claim no more than that the direct evidence for the existence of a physical object is always the occurrence of some sense-datum. But if this were all there would be nothing to discuss. For, as I have already shown, the term "sense-datum" may be defined in such a way that if anyone is perceiving a physical object it *follows* that he is sensing a sense-datum: and not only that but that all that his senses reveal to him is the presence of sense-data. This does not mean that his sensory experiences must be of the sort that we are all familiar with: they might be very queer indeed: but however queer they were they would still be experiences of sense-data. Now it is not to be disputed that the direct evidence for the existence of physical objects is sensory evidence: for any evidence that was not sensory would not be called direct. And clearly if you decide to call obtaining such evidence "sensing sense-data" it will follow that you can obtain such evidence only by sensing sense-data. The only question then is whether you agree with the proposal to use the *word* "sense-datum." But surely those who have taken, or accepted, the title of phenomenalists have thought that they were doing more than extending their patronage to a word.

Yes, but what more? What is the point of introducing the sense-datum vocabulary? The idea is that it helps you to learn something about the nature of physical objects, not indeed in the way that doing science does, but that you come to understand better what is meant by propositions about physical objects, what these propositions amount to, what their "cash-value" is, by restating them in terms of sense-data. That is, the fact that you *can* restate them in this way, *if* you can, tells you something important about them. Furthermore, it is claimed that if you talk in terms of sense-data you are somehow getting deeper than if you are content to talk, as we all do in everyday life, in terms of physical objects. The naive realist is not in error. Naive realism is not a false theory of perception: it is a refusal to play this sort of game. And if a man will not play he cannot lose. But one is inclined to say that the naive realist is missing something by refusing to play: that he is not getting to the root of the matter. And the justification for this is that there is a sense in which the sense-datum language is logically prior to the physical object language. For it is impossible that a physical object should be perceived without its being true that some dense-datum is being sensed: but it is not impossible that any number of sense-data should be sensed without its ever being true that any physical object is perceived. For the relations between sense-data in virtue of which we are justified in claiming that we perceive physical objects are contingent: they might conceivably not have obtained.

But now it turns out that for the reasons I have given, statements about physical objects cannot be translated into statements about sense-data. Consequently, the phenomenalist is obliged to give up his original position. But he need modify it only slightly. He cannot show precisely what you are saying about sense-data when you make a given statement about a physical object, because you are not saying anything precise about sense-data. Nevertheless, he will maintain, what you are saying, though vague, still refers ultimately to sense-data and does not refer to anything other than sense-data. Consequently, he can hope to give a suitably vague translation. It should be possible to indicate at least what sort of thing we are saying about sense-data when we make a statement like "there is a match-box on the table." And if the phenomenalist can do this he may be allowed to have proved his case.

The *a priori* argument for supposing that this must be possible is that if we are not referring to sense-data, and exclusively to sense-data, when we talk about physical objects, it is difficult to see what we can be referring to. "Physical objects," is the unkind answer; and, of course, it is a correct answer, correct but unhelpful. For if we use the sense-datum language— and we have not found any good reason why we should not use it; it has not been shown that it necessarily involves any assumptions that are either logically or empirically mistaken—then it looks as if we are using it as a substitute for the physical-object language. The world does not contain sense-data *and* physical objects, in the sense in which it contains chairs *and* tables, or in the sense in which it contains colors *and* sounds. One is inclined to say, therefore, that phenomenalism must be true, on the ground that the only alternative to it, once we have agreed to use the sense-datum terminology, is the iron-curtain theory of perception: that physical objects are there sure enough but we can never get at them, because all we can observe is sense-data: and surely this theory at least can be shown to be untenable.

IV.

All the same, there are difficulties in the way of the phenomenalists. One, which I shall now try to meet, concerns the question of causation. Regarded by Professor Stout as a fatal objection to phenomenalism,[1] it led Professor Price to postulate, as the owners of causal properties, a set of

[1] G. F. Stout, "Phenomenalism." Proceedings of the Aristotelian Society, 1938–9.

unobservable entities to which he gives the name of "physical occu-
pants"[2] a piece of mythology which I understand that he has since
repudiated—and it has recently been restated with force and clarity by Mr.
W. F. R. Hardie.[3] The difficulty is this:

Our perceptions are fragmentary. We do not perceive all the physical
objects that there are all the time: and yet we believe, and often have good
reason to believe, that some of them exist when no one is perceiving them.
And not only this, but we often have good reason to believe that they are
causally efficacious when no one is perceiving them. An example that Price
gives is that of a concealed magnet which causes the observed deflection of
a compass needle. Now it may be held that what are described as causal
relations between physical objects, or physical events, are analyzable in
terms of regularities among sense-data. But the trouble is that in a great
many cases in which we postulate causal relationships, the required sensory
regularities are not observed. Assuming that I perceive the deflection of
Price's compass needle, then I am sensing certain visual sense-data, and the
occurrence of these sense-data may, it is said, be described as an event. But
the existence of the magnet throughout the relevant period of time is not
an event in the same sense. For *ex hypothesi* no sense-data "belonging to"
the magnet are occurring. You may analyze the statement that the magnet
exists into a hypothetical statement to the effect that if certain conditions
were fulfilled, sense-data characteristic of the appearance of the magnet
would be obtained. But since the conditions in question are not in fact
fulfilled, the statement that the magnet exists does not, when analyzed in
sensory terms, describe any actual event. It does not, when so analyzed, say
that anything exists, but only, to quote Mr. Hardie, that given certain
conditions something would exist which actually does not. But this is to
fall into the absurdity, as Stout calls it, of supposing that "actual occurrences depend upon mere possibilities." For surely it is self-evident that
actual events have actual causes. A mere possibility cannot be a cause.

Let me try to state this objection more clearly. The argument may be
set out in the following way. "It makes sense to say that physical objects
exist and are causally efficacious at times when no one is perceiving them.
There may, therefore, be unobserved physical events and they may stand in
causal relations to other unobserved events, or to observed events. Now, if
the phenomenalists are right, an unobserved physical event is reducible to
a set of possible sensory events. But on an "agency" view of causation this
is incompatible with its being the cause, since a mere set of possibilities

2 H. H. Price, "Perception," ch. IX and X.
3 W. F. R. Hardie, "The Paradox of Phenomenalism." Proceedings of the Aristotelian
Society, 1945–6.

cannot *do* anything. And the same is true even on a "regularity" view of causation: for a possible sensory occurrence is not an event in the sense in which an actual sensory occurrence is an event, and the regularities must be assumed to hold between events of the same type. It is impossible therefore for the phenomenalists to explain how unobserved physical events can be causes. Consequently phenomenalism is false."

As Mr. Hardie has pointed out to me, the argument may be made independent of the empirical premiss that our perceptions are fragmentary, or, in other words, that some physical events are unobserved. For whether or not a physical event is observed, the observation of it is not logically necessary to its occurrence. That is to say, the statement that it occurs does not entail the statement that it is observed to occur. Consequently, the phenomenalist's analysis of a statement which describes the occurrence of a physical event need refer only to possible sense-data, though actual sense-data may have to be brought in if the statement at the physical level itself involves a reference to a percipient. Furthermore the causal properties of physical objects adhere to them whether they are observed or not. If, therefore, the phenomenalist is to allow that any physical events are causes he must maintain that a set of possibilities can be a cause. And this, in the eyes of those who raise this objection, is a manifest absurdity.

This argument has convinced many people, but I think that it is fallacious, and that the fallacy lies partly in a confusion over the use of the word "cause," and partly in an ambiguity in the use of the word "event." I am perfectly willing to admit that an actual event, if it has a cause at all, must have an actual cause, though even here there is a play on the word "actual," since in many cases what is called the cause will be a past event, and so, in a sense, no longer "actual." Still I will grant that, if an event has a cause, that cause must itself be an event which is "actual" in the sense that it either is actually occurring or has at some time actually occurred. But in this proposition the word "event" is being used as a term at the physical level. I do not mean by this that an event, in this sense of the word, must be physical: it may also be mental: but it is at the physical level inasmuch as it occupies a position in physical time, as opposed to sensory time, and inasmuch as it occupies a position in physical space, as opposed to sensory space, if it is spatially located at all. In this sense both the deflection of the needle, to recur to Price's example, and the state of the magnet are actual events, whether they are observed or not. The magnet actually exercises the causal properties in virtue of which the needle is deflected: that is to say, the deflection of the needle can be explained by reference to the properties of the magnet. But this is in no way incompatible with the phenomenalist's view that a proposition asserting the existence of the magnet and describing its causal properties is equivalent to a set of purely hypothetical properties about sense-data. Again, the actual event which is my observing the deflection of the compass needle also has actual causes, including certain processes in my nervous system, which are not themselves observed. Or, in other words, the truth of the proposition that I am observing a compass needle is connected by a well-established theory with the truth of certain other propositions, themselves not directly verified on this occasion, which refer among other things to processes in my nervous system. These propositions are all at the physical level. They are categorical, and consequently they describe actual events, in the appropriate sense of "event." But once more this is perfectly compatible with their being analyzable into hypothetical propositions about sense-data. Only—and this is the important point—the sense-datum propositions, even those that are categorical, do not describe events in the same sense of the word "event." The "events" that they describe are not in physical time or in physical space. And it is only at the physical level that causal relations hold between actual events. It is indeed only at the physical level that events can properly be said to have causes at all.

This being so, the trouble arises when, instead of asking what is the cause of my observing the compass needle, which is a legitimate question, or even what is the cause of my sensing sense-data "belonging to" the compass needle, which is still a legitimate question, so long as "my sensing the sense-data" is taken as the description of a process which takes place in physical time, we ask what is the cause of the sense-data themselves. For this is a nonsensical question. It is nonsensical because the sense-data are not events in the sense in which the deflection of the needle is an event, so that the term "cause" which is understood as a relation between events at the physical level, does not apply to them. Unfortunately phenomenalists, among whom I must here include myself, have usually failed to see this and so have fallen into the trap of meeting the question "What is the cause of these sense-data?" with the answer "Other sense-data." And in this way they have gratuitously laid themselves open to the sort of objection that Stout and Hardie raise.

To make it clear that such objections are invalid, we may restate the phenomenalist's answer as follows: "There are well-established theories, or hypotheses, which connect different propositions at the physical level. There is, for example, a well-established theory of electro-magnetics through which a proposition describing the deflection of a compass needle can be connected with a proposition describing the state of a magnet; that is, the proposition referring to the needle will, given certain conditions, be deducible from the proposition about the magnet in conjunction with the propositions of the theory. When this is so, then, if the hypotheses in question are of certain specifiable types, we say that the event described by one of these propositions is a cause of the event described by the other. This is not by any means the only sense in which we use the word "cause," but it is the sense that is relevant to the present argument. Both events are actual, in the sense that the propositions which describe them are categorical, but these propositions, which are categorical at the physical level, are reducible to hypothetical propositions about sense-data. This may be expressed by saying that the physical events in question are analyzable into sets of possible sensory occurrences; but these sensory occurrences are not events, in the same sense of "event"; neither can they have, or be, causes in the same sense of "cause." It is therefore misleading to say that sense-data depend upon one another: for this suggests that they can possess causal properties in the same way as physical objects, which is not the case. They can, however, be correlated with one another, and it is only because they can be so correlated that we have any reason to believe in the existence of causal connections between physical events. Indeed to say that there is a causal connection between physical events is, in the last analysis, to make a very complicated statement about correlations between sense-data. The sense-data which are correlated may be actual, but they need not be. For the basis of the correlation is always a hypothetical proposition to the effect that a sense-datum of a certain sort occurs if in certain conditions a sense-datum of a certain other sort occurs, and it is not necessary for the truth of such a proposition either that the protasis or that the apodosis should be actually fulfilled. Thus a proposition of the form "if, if p then q, then, if r then s" may very well be true even though p, q, r, and s are all false. Consequently in the case of sense-data, there is no absurdity in making actual occurrences "depend upon" mere possibilities: for there is no absurdity in saying that a categorical proposition would not be true unless some hypothetical proposition were true. This hypothetical proposition states that such and such an event would occur if certain conditions were fulfilled, and there is no absurdity in holding that it may still be true even if the requisite conditions happen not to be fulfilled. But this is all that the "dependence" of actual upon possible sense-data comes to. What makes it seem an absurdity is the misleading terminology of "causes" and "events."

V.

So far, I hope, so good: but the conception of "possible sense-data" still involves certain difficulties. It is usually illustrated by some such example as "the 'family' of sense-data which constitutes the table in the next room is possible in the sense that if I were there I should be sensing one of its members": and with that we are supposed to be content. But I do not think that we should be content with anything so simple as that. To begin with, the choice of such an example covers two very important assumptions. It is assumed both that the introduction of myself as an observer would not affect what I am supposed to observe; and that the conditions would be such as to allow of my observing: and neither of these assumptions will be justified in all cases. Consider, for example, the proposition that Dr. Crippen murdered his wife in his house in Camden Town in the year 1910. Now the suggestion is that this means that if I had been there at the appropriate time I should have sensed certain sense-data, namely such as would constitute a sensory manifestation of a man, answering to the description of Dr. Crippen, engaged in murdering his wife. But even allowing that there is sense in which I logically *could* have been there, although in actual fact I was not yet born, the answer is that even if I had been there I almost certainly should not have sensed anything of the kind. It is most unlikely that Dr. Crippen would have murdered his wife while I was looking on. But here it may be objected that the word "I" in this context does not refer explicitly to me. It is a variable, not a constant. What is meant is that if *anybody* had been there, he would have sensed the requisite sense-data. But it is most unlikely that Dr. Crippen would have murdered his wife while anybody, other than an accomplice, was looking on. Besides why do we have to say "If anybody had been there." Somebody *was* there. Dr. Crippen was. And he must have sensed a host of sense-data while he was murdering his wife and subsequently dismembering her. So, up to a certain point in the story, did his wife. So why should we not just say that a number of interesting sense-data occurred in such and such a part of Camden Town on such and such a day in the year 1910? We shall see later on why this will not do either.

Again, take the proposition that the sun, though it may look no larger than a man's hand, is really very large indeed, so many thousand miles in diameter. Does this mean that if I were very close to it I should see it stretching out enormously in all directions, or that if I laid measuring rods along it of the requisite sort I should sense the required coincidences of sense-data? But if I were very close to it, I should not see anything at all, I should be shrivelled up: and my operation with the measuring rods could not be carried out. Of course it is possible to carry out some operations with a view to determining the dimensions of the sun: for how else should we in fact determine them? But these operations are ordinarily thought to provide only indirect, and not direct, evidence for the conclusions that they establish. Whereas what the phenomenalist is seeking to describe is an observation that would constitute direct evidence: and the objection is that in the conditions that he postulates such direct evidence may not be physically obtainable.

Professor Price has suggested to me that these difficulties can be overcome by making suitable assumptions about the character of the observer. Thus it is not necessary, he supposes, that the hypothetical witness of Dr. Crippen's act should be a human being; it might be a mouse. Or, if a human being be insisted upon, the observer might be assumed to be looking through the keyhole, or surveying the proceedings from afar through a telescope. Or it might be made a supplementary condition that Dr. Crippen should be affected with psychic blindness, so that he would have gone about his business just as if no intruder had been there, in exactly the way, in fact, in which he *did* go about his business, since no intruder *was* there. Similarly, in the example of the sun, I might credit myself hypothetically with an uninflammable body, so that I could make my observations without being shrivelled up. And in this case it can also be argued that all that is required is that the observations should be "possible in principle": so that it is not a fatal objection to the analysis that they would not be made in fact.

But if the fact is that the desired observations would not be made in the stated conditions then the hypothetical propositions in which it is affirmed that they would be made are false: and since the categorical position of which they are offered as an analysis may nevertheless be true, the analysis is incorrect. To say that the observations are "possible in principle" is merely to say that one can conceive of the conditions being such that they would be made: but it is just the specification of the conditions that constitutes our problem. Neither do I think that the difficulty can be met in the sort of way that Price suggests. For, in his examples, the truth of the hypothetical proposition is dependent upon the truth of some physical or psychological law, as that murderers are not deterred by the presence of mice or that gaseous bodies are not shrivelled by great heat: and while these laws may be valid, their validity is not involved in that of the propositions which we are trying to analyze. After all, Dr. Crippen *might* have been put off by the presence of a mouse: it *might* be the case that when Professor Price approached the sun in his gaseous body he still could not make the required observations. But, however this might be, it would remain true that Dr. Crippen *did* murder his wife, and that the sun has the diameter that it has. And this means that even if we recast our hypothetical propositions in such agreeably fantastic forms as Price suggests, they will still not be equivalent to the propositions of which they are supposed to be the analyses.

Neither is this the only difficulty. So far, in referring to the conditions which go to constitute the "possibility" of sense-data, in any given case, I have used such phrases as "if I were in the next room," or "if any observer had been there": and it is in such terms as these that phenomenalists do usually talk when they try to indicate the sort of way in which they would analyze propositions about unperceived physical objects. Thus Berkeley, for once ignoring God, says that "the question whether the earth moves amounts in reality to no more than this, to wit, whether we have reason to conclude from what has been observed by astronomers, that if we were placed in such and such circumstances, and such or such a position and distance, both from the earth and sun, we should perceive the former to move." [4] But to speak of "my" or "our" being in a certain position is to speak about a physical object, namely a human body, and to speak of its position involves a reference to other physical objects, in Berkeley's example the earth and the sun. No doubt he is "speaking with the vulgar": he has to in order to make himself intelligible; so do we all. But how do "the learned" speak in this case? If the phenomenalist is to make good his claim that categorical propositions about physical objects are reducible to hypothetical propositions about sense-data, it is not enough that he should indicate what the apodoses of his hypotheticals come to in sensory terms: he must do the same with the protases also. But how is this to be done?

Professor Price deals with this point in the fifth chapter of his book on "Hume's Theory of the External World." He remarks truly that the phenomenalistic analysis of any "material-object statement" is extremely complex, since it involves in each case an indefinite number of statements to the effect that if someone were at a place P, he would be sensing a sense-datum S, if he were at place P_2 he would be sensing S_2 . . . . . if he were at place P_n he would be sensing S_n, and he goes on to consider what the phenomenalist must mean by someone's being at a place P_1. His answer is that he must mean "so far from here" and "in such and such a direction" and that these expressions "refer to the sensational route, so to speak, which anyone would have to traverse if he were to pass from P, to the place where the speaker is." "Thus the phenomenalistic analysis of 'x is at P,' will be something like the following: 'X is sensing a visual or tactual field such that *if* he had replaced it by another spatially adjoined to it, and *if* he had replaced that by another spatially adjoined to it, and if he had replaced that in turn by still another, and so on, then eventually he

4 Principles of Human Knowledge. LVIII.

would have been sensing the visual or tactual field which is actually being sensed by the speaker at this moment." Presumably some reference to kinaesthetic data would be needed to bring out the point that it is the person X that is supposed to be moving: and certainly one would require some description of the contents of the visual and tactual fields "through" which X is supposed to pass. For otherwise neither his starting point nor his route would be identifiable.

A similar treatment is given to the question of position in time. "The first stage of the analysis will yield hypothetical propositions such as "If anyone had been at place P_1, at time t, he would have sensed S_1, if anyone had been at place P_2 at time t_2: he would have sensed S_2. . . ." And here "at time t," will mean according to Price, "so many minutes or hours, or days before *now*," which again must be "analyzed in terms of a sensational route." So, " 'X had a sense-experience at a past date t' (e.g., 3,000 years ago) must be equivalent to something like the following: 'he sensed a sense-field such that *if* he had been going to sense a later one spatio-temporally adjoining it, and if he had been going to sense a still later one spatio-temporally adjoining that one and so on, then eventually he *would* have been going to sense the sense-field which is at present being sensed by the speaker.' "

Price goes on to make the further point that the observer must be supposed *really* to travel along his sensational route, both in space and time, and not merely to dream or have a hallucinatory experience of doing so. And this means that the phenomenalist must include in his analysis the possibility of obtaining innumerable bye-series "branching off from the main one" as a guarantee that the main series is veridical. Accordingly, Price concludes that although he may not have shown that the phenomenalistic analysis is false he has at least shown it to be very much more complex than is usually realized.

But is it only a question of complexity? I think that the analysis which Price attributes to the phenomenalist is open to a far more serious objection. For it implies that the description of any event which is remote in space or time from the speaker contains as part of its meaning not only a description of the sense-field that the speaker is actually sensing, but also a description of a long series of intervening sense-fields. And surely this is incorrect. Suppose, for example, that I make some remark about the South Pole, say that there is a colony of penguins so many miles to the north of it, engaged in some activity or other. It seems clear that this remark will not contain any reference whatsoever either to what I am sensing now or to what I should sense on my way to the place in question. I have, indeed, only a very vague idea of the way to get from here to the South Pole, and a still vaguer idea of what I should observe on my journey, but I do not think that this impairs my understanding of my original proposition. Of course, if I am allowed to take an airplane it will be easier: there will be fewer sense-fields to traverse and they are likely to be more homogeneous in content, assuming that the airplane does not crash. But even airplanes take time to travel, and by the time I get to the South Pole the colony of penguins may have dispersed. So I shall have to make myself start earlier. "If I had taken an airplane so many hours ago"—whatever this may come to in sensory terms—"then I should now be sensing sense-data characteristic of the appearance of penguins, preceded by sense-data . . ." and here there follows a step by step description in reverse of all my experiences *en route*. Surely as an analysis of my original proposition this is most unplausible.

Again, it is to be noticed that Price's phenomenalistic analysis of the proposition about someone's having an experience in the past ends with the words: "eventually he would have been going to sense the sense-field which is at present being sensed by the speaker." But it is characteristic of the sense-field that is now being sensed by me, the speaker, that it is somato-centric to my body: and for anyone to sense it he must, as it were, be "in" my body. That is, he must be having sense-data that are identical with those that are now being obtained "from" my body. And this adds a further touch of strangeness to what is already a very strange fashion of dealing with the past. Consider, for example, the proposition that Julius Caesar crossed the Rubicon in the year 49 B.C. Resurrecting Caesar after the Ides of March, or ignoring the Ides of March altogether, which we are presumably entitled to do since the whole of our story will be hypothetical, we carry him through two thousand years of history, second by second or minute by minute, according to our estimate of the average duration of a sense-field, and finally bring his wanderings to an end by making him occupy my body. I cannot believe that when I say that Julius Caesar crossed the Rubicon in the year 49 B.C. I am implying quite so much as this.

VI.

These are serious difficulties: and they might well be thought to be fatal to the phenomenalist, if he were committed to holding the views that Price attributes to him: but I do not think that he is. I do not think that he is bound to claim that the analysis of a proposition referring to an event which is remote in space or time from the speaker involves tracing the sensory route from "there" and "then" to "here" and "now." There would in any case be no *one* sensory route to trace. I think rather that he would hope to describe the "setting" of the event directly in sensory terms, without including what would have to happen for this setting to become the speaker's own. Thus he would try to reproduce "being at the South Pole" in sensory terms without saying anything about *this* sense-field, or about the other sense-fields that, in a suitably Pickwickian sense of "between," may lie between this sense-field and the sense-field that "presents" the South Pole. Similarly, he would try to give a sensory version of "Caesar crossed the Rubicon in 49 B.C.," without referring to *this* sense-field or to the long series of sense-fields that might be supposed to fill the gap between that time and this. But how could this be done? The answer is, I think, that one would have to describe both places and times in terms of the local scenery. Thus it should be possible to indicate a series of sensory experiences which were such as would entitle anyone who had them to assert "I am so many miles north of the South Pole," and in that case the analysis of our proposition about the penguins would be that if such sensory experiences were occurring they would be accompanied by other sense-experiences which were such as would entitle anyone who had them to assert "here is a colony of penguins, behaving in such and such a fashion." It is true, indeed, that not all places are identifiable by obvious landmarks—I imagine, for example, that the South Pole looks very much like the North Pole—so that the description of the "local scenery" would often have to be rather complicated. In the case of the South Pole I suppose that it would involve a hypothetical reference to the results of making certain measurements. But the fact remains that people do contrive to orient themselves, and that they do so by having certain sense-experiences. Consequently it seems reasonable for the phenomenalist to set out to define positions in space in terms of the sense-experiences by which they would actually be identified.

There is, however, still a difficulty about time. For the expression "if such and such sense-experiences were occurring" means "if they were occurring *now*," and the use of the word "now" involves a reference to physical time. Consequently, some phrase will have to be added to the effect that these sense-experiences are, or rather would be, sensibly contemporaneous with some standard sense-experiences which fix the moment of time. And this too will be rather complicated. "Given such sense-experiences as would entitle anyone who had them to assert that he was looking at a watch, and given such sense-experiences as would entitle anyone who had them to assert that the watch was going properly, and given such sense-experiences as would entitle anyone who had them to assert that the watch showed such and such a reading and given that these last experiences were sensibly contemporaneous with the experiences described in the final apodosis of the long series of "if-clauses" involved in the identification of the place, then (there would be) such sense-experiences as would entitle anyone who had them to assert that there was "there and then" a colony of penguins, behaving in such and such a fashion. And even this is a considerable over-simplification since each of the hypothetical clauses conceals an indefinite number of subsidiary hypotheticals. But once again the phenomenalist might appeal to the fact that people do identify times and that they do so by having certain sense-experiences. And an analysis of this sort though very far from simple is at any rate not quite so complex as the analysis in terms of sensory routes.

The same problem arises in the case of propositions about the past. Take Dr. Crippen again. I suppose that one could describe a series of experiences which would be such as to justify the assertion "this is the year 1910 A.D.," without having to go back to the birth of Christ, which anyhow is wrongly dated. One might, for example, invoke calendars or newspapers, though this would not do so well for such a date as 49 B.C. Still we do manage to determine dates without having to refer explicitly to history or astronomy, though there is a sense in which dating involves both. Consequently, the phenomenalist might try to deal with Crippen on the following lines. "If a certain set of sense-experiences, namely such as would entitle anyone who had them to assert 'this is such and such a room in such and such a street in Camden Town' had been sensibly contemporaneous with a series of sense-experiences of such a character as would entitle anyone who had them to assert 'this is such and such an hour of such and such a day in the year 1910,' they would have been accompanied by a series of sense-experiences of such a character as would entitle anyone who had them to assert 'here is a man called Dr. Crippen engaged in murdering his wife.' But the defect of this formulation is that it provokes the question: When would all this have happened? to which the only answer is that the question is illegitimate. For all the wheres and whens are supposed to be included in the sensory story: so that there can be no where and when of the story. It was for this reason that in dealing just now with my example of the penguins at the South Pole I introduced the conditional clauses with the word 'given' instead of the customary 'if.' My object was to avoid the use of verbs which, by reason of their tenses, would have referred unwarrantably to physical time."

Another defect of the formulation: "If a series A of sense-experiences had been sensibly contemporaneous with a series B, they would have been accompanied, or followed, by a series C" is that in certain cases it may be that they were so accompanied so that it is idle to say that they would have been. Thus, in the Crippen example, it may be objected, as I remarked before, that it is silly to say "*if* anybody were to have had certain experiences" when we can reasonably assume that somebody, namely Crippen himself, *did* have them. But the answer to this is that it is a mistake to say either that certain sense-experiences *were* obtained, or that they would have been obtained, if this is understood, as it naturally would be, to involve a reference to physical time. The protosis of our hypothetical is supposed to describe in sensory terms, the "setting" of the event of which the apodosis contains the sensory description. Consequently, there is no need to put the setting itself into space and time: and not only is there no need to do this, but the attempt to do it leads to a vicious confusion of the physical and sensory levels of language.

A similar confusion arises if it is said, or implied, that the sense-data, which supply the phenomenalist with the materials for his analyses, are, or would be, sensed *by* anyone, whether it be myself, the speaker, or anybody else. For not only does this involve an illegitimate reference to physical bodies, and so to physical space and time, but it leads also to the difficulties which I mentioned earlier, concerning the possibility of physical interaction between the observer and the event that he is put there to observe. The way to meet these difficulties, I now suggest, is not to choose some apparently inoffensive observer, such as a mouse, or a man with a telescope, but to exclude from the analysis any reference to an observer at all. Admittedly, it is necessary, in practice, to refer to an observer in order to explain what is meant by a sense-datum: for it is only in terms of what is relatively familiar that an unfamiliar term can be understood. But once the sense-datum language has been accepted as basic, then observers, like everything else at the physical level, must be reduced to sense-data. For to allow them to stand outside "having" or "sensing" the sense-data would be to bring sense-data themselves up to the physical level and so vitiate the whole phenomenalistic program.

That no explicit reference to a physical body should occur in the phenomenalist's analysis would be generally admitted: but it seems usually to have been thought that an observer of some sort must always figure in the protases, not indeed baldly as his physical self, but in the correct sensory disguise. It does not appear to me, however, that this is necessary. I do not see, for example, why the phenomenalist's version of such a proposition as "there is a bookcase in the dining-room" should contain the description of any sensory manifestation of a human body. It has to identify the dining-room in question and also to specify some period of time, but that should be enough. It may, indeed, be argued that unless some human body were present no sense-experiences would occur at all. But the analysis does not state that any sense-experiences do occur: only that given certain sense-experiences, then . . . certain others. That no experiences at all would be "given" unless there were an observer is indeed a physical fact: but there is no reason why that physical fact should be prefixed to every sensory analysis. On the contrary, the phenomenalist must hold that it is itself to be analyzed in purely sensory terms. The only cases, therefore, in which the analysis will contain a sensory description of an observer are those in which there is some reference to an observer in the proposition which is to be analyzed. In such case the observer will figure *in* the sensory story, but in no case will there be an observer *of* the story. The phenomenalist's tale does not include the author: it is, in that respect, a tale that tells itself.

VII.

I suggest then that the phenomenalist's analysis of a simple proposition about a physical object, say a proposition to the effect that there exists a physical object of a certain sort in a certain place throughout a certain period of time, should take the following form. A protasis, which will itself include a number of subsidiary hypotheticals, describing such sense experiences as would be sufficient to identify the place and time in question, or in other words, to put the physical object in its proper setting: followed by an apodosis which would describe such sense-experiences as would be sufficient to verify the presence of the physical object in question: and this apodosis will also have to contain a number of subsidiary hypotheticals to rule out the possibility of an illusion. If this were done, the truth of the whole hypothetical might, I think, pass as a sufficient condition of the truth of the proposition which it was intended to analyze. It would not, however, be a necessary condition because of the relative indefiniteness of the proposition at the physical level. But as has already been shown, to formulate a sufficient condition in purely sensory terms is the most that the phenomenalist can reasonably hope for: and I cannot claim to have done more than give a very rough sketch of the way in which this might be achieved.

The fact is that so long as he confines himself to giving a *general* account of the way in which physical objects are "constructed" out of sense-data, or a *general* account of the way in which physical space and time are "constructed" out of sensory spaces and times, the phenomenalist does not appear to meet any insuperable obstacles. But directly he tries to reduce any particular statement about a physical object, even the simplest, to a statement, or set of statements, about sense-data, he runs into difficulties which, however he may make light of them in theory, in practice overwhelm him. The reason for this may lie only in the extreme complexity of his undertaking. But I think that there may be a more serious reason. I think that it might be argued that he was setting himself a task that could not, by its very nature, be satisfactorily fulfilled. For the language in which we refer to physical objects has its own logic. Now the sensory language to which the phenomenalist seeks to reduce the other must also have its logic, and this logic must be either the same as that of the physical language or different. If it is made the same—if, for example, the phenomenalist allows himself to speak of "sensibilia" having a continued and distinct existence in space and time—then we are inclined to say that he has not carried out his program, because these sensibilia are only physical objects, or attenuated physical objects, in disguise. But if the logic of the sensory language is different, then we are inclined to say that the statements which are expressed in it are not perfect translations of the statements at the physical level, just because their logic is different. So what is the phenomenalist to do?

If this line of argument is correct, then the solution of the "problem of perception" may be to treat our beliefs about physical objects as constituting a theory, the function of which is to explain the course of our sensory experiences. The statements which are expressed in terms of the theory may not then be capable of being reproduced exactly as statements about sense-data: that is, it may not be possible wholly to rewrite them as statements about sense-data. Nevertheless, they will function only as means of grouping sense-data: and it will be a contingent fact that sense-data are so organized that the theory is valid. It may then be required of the philosopher to make clear in what this organization consists: that is, to show in a general way what relations must obtain between sense-data for the demands of the theory to be met. Thus, to echo Kent, he may be represented as trying to answer the question: How is the physical object language possible? And to this question the phenomenalist has, I think, the makings of a satisfactory answer.

THE SENSE-DATUM FALLACY

H. A. Prichard (1871–1947)

When Berkeley asserted that the things which we perceive depend on our perception of them, he was undoubtedly using the term "perceive" in its ordinary sense. By "its ordinary sense" I mean that for which in recent times the term "sense" is sometimes substituted, i.e., the sense in which it is used to stand for a certain generic mental activity or state of which, when we reflect, we think seeing, feeling or touching, hearing, tasting, and smelling to be species. And in considering the use of the term "sense-datum" this is the only sense in which I shall use the term "perceive." No doubt there are two other senses in which some writers on perception use the term which have to be distinguished from the ordinary sense, viz., those to which Professor Price refers in the second chapter of his *Perception*.[1] Of these other senses one is that in which the phrase "my perceiving a certain body" is used to stand for what is really my thinking, .i.e., thinking without question, that I am perceiving that body—a sense for which Professor Price substitutes the phrase "my being perceptually conscious of the body." In this sense I am in a case of double vision perceiving, for instance, two candles, although in fact there is only one candle to be perceived. The other of these senses is that in which, as Professor Price in effect says, the phrase "my perceiving a certain body" is used to stand not for a mental activity or state but for a combination of three things, which together are asserted, by those who use the term thus, to be a situation in which I am, viz., (1) my perceiving, in the ordinary sense, some secondary quality, (2) a peculiar relation of that quality to the body, and (3) the absence of any such relation of it to any other body. But the first of these senses is open to the objection that it is misleading to designate as perceiv-

From *Knowledge and Perception* (1950), pp. 200–14. Originally published in Aristotelian Society, Supplementary Volume XVII, 1938. Reprinted by the courtesy of the Editor of the Aristotelian Society. Copyright 1938 The Aristotelian Society.
[1] pp. 22–4.

ng what avowedly has to be distinguished from perceiving in the ordinary
sense, as being thinking. And to the latter it can be objected that it is still
more misleading to use the term "perceiving" for something which is
avowedly not a mental state or activity, and also, that as the thing meant is
a combination of three, or rather, to speak strictly, a very large number, of
things which have no unity or connectedness, the term so used is simply
arbitrary—just as a term invented for a combination of a sunspot and a
sneeze would be arbitrary. And for these reasons it seems to me dangerous
to use the term "perceive" in any but its ordinary sense. In any case, however, it is clear that Berkeley was not using the term in either of those
other senses.

   If, using the term "perceive" in its ordinary sense, we ask, "Of what
sort or sorts are the various things which we perceive?," we all, of course, at
first give what has been called the Naive Realist answer, viz., that what we
perceive is in all cases a body, that what we see, for instance, is a table, that
what we hear is a bell, and so on. If, having given this answer, we then go
on to ask a second question, viz., "Does what we perceive depend on our
perception of it?," we necessarily answer that it does not. For unless we use
the phrase "a body" in a Pickwickian sense, or else adopt the device of putting it into inverted commas to avoid responsibility for meaning anything
in particular by it, we mean by "a body" a something of a certain kind,
which, as we discover when we reflect, cannot by its very nature depend on
our perception of it. Berkeley, however, answered the first question differently. He maintained that what we see is a color, that what we hear is a
sound, that what we feel is a feeling of resistance, that what we taste is a
flavor, and that what we smell is an odor; and thinking, when he reflected
on these things, that they have a certain common character, that of being
sensations, he maintained generally that what we perceive is a sensation.
And he then went on to answer the second question by asserting that since
a sensation is by its very nature something inseparable from the perception
of it, what we perceive necessarily depends on our perception of it, his conclusion when properly stated in his own language being that the *esse* of
what we perceive *involves* (not *is*) *percipi*.

   Now there have been several writers recently who, though they may
express themselves differently, really agree, and, in my opinion, rightly
agree, with Berkeley to the extent of thinking that the object of perception
in the ordinary sense of "perception" is not a body but a secondary quality
of the kind corresponding to the special kind of perception. But among
them there have been some who have objected to Berkeley's statement
that the secondary quality perceived is a sensation, and have substituted for
it the statement that it is a sense-datum; and in consequence they have

been led to ask certain questions about the various secondary qualities which we perceive, as questions about sense-data. And the object of this paper is to urge that this substitution is fallacious, as being based on the mistaken idea that perceiving is a form of knowing; and that, in consequence of the mistakenness of this idea, the questions thus raised about the various secondary qualities which we perceive are also fallacious.

I do not of course mean to suggest that the idea which I have implied to be mistaken is confined to those who use the term "sense-datum." It certainly is not. And in any case, to give rise to the term, the idea must have arisen independently of it. Yet once a mistake has received expression in a term or phrase it is more insidious, because a new-comer to the subject, finding the term in existence, is apt simply to take for granted the truth of the idea which has given rise to it.

To prepare the ground I propose first to refer to the idea in question and to its consequences, apart from the use of the term to express it.

The idea that perceiving is a species of knowing has recently become prominent in an alleged refutation of Berkeley which has not infrequently been advanced of late years, and notably by Professor Moore, Mr. Bertrand Russell, and Professor Kemp Smith. Of these the last mentioned, referring to Berkeley's argument that the objects of perception are subjective because they are sensations, states the refutation thus: "Even without questioning that the objects known (i.e., known in perception) are sensations, we may dispute the inference that they are therefore subjective. Thanks to Ward, Moore, Stout, and others, it is now very generally recognized that 'sensation' is an ambiguous term. It is used with two very different meanings, as process of apprehension and as object apprehended. If sensation is mental process, then for this sufficient reason it must fall on the subjective side. But if, on the other hand, sensations have to be regarded not as mental processes, but as objects revealed in and through such processes, this argument will fall to the ground. Though red is known only as sensation, it is undoubtedly an objective content. It is not a state of the subject, but an object to the subject. Similarly, a sound or an odor or a taste is an object apprehended by the mind, and is therefore distinct from the processes in which such apprehension consists. . . . The subjectivist argument, that objects as known are sensations, and therefore are subjective, makes use of this fundamental ambiguity. Only by interpreting sensations as signifying objective contents can it justify the assertion that objects are known as sensations; and yet only by regarding sensations as mental processes can it legitimate the inference that they are therefore subjective. The ground of the argument involves one interpretation of the term 'sensation,' the conclusion implies the other. It is open to us to propound the counter-argument. Since sensations are only known as objects they are distinct from mental processes, and cannot be mental or subjective." ²

Here Professor Kemp Smith is tacitly agreeing with Berkeley that in the case of each kind of perception the object of perception is not a body but a secondary quality of the sort corresponding to the kind of perception; but he is maintaining against Berkeley that the statement, for instance, that some color which we are seeing is a sensation is ambiguous, on the ground that the phrase "a sensation" sometimes means an object of apprehension and sometimes an apprehending of something. And he is adding that while we shall only think the statement true, if in it "a sensation" means an object of apprehension, we shall only think it conclusive if in it the phrase means an apprehending of something. He concludes that such plausibility as Berkeley's argument has comes from failure to distinguish these meanings, and disappears as soon as we distinguish them, as we do when we use different phrases for each, such as "a sensum" or "a sensing." Finally, he is asserting that once the ambiguity is detected we can advance the counter-argument, viz., that a color which we see, just because it is an object of apprehension and not an apprehension of something, cannot be subjective, i.e., dependent on its being sensed, i.e., perceived, by us.

Here the basis of Professor Kemp Smith's criticism is clear. It is the idea that seeing a certain color, for instance, or hearing a certain sound, is an apprehending, a knowing, or a being aware of, that color or sound. For he is expressly maintaining that when we see the color, for instance, the color is an object of apprehension; and he certainly does not mean by this that along with our seeing the color, and to be distinguished from it, there is also our apprehending that color. He is, therefore, implying the idea that seeing that color *is* an apprehending of it. Further, if he had been asked, "Of what kind is the apprehending?" he certainly would have had to answer, "Of that special kind which is perceiving and which differs from other kinds, such as remembering and self-consciousness, by being perceiving—seeing, hearing, &c., being species of this kind of knowing." He is, therefore, implying the idea that perceiving in its various forms is a special kind of knowing, this idea being what he is using in order to refute Berkeley.

Further, this being so, it is also clear that Professor Kemp Smith should in consistency have gone further and contended not merely that Berkeley fails to establish his conclusion but also that the contrary conclusion is true, viz., that the colors we see, the sounds we hear, &c., are independent of our seeing or hearing them. For we all, including Professor Kemp Smith, think that the existence of what we know is independent of

² *Prolegomena to an Idealist Theory of Knowledge*, pp. 44–5.

our knowledge of it, on the ground that otherwise our knowledge of it would not be knowledge. Consequently, Professor Kemp Smith, holding as he does that, for instance, to see some color is to know it in a particular way, should have maintained that the colors or the other secondary qualities which we perceive exist independently of our perceiving them.

Professor Moore, in his Refutation of Idealism, in effect offers the same criticism of Berkeley, though perhaps I should have said "seems to offer" rather than "offers" because I confess that I find this article extremely obscure. And it is because of this obscurity that I have not referred to his formulation of the refutation first, although it may have been what originally suggested the refutation to Professor Kemp Smith. Professor Moore speaks of having shown that the Idealist's assertion "Esse is percipi," if it is to be true, must mean "whatever is experienced also *must* be experienced," [3]—the term "experienced" here being plainly Professor Moore's equivalent for Berkeley's "perceived." And if I follow him rightly, he holds that this statement can be refuted by considering the nature of a sensation. He implies that a sensation is always a sensation of a secondary quality, for instance, of a blue color or of a green color. And he holds that every sensation has two elements or constituents, viz., (1) consciousness in respect of which all sensations are alike, (2) the object of the sensation in respect of which one differs from another.[4] By the term "consciousness" he afterwards explains that he means the "knowing" or "being aware of" or "experiencing" something, a sensation, he says, being really a case of "knowing" or being "aware of" or "experiencing" something.[5] And by "the object of a sensation," e.g., a blue color, he implies that he means the object of that knowing or experiencing. How, holding as he does that, for instance, the sensation of a blue color is a knowing that color, he can also maintain that the color known is a constituent of that knowing, it is difficult to understand. But at least we must allow that he is maintaining that what he calls our having a sensation of a blue color, i.e., that what Berkeley called, and what is, our seeing a blue color, is a kind of knowing that color. And it is this idea which Professor Moore uses to refute Berkeley in a passage the last part of which Professor Kemp Smith quotes with approval.

> Idealists [Professor Moore says] admit that some things really exist of which they are not aware. . . . They are, therefore [they hold], sometimes aware of something which is *not* an inseparable aspect of their own experience. . . . And what my analysis of

[3] *Philosophical Studies*, p. 16.
[4] Ibid., pp. 17, 25.
[5] Ibid., p. 24. The inverted commas are Professor Moore's.

sensation has been designed to show is, that whenever I have a mere sensation or idea, the fact is that I am then aware of something which is equally and in the same sense *not* an inseparable aspect of my experience. . . . There is, therefore, no question of how we are to "get outside the circle of our own ideas and sensations." Merely to have a sensation is already to be outside that circle.[6]

Consequently Professor Moore's refutation of the Idealists, i.e., of Berkeley and his followers, is the same as Professor Kemp Smith's.

We may now consider the consequences of the idea that perceiving is a species of knowing for anyone who, like Professor Moore or Professor Kemp Smith, agrees with Berkeley that what we perceive is in the case of each kind of perception a secondary quality of the corresponding sort. Since, to take the case of hearing, he thinks that when we are hearing something on a given occasion, what we are hearing is a sound, and also that for us to hear something is to know or apprehend it in a particular kind of way, he will necessarily come to think of the sound which he thinks of as what we are hearing as something the existence, and therefore also the nature, of which is independent of our hearing it, since otherwise our hearing it would not be knowing it. And for the corresponding reason he will come to think generally of any secondary quality which he thinks of as being what we are perceiving, as independent of our perceiving it, though possibly dependent on us in some other way. He will therefore be led to ask questions about the various secondary qualities which he considers are what various individuals perceive on various occasions, on the assumption that, though they are perceived, their existence and their character is independent of their being perceived. And as he will think that, since these secondary qualities do not require to be perceived, no others can require it, he will necessarily come to think of the secondary qualities generally as not depending on being perceived for their existence and their character. Hence, he will further be led to ask questions about the secondary qualities such as we ask about things of any kind the existence of which we think we know, and so which we think of as existing independently of our and of others knowing them. Of these questions, one, strictly speaking, concerns not the qualities themselves but our power of perceiving them. It is the question: "Can, for instance, some sound which I am hearing be heard by another, or must it be different from any sound which another hears?" The question is usually expressed in the form: "Are the various secondary qualities which we perceive private to us, or are they public?," i.e., really, "Is the

6 Ibid., pp. 26–7.

perceiving some sound which I am perceiving private to me, i.e., possible only for me, or is it public, i.e., possible for anyone?" And it is inevitably raised by anyone who thinks of perceiving as a species of knowing, because on the one hand, since he thinks of the sound which I am hearing as independent of my hearing it, it does not seem to him something which it is *impossible* for another to hear, and on the other hand, he finds it hard to believe that sounds heard by two people can be numerically identical. At the same time it should be noted that the only answer which he is *entitled* to give is that the secondary qualities are public, since it cannot be impossible for what exists independently of my perceiving it to be perceived by another. Of the remaining questions one concerns the nature of a secondary quality which we perceive, and the other its cause, if it has a cause. The former is the question: "What sort of a thing is it?" "Is it, for instance, an event either in the mind or in the brain, and so something transitory, or is it something permanent?" "Is it a substance, or a phase of a substance?" "Is it physical or mental?" Again, if it be decided that it is an event, the question is inevitably asked: "How does it originate, i.e., how is it caused?" This question is sometimes asked in the form: "What is the cause of a sensation?.," and it comes to be sharply distinguished from the question: "What is the cause of our apprehension of a sensation in perception?"

Consequently we are not surprised to find Professor Kemp Smith raising and considering these questions in a chapter which he significantly entitles "The *ontological* [7] status of the secondary qualities." He asks, for instance, whether the secondary qualities [i.e., really the secondary qualities which we perceive] are in themselves transitory,[8] and he maintains that the question raises many of the most difficult problems of metaphysics. Again, he asks whether they are physical or psychical, and finds that the question admits of no direct answer. He also asks in effect whether those which we perceive are private to us, and gives an answer which from his point of view is surprising, viz., that they are. He also asks how the secondary qualities which we perceive are generated, and implies that it is important to distinguish the physiological conditions on which their generation depends from those on which our perception of them depends.

For the same reason we are not surprised to find that Professor Price, who also holds that what he calls sensing, i.e., perceiving in the ordinary sense, is a kind of knowing, considers these and cognate questions about the secondary qualities which we perceive, in chapters in *Perception* which are stated to deal respectively with the nature of sense-data, their relation

[7] The italics are mine.
[8] *Prolegomena to an Idealist Theory of Knowledge*, p. 70.

to one another, their relation to matter, and their origination. And the importance which he attaches to these questions may be gauged from the fact that his discussion of them occupies almost half of the whole book.

On the other hand, for anyone who holds Berkeley's view these questions are questions which do not arise at all, and which, if asked, are asked under a mistake and can only receive an erroneous answer. For according to him, since a sound, for instance, which we are hearing is inseparable from our hearing it, it is something the hearing of which by another is impossible, and since there is no such thing as a sound which is independent of its being heard, there is nothing of which to ask, "What sort of a thing is it?" and, "How is it caused?," so that the very questions are mistaken, and if asked, can for this reason only receive a false answer.

If, however, we now go on to consider the truth of the idea which leads to these questions, we find that the idea is mistaken, and, what is more, that the mistake is due to failure to recognize that Berkeley was after all right in contending that the various secondary qualities which we perceive depend on our perceiving them.

We have to admit that Berkeley and his modern opponents are right in thinking that what we perceive in the case of each kind of perception is a secondary quality of the corresponding sort. We have also to admit that Berkeley is right in contending that the various secondary qualities which we perceive are by their very nature dependent on our perceiving them. We must, for instance, in the end admit that it is self-evident that some sound which we are hearing depends on our hearing it. This being so, we have to admit that it at once follows that to perceive something is *not* to know it in a special kind of way, since if it were, the thing perceived could not depend on our perceiving it, as in fact it does. The argument is simple enough: "What we perceive is always some secondary quality or qualities. Any secondary quality which we perceive depends on our perceiving it. Consequently to perceive something cannot be to know it, because if it were, the thing perceived would be independent of our perceiving it, and yet, being a secondary quality, it is not." To this argument another can be added which also is conclusive. This is that if perceiving were a kind of knowing, mistakes about what we perceive would be impossible, and yet they are constantly being made, since at any rate in the cases of seeing and feeling or touching we are almost always in a state of thinking that what we are perceiving is various bodies, although we need only reflect to discover that in thinking this we are mistaken.

Further, once we reach the conclusion that perceiving is not a kind of knowing, there are various other conclusions which we are forced to draw. One is that Berkeley's opponents are really arguing the wrong way round.

Instead of arguing, as they should, that because the secondary qualities which are what we perceive necessarily depend on our perceiving them, perceiving cannot be a kind of knowing, they are arguing that because perceiving is a kind of knowing, the secondary qualities which are what we perceive cannot depend on our perceiving them. And to discover their mistake we need only recognize, as in the end we must, that the secondary qualities which are what we perceive do depend on our perceiving them. A second is that the alleged refutation of Berkeley does not establish the contrary of his conclusion, simply because its premise that perceiving is a kind of knowing is false. A third is that the alleged refutation fails to refute Berkeley's argument. For a supporter of the argument can reply thus:

> When, following Berkeley, I say, for instance, that a sound which I am hearing is a sensation, I do *not* mean by "a sensation" either of the things one of which you say it must mean. I do not mean by it either a something which is being apprehended or an apprehending of something. I mean by it a something having a certain character which we recognize as common to the various secondary qualities which we perceive and which is such as to involve that what has it is perceived. And I am not refuted by the assertion that perceiving is a kind of knowing, because it is not.

Lastly, we have to conclude that since Berkeley was after all right in contending that the objects of perception as being sensations depend on their being perceived, all the questions recently referred to about the secondary qualities which we perceive which are based on the idea that they are independent of perception are based on a mistake, and that, in consequence, if they are answered, they can only receive a false answer.

We are now in a position to consider the use of the term "sense-datum." To do this, I propose to refer mainly to Mr. Bertrand Russell's *Problems of Philosophy*, in which, so far as I am aware, the term first occurs. For unless I am mistaken, with one exception, the others who use it do so in the same way. In particular, Professor Price, finding the term ready to hand, introduces [9] it in a similar way, differing from Mr. Russell only in using the term "sensing" instead of "immediately experiencing" for perceiving. Consequently what can be said of Mr. Russell can also be said of Professor Price. The one exception to which I have referred is Professor Moore in his article entitled "The status of sense-data." [10] But as in my opinion his use of the term is open to the same comments as those to

[9] *Perception*, p. 3 [this volume p. 205].
[10] *Philosophical Studies*, ch. v.

which the usual use of the term is open, as well as to an objection peculiar to it, I do not propose to refer specially to it.

Mr. Russell, after giving reasons for holding that when we seem to ourselves to be seeing a table in front of us, the table, if there be one, is not what we immediately experience by sight, or touch, or hearing, says: "The real table, if there is one, is not *immediately* known to us at all, but must be an inference from what is immediately known. Hence two very difficult questions at once arise; namely, (1) Is there a real table at all? (2) If so, what sort of object can it be?" And he then goes on to say: "It will help us in considering these questions to have a few simple terms of which the meaning is definite and clear. Let us give the name of 'sense-data' to the things that are immediately known in sensation: such things as colors, sounds, smells, hardnesses, roughnesses, and so on. We shall give the name 'sensation' to the experience of being immediately aware of these things. Thus whenever we see a color, we have a sensation *of* the color, but the color itself is a sense-datum, not a sensation. The color is that *of* which we are immediately aware, and the awareness itself is the sensation." [11]

Here certain things are clear: (1) The phrase "immediately experience by sight or touch or hearing" is Mr. Russell's phrase for "perceive" in the ordinary sense. Also (2) he is implying that what we thus experience, i.e., what we perceive, is one of the secondary qualities, i.e., a color in the case of seeing, a sound in the case of hearing, and so on. Hence (3) he is showing himself here at one with Professor Moore and Professor Kemp Smith in agreeing with Berkeley that what we perceive is not, as we ordinarily think, a body, but a secondary quality. (4) Since he implies that what we immediately experience by sight or touch or hearing, i.e., that what we perceive, is a secondary quality, and since he speaks of our immediately experiencing something, i.e., some secondary quality, as our being immediately *aware of* that quality, he is also showing himself at one with Professor Moore and Professor Kemp Smith in thinking perceiving to be a special kind of knowing, his term for the special kind being "immediately knowing in sensation." (5) He is saying that it will help the consideration of the questions raised about the table if we choose the term "sense-data" to stand for the things that are immediately known in sensation. But (6) here the phrase "*the* things that are immediately known in sensation" must be a slip for "*things* immediately known in sensation." For he says of some color which we are seeing that it is *a* sense-datum, and to say this is to imply that "sense-data" is a term not for what is really only a certain numerical group consisting of all the things which are being immediately known in sensation at a

[11] *The Problems of Philosophy*, pp. 16–17.

given moment, but for things of a certain sort, viz., things being thus apprehended. Mr. Russell therefore is here really giving "sense-data" the meaning of *things* immediately known in sensation. (7) In giving this term this meaning he is, of course, taking for granted the existence of the thing meant, since otherwise he would consider it useless to invent a term for it. But (8) there cannot really be such a thing as the thing meant, viz., things immediately known in sensation, unless there really is such a thing as immediately knowing in sensation, i.e., unless immediately experiencing, i.e., perceiving, something really is knowing it in the special way called immediately knowing in sensation. Hence the introduction and use of the term "sense-data" cannot be justified unless Mr. Russell is right in agreeing with Professor Moore and Professor Kemp Smith that perceiving is a special kind of knowing. And although here Mr. Russell is ostensibly only inviting his readers to accept a piece of terminology, he is in fact at the same time inviting them to accept a certain theory, viz., the theory that perceiving is a kind of knowing, a theory apart from which the use of the term is illegitimate.

This, however, is not all. For when we consider the matter we find that even if this theory were true, there could not be such a thing as a sense-datum, as Mr. Russell, and therefore also as Professor Price, uses the term. For grant for the sake of argument that on some occasion I am apprehending in the form of perceiving a particular color, a particular sound, and a particular feeling of roughness. Then, no doubt, any one of them is being thus apprehended by me. Nevertheless it is not a something which is being thus apprehended. If I am eating a number of things, say, some cheese, some bread, and some salt, they together form a certain numerical group, viz., the totality of the things which I am eating. But their membership of this group does not constitute them things having a certain common character, and so things of a certain sort for which the term would have to be "things which I am eating," or "things which are being eaten by me," or perhaps "things which are being eaten by someone." There is no such sort. The things which I am eating are united simply by my eating them; and my eating them does not constitute them things of a certain sort. Indeed to speak of *a* something which is being eaten by me, or of *a* something which is being eaten by someone, is merely verbal, because to be being eaten is not a character of anything. Similarly the color, the sound, and the feeling of roughness which I am thus apprehending are united solely by my thus apprehending them; and though each is one of the things which are being thus apprehended by me, none is *a* something which is being thus apprehended by me. There is no such thing as a thing which is being thus apprehended by me, nor again such a thing as a thing which is being thus apprehended by someone.

The truth is, of course, that when Mr. Russell and Professor Price state, as they do, that some color which I am seeing is a sense-datum—and the statement is typical of their use of the term—they are not really expressing, as ostensibly they are, an idea of theirs about the color which I am seeing; they are expressing an idea about my perceiving it, viz. that it is knowing it in a special kind of way; and they are expressing it in a misleading way, by expressing it as if it were an idea about the color. Consequently if we go behind the mere verbal form of the statement: "The color which I see is a sense-datum," we have to allow that it is only a misleading way of saying: "My seeing the color which I am seeing is a special kind of way of knowing it." And, this being so, the question: "Is it legitimate to assert of some color, for instance, which I am seeing that it is a sense-datum?" reduces to the question: "Is perceiving a kind of knowing?"

We can now notice a radical difference between Berkeley's statement that the various secondary qualities which we perceive are sensations and the statement which Mr. Russell and Professor Price prefer as a substitute, viz., that they are sense-data. While the former attributes to them a certain common character, the latter does not; and it even leaves the question open whether they have a common character. All that it does is to state that in perceiving them we are knowing them. Indeed, Professor Price is not only aware of this difference, but regards it as an important reason for preferring the latter statement. He says that the admission that there are sense-data (i.e., really, that the secondary qualities which we sense [i.e., perceive] are sense-data), commits us to very little; and that in particular it does not commit us to any view about what is called "the status" of sense-data in the universe, i.e., as to whether they are events, or substances, or states of substances, or as to whether they are physical or mental or neither, or, again, to any view about their origin, i.e., as to whether they result from physical or from mental processes or from both.[12] He then adds: "The term 'sense-datum' is meant to be a *neutral* term. The use of it does not imply the acceptance of any particular theory. The term is meant to stand for something whose existence is indubitable (however fleeting), something from which all theories of perception ought to start, however much they may diverge later." He considers that all past theories have in fact started from the idea that there are sense-data; and he maintains that Locke and Berkeley in calling them *ideas of sensation*, Hume in calling them *impressions*, and Kant in calling them *Vorstellungen*, were using

12 *Perception*, pp. 18–19 [this volume pp. 218–19].

question-begging terms, and that in particular that they were thereby committing themselves to the view that sense-data (i.e., really, the secondary
qualities which we perceive) are mental events.

This ground for preference, however, seems to me wholly unjustified.
In Professor Price's sense of "begging the question," viz., that of committing oneself to a certain view, undoubtedly when Berkeley asserted of some
color which we are seeing that it is a sensation, he is begging the question
both about its character and about its relatedness to our perception of it.
And undoubtedly when Professor Price states, as in effect he does,[13] that
the color is a sense-datum, he is at least not begging the question in this
sense about its character. But also undoubtedly, though he fails to notice
it, he, in making this statement, is equally with Berkeley begging the other
and the really important question, viz., that about its relatedness to our
perception of it. For as he is really saying that our seeing the color is *knowing* it in a particular way, and so is implying that the color seen is independent of our perception, he is just as much begging the main question at
issue between Berkeley and his opponents as is Berkeley when he asserts
that it is a sensation, although, of course, he is begging it in the opposite
direction.

Further, since, as we must allow, perceiving is not a kind of knowing,
Professor Price and Mr. Russell, in asserting that a color which we see is a
sense-datum, are not only begging the main question, but begging it in the
wrong direction. Indeed, any such statement must be false; and to discover
that it is false we need only consider what those who make it really mean by
it. So far then from its being, as Professor Price asserts,[14] certain that there
are sense-data, it is certain that there are not. Consequently, too, to refer,
as Mr. Russell and Professor Price do, to the various qualities which we
perceive as sense-data, and to ask and to answer questions about them, as
Professor Price and certain others do, as questions about sense-data, is to
be involved in a mistake, that of thinking of perceiving as a kind of knowing. The procedure, therefore, is one which needs to be abandoned altogether.

One remark may be added by way of conclusion. Readers of Mr. Russell and Professor Price can hardly fail to be struck by their readiness to
admit the existence of unperceived secondary qualities—an admission of
which they make use when, not satisfied that there really are such things as
bodies, and yet wanting to find a substitute for them which can be represented as that with which physics deals, they seek to find it in certain com-
binations of perceived and unperceived secondary qualities. This readiness

13 Ibid., p. 3 [this volume p. 204].
14 Ibid., p. 282.

is shown by Mr. Russell in the passage already quoted from his *Problems of Philosophy*. For there he illustrates sense-data, not as we should expect by colors we are seeing, and sounds we are hearing, but by colors and sounds, i.e., by colors and sounds whether perceived or not, and even if we ignore the inconsistency, since even on his own view an unseen color cannot be something which is being immediately known in sensation, we must allow that since here he is including unperceived secondary qualities among sense-data, he is admitting their existence. This readiness, however, is more obvious in his *Mysticism and Logic*,[15] where after illustrating sense-data by particular patches of color and particular sounds, he says: "I shall give the name *sensibilia* to those objects which have the same metaphysical and physical status as sense-data, without necessarily being data to any mind." Professor Price, too, shows this readiness when he allows the reality of certain what he calls "possible" or "obtainable" sense-data as, together with certain actual sense-data, forming a family of sense-data.[16] For although he explains that he means by "a possible sense-datum" a sense-datum which would be actual if certain events occurred in the observer, and so something which is not actual, and although he even says that obtainable sense-data do not exist at all,[17] he is there implying the reality of what he refers to as those obtainable sense-data which are members of families of sense-data. And plainly what he is here referring to, and implying the reality of, is certain secondary qualities which, conditions being what they are, are not, and indeed cannot be, being perceived. He is, therefore, here tacitly admitting the reality of certain secondary qualities which are not being perceived. This readiness, no doubt, at first strikes us as surprising. But, in view of what has been said, the explanation is surely obvious. For once anyone who thinks that the object of perception is always a secondary quality has convinced himself that perceiving is a kind of knowing, it is inevitable that he will go on to think of a secondary quality as independent of perception. Indeed Professor Price himself practically says this when he says of the secondary qualities: "Of course there was never any reason for thinking that these entities depended in any manner upon the sensing of them, for sensing is a form of knowing." [18]

---

[15] p. 148.
[16] *Perception*, pp. 262–3, 53.
[17] Ibid., p. 284.
[18] Ibid., p. 41.

IS THERE A PROBLEM ABOUT SENSE-DATA?

G. A. Paul (1912–1962)

The problem with which we shall be principally concerned is "Are there such things as sense-data?" We shall go on to consider also the questions, supposing there are such things, whether they are private, whether they can exist unsensed, and whether they can continue to exist throughout a period of time or are merely momentary.

About these last problems I shall perhaps be able to say something definite, but about the first I am unable to come to any decision. The difficulty about it is not that there is a problem which we can understand and to which we are unable to find the answer; the difficulty is on the contrary to find out clearly what the problem is itself. It is the difficulty of understanding what anyone is saying who says that there *are* such things as sense-data, and is due partly to the fact that not all the words used occur in everyday speech, a new technical term "sense-datum" having been brought into use. It is not, however, due solely to the fact that a word is being introduced which has not been used before, for there are many cases in which this is done where there is no such difficulty. For example the physiologists who wished to introduce the word "fovea" to describe a certain peculiarity of the structure of the eye can have encountered no such difficulty. They could say that they were using "fovea" as a name for the slight depression in the retina diametrically opposite to the pupil, and by dissecting eyes could point to instances of this depression. When they had done this no one would have any difficulty in answering the question "Are there such things as foveas?" This is the sort of question with which, because of its linguistic similarity, we are apt to compare our question "Are there such things as sense-data?" and in case we should be misled by this similarity we require to point out the differences which also exist between them. Once

From Aristotelian Society, Supplementary Volume XV (1936), pp. 61–77. Reprinted by courtesy of the Editor of The Aristotelian Society. Copyright 1936 The Aristotelian Society.

we know that "fovea" is being used to mean "the slight depression in the retina diametrically opposite to the pupil" we can find the answer to Qf [1] by dissecting some eyes and finding in each case whether there is an object which answers to this description. Before we even start the experiment of dissecting we have some idea of what it will be like to find such a depression and of what it will be like to be unable to find such a depression or to find that there is no such depression.

On the other hand if we are to find whether there are such things as sense-data we need make no experiment, and no experiment of any kind will help us. Sense-data, if there are such things, are objects which, so far from needing to seek by making an experiment, we cannot help seeing every time we see anything at all. It is sometimes said that we have only to inspect what happens whenever we have any visual experience of any kind to become aware that on such occasions we always do see an object of the sort which is being called the "sense-datum" sort. For example, it is said, you know what it is to look from an angle at the top surface of a penny lying flat on a table; in such a case the surface which you can see of the penny is round but you see it by means of an object which is not round but elliptical. A great difference becomes quickly obvious between this and the answer to Qf, where the point of asking whether there were such things as foveas was that you would know what it was like to discover a retina which lacked a depression opposite to the lens, whereas in this case you do not know what it would be like to be seeing anything whatever and not be perceiving an object of the sort in question. It then seems that either there was no point in asking Qs [2] (since you can have no idea what it would be like for the answer to be "No") or that the point of asking such a question is very different from the point of asking such a question as Qf. If this is not obvious, we can try to make it so by further consideration of the situation where you look at a penny from an angle. Sometimes in such a case it is true to say "I see the round top surface of this penny, and I see that it is round, but it looks elliptical," and what some philosophers say is that you can become aware on inspection that it is true not only that you are seeing a round object but also that you are seeing an object which is elliptical (the elliptical object being related to the round object in a certain intimate way which we have expressed by saying that the round object is seen "by means of it").

Some people have claimed that they are unable to find such an object, and others have claimed that they do not understand how the existence of such an object can be doubted, which drives one to ask what it would be

[1] "Qf" = "the question 'Are there such things as foveas?'"
[2] "Qs" = "the question 'Are there such things as sense-data?'"

like to be unable to find such an object and what it is like to find one. A clue is given by the fact that the claim generally made is not what would sometimes be called the "more moderate" one that whenever we see a physical object we do in fact see a sense-datum but the "less moderate" claim that it is logically impossible that we should see a physical object and not see a sense-datum. To call one the "more" and the other the "less" moderate claim is misleading, for it obscures the fact that while the "more" moderate would be a simple empirical statement the "less" moderate is a statement that so and so is logically impossible, i.e., in this case, a statement about the way a certain expression is to be used, viz., that "I saw a circular penny, and I saw an elliptical object (by means of which I saw it)" is to be another way of saying "I saw a round penny, and it looked elliptical to me."

Is there any test which would be relevant to whether it is true that in such a case there is an object which is round and also that there is an object which is elliptical?

This brings us to the question what it means to say of a sense-datum that it is an object. To say that there are such objects as foveas is to say that in eyes there is a shallow depression opposite to the lens; to say that a fovea is an object is to say that it is a physical object or at least a depression in a physical object, that it is the sort of thing that several people can see at once, and can be pointed to by, for example, placing a probe in it. It is not in the same way clear what is meant by saying of a *sense-datum* that it is an object, for people ask about it "is it a physical part of a physical object?," "is it private to one percipient?," "is it the sort of thing one can point to?" Such questions have the usual empirical look, but if we consider what facts we should consider relevant to their truth or falsity we see that they are not asking for information about "objects" but about the uses of words, viz., is "observed surface" of a physical object replaceable in all sentences in which it occurs by "corresponding sense-datum"?, "does it mean anything to say 'More than one person is seeing the same sense-datum at the same time'?," "is there anything which is (to be) called 'pointing to a sense-datum'?" In saying that the word "fovea" is to stand for a *thing* of a certain sort, meaning a *physical* thing, and at the same time *pointing* to an instance of a fovea, we say a great deal about the way the word is to be used—in fact we say all that any physiologist requires in order to be able to use the word successfully, i.e., from our pointing only to one instance of a fovea and calling it "fovea" he knows at once what is meant by saying ever so many things about foveas, e.g., that there are and have been foveas which no one ever has or will see, that a given fovea is the same one as we examined yesterday, that it continued to exist overnight when no one was looking at it, that the person standing beside me is looking at the same fovea as I am, that it is turning a deeper yellow, and so on. This is a simple thing to point out, but it is of importance here. All that seems to happen is that someone points to an object, and says the name of the object, whereupon by watching the behavior of the object we are enabled to make all sorts of true statements about it. Similarly it seems in telling us what sense-data are, someone refers to a situation with which we are all familiar, viz., seeing a penny obliquely, and says "the elliptical object which is related in such and such a way to the observed surface of the penny is a sense-datum." One is thereupon inclined to behave in the way one is justified in doing when such a thing as a fovea is pointed out to one, viz., to suppose that one knows what is to be meant by saying of such an object that, for example, objects of the same sort have existed which no one ever has or will see, that this object is the same one as I saw a short time ago, that it does or does not continue to exist when no one is looking at the penny from this angle, that it is turning a darker brown, and so on. That is, one is inclined to go on and talk as if one had just learned the name of some new kind of physical object which has just been brought to light. We know in the case of physical objects what it means to say *"this object* has such and such properties," and when someone tries to point out to us an object of the sort that is to be called a "sense-datum" we go on as if we knew in the same way what it means to say *"this object* has such and such properties," "this sense-datum has such and such properties." But in fact the case is very different: the word "fovea" was introduced as a name for a physical object, and we know how to use it in new cases because we know in general how words for physical objects are used in English. This statement is the crux of the present paper. There are certain general criteria which ordinarily enable us to decide whether a given physical object is the same object as we saw at a given previous time, whether it is the same object even though many of its properties are different, whether it is a different object from one we saw previously although it has very much the same properties, whether it is now changing its color and shape, and so on. This being so, we are apt to think that all we have to do is to give a name to an object and then examine this object and watch its behavior in order to be able to make up true statements about it in which this name occurs: we forget that the name-word is being brought into use as a member of a class of words whose use in certain contents is already given. E.g., everyone can imagine circumstances in which it would be true to say "He opened his eyes, saw a certain fovea, closed his eyes and did not see it for five seconds, opened them again and saw *the same fovea* again," and circumstances in which it would be false to say this (e.g., if during the five seconds someone cunningly replaced the eye-dissection he had been examining by another exactly similar). On the other hand, can anyone describe or imagine circumstances in which it would be true to say "He saw a certain sensedatum, ceased to see it for five seconds, and then saw *the same sensedatum* again"? Would it be true to say this, for example, if it were true to say "He saw a certain penny from a certain angle, and it looked elliptical to him, he closed his eyes and did not see it for five seconds, opened them again and saw the same penny looking exactly the same to him"? The answer is that no examination of such a situation will provide us with an answer: in the one case it seems that examination of the situation in question *will* provide an answer; in the other that it will not. It seems that in one case examination of the object in question will tell us whether it continued to exist throughout a period; but that in the other it will not. In a sense it does not do so in either case; but in the case where we introduce the word "fovea" by pointing to one or more foveas everyone does as a matter of fact know under what conditions it is to be true to say that this is the same fovea as I saw five seconds ago, this fovea has been on this table for the last half-hour although no one has been in the room, and so on. They know this because they know under what circumstances it is true to say such things of other physical objects; but it is not *necessary* that the word "fovea" should behave like other words for physical objects. We might, for example, say "No fovea lasts longer than a single specious present" meaning this not as an empirical statement but as a statement of how the word fovea is to be used. We might have some good reason for adopting such a way of speaking; e.g., suppose certain minute structures in the fovea were, we discovered, annihilated and replaced every five minutes, then we might very well say "During the last half-hour I have observed five foveas succeed one another here, each differing from the last one in respect of the minute structures (M)" or "During the last half-hour I have observed the same fovea, the minute structures (M) in it being replaced every five minutes" and mean the same by these two statements.

The word "sense-datum" as people have employed it does not fall into a fully-prepared scheme for its usage as a word for a physical object does, but its usage is not purely arbitrary. By this I mean that its use is connected with the use of certain words which *are* in ordinary language, e.g., "looks," "appears," "appearance," and with certain uses of "this," "after-image," and "image." We shall now consider some uses of such words with which it is connected, and how it is connected with them.

We so use language that whenever it is true that I am seeing the round top surface of a penny, and know that it is round, it is true to say that the penny *looks* (e.g.) elliptical to me, in a sense in which this does not entail that I am in any way deceived about the real shape of the penny. (I shall indicate this sense by means of a suffix:—"looks[1].") The rule which has generally been adopted is that the sense-datum is correctly said to have whatever shape and color-property the corresponding surface of the physical object looks[1] to me to have. E.g., suppose a red light is cast upon the penny as I view it obliquely, then if it is true that the surface which I see is round and brown, and looks[1] to be elliptical and red, then according to our rule it is true to say that the corresponding sense-datum *is* elliptical and red.

Those who have in practice used the word "sense-datum" have not spoken as if what they were doing was introducing *merely* an alternative way of saying this same thing over again, but as if this new sentence which they substitute were in some way nearer to the facts. They have the idea that in some sense when a physical object looks[1] red to someone then something really is red, i.e., that there really are in such cases two *objects*, one which looks[1] red and one which *is* red, and that somehow the one which *is* red has generally been overlooked, and its existence has now for the first time been recognized. It is said that its existence cannot be doubted, for if we carefully inspect what happens when a physical object appears red to us we shall come to realize that we can see this object, and further that, while in every such case it is academically possible to doubt whether there really is a physical object which is appearing red, it is academically impossible to doubt that there is an object which *is* red. The point is that although I may have been mistaken in supposing that there was a round surface of a penny looking[1] elliptical to me, yet it is quite certain that there was an elliptical appearance (and that it is logically impossible that this appearance should merely have *looked* elliptical to me). I shall only point out that another way of describing the same situation is "I thought I was seeing a round surface of a penny, which was looking elliptical to me, but in fact there was no penny there at all." It is then asked: "If there was no penny there at all, what was really happening? what were the elements of the situation?" and it is answered that what I was really seeing was a sense-datum which was elliptical, but was not a sense-datum "of" a physical object (or at least not "of" a penny). It is an equally good answer to say "It only seemed to me as if there was a round penny which looked[1] elliptical. I was really not seeing anything at all." This says just the same as the statement which contained the word "sense-datum," and there is no question of the one saying it less or more adequately than the other.

Sometimes people explain how they are going to use "sense-datum" by taking the case when I have an after-image with my eyes closed, in which case it is quite certain that there is no external object which is appearing, say, red. They then say that a sense-datum is any object which is seen in the sense in which the after-image is seen, and ask us to notice that whenever we see a physical object we see[1] an object (in this sense, which I am going to call "see[1] "). It is, however, not at all clear what this means. For it is not certain that whenever I see a physical object I see any *other* object in any sense of see. What is certain is that, suppose the physical object looks[1] red, there is nothing to prevent me from expressing that by saying that an object which is red corresponds to the physical object, and nothing to prevent me from saying that I see[1] that object. Such a notation might be convenient for certain purposes, and is unlikely to mislead, because (1) it makes no sense to say of an after-image that it looks different from what it really is, and we are not tempted to say such a thing of a sense-datum, and certainly have not given any meaning to saying it of a sense-datum, and (2) it is possible, and may sometimes happen, that what we took to be an after-image turns out to be an appearance of a physical object, and *vice versa*. This way of talking at once suggests that there really is in such a case an object (viz., a sense-datum) about which it is doubtful whether it is an after-image, or an appearance (sense-datum) of a physical object.

My intention has not been to deny that there are sense-data, if by that is meant that (1) we can understand, to some extent at least, how people wish to use the word "sense-datum" who have introduced it in philosophy, and that (2) sometimes statements of a certain form containing the word "sense-datum" are true, e.g., "I am seeing[1] an elliptical sense-datum 'of' a round penny." Nor do I wish to deny that the introduction of this terminology may be useful in helping to solve some philosophical problems about perception; but I do wish to deny that there is any sense in which this terminology is nearer to reality than any other which may be used to express the same facts; in particular I wish to deny that in order to give a complete and accurate account of any perceptual situation it is necessary to use a noun in the way in which "sense-datum" is used,[3] for this leads to the notion that there are entities of a curious sort over and above physical objects which can "have" sensible properties but cannot "appear to have" sensible properties which they have not got.

We shall consider now certain puzzles to which the use of "sense-datum" has given rise.

There is first the idea of the sense-datum as a sort of barrier, an entity which gets between us and the physical object. In trying to overcome the

---

[3] I.e., there are no facts of visual experience in order to express which it is necessary to use a noun functioning in the way "sense-datum" does.

idea of its being a barrier people ask "Is the corresponding sense-datum identical with the observed surface of the physical object?" An answer to this question is relevant to many questions commonly asked, viz., are sense-data mental or physical, are they private or public, do they exist only when someone is seeing[1] them or can they exist while no one is seeing[1] them, are they merely momentary or can they continue to exist throughout a time? In order to be able to answer "Yes" to it philosophers have even been prepared to alter their use of "sense-datum" so that it makes sense to say that such and such a sense-datum appears to have sensible qualities it does not in fact have [4]; for if the answer were "Yes," not only would the idea of a barrier be overcome, but also the second of each of these alternatives would be true, for we should say that what is a part of the surface of a physical object in this sense is physical, and we know what it is for more than one person to see the same part of the surface of a physical object, and for such a part to exist while no one is perceiving it, and for it to continue to exist throughout a period of time. The question whether a given sense-datum is identical with the corresponding surface has the air of being a question about two objects (or about one object) which is to be settled by inspecting the object or objects. Actually it is to be settled by examining not an object but our use of the two words "sense-datum" and "surface"; if we find some sentence which says something true about the sense-datum such that if the sentence which results from replacing the word "sense-datum" in that sentence by the word "surface" is either false or meaningless, that is what we shall call the sense-datum and the surface being not identical. Thus if *ex hypothesi* the corresponding surface is really round, and the sense-datum I see of it is elliptical, to say "the sense-datum is round" is either false or nonsense; and so is "the corresponding surface is elliptical." This is what we call the sense-datum and the surface being not identical. Thus it is not true to say that in this case the sense-datum is physical if we mean by that that it is a part of the surface of a physical object in the sense in which the corresponding part of the surface is a part of the surface of a physical object.

It is suggested that in certain favored cases it may yet be true that the sense-datum is identical with the corresponding surface. E.g., suppose I am looking at the penny in such a way that it looks[1] to me the same shape as it really is, i.e., the corresponding surface is round and the sense-datum of it is round. We have now to try and show a further difference between the way the two words behave, and at this point the most useful thing to consider is that future experience might lead us to believe that the surface in question had not been really round, whereas this same evidence would not

4 E.g., John Wisdom "Problems of Mind and Matter" pp. 156–7, and ch. IX passim.

lead us to doubt that it had looked[1] round to me, i.e., that the sense-datum I saw of it had been round. That is, what is evidence in such a case against the truth of "the surface is round" is not evidence against the truth of "the sense-datum is round."

It is, however, not impossible to hold that in such a case it is the same object which is being called "round," but that it is being called "round" in two different senses, and that all that has been shown is that it is not round in one sense but may yet be round in the other.

This urges us to try to point out further differences in usage between the two words, and so we come to a problem which is thorny indeed. It is suggested that, say, a minute ago the surface, in question, of the penny was in existence but the sense-datum was not, that it only came into existence when I looked at the penny. If one takes one's cue for the use of "sense-datum" from the use of "looks[1]" this is the natural thing to say. Suppose that a minute ago the penny was in my pocket out of sight, then it is not true that "the penny really was round and looked[1] ø to so and so," and we incline to say that if it was not looking[1] ø to anybody then there was no sense-datum of it. We ask "How *can* there be a sense-datum which no one is seeing?" and get the answer "A sense-datum is an object which you see. You know that other objects which you see exist while no one is seeing them. So why should not sense-data do so likewise?" We may then say: "Sense-data are only products, which are made by certain physical processes involved in seeing. They can have no existence apart from such processes." To this it will perhaps be answered "There is no reason to suppose that sense-data are manufactured by these processes. We may suppose that our sense-data exist unsensed and that all that the processes involved in seeing do is to select from among those already there." This sort of argument arises from considering sense-data as if they were a sort of physical objects. We know what it is for physical objects, which we see, to exist during times when we are not seeing them. We often do things which we call observing that a given physical object has continued to exist unperceived throughout a given period of time; but there is nothing which we similarly call observing that a given sense-datum has continued to exist unperceived throughout a given period of time. There are certain criteria which are ordinarily used as criteria for whether a physical object has gone on existing unperceived throughout a time; but there is nothing which is a criterion of this in the case of sense-data. We may if we care introduce such criteria, i.e., we may describe what we are going to call "observing that a sense-datum has gone on existing unperceived throughout such and such a time"; but probably we are strongly disinclined to do so, because we incline to take our use of the word "sense-datum" from that of "looks[1]," "appears," and "appearance."

It does not *make* sense to say that a sense-datum has existed unperceived; in giving the usage of the word we have not given a use to this, but it is open to us to do so if we care.

Perhaps it will be useful here to give an example of something which similarly does not make sense, but which we require to contemplate a little before we become quite clear that it doesn't. Whether rightly or wrongly there is attributed to the President [5] of this session the remark "It is not true that I sleep *more* than other people, I only sleep *more slowly*." It takes just a moment or two to see that sleeping is not the sort of thing that one *can* do more slowly than other people, and perhaps another moment or two to see that this means that to say that one person sleeps more slowly than another is to say something which has no meaning. The world being as it is we are not inclined to give a use to this phrase; on the other hand it is easy to describe circumstances in which we would be so inclined. Suppose, for example, that human beings were clearly divided into two kinds, those who walked and ate slowly and required a long sleep to recover from a given amount of exercise, and those who walked and ate quickly and required only a short sleep to recover from a given amount of exercise, then we should be very inclined to say that people of the first kind slept more slowly than people of the second kind.

Similarly, to say that a sense-datum has existed unperceived is to say something to which no meaning is given, but to which in certain circumstances we might be strongly inclined to give meaning. It is worth pointing out, for example, that sometimes we speak of an "appearance" of a thing which is not an appearance to anyone. E.g., "What a fine sunset. It must present a wonderful appearance from the top of Mochrum hill" does not imply that there is anyone there to whom it would be presented. On the other hand, we frequently use "appearance" in a different way. E.g., suppose I look at the round surface of the penny from a certain angle, then shut my eyes or go away for five minutes, then look at it again under similar conditions from the same place, we might describe this correctly by saying that "I saw two different appearances of it which were exactly the same in shape and color." We do not describe it by saying that "I saw twice the same appearance which continued to exist during the period when I was not seeing it." Whether we are to say that in this case I saw numerically the same sense-datum twice or that I saw two sense-data which had the same qualities is a matter of indifference, and perhaps we will never require

[5] [Professor G. F. Stout—ed. note.]

to use "sense-datum" in such a case and so need never make any decision on the matter. The important point is that whatever we do is not demanded by the nature of objects which we are calling "sense-data," but that we have a choice of different notations for describing the same observations, the choice being determined only by the greater convenience of one notation, or our personal inclination, or by tossing a coin.

Whether the sense-datum in question is to be said to have existed between the times when it was observed is also, as I have tried to show, a matter for the people who wish to use the terminology to decide, should occasion arise. What is important is that whatever criteria are laid down for the existence of a sense-datum during a time when it is unobserved, to say that since these criteria are fulfilled *therefore* it is the case that there is an object exactly like a sense-datum, only that it is unobserved, is misleading. That there is such an object is not a further fact inferred from them. It is better to say that these criteria being fulfilled is what we *call* a sense-datum's existing unobserved. This is particularly important in considering theories which say that an unsensed sense-datum exists at a certain place if an observer at that place would see a sense-datum answering to the given description. We may use the fact that if an observer were to be at a given place he would see a sense-datum of a given sort as a criterion for there existing an unsensed sense-datum of that sort; but if that is all we use, the fact that an observer at that place would see such and such a sense-datum is what we *call* a sense-datum of that sort's existing at that time. This is extremely important in considering the kind of view which tries to "mitigate the severities of phenomenalism" by saying that physical objects are groups of actual and possible (or unsensed) sense-data. The attractiveness of such a view fades when one considers what is the criterion which is being used for the existence of unsensed sense-data, and what is the relation between the criterion and the object of whose existence it is a criterion.

It is also important in considering another thing which is said, viz., that sense-data are a sort of things which only one person can ever see, i.e., that it is impossible that you should ever see my sense-data, i.e. that you should ever see a sense-datum which I see, and vice versa. People have the idea of sense-data as sort of private physical objects which each person keeps behind a high wall, and that although two people never see the same sense-datum the order in which I see my sense-data is connected in a fortunate fashion with the order in which you see yours and other people see theirs; but it is with a feeling of regret that people say "content can't be communicated, only structure can," and it is with a feeling of discomfort that they contemplate the possibility that although when an object looks to me green, I have a green sense-datum, yet it may always be the case that when an object looks to *you* green you may have a red sense-datum, and so long as the error is systematic it is undiscoverable.

In the first place we have to consider what is meant by saying that "content can't be communicated." This suggests that there is some process which we can describe but can't do, viz., communicate content. It suggests that the walls between our private collections of sense-data are so high that we can't see over, but that it is not inconceivable that we should. That, however, is misleading. It makes us feel "If only I could show you my sense-datum, we could decide whether we see the same or not." But in fact there is nothing I can't do. I could show you all my sense-data if the words "showing you a sense-datum of mine" had any meaning. To say that content can't be communicated is to say that "one person has communicated the content of his sense-experiences to another" means nothing at all. To suppose otherwise is to treat sense-data as if they were a sort of physical objects, and so to assume that it makes sense to say that two people see the same sense-datum.

Ingenious circumstances have been described in which we *should* feel urged to say that one person was having another's sense-datum; but I do not propose to give such an example here. I wish to consider only two things:—(1) suppose I look over your shoulder at a gas fire some feet in front of us both, and suppose that when I move my head into the position where yours is there is no difference in the way the fire looks[1] to me, and suppose when you move your head into the place where mine was you say that there is no difference in the way the fire looks[1] to you. Now suppose that we both have good eyes and have shown no signs of abnormal color-vision. Then it is true that the gas fire looks[1] the same to both of us, and there is a sense in which it is true that it presents the same appearance to both of us; but do we see the same sense-datum of the fire? I.e., numerically the same sense-datum of it? Most people who have used the term "sense-datum" would with little hesitation say that the sense-datum you see is not identical with the sense-datum I see. Why? Not because they see something about the nature of such objects which shows that they are not numerically the same, but simply because no meaning is given to "two people are seeing the same sense-datum."

(2) This raises the problem, what is meant by saying of *someone else* that he is seeing a sense-datum of a certain sort? When we think of such a thing we all think of a sort of inner vision inside the man's head directed on an object which we picture as a sort of screen, the whole thing being cut off from the outside world by a high barrier. We think that a man's behaving or not behaving in such and such ways is a symptom of some inner

condition, viz., whether he has in fact such an object before his inner eye behind the barrier, and we regard this thing of which his behavior is a symptom as something which we can never directly observe, but as something which might conceivably not exist even if his behavior were exactly what it is. Such imagery is pointless. If this entity which he alone sees did not exist and his behavior were no different from what it is, the world would appear to us to go on just the same, except that he would never really see things as they are, but only appear to. This shows that we have made a mistake about the use of such a phrase as "other people see sense-data similar to mine." The mistake is, as before, the one about the relation between the criterion for a thing's existence and the thing's existence. What we call someone else's seeing a sense-datum is his behaving in certain ways in certain situations, his reacting in certain ways to certain stimuli. A man's being color-blind is not his having pictures of *only* certain sorts in his private collection, at whose absence we can guess more or less reliably by certain tests. His being color-blind is his behaving in certain ways. Similarly your seeing the same color as I do on looking at a certain object, or seeing a different color when we should expect to see the same, is not my having in my collection a differently colored picture from what you have in yours, but my behaving in a certain way. We could easily mention tests which would ordinarily be taken as tests for deciding whether people have the same (i.e., exactly similar) sense-data under such and such conditions. (E.g., color-choosing tests for color-blindness.)

I do not deal with *the* problem about sense-data, which gives point to the introduction of the word at all. I mean "How are sense-data related to physical objects?" I.e., how does our use of the word "sense-datum" compare with our use of our words for physical objects? and does the use of the word "sense-datum" help to free us from any of the difficulties we get into about our use of words for physical objects?

And I have not touched upon how our use of the word "sense-datum" is related to our use of the word "sensation."

All I have done is to consider a number of questions about the way "sense-datum" is brought into use, which it seems to me must be considered before anything is said about the larger problems it was introduced to deal with.

SEEING

G. J. Warnock (1923–)

It is in some ways an unfortunate fact that many, perhaps most, of those philosophers who have written about perception have in fact been primarily interested in knowledge—in the principles of human knowledge, in our knowledge of the external world, in the foundations of empirical knowledge. It may be that the theory of knowledge presents more interesting problems than perception does, but in discussing them perception itself cannot be ignored, and ought not to be treated in too perfunctory a manner. In this paper I wish to call attention to some points about seeing which have not perhaps been sufficiently remarked. Indeed, in the discussions of perceiving, observing sensing, apprehending and the rest, it appears that simple seeing has often been neglected.

In the actual employment of the verb "to see" there appears at first sight to be a mere chaos of constructions and indeed of categories. In the case of most transitive verbs there are fairly clear and fairly close restrictions on the types of expressions which can properly occur as their objects, or on the other constructions, if any, by which they can be followed. By contrast one is inclined to say [1] that one may be said to see at least (1) things (not necessarily material objects); (2) events, happenings, perfor-

From *Proceedings of the Aristotelian Society*, Vol. 55 (1954–55), pp. 201–18. Reprinted by courtesy of the author and of the Editor of the Aristotelian Society. Copyright 1955 The Aristotelian Society.

[1] I say only that one is *inclined* to say this, since it is not clearly a proper thing to say. One may say that, e.g., I saw the color of his tie, that the color of his tie is a quality of his tie, and hence that I saw a quality, or that I saw the untidiness of his room, i.e., the untidy state of his room, and hence that I saw a state. But the reverse argument that one may see a quality, that redness is a quality, and hence that one may see redness, seems to lead to an uncomfortable conclusion. Similarly, that one may see the relation between the windows and the door suggests that one may see a relation, but one does not wish to say that one sees, say, proximity. The rather bald expressions in the text should be interpreted in terms of the various constructions which we do employ, not as licensing constructions which we do not. The need for caution here was pointed out to me by Mr. H. P. Grice, to whom I am indebted also at many other points.

mances; (3) qualities; (4) relations; (5) states or conditions; and (6) facts (including negative facts). One may further be said to see where things are, how things are done or how to do things, why things happen, and whether things are happening. The list is not exhaustive, but it seems to me to be already extensive enough to make it clear that the verb "to see" is in some way an oddity; we need to investigate its seeming grammatical and categorical sprawl. It will appear also that the implications of its uses are by no means simple.

I.

1. Consider first the statement that I once saw Lloyd George. Now if we take Lloyd George to have been what Prichard used to call a body, this statement entails that on at least one occasion I saw a body. It is now relevant to consider one of the reasons for which Prichard, and others, used to maintain that such a statement "will not stand examination." It was urged that, if ever a body were "really seen," it would necessarily appear as it really was; there are however admittedly cases in which this is not so, and by a rather indefinite appeal to some sort of "continuity," it was concluded that in no case is it really so. Similarly Broad has maintained (in *Philosophy*, Jan. 1952) that "in view of the continuity between the most normal and the most abnormal cases of seeing," it is necessary to conclude that in no case at all is seeing really "prehensive of bodies," or of the surfaces of bodies; and it appears that this conclusion is taken to refute any ordinary claim to see a body, at least as that claim would be commonly understood.

If I understand these arguments rightly, they turn on the point that, if A really prehends (or apprehends) X, it is impossible that X should appear to him as it is not; I am not sure whether it would have been asserted also, what is not the same thing, that it is impossible that A should take X to be what it is not. Broad appears to incline to this latter assertion, since he does not think it clearly mistaken to suggest that "prehending might properly be described as a form of 'knowing' "; but Prichard, at some apparent risk of inconsistency, maintains that we do habitually *mis*take the entities that we apprehend for bodies. However, we need not settle this point precisely; for it is in any case now possible to conclude that seeing is in fact neither prehending nor apprehending, nor is it commonly thought to be so. For, so far from its being impossible that, if I really saw Lloyd George, he should have appeared to me otherwise than he really was, perhaps impossible also that I should have been mistaken as to his identity or character, there is no need to deny that I saw Lloyd George even if every possible mistake [2] were actually made, or even if he appeared in the most unnatural guise.

Suppose for example, that I saw Lloyd George standing lost in meditation in Madame Tussaud's, and mistook him for a wax model of Winston Churchill; suppose, if you like, that he was actually pretending to be a wax model of Winston Churchill, and had disguised himself for the purpose; there would be in all this no reason at all to deny that I then saw Lloyd George. For to say that I saw Lloyd George does not entail either that I was then, or that I am now, able to describe his appearance correctly or even at all, that at the time I identified him correctly or even at all; it does not entail that he appeared to me to be Lloyd George, or that he appeared as Lloyd George normally did. Certainly if I now say that I saw Lloyd George, I do at least claim to have now, by whatever means and in spite of whatever disguises, identified as Lloyd George the person that I saw; but others might truly say of me, even though I would not say of myself, that I saw Lloyd George, even if I have not now, and had not then, any notion that it was Lloyd George that I saw. We may consider a more extreme case still. Suppose that, when I saw Lloyd George, I made no mistake only through making no judgment whatever, that I was not misled by appearances only because I was not led by appearances at all; suppose that I was an infant in arms. Even so, so long as there is reason to hold that I did, as we might say, "set eyes on" the man who was in fact Lloyd George, then there is reason to say that I saw him, even though I then neither made, nor could have made, any judgment at all, either right or wrong, about who or what it was that I saw.

2. I suspect that some philosophers have been misled in this matter by confining their attention to uses of the verb "to see" in the present tense and the first person singular. It has been rightly emphasized that the statement that one sees, say, a fox, is true only if there is a fox to be seen, and if what is seen is actually a fox. It follows from this that I would myself ordinarily say that I see a fox only if I not only believe with some reason, but believe that I know, that what I see is a fox. But the question whether I actually do see a fox is not the same question as whether I myself would say that I do. Not only might I falsely say that I do when I do not; others might truly say of me that I do, even though I would not say this or would actually deny it. If I say that I see a fox and am asked how I know that it is a fox, I cannot consistently say "I don't know—perhaps it isn't"; but if I

---

[2] This is, I fear, a rhetorical exaggeration. Mistakes exceeding a certain degree of wildness would justify the view that I was the victim of hallucination or in some other way in no fit state to see things.

say of someone else that he sees a fox and am asked how he knows that it is a fox, I may properly say "He doesn't know—he thinks it's a dog"— though of course I still imply that I know that it is a fox. Similarly with the past tense; if I now say that I saw a fox, although I thus purport to know now that it was a fox that I saw, I may quite properly deny that I knew this when I saw it. One who says that he sees purports to know; but one who does not know does not, for that reason, not see.

It is of course true that very often the best way to identify something, or to put one's self in a position to describe it correctly, is to see it, to have a look at it; it is however a mistake to suppose that seeing things essentially involves knowing, or getting to know, what they are, or what they are like, or even how they appear.

3. We must now consider some of the qualifications required by this rather bald conclusion. We need not go into the question whether it is necessary that one who is to be said to see should have eyes (though of course it is in any case a highly important fact that we do have eyes, that we have two of them, that they are as they are, and that they both point the same way); for without answering this question, we may say for a start that one who sees must have a field of vision, and that what he may rightly be said to see must be in it. Now what more than this ought we to say?

(a) The obvious point that one who sees must not only have his eyes open and in working order, but must also be conscious, is not quite so simple as it might seem. The infant of whom we say rightly that he saw Lloyd George doubtless set eyes on him in a normal, though non-adult, condition of consciousness; it is however clearly not necessary that the condition of consciousness should be normal. The taker of mescalin presumably sees what he looks at; but the open-eyed sleep-walker presumably does not; and there is room for many intermediate conditions. How far, then, may one deviate from normal conditions of consciousness without its for that reason being called in question whether one sees those things on which one's eyes are set? I do not know what can be said in general on this point, if anything can; it may be that only *ad hoc*, and probably sometimes rather arbitrary, decisions are possible for particular cases.

(b) It would, I imagine, be easily admitted, though some philosophers have seemed to deny, that the truth of the statement that Jones saw a fox is not impugned by Jones' misidentification of what he saw, nor by his failing either to identify or misidentify it, nor by his being mistaken as to its character or qualities. But, it might be said, not only must one who sees be conscious, he must in some way and degree be conscious *of* what he sees. If Jones sees a fox, he must at least be conscious of a—perhaps by him unidentified and unconsidered—*something* in his field of vision; if not, it must surely be absurd to say that he sees it.

Now let us widen the scope of this question by bringing in the notion of noticing. "Notice" appears to have at least two (relevant) uses; roughly, it means sometimes "to be struck by," sometimes "to pick out." Suppose that I am asked "Did you notice his tie?," in a context such that the question suggests that there was something noteworthy about it. Now I might be in no doubt that I did see his tie, but if I was not particularly struck by and perhaps cannot recall anything about it, I might answer the question in the words "No, not particularly." On the other hand, if asked "Did you see Lloyd George?" (e.g., in the audience) I might reply that I did not, for the reason that I had not noticed him, picked him out in the crowd. It seems to me to follow from this that it scarcely makes sense to ask *in general* whether one who sees also notices. It is, I suppose, not inconceivable that a person should be of so enthusiastic or sensitively observant a nature that he noticed, was in some degree struck by, absolutely everything that he saw; but this is certainly not the common case, and indeed one might say that for most of us there is, about most of the things that we see, simply nothing to notice (particularly). It is even clearer that not every case of seeing is a case of picking something out; in this sense, when for instance one sees a large building from close at hand, one neither notices it nor fails to do so. Thus, when it is true that X saw Y, the question whether X noticed Y may not be in place at all; if it is in place, the answer may be Yes or No, depending on the sense in which the question is to be understood.

What then of "being conscious of"? Clearly there are some cases, and some senses, in which one may be said to see what one is not conscious of. One may, for instance, be quite unconscious of the dust on one's furniture, idiomatically "blind" to it, but one need not be said not to see it; one may indeed become unconscious of it precisely because one sees it so often. I think too that it would be intelligible to say that someone's attention was occupied so exclusively with, e.g., what he was listening to, that he was quite unconscious of what he saw; perhaps also one may be said sometimes to remember seeing something that one was not conscious of at the time. But in absolutely ordinary cases the question is certainly obscure and perhaps unreal; if I report that Jones saw Lloyd George at a meeting yesterday, what could prompt you to ask me "Was Jones conscious of him?"? If Jones were an ambitious Liberal of the appropriate date, it might indeed be said of him that he was agreeably conscious of his leader's presence in the front row; but one is not in this sense conscious of all that one sees, nor indeed is it necessary that one should see what one is thus conscious of.

I suspect that, if there is a sense of "being conscious of" so different from that of "noticing" that one is in general and always conscious of what one sees, it is such that it is to be simply analytic that what one sees one is conscious of; but whether there is any utility in such a sense seems to me doubtful. One might be inclined to sponsor such a use of "conscious of" in the hope of evading an apparent dilemma: if one abandons, as clearly one must abandon, the idea that one who sees must have actual knowledge of what is before his eyes, it may appear that seeing is in peril of becoming attenuated to the object's merely being before his eyes; it is however a mere physical fact that this is so, and it is rightly felt that seeing must amount to more than this. At this point, then, one may be inclined to say that one must be conscious of what one sees, thus bringing in more than the thing's merely being before one's eyes, yet less than one's having actual knowledge of it. This is, however, too obscure to be the solution of any difficulty, and should be regarded only as an incentive to the examination of particular cases. Certainly, if someone appears to be, and later sincerely asserts that he was, unconscious of something clearly before his eyes, there must always be a serious question whether he saw it; but such cases will differ, and we should not assume that in all it must be impossible so to explain his being unconscious of it as not necessarily to exclude saying also that he saw it.

(c) There is a variety of curious questions which might be raised about the thing seen, turning upon the question, where this is appropriate, *how much* of it must be seen for it to be true that simply the thing itself is seen. It used at one time to be urged that one never sees, at a given moment, the whole of any object at which one looks, and hence that one cannot be said simply to see it. This contention appears to overlook the seeing of, for example, rainbows. More seriously, it seems to confuse seeing only part of (the proper contrast with the whole of) an object, with seeing it only from one point of view—seeing only Lloyd George's left leg, for example, with seeing him only from the side. This is not unimportant, for whereas one might well hesitate to say that one had seen Lloyd George if one had seen, unfortunately, only his left leg, one would not so hesitate if one had seen him, naturally enough, only from one's place in the auditorium. It would be minute and tedious to elaborate this question very far; I would like to make only four general comments upon it. (i) It is clearly not in general necessary that one should see the whole of what one sees, even in cases where to speak thus is appropriate, for it to be simply true that one sees it. I have never seen the whole of Blenheim Palace, but there is no question that I have seen it. (ii) It is important to bear in mind the conditions in which particular types of things are customarily seen. We are accustomed to seeing people, for instance, partly covered by clothing, but do not feel inclined, since this is how we ordinarily see them, to complain that we see only part of them. Even if they were totally covered up, still, so long as what they were covered with was clothing or at least something commonly worn such as armor, we might say that we had seen them without qualification. The case would be altered if they were encased in boxes, particularly if these were quite rigid, and it is of course different also for objects which are not ordinarily covered at all. (iii) Some parts of some objects are more significant than others. One would be readier to say simply that one had seen Lloyd George, if one had seen only his face, than if one had seen only his feet. (iv) The question what it is proper to say will often depend also on the conversational context. For example, where the task is to find some object, it will not mislead to say that one sees it as soon as one has located it; but where the interest is in an object's appearance, inability to give an account of this might call for qualification of the claim to have seen it. Thus, if one were trying to locate the cricket pavilion on a very dark night, one might say that one saw it (implying "Now I know where it is") on seeing only a very small though recognizable part; but if one had seen only the top left-hand corner of a painting otherwise completely covered, to say simply that one had seen it (suggesting "I know what it looks like") would be improper. This is not of course to say that inability to describe an object's appearance is *always* a reason for qualifying the claim to have seen it.

So far, we have been considering the seeing of things, objects—not necessarily, of course, material objects. The case of seeing happenings, events, occurrences must be briefly dealt with, and in any case is similar in most respects, not quite in all. If, for example, I say truly that Smith saw the robbery committed, it does not follow that he then knew, or now knows, that that is what he saw happening, that any robbery was committed. He may have failed to realize, or perhaps not particularly noticed, what was going on; if so, he will not be a good witness to the event, but he still was a witness of it—he did see it happen. Again, one might properly say that the only witness of some occurrence was, unluckily, an infant, who had no idea what was going on and could not give any account of what he saw. The only important new point, I think, is this: one may not only fail to realize the nature of, or fail to notice, an event that occurs before one's eyes—it may be that the event occurs too quickly to be seen at all; so that even if warned and watching, and although the event does certainly occur before one, one cannot say that one sees it happen, or happening. It might reasonably be suggested, however, that there is an analogue to this in the case of an object which is in one's field of vision too briefly to be seen; in such a case it is clear that one simply does not see it; it is not a case of seeing but failing to notice. The conjuror sometimes eludes one's vigilance by diverting one's attention; but sometimes the quickness of the hand defeats the eye.

The argument so far can be summed up as follows. In any of the cases so far considered, we may take it that, if it is to be true that A saw X, then at least A must have set eyes on X, being conscious and with eyes in reasonable working order. It may in some cases be further required that A should have noticed X, picked X out; but this point does not arise in every case; and certainly it cannot be always required that A should have taken particular note of X. It may be that in some sense—which deserves more consideration than I have given it—it must be true that A was conscious of X; however, there is certainly *a* sense in which this is not necessary. It is in no case necessary that A should have identified X, or made a correct judgment of X's character or qualities, or even that he should have known how X appeared to him; on this last point, one might say vaguely that he always could have known this, but certainly he need not actually have done so.

It seems to me that these contentions have often been denied, perhaps inadvertently, and indeed that they must be denied in most attempts to exhibit seeing as consisting in, or even including, any sort of "apprehending" or "direct awareness"; for these latter expressions have commonly been defined by reference to what the percipient knows, in some cases "incorrigibly," to be true. One who sees, however, need not know anything at all.

II.

1. The case is radically altered when we pass to the other constructions which I listed at the beginning. This is most obviously so in the case of (6), the seeing of facts; and this case can usefully be contrasted with those that we have just been considering. Suppose that I, who do not play chess, and a competent chess-player are watching together a game in progress. It is clear that, in the senses so far considered, he sees what I see, no more and no less; we both see the board, the pieces, the players, the movements made. But suppose that at a certain stage of the game my companion sees that White's bishop is dangerously exposed. Now although in a sense I still see what he sees, I certainly do not see this; and clearly the reason for saying that I do not see it is that I do not realize, and in my ignorance am not in a position to realize, that the piece in question is dangerously exposed. The facts that it is so, and that I have a good view of the

game in which that is true, do not together add up to my seeing that it is so; for in this there would be essentially involved my noticing, realizing, getting to know that it is so. Nor, if I later learn how to play chess, can I say retrospectively that I saw that White's bishop was dangerously exposed; for I did not realize this at the time, and hence did not then see it.

One can say "I saw a fox but I did not know that it was one," or "He sees a fox but he does not know that it is one." By contrast one cannot say either "I saw that it was raining but I did not realize that it was," or "He sees that it is raining but he does not realize that it is."

2. Now of the other cases not yet considered I think one can say, not only that they share this feature, but also that they share it in virtue of being essentially variants of the same case. Consider a simple case of what we called, with hesitation, seeing a quality, for example seeing the color of Lloyd George's tie. It is clear that one could not rightly say that one saw the color of his tie, if one did not get to know at the time what color it was. At first sight this might seem anomalous. Why, one might ask, if I can rightly say that I saw the tie though I did not know what it was, can I not say that I saw the color of the tie though I did not realize what it was? I imagine that the answer to this question—the question why we should speak in this way—would be that, unless I noticed the color of his tie and hence knew what color it was, there would be no point in making particular mention of the color in saying what I saw. Similarly, there would be no point in asking the particular question "Did you see the color of his tie?," if an affirmative answer to this question were compatible with the answerer's not knowing what color it was. It is worth noticing that, if asked whether one could see, say, the shape of a building, it would be natural to reply in the words "No, I could not really *tell* from where I was standing." It would by contrast be plainly outrageous to reply "Yes, but I could not tell what shape it was."

Similar considerations apply to the seeing of relations, and states or conditions. To say "I thought he was a very tidy person until I saw the state of his room" is clearly to imply that I saw *that* his room was untidy; the point of making particular mention of the *state* of his room would be lost unless I meant to convey that I got to know what his room was like. Similarly, a newly immigrant Eskimo taken on a tour of my garden might certainly be said to see my garden, but hardly the neglected condition of my garden; for his general ignorance of gardens would preclude him from realizing that it was, by comparison with other gardens, neglected. An expert who looks at the engine of a car might possibly see its condition at a glance, but I, though I see the same engine, do not see this. Again, suppose that an architect directs one's attention to the relation between the upper and lower windows of a façade; if one does not know what he has in mind, what exactly it is that he sees to be true of these windows, one would be guilty of some dishonesty if one claimed to see the relation in question. One might indeed say simply "No, I don't see it."

We may simplify the remaining cases by saying briefly: to see why the engine stopped is to see *that* it stopped for a particular reason; to see where the fault was is to see *that* it was in a particular place; to see how to cure it is to see *that* it could be cured in a particular way; to see whether there is petrol in the tank is to see *that* there is some (or is not). In effect, in all these instances alike it is the "see that . . ." construction which must be regarded as fundamental. It thus becomes important to examine this construction more closely. Perhaps it will be useful to consider the ways in which a claim to see that so-and-so might be attacked, since this should serve to bring out what it is that is claimed.

3. First, then, and very obviously, any such claim might be attacked by denying or questioning the fact alleged in the subordinate clause. If for instance I say "I had hoped to have a word with Jones, but I see that he isn't here," I would be conclusively shown to have been mistaken if it were shown that in fact Jones was present. One cannot claim or be said to see that *p*, if not-*p*, just as in such a case one cannot rightly claim or be said to know that *p*; and this is of course more than a chance analogy.

Next, such a claim might be attacked on the ground that although what one claims to see to be the case is the case, yet one does not know that it is the case. Suppose that I say "I saw at once that he was seriously ill." It might be objected that I had not in fact realized this. "You did nothing about it for days; I don't believe you knew"; or that I lacked the necessary qualifications—"You're not a doctor; how could you have told that he was seriously ill?"; or that nobody could have known—"There weren't any particular symptoms at that time"; or again, that I ought not to speak so confidently—"You couldn't possibly have been sure." It is not in these cases disputed either that I saw him, or that he was ill; it is contended that, when I saw him, I did not or could not have *known*, and hence did not see, that he was ill.

Slightly different from this is the further objection that, although what one claims to see to be the case is the case, and although one may know that it is the case, still one does not *see* that it is the case. For example: "You knew he was ill from what the nurse told you; there weren't any visible symptoms." Similarly, if someone were to make the absurd remark "I see that the moon is 250,000 miles away" (and were to say this as if making a judgment of distance by eye, not reporting something that he had read), it would not be necessary to question either the fact or his knowledge of the fact; the absurdity would consist in the impossibility of discovering, or even estimating, just by looking, the distance away of such a distant object.

Thus the claim to see that *p*—*mutatis mutandis* for other tenses—appears to involve (i) that *p* is the case; (ii) that the claimant knows that *p* is the case; (iii) that there are in what he sees sufficient grounds for concluding that *p*; and (iv) that he so concludes on those grounds.

4. It will be advisable to correct at once a possible wrong impression that might be conveyed by speaking, almost unavoidably, of "grounds" and "conclusions." We tend no doubt, and in general quite properly, to think of the grounds for a conclusion as being appreciably different from the conclusion, and of a conclusion as being drawn, reached, or arrived at, after at least some thought. In the discussion of seeing that *p*, however, all this may be inappropriate. The "ground" for saying, for instance, "I saw that he was mowing the lawn" may be simply that one saw him mowing the lawn; and in such a case that he was mowing the lawn would not be a "conclusion" drawn at length or with difficulty—nor, one might add, arrived at by inference. If the question be raised why in this case one should bother to say "I saw that he was mowing the lawn" at all, when one might have said simply "I saw him mowing the lawn," an important part of the answer would be that, however verbally alike, these constructions may have very different conversational points. Roughly, if what is of concern is what happened to the lawn, the former construction is the more natural; if what is of concern is what he was doing, then the latter. There would often be hardly anything to choose between them, but this is not to say that there would never be any reason to pick one rather than the other.

Furthermore, in spite of the close verbal similarity between "I saw that he was mowing the lawn" and "I saw him mowing the lawn," there are important logical differences. Certainly neither sentence entails the other. For if he had a very strange sort of mowing machine I might see him mowing the lawn without seeing that that was what he was doing; and I might possibly, on seeing, say, cut grass flying into the air on the other side of a wall, be justified in saying that I saw that he was mowing the lawn, though it would scarcely be proper to say that I saw him mowing it.

Of course the "conclusion" *may* sometimes be quite remote from the "grounds." For example, on seeing chairs, tables, crockery, etc., being carried out into my neighbor's garden at about 4 p.m., I might say "I see that they're going to have tea in the garden." On seeing the flag at half-mast I might say "I see that someone has died." And there is also the rather special case of, for instance, seeing in the newspaper that income tax is to be raised.

5. This last case raises a question of some interest. One can well imagine the protest being made "But you don't literally *see* that income tax is to be raised." But why not? It might be said that all one literally sees is that the paper says so. But what if the paper is absolutely reliable, so that one can reasonably claim to know that what it says is true? Or again it might be said that all one literally sees are the *words* "Income tax is to be raised." But does one not literally see that those words are on the page? And if one sees this and knows what they mean, does one not see that a certain assertion is made, and hence—if the paper is known to be reliable —that something is the case? Or if the extreme position is taken that one literally sees only black marks on a white ground, one might ask why, if these marks are in fact printed words, it should be non-literal to say that one sees the words. There is surely nothing non-literal in the statement that one sees, say, a drawing of Lloyd George, though this too may consist only of black marks on paper.

I believe that what this train of argument shows is, not perhaps that it either is or is not correct to say that one literally sees that income tax is to be raised, but rather that the distinction here between literal and non-literal uses is less clear, or more arbitrary, than one might have supposed. No doubt it would be safe to say that such locutions as "seeing the solution," "seeing no hope," or "seeing prosperity ahead" are simply visual metaphors, that here there is no question of literal seeing. One might on the other hand be tempted to say that only visible objects can be literally seen. To say this, however, is not safe at all; for it appears to entail that *all* cases of "seeing that . . ." are cases only of metaphorical seeing; and this is too extreme. But if one accepts some such cases as cases of literal seeing, a series could be devised from these to the metaphorical cases a fair stretch of which would be indeterminate. To see Jones mowing his lawn gives so plain a reason for saying that he is mowing his lawn that one must surely concede that one literally sees that he is doing so; to see certain words in a newspaper gives a very different sort of reason for saying, for instance, that income tax is to be raised; but there are other sorts of reasons from which it is not so different, and it is also a reason which a blind man could not have.

It is less important perhaps, to settle this question than to notice how this sort of doubt as to the propriety of saying "I see that . . ." differs from other sorts. It might be objected that, whatever sort of reason seeing certain words in a newspaper may give, it in no case gives a sufficiently good reason for saying that one sees that income tax is to be raised. But to say this would be to object to the statement as being credulous, ill-founded, unwarranted, not as being non-literal. This is of course an entirely different objection, which would be rebutted, if at all, on quite different grounds; the dispute would concern, not linguistic propriety, but the strength of evidence.

My aim in this paper has been to call attention in the first instance to the wide variety of constructions in which the verb "to see" can occur, and then to clarify so far as possible the complex and confusing picture thus displayed at first sight. I have concentrated mainly on establishing one distinction, which can be briefly summed up as follows. If there is a sense, as there is, in which we speak of the ability to see as a physical capacity, in which to be able to see better than others is not to enjoy any superiority of wits, skill, talent, or experience, then there must be a sense in which seeing does not involve the acquired abilities to identify, recognize, name, describe, and so on. The recruit to the Observer Corps must learn how to identify aircraft, but he is already as well able to see them as he ever will be. By contrast, if only the comparatively expert is able to see why the engine stopped, what is wrong with the carburetor, how to put it right, and so on, then there must be as it were another sort of seeing in which the wits are essentially exercised, which requires experience or judgment, talent or skill. There is on either side of this broad division considerable complexity and some flexibility, distinctions which should certainly not be neglected; but I believe that those distinctions are neither so great nor so sharp as is the main distinction itself, nor so liable to generate confusion, if they are ignored, in philosophical argument about perception and knowledge.

I would like to append two final remarks. First, it is clear that much of what I have said of seeing could *not* be truly said of hearing or smelling, tasting or feeling. And second, it is a curious fact that, if I am right, the familiar philosophical distinction between sensing and observing does not fit the case of seeing at all; for though there are doubtless many cases in which seeing is a good deal more than sensing, there are many also in which it is much less than observing.

A PRIORI AND EMPIRICAL KNOWLEDGE

Immanuel Kant (1724–1804)

I. THE DISTINCTION BETWEEN PURE AND EMPIRICAL KNOWLEDGE

There can be no doubt that all our knowledge begins with experience. For how should our faculty of knowledge be awakened into action did not objects affecting our senses partly of themselves produce representations, partly arouse the activity of our understanding to compare these representations, and, by combining or separating them, work up the raw material of the sensible impressions into that knowledge of objects which is entitled experience? In the order of time, therefore, we have no knowledge antecedent to experience, and with experience all our knowledge begins.

But though all our knowledge begins with experience, it does not follow that it all arises out of experience. For it may well be that even our empirical knowledge is made up of what we receive through impressions and of what our own faculty of knowledge (sensible impressions serving merely as the occasion) supplies from itself. If our faculty of knowledge makes any such addition, it may be that we are not in a position to distinguish it from the raw material, until with long practice of attention we have become skilled in separating it.

This, then, is a question which at least calls for closer examination, and does not allow of any off-hand answer:—whether there is any knowledge that is thus independent of experience and even of all impressions of the senses. Such knowledge is entitled *a priori*, and distinguished from the *empirical*, which has its sources *a posteriori*, that is, in experience.

The expression "*a priori*" does not, however, indicate with sufficient

From *Critique of Pure Reason* (1st ed., 1781; 2nd ed., 1787), sections I–V of the Introduction to the *second* edition. Translated from the German by Norman Kemp Smith (1929). Translation used by permission of Macmillan & Co. Ltd., London; St. Martin's Press, Inc., New York; and The Macmillan Company of Canada, Limited. The title of this selection has been supplied by the editors.

precision the full meaning of our question. For it has been customary to say, even of much knowledge that is derived from empirical sources, that we have it or are capable of having it *a priori*, meaning thereby that we do not derive it immediately from experience, but from a universal rule—a rule which is itself, however, borrowed by us from experience. Thus we would say of a man who undermined the foundations of his house, that he might have known *a priori* that it would fall, that is, that he need not have waited for the experience of its actual falling. But still he could not know this completely *a priori*. For he had first to learn through experience that bodies are heavy, and therefore fall when their supports are withdrawn.

In what follows, therefore, we shall understand by *a priori* knowledge, not knowledge independent of this or that experience, but knowledge absolutely independent of all experience. Opposed to it is empirical knowledge, which is knowledge possible only *a posteriori*, that is, through experience. *A priori* modes of knowledge are entitled pure when there is no admixture of anything empirical. Thus, for instance, the proposition, "every alteration has its cause," while an *a priori* proposition, is not a pure proposition, because alteration is a concept which can be derived only from experience.

II. WE ARE IN POSSESSION OF CERTAIN MODES OF *A PRIORI* KNOWLEDGE, AND EVEN THE COMMON UNDERSTANDING IS NEVER WITHOUT THEM

What we here require is a criterion by which to distinguish with certainty between pure and empirical knowledge. Experience teaches us that a thing is so and so, but not that it cannot be otherwise. First, then, if we have a proposition which in being thought is thought as *necessary*, it is an *a priori* judgment; and if, besides, it is not derived from any proposition except one which also has the validity of a necessary judgment, it is an absolutely *a priori* judgment. Secondly, experience never confers on its judgments true or strict, but only assumed and comparative *universality*, through induction. We can properly only say, therefore, that, so far as we have hitherto observed, there is no exception to this or that rule. If, then, a judgment is thought with strict universality, that is, in such manner that no exception is allowed as possible, it is not derived from experience, but is valid absolutely *a priori*. Empirical universality is only an arbitrary extension of a validity holding in most cases to one which holds in all, for instance, in the proposition, "all bodies are heavy." When, on the other hand, strict universality is essential to a judgment, this indicates a special source of knowledge, namely, a faculty of *a priori* knowledge. Necessity and strict universality are thus sure criteria of *a priori* knowledge, and are inseparable from one another. But since in the employment of these criteria the contingency of judgments is sometimes more easily shown than their empirical limitation, or, as sometimes also happens, their unlimited universality can be more convincingly proved than their necessity, it is advisable to use the two criteria separately, each by itself being infallible.

Now it is easy to show that there actually are in human knowledge judgments which are necessary and in the strictest sense universal, and which are therefore pure *a priori* judgments. If an example from the sciences be desired, we have only to look to any of the propositions of mathematics; if we seek an example from the understanding in its quite ordinary employment, the proposition, "every alteration must have a cause," will serve our purpose. In the latter case, indeed, the very concept of a cause so manifestly contains the concept of a necessity of connection with an effect and of the strict universality of the rule, that the concept would be altogether lost if we attempted to derive it, as Hume has done, from a repeated association of that which happens with that which precedes, and from a custom of connecting representations, a custom originating in this repeated association, and constituting therefore a merely subjective necessity. Even without appealing to such examples, it is possible to show that pure *a priori* principles are indispensable for the possibility of experience, and so to prove their existence *a priori*. For whence could experience derive its certainty, if all the rules, according to which it proceeds, were always themselves empirical, and therefore contingent? Such rules could hardly be regarded as first principles. At present, however, we may be content to have established the fact that our faculty of knowledge does have a pure employment, and to have shown what are the criteria of such an employment.

Such *a priori* origin is manifest in certain concepts, no less than in judgments. If we remove from our empirical concept of a body, one by one, every feature in it which is [merely] empirical, the color, the hardness or softness, the weight, even the impenetrability, there still remains the space which the body (now entirely vanished) occupied, and this cannot be removed. Again, if we remove from our empirical concept of any object, corporeal or incorporeal, all properties which experience has taught us, we yet cannot take away that property through which the object is thought as substance or as inhering in a substance (although this concept of substance is more determinate than that of an object in general). Owing, therefore, to the necessity with which this concept of substance forces itself upon us, we have no option save to admit that it has its seat in our faculty of *a priori* knowledge.

III. PHILOSOPHY STANDS IN NEED OF A SCIENCE WHICH SHALL DETERMINE THE POSSIBILITY, THE PRINCIPLES, AND THE EXTENT OF ALL A *PRIORI* KNOWLEDGE

But what is still more extraordinary than all the preceding is this, that certain modes of knowledge leave the field of all possible experiences and have the appearance of extending the scope of our judgments beyond all limits of experience, and this by means of concepts to which no corresponding object can ever be given in experience.

It is precisely by means of the latter modes of knowledge, in a realm beyond the world of the senses, where experience can yield neither guidance nor correction, that our reason carries on those inquiries which owing to their importance we consider to be far more excellent, and in their purpose far more lofty, than all that the understanding can learn in the field of appearances. Indeed we prefer to run every risk of error rather than desist from such urgent inquiries, on the ground of their dubious character, or from disdain and indifference. These unavoidable problems set by pure reason itself are *God, freedom,* and *immortality.* The science which, with all its preparations, is in its final intention directed solely to their solution is metaphysics; and its procedure is at first dogmatic, that is, it confidently sets itself to this task without any previous examination of the capacity or incapacity of reason for so great an undertaking.

Now it does indeed seem natural that, as soon as we have left the ground of experience, we should, through careful inquiries, assure ourselves as to the foundations of any building that we propose to erect, not making use of any knowledge that we possess without first determining whence it has come, and not trusting to principles without knowing their origin. It is natural, that is to say, that the question should first be considered, how the understanding can arrive at all this knowledge a *priori*, and what extent, validity, and worth it may have. Nothing, indeed, could be more natural, if by the term "natural" we signify what fittingly and reasonably ought to happen. But if we mean by "natural" what ordinarily happens, then on the contrary nothing is more natural and more intelligible than the fact that this inquiry has been so long neglected. For one part of this knowledge, the mathematical, has long been of established reliability, and so gives rise to a favorable presumption as regards the other part, which may yet be of quite different nature. Besides, once we are outside the circle of experience, we can be sure of not being *contradicted* by experience. The charm of extending our knowledge is so great that nothing short of encountering a direct contradiction can suffice to arrest us in our course; and this can be avoided, if we are careful in our fabrications—which nonetheless will still remain fabrications. Mathematics gives us a shining example of how far, independently of experience, we can progress in *a priori* knowledge. It does, indeed, occupy itself with objects and with knowledge solely in so far as they allow of being exhibited in intuition. But this circumstance is easily overlooked, since this intuition can itself be given *a priori*, and is therefore hardly to be distinguished from a bare and pure concept. Misled by such a proof of the power of reason, the demand for the extension of knowledge recognizes no limits. The light dove, cleaving the air in her free flight, and feeling its resistance, might imagine that its flight would be still easier in empty space. It was thus that Plato left the world of the senses, as setting too narrow limits to the understanding, and ventured out beyond it on the wings of the ideas, in the empty space of the pure understanding. He did not observe that with all his efforts he made no advance—meeting no resistance that might, as it were, serve as a support upon which he could take a stand, to which he could apply his powers, and so set his understanding in motion. It is, indeed, the common fate of human reason to complete its speculative structures as speedily as may be, and only afterwards to inquire whether the foundations are reliable. All sorts of excuses will then be appealed to, in order to reassure us of their solidity, or rather indeed to enable us to dispense altogether with so late and so dangerous an inquiry. But what keeps us, during the actual building, free from all apprehension and suspicion, and flatters us with a seeming thoroughness, is this other circumstance, namely, that a great, perhaps the greatest, part of the business of our reason consists in analysis of the concepts which we already have of objects. This analysis supplies us with a considerable body of knowledge, which, while nothing but explanation or elucidation of what has already been thought in our concepts, though in a confused manner, is yet prized as being, at least as regards its form, new insight. But so far as the matter or content is concerned, there has been no extension of our previously possessed concepts, but only an analysis of them. Since this procedure yields real knowledge *a priori*, which progresses in an assured and useful fashion, reason is so far misled as surreptitiously to introduce, without itself being aware of so doing, assertions of an entirely different order, in which it attaches to given concepts others completely foreign to them, and moreover attaches them *a priori*. And yet it is not known how reason can be in position to do this. Such a question is never so much as thought of. I shall therefore at once proceed to deal with the difference between these two kinds of knowledge.

IV. THE DISTINCTION BETWEEN ANALYTIC AND SYNTHETIC JUDGMENTS

In all judgments in which the relation of a subject to the predicate is thought (I take into consideration affirmative judgments only, the subsequent application to negative judgments being easily made), this relation is possible in two different ways. Either the predicate B belongs to the subject A, as something which is (covertly) contained in this concept A; or B lies outside the concept A, although it does indeed stand in connection with it. In the one case I entitle the judgment analytic, in the other synthetic. Analytic judgments (affirmative) are therefore those in which the connection of the predicate with the subject is thought through identity; those in which this connection is thought without identity should be entitled synthetic. The former, as adding nothing through the predicate to the concept of the subject, but merely breaking it up into those constituent concepts that have all along been thought in it, although confusedly, can also be entitled explicative. The latter, on the other hand, add to the concept of the subject a predicate which has not been in any wise thought in it, and which no analysis could possibly extract from it; and they may therefore be entitled ampliative. If I say, for instance, "All bodies are extended," this is an analytic judgment. For I do not require to go beyond the concept which I connect with "body" in order to find extension as bound up with it. To meet with this predicate, I have merely to analyze the concept, that is, to become conscious to myself of the manifold which I always think in that concept. The judgment is therefore analytic. But when I say, "All bodies are heavy," the predicate is something quite different from anything that I think in the mere concept of body in general; and the addition of such a predicate therefore yields a synthetic judgment.

Judgments of experience, as such, are one and all synthetic. For it would be absurd to found an analytic judgment on experience. Since, in framing the judgment, I must not go outside my concept, there is no need to appeal to the testimony of experience in its support. That a body is extended is a proposition that holds *a priori* and is not empirical. For, before appealing to experience, I have already in the concept of body all the conditions required for my judgment. I have only to extract from it, in accordance with the principle of contradiction, the required predicate, and in so doing can at the same time become conscious of the necessity of the judgment—and that is what experience could never have taught me. On the other hand, though I do not include in the concept of a body in general the predicate "weight," nonetheless this concept indicates an object of experience through one of its parts, and I can add to that part other parts of this same experience, as in this way belonging together with the concept. From the start I can apprehend the concept of body analytically through the characters of extension, impenetrability, figure, etc., all of which are thought in the concept. Now, however, looking back on the experience from which I have derived this concept of body, and finding weight to be invariably connected with the above characters, I attach it as a predicate to the concept; and in doing so I attach it synthetically, and am therefore extending my knowledge. The possibility of the synthesis of the predicate "weight" with the concept of "body" thus rests upon experience. While the one concept is not contained in the other, they yet belong to one another, though only contingently, as parts of a whole, namely, of an experience which is itself a synthetic combination of intuitions.

But in *a priori* synthetic judgments this help is entirely lacking. [I do not here have the advantage of looking around in the field of experience.] Upon what, then, am I to rely, when I seek to go beyond the concept A, and to know that another concept B is connected with it? Through what is the synthesis made possible? Let us take the proposition, "Everything which happens has its cause." In the concept of "something which happens," I do indeed think an existence which is preceded by a time, etc., and from this concept analytic judgments may be obtained. But the concept of a "cause" lies entirely outside the other concept, and signifies something different from "that which happens," and is not therefore in any way contained in this latter representation. How come I then to predicate of that which happens something quite different, and to apprehend that the concept of cause, though not contained in it, yet belongs, and indeed necessarily belongs, to it? What is here the unknown = X which gives support to the understanding when it believes that it can discover outside the concept A a predicate B foreign to this concept, which it yet at the same time considers to be connected with it? It cannot be experience, because the suggested principle has connected the second representation with the first, not only with greater universality, but also with the character of necessity, and therefore completely *a priori* and on the basis of mere concepts. Upon such synthetic, that is, ampliative principles, all our *a priori* speculative knowledge must ultimately rest; analytic judgments are very important, and indeed necessary, but only for obtaining that clearness in the concepts which is requisite for such a sure and wide synthesis as will lead to a genuinely new addition to all previous knowledge.

V. IN ALL THEORETICAL SCIENCES OF REASON
SYNTHETIC A *PRIORI* JUDGMENTS
ARE CONTAINED AS PRINCIPLES

1. *All mathematical judgments, without exception, are synthetic.* This fact, though incontestably certain and in its consequences very important, has hitherto escaped the notice of those who are engaged in the analysis of human reason, and is, indeed, directly opposed to all their conjectures. For as it was found that all mathematical inferences proceed in accordance with the principle of contradiction (which the nature of all apodeictic certainty requires), it was supposed that the fundamental propositions of the science can themselves be known to be true through that principle. This is an erroneous view. For though a synthetic proposition can indeed be discerned in accordance with the principle of contradiction, this can only be if another synthetic proposition is presupposed, and if it can then be apprehended as following from this other proposition; it can never be so discerned in and by itself.

First of all, it has to be noted that mathematical propositions, strictly so called, are always judgments *a priori*, not empirical; because they carry with them necessity, which cannot be derived from experience. If this be demurred to, I am willing to limit my statement to *pure* mathematics, the very concept of which implies that it does not contain empirical, but only pure *a priori* knowledge.

We might, indeed, at first suppose that the proposition $7 + 5 = 12$ is a merely analytic proposition, and follows by the principle of contradiction from the concept of a sum of 7 and 5. But if we look more closely we find that the concept of the sum of 7 and 5 contains nothing save the union of the two numbers into one, and in this no thought is being taken as to what that single number may be which combines both. The concept of 12 is by no means already thought in merely thinking this union of 7 and 5; and I may analyze my concept of such a possible sum as long as I please, still I shall never find the 12 in it. We have to go outside these concepts, and call in the aid of the intuition which corresponds to one of them, our five fingers, for instance, or, as Segner does in his *Arithmetic*, five points, adding to the concept of 7, unit by unit, the five given in intuition. For starting with the number 7, and for the concept of 5 calling in the aid of the fingers of my hand as intuition, I now add one by one to the number 7 the units which I previously took together to form the number 5, and with the aid of that figure [the hand] see the number 12 come into being. That 5 should be added to 7, I have indeed already thought in the concept of a sum $= 7 + 5$, but not that this sum is equivalent to the number 12. Arithmetical propositions are therefore always synthetic. This is still more evident if we take larger numbers. For it is then obvious that, however we might turn and twist our concepts, we could never, by the mere analysis of them, and without the aid of intuition, discover what [the number is that] is the sum.

Just as little is any fundamental proposition of pure geometry analytic. That the straight line between two points is the shortest, is a synthetic proposition. For my concept of *straight* contains nothing of quantity, but only of quality. The concept of the shortest is wholly an addition, and cannot be derived, through any process of analysis, from the concept of the straight line. Intuition, therefore, must here be called in; only by its aid is the synthesis possible. What here causes us commonly to believe that the predicate of such apodeictic judgments is already contained in our concept, and that the judgment is therefore analytic, is merely the ambiguous character of the terms used. We are required to join in thought a certain predicate to a given concept, and this necessity is inherent in the concepts themselves. But the question is not what we *ought* to join in thought to the given concept, but what we *actually* think in it, even if only obscurely; and it is then manifest that, while the predicate is indeed attached necessarily to the concept, it is so in virtue of an intuition which must be added to the concept, not as thought in the concept itself.

Some few fundamental propositions, presupposed by the geometrician, are, indeed, really analytic, and rest on the principle of contradiction. But, as identical propositions, they serve only as links in the chain of method and not as principles; for instance, $a = a$; the whole is equal to itself; or $(a + b) > a$, that is, the whole is greater than its part. And even these propositions, though they are valid according to pure concepts, are only admitted in mathematics because they can be exhibited in intuition.

2. *Natural science (physics) contains* a priori *synthetic judgments as principles.* I need cite only two such judgments: that in all changes of the material world the quantity of matter remains unchanged; and that in all communication of motion, action and reaction must always be equal. Both propositions, it is evident, are not only necessary, and therefore in their origin a *priori*, but also synthetic. For in the concept of matter I do not think its permanence, but only its presence in the space which it occupies. I go outside and beyond the concept of matter, joining to it a *priori* in thought something which I have not thought *in* it. The proposition is not, therefore, analytic, but synthetic, and yet is thought a *priori*; and so likewise are the other propositions of the pure part of natural science.

3. *Metaphysics,* even if we look upon it as having hitherto failed in all

its endeavors, is yet, owing to the nature of human reason, a quite indispensable science, and *ought to contain* a priori *synthetic knowledge*. For its business is not merely to analyze concepts which we make for ourselves *a priori* of things, and thereby to clarify them analytically, but to extend our *a priori* knowledge. And for this purpose we must employ principles which add to the given concept something that was not contained in it, and through *a priori* synthetic judgments venture out so far that experience is quite unable to follow us, as, for instance, in the proposition, that the world must have a first beginning, and such like. Thus metaphysics consists, at least *in intention*, entirely of *a priori* synthetic propositions.

❖ 33 ❖

THE A PRIORI

A. J. Ayer (1910–   )

The view of philosophy which we have adopted may, I think, fairly be described as a form of empiricism. For it is characteristic of an empiricist to eschew metaphysics, on the ground that every factual proposition must refer to sense-experience. And even if the conception of philosophizing as an activity of analysis is not to be discovered in the traditional theories of empiricists, we have seen that it is implicit in their practice. At the same time, it must be made clear that, in calling ourselves empiricists, we are not avowing a belief in any of the psychological doctrines which are commonly associated with empiricism. For, even if these doctrines were valid, their validity would be independent of the validity of any philosophical thesis. It could be established only by observation, and not by the purely logical considerations upon which our empiricism rests.

Having admitted that we are empiricists, we must now deal with the objection that is commonly brought against all forms of empiricism; the objection, namely, that it is impossible on empiricist principles to account for our knowledge of necessary truths. For, as Hume conclusively showed,

From *Language, Truth and Logic* (1936; 2nd ed., 1946), chapter IV. Used by permission of Victor Gollancz, Ltd., London. (Published in the United States by Dover Publications, Inc., New York.)

no general proposition whose validity is subject to the test of actual experience can ever be logically certain. No matter how often it is verified in practice, there still remains the possibility that it will be confuted on some future occasion. The fact that a law has been substantiated in $n - 1$ cases affords no logical guarantee that it will be substantiated in the nth case also, no matter how large we take n to be. And this means that no general proposition referring to a matter of fact can ever be shown to be necessarily and universally true. It can at best be a probable hypothesis. And this, we shall find, applies not only to general propositions, but to all propositions which have a factual content. They can none of them ever become logically certain. This conclusion, which we shall elaborate later on, is one which must be accepted by every consistent empiricist. It is often thought to involve him in complete skepticism; but this is not the case. For the fact that the validity of a proposition cannot be logically guaranteed in no way entails that it is irrational for us to believe it. On the contrary, what is irrational is to look for a guarantee where none can be forthcoming; to demand certainty where probability is all that is obtainable. . . . We shall discover that there is nothing perverse or paradoxical about the view that all the "truths" of science and common sense are hypotheses; and consequently that the fact that it involves this view constitutes no objection to the empiricist thesis.

Where the empiricist does encounter difficulty is in connection with the truths of formal logic and mathematics. For whereas a scientific generalization is readily admitted to be fallible, the truths of mathematics and logic appear to everyone to be necessary and certain. But if empiricism is correct no proposition which has a factual content can be necessary or certain. Accordingly the empiricist must deal with the truths of logic and mathematics in one of the two following ways: he must say either that they are not necessary truths, in which case he must account for the universal conviction that they are; or he must say that they have no factual content, and then he must explain how a proposition which is empty of all factual content can be true and useful and surprising.

If neither of these courses proves satisfactory, we shall be obliged to give way to rationalism. We shall be obliged to admit that there are some truths about the world which we can know independently of experience; that there are some properties which we can ascribe to all objects, even though we cannot conceivably observe that all objects have them. And we shall have to accept it as a mysterious inexplicable fact that our thought has this power to reveal to us authoritatively the nature of objects which we have never observed. Or else we must accept the Kantian explanation which, apart from the epistemological difficulties which we have already touched on, only pushes the mystery a stage further back.

It is clear that any such concession to rationalism would upset the main argument of this book. For the admission that there were some facts about the world which could be known independently of experience would be incompatible with our fundamental contention that a sentence says nothing unless it is empirically verifiable. And thus the whole force of our attack on metaphysics would be destroyed. It is vital, therefore, for us to be able to show that one or other of the empiricist accounts of the propositions of logic and mathematics is correct. If we are successful in this, we shall have destroyed the foundations of rationalism. For the fundamental tenet of rationalism is that thought is an independent source of knowledge, and is moreover a more trustworthy source of knowledge than experience; indeed some rationalists have gone so far as to say that thought is the only source of knowledge. And the ground for this view is simply that the only necessary truths about the world which are known to us are known through thought and not through experience. So that if we can show either that the truths in question are not necessary or that they are not "truths about the world," we shall be taking away the support on which rationalism rests. We shall be making good the empiricist contention that there are no "truths of reason" which refer to matters of fact.

The course of maintaining that the truths of logic and mathematics are not necessary or certain was adopted by Mill. He maintained that these propositions were inductive generalizations based on an extremely large number of instances. The fact that the number of supporting instances was so very large accounted, in his view, for our believing these generalizations to be necessarily and universally true. The evidence in their favor was so strong that it seemed incredible to us that a contrary instance should ever arise. Nevertheless it was in principle possible for such generalizations to be confuted. They were highly probable, but, being inductive generalizations, they were not certain. The difference between them and the hypotheses of natural science was a difference in degree and not in kind. Experience gave us very good reason to suppose that a "truth" of mathematics or logic was true universally; but we were not possessed of a guarantee. For these "truths" were only empirical hypotheses which had worked particularly well in the past; and, like all empirical hypotheses, they were theoretically fallible.

I do not think that this solution of the empiricist's difficulty with regard to the propositions of logic and mathematics is acceptable. In discussing it, it is necessary to make a distinction which is perhaps already enshrined in Kant's famous dictum that, although there can be no doubt that all our knowledge begins with experience, it does not follow that it all arises out of experience.[1] When we say that the truths of logic are known independently of experience, we are not of course saying that they are innate, in the sense that we are born knowing them. It is obvious that mathematics and logic have to be learned in the same way as chemistry and history have to be learned. Nor are we denying that the first person to discover a given logical or mathematical truth was led to it by an inductive procedure. It is very probable, for example, that the principle of the syllogism was formulated not before but after the validity of syllogistic reasoning had been observed in a number of particular cases. What we are discussing, however, when we say that logical and mathematical truths are known independently of experience, is not a historical question concerning the way in which these truths were originally discovered, nor a psychological question concerning the way in which each of us comes to learn them, but an epistemological question. The contention of Mill's which we reject is that the propositions of logic and mathematics have the same status as empirical hypotheses; that their validity is determined in the same way. We maintain that they are independent of experience in the sense that they do not owe their validity to empirical verification. We may come to discover them through an inductive process; but once we have apprehended them we see that they are necessarily true, that they hold good for every conceivable instance. And this serves to distinguish them from empirical generalizations. For we know that a proposition whose validity depends upon experience cannot be seen to be necessarily and universally true.

In rejecting Mill's theory, we are obliged to be somewhat dogmatic. We can do no more than state the issue clearly and then trust that his contention will be seen to be discrepant with the relevant logical facts. The following considerations may serve to show that of the two ways of dealing with logic and mathematics which are open to the empiricist, the one which Mill adopted is not the one which is correct.

The best way to substantiate our assertion that the truths of formal logic and pure mathematics are necessarily true is to examine cases in which they might seem to be confuted. It might easily happen, for example, that when I came to count what I had taken to be five pairs of objects, I found that they amounted only to nine. And if I wished to mislead people I might say that on this occasion twice five was not ten. But in that case I should not be using the complex sign "$2 \times 5 = 10$" in the way in which it is ordinarily used. I should be taking it not as the expression of a purely mathematical proposition, but as the expression of an empirical generalization, to the effect that whenever I counted what appeared to me to be five

[1] *Critique of Pure Reason*, 2nd ed., Introduction, section i.

pairs of objects I discovered that they were ten in number. This generalization may very well be false. But if it proved false in a given case, one would not say that the mathematical proposition "$2 \times 5 = 10$" had been confuted. One would say that I was wrong in supposing that there were five pairs of objects to start with, or that one of the objects had been taken away while I was counting, or that two of them had coalesced, or that I had counted wrongly. One would adopt as an explanation whatever empirical hypothesis fitted in best with the accredited facts. The one explanation which would in no circumstances be adopted is that ten is not always the product of two and five.

To take another example: if what appears to be a Euclidean triangle is found by measurement not to have angles totalling 180 degrees, we do not say that we have met with an instance which invalidates the mathematical proposition that the sum of the three angles of a Euclidean triangle is 180 degrees. We say that we have measured wrongly, or, more probably, that the triangle we have been measuring is not Euclidean. And this is our procedure in every case in which a mathematical truth might appear to be confuted. We always preserve its validity by adopting some other explanation of the occurrence.

The same thing applies to the principles of formal logic. We may take an example relating to the so-called law of excluded middle, which states that a proposition must be either true or false, or, in other words, that it is impossible that a proposition and its contradictory should neither of them be true. One might suppose that a proposition of the form "x has stopped doing y" would in certain cases constitute an exception to this law. For instance, if my friend has never yet written to me, it seems fair to say that it is neither true nor false that he has stopped writing to me. But in fact one would refuse to accept such an instance as an invalidation of the law of excluded middle. One would point out that the proposition "My friend has stopped writing to me" is not a simple proposition, but the conjunction of the two propositions "My friend wrote to me in the past" and "My friend does not write to me now": and, furthermore, that the proposition "My friend has not stopped writing to me" is not, as it appears to be, contradictory to "My friend has stopped writing to me," but only contrary to it. For it means "My friend wrote to me in the past, and he still writes to me." When, therefore, we say that such a proposition as "My friend has stopped writing to me" is sometimes neither true nor false, we are speaking inaccurately. For we seem to be saying that neither it nor its contradictory is true. Whereas what we mean, or anyhow should mean, is that neither it nor its apparent contradictory is true. And its apparent contradictory is really only its contrary. Thus we preserve the law of excluded middle by showing that the negating of a sentence does not always yield the contradictory of the proposition originally expressed.

There is no need to give further examples. Whatever instance we care to take, we shall always find that the situations in which a logical or mathematical principle might appear to be confuted are accounted for in such a way as to leave the principle unassailed. And this indicates that Mill was wrong in supposing that a situation could arise which would overthrow a mathematical truth. The principles of logic and mathematics are true universally simply because we never allow them to be anything else. And the reason for this is that we cannot abandon them without contradicting ourselves, without sinning against the rules which govern the use of language, and so making our utterances self-stultifying. In other words, the truths of logic and mathematics are analytic propositions or tautologies. In saying this we are making what will be held to be an extremely controversial statement, and we must now proceed to make its implications clear.

The most familiar definition of an analytic proposition, or judgment, as he called it, is that given by Kant. He said [2] that an analytic judgment was one in which the predicate B belonged to the subject A as something which was covertly contained in the concept of A. He contrasted analytic with synthetic judgments, in which the predicate B lay outside the subject A, although it did stand in connection with it. Analytic judgments, he explains, "add nothing through the predicate to the concept of the subject, but merely break it up into those constituent concepts that have all along been thought in it, although confusedly." Synthetic judgments, on the other hand, "add to the concept of the subject a predicate which has not been in any wise thought in it, and which no analysis could possibly extract from it." Kant gives "all bodies are extended" as an example of an analytic judgment, on the ground that the required predicate can be extracted from the concept of "body," "in accordance with the principle of contradiction"; as an example of a synthetic judgment, he gives "all bodies are heavy." He refers also to "$7 + 5 = 12$" as a synthetic judgment, on the ground that the concept of twelve is by no means already thought in merely thinking the union of seven and five. And he appears to regard this as tantamount to saying that the judgment does not rest on the principle of contradiction alone. He holds, also, that through analytic judgments our knowledge is not extended as it is through synthetic judgments. For in analytic judgments "the concept which I already have is merely set forth and made intelligible to me."

I think that this is a fair summary of Kant's account of the distinction between analytic and synthetic propositions, but I do not think that it suc-

[2] *Critique of Pure Reason*, 2nd ed., Introduction, sections iv and v.

ceeds in making the distinction clear. For even if we pass over the difficulties which arise out of the use of the vague term "concept," and the unwarranted assumption that every judgment, as well as every German or English sentence, can be said to have a subject and a predicate, there remains still this crucial defect. Kant does not give one straightforward criterion for distinguishing between analytic and synthetic propositions; he gives two distinct criteria, which are by no means equivalent. Thus his ground for holding that the proposition "$7 + 5 = 12$" is synthetic is, as we have seen, that the subjective intension of "$7 + 5$" does not comprise the subjective intension of "12"; whereas his ground for holding that "all bodies are extended" is an analytic proposition is that it rests on the principle of contradiction alone. That is, he employs a psychological criterion in the first of these examples, and a logical criterion in the second, and takes their equivalence for granted. But, in fact, a proposition which is synthetic according to the former criterion may very well be analytic according to the latter. For, as we have already pointed out, it is possible for symbols to be synonymous without having the same intensional meaning for anyone: and accordingly from the fact that one can think of the sum of seven and five without necessarily thinking of twelve, it by no means follows that the proposition "$7 + 5 = 12$" can be denied without self-contradiction. From the rest of his argument, it is clear that it is this logical proposition, and not any psychological proposition, that Kant is really anxious to establish. His use of the psychological criterion leads him to think that he has established it, when he has not.

I think that we can preserve the logical import of Kant's distinction between analytic and synthetic propositions, while avoiding the confusions which mar his actual account of it, if we say that a proposition is analytic when its validity depends solely on the definitions of the symbols it contains, and synthetic when its validity is determined by the facts of experience. Thus, the proposition "There are ants which have established a system of slavery" is a synthetic proposition. For we cannot tell whether it is true or false merely by considering the definitions of the symbols which constitute it. We have to resort to actual observation of the behavior of ants. On the other hand, the proposition "Either some ants are parasitic or none are" is an analytic proposition. For one need not resort to observation to discover that there either are or are not ants which are parasitic. If one knows what is the function of the words "either," "or," and "not," then one can see that any proposition of the form "Either p is true or p is not true" is valid, independently of experience. Accordingly, all such propositions are analytic.

It is to be noticed that the proposition "Either some ants are parasitic or none are" provides no information whatsoever about the behavior of ants, or, indeed, about any matter of fact. And this applies to all analytic propositions. They none of them provide any information about any matter of fact. In other words, they are entirely devoid of factual content. And it is for this reason that no experience can confute them.

When we say that analytic propositions are devoid of factual content, and consequently that they say nothing, we are not suggesting that they are senseless in the way that metaphysical utterances are senseless. For, although they give us no information about any empirical situation, they do enlighten us by illustrating the way in which we use certain symbols. Thus if I say, "Nothing can be colored in different ways at the same time with respect to the same part of itself," I am not saying anything about the properties of any actual thing; but I am not talking nonsense. I am expressing an analytic proposition, which records our determination to call a color expanse which differs in quality from a neighboring color expanse a different part of a given thing. In other words, I am simply calling attention to the implications of a certain linguistic usage. Similarly, in saying that if all Bretons are Frenchmen, and all Frenchmen Europeans, then all Bretons are Europeans, I am not describing any matter of fact. But I am showing that in the statement that all Bretons are Frenchmen, and all Frenchmen Europeans, the further statement that all Bretons are Europeans is implicitly contained. And I am thereby indicating the convention which governs our usage of the words "if" and "all."

We see, then, that there is a sense in which analytic propositions do give us new knowledge. They call attention to linguistic usages, of which we might otherwise not be conscious, and they reveal unsuspected implications in our assertions and beliefs. But we can see also that there is a sense in which they may be said to add nothing to our knowledge. For they tell us only what we may be said to know already. Thus, if I know that the existence of May Queens is a relic of tree-worship, and I discover that May Queens still exist in England, I can employ the tautology "If p implies q, and p is true, q is true" to show that there still exists a relic of tree-worship in England. But in saying that there are still May Queens in England, and that the existence of May Queens is a relic of tree-worship, I have already asserted the existence in England of a relic of tree-worship. The use of the tautology does, indeed, enable me to make this concealed assertion explicit. But it does not provide me with any new knowledge, in the sense in which empirical evidence that the election of May Queens had been forbidden by law would provide me with new knowledge. If one had to set forth all the information one possessed, with regard to matters of fact, one would not write down any analytic propositions. But one would make use of analytic propositions in compiling one's encyclopedia, and would thus come to include propositions which one would otherwise have overlooked. And, besides enabling one to make one's list of information complete, the formulation of analytic propositions would enable one to make sure that the synthetic propositions of which the list was composed formed a self-consistent system. By showing which ways of combining propositions resulted in contradictions, they would prevent one from including incompatible propositions and so making the list self-stultifying. But in so far as we had actually used such words as "all" and "or" and "not" without falling into self-contradiction, we might be said already to know what was revealed in the formulation of analytic propositions illustrating the rules which govern our usage of these logical particles. So that here again we are justified in saying that analytic propositions do not increase our knowledge.

The analytic character of the truths of formal logic was obscured in the traditional logic through its being insufficiently formalized. For in speaking always of judgments, instead of propositions, and introducing irrelevant psychological questions, the traditional logic gave the impression of being concerned in some specially intimate way with the workings of thought. What it was actually concerned with was the formal relationship of classes, as is shown by the fact that all its principles of inference are subsumed in the Boolean class-calculus, which is subsumed in its turn in the propositional calculus of Russell and Whitehead.[3] Their system, expounded in *Principia Mathematica*, makes it clear that formal logic is not concerned with the properties of men's minds, much less with the properties of material objects, but simply with the possibility of combining propositions by means of logical particles into analytic propositions, and with studying the formal relationship of these analytic propositions, in virtue of which one is deducible from another. Their procedure is to exhibit the propositions of formal logic as a deductive system, based on five primitive propositions, subsequently reduced in number to one. Hereby the distinction between logical truths and principles of inference, which was maintained in the Aristotelian logic, very properly disappears. Every principle of inference is put forward as a logical truth and every logical truth can serve as a principle of inference. The three Aristotelian "laws of thought," the law of identity, the law of excluded middle, and the law of non-contradiction, are incorporated in the system, but they are not considered more important than the other analytic propositions. They are not reckoned among the premises of the system. And the system of Russell and Whitehead itself is probably only one among many possible logics, each

---

[3] *Vide* Karl Menger, "Die Neue Logik," *Krise und Neuaufbau in den Exakten Wissenschaften*, pp. 94–6; and Lewis and Langford, *Symbolic Logic*, Chapter v.

of which is composed of tautologies as interesting to the logician as the arbitrarily selected Aristotelian "laws of thought." [4]

A point which is not sufficiently brought out by Russell, if indeed it is recognized by him at all, is that every logical proposition is valid in its own right. Its validity does not depend on its being incorporated in a system, and deduced from certain propositions which are taken as self-evident. The construction of systems of logic is useful as a means of discovering and certifying analytic propositions, but it is not in principle essential even for this purpose. For it is possible to conceive of a symbolism in which every analytic proposition could be seen to be analytic in virtue of its form alone.

The fact that the validity of an analytic proposition in no way depends on its being deducible from other analytic propositions is our justification for disregarding the question whether the propositions of mathematics are reducible to propositions of formal logic, in the way that Russell supposed.[5] For even if it is the case that the definition of a cardinal number as a class of classes similar to a given class is circular, and it is not possible to reduce mathematical notions to purely logical notions, it will still remain true that the propositions of mathematics are analytic propositions. They will form a special class of analytic propositions, containing special terms, but they will be none the less analytic for that. For the criterion of an analytic proposition is that its validity should follow simply from the definition of the terms contained in it, and this condition is fulfilled by the propositions of pure mathematics.

The mathematical propositions which one might most pardonably suppose to be synthetic are the propositions of geometry. For it is natural for us to think, as Kant thought, that geometry is the study of the properties of physical space, and consequently that its propositions have factual content. And if we believe this, and also recognize that the truths of geometry are necessary and certain, then we may be inclined to accept Kant's hypothesis that space is the form of intuition of our outer sense, a form imposed by us on the matter of sensation, as the only possible explanation of our *a priori* knowledge of these synthetic propositions. But while the view that pure geometry is concerned with physical space was plausible enough in Kant's day, when the geometry of Euclid was the only geometry known, the subsequent invention of non-Euclidean geometries has shown it to be mistaken. We see now that the axioms of a geometry are simply definitions, and that the theorems of a geometry are simply the logical

---

[4] *Vide* Lewis and Langford, *Symbolic Logic*, Chapter vii, for an elaboration of this point.
[5] *Vide Introduction to Mathematical Philosophy*, Chapter ii.

consequences of these definitions.[6] A geometry is not in itself about physical space; in itself it cannot be said to be "about" anything. But we can use a geometry to reason about physical space. That is to say, once we have given the axioms a physical interpretation, we can proceed to apply the theorems to the objects which satisfy the axioms. Whether a geometry can be applied to the actual physical world or not, is an empirical question which falls outside the scope of the geometry itself. There is no sense, therefore, in asking which of the various geometries known to us are false and which are true. In so far as they are all free from contradiction, they are all true. What one can ask is which of them is the most useful on any given occasion, which of them can be applied most easily and most fruitfully to an actual empirical situation. But the proposition which states that a certain application of a geometry is possible is not itself a proposition of that geometry. All that the geometry itself tells us is that if anything can be brought under the definitions, it will also satisfy the theorems. It is therefore a purely logical system, and its propositions are purely analytic propositions.

It might be objected that the use made of diagrams in geometrical treatises shows that geometrical reasoning is not purely abstract and logical, but depends on our intuition of the properties of figures. In fact, however, the use of diagrams is not essential to completely rigorous geometry. The diagrams are introduced as an aid to our reason. They provide us with a particular application of the geometry, and so assist us to perceive the more general truth that the axioms of the geometry involve certain consequences. But the fact that most of us need the help of an example to make us aware of those consequences does not show that the relation between them and the axioms is not a purely logical relation. It shows merely that our intellects are unequal to the task of carrying out very abstract processes of reasoning without the assistance of intuition. In other words, it has no bearing on the nature of geometrical propositions, but is simply an empirical fact about ourselves. Moreover, the appeal to intuition, though generally of psychological value, is also a source of danger to the geometer. He is tempted to make assumptions which are accidentally true of the particular figure he is taking as an illustration, but do not follow from his axioms. It has, indeed, been shown that Euclid himself was guilty of this, and consequently that the presence of the figure is essential to some of his proofs.[7] This shows that his system is not, as he presents it, completely rigorous, although of course it can be made so. It does not show that the presence of

---

[6] Cf. H. Poincaré, *La Science et l'Hypothèse*, Part II, chapter iii.
[7] Cf. M. Black, *The Nature of Mathematics*, p. 154.

the figure is essential to a truly rigorous geometrical proof. To suppose that it did would be to take as a necessary feature of all geometries what is really only an incidental defect in one particular geometrical system.

We conclude, then, that the propositions of pure geometry are analytic. And this leads us to reject Kant's hypothesis that geometry deals with the form of intuition of our outer sense. For the ground for this hypothesis was that it alone explained how the propositions of geometry could be both true *a priori* and synthetic: and we have seen that they are not snythetic. Similarly our view that the propositions of arithmetic are not synthetic but analytic leads us to reject the Kantian hypothesis [8] that arithmetic is concerned with our pure intuition of time, the form of our inner sense. And thus we are able to dismiss Kant's transcendental aesthetic without having to bring forward the epistemological difficulties which it is commonly said to involve. For the only argument which can be brought in favor of Kant's theory is that it alone explains certain "facts." And now we have found that the "facts" which it purports to explain are not facts at all. For while it is true that we have *a priori* knowledge of necessary propositions, it is not true, as Kant supposed, that any of these necessary propositions are synthetic. They are without exception analytic propositions, or, in other words, tautologies.

We have already explained how it is that these analytic propositions are necessary and certain. We saw that the reason why they cannot be confuted in experience is that they do not make any assertion about the empirical world. They simply record our determination to use words in a certain fashion. We cannot deny them without infringing the conventions which are presupposed by our very denial, and so falling into self-contradiction. And this is the sole ground of their necessity. As Wittgenstein puts it, our justification for holding that the world could not conceivably disobey the laws of logic is simply that we could not say of an unlogical world how it would look.[9] And just as the validity of an analytic proposition is independent of the nature of the external world, so is it independent of the nature of our minds. It is perfectly conceivable that we should have employed different linguistic conventions from those which we actually do employ. But whatever these conventions might be, the tautologies in which we recorded them would always be necessary. For any denial of them would be self-stultifying.

We see, then, that there is nothing mysterious about the apodeictic certainty of logic and mathematics. Our knowledge that no observation can

[8] This hypothesis is not mentioned in the *Critique of Pure Reason*, but was maintained by Kant at an earlier date.
[9] *Tractatus Logico-Philosophicus*, 3.031.

ever confute the proposition "$7 + 5 = 12$" depends simply on the fact that the symbolic expression "$7 + 5$" is synonymous with "12," just as our knowledge that every oculist is an eye-doctor depends on the fact that the symbol "eye-doctor" is synonymous with "oculist." And the same explanation holds good for every other a priori truth.

What is mysterious at first sight is that these tautologies should on occasion be so surprising, that there should be in mathematics and logic the possibility of invention and discovery. As Poincaré says: "If all the assertions which mathematics puts forward can be derived from one another by formal logic, mathematics cannot amount to anything more than an immense tautology. Logical inference can teach us nothing essentially new, and if everything is to proceed from the principle of identity, everything must be reducible to it. But can we really allow that these theorems which fill so many books serve no other purpose than to say in a roundabout fashion 'A = A'?" [10] Poincaré finds this incredible. His own theory is that the sense of invention and discovery in mathematics belongs to it in virtue of mathematical induction, the principle that what is true for the number 1, and true for $n + 1$ when it is true for n,[11] is true for all numbers. And he claims that this is a synthetic a priori principle. It is, in fact, a priori, but it is not synthetic. It is a defining principle of the natural numbers, serving to distinguish them from such numbers as the infinite cardinal numbers, to which it cannot be applied.[12] Moreover, we must remember that discoveries can be made, not only in arithmetic, but also in geometry and formal logic, where no use is made of mathematical induction. So that even if Poincaré were right about mathematical induction, he would not have provided a satisfactory explanation of the paradox that a mere body of tautologies can be so interesting and so surprising.

The true explanation is very simple. The power of logic and mathematics to surprise us depends, like their usefulness, on the limitations of our reason. A being whose intellect was infinitely powerful would take no interest in logic and mathematics.[13] For he would be able to see at a glance everything that his definitions implied, and, accordingly, could never learn anything from logical inference which he was not fully conscious of already. But our intellects are not of this order. It is only a minute proportion of the consequences of our definitions that we are able to detect at a glance. Even so simple a tautology as "$91 \times 79 = 7189$" is beyond

---

[10] La Science et l'Hypothèse, Part I, chapter i.

[11] This was wrongly stated in previous editions as "true for n when it is true for $n + 1$."

[12] Cf. B. Russell's Introduction to Mathematical Philosophy, chapter iii, p. 27.

[13] Cf. Hans Hahn, "Logik, Mathematik und Naturerkennen," Einheitswissenschaft, Heft II, p. 18. "Ein allwissendes Wesen braucht keine Logik und keine Mathematik."

the scope of our immediate apprehension. To assure ourselves that "7189" is synonymous with "91 × 79" we have to resort to calculation, which is simply a process of tautological transformation—that is, a process by which we change the form of expressions without altering their significance. The multiplication tables are rules for carrying out this process in arithmetic, just as the laws of logic are rules for the tautological transformation of sentences expressed in logical symbolism or in ordinary language. As the process of calculation is carried out more or less mechanically, it is easy for us to make a slip and so unwittingly contradict ourselves. And this accounts for the existence of logical and mathematical "falsehoods," which otherwise might appear paradoxical. Clearly the risk of error in logical reasoning is proportionate to the length and the complexity of the process of calculation. And in the same way, the more complex an analytic proposition is, the more chance it has of interesting and surprising us.

It is easy to see that the danger of error in logical reasoning can be minimized by the introduction of symbolic devices, which enable us to express highly complex tautologies in a conveniently simple form. And this gives us an opportunity for the exercise of invention in the pursuit of logical inquiries. For a well-chosen definition will call our attention to analytic truths, which would otherwise have escaped us. And the framing of definitions which are useful and fruitful may well be regarded as a creative act.

Having thus shown that there is no inexplicable paradox involved in the view that the truths of logic and mathematics are all of them analytic, we may safely adopt it as the only satisfactory explanation of their *a priori* necessity. And in adopting it we vindicate the empiricist claim that there can be no *a priori* knowledge of reality. For we show that the truths of pure reason, the propositions which we know to be valid independently of all experience, are so only in virtue of their lack of factual content. To say that a proposition is true *a priori* is to say that it is a tautology. And tautologies, though they may serve to guide us in our empirical search for knowledge, do not in themselves contain any information about any matter of fact.

❖ **34** ❖

A DEFENCE OF
"SYNTHETIC NECESSARY TRUTH"
Stephen Toulmin (1922–   )

I

There is a certain class of propositions (which, in order to avoid begging any questions, I shall refer to as "Type-Q" propositions) about whose logical status contemporary philosophers have come to hold radically-opposed opinions, opinions separated by an apparently unbridgeable gulf. Typical of the class are the two propositions,

> "Seven and five make twelve" and
> "Nothing can be both red and green all over." [1]

Others which have at one time or another been suggested as belonging to the class are the propositions,

> "Such and such a type of intention or emotion would necessarily be fitting (or unfitting) to such and such a kind of situation," [2] and
> "One ought always so to choose that the same volition shall comprehend the maxims of one's choice as a universal law." [3]

It is generally agreed that the most typical propositions of this class are "necessary," i.e., that the accumulation of evidence from experiments or observations is neither required for, nor relevant to the establishment of their truth or falsity; but beyond this point there is no general agreement. Some philosophers hold that they are "synthetic," i.e., that their truth does not follow from the definitions of the terms involved alone, and that

---

Reprinted from *Mind*, Vol. 58, 1949, by permission of the author and of the editor of *Mind*.
[1] See A. C. Ewing on "The Linguistic Theory of A Priori Propositions," *Proc. Aristot. Soc.*, 1939–40, pp. 207–244: I shall refer to this paper as "E."
[2] C. D. Broad, *Five Types of Ethical Theory*, p. 282.
[3] Immanuel Kant, *Fundamental Principles of the Metaphysics of Morals*, tr. Abbott, p. 71.

309

they are known by "*a priori* insight," [4] "immediate apprehension," [5] or "intuitive induction." [6] (This opinion I shall refer to as the "Synthetic Theory.") Such philosophers find nothing obnoxious in the idea of propositions which are both "synthetic" and "necessary." Their opponents, on the other hand, seem to regard the phrase "synthetic necessary proposition" as a contradiction in terms; for they hold it to be demonstrable that there can be no such propositions, and *a fortiori* that "type-Q" propositions are not both synthetic and necessary. Any necessary proposition which seems on a superficial examination to be also "synthetic," they declare, will be found on closer inspection to be "analytic"—true "by definition," or by "linguistic convention"—after all:

> "Our knowledge that no observation can ever confute the proposition '7 + 5 = 12' depends simply on the fact that the symbolic expression '7 + 5' is synonymous with '12,' just as our knowledge that every oculist is an eye-doctor depends on the fact that the symbol 'eye-doctor' is synonymous with 'oculist.' And the same explanation holds good for every other *a priori* truth." [7]

(This opinion I shall call the "Analytic Theory.")

In this paper, I want to reconcile these opposing views. I shall argue that there is nothing self-contradictory in talking of "synthetic necessary propositions." With the help of an example more familiar in everyday life than in philosophical discussions, I shall try to throw fresh light on to the logical status of "type-Q" propositions. I shall point out that the issue has been given a delusive sharpness by the introduction of certain irrelevant "epistemological" arguments; namely, attempts to answer the conundrum, "How do we 'know' synthetic necessary truths?" as though it were like the question, "How do cats see in the dark?" Leaving these aside, I shall attempt to reconstruct the source of the Analytic Theory's plausibility, and at the same time to discover why supporters of the Synthetic Theory are led to get so hot under the collar at the prospect of the Analytic Theory ("a doctrine which must encourage the widespread depreciation of reason in so far as it has any influence at all" [8]).

II

The Analytic Theory, or at any rate the most usually published form of it, as interpreted in the most natural and literal senses of the terms employed,

[4] See, for example, E, p. 213.
[5] See, for example, D. D. Raphael, *The Moral Sense*, p. 34.
[6] Broad, *loc. cit.*; Raphael, *op. cit.*, p. 193, etc.
[7] A. J. Ayer, *Language, Truth and Logic*, 1st ed., p. 115. [p. 306–7 this volume.]
[8] E, p. 209.

has defects which supporters of the Synthetic Theory have pointed out ably and at length: these defects I intend only to summarize. To begin with, although it can be agreed that the truth of type-Q propositions "depends wholly on the meaning of the terms used" [9]—supporters of the Synthetic Theory neither need to, nor do dispute this—this is not the same as saying that they are true or false in virtue of the *definitions* of the terms used. Their truth certainly does not depend on anything which anyone but a philosopher with an axe to grind would call "definitions" or linguistic "rules": books of grammar and dictionaries [10] do not suffice to establish typical type-Q propositions any more than they do matters of fact. Further, it is quite certain that, whatever language a type-Q proposition were expressed in, it must always remain logically unaffected: it must be as true or as false in Chinese, Afghan or Malay as it is when expressed in languages we can understand.[11] This fact is concealed by those who claim that the truth of type-Q propositions is based on "linguistic conventions"; and the use of this phrase also gives such propositions a misleading air of arbitrariness ("conventionality"), which supporters of the Synthetic Theory understandably find offensive.[12]

Now it seems to me that supporters of the Analytic Theory ought to grant that these are perfectly valid objections to their view, certainly in the forms in which it has been expressed up to now. Indeed, I suspect that they only hesitate to grant this because they believe that to do so must commit them to the Synthetic Theory *as a whole*. Such a belief is mistaken: they can quite well afford to allow that there is some value in Kant's division of necessary propositions into "analytic" and "synthetic," and even agree to say, for the purposes of argument, that there can be such things as "synthetic necessary propositions," without finding themselves forced to swallow, willy-nilly, all that seems to them unpalatable in the usual expositions of the Synthetic Theory. For what is pernicious in these expositions, is, surely, not so much the decision to apply the title "synthetic necessary proposition" to certain propositions, as the doctrine that, granted the existence of "synthetic necessary truths," we must "know" them by "intuition," by "*a priori* insight," by a "rational faculty of immediate apprehension" ("Something accompanying and behind all the senses, [which] receives *some* new ideas by itself and without the medium of sensation" [13]). This doctrine I shall refer to as "the Doctrine of the Inner Eye."

[9] Cf., E, pp. 231–232.
[10] E, p. 213.
[11] E, pp. 217–219.
[12] E, pp. 209, 232, 240–241.
[13] Raphael, pp. 2–3, 34, etc.

It is my first task to show that behind Kant's division of necessary propositions there lies an indisputable distinction, which is conveniently marked by the use of his terms, "analytic" and "synthetic"; but that to grant this is not necessarily to grant the Doctrine of the Inner Eye.

III

I can best do this with the help of examples taken from an everyday activity, that of running a regatta, consisting of a number of "knock-out" competitions. Here (away from the blinding dust of the philosophical arena) we can recognize the distinction between "synthetic" and "analytic necessaries" without getting entangled in epistemological side-issues; and we can carry back the lessons learned when we return and reconsider the more complicated and contentious "type-Q" propositions.

Suppose, then, that eight crews enter for the Visitors' Challenge Cup, and that the draw comes out as follows:—

King's
Lady Margaret   } Heat 1 }   First
Jesus   } Semi-Final
Christ Church   } Heat 2 }   } Final
Oriel
New College   } Heat 3 }   Second
Corpus Christi }   } Semi-Final
Pembroke   } Heat 4 }

I may now have occasion to say:

(a) "King's can't get into the final,"

(b) "King's can't get into the second semi-final," or

(c) "King's and Lady Margaret can't both get into the final."

Of these propositions, (a) is unquestionably "empirical." If called upon to justify my belief I shall appeal to past form as evidence, saying "Their stroke is too short," "Their blade-work is ragged," or "The other crews in the top half of the draw are too fast for them." No such considerations are, on the other hand, relevant to the truth of (b) and (c).

There are, however, other grounds on which (b) and (c) may be called "empirical," for King's and Lady Margaret might very well have been drawn elsewhere. (By exchanging King's and any of the four bottom crews, you falsify both (b) and (c). In order to discount this empirical element—what we call "the luck of the draw"—let us consider instead the two propositions,

(d) "The first crew in the draw can't get into the second semi-final," and

(e) "The first two crews in the draw can't both get into the final."
These propositions, I suggest, can fairly be called both "necessary" and "synthetic."

In order to confirm that (d) and (e) are necessary, notice that no observation or experience could ever confute them. We do not need to go to more and more and more regattas in order to make sure of their truth: we know very well that they are true without that. If, for instance, a semi-final in which the first crew in the draw competed took place later in time than that between crews from the bottom half, that would not falsify (d). It would only show that the "second semi-final" had been rowed before the "first semi-final."

But, granted that the propositions (d) and (e) are "necessary," are they not perhaps also "analytic"? I think it would be an unnatural extension of the term to call them "analytic." It would certainly be an unnatural extension of the terms "definition" and "convention" to say that they were true "by definition" or "by linguistic convention." Nothing which it would be at all natural to give as "definitions" of the terms "crew," "draw," "heat," "final," etc., (e.g., the definitions in the *Oxford English Dictionary*) would be sufficient to establish the truth of (d) and (e). In protesting against the Analytic Theory on these grounds, supporters of the Synthetic Theory, such as Dr. Ewing,[14] seem to me to be entirely in the right. If it *is* from "conventions" or "rules" that the truth of (d) and (e) follows, it is not from "linguistic" rules or conventions: it is from *the rules for running a regatta*; and these are something quite different from the definitions of "crew," "draw," "heat," "final," etc.

Advocates of the Analytic Theory may, of course, reply that to say this is only to make the truth of (d) and (e) follow, in addition, from the definitions of the terms "knock-out competition" and "regatta," and in a sense this is true; but, at the same time, it both is true in a misleading way and concedes the crucial point. To explain this: it is conceivable that one might come across people engaged in an activity closely resembling that which we call "running a regatta," who denied the propositions (d) and (e). It might be that we found, for example, that among these people the race between the first two crews in the draw was taken as the "decider" (so falsifying (e) in a practical manner), the winner of this race being given the prize and treated as "the champion crew." And, if this were to happen, we should no doubt want to say (according to the circumstances) that

14 Cf., the paper (E) quoted above.

what they were running was "a misconducted regatta," "a different kind of regatta," or even "not a regatta at all," certainly "not what *we* call a regatta." But suppose that considerations like these were held to show that the truth of the propositions (*d*) and (*e*) does, after all, depend on "definitions" or "linguistic conventions" (since their being true is part of what we should require before agreeing to apply the terms "knock-out competition" and "regatta" to any activity); then we must give a two-fold answer:—

(i) The "definitions" at issue are not those of the terms involved in (*d*) and (*e*) *alone*, for the words "regatta" and "knock-out competition" do not occur in either of these propositions. That fact alone, on the definition of "synthetic" adopted in this paper, is enough to justify calling them "synthetic": the crucial point is therefore conceded.

(ii) Even granted that the truth of (*d*) and (*e*) follows from all these "definitions" taken together, the "definition" of "regatta" to which we must appeal is no arbitrary one. There is all the difference in the world between saying, "That's not what we call a 'regatta': the word for that is 'raffle,'" (so asserting a purely linguistic matter) and saying, "That's not what we call a regatta; that's hardly more than a raffle!" meaning, "That kind of competition is no test of the skill of the competitors: winning it is hardly more than a matter of pure chance, so it doesn't serve the purpose of a regatta at all!" The distinction between the *usages* of the terms "regatta" and "raffle" may be a linguistic convention, but it is (to put it at the best) hopelessly misleading to talk of the difference in *purpose* between a raffle and a regatta either as "conventional" or as "a matter of words."

Let me sum up the lessons to be learned from this example. There is an indisputable distinction to be drawn between necessary propositions of two kinds: those like "An oculist is an eye-doctor," whose truth follows from the definitions of the terms involved alone, and those like "The first two crews in the draw can't both get into the final," which cannot be proved true without a further appeal. This distinction is conveniently marked by calling propositions of the first kind "analytic" and those of the second "synthetic." (I shall argue in a moment that this use of the terms "synthetic and "analytic" reflects Kant's own practice, if not perhaps his intentions, and that, in adopting it, we shall be doing him more justice than do the advocates of the Doctrine of the Inner Eye.) Those philosophers, such as Ayer, who have in the past supported a "purely analytic" theory of necessary propositions, need not be afraid of recognizing this distinction; for, in order to justify what on these standards we shall call "synthetic necessary propositions," we need not appeal to the evidence of any mysterious "sixth sense," "insight" or "intuition," but only to our understanding of the nature of the subject-matter under discussion, that is, to the "logical type" of the concepts involved. Still, the definitions of the terms involved are, by themselves, not enough. In order, for instance, to prove the truth of (d) and (e), we have to know not only the definitions of "crew," "final," "draw," etc.: we have also to know (and, it is important to note, in considerable detail) what it is to run a "regatta," as opposed to a "sweepstake," a "championship competition," etc. If we are to prove (d) and (e), "we must," to use Kant's own words, "advance beyond the cognition of the objects to a critical examination of the subject." [15]

IV

It is interesting to find Kant making a remark like this. His intentions are often obscure, and the way in which he uses terms like "subject" is, as a result, consistently ambiguous. (Does he mean "thinker" or "subject-matter"?) If, however, we discount the mock-psychological facade, and examine the logical structure behind it, we shall find that his position is not widely different from ours.

Consider, for example, his "principle of the autonomy of the will," the "synthetical and necessary proposition" in elucidating which he makes the remark just quoted. This principle he states in the words,

"Always so to choose that the same volition shall comprehend the maxims of our choice as a universal law." [16]

After stripping away the psychological trappings, I want to reinterpret it in the form,

(f) "The only principles to which one ought to appeal in justification of one's decisions and actions are ones which apply universally—not to me rather than you, now rather than another time, etc."

(This may not be what Kant said, but it seems to me to have something very closely to do with what Kant said, and to be a proposition well worth discussing.)

Proposition (f) is, in my sense of the phrase, a "synthetic necessary" proposition. We do not discover its truth by observation or experiment, as we go along: it is "necessary" or nothing. At the same time, its truth could hardly be said to follow from anything one would naturally give as "definitions" of the terms involved *alone*: it is, therefore, "synthetic." But, bearing in mind the lessons of the regatta example, it is not hard to discover what else it is that the truth of (f) *does* depend on. For, just as in the case of (d) and (e) it is taken for granted that we are talking about a "knock-

[15] *Loc. cit.*
[16] *Loc. cit.*

out competition" and a "regatta," so (f) has to be understood as referring
to the "moral" justification of our decisions and actions. It is true that, if
people stopped talking about what they ought "morally speaking" to do,
that is, if they ceased to take "moral" considerations into account in
making up their minds, the truth of (f) might be forgotten or denied. But,
if that were to happen, we should have to say that they were no longer
talking about the same kind of thing as before; that it was appeals to
"privilege," to "expediency," to "authority," with which they were concerned, rather than appeals to "morality"; and this would make nonsense
of (f), rather than falsifying it, since, in the absence of any qualification,
we understand "ought" as meaning "ought (morally speaking)."

The truth of (f) depends, therefore, not only on the definitions of the
terms involved, but in addition on what we mean by "morality," as opposed to "privilege," "expediency," etc. Appealing to universal principles is
a part of what we mean by "appealing to morality," and "by speaking morally." Once again, we cannot question the truth of the synthetic necessary proposition (f), so long as we understand and accept the nature of the
subject-matter under discussion; namely, that it is a question of "morality."
And, once again, to claim that this proposition is true "by linguistic convention," or "by definition," after all (even if it does not actually follow
from the definitions of the terms involved alone) is hopelessly misleading:
the distinction we draw between "morality" and "privilege" is in most
situations more than "a matter of words."

Before leaving Kant, may I interject a few remarks about the *Critique
of Pure Reason?* When Kant declares that we cannot help thinking in
terms of spatial, temporal and causal notions, he seems to be concerning
himself with a kind of super-empirical psychology; and this raises endless
problems. But there is logical backing for what he says, as we can recognize
if we recall his preoccupation with the question, "How is knowledge possible?" [17]

Consider the proposition,

(g) "One cannot help thinking in terms of spatial, temporal and
causal notions."

As it is expressed, this is certainly no analytic truism; but, if we add the
clause, "If it's knowledge one is after," we can trace the source of its necessary truth. If you forswore the use of all spatial, temporal and causal notions, nothing which you said would be very informative, or would communicate anything which could properly be called "knowledge." It is true
that you might still be able to say. "Something happened to me some-

[17] This was pointed out to me by Professor von Wright in discussion.

where sometime." Yet even this might have to be ruled out, since the words "somewhere" and "sometime" could only be used correctly by one who understood words like "here" and "now"; in which case you could only exclaim, "Man!" or "Ow!" or "Hurrah!" Now, supposing that this *were* all that you could say to me, I should be entitled to reply, "That's not 'knowledge'!" By this I should mean, not "The word for that is 'rumor' or 'hokum' or 'exclamation,' not 'knowledge,'" but rather, "That gives me none of the kind of help needed in this situation, such as you would have given me by saying, 'A tall man in a mackintosh jumped out from behind the gate as I was walking past it five minutes ago and struck me on the head, breaking my spectacles.'" One might, therefore, argue very plausibly that proposition (g) is both true, and necessarily true, though its proof requires us to appeal not only to the definitions of the terms involved, but also to the nature of the subject at issue; that is, to the distinction between what can and what cannot properly be called "knowledge."

V

It should now be possible to explain both the source of the Analytic Theory's plausibility, and the horror which it so often arouses in opponents.

First, then, what is it that has led philosophers to advocate the Analytic Theory, despite the comparatively obvious fallacies involved? Recall the lessons of the examples we have examined. There is a slightly eccentric sense of "follow" such that type-Q propositions may be said to follow from certain "definitions," or rather from the nature of certain distinctions which we are in the habit of making (and for very good reasons); such as that between a "regatta" and a "raffle," that between "morality" and "privilege," and that between what can and what cannot properly be called "knowledge." (These distinctions, however, define not the terms but the logical type, or the nature of the subject-matter of the type-Q propositions concerned.) In consequence, there is another class of propositions with which type-Q propositions may easily be confused. This class is made up as follows: for every type-Q proposition, we may construct a corresponding proposition in which the nature of the subject-matter is made explicit. In place of

(e) "The first two crews in the draw can't both get into the final," we may consider

(e') "In a 'knock-out competition' in a 'regatta,' the first two crews in the 'draw' can't both get into the 'final.'"
In place of

(*f*) "The only principles to which one ought to appeal are universal ones. . . ,"
we may consider

(*f'*) "When taking 'moral' considerations into account, the only 'principles' to which we 'ought' to appeal are universal ones . . ."
In place of

(*g*) "One cannot help thinking in terms of spatial, temporal and causal notions,"
we may consider

(*g'*) "If one is to obtain 'knowledge,' one cannot help thinking in terms of spatial, temporal and causal notions."
And likewise, in place of

(*h*) "Seven and five make twelve,"
we may consider

(*h'*) "In 'the arithmetic of natural numbers,' seven and five make twelve."

It is reasonable enough to call the propositions (*e'*) to (*h'*) "analytic necessaries." And, since these propositions only make explicit what is already implicit in the type-Q propositions (*e*) to (*h*), the advocates of the Analytic Theory may have argued that (*e*) to (*h*) must therefore also be classed as "analytic necessaries." "In any case," they may say, "we know nowadays how much more complicated definitions may be than used to be suspected: it is therefore pardonable to confuse, or rather to ignore the differences between the two classes of proposition." But, whatever may be said in their defence, and however much one may sympathize with them in their distaste for the Doctrine of the Inner Eye, the differences between the propositions (*e*) to (*h*) and the propositions (*e'*) to (*h'*) remain; and it remains an extension of the notion of a "definition" far beyond its everyday limits to pack into it everything needed to prove the truth of type-Q propositions from the "definitions" of their terms alone, for this means including in every "definition" all those things which distinguish a notion of one type from notions of *other* logical types as well as everything marking it off from other notions of the *same* type, all those things which make red a "color" as well as everything marking it off from green, blue, brown, etc.

So much for the fallacies behind the Analytic Theory. But what makes it seem to so many of its opponents not just false but outrageous? One of the lessons of the regatta example was the difference between two similar-looking classes of propositions:—

(i) "That's not a 'regatta'; that's a 'raffle.' "
  "That's not an 'oculist'; that's an 'optician.' "

(The issue in these cases is purely "linguistic." The proposition is intended to correct someone's usage, and the second half can in each case be read as "the word for that is 'raffle,' 'optician,' etc.")

    (ii) "That's not a regatta: that's hardly more than a raffle!"

           "That's not an appeal to morality: that's an appeal to privilege!"

           "You can't call that knowledge!"

           "That's a funny kind of arithmetic!"

(The issue in these cases is far from being purely linguistic. The proposition is intended not just to correct someone's usage, but to make him think and behave very differently. The issue can, therefore, hardly be called either "conventional" or "a matter of words.")

Quite apart from confusing the propositions (e) to (h) and (e') to (h'), advocates of the Analytic Theory have to assimilate all the members of class (ii) to class (i). Only by treating the members of class (ii) as "matters of words," like those in class (i), can they justify themselves in calling type-Q propositions "analytic," true "by definition," true "by linguistic convention." And to do this is clearly to misrepresent both the nature of class (ii) propositions, and that of the type-Q propositions dependent on them. In view of this, we need hardly be surprised at the feelings of outrage which supporters of the Synthetic Theory express when faced with the Analytic Theory. (Even so, we may feel that they are hardly justified in suggesting that belief in the truth of the Analytic Theory should lead one to abandon discussion in favor of violence as a means of settling disputes! [18])

VI

A few remarks, in conclusion, about the Doctrine of the Inner Eye, since this is the real bone of contention between supporters of the two theories. It should be clear by now that the existence of "synthetic necessary" propositions and the "synthetic" nature of type-Q propositions are questions wholly independent of this doctrine. There is not much temptation to invoke any "intuition" or other "rational faculty" to justify one's certainty of the truth of the proposition (e), "The first two crews in the draw can't both get into the final": it is clear, in this case, that a knowledge of what it is "to run a regatta" is all that we need to appeal to. The question we now have to ask is why this independence should be any less obvious in the case of more typical type-Q propositions. How is it, then, that so many philosophers have come to think that some special "faculty," "insight" or "intuition" was needed to inform us of the truth of type-Q propositions?

[18] See E, pp. 240–241.

I can, at the moment, suggest only the beginnings of an answer to this question. Notice to begin with two kinds of proposition of which it is possible to be "absolutely certain." On the one hand, (1) there are those propositions (for example, "The ace of hearts is in my hand") of whose truth we are certain without there being any question of our adducing "reasons": if challenged, we can only appeal to "the evidence of our senses." On the other hand, (2) there are those propositions whose truth we cannot question if we understand the nature of the subject-matter at all. Type-Q (synthetic necessary) propositions belong, as I have been trying to explain, to the second class: advocates of the Doctrine of the Inner Eye talk as though they belonged to the first.

Consider the following passage written by a supporter of the Synthetic Theory (incidentally, by one who claims [19] not to "postulate some mysterious faculty" to explain our knowledge of synthetic necessary truths) :—

> "It is surely plain that some *a priori* propositions, e.g. everything which has shape has size, a thing cannot be both red and green, if one thing is above another and the second is above a third the first is above the third, all three-sided rectilinear figures have three angles, could be seen to be true without the use of language. A person who was capable of forming visual images might quite well see the truth of any of these propositions without having to put them into words, and therefore their truth cannot possibly depend on the structure of language." [20]

The crucial and ensnaring phrases in this passage are "seen to be true" and "see the truth of." Certainly, when talking about propositions of class (1), we are accustomed to using phrases of the form "seeing the ace of hearts in my hand," "seeing that the ace of hearts is in my hand," "seeing that the proposition 'The ace of hearts is in my hand' is true" and "seeing the truth of the proposition 'The ace of hearts is in my hand,'" interchangeably. But this practice can be extended to propositions of class (2) only through a misunderstanding. If this *is* done, however, the Doctrine of the Inner Eye acquires considerable plausibility. For then, having noticed that seeing the ace of hearts in your hand is much the same as seeing the truth of the proposition, "The ace of hearts is in my hand," you may all too easily begin looking for the experience whose description is interchangeable with the phrase "seeing the truth of the proposition, 'Nothing can be both red and green all over.'"

Once begun, this search need never end, for no answer can be at all satisfactory. No experience will do for the propositions, "Nothing can be

[19] E, p. 243.
[20] E, p. 217.

both red and green all over" and "The first two crews in the draw can't both get into the final," what seeing the ace of hearts in your hand does for the proposition, "The ace of hearts is in my hand." "Use your eyes," is a fair answer to the question, "How am I to know that the ace of hearts is in my hand?": the answers to the questions, "How am I to know that the first two crews can't both get into the final?" and "How am I to know that nothing can be both red and green all over?" are to be given, not by any appeal to a "sixth sense" or to "visual imagery," but by reference to the way in which regattas are run, the purpose of regattas, etc., and to the nature of color-concepts, the purpose of classification by colors, etc. One can conjure up a visual image of the ace of hearts in one's hand, and to do this is (if you like to call it that) "to see what is meant by the words 'The ace of hearts is in my hand.'" But, conjure up what visual images you choose, you will never find one which shows you "what is meant by the words 'Nothing can be both red and green all over'": all you can imagine is *red and green objects*. Nor is visualizing three dots, one above the other, in any sense the same as "seeing the truth of the proposition, 'If one thing is above another, and the second is above a third, the first is above the third'": the most such a visual image could ever be said to do would be to *remind* you or to *convince* you of the truth of that proposition.

To resort to "intuition," "rational faculties," "visual images" and so on is to overlook or forget the fact that "seeing the truth of a type-Q proposition" is not a matter of "having the right experiences," as it would be if type-Q propositions belonged to class (1), but is a matter of "understanding the nature of the subject-matter." And understanding the nature of the subject-matter is (to adapt Professor Ryle's illuminating distinction [21]) as much "knowing how . . ." or "knowing what it is to . . ." as it is "knowing that . . ." The natural thing, for example, to say about a man who knows that seven and five make twelve is that (unlike some) he knows "how to count"; not that he has access, which others are denied, to certain mysteriously ultimate and ineluctable facts about the universe (or what Dr. Ewing inscrutably calls "the real" [22]). Likewise, the man who knows that p and q together entail r is a man who knows "how to make inferences."

What we commonly call "insight" may help mathematicians like Fermat and Ramanujan and logicians like Russell to get their answers more quickly than other people, and even to get answers which they would not have reached without it; but it is no substitute for a proof. "A priori

---

[21] See G. Ryle, "Knowing How and Knowing That," *Proc. Aristot. Soc.*, 1945–46, pp. 1–16 [pp. 167–80 this volume.

[22] E, p. 211.

insight," again, might *help* one to see the truth of complicated type-Q propositions; but it is no substitute for a discursive analysis of the types of situation and activity in connection with which the propositions are used, and the functions they perform in those situations. Intuition, visual imagery, insight and what-you-like may be short cuts to confidence in the truth of synthetic necessary propositions, but they cannot constitute a proof.

❖   **35**   ❖

INDUCTION AND EXPERIENCE
David Hume (1711–1776)

I.

All the objects of human reason or inquiry may naturally be divided into two kinds, to wit, *Relations of Ideas*, and *Matters of Fact*. Of the first kind are the sciences of Geometry, Algebra, and Arithmetic; and in short, every affirmation which is either intuitively or demonstratively certain. *That the square of the hypothenuse is equal to the square of the two sides*, is a proposition which expresses a relation between these figures. *That three times five is equal to the half of thirty*, expresses a relation between these numbers. Propositions of this kind are discoverable by the mere operation of thought, without dependence on what is anywhere existent in the universe. Though there never were a circle or triangle in nature, the truths demonstrated by Euclid would forever retain their certainty and evidence.

Matters of fact, which are the second objects of human reason, are not ascertained in the same manner; nor is our evidence of their truth, however great, of a like nature with the foregoing. The contrary of every matter of fact is still possible; because it can never imply a contradiction, and is conceived by the mind with the same facility and distinctness, as if ever so conformable to reality. *That the sun will not rise tomorrow* is no less intelligible a proposition, and implies no more contradiction than the affirmation, *that it will rise.* We should in vain, therefore, attempt to demonstrate

From *An Enquiry Concerning Human Understanding* (1748), section 4. The title of this selection has been supplied by the editors.

its falsehood. Were it demonstratively false, it would imply a contradiction, and could never be distinctly conceived by the mind.

It may, therefore, be a subject worthy of curiosity, to inquire what is the nature of that evidence which assures us of any real existence and matter of fact, beyond the present testimony of our senses, or the records of our memory. This part of philosophy, it is observable, has been little cultivated, either by the ancients or moderns; and therefore our doubts and errors, in the prosecution of so important an inquiry, may be the more excusable; while we march through such difficult paths without any guide or direction. They may even prove useful, by exciting curiosity, and destroying that implicit faith and security, which is the bane of all reasoning and free inquiry. The discovery of defects in the common philosophy, if any such there be, will not, I presume, be a discouragement, but rather an incitement, as is usual, to attempt something more full and satisfactory than has yet been proposed to the public.

All reasonings concerning matter of fact seem to be founded on the relation of *Cause and Effect.* By means of that relation alone we can go beyond the evidence of our memory and senses. If you were to ask a man, why he believes any matter of fact, which is absent; for instance, that his friend is in the country, or in France; he would give you a reason; and this reason would be some other fact; as a letter received from him, or the knowledge of his former resolutions and promises. A man finding a watch or any other machine in a desert island, would conclude that there had once been men in that island. All our reasonings concerning fact are of the same nature. And here it is constantly supposed that there is a connection between the present fact and that which is inferred from it. Were there nothing to bind them together, the inference would be entirely precarious. The hearing of an articulate voice and rational discourse in the dark assures us of the presence of some person: Why? because these are the effects of the human make and fabric, and closely connected with it. If we anatomize all the other reasonings of this nature, we shall find that they are founded on the relation of cause and effect, and that this relation is either near or remote, direct or collateral. Heat and light are collateral effects of fire, and the one effect may justly be inferred from the other.

If we would satisfy ourselves, therefore, concerning the nature of that evidence, which assures us of matters of fact, we must inquire how we arrive at the knowledge of cause and effect.

I shall venture to affirm, as a general proposition, which admits of no exception, that the knowledge of this relation is not, in any instance, attained by reasonings a priori; but arises entirely from experience, when we find that any particular objects are constantly conjoined with each other.

Let an object be presented to a man of ever so strong natural reason and abilities; if that object be entirely new to him, he will not be able, by the most accurate examination of its sensible qualities, to discover any of its causes or effects. Adam, though his rational faculties be supposed, at the very first, entirely perfect, could not have inferred from the fluidity and transparency of water that it would suffocate him, or from the light and warmth of fire that it would consume him. No object ever discovers, by the qualities which appear to the senses, either the causes which produced it, or the effects which will arise from it; nor can our reason, unassisted by experience, ever draw any inference concerning real existence and matter of fact.

This proposition, *that causes and effects are discoverable, not by reason but by experience,* will readily be admitted with regard to such objects, as we remember to have once been altogether unknown to us; since we must be conscious of the utter inability, which we then lay under, of foretelling what would arise from them. Present two smooth pieces of marble to a man who has no tincture of natural philosophy; he will never discover that they will adhere together in such a manner as to require great force to separate them in a direct line, while they make so small a resistance to a lateral pressure. Such events, as bear little analogy to the common course of nature, are also readily confessed to be known only by experience; nor does any man imagine that the explosion of gunpowder, or the attraction of a loadstone, could ever be discovered by arguments *a priori.* In like manner, when an effect is supposed to depend upon an intricate machinery or secret structure of parts, we make no difficulty in attributing all our knowledge of it to experience. Who will assert that he can give the ultimate reason, why milk or bread is proper nourishment for a man, not for a lion or a tiger?

But the same truth may not appear, at first sight, to have the same evidence with regard to events, which have become familiar to us from our first appearance in the world, which bear a close analogy to the whole course of nature, and which are supposed to depend on the simple qualities of objects, without any secret structure of parts. We are apt to imagine that we could discover these effects by the mere operation of our reason, without experience. We fancy, that were we brought on a sudden into this world, we could at first have inferred that one Billiard-ball would communicate motion to another upon impulse; and that we needed not to have waited for the event, in order to pronounce with certainty concerning it. Such is the influence of custom, that, where it is strongest, it not only covers our natural ignorance, but even conceals itself, and seems not to take place, merely because it is found in the highest degree.

But to convince us that all the laws of nature, and all the operations of bodies without exception, are known only by experience, the following reflections may, perhaps, suffice. Were any object presented to us, and were we required to pronounce concerning the effect, which will result from it, without consulting past observation; after what manner, I beseech you, must the mind proceed in this operation? It must invent or imagine some event, which it ascribes to the object as its effect; and it is plain that this invention must be entirely arbitrary. The mind can never possibly find the effect in the supposed cause, by the most accurate scrutiny and examination. For the effect is totally different from the cause, and consequently can never be discovered in it. Motion in the second Billiard-ball is a quite distinct event from motion in the first; nor is there anything in the one to suggest the smallest hint of the other. A stone or piece of metal raised into the air, and left without any support, immediately falls: but to consider the matter *a priori*, is there anything we discover in this situation which can beget the idea of a downward, rather than an upward, or any other motion, in the stone or metal?

And as the first imagination or invention of a particular effect, in all natural operations, is arbitrary, where we consult not experience; so must we also esteem the supposed tie or connection between the cause and effect, which binds them together, and renders it impossible that any other effect could result from the operation of that cause. When I see, for instance, a Billiard-ball moving in a straight line towards another; even suppose motion in the second ball should by accident be suggested to me, as the result of their contact or impulse; may I not conceive, that a hundred different events might as well follow from that cause? May not both these balls remain at absolute rest? May not the first ball return in a straight line, or leap off from the second in any line or direction? All these suppositions are consistent and conceivable. Why then should we give the preference to one, which is no more consistent or conceivable than the rest? All our reasonings *a priori* will never be able to show us any foundation for this preference.

In a word, then, every effect is a distinct event from its cause. It could not, therefore, be discovered in the cause, and the first invention or conception of it, *a priori*, must be entirely arbitrary. And even after it is suggested, the conjunction of it with the cause must appear equally arbitrary; since there are always many other effects, which, to reason, must seem fully as consistent and natural. In vain, therefore, should we pretend to determine any single event, or infer any cause or effect, without the assistance of observation and experience.

Hence we may discover the reason why no philosopher, who is rational and modest, has ever pretended to assign the ultimate cause of any natural operation, or to show distinctly the action of that power, which produces any single effect in the universe. It is confessed, that the utmost effort of human reason is to reduce the principles, productive of natural phenomena, to a greater simplicity, and to resolve the many particular effects into a few general causes, by means of reasonings from analogy, experience, and observation. But as to the causes of these general causes, we should in vain attempt their discovery; nor shall we ever be able to satisfy ourselves, by any particular explication of them. These ultimate springs and principles are totally shut up from human curiosity and inquiry. Elasticity, gravity, cohesion of parts, communication of motion by impulse; these are probably the ultimate causes and principles which we shall ever discover in nature; and we may esteem ourselves sufficiently happy, if, by accurate inquiry and reasoning, we can trace up the particular phenomena to, or near to, these general principles. The most perfect philosophy of the natural kind only staves off our ignorance a little longer: as perhaps the most perfect philosophy of the moral or metaphysical kind serves only to discover larger portions of it. Thus the observation of human blindness and weakness is the result of all philosophy, and meets us at every turn, in spite of our endeavors to elude or avoid it.

Nor is geometry, when taken into the assistance of natural philosophy, ever able to remedy this defect, or lead us into the knowledge of ultimate causes, by all that accuracy of reasoning for which it is so justly celebrated. Every part of mixed mathematics proceeds upon the supposition that certain laws are established by nature in her operations; and abstract reasonings are employed, either to assist experience in the discovery of these laws, or to determine their influence in particular instances, where it depends upon any precise degree of distance and quantity. Thus, it is a law of motion, discovered by experience, that the moment or force of any body in motion is in the compound ratio or proportion of its solid contents and its velocity; and consequently, that a small force may remove the greatest obstacle or raise the greatest weight, if, by any contrivance or machinery, we can increase the velocity of that force, so as to make it an overmatch for its antagonist. Geometry assists us in the application of this law, by giving us the just dimensions of all the parts and figures which can enter into any species of machine; but still the discovery of the law itself is owing merely to experience, and all the abstract reasonings in the world could never lead us one step towards the knowledge of it. When we reason *a priori*, and consider merely any object or cause, as it appears to the mind, independent of all observation, it never could suggest to us the notion of any distinct object, such as its effect; much less, show us the inseparable and inviolable connection between them. A man must be very sagacious who could discover by reasoning that crystal is the effect of heat, and ice of cold, without being previously acquainted with the operation of these qualities.

II.

But we have not yet attained any tolerable satisfaction with regard to the question first proposed. Each solution still gives rise to a new question as difficult as the foregoing, and leads us on to farther inquiries. When it is asked, *What is the nature of all our reasonings concerning matter of fact?* the proper answer seems to be, that they are founded on the relation of cause and effect. When again it is asked, *What is the foundation of all our reasonings and conclusions concerning that relation?* it may be replied in one word, Experience. But if we still carry on our sifting humor, and ask, *What is the foundation of all conclusions from experience?* this implies a new question, which may be of more difficult solution and explication. Philosophers, that give themselves airs of superior wisdom and sufficiency, have a hard task when they encounter persons of inquisitive dispositions, who push them from every corner to which they retreat, and who are sure at last to bring them to some dangerous dilemma. The best expedient to prevent this confusion, is to be modest in our pretensions; and even to discover the difficulty ourselves before it is objected to us. By this means, we may make a kind of merit of our very ignorance.

I shall content myself, in this section, with an easy task, and shall pretend only to give a negative answer to the question here proposed. I say then, that, even after we have experience of the operations of cause and effect, our conclusions from that experience are *not* founded on reasoning, or any process of the understanding. This answer we must endeavor both to explain and to defend.

It must certainly be allowed, that nature has kept us at a great distance from all her secrets, and has afforded us only the knowledge of a few superficial qualities of objects; while she conceals from us those powers and principles on which the influence of those objects entirely depends. Our senses inform us of the color, weight, and consistence of bread; but neither sense nor reason can ever inform us of those qualities which fit it for the nourishment and support of a human body. Sight or feeling conveys an idea of the actual motion of bodies; but as to that wonderful force or power, which would carry on a moving body forever in a continued change of place, and which bodies never lose but by communicating it to others; of this we cannot form the most distant conception. But notwithstanding this ignorance of natural powers [1] and principles, we always presume, when we see like sensible qualities, that they have like secret powers, and expect that effects, similar to those which we have experienced, will follow from them. If a body of like color and consistence with that bread, which we have formerly eat, be presented to us, we make no scruple of repeating the experiment, and foresee, with certainty, like nourishment and support. Now this is a process of the mind or thought, of which I would willingly know the foundation. It is allowed on all hands that there is no known connection between the sensible qualities and the secret powers; and consequently, that the mind is not led to form such a conclusion concerning their constant and regular conjunction, by anything which it knows of their nature. As to past *Experience*, it can be allowed to give *direct* and *certain* information of those precise objects only, and that precise period of time, which fell under its cognizance: but why this experience should be extended to future times, and to other objects, which for aught we know, may be only in appearance similar; this is the main question on which I would insist. The bread, which I formerly eat, nourished me; that is, a body of such sensible qualities was, at that time, endued with such secret powers: but does it follow, that other bread must also nourish me at another time, and that like sensible qualities must always be attended with like secret powers? The consequence seems nowise necessary. At least, it must be acknowledged that there is here a consequence drawn by the mind; that there is a certain step taken; a process of thought, and an inference, which wants to be explained. These two propositions are far from being the same, *I have found that such an object has always been attended with such an effect*, and *I foresee, that other objects, which are, in appearance, similar, will be attended with similar effects*. I shall allow, if you please, that the one proposition may justly be inferred from the other: I know, in fact, that it always is inferred. But if you insist that the inference is made by a chain of reasoning, I desire you to produce that reasoning. The connection between these propositions is not intuitive. There is required a medium, which may enable the mind to draw such an inference, if indeed it be drawn by reasoning and argument. What that medium is, I must confess, passes my comprehension; and it is incumbent on those to produce it, who assert that it really exists, and is the origin of all our conclusions concerning matter of fact.

This negative argument must certainly, in process of time, become altogether convincing, if many penetrating and able philosophers shall turn their inquiries this way and no one be ever able to discover any connecting

[1] The word, Power, is here used in a loose and popular sense. The more accurate explication of it would give additional evidence to this argument.

proposition or intermediate step, which supports the understanding in this conclusion. But as the question is yet new, every reader may not trust so far to his own penetration, as to conclude, because an argument escapes his inquiry, that therefore it does not really exist. For this reason it may be requisite to venture upon a more difficult task; and enumerating all the branches of human knowledge, endeavor to show that none of them can afford such an argument.

All reasonings may be divided into two kinds, namely, demonstrative reasoning, or that concerning relations of ideas, and moral reasoning, or that concerning matter of fact and existence. That there are no demonstrative arguments in the case seems evident; since it implies no contradiction that the course of nature may change, and that an object, seemingly like those which we have experienced, may be attended with different or contrary effects. May I not clearly and distinctly conceive that a body, falling from the clouds, and which, in all other respects, resembles snow, has yet the taste of salt or feeling of fire? Is there any more intelligible proposition than to affirm, that all the trees will flourish in December and January, and decay in May and June? Now whatever is intelligible, and can be distinctly conceived, implies no contradiction, and can never be proved false by any demonstrative argument or abstract reasoning *a priori*.

If we be, therefore, engaged by arguments to put trust in past experience, and make it the standard of our future judgment, these arguments must be probable only, or such as regard matter of fact and real existence, according to the division above mentioned. But that there is no argument of this kind, must appear, if our explication of that species of reasoning be admitted as solid and satisfactory. We have said that all arguments concerning existence are founded on the relation of cause and effect; that our knowledge of that relation is derived entirely from experience; and that all our experimental conclusions proceed upon the supposition that the future will be conformable to the past. To endeavor, therefore, the proof of this last supposition by probable arguments, or arguments regarding existence, must be evidently going in a circle, and taking that for granted, which is the very point in question.

In reality, all arguments from experience are founded on the similarity which we discover among natural objects, and by which we are induced to expect effects similar to those which we have found to follow from such objects. And though none but a fool or madman will ever pretend to dispute the authority of experience, or to reject that great guide of human life, it may surely be allowed a philosopher to have so much curiosity at least as to examine the principle of human nature, which gives this mighty authority to experience, and makes us draw advantage from that similarity which nature has placed among different objects. From causes which appear *similar* we expect similar effects. This is the sum of all our experimental conclusions. Now it seems evident that, if this conclusion were formed by reason, it would be as perfect at first, and upon one instance, as after ever so long a course of experience. But the case is far otherwise. Nothing so like as eggs; yet no one, on account of this appearing similarity, expects the same taste and relish in all of them. It is only after a long course of uniform experiments in any kind, that we attain a firm reliance and security with regard to a particular event. Now where is that process of reasoning which, from one instance, draws a conclusion, so different from that which it infers from a hundred instances that are nowise different from that single one? This question I propose as much for the sake of information, as with an intention of raising difficulties. I cannot find, I cannot imagine any such reasoning. But I keep my mind still open to instruction, if any one will vouchsafe to bestow it on me.

Should it be said that, from a number of uniform experiments, we *infer* a connection between the sensible qualities and the secret powers; this, I must confess, seems the same difficulty, couched in different terms. The question still recurs, on what process of argument this *inference* is founded? Where is the medium, the interposing ideas, which join propositions so very wide of each other? Is it confessed that the color, consistence, and other sensible qualities of bread appear not, of themselves, to have any connection with the secret powers of nourishment and support. For otherwise we could infer these secret powers from the first appearance of these sensible qualities, without the aid of experience; contrary to the sentiment of all philosophers, and contrary to plain matter of fact. Here, then, is our natural state of ignorance with regard to the powers and influence of all objects. How is this remedied by experience? It only shows us a number of uniform effects, resulting from certain objects, and teaches us that those particular objects, at that particular time, were endowed with such powers and forces. When a new object, endowed with similar sensible qualities, is produced, we expect similar powers and forces, and look for a like effect. From a body of like color and consistence with bread we expect like nourishment and support. But this surely is a step or progress of the mind, which wants to be explained. When a man says, *I have found, in all past instances, such sensible qualities conjoined with such secret powers:* And when he says, *Similar sensible qualities will always be conjoined with similar secret powers,* he is not guilty of a tautology, nor are these propositions in any respect the same. You say that the one proposition is an inference from the other. But you must confess that the inference is not intuitive; neither is it demonstrative: Of what nature is it, then? To say it is experimental, is begging the question. For all inferences from experiences suppose, as their foundation, that the future will resemble the past, and that similar powers will be conjoined with similar sensible qualities. If there be any suspicion that the course of nature may change, and that the past may be no rule for the future, all experience becomes useless, and can give rise to no inference or conclusion. It is impossible, therefore, that any arguments from experience can prove this resemblance of the past to the future; since all these arguments are founded on the supposition of that resemblance. Let the course of things be allowed hitherto ever so regular; that alone, without some new argument or inference, proves not that, for the future, it will continue so. In vain do you pretend to have learned the nature of bodies from your past experience. Their secret nature, and consequently all their effects and influence, may change, without any change in their sensible qualities. This happens sometimes, and with regard to some objects: Why may it not happen always, and with regard to all objects? What logic, what process of argument secures you against this supposition? My practice, you say, refutes my doubts. But you mistake the purport of my question. As an agent, I am quite satisfied in the point; but as a philosopher, who has some share of curiosity, I will not say skepticism, I want to learn the foundation of this inference. No reading, no inquiry has yet been able to remove my difficulty, or give me satisfaction in a matter of such importance. Can I do better than propose the difficulty to the public, even though, perhaps, I have small hopes of obtaining a solution? We shall at least, by this means, be sensible of our ignorance, if we do not augment our knowledge.

I must confess that a man is guilty of unpardonable arrogance who concludes, because an argument has escaped his own investigation, that therefore it does not really exist. I must also confess that, though all the learned, for several ages, should have employed themselves in fruitless search upon any subject, it may still, perhaps, be rash to conclude positively that the subject must, therefore, pass all human comprehension. Even though we examine all the sources of our knowledge, and conclude them unfit for such a subject, there may still remain a suspicion, that the enumeration is not complete, or the examination not accurate. But with regard to the present subject, there are some considerations which seem to remove all this accusation of arrogance or suspicion of mistake.

It is certain that the most ignorant and stupid peasants—nay infants, nay even brute beasts—improve by experience, and learn the qualities of natural objects, by observing the effects which result from them. When a child has felt the sensation of pain from touching the flame of a candle, he will be careful not to put his hand near any candle; but will expect a similar effect from a cause which is similar in its sensible qualities and appearance. If you assert, therefore, that the understanding of the child is led into this conclusion by any process of argument or ratiocination, I may justly require you to produce that argument; nor have you any pretence to refuse so equitable a demand. You cannot say that the argument is abstruse, and may possibly escape your inquiry; since you confess that it is obvious to the capacity of a mere infant. If you hesitate, therefore, a moment, or if, after reflection, you produce any intricate or profound argument, you, in a manner, give up the question, and confess that it is not reasoning which engages us to suppose the past resembling the future, and to expect similar effects from causes which are, to appearance, similar. This is the proposition which I intended to enforce in the present section. If I be right, I pretend not to have made any mighty discovery. And if I be wrong, I must acknowledge myself to be indeed a very backward scholar; since I cannot now discover an argument which, it seems, was perfectly familiar to me long before I was out of my cradle.

❖ 36 ❖

OF INDUCTION

Richard Whately (1787–1863)

1.

Much has been said by some writers of the superiority of the Inductive to the Syllogistic method of seeking truth; as if the two stood opposed to each other; and of the advantage of substituting the Organon of Bacon for that of Aristotle, etc. which indicates a total misconception of the nature of both. There is, however, the more excuse for the confusion of thought which prevails on this subject, because eminent Logical writers have treated, or at least have appeared to treat, of Induction as a kind of Argument distinct from the Syllogism; which if it were, it certainly might be contrasted with the Syllogism: or rather, the whole Syllogistic theory

From *Elements of Logic* (1826), Book IV, chapter 1.

would fall to the ground, since one of the very first principles it establishes, is that *all* Reasoning, on whatever subject, is one and the same process, which may be clearly exhibited in the form of Syllogisms. It is hardly to be supposed, therefore, that was the deliberate meaning of those writers; though it must be admitted that they have countenanced the error in question, by their inaccurate expressions.

This inaccuracy seems chiefly to have arisen from a vagueness in the use of the word Induction; which is sometimes employed to designate the process of *investigation* and of its collecting facts; sometimes, the deducing of an inference *from* those facts. The former of these processes (viz. that of observation and experiment) is undoubtedly *distinct* from that which takes place in the Syllogism; but then it is not a process of *argumentation;* the latter again *is* an argumentative process; but then it is, like all other arguments, capable of being Syllogistically expressed. And hence Induction has come to be regarded as a *distinct* kind of *argument* from the Syllogism. This Fallacy cannot be more concisely or clearly stated, than in the technical form with which we may now presume our readers to be familiar.

"Induction is distinct from Syllogism:
 Induction is a process of Reasoning"; therefore
"There is a process of Reasoning distinct from Syllogism."

Here "Induction," which is the Middle-Term, is used in different senses in the two Premisses.

Induction, so far forth as it is an *argument,* may, of course, be stated Syllogistically: but so far forth as it is a *process of inquiry* with a view to obtain the Premisses of that argument, it is, of course, out of the province of Logic: and the latter is the original and strict sense of the word. Induction means properly, not the inferring of the conclusion, but the *bringing in,* one by one, of instances, bearing on the point in question, till a sufficient number has been collected. The ambiguity, therefore, above alluded to, and which has led to much confusion, would be best avoided by saying that we do not, strictly speaking, reason *by* Induction, but reason *from* Induction: i.e., *from* our observations on one, or on several individuals, we draw a conclusion respecting the Class they come under: or, in like manner, from several Species, to the Genus which comprehends them:—in logical language, what we have predicated of certain *singular* terms, we proceed to predicate of a *common* term which comprehends them;—or proceed in the same manner from Species to Genus. E.g., "The Earth moves round the Sun in an elliptical orbit; so does Mercury; and Venus; and Mars, etc.: therefore a *Planet* (the common term comprehending these singulars) moves round," etc. "Philip was reckless of human life; so was Alexander, and J. Caesar; and Augustus, etc.: therefore this is the general character of a *Conqueror*."

Now it appears as if the most obvious and simplest way of filling up such enthymemes as these, expressed as they are, would be in the *third* figure; having of course a *particular* Conclusion:

> "Earth, Mercury, Venus, etc. move, etc.
> *Mi*. These are planets; therefore
> *Some* planets move, etc."

But when we argue from Induction we generally mean to infer more than a particular conclusion; and accordingly most logical writers present to us the argument in the form of a syllogism in *Barbara*; inserting, of course, a different minor premiss from the foregoing, viz.: the simple converse of it. And if I am allowed to assume, not merely that "Mercury, Venus, and whatever others I may have named, are Planets," but also, that "All Planets are these,"—that these are the *whole* of the individuals comprehended under the Term Planet,—I am no doubt, authorized to draw a universal conclusion. But such an assumption would, in a very great majority of cases where Induction is employed, amount to a palpable falsehood, if understood literally. For it is but seldom that we find an instance of what Logicians call a "perfect induction;" viz. where there is a complete enumeration of all the individuals, respecting which we assert collectively what we had before asserted separately; as "John is in England; and so is Thomas; and so is William; and all the sons of such a one are John, Thomas, and William; therefore all his sons are in England." Such cases, I say, seldom occur; and still more rarely can such an Induction (which Bacon characterizes as "res puerilis" [1])—since it does not lead the mind from what is better-known to what is less-known—serve any important purpose.

But in such Inductions as are commonly employed, the assumption of such a minor-premiss as in the above-example would be, as I have said, strictly speaking, a false assumption. And accordingly those logicians who state an argument from Induction in the above form, mean, I apprehend, that it is to be understood with a certain latitude; i.e., that, in such propositions as "all planets are Mercury, Venus, etc." or "all conquerors are Philip, Alexander, and Caesar," they mean, (by a kind of logical fiction) to denote that "all Conquerors are *adequately represented* by Philip, Alex-

---

[1] It may very well happen too, that (as in the example above) a certain circumstance may, in fact, belong to each individual of a certain class, and yet may have no connection, except accidentally, with the *Class itself, as such*; i.e., with the *description* of it, and that which *constitutes* it a Class . . . ["Res puerilis" means "a childish thing"— ed. note.]

ander, etc."—that these individual persons or cases are a sufficient *sample*, in respect of the matter in question, of the Class they belong to.

I think it clearer, therefore, to state simply and precisely what it is that we do mean to assert. And in doing this, we shall find that the expressed premiss of the enthymeme, viz.: that which contains the statement respecting the individuals—is the *Minor*; and that it is the Major that is suppressed, as being in all cases substantially the same: viz. that *what belongs to the individual or individuals we have examined, belongs* (certainly, or probably, as the case may be) *to the whole class under which they come.* E.g., From finding on examination of several sheep, that they each ruminate, we conclude that the same is the case with the *whole Species* of sheep: and from finding on examination of the sheep, ox, deer, and other animals deficient in upper cutting-teeth, that they each ruminate, we conclude (with more or less certainty) that quadrupeds thus deficient are ruminants: the hearer readily supplying, in sense, the suppressed major premiss; viz. that "what belongs to the individual sheep we have examined, is likely to belong to the whole species," etc.

Whether that which is properly called Induction (viz. the inquiry respecting the several individuals or species) be sufficiently ample, i.e., takes in a sufficient number of individual, or of specific cases,—whether the character of those cases has been correctly ascertained—and how far the individuals we have examined are *likely to resemble*, in this or that circumstance, *the rest* of the class, etc. etc., are points that require indeed great judgment and caution; but this judgment and caution are not to be aided by Logic; because they are, in reality, employed in deciding whether or not it is fair and allowable to *lay down your Premisses*; i.e., whether you are authorized or not, to assert, that "what is true of the individuals you have examined, is true of the whole class: " and that this or that *is* true of those individuals. Now, the rules of Logic have nothing to do with the truth or falsity of the Premisses; except, of course, when they are the conclusions of former arguments; but merely teach us to decide, not, whether the Premisses are *fairly laid down*, but whether the Conclusion *follows fairly from* the Premisses or not.

It has however been urged that what are described as the Major premisses in drawing inferences from Inductions, are resolvable ultimately into an assertion of the "Uniformity of the laws of Nature," or some equivalent proposition; and that this is, itself, obtained by *Induction*; whence it is concluded that there must be at least *one* Induction—and that, the one on which all others depend—incapable of being exhibited in a Syllogistic form.

But it is evident, and is universally admitted, that in *every* case where

an inference is drawn from Induction (unless that name is to be given to a
mere random guess without any grounds at all) we must form a judgment
that the instance or instances adduced are *"sufficient* to authorize the
Conclusion";—that it is *"allowable"* to take these instances as a sample
warranting an inference respecting the whole Class. Now the expression of
this judgment in words, is *the very Major premiss* alluded to. To acknowledge this, therefore, is to acknowledge that all reasoning from Induction
without exception does admit of being exhibited in a syllogistic form; and
consequently that to speak of one Induction that does *not* admit of it, is a
contradiction.

Whether the belief in the constancy of Nature's laws,—a belief of
which no one can divest himself—be intuitive and a part of the constitution of the human mind, as some eminent metaphysicians hold, or
acquired, and in what way acquired, is a question foreign to our present
purpose. For *that,* it is sufficient to have pointed out that the necessity of
assuming a universal Major premiss, expressed or understood, in order to
draw any legitimate inference from Induction, is virtually acknowledged
even by those who endeavor to dispute it.

2.

Whether then the Premiss may fairly be assumed, or not, is a point which
cannot be decided without a competent knowledge of the *nature of the
subject.* E.g., in most branches of Natural Philosophy, in which the circumstances that in any case affect the result, are usually far more clearly
ascertained than in human affairs, a *single instance* is usually accounted a
sufficient Induction; e.g. having once ascertained that an individual magnet
will attract iron, we are authorized to conclude that this property is universal. In Meteorology, however, and some other branches of Natural-
philosophy, in which less advancement has been made, a much more
copious Induction would be required. And in respect of the affairs of
human life, an inference from a single instance would hardly ever be
deemed allowable.

But it is worth remarking, that in all cases alike, of reasoning from
Induction, the greater or less degree of confidence we feel is always pro-
portioned to the belief of our having more or less completely *ascertained
all the circumstances* that bear upon the question. All men practically
acknowledge this to hold good in all cases alike, physical or moral, by
invariably attributing any *failure* in their anticipations in any case, to some
ignorance or miscalculation respecting some circumstances connected
with the case. . . .

In some subjects, however, there will usually be more of these circumstances difficult to be accurately ascertained, than in others; and the degree of certainty belonging to the Major premiss, will vary accordingly. But universally, the *degree of evidence* for any proposition we set out with as a Premiss (whether the expressed or the suppressed one) is not to be learned from mere Logic, nor indeed from *any one distinct* Science; but is the province of whatever Science furnishes the subject-matter of your argument. None but a Politician can judge rightly of the degree of evidence of a proposition in Politics; a Naturalist, in Natural History, etc.

E.g., from examination of many horned animals, as sheep, cows, etc., a Naturalist finds that they have cloven feet; now his *skill as a Naturalist* is to be shown in judging whether these animals are likely to resemble in the form of their feet all other horned animals; and it is the exercise of this judgment, together with the examination of individuals, that constitutes what is usually meant by the *Inductive process*; which is that by which we gain, what are properly, *new truths*; and which is not connected with Logic; being not what is strictly called *Reasoning*, but *Investigation*. But when this major Premiss is granted him, and is combined with the minor, viz. that the animals he has examined have cloven feet, then he *draws the Conclusion logically*; viz. that "the feet of all horned animals are cloven." [2] Again, if from several times meeting with ill-luck on a Friday, any one concluded that Friday, universally, is an unlucky day, one would object to his *Induction*; and yet it would not be, as an *argument, illogical*; since the Conclusion *follows* fairly, *if* you *grant* his implied Premiss; viz; that the events which happened on those particular Fridays are such as must happen, or are especially likely to happen, on all Fridays: but we should object to his *laying down this* Premiss; and therefore should justly say that his *Induction* is faulty, though his *argument* is correct.

And here it may be remarked, that the ordinary rule for fair argument, viz. that in an Enthymeme the suppressed Premiss should be always the one of whose truth *least doubt* can exist, is not observed in Induction: for the Premiss which is usually the more doubtful of the two, is, in the case, the *major*; it being in many cases not quite certain that the individuals, respecting which some point has been ascertained, are to be fairly regarded as a sample of the whole class: and yet the major Premiss is seldom expressed; for the reason just given, that it is easily understood; as being (*mutatis mutandis*) the *same* in every Induction.

What has been said of Induction will equally apply to Example;

[2] I have selected an Instance in which Induction is the *only* ground we have to rest on; no reason, that I know of, having ever been assigned that could have led us to conjecture this curious fact *a priori*.

which differs from it only in having a *singular*, instead of a general conclusion; and that, from a *single* case. E.g., in one of the instances above, if
the conclusion had been drawn, not respecting conquerors in general, but
respecting *this or that* conqueror, that he was not likely to be careful of
human life, *each* of the cases adduced to prove this would have been called
an Example. (See *Elements of Rhetoric*, Part I. ch. ii. § 6.)

Some have maintained that in employing an Example we proceed at
once from one individual case to another, without the intervention of any
universal premiss. But whether we are fairly *authorized* or not to draw an
inference from any example, must depend on what is called the PARAL-
LELISM of the two cases; i.e., their being likely to agree in respect of the
point in question: and the assertion, in words, of this parallelism, is a
universal proposition. He who has in his mind this proposition, has virtually asserted such a major premiss as I have been speaking of: and he who
has it not, if he should be right in the inference itself that he draws, is,
confessedly right only by chance.

From what has been said in this, . . . it will be seen, I trust, how
untenable are the objections which have of late years been urged, with an
air of triumph, against the above explanations of the process of reasoning
from Induction and Example. Those objections, though having, at the first
glance, an air of philosophical ingenuity, are found, on a closer examination, utterly unmeaning and self-destructive; since they imply a complete
admission, though in different words, of the very principle objected to.

❖ 37 ❖

ON INDUCTION

Bertrand Russell (1872–   )

. . . What things are there in the universe whose existence is known to us
owing to our being acquainted with them? So far, our answer has been that
we are acquainted with our sense-data, and, probably, with ourselves.

Chapter 6 of Bertrand Russell's *The Problems of Philosophy* (1912). Reprinted by
permission of the Clarendon Press, Oxford.

'hese we know to exist. And past sense-data which are remembered are
.nown to have existed in the past. This knowledge supplies our data.

But if we are to be able to draw inferences from these data—if we are
o know of the existence of matter, of other people, of the past before our
1dividual memory begins, or of the future, we must know general princi-
•les of some kind by means of which such inferences can be drawn. It
nust be known to us that the existence of some one sort of thing, A, is a
ign of the existence of some other sort of thing, B, either at the same
ime as A or at some earlier or later time, as, for example, thunder is a sign
•f the earlier existence of lightning. If this were not known to us, we could
1ever extend our knowledge beyond the sphere of our private experience;
nd this sphere, as we have seen, is exceedingly limited. The question we
1ave now to consider is whether such an extension is possible, and if so,
1ow it is effected.

Let us take as an illustration a matter about which none of us, in fact,
eel the slightest doubt. We are all convinced that the sun will rise tomor-
ow. Why? Is this belief a mere blind outcome of past experience, or can it
•e justified as a reasonable belief? It is not easy to find a test by which to
udge whether a belief of this kind is reasonable or not, but we can at least
1scertain what sort of general beliefs would suffice, if true, to justify the
1dgment that the sun will rise tomorrow, and the many other similar
1dgments upon which our actions are based.

It is obvious that if we are asked why we believe that the sun will rise
omorrow, we shall naturally answer, "Because it always has risen every
lay." We have a firm belief that it will rise in the future, because it has
isen in the past. If we are challenged as to why we believe that it will
ontinue to rise as heretofore, we may appeal to the laws of motion: the
:arth, we shall say, is a freely rotating body, and such bodies do not cease
o rotate unless something interferes from outside, and there is nothing
1utside to interfere with the earth between now and tomorrow. Of course it
night be doubted whether we are quite certain that there is nothing out-
;ide to interfere, but this is not the interesting doubt. The interesting
loubt is as to whether the laws of motion will remain in operation until
:omorrow. If this doubt is raised, we find ourselves in the same position
1s when the doubt about the sunrise was first raised.

The *only* reason for believing that the laws of motion will remain in
1peration is that they have operated hitherto, so far as our knowledge of the
past enables us to judge. It is true that we have a greater body of evidence
from the past in favor of the laws of motion than we have in favor of the
;unrise, because the sunrise is merely a particular case of fulfilment of the
laws of motion, and there are countless other particular cases. But the real

question is: Do *any* number of cases of a law being fulfilled in the past afford evidence that it will be fulfilled in the future? If not, it becomes plain that we have no ground whatever for expecting the sun to rise tomorrow, or for expecting the bread we shall eat at our next meal not to poison us, or for any of the other scarcely conscious expectations that control our daily lives. It is to be observed that all such expectations are only *probable*; thus we have not to seek for a proof that they *must* be fulfilled, but only for some reason in favor of the view that they are *likely* to be fulfilled.

Now in dealing with this question we must, to begin with, make an important distinction, without which we should soon become involved in hopeless confusions. Experience has shown us that, hitherto, the frequent repetition of some uniform succession or coexistence has been a *cause* of our expecting the same succession or coexistence on the next occasion. Food that has a certain appearance generally has a certain taste, and it is a severe shock to our expectations when the familiar appearance is found to be associated with an unusual taste. Things which we see become associated, by habit, with certain tactile sensations which we expect if we touch them; one of the horrors of a ghost (in many ghost-stories) is that it fails to give us any sensations of touch. Uneducated people who go abroad for the first time are so surprised as to be incredulous when they find their native language not understood.

And this kind of association is not confined to men; in animals also it is very strong. A horse which has been often driven along a certain road resists the attempt to drive him in a different direction. Domestic animals expect food when they see the person who usually feeds them. We know that all these rather crude expectations of uniformity are liable to be misleading. The man who has fed the chicken every day throughout its life at last wrings its neck instead, showing that more refined views as to the uniformity of nature would have been useful to the chicken.

But in spite of the misleadingness of such expectations, they nevertheless exist. The mere fact that something has happened a certain number of times causes animals and men to expect that it will happen again. Thus our instincts certainly cause us to believe that the sun will rise tomorrow, but we may be in no better a position than the chicken which unexpectedly has its neck wrung. We have therefore to distinguish the fact that past uniformities *cause* expectations as to the future, from the question whether there is any reasonable ground for giving weight to such expectations after the question of their validity has been raised.

The problem we have to discuss is whether there is any reason for believing in what is called "the uniformity of nature." The belief in the uniformity of nature is the belief that everything that has happened or will happen is an instance of some general law to which there are *no* exceptions. The crude expectations which we have been considering are all subject to exceptions, and therefore liable to disappoint those who entertain them. But science habitually assumes, at least as a working hypothesis, that general rules which have exceptions can be replaced by general rules which have no exceptions. "Unsupported bodies in air fall" is a general rule to which balloons and airplanes are exceptions. But the laws of motion and the law of gravitation, which account for the fact that most bodies fall, also account for the fact that balloons and airplanes can rise; thus the laws of motion and the law of gravitation are not subject to these exceptions.

The belief that the sun will rise tomorrow might be falsified if the earth came suddenly into contact with a large body which destroyed its rotation; but the laws of motion and the law of gravitation would not be infringed by such an event. The business of science is to find uniformities, such as the laws of motion and the law of gravitation, to which, so far as our experience extends, there are no exceptions. In this search science has been remarkably successful, and it may be conceded that such uniformities have held hitherto. This brings us back to the question: Have we any reason, assuming that they have always held in the past, to suppose that they will hold in the future?

It has been argued that we have reason to know that the future will resemble the past, because what was the future has constantly become the past, and has always been found to resemble the past, so that we really have experience of the future, namely of times which were formerly future, which we may call past futures. But such an argument really begs the very question at issue. We have experience of past futures, but not of future futures, and the question is: Will future futures resemble past futures? This question is not to be answered by an argument which starts from past futures alone. We have therefore still to seek for some principle which shall enable us to know that the future will follow the same laws as the past.

The reference to the future in this question is not essential. The same question arises when we apply the laws that work in our experience to past things of which we have no experience—as, for example, in geology, or in theories as to the origin of the Solar System. The question we really have to ask is: "When two things have been found to be often associated, and no instance is known of the one occurring without the other, does the occurrence of one of the two, in a fresh instance, give any good ground for expecting the other?" On our answer to this question must depend the validity of the whole of our expectations as to the future, the whole of the results obtained by induction, and in fact practically all the beliefs upon which our daily life is based.

It must be conceded, to begin with, that the fact that two things have been found often together and never apart does not, by itself, suffice to *prove* demonstratively that they will be found together in the next case we examine. The most we can hope is that the oftener things are found together, the more probable it becomes that they will be found together another time, and that, if they have been found together often enough, the probability will amount *almost* to certainty. It can never quite reach certainty, because we know that in spite of frequent repetitions there sometimes is a failure at the last, as in the case of the chicken whose neck is wrung. Thus probability is all we ought to seek.

It might be urged, as against the view we are advocating, that we know all natural phenomena to be subject to the reign of law, and that sometimes, on the basis of observation, we can see that only one law can possibly fit the facts of the case. Now to this view there are two answers. The first is that, even if *some* law which has no exceptions applies to our case, we can never, in practice, be sure that we have discovered that law and not one to which there are exceptions. The second is that the reign of law would seem to be itself only probable, and that our belief that it will hold in the future, or in unexamined cases in the past, is itself based upon the very principle we are examining.

The principle we are examining may be called the *principle of induction,* and its two parts may be stated as follows:

(*a*) When a thing of a certain sort A has been found to be associated with a thing of a certain other sort B, and has never been found dissociated from a thing of the sort B, the greater the number of cases in which A and B have been associated, the greater is the probability that they will be associated in a fresh case in which one of them is known to be present;

(*b*) Under the same circumstances, a sufficient number of cases of association will make the probability of a fresh association nearly a certainty, and will make it approach certainty without limit.

As just stated, the principle applies only to the verification of our expectation in a single fresh instance. But we want also to know that there is a probability in favor of the general law that things of the sort A are *always* associated with things of the sort B, provided a sufficient number of cases of association are known, and no cases of failure of association are known. The probability of the general law is obviously less than the probability of the particular case, since if the general law is true, the particular case must also be true, whereas the particular case may be true without the general law being true. Nevertheless the probability of the general law is increased by repetitions, just as the probability of the particular case is. We may therefore repeat the two parts of our principle as regards the general law, thus:

(a) The greater the number of cases in which a thing of the sort A has been found associated with a thing of the sort B, the more probable it is (if no cases of failure of association are known) that A is always associated with B;

(b) Under the same circumstances, a sufficient number of cases of the association of A with B will make it nearly certain that A is always associated with B, and will make this general law approach certainty without limit.

It should be noted that probability is always relative to certain data. In our case, the data are merely the known cases of coexistence of A and B. There may be other data, which *might* be taken into account, which would gravely alter the probability. For example, a man who had seen a great many white swans might argue, by our principle, that on the data it was *probable* that all swans were white, and this might be a perfectly sound argument. The argument is not disproved by the fact that some swans are black, because a thing may very well happen in spite of the fact that some data render it improbable. In the case of the swans, a man might know that color is a very variable characteristic in many species of animals, and that, therefore, an induction as to color is peculiarly liable to error. But this knowledge would be a fresh datum, by no means proving that the probability relatively to our previous data had been wrongly estimated. The fact, therefore, that things often fail to fulfill our expectations is no evidence that our expectations will not *probably* be fulfilled in a given case or a given class of cases. Thus our inductive principle is at any rate not capable of being *disproved* by an appeal to experience.

The inductive principle, however, is equally incapable of being *proved* by an appeal to experience. Experience might conceivably confirm the inductive principle as regards the cases that have been already examined; but as regards unexamined cases, it is the inductive principle alone that can justify any inference from what has been examined to what has not been examined. All arguments which, on the basis of experience, argue as to the future or the unexperienced parts of the past or present, assume the inductive principle; hence we can never use experience to prove the inductive principle without begging the question. Thus we must either accept the inductive principle on the ground of its intrinsic evidence, or forgo all justification of our expectations about the future. If the principle is unsound, we have no reason to expect the sun to rise tomorrow, to expect bread to be more nourishing than a stone, or to expect that if we throw ourselves off the roof we shall fall. When we see what looks like our best friend approaching us, we shall have no reason to suppose that his body is not inhabited by the mind of our worst enemy or of some total stranger. All our conduct is based upon associations which have worked in the past, and which we therefore regard as likely to work in the future; and this likelihood is dependent for its validity upon the inductive principle.

The general principles of science, such as the belief in the reign of law, and the belief that every event must have a cause, are as completely dependent upon the inductive principle as are the beliefs of daily life. All such general principles are believed because mankind have found innumerable instances of their truth and no instances of their falsehood. But this affords no evidence for their truth in the future, unless the inductive principle is assumed.

Thus all knowledge which, on a basis of experience tells us something about what is not experienced, is based upon a belief which experience can neither confirm nor confute, yet which, at least in its more concrete applications, appears to be as firmly rooted in us as many of the facts of experience. The existence and justification of such beliefs—for the inductive principle, as we shall see, is not the only example—raises some of the most difficult and most debated problems of philosophy. . . .

✧   38   ✧

IS THERE A PROBLEM OF INDUCTION?

Frederick L. Will (1909–   )

The problem of induction, as it is usually understood, concerns all our beliefs about matters of fact which go beyond our experience or observation, whether these beliefs are about past events, unobserved present events, or events in the future. It concerns all those cases where on the basis of observations now made, or remembered to have been made, one concludes that events or things which are not now observed have some

Reprinted from *The Journal of Philosophy*, Vol. XXXIX (1942), pp. 505–13, with the kind permission of the author and of the editors of *The Journal of Philosophy*.

specified character. For purposes of simplicity it seems advisable to restrict the consideration of the problem to just one of its temporal phases, namely, to beliefs concerning the future. As so restricted the problem still includes the question of the validity of scientific laws, since they are all statements about the future, as well as about the present and the past, which is the aspect of induction which has always appeared to philosophers as most challenging and fundamental. It is assumed that if the philosophical questions raised concerning induction can be disposed of in the case of beliefs about the future, the same disposition will apply, with little alteration, to questions about induction as a whole.[1]

I

The central question concerning inductive procedures in their reference to the future is whether they are capable at all of yielding genuine knowledge about future events. Those who find some special problem in induction, based upon some general inadequacy in inductive methods as a whole, answer that these methods do not and cannot produce such results. Now if someone is sure that, no matter how careful the employment of inductive procedures may be, they yet can never give us knowledge of the future, he must have some idea of what it would be like to know the future even though this knowledge is, as he believes, inductively unattainable. Of those philosophers, therefore, who say that we do not really know statements about the future it is legitimate and valuable to ask what, according to them, it would be like to know such statements. What kind of knowledge have they in mind which according to them is desirable but unattainable through inductive methods? What does it mean really to know the future?

In the case of some refined philosophical doubts, as John Wisdom has pointed out in his paper on "Philosophical Perplexity," [2] it is impossible to answer such direct fundamental questions; and this impossibility, this inability to describe at all what it would be like really to know what is in question eloquently testifies that although the verbal forms are closely similar to those commonly employed in expressing doubt or indecision, they do not in these cases express a legitimate doubt. In the case of induction, however, the matter is not so simple. Here the person expressing what seems to him a doubt can give some kind of answer to the question

---

[1] For much of the stimulation to draw the conclusions expressed in this paper I am indebted to my colleagues Professors A. E. Murphy and Max Black; the conclusions are of course entirely my own responsibility.

[2] Proc. Artist. Soc., N.S., Vol. XXXVII (1937), pp. 71–88.

of what it would be like really to know statements about the future. To know such statements really, he may very well reply, would be to know such statements with the certainty with which we know the statements of mathematics and logic. These latter fields positively exemplify genuine, certain knowledge. The inadequacy of our inductive beliefs about the future, as revealed in comparison with these more perfect forms of knowledge, show how far from genuine knowledge they are, how widely they are open to doubt.

An alternative or additional answer which may be given to this question by one expressing skepticism concerning inductive procedures would refer for examples of genuine knowledge to the data of immediate experience, contrasting the immediate certainties of these with the mediacy of inductive conclusions. That it is the comparison of inductive conclusions with the statements of mathematics and logic, on the one hand, and with the data of immediate experience, on the other, which is largely responsible for the philosophical doubts concerning induction, can be seen not only in the expressions of our contemporaries, as Margaret Macdonald has shown,[3] but also, and even more clearly, in a historical examination of the appearance of these doubts in modern philosophy. We cannot now perceive what is going to happen in the future, at least in the sense in which we perceive what is happening in our present experience. To the early rationalist philosophers this appeared to be no great difficulty, since they believed that discovery of the proper method would make it possible to demonstrate statements about the future in the way that the statements of mathematics and logic are demonstrated. Although this hope did not long persist, being dissipated considerably by the time of Locke and Leibniz, those who held it believed that the criteria for the use of "know," or as they would have said, the criteria for genuine knowledge in all fields, were the same as those used in logic and the rapidly developing disciplines of mathematics. The empiricists were sufficiently in agreement with the rationalists to follow them in this matter, but they soon came to realize what Hume established so convincingly, that all causal laws, in short all the laws of nature, do not and cannot satisfy the rationalist criteria. They all can be denied without self-contradiction. It is the conjunction of this discovery with the rationalist criteria for knowledge which, in the main, produced the skepticism which seemed to arise from Hume's examination of the causal relation. The only kind of knowledge recognized as genuine was either direct perceptual knowledge or demonstrative knowledge based on

[3] *Arist. Soc.*, Supp. Vol. XVI (1937), pp. 20–35. This same point has been made more recently by Norman Malcolm in "Certainty and Empirical Statements," *Mind*, N.S., Vol. LI (1942), pp. 18–46 [pp. 360–87 this volume].

the necessity of avoiding contradiction. The laws of nature, and indeed all statements about the future, fall in neither of these classes. Therefore none of these things can be known.

While the considerations just mentioned can well account for the skepticism expressed by some philosophers concerning induction, they fortunately do not justify it. It is entirely possible to admit all the evidence adduced by these skeptical philosophers, and to understand how that evidence has led them to express what appears to them as legitimate doubt, without admitting that the doubt is as sound as they believe. It may be granted willingly that one cannot perceive future events in the way that he perceives his present sense-data. It may be granted also, and even insisted upon, since there are still philosophers to be convinced on this point, that it is impossible to demonstrate statements about the future in the way in which it is possible to demonstrate a statement of mathematics or logic. Now quite clearly if the word "know" is to be restricted to immediately perceived events and logical demonstrations, then one cannot be properly said to know any statement about the future. But the sting of this conclusion is removed when one realizes that in this argument and conclusion the word "know" is used in a very special and unusual sense. If someone has reasons for wishing to restrict the word "cold" to temperatures below $-50°$ F., then it clearly follows that in his language the weather in the United States is seldom cold, or, as he might be tempted sometimes to put it, that it is seldom *really* cold. And if he were met by an objection from someone using this word in a more ordinary way and who consequently insisted that temperatures of as low as $+ 10°$ F., frequently found in the United States, are really cold, it would be obvious that these people are disputing about the use or definition of a word and not about actual temperatures or states of affairs in the United States. Though not so obviously, indeed in a much more complicated and perplexing way, this dispute over whether we really know any statements about the future is at bottom a dispute between those who wish and those who do not wish to restrict the use of "know" and other similar words in the above described ways. It does not of course make the slightest difference in the reliability of our inductive beliefs concerning the future whether we call them "knowledge," or "belief," or even "opinion." Whether we should continue to call them knowledge or not is a matter, like all other questions of linguistic usage, to be decided upon the basis of the relative convenience or usefulness of the alternative usages proposed. Unfortunately, however, statements which are legitimate only when interpreted in a very unusual way have a pernicious tendency to pass under their more ordinary interpretation. And it is apparently due to this that the statement that we do not know inductive conclusions about the future, though entirely legitimate when the word "know" is employed in the extraordinary sense noted above, has come to impose upon some philosophers, those who state it as well as those who hear it stated, as a statement about knowing and not knowing in a more ordinary sense of these terms, and hence as an expression of legitimate skepticism concerning inductive beliefs. Such is the origin of that peculiarly insoluble and tantalizing and wholly gratuitous pseudo-problem, the so-called Problem of Induction.

II

How this illegitimate skepticism and this pseudo-problem are the products of linguistic confusion may better be understood by returning to the original statement that we do not know, or do not *really* know, statements about the future. Suppose a philosopher has been rightly convinced, as described above, that we cannot perceive directly, nor can we logically demonstrate, what is going to happen in the future. And suppose further that this philosopher resolves that no matter what course others may take, he is going to use the word "know" just for the perceptions of immediate experience and the demonstrations of logic and mathematics, and that hence, whatever their status, inductive conclusions cannot literally be called knowledge. Very well. This philosopher is proposing, at least for himself, a radical alteration in the use of the word "know," its synonyms and their derivatives. In evaluating this proposal, as has been indicated, it is necessary to inquire what consequences it involves, how much and in what respects usage would be changed if it were adopted, and whether the new usage would be convenient or inconvenient, useful or not.

One very important consequence which the proposal involves, and which is only sometimes seen by its advocates, is that a consistent adoption of it requires that the word "know," and of course the other related ones, cannot be applied to any statement of fact whatever. The only statement which we should properly be said to know in the new usage would be the statements of mathematics and logic. Inductive conclusions about the present and past, as well as those about the future, may not be termed knowledge, for they do not fall in the two restricted classes of direct perception and demonstration. And although the immediate data of experience have been admitted into the class of knowledge, it can be shown that this class does not include also *statements* about these data. For all statements about these data, even statements which are intended to be just descriptions of the data themselves, are also by the very conditions of the use of terms, statements about other things not immediately perceived;

and this latter aspect of the affirmation has been strictly excluded from the class termed knowledge. If I say only, referring to my present immediate experience, "This is a yellow patch," I am stating, among other things, that there is some similarity between this patch and other colored patches which I have in the past perceived; and this similarity is not something immediately given and perceived as the color of the patch is given and perceived. The assertion of it, therefore, is a statement clearly not embraced in the restricted definition of knowledge, but one which can probably be defended and established, should any question arise concerning its correctness, only by the inductive methods already excluded from the class of things yielding strictly defined knowledge.

The philosopher proposing this alteration in the use of "know" may be prepared to accept these consequences. The restriction may be more confining than he at first realized, involving as a consequence that no one can be properly said to know any statement of fact, but he may nevertheless be willing to stand by his previous definition. But consider for a moment two of the phrases which were just used in attempting to describe accurately the consequences in use of this definition. It was said that inductive methods were "already excluded from the class of things yielding strictly defined knowledge," and, also, that in the usage proposed "no one can be properly said to know any statement of fact." Notice how similar these phrases are to phrases ordinarily employed to express genuine doubt and skepticism, and notice how easily they slide over into statements even more similar. How easy it would be to say, instead of "excluded from the class yielding strictly defined knowledge," "excluded from the class yielding *genuine* knowledge"; or instead of "no one can be properly said to know any statement of fact" to say "no one can *really* know any statement of fact." In a sense these latter phrases are entirely legitimate, so long as one is clear that what he means is that this or that kind of method, or statement, does not fall under a certain definition. But it is difficult to remain clear on this point when the expressions are so similar in form to expressions of a very different kind, and where they constantly mislead one by virtue of their similarity into thinking that he is making a very different statement from that which he started out to make, and from that which is justified by his premises.

For if one says that we do not really know statements about the future, or that such statements do not contain genuine knowledge, meaning by that simply that such statements do not fall in the class defined as containing only the data of immediate experience and the demonstrations of logic and mathematics, his statement, though true, is apt to be very misleading. For this is not what these words ordinarily mean. The point of his statement, which is that there is a genuine distinction between the methods used in establishing a belief about the future and those used in establishing some other kinds of data and belief, is presented in linguistic forms which are usually employed to express a distinction between beliefs which are *well*-established and those which are not, i.e., between what we know and what we do not know, not in the above specially defined sense of "know," but in the more normal sense of having well-grounded and true belief. Because the use of "know" or "knowledge" in either of these two statements is a highly unusual one, there is a constant tendency for them to be interpreted in their more normal senses; and the effect upon the statements is thus, unless they are constantly circumscribed, that as they sound exactly like ordinary expressions of doubt, so they come to be interpreted, almost inevitably, as expressing a doubt concerning the adequacy of all our knowledge, or rather, all our beliefs, about the future. Compare, for example, the two statements, "We don't really know how many German soldiers are in Libya," and, "We don't really know statements about the future." Of course the former statement, and countless like it, are expressions of genuine doubt, or gaps in our knowledge, as the latter term is commonly used. Affected by the great similarity of form one reacts also to the latter statement with a feeling of doubt and uneasiness altogether unwarranted by the state of affairs. "So we don't really know any statement about the future? Then all such statements, all scientific laws, are open to doubt." There is, then, some general problem of justifying all these inductive beliefs. Since the inductive methods alone do not give genuine knowledge, some further support must be found for our beliefs about the future which will rescue them from their dubious state. A Principle of the Uniformity of Nature must be established, or a transcendental method of proof devised in order to ensure the validity of the causal category for all possible experience. Somehow the future must be made safe for inductive prediction.

All the uneasiness, the pseudo-skepticism and the pseudo-problem of induction, would never appear if it were possible to keep clear that "know" in the statement that we do not know statements about the future is employed in a very special sense, not at all its ordinary one. Unless it is employed in a special sense the statement is outrageously false, for in the ordinary sense of "know" we do of course know countless things about the future. When "know" is employed in the special sense described above, the statement that we do not know statements about the future is undeniable, but also it involves no doubt or skepticism whatever. It is just when the statement has been established in its extraordinary sense, and by the tricks of language comes to be employed and affirmed in a more ordinary sense, without the appreciation that with the shift of meaning all substantiation has disappeared, that it appears to be a convincing expression of skepticism. Then it is that some philosophers begin to think and say, in spite of themselves, that perhaps after all the future may not be like the present and the past, that the general Order of Nature, whatever that is, may change, bringing down around our ears our world and our science.

III

There are many more things to be said, and said in greater and more convincing detail, concerning the causes and cure of the Problem of Induction than has been possible in this brief paper. What has been said concerning the genesis of this false problem in linguistic confusion has been prepared with the intention of helping those afflicted with the problem by enabling them to perceive that their difficulty is a linguistic one, and not one of our inability to know any facts, a difficulty, that is, about how to speak about inductive beliefs, and not one, though it appears to be, of the over-all insecurity of these beliefs. Yet it is possible that the statement of the position is so compressed and the arguments so abbreviated that they are more likely to irritate than persuade and help anyone genuinely puzzled by this problem. The statement that we do not know statements about the future has been assayed as valid only when the word "know" is defined in a very unusual and restricted way. Why there should be people with such strong, and in the end misleading, preferences in the definition of this word has undoubtedly not been made sufficiently clear. Although the outlines of the explanation, in terms of centuries of rationalist and intuitionist prejudice, accumulated and congealed before the inductive methods of modern science had begun to show their character and their power, seem substantially correct, a convincing proof of their correctness requires a much fuller account than could be given here of the Problem of Induction both as it arose in modern philosophy and as it is now stated by contemporaries who find the problem compelling and have tried to solve it. Finally there is need for a detailed treatment and effective disposition of that phase of the problem which inevitably appears in the form of the questions whether the future will be like the past, whether Nature is after all uniform, and whether this must not be established in some non-inductive manner before the conclusions of any inductive procedure can be adopted as a reasonable belief. This is one phase of the Problem of Induction which even to its most confirmed addicts must sometimes seem suspicious and false, and it is one which most readily and completely yields to the kind of resolving analysis which has here been presented. It is impossible to begin here to show how this specific form of the pseudo-skepticism can be diagnosed and removed, but in closing it may be valuable to suggest very briefly what, when the analysis has been performed, the positive, correct conclusions about the matter seem to be.

We do know statements about the future. Not only is it true that we know such statements in the ordinary sense of "know"; we also know them in the only sense in which it is appropriate, in which at bottom it is meaningful at all, to speak of knowing the future or knowing statements about it. What the arguments of the skeptics prove is not only that we do not know statements about the future in either of the senses to which the term "know" is restricted by them, but further that it is literally senseless and contradictory to speak of knowing them in either of these two ways. For future events, being by definition ones which have not yet occurred, cannot by that very condition be perceived like sense-data; and logically demonstrable sentences, being by definition tautologous or analytic, by that condition make no assertions about any events, whether past, present, or future. Nor does knowing statements about the future by inductive methods involve any over-all assumption about how the future will be like the present and past, about the so-called Uniformity of Nature. To say that inductive conclusions are uncertain because we do not know whether the future will be like the present and past simply begs the whole question. The progress of science is in good part progress in discovering just how much similarity with the present and past can be expected in the future. Every day, as scientists extend their inductive procedures further and further, we learn more and more about the similarity which the future will have with the present and past. This slow, step by step process cannot be circumvented or cut short, as the history of philosophy and science should show by now, by loose talk concerning the uniformity of nature or by some transcendental deduction of the categories of all possible experience. It cannot be denied that many of the statements of science and everyday life, scientific laws and predictions about the future, are not as well-founded as could be desired. But in so far as they are scientifically or inductively established at all, they have the only kind of establishment which they can get, the only kind of which it is even meaningful to speak, and, fortunately, and this is no mean consideration, the only kind that for the practical purposes of life they seem to need.

DISCRIMINATION OF CERTAINTY
AND PROBABILITY

W. Stanley Jevons (1835–1882)

We can never recur too often to the truth that our knowledge of the laws and future events of the external world is only probable. The mind itself is quite capable of possessing certain knowledge, and it is well to discriminate carefully between what we can and cannot know with certainty. In the first place, whatever feeling is actually present to the mind is certainly known to that mind. If I see blue sky, I may be quite sure that I do experience the sensation of blueness. Whatever I do feel, I do feel beyond all doubt. We are indeed very likely to confuse what we really feel with what we are inclined to associate with it, or infer inductively from it; but the whole of our consciousness, as far as it is the result of pure intuition and free from inference, is certain knowledge beyond all doubt.

In the second place, we may have certainty of inference; the fundamental laws of thought, and the rule of substitution are certainly true; and if my senses could inform me that A was indistinguishable in color from B, and B from C, then I should be equally certain that A was indistinguishable from C. In short, whatever truth there is in the premises, I can certainly embody in their correct logical result. But the certainty generally assumes a hypothetical character. I never can be quite sure that two colors are exactly alike, that two magnitudes are exactly equal, or that two bodies whatsoever are identical even in their apparent qualities. Almost all our judgments involve quantitative relations, and we can never attain exactness and certainty where continuous quantity enters. Judgments concerning discontinuous quantity or numbers, however, allow of certainty; I may establish beyond doubt, for instance, that the difference of the squares of 17 and 13 is the product of $17 + 13$ and $17 - 13$, and is therefore 30×4, or 120.

From *The Principles of Science* (1st ed., 1874; 2nd ed., 1877) (London: Macmillan and Co., 1892, pp. 235–39), chapter XI, section 11.

Inferences which we draw concerning natural objects are never certain except in a hypothetical point of view. It might seem to be certain that iron is magnetic, or that gold is incapable of solution in nitric acid; but, if we carefully investigate the meanings of these statements, they will be found to involve no certainty but that of consciousness and that of hypothetical inference. For what do I mean by iron or gold? If I choose a remarkable piece of yellow substance, call it gold, and then immerse it in a liquid which I call nitric acid, and find that there is no change called solution, then consciousness has certainly informed me that, with my meaning of the terms, "Gold is insoluble in nitric acid." I may further be certain of something else; for if this gold and nitric acid remain what they were, I may be sure there will be no solution on again trying the experiment. If I take other portions of gold and nitric acid, and am sure that they really are identical in properties with the former portions, I can be certain that there will be no solution. But at this point my knowledge becomes purely hypothetical; for how can I be sure without trial that the gold and acid are really identical in nature with what I formerly called gold and nitric acid. How do I know gold when I see it? If I judge by the apparent qualities—color, ductility, specific gravity, etc., I may be misled, because there may always exist a substance which to the color, ductility, specific gravity, and other specified qualities, joins others which we do not expect. Similarly, if iron is magnetic, as shown by an experiment with objects answering to those names, then all iron is magnetic, meaning all pieces of matter identical with my assumed piece. But in trying to identify iron, I am always open to mistake. Nor is this liability to mistake a matter of speculation only.[1]

The history of chemistry shows that the most confident inferences may have been falsified by the confusion of one substance with another. Thus strontia was never discriminated from baryta until Klaproth and Haüy detected differences between some of their properties. Accordingly chemists must often have inferred concerning strontia what was only true of baryta, and *vice versa*. There is now no doubt that the recently discovered substances, cesium and rubidium, were long mistaken for potassium.[2] Other elements have often been confused together—for instance, tantalum and niobium; sulphur and selenium; cerium, lanthanum, and didymium; yttrium and erbium.

Even the best known laws of physical science do not exclude false inference. No law of nature has been better established than that of uni-

[1] Professor Bowen has excellently stated this view. *Treatise on Logic.* Cambridge, U.S.A., 1866, p. 354.
[2] Roscoe's *Spectrum Analysis*, 1st edit., p. 98.

versal gravitation, and we believe with the utmost confidence that any body capable of affecting the senses will attract other bodies, and fall to the earth if not prevented. Euler remarks that, although he had never made trial of the stones which compose the church of Magdeburg, yet he had not the least doubt that all of them were heavy, and would fall if unsupported. But he adds, that it would be extremely difficult to give any satisfactory explanation of this confident belief.[3] The fact is, that the belief ought not to amount to certainty until the experiment has been tried, and in the meantime a slight amount of uncertainty enters, because we cannot be sure that the stones of the Magdeburg Church resemble other stones in all their properties.

In like manner, not one of the inductive truths which men have established, or think they have established, is really safe from exception or reversal. Lavoisier, when laying the foundations of chemistry, met with so many instances tending to show the existence of oxygen in all acids, that he adopted a general conclusion to that effect, and devised the name oxygen accordingly. He entertained no appreciable doubt that the acid existing in sea salt also contained oxygen;[4] yet subsequent experience falsified his expectations. This instance refers to a science in its infancy, speaking relatively to the possible achievements of men. But all sciences are and ever will remain in their infancy, relatively to the extent and complexity of the universe which they undertake to investigate. Euler expresses no more than the truth when he says that it would be impossible to fix on any one thing really existing, of which we could have so perfect a knowledge as to put us beyond the reach of mistake.[5] We may be quite certain that a comet will go on moving in a similar path *if* all circumstances remain the same as before; but if we leave out this extensive qualification, our predictions will always be subject to the chance of falsification by some unexpected event, such as the division of Biela's comet or the interference of an unknown gravitating body.

Inductive inference might attain to certainty if our knowledge of the agents existing throughout the universe were complete, and if we were at the same time certain that the same Power which created the universe would allow it to proceed without arbitrary change. There is always a possibility of causes being in existence without our knowledge, and these may at any moment produce an unexpected effect. Even when by the theory of probabilities we succeed in forming some notion of the compara-

[3] Euler's *Letters to a German Princess*, translated by Hunter. 2nd ed., Vol. ii. pp. 17, 18.
[4] Lavoisier's *Chemistry*, translated by Kerr. 3rd ed., pp. 114, 121, 123.
[5] Euler's *Letters*, vol. ii. p. 21.

tive confidence with which we should receive inductive results, it yet appears to me that we must make an assumption. Events come out like balls from the vast ballot-box of nature, and close observation will enable us to form some notion . . . of the contents of that ballot-box. But we must still assume that, between the time of an observation and that to which our inferences relate, no change in the ballot-box has been made.

❖   40   ❖

CERTAINTY AND INDUCTION

Thomas Fowler (1832–1904)

Since the publication of my second edition, there has appeared an important work on Scientific Method, entitled "The Principles of Science," by Professor Stanley Jevons, of Owens College, Manchester. To this I have made occasional references in the footnotes to my present edition. But, as I differ entirely from Professor Jevons on the fundamental question of the validity of our inductive inferences, I think it desirable to offer a few remarks on this point in the present place, rather than to introduce controversial matter into the body of the work.

Mr. Jevons over and over again asserts the uncertainty, or the mere probability, of all inductive inferences. Thus, for instance, in his chapter on the Philosophy of Inductive Inference, he says:—"I have no objection to use the words cause and causation, provided they are never allowed to lead us to imagine that our knowledge of nature can attain to certainty." [1] And again: "We can never recur too often to the truth that our knowledge of the laws and future events of the external world is only probable." [2] Once more: "By induction we gain no certain knowledge; but by observation, and the inverse use of deductive reasoning, we estimate the probability that an event which has occurred was preceded by conditions of specified character, or that such conditions will be followed by the event." [3]

From the Preface to the 3rd edition (1876) of *The Elements of Inductive Logic*. The title of this selection has been supplied by the editors.

[1] Vol. i, p. 260.
[2] Ibid., p. 271 [p. 353 this volume].
[3] Ibid., p. 257.

At the same time, I am quite unable to reconcile with these passages other passages, such as those in which Mr. Jevens says: "We know that a penny thrown into the air will certainly fall upon a flat side, so that either the head or tail will be uppermost," [4] or, "I can be certain that nitric acid will not dissolve gold, provided I know that the substances employed really correspond to those on which I tried the experiment previously." [5]

But, waiving the question of inconsistency, I maintain as against Mr. Jevons that many of our inductive inferences have all the certainty of which human knowledge is capable. Is the law of gravitation one whit less certain than the conclusion of the 47th Proposition of the First Book of Euclid? Or is the proposition that animal and vegetable life cannot exist without moisture one whit less certain than the truths of the multiplication table? Both these physical generalizations are established by the Method of Difference, and, as *actual* Laws of Nature, admit, I conceive, of no doubt. But it may be asked if they will always continue to be Laws of Nature? I reply that, unless the constitution of the Universe shall be changed to an extent which I cannot now even conceive, they will so continue, and that no reasonable man has any practical doubt as to their continuance. And why? Because they are confirmed by the whole of our own experiences, which in both these cases is of enormous extent and variety, by the experience of our ancestors, and by all that we can ascertain of the past history of nature, while their reversal would involve the reversal of almost all the other laws with which we are acquainted. Still, it must be confessed that all our inferences from the present to the future are, in one sense, hypothetical, the hypothesis being that the circumstances on which the laws themselves depend will continue to be the same as now, that is, in the present case, that the constitution of nature, in its most general features, will remain unchanged; or, to put it in still another form, that the same causes will continue to produce the same effects. What would happen if this expectation were ever frustrated, it is absolutely impossible for us to say, so completely is it assumed in all our plans and reasonings.

We may say, then, that there are many inductions as to the *actual* constitution of nature which we may accept with certainty, while, with respect even to the distant future, we may accept them with equal certainty, on the hypothesis that the general course of nature will not be radically changed. And if the general course of nature were changed, might not the change affect our faculties as well as the objects of our knowledge; and, in that case, are we certain that we should still regard things that are

[4] Ibid., p. 228. Mr. Jevons, however, curiously enough is not certain about the truth of the Law of Gravitation. See below.
[5] Ibid., p. 270.

equal to the same thing as equal to one another, or assume that a thing cannot both be and not be in the same place at the same time? There is, in fact, no limit to the possibility of skepticism with regard to the persistency either of the laws of external nature or of the laws of mind. But all our reasonings depend on the hypothesis that the most general laws of matter and the most general laws of mind will continue to be what they are, and of the truth of this hypothesis no reasonable man entertains any practical doubt.[6]

There is, then, I contend, no special uncertainty attaching to the truths arrived at by induction. They are, indeed, like all other truths, relative to the present constitution of nature and the present constitution of the human mind, but this is a limitation to which all our knowledge alike is subject, and which it is vain for us to attempt to transcend. Syllogistic reasoning implies a particular constitution of the mind, as much as inductive reasoning implies a particular constitution of nature. Both mind and nature might, of course, be radically changed by an omnipotent power, but what the consequences of that change might be it is utterly impossible for us to say.

The uniformity of nature, the trustworthiness of our own faculties—these are the ultimate generalizations which lie at the root of all our beliefs, and are the conditions of all our reasonings. It is, of course, always possible to insinuate doubts as to either, but, however curious and entertaining such doubts may be, they have no practical influence even on those who originate them. Even Mr. Jevons himself, we have seen, when not under the dominion of his theory, speaks of some of the results of induction as certain, and we can hardly conceive men of science commonly speaking of the most firmly established generalizations of mechanics, optics, or chemistry, simply as conclusions possessing a high degree of probability.

Still, Mr. Jevons, appearing not in the character of a physicist, but of a logician, tells us that "the law of gravitation itself is only probably true." [7] It would be interesting to learn what is the exact amount of this "probability," or, if it be meant that we can only be certain that the force of gravity is acting here and now, it would be an interesting inquiry to ascertain what is the exact value of the "probability" that it is at this moment acting in Manchester as well as in Oxford, or that it will be acting at this time tomorrow as well as today.

---

[6] Thus Mr. Jevons, who, when he begins to theorize, has doubts as to the truth of the law of gravitation, has no doubt, when he throws a penny up into the air, that it will fall on a flat side.

[7] Ibid., p. 300.

But, if the conclusions of Induction are thus uncertain, where, according to Mr. Jevons, are we to find certainty? "Certainty belongs only to the deductive process and to the teachings of direct intuition." [8] Does it then belong to the conclusions of deduction? Apparently not, for, at the very beginning of the work,[9] we are told that "in its ultimate origin or foundation, all knowledge is inductive," and Mr. Jevons is, of course, too practiced a logician to suppose that the conclusion can be more certain than the premises. The conclusions of geometry, therefore, partake of the same "uncertainty" as the results of the physical sciences, and the region of "certainty" is confined to our direct intuitions and to the rules of syllogism (supposing, that is, a difference to be intended between the "deductive process" and deductive results). We venture to suggest that this small residuum of "certainty" would soon yield to solvents as powerful as those which Mr. Jevons has applied to the results of induction (and apparently also of deduction); and that, therefore, its inherent "uncertainty" is no special characteristic of that method, but one which it shares with all our so-called knowledge.

The fact is that in all reasoning, whether inductive or deductive, we make, and must make, assumptions which may theoretically be questioned, but of the truth of which no man, in practice, entertains the slightest doubt. Thus, in syllogistic reasoning, we assume at every step the trustworthiness of memory; we assume, moreover, the validity of the premises, which, as Mr. Jevons acknowledges, must ultimately be guaranteed either by induction or direct observation; lastly, we assume the validity of the primary axioms of reasoning, which, according to different theories, are either obtained by induction or assumed to be necessary laws of the human mind. In this sense, all reasoning and all science is hypothetical, and the assumption of the Uniformity of Nature does not render inductive reasoning hypothetical in any special sense of the term. For, if the Laws of the Uniformity of Nature and of Universal Causation admit of exceptions or are liable to ultimate frustration, so, for aught we know, may the axioms of syllogistic reasoning or the inductions by which we have established the trustworthiness of our faculties. And, if the conceptions of uniformity and causation be purely relative to man, so, for aught we know, may be the so-called laws of thought themselves.[10] Induction would only be hypothetical

[8] Ibid., p. 309.
[9] Ibid., p. 14.
[10] According to the view of the nature and ultimate origin of human knowledge, accepted both by Mr. Jevons and myself, it is, in fact, no paradox but a mere truism to say that the fundamental axioms of reasoning are themselves only particular uniformities of nature, arrived at by the same evidence and depending for their justification on the same grounds as those ultimate generalizations on causation to which we give

in a special sense, if we had any reasonable ground for doubting the truth of the hypotheses [11] on which it rests.

But, as "in its ultimate origin or foundation, all knowledge" (including, of course, that of the laws which govern the syllogistic process itself) "is inductive," Professor Jevons must either employ the word "certain" in a variety of senses, or he must be prepared with the philosophers of the New Academy to maintain the uncertainty of all knowledge whatsoever.

❖ 41 ❖

CERTAINTY AND EMPIRICAL STATEMENTS
Norman Malcolm (1911–   )

I.

It is a view commonly held by present-day philosophers, that it can never be known with absolute certainty that any empirical statement is true. Ordinarily they wish to include among empirical statements every statement which implies the existence of a material thing, every statement which implies that some other person is having some sensation, feeling or experience, and every statement which implies the existence of something in the past. Professor C. I. Lewis has said that ". . . all empirical knowledge is probable only." [1] Mr. A. J. Ayer has said that "no genuine synthetic proposition . . . can be absolutely certain." [2] And more recently, ". . .

Reprinted from *Mind*, Vol. LI (1942), with the permission of the author and of the editor of *Mind*.

---

the special names of the Law of Universal Causation and the Law of the Uniformity of Nature.

[11] I need hardly say that I am not here using the word "hypothesis" in the sense of an unverified assumption. Reasoning, both inductive and deductive, is found on analysis to depend, in the last resort, on certain assumptions or hypotheses, but then the truth of these assumptions or hypotheses is guaranteed by the whole experience of the human race, past and present, and beyond this guarantee we conceive that there is no other attainable. In other words, all truth is relative to our faculties of knowing, and this condition it is in vain for us to attempt to transcend.

[1] *Mind and the World-Order*, 1929, p. 309.

[2] *Language, Truth, and Logic*, 1936, p. 127.

statements about material things are not conclusively verifiable." ³ Mr. Bertrand Russell has said, "Let us take first the belief in common objects such as tables and chairs and trees. We all feel quite sure about these in ordinary life, and yet our reasons for confidence are really very inadequate." ⁴ And more recently, ". . . we can never be completely certain that any given proposition is true." ⁵

It is well known that Professor G. E. Moore stoutly repudiates all such "skeptical" assertions. In his "A Defence of Common Sense," ⁶ Moore said that he knew *with certainty* that the earth has existed for a long time; that there have been many other human beings upon it both before and during his lifetime; that those other human beings have had many thoughts, experiences and feelings; and that many human beings beside himself have known with certainty the truth of these statements. In a recent unpublished paper, Moore, in referring to some remarks made by John Wisdom, makes the following statement, "He says that he sometimes *knows for certain* that a thing he points at is cheese; and therefore *knows in the strict sense* that he won't have to correct himself tomorrow; and goes on to say that it is often *absolutely* certain that what he points at is cheese. . . . About all this . . . I quite agree with him. It is, I should say, *absolutely* certain that this is a piece of paper with writing on it." In his "Proof of an External World," ⁷ Moore says that he can prove that there are material things. "How? By holding up my two hands, and saying, as I make a certain gesture with my right hand, 'Here is one hand,' and adding, as I make a certain gesture with the left, 'and here is another.' " ⁸ He goes on to say that his proof satisfies several conditions of a rigorous proof. One condition which a rigorous proof must satisfy, is that the premise must be known to be true. And "I certainly did at the moment know that which I expressed by the combination of certain gestures with saying the words 'there is one hand and here is another.' I *knew* that there was one hand in the place indicated by combining a certain gesture with my first utterance of 'here' and that there was another in the different place indicated by combining a certain gesture with my second utterance of 'here.' How absurd it would be to suggest that I did not know it, but only believed it, and that perhaps it was not the case. You might as well suggest that I do not know that I am now standing up and talking—that perhaps

³ Ayer, *The Foundations of Empirical Knowledge*, 1940, p. 239.
⁴ *Philosophy*, 1927, p. 3.
⁵ *An Inquiry into Meaning and Truth*, 1940, p. 166.
⁶ *Contemporary British Philosophy*, Second Series, edited by J. H. Muirhead.
⁷ *Proceedings of the British Academy*, Volume XXV, 1939.
⁸ Op. cit., p. 25.

after all I'm not, and that it's not quite certain that I am." [9] In general, Moore would maintain that vast numbers of empirical statements are known with certainty; and he would maintain that among the empirical statements that are known with certainty are statements about material things, statements about other minds, and statements about the past.

I wish to say that what Moore says is true, and that what is said by the numerous philosophers whom he opposes is false. My main interest is, however, not in showing this, but in clarifying the nature of the dispute. I want to examine the powerful temptations that have led those philosophers to assert such a striking paradox as that no empirical statements are known with certainty. I want to consider to what extent their contention is philosophically illuminating, and to what extent it is pointless and misleading.

Let us notice first of all the non-empirical character of the dispute. When Moore holds up his hand in front of the philosopher and says that it is absolutely certain that here is a hand, and the philosopher says that it is not absolutely certain, there is no empirical evidence which Moore could produce which would make the philosopher agree with him. It would be useless for Moore to tell the philosopher to step up closer or to touch it. This shows that Moore and the philosopher do not disagree about any question of empirical fact. It may be said that what the philosopher thinks is that it is not absolutely certain that they are not dreaming or having an hallucination, while Moore thinks it *is* absolutely certain that they are not; and this, it may be said, is an empirical dispute. But the answer to this is that there is not any sort nor any amount of empirical evidence which could be submitted to the philosopher, in the face of which he would give up his contention, and agree that it is absolutely certain that they are not dreaming, and are seeing a real hand. In other words, when the philosopher says that it is not absolutely certain that Moore is showing him a hand, he is not making any empirical claim, i.e., any claim which could be substantiated or refuted by empirical evidence. And the arguments which he gives for his view are not empirical arguments but philosophical ones.

Let us now examine one of the most tempting of these arguments. I shall quote from Professor Lewis:—

"Obviously in the statement 'this penny is round' I assert implicitly *everything the failure of which would falsify the statement.* The implicit prediction of *all* experience which is essential to its *truth* must be contained in the original judgment. Otherwise, such experience would be irrelevant. All that further experience the failure of which would lead to the repudiation of the apprehension as illusory or mistaken is predicted in

[9] Ibid., p. 26.

the judgment made. Now suppose we ask: How long will it be possible to verify in some manner the fact that this penny is round? What totality of experience would verify it completely beyond the possibility of necessary reconsideration? . . . it seems to be the fact that *no* verification would be absolutely complete; that all verification is partial and a matter of degree. . . . Is it not the case that the simplest statement of objective particular fact implicitly asserts something about possible experience throughout all future time; that theoretically every objective fact is capable of some (partial) verification at any later date, and that no totality of such experience is absolutely and completely sufficient to put our knowledge of such particulars beyond all possibility of turning out to be in error? So far as this is true, *all interpretation of particulars and all knowledge of objects is probable* only, however high the degree of probability. Every such judgment about the real external world remains forever at the mercy of future possible experience. Between the immediate awareness, 'this looks round,' and the objective interpretation, 'this is round,' there lies all the difference between this present moment and all time; between an experience which is now complete and *had*, and a totality of possible experience which is unlimited and inexhaustible." [10]

I wish to call attention to an important feature of this line of argument. Lewis declares that no judgment about the objective character of a particular object is capable of *complete* verification. And this is because a complete verification would consist of a "totality of experience" acquired "throughout all future time." No experience acquired in a finite course of time would comprise a *complete* verification, for "the verifiable consequences of any fact last as long as time itself." [11] We might put the point in this way: No empirical statement can be completely verified because a "complete" verification would consist of an *infinite* number of verification tests. Any verification which comprises less than an infinite number of tests is only a "partial" verification, and can make the truth of the statement only probable, never certain.

We can see that if "*p* is completely verified" means "an infinite number of favorable verification tests have been performed with regard to *p*," then it certainly is the case that no proposition has ever been, or ever will be, completely verified. The reason this is so, is that it is *self-contradictory* to say that an infinite number of tests have been performed, or will be performed. It is self-contradictory to say with regard to a given proposition, *p*, that certain people began at a definite time, t_1, to make verification tests, and at a certain definite time, t_2, they ceased to make

[10] Op. cit., pp. 279–281.
[11] Ibid., p. 282.

tests, and between t_1 and t_2 they performed an infinite number of tests. The reason, then, that Professor Lewis is sure that no empirical proposition can be completely verified, is that he *gives* such a meaning to the phrase "complete verification," that it would be self-contradictory to say that any proposition is completely verified. And he gives such a meaning to the phrase "partial verification," that it is *tautological* to say of any empirical proposition that it can only be partially verified; for this simply means that any number of tests which are performed with regard to it will be a finite number. If now the philosopher identifies "it is probable that p" with "p is partially verified," and "it is certain that p" with "p is completely verified," he can then derive the philosophical proposition, "No empirical statement can be certain, but at best only probable."

One main source of the view that empirical statements are never certain, is that some philosophers are led to interpret the meaning of the phrase "it is certain," as applied to empirical statements, in such a way that they suppose that it is self-contradictory to say of an empirical statement that its truth is certain. If these philosophers were right, then it would be the case that when in ordinary life we say things like "It's quite certain that the ship was torpedoed," "I know for certain that that building to the left is the Empire State," "It's absolutely certain that he's got appendicitis," we should be saying something self-contradictory. It is indeed often the case that when people say things of this sort, what they say is false. But nothing could be more absurd than to suppose that what they say is self-contradictory. Nothing could be more absurd than to suppose that when in ordinary life a person says "It's absolutely certain that the grain in that field is oats, not wheat," what he means is that he or some other person or persons have performed an infinite number of tests to determine whether the grain is oats or wheat.

But I want to ignore for the moment the fact that the philosophers are mistaken in thinking that the meaning which they are led to attach to the expression "it is certain that" is the ordinary meaning, or even *an* ordinary meaning of it. I want to point out how misleading is their way of talking. They say that we cannot have certainty about empirical matters, that we can have only probability. This sounds as if our knowledge of empirical matters falls short of an *ideal*, as if we should have to get along as well as possible with the *inferior* sort of knowledge that we are actually able to attain. It turns out, however, that the philosophers have *defined* "certainty" in such a way that knowing with certainty about empirical matters is not an ideal at all, but a logically impossible state of affairs. The idea that we are unfortunate in having what is only second-best, which is often conveyed by the statement that our empirical knowledge is "only probable" or "merely probable," is totally misleading, because the philosophers have defined "probable" in such a way that it would not make sense, would be logically absurd, to say that the truth of an empirical statement was "more than probable." One can fall short of an ideal, only if it makes sense to speak of *attaining* the ideal. But the philosophers have defined "certainty" in such a way that it does not make sense to speak of attaining certainty. And therefore it does not make sense to speak of *failing* to attain certainty.

It is not difficult to find examples of philosophers attaching a self-contradictory meaning to an ordinary expression. Mr. Russell provided us with an example of this tendency when he said: ". . . there are reasons . . . for being more or less distrustful of memory. It is obvious that no *direct* confirmation of a belief about a past occurrence is possible, because we cannot make the past recur. We can find confirmation of an indirect kind in the revelations of others and in contemporary records." [12] This is offered as one reason for saying that "the fact that we cannot free ourselves from dependence upon memory in building up knowledge is, *prima facie*, a reason for regarding what passes for knowledge as not quite certain." [13] Russell says that we cannot directly confirm any statement about a past event "because we cannot make the past recur." This seems to show that he is attaching such a meaning to the phrase "directly confirm," that we could directly confirm the occurrence of a past event only by witnessing now that event. But we cannot witness *now* a past event, because we could witness it now only if it occurred now; and it is self-contradictory to speak of numerically the same event occurring at two different times. In other words, Russell defines "directly confirm" in such a way that it is self-contradictory to speak of directly confirming any statement about the past. Since the fact that we cannot "directly" confirm statements about the past is supposed to be a ground for proving that "what passes for knowledge is not quite certain," it appears that Russell means by "certain knowledge" something likewise self-contradictory.

It is clear that the meaning which Russell gives to the phrase "directly confirm" is no ordinary meaning of it. Suppose that it is suspected that Robinson was in the house on the night of the murder. What would ordinarily be said to indirectly confirm this suspicion, and what to directly confirm it? If there was found in an ash tray a butt of a cigarette of the rather uncommon brand that Robinson smoked, this might be called an indirect confirmation. But if several reliable witnesses reported that they had seen Robinson enter the house, we should say that this *directly* con-

[12] *Philosophy*, p. 7.
[13] Ibid., pp. 7–8.

firmed the suspicion. If the district attorney had only the cigarette butt for evidence, he might report that he had not yet been able to directly confirm the suspicion. He would regard direct confirmation as a goal to be striven for. In the ordinary sense of the words, "direct confirmation" is *superior* to "indirect confirmation." But Russell gives such a meaning to the phrase "direct confirmation" that it would be ridiculous to say that direct confirmation was superior to indirect confirmation. For direct confirmation would be something self-contradictory.

Let us notice carefully the nature of Mr. Russell's procedure in this case. He takes the two expressions "direct confirmation" and "indirect confirmation," whose ordinary meaning is such that direct confirmation of a statement about the past is superior to indirect confirmation, i.e., direct confirmation is an ideal state of evidence, which in many cases is difficult to obtain, but which it makes sense to speak of obtaining. Russell now gives a self-contradictory meaning to "direct confirmation," and thereby makes the "discovery" that we can never directly confirm any statement about the past. Whereupon, it is concluded that we are forever condemned to have only evidence of an inferior sort with regard to statements about the past, and that we shall never be justified in having complete confidence in any of them. What has happened is that Mr. Russell has been tempted to invent such meanings for the phrases "directly confirm" and "indirectly confirm," that "directly confirm" becomes self-contradictory, and "only indirectly confirm" becomes tautologous; and he has shown nothing whatever about the ordinary meanings of these expressions. Exactly the same thing happened in the case of Professor Lewis and the phrases "completely verify" and "partially verify."

This same subtle philosophical procedure may be illustrated in connection with a different class of empirical statements, i.e., statements about other minds. Philosophers are fond of saying, "You can never know for certain that another person is having an experience, or sensation, or feeling, because you can never be directly aware of another person's feelings or experiences. You can only be directly aware of your own." It then turns out that by being "directly aware" of Jones's toothache, they mean *having* numerically the same toothache that Jones is having. And so what their declaration that "you can never know for certain that another person is having a toothache" amounts to, is that "You can never have another person's toothache, you can have only your own toothache." But this is a misleading way of saying that the expression, "I am having numerically the same toothache that someone else is having," is self-contradictory.

What the philosophers have done, is to invent a self-contradictory meaning for the expression "knowing for certain that another person is having an experience." They then announce regretfully, that we can never really know for certain that other persons have experiences, and that they are not really automatons. It should be clear that the meaning which the philosophers give to that expression is an artificial one. It would be absurd to maintain that when in ordinary life a person says "It's quite certain that Joan is not pretending. I know for certain that she really is in great pain," what he means is that he is having numerically the same pain that Joan is having. And it would be absurd to maintain that his statement is in any other way self-contradictory. We use the phrase "know for certain" in ordinary life in such a way that it makes sense to say that one knows for certain statements about other minds. Of course, in many cases one does not know for certain, but has only the sort of evidence which makes such a statement probable. The philosopher proceeds to startle us with the information that we *never* know such statements for certain. But we can recover our equanimity, when we see that he has simply altered the meaning of "know for certain." We will agree with him that in his new self-contradictory sense of "know for certain," we can never know for certain statements about other minds. But we shall insist that in the old, ordinary sense of "know for certain," we can and frequently do know such statements with certainty.

II.

Mr. Ayer makes some remarks about this problem of empirical certainty which serve to throw some light upon it. He says, "Can we, in virtue of our sense-experiences, ever be sure of the truth of any proposition that implies the real existence of a material thing? . . . The answer is that if what we require to make us sure is a logical demonstration, then we cannot ever be sure. . . . We do indeed verify many such propositions to an extent that makes it highly probable that they are true; but since the series of relevant tests, being infinite, can never be exhausted, this probability can never amount to logical certainty. . . .

"It must be admitted then that there is a sense in which it is true to say that we can never be sure, with regard to any proposition implying the existence of a material thing, that we are not somehow being deceived; but at the same time one may object to this statement on the ground that it is misleading. It is misleading because it suggests that the state of "being sure" is one attainment of which is conceivable, but unfortunately not within our power. But, in fact, the conception of such a state is self-contradictory. For in order to be sure, in this sense, that we were not being deceived, we should have to have completed an infinite series of verifications; and it is an analytic proposition that one cannot run through all the members of an infinite series. . . . Accordingly, what we should say, if we wish to avoid misunderstanding, is not that we can never be certain that any of the propositions in which we express our perceptual judgments are true, but rather that the notion of certainty does not apply to propositions of this kind. It applies to the *a priori* propositions of logic and mathematics, and the fact that it does apply to them is an essential mark of distinction between them and empirical propositions." [14]

Mr. Ayer's remarks have the virtue of pointing out that, in the sense of the word "certain" of which he is thinking, it is self-contradictory to say of any empirical statement that its truth is certain; and of recognizing how misleading it is, therefore, for the philosopher to say, as if it were a matter for regret, that empirical statements are never certain. But he makes a gross mistake when he goes on to say that *the notion of certainty* does not apply to empirical propositions, but instead to *a priori* propositions.

What is true is that the sense of the word "certain" in which *a priori* statements are certain does not apply to any empirical statement; for if it did, we should not call the statement an *empirical* statement. But it does not follow in the least that there is not *a* sense of the word "certain" in which it does apply to empirical statements. Suppose that a person were to reprove someone for calling an argument *circular*, saying to him that the motion of circularity does not apply to arguments, but only to material things. His remark would be entirely analogous to what Ayer says about "the notion of certainty." It is true that the word "circular" does not have an application to arguments in the same sense in which it has an application to material things. But it does have an application to arguments. And the word "certain" does have an application to empirical statements.

Ayer has somehow been led to suppose that there is only one sense, or only one "proper" sense, of the word "certain." And there seems to be a tendency among philosophers to suppose this. I shall try to show later that there are three senses of the expression "it is certain that" which are important in connection with this problem. But it should be plain to anyone who reflects for a moment, that there is an extremely common usage of the phrase "it's certain that," in which it applies to empirical statements. Hardly a one of us ever goes through a day without applying that phrase to some empirical statement. It is not easy to describe the criteria which regulate this usage of the phrase, but the fact that it is not easy to do this should not lead us to say that it does not *have* a well-established usage in which it is applicable to empirical statements.

[14] *The Foundations of Empirical Knowledge,* pp. 43–45.

III.

I wish to discuss now an important confusion which has helped to produce the view that empirical statements can never be known with certainty. The confusion I refer to is the confusion of logical possibility with empirical possibility. Let me cite an example of it in some remarks made by Mr. Russell. In discussing whether our confidence in statements about the past is justified, he says, "Now, apart from arguments as to the proved fallibility of memory, there is one awkward consideration which the skeptic may urge. Remembering, which occurs now, cannot possibly—he may say—prove that what is remembered occurred at some other time, because the world might have sprung into being five minutes ago, exactly as it then was, full of acts of remembering which were entirely misleading. . . . There is no logical impossibility in the view that the world was created five minutes ago, complete with memories and records. This may seem an improbable hypothesis, but it is not logically refutable.

"Apart from this argument, which may be thought fantastic, there are reasons of detail for being more or less distrustful of memory." [15]

It seems clear from these remarks, that Russell was inclined to regard the fact that it is logically possible that the world was created five minutes ago, as a *reason* for "being more or less distrustful of memory." And to say that it is a reason for being "distrustful of memory" can only mean that it shows that there is *some possibility* that the world was created five minutes ago. I want to say that this is absolutely false. I hold that it is an absolute confusion to say that because it is logically possible that the world was created five minutes ago, therefore there is *some* possibility that the world was created five minutes ago.

I wish to call attention to two totally different uses of the expressions "it is possible," "it might be," "perhaps it is," "it could be"; and of the corresponding negative expressions, "it is impossible," "it cannot be," "it could not be." One use of these expressions, although by no means the more frequent, is when they express logical possibility and logical impossibility. Now to say that it is logically possible that p is true, is to say nothing more or less than that the statement, "p," is *not* self-contradictory. And to say that it is logically impossible that p is true is to say nothing more or less than that the statement, "p," is self-contradictory. When these expressions are being used to refer to logical possibility, to say that it is possible, or that it might be, or that perhaps it is the case, that the world began to exist five

15 *Philosophy*, p. 7.

minutes ago, is simply to say that the statement, "the world began to exist five minutes ago," is not self-contradictory.

But by far the more frequent use of these expressions, is a use in which they do not express logical possibility or impossibility. Let me give some examples of this other use. The doctor says, "With your leg in that condition it would be impossible for you to march in the parade today; but perhaps in three days you will be able to get about all right." The doctor certainly does not mean that the statement, "you will march in the parade today," is self-contradictory. And he certainly does not mean by his second statement, merely that it is *logically* possible that you will get about all right in three days. Or again: Something is approaching you from a distance. After straining your eyes to make it out, you say, "It could be a man on a bicycle." You certainly do not mean to be stating that "There's a man on a bicycle there" is not self-contradictory. Or again: Someone, pointing at a rushing river, may say, "None of us could possibly swim it. But we might be able to get across in our canoe." It is obvious that logical possibility and impossibility are not being talked about in this connection.

It is quite clear that the expressions "it is possible," "it might be," etc., are used in a sense in which they do not refer to logical possibility. I shall not try to define the meaning of the expressions in this use. But it is a meaning with which we are all perfectly familiar. I shall merely give it a name, by saying that when the expressions are used in this sense they refer to "empirical possibility"; and that the corresponding negative expressions refer to "empirical impossibility."

I wish to point out an important difference in the use of these expressions, when they refer to empirical possibility, from their use when they refer to logical possibility. When one is talking about empirical possibility, it makes sense to say, "there is a slight possibility," "there is a considerable possibility," "there is some possibility," "it is barely possible," "there is hardly any possibility," "there was a possibility of it, but there isn't any more," "that has been possible for a long time," "there is still a possibility," etc. But when you are talking about logical possibility, it does not make sense to say any of these things. The point might be expressed by saying that empirical possibility admits of *degree*, and also admits of *tense*. Logical possibility admits neither of degree nor of tense. It is all right to say, "There is some possibility, although not very much, that we shall go to California"; "There is a greater possibility that we shall go to Maine." But if what you wanted to say was that it is *logically* possible that you will go to California, this would be a totally incorrect way to express it. For what you say when you say that it is logically possible that p, is that "*p*," is not self-contradictory. And there are no *degrees* of being self-contradictory. One statement cannot be more or less self-contradictory than another. Likewise, in discussing your plans for the summer, you could say, "There is *still* the possibility that we shall go to California." Or: "A year ago it wasn't possible for us to go to California. But now it is." But you could not correctly use that sentence to express the fact that it is logically possible that you will go to California. For it does not make sense to talk about one and the same statement having been self-contradictory at one time and not at another, or *continuing* to be self-contradictory, in the way in which a watch may continue to keep good time.

The reason it is important to make these distinctions is this: Philosophers are commonly led to confuse these two entirely different uses of the expressions we are considering. For example, they conclude from the fact that so and so is possible, where this expresses *logical* possibility, that therefore there is *some* possibility that so and so is the case. Now the statement, "There is some possibility that *p*," *entails* the statement, "It is not absolutely certain that not-*p*." In this way the philosophers obtain an argument for saying that no empirical statements are absolutely certain; for they can truly say of any empirical statement that its falsehood is possible, in the sense of logically possible.

When Mr. Russell was inclined to regard the fact that there is no logical impossibility in the view that the world sprang into being five minutes ago, as a reason for "being more or less distrustful of memory," he presented a flagrant example of the fallacy of confusing logical and empirical possibility. He seems to have thought that he could infer from the fact that the world *might* (logically possible) have sprung into existence five minutes ago, that there is *some* possibility that it actually did. I have tried to show that this is a completely fallacious inference. With regard to any proposition whatever, it does not *follow* from the fact that *p* is logically possible that there is the least possibility that not-*p* is false.

Let us notice another illustration of the commission of this fallacy. Mr. Ayer discusses the question of whether I can at any time be sure that I am not dreaming. He says "the answer is that if what is here meant by 'being sure' is 'being able to give a conclusive demonstration,' then it is true that I cannot at any time be sure that I am not dreaming. I am able, in fact, to convince myself that I am not, by putting my perceptual judgments to the test of further experience and finding that they are substantiated. But since there is no theoretical limit to this process of testing, it is *always* logically possible that I am mistaken. However many favorable tests I may make, *the possibility still remains* that my subsequent experiences will consistently be such as to make me conclude that the perceptions that I had to my own satisfaction proved to be veridical were not so really, and that I was dreaming after all." [16]

Mr. Ayer has slipped from the language of logical possibility to the language of empirical possibility. It is true that the statement "I am dreaming" is not self-contradictory. *That is what it means* to say that it is logically possible that I am mistaken in thinking that I am not dreaming. It does not make sense to say that this possibility *always* exists, because it does not make sense to talk of its *ceasing* to exist. The extent to which I verify the statement "I am not dreaming" is *irrelevant* to the existence of this logical possibility. There is no connection between verification and logical possibility or impossibility. Thus Ayer speaks most misleadingly when he says, "However many favorable tests I may make, the possibility (logical) still remains," etc. For his remark seems to imply that the number of tests *could* have a bearing on the existence of the sort of possibility of which he is speaking. But, furthermore, he speaks incorrectly when he says that "the possibility still remains," etc. He has lapsed into language which is appropriate only to empirical possibility.

From the statement that it is logically possible that I am dreaming now, Ayer moves to the statement that the possibility still remains that I am dreaming now. But this is an illegitimate move. For the latter statement implies that there is *some* possibility, or *a* possibility that I am dreaming now. And it does not follow from the fact that it is logically possible that I am dreaming now, that there is *any* possibility that I am dreaming now. And it is, in fact, the case at this moment that there is not the least possibility that I am dreaming. To point out that the statement "I am dreaming" is not self-contradictory, is to point out something entirely irrelevant to this fact.

This source of philosophical confusion might be removed if philosophers were to substitute the language of "self-contradictory" for the language of "logically possible." What I mean is that instead of saying "it is logically possible that p," or "it might be that p," or "perhaps p," it might be better to say "p is not self-contradictory." Because of the great similarity in the form of the expressions, there is a strong temptation to move illegitimately from "it is logically possible that p," or "it might be (logically) that p," to "there is some possibility that p." And from this one infers, properly, that it is not certain that not-p. This source of error would be removed if philosophers possessed only *one* language of possibility, i.e., the language of empirical possibility.

If instead of talking about logical possibility and impossibility, philos-

16 *The Foundations of Empirical Knowledge*, pp. 42–43. My italics.

ophers talked about statements being self-contradictory or not self-contradictory they would not be so inclined to say that no empirical statements are *completely verifiable.* From the fact that there is *still a* possibility that not-*p*, it *follows* that *p* has not been completely verified. Philosophers are tempted to infer from the fact that it is logically possible that not-*p*, that there is *still a* possibility that not-*p*. They then generalize this argument to show that no empirical statement is completely verifiable. But if, instead of saying that it is logically possible that not-*p*, they simply said that not-*p* is not self-contradictory, perhaps they would not be so likely to infer that there is *a* or *some* possibility that not-*p*; and to conclude therefore that *p* is not completely verified.

In any case, it *should* be clear that *verification* applies only to empirical statements. Since verification applies to empirical statements, *complete* verification applies to empirical statements. It should be clear, too, that a statement is not an *empirical* statement unless it has a negative which is not self-contradictory. It *follows* from the fact that *p* is an empirical statement that not-*p* is not self-contradictory. And it *follows* from the fact that *p* is an empirical statement that *p* is capable (logically) of complete verification. Thus it is fallacious to argue that because not-*p* is not self-contradictory, therefore *p* cannot be completely verified. And this is the fallacy that the philosophers commit when they argue that no empirical statement can ever be completely or conclusively verified, because *no matter* to *what* extent it has been verified, it is "always" possible or "the possibility still remains" that the statement is false.

IV.

A. The phrase "it is certain that" has an application to three different sorts of statements, i.e., to sense-statements, to *a priori* statements, and to empirical statements. To bring out the differences in these applications of the phrase, will help to explain the existence of the view that empirical statements are never known with certainty.

By "sense-statements" I mean statements of the sort, "I have a pain," "I am tasting a sweetish taste," "This looks brown to me," "This feels soft to me." They are to be opposed to statements of the sort, "I have a bad tooth," "This has a sweetish taste," "This is brown," "This is soft." When philosophers say that no empirical statements are known with certainty they are not generally referring to statements of the first sort. They generally use the phrase "empirical statement" in such a way that statements of the second sort would be included among empirical statements, while sense-statements would not be included among empirical statements. It is in this way that I am using the phrases "empirical statement" and "sense-statement."

By "sense-statements" I mean statements of the kind to which philosophers have referred by such descriptions as "statements which report what is immediately given in experience," which "report a present datum," and "cannot be refuted by subsequent experience." Empirical statements, on the other hand, they have characterized as containing "predictions as to what future experience will give," and as "going beyond the present datum." [17] It has also been said of sense-statements that they are "incorrigible." By this is meant that when you say "I have a pain," or make some other sense-statement, you cannot be mistaken about the facts. You may commit the linguistic error of expressing your meaning with the wrong words. But if you do express your meaning with the right words, and if you are not telling a lie, then it follows that your sense-statement is true. Empirical statements, on the contrary, are "corrigible." By this is meant that when you make an empirical statement you *can* be mistaken about the facts. Even if you express your meaning correctly and are not lying, it does not follow that your empirical statement is true. For you can be mistaken in thinking that what you assert to be the case is in fact the case. Sense-statements are not open to this type of error, and that is why they are called "incorrigible."

Now many philosophers would say this sort of thing: that you can know with absolute certainty that you have the sort of pain ordinarily called toothache, but that you cannot ever be certain that you have a tooth in bad condition; that you can know for certain that something *looks* brown to you, but you can never know for certain that it *is* brown; that you can know with perfect certainty that something feels soft to you, but you can never know with perfect certainty that it *is* soft. That, in short, you can know sense-statements, with certainty.

Let us consider a little further what is meant by the "incorrigibility" of sense-statements. To say that sense-statements are incorrigible means that when you make a sense-statement you *cannot* be mistaken about the facts. But in what sense is "cannot" used here? Is it the sense of "cannot" in which it is true that a man cannot swim the Atlantic? Not at all. For although it would be false, it would *make sense* to say, "So and so swam the Atlantic yesterday." In the true statement "A man cannot swim the Atlantic," the "cannot" is used in a *factual* sense. And the absurdity of

---

[17] When Mr. Russell speaks of "basic propositions," he means to be referring, I am sure, to statements of the sort that I call sense-statements; but it seems to me that all of his definitions of the expression "basic proposition," are unsatisfactory. Cf. *An Inquiry into Meaning and Truth*, pp. 171–174, 187–190.

which one would be guilty in supposing that someone swam the Atlantic yesterday would be a *factual* absurdity.

But to say that when one makes a sense-statement such as "I have a sharp pain," one *cannot* be mistaken about the facts is to use "cannot" in a *logical* sense. For what this statement means is that *it does not make sense* to say, "I think I have a sharp pain, but perhaps I am mistaken"; or to say, "So and so says that he has a severe headache, but perhaps he is mistaken." The absurdity of which one would be guilty if one said these things would be a *logical* absurdity. What is meant by saying that a person *cannot* be mistaken as to the truth of a sense-statement is less ambiguously expressed by the statement, that it is *nonsensical* to say that perhaps a person is mistaken as to the truth of the sense-statement he has uttered. To say, therefore, that sense-statements are "incorrigible" is to say that it does not make sense to question them. To say this is to state the defining characteristic of sense-statements.

When the philosopher says that sense-statements can be known with certainty, but that empirical statements cannot, what he is doing is restricting the use of the phrase "known with certainty" in such a way that a statement will be capable of being known with certainty, if and only if it is an incorrigible statement. In other words, he is proposing to use the phrase "is known with certainty" in such a way that it will be *equivalent* to the phrase "is incorrigible." But then we see that his pronouncement that sense-statements can be known with certainty, but empirical statements cannot, is a plain truism. For it amounts to saying that sense-statements are incorrigible, and empirical statements are corrigible. And incorrigibility is the defining characteristic of sense-statements, while corrigibility is a defining characteristic of empirical statements. Of course, no empirical statement can be incorrigible, for if any statement were incorrigible, we should not call it an empirical statement. The philosopher's pronouncement really amounts to saying that empirical statements are not sense-statements— which is, of course, true. If it were the case that the only proper use of the phrase "is known with certainty" was such that its meaning was equivalent to that of the phrase "is incorrigible," then no person could say that an empirical statement was known with certainty, and say something true. For he would be saying that an empirical statement was incorrigible, which would be logically absurd.

Let us turn for a moment to the philosophers who say that *a priori* statements can be known with certainty, but not empirical statements. They may argue the point by saying that *a priori* statements *cannot* be false, while empirical statements *can* be false. But they express their meaning ambiguously; for there is a perfectly proper and ordinary sense of "cannot" in which many empirical statements cannot be false, e.g., "it cannot be false that the military disaster which France suffered in 1940 has brought unhappiness to many persons." What the philosophers mean when they say that an *a priori* statement cannot be false is better expressed by saying that the negative of an *a priori* statement is self-contradictory. Their declaration that only *a priori* statements can be known with certainty is a disguised recommendation that the phrase "it is certain that" be applied to a statement if and only if the statement has a self-contradictory negative. It is a proposal to use the phrase "it is certain that *p*," so that it will be *equivalent* to the phrase "*p* has a self-contradictory negative." And this is the way that the philosophers are using the word "certain" when they say that no empirical statement is ever certain, but only *a priori* statements are. So what they are really saying is that no empirical statement has a self-contradictory negative, while every *a priori* statement does have a self-contradictory negative. And this is an absolute tautology. For it is the defining characteristic of an *a priori* statement that it has a self-contradictory negative, and it is a defining characteristic of an empirical proposition that it does not have a self-contradictory negative.

B. We have seen that an important source of the philosophical view that empirical statements are never certain, lies in the fact that the philosophers compare empirical statements with *a priori* statements and with sense-statements. Certain striking differences between empirical statements and statements of the other two types makes them want to predicate certainty of the latter only. In other words, they want to use the word "certain" in such a way that a statement will be called "certain" only if it is either a sense-statement, or an *a priori* statement. They want to abolish the use of the word "certain," in which it is applied to empirical statements. They want to abolish one of the three uses of the word, and retain the other two.

What I wish to point out is that the two uses of the word "certain" which they want to retain are *degenerate* uses, and that the use they want to abolish is *non*-degenerate. Let me explain this. When it is said that a sense-statement is certain, what this means is that it does not make sense to doubt or question it. And when it is said that an *a priori* statement is certain, what this means is that the negative of it is self-contradictory. Now the defining characteristic of a sense-statement is that it does not make sense to question it. And the defining characteristic of an *a priori* statement is that it has a self-contradictory negative. Therefore to say of a sense-statement that its truth is certain is to say nothing more nor less than that it is a sense-statement; and to say of an *a priori* statement that its truth is certain, is simply to say that it is an *a priori* statement. The proposition "*p* is a sense-statement and *p* is absolutely certain," is a flat tautology. And so is the proposition "*p* is an *a priori* statement and *p* is absolutely certain." In both cases the phrase "*p* is absolutely certain" adds nothing whatever. To say of an *a priori* statement, or of a sense-statement, that its truth is certain is to say something trivial and non-informative. That is what I meant by saying that the uses of the word "certain," in which it is applied to statements of these two types, are degenerate.

But the use of the word "certain" in which it is applied to empirical statements is by no means degenerate. The proposition "*p* is an empirical statement and *p* is absolutely certain" is far from being a tautology. To say of an empirical statement that it is certain is to say something highly informative. It is informative on two grounds. First, it says that the empirical statement is *true*, and not false. Some empirical statements are true and some false, and nothing could be more informative than to say to which class it belongs. Second, to say that the statement is certain is to say that it is not merely probable. Saying this, describes to some extent the nature of the *evidence* for the statement. It tells us something which we could not possibly know, by merely knowing that the statement is an empirical one.

Thus the philosophers who wish to abolish the application of the word "certain" to empirical statements are in a very queer position. For what they propose to do is to take away the use of the word "certain," in which to say that a statement is certain is to say something significant and worth listening to. And they propose to keep only uses of the word, in which to say that a statement is certain is to say something absolutely trivial. If we followed out their recommendation, the word "certain" would become a worthless word.

Some philosophers, who admit that there is a perfectly proper sense of "certain," in which empirical statements can be certain, are inclined, nevertheless, to talk as if sense-statements or *a priori* statements have a *superior* kind of certainty. I think that it is rather senseless to speak of the certainty of empirical statements as being either "inferior" or "superior" to the certainty of sense-statements or of *a priori* statements, since entirely different senses of the word "certain" are being talked about. But if I were compelled to say one or the other, I should prefer to say that empirical certainty is the superior certainty. And the reason which I should give is that to say of either a sense-statement or an *a priori* statement that its truth is certain is to say something tautological and utterly trivial. While to say of an empirical statement that its truth is certain, is to say something significant and informative.

C. Let us consider another aspect of the recommendation to discontinue the application of "certain" to empirical statements. What the philosophers want us to do is to substitute for the word "certain," the expressions "probable" or "highly probable." No matter how satisfactory is the evidence for p, we are always to say "it is probable that p," never "it is certain that p." The question I wish to raise is, supposing that we did adopt the recommended alteration in our language, should we have gained anything by it?

It is necessary to remind ourselves of the important differences between the cases which we, in our present language, describe as cases of certainty, and the cases which we at present describe as cases of probability. Consider this example: your car begins to choke, sputter and lunge in the way it does when it is out of gas. You say, "Probably the gas tank is empty." You then get out and test the tank with a measuring stick which comes out dry. You say, "It's certainly bone dry." The philosophers would have us still say "probable" in the latter case; and even if the tank had a removable top, which we removed and saw by the broad daylight that it was empty, they would allow us to say nothing more than "It's highly probable that it's empty." Or again: A doctor observes the symptoms of pain, fever, and the way the abdomen of his patient feels. He writes in his report, "Ruptured appendix highly probable." He then operates, and sees the ruptured condition of the appendix with his eyes. Is he then to announce to the students in the amphitheatre, that it is "highly probable" that this is a case of ruptured appendix? Or again: Your wife frowns and walks out of the room. You say, "Very likely she's displeased with me." Compare this with the case where she screams, sobs, goes home to mother, and institutes divorce proceedings. The philosophers would have you describe the latter situation, too, by saying, "It's very likely that she's displeased with me." Or again: On the basis of knowledge of past performance, you say, "It's highly probable that Joe Louis won by a knockout last night." Later you see the newspapers and talk with dozens of people who saw the fight. Are you to continue to say that it is "highly probable" that Louis won by a knockout?

The point of these examples is to emphasize the striking differences between the cases which we ordinarily call cases of probability, and the cases which we ordinarily call cases of certainty. How different is the doctor's evidence for saying that the patient has a ruptured appendix, when he has only observed the pain and fever symptoms and felt the abdomen, from his evidence for saying it when he has opened the abdomen and seen the ruptured appendix! What a difference there is in the nature of the evidence for saying that Joe Louis won last night, when in one case the evidence is Louis's many victories in the past and the mediocre past performance of his opponent, and in the other case the evidence is that 20,000 people saw the knockout blow! *The function of the distinction*, in ordinary language, between *probability* and *certainty*, *is just to describe such differences.* If we were to abolish this distinction, we should have abandoned an important piece of our descriptive language.

What the philosophers' recommendation amounts to, is that we should *stretch* the application of the phrase "highly probable," so that it would apply to not only statements of the sort which we now call highly probable, but also to statements of the sort which we now call certain. But if we adopted this proposal, how then could we express the differences between what we *now* say is "highly probable but not quite certain," and what we now say is "absolutely certain"? If an anxious parent wanted to know whether his child had a ruptured appendix, and the doctor said that it was "highly probable" that it was ruptured, he would want to know whether it was highly probable in the *old* sense, or "highly probable" in the *new* sense. In our revised language, it would be impossible to tell him which it was. We could tell him only if we *invented a new word* which took the place of the banished word "certain." We should have to invent a new word which would enable us to express the same old distinction between probability and certainty, that we had tried to abolish. Thus we should have gained nothing by attempting to alter ordinary language.

There are words in our language that operate in *pairs*. For example, there is "large" and "small," "hot" and "cold," "fast" and "slow," "probable" and "certain." Suppose that we banished the word "small" from the language, and applied the word "large" to everything, both large and small. It is obvious that if in describing an object to someone you said that it was "large" that would convey no information to him at all about the size of the object. The word "large" would drop out of the language, because it would be a *useless* word. It is essential to the meaning of "large," as it is now used, that large is *contrasted* with small. If large ceases to be contrasted with small, the word "large" loses its meaning.

Similarly, if "it's probable" or "it's highly probable" were to precede *every* empirical statement, these expressions would lose their meaning. For it is essential to the meaning of "probable" and "highly probable," that probability is *contrasted* with certainty. That is why it makes sense to say, "It's highly probable but not quite certain." If the application of "certain" to empirical statements was abolished, the word "probable" would also cease to be applied to them. For it would have become a useless piece of language, a word which conveyed no information.

It would be fruitless to argue that probability would be contrasted with certainty, in the sense of "certain" in which sense-statements and *a priori* statements are certain. For we have seen that to say that a sense-statement is certain, simply means that it is a sense-statement; and to say that an *a priori* statement is certain, simply means that it is an *a priori* statement. If we altered our language in the way that the philosophers want, then to say that a statement was certain would simply mean that it was not an empirical statement, but was either a sense-statement or an *a priori* statement. And to say that a statement was "probable" would simply mean that it was an *empirical* statement. But the words "probable" and "certain" would no longer be capable of being used to call attention to differences *within* the class of empirical statements. Those words could no longer indicate the differences in the evidence for various empirical statements. But it is important that we should have *some* set of words which would indicate these differences. And if that function were taken away from the words "probable" and "certain," we should have to invent a new pair of words which would perform that same function.

V.

In this concluding section, I wish to discuss the chief sources of the philosophical view that no empirical statements are known with certainty, but are at best only probable.

A. One of the main things which has led philosophers to say that the statements which we call certain are really only highly probable, has been the desire to point out that the differences in the evidence for statements that we call probable and for statements that we call certain are only differences of *degree*. Their point can best be brought out by the aid of examples. Suppose that a small child says that it saw a lion in the street. You might dismiss this as a fancy, or as the wrong use of a word. But then several other older children say they saw it too, and insist that it was a lion. You might then be inclined to say that there was some probability that they saw a lion. Then you find that a thousand adults swear that they saw a lion in the street, and that their stories and descriptions are in perfect agreement. You would say then that it is absolutely certain that there was a lion in the street. Now the philosophers wish to say that differences in the *maturity* of the observers, and differences in the *number* of observers are differences of degree only—that there is no difference of *kind* between the case where you say that the evidence is conclusive and the case where you say that the evidence is not conclusive. Or consider this example: You hear a familiar voice outside the window, and exclaim, "That is probably Charles!" He then walks into the room, and you say, "It certainly is

Charles!" Now what the philosophers want to say is this: In the case of mere probability, what you had for evidence was some of the auditory data associated with Charles. In the case of "certainty" you had the visual data associated with Charles, in addition to the auditory data. But the difference between the two cases is really only a difference in the *amount* of data—it is really only a difference of degree.

The philosophers' claim might be generalized in this way: The differences between what we call probability and what we call certainty are differences in the number of observers, or the number of observations, or the amount of data. The difference between "partial verification" and "complete verification," as we use these expressions in ordinary language, consists principally in a difference in the number of favorable tests. Likewise, the difference between "conclusive" and "inconclusive" evidence is of this sort. But differences in the number of observers or tests, or in the amount of data, are only differences of degree. No line can be drawn which will sharply separate cases of "conclusive" evidence from cases of "inconclusive" evidence, cases of "certainty" from cases of "probability." The differences are not differences of *kind*. Therefore, why can it not be said that the cases of what we call "certainty" are really cases of very high probability?

I agree, on the whole, with this way of describing the nature of the differences between the sort of evidence which makes a statement probable, and the sort of evidence which makes it certain. I think that this way of describing it may even be illuminating. If one had the idea that certainty is a mysterious quality, which inexplicably belongs to some statements and not to others, then it would be salutary to argue that the difference between certainty and probability is only one of degree. When Professor Moore is engaged in maintaining, correctly, with regard to some empirical statement, that its truth is absolutely certain, and is asked by a philosopher *how* he knows that it is absolutely certain; his frequent reply is, that he doesn't know *how* he knows, but he certainly *does* know. People, listening to Moore, sometimes get the impression that Moore thinks that it is by some sort of *intuition* that he discovers whether the truth of a statement is certain. They get the impression that Moore thinks that certainty is a simple, indefinable quality like yellow, which unaccountably attaches to some statements and not to others. If anybody ever does think this, then it would be well to give him the above line of talk, about the nature of the differences between probability and certainty.

But I want to point out how *arbitrary* it is to say that the differences between probability and certainty are not differences of *kind*. Why not say that the difference between the evidence which you have for the presence of Charles, when you only hear a familiar voice at the window, and the evidence which you have when you see him enter the room, is a difference in the *kind* of evidence? Why not say that the difference between the testimony of one child, and the testimony of a thousand adults, is a difference in the *kind* of evidence? What lies behind this arbitrary use of the word "kind" is that the philosophers want to say that a difference in the nature of the evidence for two statements is a difference in "kind," if and only if the "evidence" for one statement is a *demonstrative proof*, and the evidence for the other statement is *not* a demonstrative proof. To give a demonstrative proof of a statement would consist in showing that the statement is logically deducible from *a priori* premises. When the philosophers say that the difference between certainty and probability is not a difference in *kind*, what they mean is that the evidence for a statement, the truth of which is "certain," does not consist of a demonstrative proof; any more than does the evidence for a statement, the truth of which is only probable, consist of a demonstrative proof. And of course this is true. If any statement is capable of demonstrative proof, then it is not an *empirical* statement, but an *a priori* statement. So what the philosophers are saying, when they say that the difference between certainty and probability is not a difference in kind, is that the statements which are "certain," as well as the statements which are "probable," have, after all, only the sort of evidence that empirical statements can have. And this is a truism. The philosophers' statement that the difference between probability and certainty is not one of kind, presents, in a disguised way, the familiar recommendation that we should restrict the application of the word "certain" to *a priori* statements.

Suppose, however, that we agreed to say that, since the differences between probability and certainty are only differences in the number of observers, number of tests, amount of data, etc., therefore the differences are of *degree* only. Would it follow that statements which we call "certain" are *really* only probable? It is easy to see that it does not follow in the least. In exactly the same sense of "difference of degree," the difference between being bald and having a full head of hair is only a difference of degree. That is, it is a difference in the *number* of hairs on the head. To argue that, because the difference between "certain" and "probable" is only one of *degree*, therefore all empirical statements are probable only—is exactly analogous to arguing that, because the difference between "being bald" and "having a full head of hair" is only one of degree, therefore all men are really bald. The point is, that it is the *function* of the words "certain" and "probable," in ordinary language, to describe those differences of degree in the evidence for various statements—just as it is the function of "bald" and "full head of hair" to describe the analogous differences of degree. The philosophers show an inclination to argue that since they are "merely" differences of degree, therefore they are not really important. But the fact is that differences of degree are extremely important, as any bald-headed man will tell you.

B. The question which I wish to discuss now is suggested by some remarks made by Mr. Russell. They are as follows: "We have therefore inductive grounds for holding (on a common-sense basis) that when I 'see a cat' there probably is a cat. We cannot go beyond 'probably,' since we know that people sometimes see cats that are not there, for instance in dreams." [18] There is no doubt that Mr. Russell intended this argument to be a perfectly general one. He meant to say that whenever a person makes any perceptual judgment, e.g., that he sees a house or a table, or he hears a bell, his judgment can be no more than *probably* true, *because* people have sometimes "seen" and "heard" things of that sort in dreams, or in hallucinations.

If we take this argument at its face value, it seems to me to be an extremely bad one. It is simply absurd to argue that *no* perceptual judgment is certain, on the grounds that *sometimes* when people have made perceptual judgments they have been mistaken, or that *sometimes* people have had "perceptual experiences," in dreams or hallucinations, which seemed veridical but were not. An analogous line of argument would be to say that it is not certain that I am now alive, because *some* people have died; or to say that it is not certain that I am not standing on my head now, because *sometimes* in the past other people and myself have stood on our heads; or to say that it is not certain that I did not have fish for breakfast, because *sometimes* people have fish for breakfast. If Russell's argument is taken at its face value, it seems to be a grotesque perversion of valid inductive argument.

But I think that Russell was trying to state a very real and serious difficulty, which he did not clearly express. He wanted to say, I believe, what many philosophers have been inclined to say—namely, that a non-veridical perceptual experience may exactly resemble a veridical perceptual experience. But if there need be no "intrinsic difference" (a favorite expression) between veridical and non-veridical experiences, then how can you tell, at any given time, whether your perceptual experience is veridical or non-veridical? Plato expressed the problem very well in the *Theaetetus*:

"*Socrates.* A question which I think that you must often have heard persons ask: How can you determine whether at this moment we are

18 *An Inquiry into Meaning and Truth*, p. 151.

sleeping, and all our thoughts are a dream; or whether we are awake, and talking to one another in the waking state?

"*Theaetetus.* Indeed, Socrates, I do not know how to prove the one any more than the other, for in both cases the facts precisely correspond; and there is no difficulty in supposing that during all this discussion we have been talking to one another in a dream; and when in a dream we seem to be narrating dreams, the resemblance of the two states is quite astonishing." [19]

The philosophically accepted answer to the question, how can you tell whether a given perceptual experience is veridical or non-veridical, is that you *cannot* tell, *at the time you are having the perceptual experience* in question. (Some philosophers would say that you can tell *afterwards*, by seeing how the experience in question is related to subsequent experiences.) And this view helps to produce the theory that the truth of an empirical statement is never certain. The answer I propose to make to the question, Can you at the time you are having a perceptual experience know whether that experience is veridical? is that *sometimes you can and sometimes you can't.* This is a perfectly common-sense answer and, it seems to me, an obviously true one.

Knowing that a certain proposition is true, does not consist in having some peculiar sort of feeling. You *know* that p is true if, first, you have evidence of a certain sort for accepting p, and, second, p is true. The difference between knowing that p is probably true, and knowing that p is certainly true, is that your evidence in the latter case must be of a higher sort, i.e., must be more conclusive; in the latter case, furthermore, p must be true.

Now what I am saying is that sometimes when you are having a perceptual experience, you have conclusive evidence that it is veridical; sometimes you do not have conclusive evidence that it is veridical; and sometimes you have conclusive evidence that it is not veridical. If, for example, you have just entered an unfamiliar room for the first time, and have not had a chance to find out whether there is a doorway or a mirror in the wall facing you—then if it should *look* as if it were someone approaching you from the front, you would not *know* whether someone was actually approaching from the front. But if in the next few moments you were able to inspect the wall, to see that there was a mirror in it, not a door, and to look about you, then you would know that no one was approaching you from the front, but that someone was approaching from behind. In those few moments you were able to obtain conclusive evidence that no one was approaching from the front.

[19] *Plato,* "Selections" (ed. by R. Demos), Scribners, p. 319. My italics.

If you have some astonishing perceptual experience, such as seeing a sudden wind hurl a house into the air, you may actually be in doubt, for a moment, as to whether you are having a dream or an hallucination. But if you collect your thoughts and look about you; get the feel of your body, and notice that your sensory reactions are normal and in agreement; observe that your surroundings (other than the house) are what they should be, your recollections being what they are; see that other people are behaving in a way which shows that they are having perceptual experiences similar to yours—then you will know that you are actually seeing a house being thrown about in the air. During the course of this perceptual experience, you would have collected conclusive evidence that it was veridical.

One question which causes some trouble in this connection is, *how long* does one "perception," or one "perceptual experience" last? When you see a man walk across the room, is that *one* perceptual experience, or a series of perceptual experiences? Or if you look slowly around a room, noticing the furniture and observing the people in the room, is that one perception or several perceptions? Can a single perceptual experience last several seconds or even minutes? or can it last no longer than a fraction of a second? This is a question as to how we are to use the expressions "perception" or "perceptual experience." But the answer to it determines in part the answer to our main question. For if we say that a perceptual experience may last several seconds or even minutes, then it is the case with regard to many a perceptual experience, that it contains its own verification within itself. That is to say, one often obtains conclusive evidence that a perceptual experience is veridical, during the course of that very perceptual experience. While if we say that a perceptual experience can last no longer than a fraction of a second, then it is perhaps the case that no one ever obtains conclusive evidence that a perceptual experience is veridical, during the course of that experience. But it does not follow that one could not know that a given perceptual experience was veridical, at the time one was having it. For you might easily have obtained, *previous* to the occurrence of the perception in question, conclusive evidence that the perception was veridical. For example, you might conclusively verify, by examining it, that the thing in the corner which looked at first like a chest of drawers, is really a radio. Having once established the fact that it is a radio, if you looked at it again a moment later, you would know that you were really seeing a radio.

In whichever of these two ways one uses the phrase "perceptual experience," therefore, it is the case that one can know that a given perceptual experience is veridical, at the time one is having the experience. That is to say, it is possible for you to know with certainty, when you are seeing an elephant, that you do see an elephant; and it is possible for you to know with certainty, when you are hearing a dog's bark, that you do hear a dog's bark. It may be said that it is *logically* possible, in each such case, that you are mistaken. And this is true. But it does not, in the least, follow from the fact that it is logically possible that you are mistaken, that you do not know with certainty that you are not mistaken.

Let us consider the possibility that two perceptual experiences, one veridical, the other non-veridical, may be "intrinsically similar"; or, to put it as Plato did, it may be that in both cases "the facts precisely correspond." This is supposed to raise a difficulty as to how one can know whether a given experience is veridical or non-veridical. It seems to me that the difficulty arises because the phrases "the facts precisely correspond" and "intrinsically similar" are confusing. Suppose that it looks to you as if there were a man in front of you walking toward you. Then you discover that it is not a door you are facing but a mirror, and that the man is approaching from the rear. Suppose that a few moments later, the man walks toward you again as you are facing the mirror. Your visual experience is the same as in the preceding case, but this time you know that you are facing a mirror, not a doorway; you have evidence in your possession, by virtue of which you know that no one is approaching you from the front.
Are we to say that in both cases "the facts precisely correspond"? Is the fact that you possess certain evidence in the second case, which you did not possess in the former case, one of "the facts"? Are the two cases "intrinsically similar"? This is a question as to how we shall use the phrases in question. If we say that the fact that you possess evidence that a perceptual experience is veridical or non-veridical is a part of the "intrinsic character" of that perceptual experience—then it follows that if a certain perceptual experience is known to be veridical it is not "intrinsically similar" to any perceptual experience which is not known to be veridical. While if we say that the fact that you possess such evidence is not a part of the "intrinsic character" of the perceptual experience in question—then it may be the case, with regard to two "intrinsically similar" perceptual experiences, that one is known to be veridical at the time it is being had, while the other is not known to be veridical, and is perhaps even illusory.

The main outline of this paper may be briefly summarized as follows:—
The doctrine that empirical statements are never known with certainty has been held by various philosophers, because these philosophers have been led to attach a self-contradictory meaning to the expression "it is certain that," as applied to empirical statements. They have held, in other

words, that there is no proper sense of the phrase "it is certain that," in which it applies to empirical statements; and we have seen that this is false. Another important source of this philosophical doctrine has been the tendency to confuse "logical possibility" with "empirical possibility." We considered the doctrine is a recommendation to restrict the application of "it is certain that" to *a priori* statements, and to sense-statements; but we saw how pointless and self-defeating it would be to adopt that recommendation. We noticed that a main source of the doctrine is the desire to point out that the differences in the nature of the evidence for empirical statements which are certain, and empirical statements which are only probable, are only differences of degree. Finally, we saw that another chief source of the doctrine is a puzzlement over the question as to whether you can tell at the time that you are having a perceptual experience, whether that perceptual experience is veridical.

PART III

TRUTH

TRUTH

Aristotle (384–322 B.C.)

In the case of that which is or which has taken place, propositions, whether positive or negative, must be true or false. Again, in the case of a pair of contradictories, either when the subject is universal and the propositions are of a universal character, or when it is individual, as has been said, one of the two must be true and the other false; whereas when the subject is universal, but the propositions are not of a universal character, there is no such necessity. We have discussed this type also in a previous chapter.

When the subject, however, is individual, and that which is predicated of it relates to the future, the case is altered. For if all propositions whether positive or negative are either true or false, then any given predicate must either belong to the subject or not, so that if one man affirms that an event of a given character will take place and another denies it, it is plain that the statement of the one will correspond with reality and that of the other will not. For the predicate cannot both belong and not belong to the subject at one and the same time with regard to the future.

Thus, if it is true to say that a thing is white, it must necessarily be white; if the reverse proposition is true, it will of necessity not be white. Again, if it is white, the proposition stating that it is white was true; if it is not white, the proposition to the opposite effect was true. And if it is not white, the man who states that it is is making a false statement; and if the man who states that it is white is making a false statement, it follows that it is not white. It may therefore be argued that it is necessary that affirmations or denials must be either true or false.

Now if this be so, nothing is or takes place fortuitously, either in the present or in the future, and there are no real alternatives; everything takes place of necessity and is fixed. For either he that affirms that it will take

De Interpretatione, Chapter 9. Translated from the Greek by E. M. Edghill. Translation reprinted from *The Problems of Philosophy*, W. D. Ross, ed., by permission of the Clarendon Press, Oxford. The title of this selection has been supplied by the editors.

place or he that denies this is in correspondence with fact, whereas if things did not take place of necessity, an event might just as easily not happen as happen; for the meaning of the word "fortuitous" with regard to present or future events is that reality is so constituted that it may issue in either of two opposite directions.

Again, if a thing is white now, it was true before to say that it would be white, so that of anything that has taken place it was always true to say "it is" or "it will be." But if it was always true to say that a thing is or will be, it is not possible that it should not be or not be about to be, and when a thing cannot not come to be, it is impossible that it should not come to be, and when it is impossible that it should not come to be, it must come to be. All, then, that is about to be must of necessity take place. It results from this that nothing is uncertain or fortuitous, for if it were fortuitous it would not be necessary.

Again, to say that neither the affirmation nor the denial is true, maintaining, let us say, that an event neither will take place nor will not take place, is to take up a position impossible to defend. In the first place, though facts should prove the one proposition false, the opposite would still be untrue. Secondly, if it was true to say that a thing was both white and large, both these qualities must necessarily belong to it; and if they will belong to it the next day, they must necessarily belong to it the next day. But if an event is neither to take place nor not to take place the next day, the element of chance will be eliminated. For example, it would be necessary that a sea-fight should neither take place nor fail to take place on the next day.

These awkward results and others of the same kind follow, if it is an irrefragable law that of every pair of contradictory propositions, whether they have regard to universals and are stated as universally applicable, or whether they have regard to individuals, one must be true and the other false, and that there are no real alternatives, but that all that is or takes place is the outcome of necessity. There would be no need to deliberate or to take trouble, on the supposition that if we should adopt a certain course, a certain result would follow, while, if we did not, the result would not follow. For a man may predict an event ten thousand years beforehand, and another may predict the reverse; that which was truly predicted at the moment in the past will of necessity take place in the fullness of time.

Further, it makes no difference whether people have or have not actually made the contradictory statements. For it is manifest that the circumstances are not influenced by the fact of an affirmation or denial on the part of anyone. For events will not take place or fail to take place because it was stated that they would or would not take place, nor is this

any more the case if the prediction dates back ten thousand years or any
other space of time. Wherefore, if through all time the nature of things
was so constituted that a prediction about an event was true, then through
all time it was necessary that that prediction should find fulfillment; and
with regard to all events, circumstances have always been such that their
occurrence is a matter of necessity. For that of which someone has said
truly that it will be, cannot fail to take place; and of that which takes place,
it was always true to say that it would be.

Yet this view leads to an impossible conclusion; for we see that both
deliberation and action are causative with regard to the future, and that, to
speak more generally, in those things which are not continuously actual
there is a potentiality in either direction. Such things may either be or not
be; events also therefore may either take place or not take place. There are
many obvious instances of this. It is possible that this coat may be cut in
half, and yet it may not be cut in half, but wear out first. In the same way,
it is possible that it should not be cut in half; unless this were so, it would
not be possible that it should wear out first. So it is therefore with all other
events which possess this kind of potentiality. It is therefore plain that it is
not of necessity that everything is or takes place; but in some instances
there are real alternatives, in which case the affirmation is no more true
and no more false than the denial; while some exhibit a predisposition and
general tendency in one direction or the other, and yet can issue in the
opposite direction by exception.

Now that which is must needs be when it is, and that which is not
must needs not be when it is not. Yet it cannot be said without qualification that all existence and non-existence is the outcome of necessity. For
there is a difference between saying that that which is, when it is, must
needs be, and simply saying that all that is must needs be, and similarly in
the case of that which is not. In the case, also, of two contradictory
propositions this holds good. Everything must either be or not be, whether
in the present or in the future, but it is not always possible to distinguish
and state determinately which of these alternatives must necessarily come
about.

Let me illustrate. A sea-fight must either take place tomorrow or not,
but it is not necessary that it should take place tomorrow, neither is it
necessary that it should not take place, yet it is necessary that it either
should or should not take place tomorrow. Since propositions correspond
with facts, it is evident that when in future events there is a real alternative, and a potentiality in contrary directions, the corresponding affirmation
and denial have the same character.

This is the case with regard to that which is not always existent or not always non-existent. One of the two propositions in such instances must be true and the other false, but we cannot say determinately that this or that is false, but must leave the alternative undecided. One may indeed be more likely to be true than the other, but it cannot be either actually true or actually false. It is therefore plain that it is not necessary that of an affirmation and a denial one should be true and the other false. For in the case of that which exists potentially, but not actually, the rule which applies to that which exists actually does not hold good. The case is rather as we have indicated.

❖   43   ❖

TRUTH AND FALSEHOOD
Bertrand Russell (1872–   )

Our knowledge of truths, unlike our knowledge of things, has an opposite, namely *error*. So far as things are concerned, we may know them or not know them, but there is no positive state of mind which can be described as erroneous knowledge of things, so long, at any rate, as we confine ourselves to knowledge by acquaintance. Whatever we are acquainted with must be something: we may draw wrong inferences from our acquaintance, but the acquaintance itself cannot be deceptive. Thus there is no dualism as regards acquaintance. But as regards knowledge of truths, there is a dualism. We may believe what is false as well as what is true. We know that on very many subjects different people hold different and incompatible opinions: hence some beliefs must be erroneous. Since erroneous beliefs are often held just as strongly as true beliefs, it becomes a difficult question how they are to be distinguished from true beliefs. How are we to know, in a given case, that our belief is not erroneous? This is a question of the very greatest difficulty, to which no completely satisfactory answer is possible. There is, however, a preliminary question which is rather less difficult, and that is: What do we *mean* by truth and falsehood? It is this preliminary question which is to be considered in this chapter.

Chapter 12 of Bertrand Russell's *The Problems of Philosophy* (1912). Reprinted by permission of the Clarendon Press, Oxford.

In this chapter we are not asking how we can know whether a belief is true or false: we are asking what is meant by the question whether a belief is true or false. It is to be hoped that a clear answer to this question may help us to obtain an answer to the question what beliefs are true, but for the present we ask only "What is truth?" and "What is falsehood?" not "What beliefs are true?" and "What beliefs are false?" It is very important to keep these different questions entirely separate, since any confusion between them is sure to produce an answer which is not really applicable to either.

There are three points to observe in the attempt to discover the nature of truth, three requisites which any theory must fulfill.

(1) Our theory of truth must be such as to admit of its opposite, falsehood. A good many philosophers have failed adequately to satisfy this condition: they have constructed theories according to which all our thinking ought to have been true, and have then had the greatest difficulty in finding a place for falsehood. In this respect our theory of belief must differ from our theory of acquaintance, since in the case of acquaintance it was not necessary to take account of any opposite.

(2) It seems fairly evident that if there were no beliefs there could be no falsehood, and no truth either, in the sense in which truth is correlative to falsehood. If we imagine a world of mere matter, there would be no room for falsehood in such a world, and although it would contain what may be called "facts," it would not contain any truths, in the sense in which truths are things of the same kind as falsehoods. In fact, truth and falsehood are properties of beliefs and statements: hence a world of mere matter, since it would contain no beliefs or statements, would also contain no truth or falsehood.

(3) But, as against what we have just said, it is to be observed that the truth or falsehood of a belief always depends upon something which lies outside the belief itself. If I believe that Charles I. died on the scaffold, I believe truly, not because of any intrinsic quality of my belief, which could be discovered by merely examining the belief, but because of an historical event which happened two and a half centuries ago. If I believe that Charles I. died in his bed, I believe falsely: no degree of vividness in my belief, or of care in arriving at it, prevents it from being false, again because of what happened long ago, and not because of any intrinsic property of my belief. Hence, although truth and falsehood are properties of beliefs, they are properties dependent upon the relations of the beliefs to other things, not upon any internal quality of the beliefs.

The third of the above requisites leads us to adopt the view—which has on the whole been commonest among philosophers—that truth consists in some form of correspondence between belief and fact. It is, however, by no means an easy matter to discover a form of correspondence to which there are no irrefutable objections. By this partly—and partly by the feeling that, if truth consists in a correspondence of thought with something outside thought, thought can never know when truth has been attained—many philosophers have been led to try to find some definition of truth which shall not consist in relation to something wholly outside belief. The most important attempt at a definition of this sort is the theory that truth consists in *coherence*. It is said that the mark of falsehood is failure to cohere in the body of our beliefs, and that it is the essence of a truth to form part of the completely rounded system which is The Truth.

There is, however, a great difficulty in this view, or rather two great difficulties. The first is that there is no reason to suppose that only *one* coherent body of beliefs is possible. It may be that, with sufficient imagination, a novelist might invent a past for the world that would perfectly fit on to what we know, and yet be quite different from the real past. In more scientific matters, it is certain that there are often two or more hypotheses which account for all the known facts on some subject, and although, in such cases, men of science endeavor to find facts which will rule out all the hypotheses except one, there is no reason why they should always succeed.

In philosophy, again, it seems not uncommon for two rival hypotheses to be both able to account for all the facts. Thus, for example, it is possible that life is one long dream, and that the outer world has only that degree of reality that the objects of dreams have; but although such a view does not seem inconsistent with known facts, there is no reason to prefer it to the common-sense view, according to which other people and things do really exist. Thus coherence as the definition of truth fails because there is no proof that there can be only one coherent system.

The other objection to this definition of truth is that it assumes the meaning of "coherence" known, whereas, in fact, "coherence" presupposes the truth of the laws of logic. Two propositions are coherent when both may be true, and are incoherent when one at least must be false. Now in order to know whether two propositions can both be true, we must know such truths as the law of contradiction. For example, the two propositions "this tree is a beech" and "this tree is not a beech," are not coherent, because of the law of contradiction. But if the law of contradiction itself were subjected to the test of coherence, we should find that, if we choose to suppose it false, nothing will any longer be incoherent with anything else. Thus the laws of logic supply the skeleton or framework within which the test of coherence applies, and they themselves cannot be established by this test.

For the above two reasons, coherence cannot be accepted as giving the *meaning* of truth, though it is often a most important *test* of truth after a certain amount of truth has become known.

Hence we are driven back to *correspondence with fact* as constituting the nature of truth. It remains to define precisely what we mean by "fact," and what is the nature of the correspondence which must subsist between belief and fact, in order that belief may be true.

In accordance with our three requisites, we have to seek a theory of truth which (1) allows truth to have an opposite, namely falsehood, (2) makes truth a property of beliefs, but (3) makes it a property wholly dependent upon the relation of the beliefs to outside things.

The necessity of allowing for falsehood makes it impossible to regard belief as a relation of the mind to a single object, which could be said to be what is believed. If belief were so regarded, we should find that, like acquaintance, it would not admit of the opposition of truth and falsehood, but would have to be always true. This may be made clear by examples. Othello believes falsely that Desdemona loves Cassio. We cannot say that this belief consists in a relation to a single object, "Desdemona's love for Cassio," for if there were such an object, the belief would be true. There is in fact no such object, and therefore Othello cannot have any relation to such an object. Hence his belief cannot possibly consist in a relation to this object.

It might be said that his belief is a relation to a different object, namely "that Desdemona loves Cassio"; but it is almost as difficult to suppose that there is such an object as this, when Desdemona does not love Cassio, as it was to suppose that there is "Desdemona's love for Cassio." Hence it will be better to seek for a theory of belief which does not make it consist in a relation of the mind to a single object.

It is common to think of relations as though they always held between *two* terms, but in fact this is not always the case. Some relations demand three terms, some four, and so on. Take, for instance, the relation "between." So long as only two terms come in, the relation "between" is impossible: three terms are the smallest number that render it possible. York is between London and Edinburgh; but if London and Edinburgh were the only places in the world, there could be nothing which was between one place and another. Similarly *jealousy* requires three people: there can be no such relation that does not involve three at least. Such a proposition as "A wishes B to promote C's marriage with D" involves a relation of four terms; that is to say, A and B and C and D all come in, and the relation involved cannot be expressed otherwise than in a form involving all four. Instances might be multiplied indefinitely, but enough has been said to show that there are relations which require more than two terms before they can occur.

The relation involved in *judging* or *believing* must, if falsehood is to be duly allowed for, be taken to be a relation between several terms, not between two. When Othello believes that Desdemona loves Cassio, he must not have before his mind a single object, "Desdemona's love for Cassio," or "that Desdemona loves Cassio," for that would require that there should be objective falsehoods, which subsist independently of any minds; and this, though not logically refutable, is a theory to be avoided if possible. Thus it is easier to account for falsehood if we take judgment to be a relation in which the mind and the various objects concerned all occur severally; that is to say, Desdemona and loving and Cassio must all be terms in the relation which subsists when Othello believes that Desdemona loves Cassio. This relation, therefore, is a relation of four terms, since Othello also is one of the terms of the relation. When we say that it is a relation of four terms, we do not mean that Othello has a certain relation to Desdemona, and has the same relation to loving and also to Cassio. This may be true of some other relation than believing; but believing, plainly, is not a relation which Othello has to *each* of the three terms concerned, but to *all* of them together: there is only one example of the relation of believing involved, but this one example knits together four terms. Thus the actual occurrence, at the moment when Othello is entertaining his belief, is that the relation called "believing" is knitting together into one complex whole the four terms Othello, Desdemona, loving, and Cassio. What is called belief or judgment is nothing but this relation of believing or judging, which relates a mind to several things other than itself. An *act* of belief or of judgment is the occurrence between certain terms at some particular time, of the relation of believing or judging.

We are now in a position to understand what it is that distinguishes a true judgment from a false one. For this purpose we will adopt certain definitions. In every act of judgment there is a mind which judges, and there are terms concerning which it judges. We will call the mind the *subject* in the judgment, and the remaining terms the *objects*. Thus, when Othello judges that Desdemona loves Cassio, Othello is the subject, while the objects are Desdemona and loving and Cassio. The subject and the objects together are called the *constituents* of the judgment. It will be observed that the relation of judging has what is called a "sense" or "direction." We may say, metaphorically, that it puts its objects in a certain *order*, which we may indicate by means of the order of the words in the sentence. (In an inflected language, the same thing will be indicated by inflections, e.g., by the difference between nominative and accusative.)

Othello's judgment that Cassio loves Desdemona differs from his judgment that Desdemona loves Cassio, in spite of the fact that it consists of the same constituents, because the relation of judging places the constituents in a different order in the two cases. Similarly, if Cassio judges that Desdemona loves Othello, the constituents of the judgment are still the same, but their order is different. This property of having a "sense" or "direction" is one which the relation of judging shares with all other relations. The "sense" of relations is the ultimate source of order and series and a host of mathematical concepts; but we need not concern ourselves further with this aspect.

We spoke of the relation called "judging" or "believing" as knitting together into one complex whole the subject and the objects. In this respect, judging is exactly like every other relation. Whenever a relation holds between two or more terms, it unites the terms into a complex whole. If Othello loves Desdemona, there is such a complex whole as "Othello's love for Desdemona." The terms united by the relation may be themselves complex, or may be simple, but the whole which results from their being united must be complex. Wherever there is a relation which relates certain terms, there is a complex object formed of the union of those terms; and conversely, wherever there is a complex object, there is a relation which relates its constituents. When an act of believing occurs, there is a complex, in which "believing" is the uniting relation, and subject and objects are arranged in a certain order by the "sense" of the relation of believing. Among the objects, as we saw in considering "Othello believes that Desdemona loves Cassio," one must be a relation—in this instance, the relation "loving." But this relation, as it occurs in the act of believing, is not the relation which creates the unity of the complex whole consisting of the subject and the objects. The relation "loving," as it occurs in the act of believing, is one of the objects—it is a brick in the structure, not the cement. The cement is the relation "believing." When the belief is *true*, there is another complex unity, in which the relation which was one of the objects of the belief relates the other objects. Thus, e.g., if Othello believes *truly* that Desdemona loves Cassio, then there is a complex unity, "Desdemona's love for Cassio," which is composed exclusively of the *objects* of the belief, in the same order as they had in the belief, with the relation which was one of the objects occurring now as the cement that binds together the other objects of the belief. On the other hand, when a belief is *false*, there is no such complex unity composed only of the objects of the belief. If Othello believes *falsely* that Desdemona loves Cassio, then there is no such complex unity as "Desdemona's love for Cassio."

Thus a belief is *true* when it *corresponds* to a certain associated complex, and *false* when it does not. Assuming, for the sake of definiteness, that the objects of the belief are two terms and a relation, the terms being put in a certain order by the "sense" of the believing, then if the two terms in that order are united by the relation into a complex, the belief is true; if not, it is false. This constitutes the definition of truth and falsehood that we were in search of. Judging or believing is a certain complex unity of which a mind is a constituent; if the remaining constituents, taken in the order which they have in the belief, form a complex unity, then the belief is true; if not, it is false.

Thus although truth and falsehood are properties of beliefs, yet they are in a sense extrinsic properties, for the condition of the truth of a belief is something not involving beliefs, or (in general) any mind at all, but only the *objects* of the belief. A mind, which believes, believes truly when there is a *corresponding* complex not involving the mind, but only its objects. This correspondence ensures truth, and its absence entails falsehood. Hence we account simultaneously for the two facts that beliefs (*a*) depend on minds for their *existence*, (*b*) do not depend on minds for their *truth*.

We may restate our theory as follows: If we take such a belief as "Othello believes that Desdemona loves Cassio," we will call Desdemona and Cassio the *object-terms*, and loving the *object-relation*. If there is a complex unity "Desdemona's love for Cassio," consisting of the object-terms related by the object-relation in the same order as they have in the belief, then this complex unity is called the *fact corrresponding to the belief*. Thus a belief is true when there is a corresponding fact, and is false when there is no corresponding fact.

It will be seen that minds do not *create* truth or falsehood. They create beliefs, but when once the beliefs are created, the mind cannot make them true or false, except in the special case where they concern future things which are within the power of the person believing, such as catching trains. What makes a belief true is a *fact*, and this fact does not (except in exceptional cases) in any way involve the mind of the person who has the belief.

Having now decided what we *mean* by truth and falsehood, we have next to consider what ways there are of knowing whether this or that belief is true or false. . . .

THE CORRESPONDENCE THEORY

Charles A. Campbell (1897–)

. . . For Absolute Idealism, Reality is a systematic whole, intelligibly continuous throughout. And just because it is intelligibly continuous throughout, there can be no barrier opposed in principle [1] to the effort of the intellect to apprehend it as it is. Since, again, there is thus absolutely no aspect of Reality which must perforce remain an "other" over against thought, the proper goal and culmination of the thought-process, which is also the attainment of Truth, must be envisaged as a state in which the distinction of thought from Reality ceases to be. For so long as any such distinction remains, Reality is presenting an aspect of otherness or opposition to thought, and so far fails to be "intelligible throughout" for the thinking subject. Truth, therefore, is to be found only in that thought which has become identical with Reality. And hence Idealists tend to speak almost indifferently of Truth *or* Reality. Such distinction as may be allowed is at most one of aspect. Truth is the character of "the one significant whole." When understood in its full and proper nature it is not, we are told, an attribute of judgments "about" Reality, but just that perfect systematic coherence which is the character of Reality itself.

Thus it is that it comes to be maintained in the Idealist theory of Truth, that Coherence is not merely the test or criterion of Truth, but also its essence, meaning, or nature. And Idealism, I think, is bound to hold this. Given its premises as to the nature of Reality, the steps to the conclusion seem fully logical. The Idealist grants, of course, that his conclusion wears a paradoxical air. When we speak of the proposition "Charles I died on the scaffold" as a "true" proposition, we certainly do not usually mean

Sections 1 (with some omissions) and 3 of Chapter III, pp. 82–4, 91–6, of *Scepticism and Construction* (1931), by C. A. Campbell. Used by permission of George Allen & Unwin Ltd. The title of this selection has been supplied by the editors.
[1] One is tempted to stress the qualification "in principle"; for there would seem to be still some who would impute to Idealism the overweening claim that the finite intelligence can *in fact* comprehend the universe in its totality.

by its being "true" that it is marked by systematic coherence. We mean, to use a rough expression at present, that what is affirmed corresponds with what did really take place. But this, the Idealist urges, is merely the illusion characteristic of an inadequate stage of thought's development. It is inevitable at the level at which there still remains an opposition between knowing mind and object to be known. But he has shown (he will proceed to tell us) that the search for truth at this dualistic level is not finally satisfied at this level, but attains what it aims at only in an experience in which the dualism breaks down in that fully coherent whole which is Truth and Reality in one. This Truth is, no doubt, Ideal Truth, never to be completely attained by man. But it is nonetheless the *real* nature of the Truth which you seek after in ordinary experience, the logical culmination of that search and strictly continuous with it. It expresses what you would attain were your search deepened and expanded to its ideal completion. Accordingly, while your view of Truth as "correspondence" with Reality is natural at a certain level, you are bound to admit that at that level at which Truth "comes into its own," fulfilling its proper nature, there is nothing "outside" for Truth to correspond with. Truth in its real meaning is one with Reality itself, and "correspondence," as an ultimate theory of its nature, must be frankly abandoned.

Now if "one-ness with Reality" is indeed the logical termination of the advance of the intellect—a consummation genuinely continuous with the process—then there does seem to me no option but to reject outright the Correspondence view of the meaning of Truth. That view will not hold good of Truth even at the human level. For if Reality is intelligibly continuous, there is no room for any distinction of principle between "human truth" and "ultimate truth." The one flows directly into the other. . . .

Our problem is, by what test are we to appraise the adequacy or inadequacy of our ideas to represent the reality which, at the phenomenological level, is taken as confronting us? Is it possible, for example, to hold that Correspondence is the "test" as well as the "meaning" of Truth? that to know whether we have got Truth we have to compare what is affirmed in the judgment with a "reality" somehow independently given? The objections to such a view are very numerous and very obvious, and it is really abundantly clear that Correspondence cannot be the "test." But since it would be overbold to suppose that this theory is, even yet, without disciples, and since, further, one does often in practice seem to oneself to be applying the "Correspondence test," it will be well to open with some observations upon it. To do so will at least serve to prepare the ground for a more satisfactory theory.

Let us take, then, the kind of instance in which we are accustomed to imagine ourselves to be testing a truth by its "correspondence" with "fact," and let us see what it is exactly that we are doing. Suppose that Smith says to us "This is a stone pillar," and that we, regarding the pillar closely and possibly feeling its texture with the hand, think or say, "Yes, that is true, for the 'facts' bear it out. Smith's judgment corresponds with the fact." Now do we really here compare Smith's judgment with what is just "fact"?

For the sake of precision we must allude first of all to an elementary point which has to be borne in mind, on whatever view one holds of the test of truth, with reference to the appraisement of the judgments of other persons. Smith's judgment is not, strictly speaking, one of the terms in our comparison. We do not compare Smith's judgment, for the simple reason that we cannot know it. The verbal expression of Smith's judgment in the proposition is what we know, and this is only an indication, capable of all degrees of inexactitude, of the real inner nature of what is being affirmed. What we do compare with the so-called "fact" is the meaning which the verbal expression of Smith's judgment provokes us to affirm, a meaning which we assume to be identical in all relevant particulars with Smith's meaning. It is quite clear that this assumption is, at least sometimes, profoundly mistaken. The sage may signify assent to the fool's declaration that "all is vanity," because the meaning these words stimulate him to affirm is in accord (as he thinks) with "fact." But if the sage were cognizant of the actual thought in the fool's mind he would in all probability tell the fool that he was talking nonsense. The assumption, then, that the judgment of another can be one term in our comparison is never strictly true, and is often false in a way which promotes serious fallacies.

This consideration, however, is relatively unimportant. It is the other term of the comparison that is our chief concern. What is the status of this "fact" with which we suppose the judgment to correspond? And let us henceforth assume, to avoid the difficulties indicated in the last paragraph, that it is our own judgment, not another person's, that we are trying to appraise. The presupposition of the theory is that the "fact" is a fragment of reality itself, a transcript of the objective world unmodified by any subjective influences. But analysis of the "fact" very soon discloses to us that such "facts" are nothing but creatures of theory. A fact exists *for us* only in the medium of judgment, and judgment is not a transparent window but a subjective function of an exceedingly complex nature. Activities of distinguishing and relating in terms of certain categorical characters are involved in the apprehension of even the meanest "fact." And the arguments which have from ancient times been led to establish this are not overthrown by being ignored. If you choose to neglect this subjective aspect of our "facts," what you are left with is not a "given reality" but a particularly vicious abstraction. It is inexcusable to assume that that which results only in connection with a complex process is itself indifferent to the fact of the process.[2]

Of course, to "recognize" this subjective aspect must not be taken to mean that we can straightway pronounce the fact as apprehended to be in disagreement with the fact as it is in the real order—the "epistemological object" (to use Dr Broad's terminology) in disagreement with the "ontological object." That is a matter which can only be settled by further investigation. But what it does mean is that in our so-called "Correspondence test" we are not comparing a judgment with some directly given reality, but simply with another judgment: with another judgment, which, for reasons not yet specified, we take to correspond with the objective reality and to be therefore "true."

As these last words indicate, what the Correspondence theory does is merely to throw the problem of the test of Truth back a stage. The "fact" with which the judgment is to correspond turns out to be itself a judgment, and "Correspondence" tells us nothing as to how we are to know when the latter judgment represents reality—when it is, in short, "true." It is evidence, then, that in order to apply the Correspondence test with any effect we must already be in possession of some independent criterion of the "true" judgment.

The fundamental vice of the Correspondence test is thus that its application really presupposes some other criterion. We may easily see that this is so even in regard to that class of instances which may fairly be said to represent the stronghold of the Correspondence theory—propositions in which something is predicted which is, apparently, borne out by the subsequent "facts." Brown says to us "There will be a thunderstorm tonight." If (to use the ordinary way of speech) "a thunderstorm does in fact occur," we naturally tend to say that Brown's judgment is proved true by the event. It accords with "fact." But what, again, is the "event" or "fact"? Insofar as I can use it as a term in my comparison, it is just a judgment of whose veridical character I entertain no misgivings. What happens is that I compare Brown's judgment (in the measure in which I apprehend it) with the judgment which I find myself making with considerable conviction (and suppose other persons similarly situated to find themselves making with like conviction) "tonight" with respect to the climatic conditions.

2 Cp. Bradley, *Appearance and Reality*, pp. 27–8.

And the truth of this latter judgment, the genuineness of *its* correspondence with reality, is clearly something that demands its own independent justification.

"But," common sense may retort, "surely such objections are purely academic? We shall admit, if you like, that the 'fact' of the thunderstorm is a fact for us only through judgment. But this judgment (and many another of kindred nature) is one which we find forced upon us by reality itself, not a 'construct' of our own. It is a judgment which, as you know very well, everyone, yourself included, would make in the given conditions, and there would be universal agreement that anyone who refused his assent to it was out of his mind—or at any rate out of his 'senses.' There is surely nothing outrageous, therefore, in speaking of the thunderstorm as an 'objective fact.' "

This response would mean, of course, the frank abandonment of Correspondence as an ultimate test: and it has the merit of permitting us to see the type of test which often underlies the ostensible adherence to Correspondence. The correspondence alleged is now granted to be one of judgment with judgment, and in assuming that the correspondence gives truth, it is assumed that the second judgment is true for reasons other than correspondence. What are these reasons? In point of fact, two distinct criteria are suggested by the statement made. And neither of them will bear a moment's scrutiny.

The sense of passivity, which is first suggested, is almost valueless. It is easy to show that there has gone to the making of a judgment such as "this is a thunderstorm" not even a little, but a very great deal of, "construction," even although the judging mind may appear to itself now to be purely receptive. And at any rate, it would be an exceedingly odd reading of experience which could find evidence for the view that the judgments in which we are relatively passive are in general the judgments in which we are most likely to be stating the truth about reality.

As to the second criterion suggested—that a judgment is true in so far as all normal people (whatever "normal" means) would make substantially the same judgment under substantially the same conditions—is Truth then to be ascertained by a mere counting of heads? If Truth is as difficult of attainment as has usually been supposed to be the case, then it may very well be that, at the present elementary level of our information about the physical world, we are one and all hopelessly wrong in what we mean to ascribe to Reality when we affirm, e.g., that a thunderstorm is taking place. What is actually going on in Reality when we make the judgment is in all probability something of quite undreamt-of complexity, something which, could we envisage it, we should declare to be not in the least like the meaning which we intended to assert in the judgment. And in this connection we may note a point which will have to receive fuller treatment later. What even the scientist (let alone Omniscience) means when he says that a thunderstorm is taking place has probably, in spite of the identity of verbal expression, far greater divergence from, than resemblance to, the meaning of the plain man: which further illustrates the hopelessness of appealing to the unanimous consent of mankind to support the veridical character of the common-sense judgment of "fact."

It is not disputed, of course, that in our everyday practice we are as a rule content to take the consensus of opinion of normal persons as sufficient warrant for the truth of perceived "facts." This is no doubt the case, but it merely illustrates the disparity of logic and life. About the only way in which there seems even a remote possibility of evading the difficulties that have been raised would be to take new ground and boldly contend that the deliverances of normal perception are not so much a *test* of fact as what is actually *meant* by fact. When we say "there will be a thunderstorm tonight," what we mean (on this view) is that tonight all normal persons in the vicinity who observe the weather conditions will pronounce that a thunderstorm is taking place. Such a view would escape the difficulty of having to show what ground there is for supposing normal perception to be in accord with reality, although not the difficulties connected with the actual variations within so-called "normal perception." But it has more than enough difficulties of its own, without our borrowing from those common to it with other theories. Above all, it clearly implies a new interpretation of the *meaning* of Truth. Truth on this view does not mean correspondence with the real order of things. It means merely correspondence with certain propositions about that order. But it is vain thus to try to eject from the conception of Truth its fundamental reference to the "real" order of things. The defect in this view is really of a piece with that which the Idealist theory of Truth exhibits, viz., conflict with what, in the persisting subject-object duality of experience, it seems inevitable for us to mean by Truth. It is surely a confusion to suppose that a person predicting a thunderstorm tonight means *merely* that tonight a certain judgment will be made upon the weather by all normal and suitably situated persons. He may *also* mean this, but what he means primarily is that physical reality will undergo a certain determinate modification. And it is only because he means this latter that it is possible for him also to mean the former.

ON TRUTH AND COHERENCE[1]

F. H. Bradley (1846–1924)

The welcome article by the Editor in *Mind*, No. 65, contains, we shall all agree, much food for reflection. Profiting, I hope, by all of it, there is nevertheless much from which I am forced to dissent. And in what follows here I shall try to deal with one point of disagreement. We can, I trust, isolate this point, at least sufficiently for a separate discussion.

Prof. Stout denies, I understand, that coherence will work as a test of truth in the case of facts due to sensible perception and memory. Mr. Russell again has taken the same line in his interesting article on Truth in the *Proceedings of the Aristotelian Society* for 1907. This is the issue to which here I confine myself, neglecting the question as to other truths whose warrant also is taken as immediate. What I maintain is that in the case of facts of perception and memory the test which we do apply, and which we must apply, is that of system. I contend that this test works satisfactorily, and that no other test will work. And I argue in consequence that there are no judgments of sense which are in principle infallible.

There is a misunderstanding against which the reader must be warned most emphatically. The test which I advocate is the idea of a whole of knowledge as wide and as consistent as may be. In speaking of system I mean always the union of these two aspects, and this is the sense and the only sense in which I am defending coherence. If we separate coherence from what Prof. Stout calls comprehensiveness, then I agree that neither of these aspects of system will work by itself. How they are connected, and whether in the end we have one principle or two, is of course a difficult question. I hope to return to this,[2] but it is impossible for me to touch on it here. All that I can do here is to point out that both of the above aspects

From *Essays on Truth and Reality* (1914) (omitting a few footnotes), Chapter VII, pp. 202–18. Used by permission of the Clarendon Press, Oxford.
[1] This chapter appeared first as an article in *Mind* for July 1909.
[2] See ch. VIII.

are for me inseparably included in the idea of system, and that coherence apart from comprehensiveness is not for me the test of truth or reality.

So much being premised, I will proceed not to argue in detail against Prof. Stout and Mr. Russell, but to endeavor to explain the real nature of that view which I advocate.[3] For the sake of clearness let me begin by mentioning some things in which I do *not* believe. I do not believe in any knowledge which is independent of feeling and sensation. On sensation and feeling I am sure that we depend for the material of our knowledge. And as to the facts of perception, I am convinced that (to speak broadly) we cannot anticipate them or ever become independent of that which they give to us. And these facts of perception, I further agree, are at least in part irrational, so far as in detail is visible. I do not believe that we can make ourselves independent of these non-rational data.

But, if I do not believe all this, does it follow that I have to accept independent facts? Does it follow that perception and memory give me truths which I must take up and keep as they are given me, truths which in principle cannot be erroneous? This surely would be to pass from one false extreme to another. Our intelligence cannot construct the world of perceptions and feelings, and it depends on what is given—to so much I assent. But that there are given facts of perception which are independent and ultimate and above criticism, is not to my mind a true conclusion. On the contrary, such facts to my mind are a vicious abstraction. We have, I should say, the aspect of datum, and we have the aspect of interpretation or construction, or what Prof. Stout calls implication (p. 27). And why, I ask, for the intelligence must there be datum without interpretation any more than interpretation without datum? To me the opposite holds good, and I therefore conclude that no given fact is sacrosanct. With every fact of perception or memory a modified interpretation is in principle possible, and no such fact therefore is given free from all possibility of error.

The reason for maintaining independent facts and infallible judgments, as I understand it, is twofold. (1) Such data, it may be said, can be actually shown. And (2) in any case they must exist, since without them the intelligence cannot work. Prof. Stout is identified,[4] I think, only with the second of these contentions.

(1) I doubt my ability to do justice to the position of the man who claims to show ultimate given facts exempt from all possible error. In the case of any datum of sensation or feeling, to prove that we have this wholly unmodified by what is called "apperception" seems a hopeless undertaking.

---

[3] In speaking of this common view as mine, I merely wish to indicate to the reader that I have no right to commit others to every detail of my case.
[4] *Mind*, No. 65, p. 28.

And how far it is supposed that such a negative can be proved I do not know. What, however, is meant must be this, that we somehow and somewhere have verifiable facts of perception and memory, and also judgments, free from all chance of error.

I will begin here by recalling a truth familiar but often forgotten, a truth of which Prof. Stout does not fail to remind us. In your search for independent facts and for infallible truths you may go so low that, when you have descended beyond the level of error, you find yourself below the level of any fact or of any truth which you can use. What you seek is particular facts of perception or memory, but what you get may be something not answering to that character. I will go on to give instances of what I mean, and I think that in every case we shall do well to ask this question, "What on the strength of our ultimate fact are we able to contradict?"

(*a*) If we take the instance of simple unrelated sensations or feelings, *a*, *b*, *c*—supposing that there are such things—what judgment would such a fact enable us to deny? We could on the strength of this fact deny the denial that *a*, *b*, and *c* exist in any way, manner or sense. But surely this is not the kind of independent fact of which we are in search.

(*b*) From this let us pass to the case of a complex feeling containing, at once and together, both *a* and *b*. On the ground of this we can deny the statement that *a* and *b* cannot or do not ever anyhow co-exist in feeling. This is an advance, but it surely leaves us far short of our goal.

(*c*) What we want, I presume, is something that at once is infallible and that also can be called a particular fact of perception or memory. And we want, in the case of perception, something that would be called a fact for observation. We do not seem to reach this fact until we arrive somewhere about the level of "I am here and now having a sensation or complex of sensations of such or such a kind." The goal is reached; but at this point, unfortunately, the judgment has become fallible, so far at least as it really states particular truth.

(*α*) In such a judgment it is in the first place hard to say what is meant by the "I." If, however, we go beyond feeling far enough to mean a self with such or such a real existence in time, then memory is involved, and the judgment at once, I should urge, becomes fallible. Thus the statement made in the judgment is liable to error, or else the statement does not convey particular truth.

(*β*) And this fatal dilemma holds good when applied to the "now" and "here." If these words mean a certain special place in a certain special series or order, they are liable to mistake. But, if they fall short of this meaning, then they fail to state individual fact. My feeling is, I agree, not subject to error in the proper sense of that term, but on the other side my feeling does not of itself deliver truth. And the process which gets from it a deliverance as to individual fact is fallible.

Everywhere such fact depends on construction. And we have here to face not only the possibility of what would commonly be called mistaken interpretation. We have in addition the chance of actual sense-hallucination. And, worse than this, we have the far-reaching influence of abnormal suggestion and morbid fixed idea. This influence may stop short of hallucination, and yet may vitiate the memory and the judgment to such an extent that there remains no practical difference between idea and perceived fact. And, in the face of these possibilities, it seems idle to speak of perceptions and memories secure from all chance of error. Or on the other side banish the chance of error, and with what are you left? You then have something which (as we have seen) goes no further than to warrant the assertion that such and such elements can and do co-exist—somehow and somewhere, or again that such or such a judgment happens—without any regard to its truth and without any specification of its psychical context. And no one surely will contend that with this we have particular fact.

The doctrine that perception gives us infallible truth rests on a foundation which in part is sound and in part fatally defective. That what is felt is felt, and cannot, so far as felt, be mistaken—so much as this must be accepted. But the view that, when I say "this," "now," "here," or "my," what I feel, when so speaking, is carried over intact into my judgment, and that my judgment in consequence is exempt from error, seems wholly indefensible. It survives, I venture to think, only because it never has understood its complete refutation.[5] That which I designate, is not and cannot be carried over into my judgment. The judgment may in a sense answer to that which I feel, but nonetheless it fails to contain and to convey my feeling. And on the other hand, so far as it succeeds in expressing my meaning, the judgment does this in a way which makes it liable to error. Or, to put it otherwise, the perceived truth, to be of any use, must be particularized. So far as it is stated in a general form, it contains not only that which you meant to say but also, and just as much, the opposite of that which you meant. And to contend for the infallibility of such a truth seems futile. On the other side so far as your truth really is individualized, so far as it is placed in a special construction and vitally related to its context, to the same extent the element of interpretation or implication is added. And, with this element, obviously comes the possibil-

---

5 I am of course referring here to Hegel. This is a matter to which I shall return (see chapters VII and IX). I am naturally not attempting to deal here with the whole subject of Error (see ch. IX).

ity of mistake. And we have seen above that, viewed psychologically, particular judgments of perception immune from all chance of error seem hardly tenable.

(2) I pass now to the second reason for accepting infallible data of perception. Even if we cannot show these (it is urged) we are bound to assume them. For in their absence our knowledge has nothing on which to stand, and this want of support results in total skepticism.

It is possible of course here to embrace both premises and conclusion, and to argue that skepticism is to be preferred to an untrue assumption. And such a position I would press on the notice of those who uphold infallible judgments of sense and memory. But personally I am hardly concerned in this issue, for I reject both the conclusion and the premises together. Such infallible and incorrigible judgments are really not required for our knowledge, and, since they cannot be shown, we must not say that they exist.

In maintaining that all sense-judgments are liable to error it would be better no doubt first to discuss the nature of error. But, since this is impossible here, let me state how much I take to be admitted or agreed on. I understand it to be admitted that some judgments of perception are fallible, and that the question is simply whether this description applies to all such judgments without exception. But, if some at least of these judgments are to be called fallible, what are we to understand by that word? We each of us have a world which we call our "real" world in space and time. This is an order, how made and based on what, it is impossible here to inquire. But facts of sense are called imaginary or erroneous, when in their offered character they do not belong to this "real" order in space or time. They all belong to it of course as facts in some one's mental history, but otherwise they do not qualify the "real" order as they claim to qualify it. We therefore relegate them to the sphere of the erroneous or the imaginary, unless we are able to modify and correct their claim so that it becomes admissible. So much as this I must take here to be admitted on both sides, though it is more than possible, I fear, that I may have thus unknowingly perverted the issue. Still, unless the question by some means is cleared, I see no way of proceeding. And the issue, as I understand it, will now be as follows. Are there any judgments of perception or memory, purporting to qualify the "real" world, which must necessarily qualify that world as they purport to qualify it? Or on the other hand are all such "facts" capable in principle of being relegated to the world of error, unless and until they are corrected?

This I take to be the issue, but there is a distinction which, before proceeding, the reader must notice, the distinction between *my* experience and *my* world and the world in general. It is one thing to say that there are truths which in and for my personal experience are fundamental and incorrigible, and it is another thing to assert that the same truths are infallible absolutely. This distinction will become clearer as we advance, for I will begin by confining the question to my personal experience. Is there any truth of perception which here is fundamental and infallible, and incapable of being banished to the world of fancy?

I agree that we depend vitally on the sense-world, that our material comes from it, and that apart from it knowledge could not begin. To this world, I agree, we have forever to return, not only to gain new matter but to confirm and maintain the old. I agree that to impose order from without on sheer disorder would be wholly impracticable, and that, if my sense-world were disorderly beyond a certain point, my intelligence would not exist. And further I agree that we cannot suppose it possible that *all* the judgments of perception and memory which for me come first, could in fact for me be corrected. I cannot, that is, imagine the world of my experience to be so modified that in the end none of these accepted facts should be left standing. But so far, I hasten to add, we have not yet come to the real issue. There is still a chasm between such admissions and the conclusion that there are judgments of sense which possess truth absolute and infallible.

We meet here a false doctrine largely due to a misleading metaphor. My known world is taken to be a construction built upon such and such foundations. It is argued, therefore, to be in principle a superstructure which rests upon these supports. You can go on adding to it no doubt, but only so long as the supports remain; and, unless they remain, the whole building comes down. But the doctrine, I have to contend, is untenable, and the metaphor ruinously inapplicable. The foundation in truth is provisional merely. In order to begin my construction I take the foundation as absolute—so much certainly is true. But that my construction continues to rest on the beginnings of my knowledge is a conclusion which does not follow. It does not follow that, if these are allowed to be fallible, the whole building collapses. For it is in another sense that my world rests upon the data of perception.

My experience is solid, not so far as it is a superstructure but so far as in short it is a system.[6] My object is to have a world as comprehensive and

---

[6] I would venture here in passing to question in principle the truth of a thesis advanced by Prof. Stout (pp. 34–5). Prof. Stout maintains that a proposition may be guaranteed by other propositions, and yet itself lend these no support. But if any proposition has a consequence which is not discordant with what we already know, this consequence is surely, so far as it goes, a support, however small, to the proposition from which it follows. I however agree that the amount of such support may be trifling.

coherent as possible, and, in order to attain this object, I have not only to reflect but perpetually to have recourse to the materials of sense. I must go to this source both to verify the matter which is old and also to increase it by what is new. And in this way I must depend upon the judgments of perception. Now it is agreed that, if I am to have an orderly world, I cannot possibly accept all "facts." Some of these must be relegated, as they are, to the world of error, whether we succeed or fail in modifying and correcting them. And the view which I advocate takes them all as in principle fallible. On the other hand, that view denies that there is any necessity for absolute facts of sense. Facts for it are true, we may say, just so far as they work, just so far as they contribute to the order of experience. If by taking certain judgments of perception as true, I can get more system into my world, then these "facts" are so far true, and if by taking certain "facts" as errors I can order my experience better, then so far these "facts" are errors. And there is no "fact" which possesses an absolute right. Certainly there are truths with which I begin and which I personally never have to discard, and which therefore remain in fact as members of my known world. And of some of these certainly it may be said that without them I should not know how to order my knowledge. But it is quite another thing to maintain that every single one of these judgments is in principle infallible. The absolute indispensable fact is in my view the mere creature of false theory. Facts are valid so far as, when taken otherwise than as "real," they bring disorder into my world. And there are today for me facts such that, if I take them as mistakes, my known world is damaged and, it is possible, ruined. But how does it follow that I cannot tomorrow on the strength of new facts gain a wider order in which these old facts can take a place as errors? The supposition may be improbable, but what you have got to show is that it is in principle impossible.[7] A foundation used at the beginning does not in short mean something fundamental at the end, and there is no single "fact" which in the end can be called fundamental absolutely. It is all a question of relative contribution to my known world-order.

"Then no judgment of perception will be more than probable?" Certainly that is my contention. "Facts" are justified because and as far as, while taking them as real, I am better able to deal with the incoming new "facts" and in general to make my world wider and more harmonious. The higher and wider my structure, and the more that any particular fact or set of facts is implied in that structure, the more certain are the structure and the facts. And, if we could reach an all-embracing ordered whole, then our

[7] A possible attempt to do this will be discussed towards the close of the chapter, [pp. 416–17 this volume].

certainty would be absolute. But, since we cannot do this, we have to remain content with relative probability. Why is this or that fact of observation taken as practically certain? It is so taken just so far as it is *not* taken in its own right. (i) Its validity is due to such and such a person perceiving it under such and such conditions. This means that a certain intellectual order in the person is necessary as a basis, and again that nothing in the way of sensible or mental distortion intervenes between this order and what is given. And (ii) the observed fact must agree with our world as already arranged, or at least must not upset this. If the fact is too much contrary to our arranged world we provisionally reject it. We eventually accept the fact only when after confirmation the hypothesis of its error becomes still more ruinous. We are forced then more or less to rearrange our world, and more or less perhaps to reject some previous "facts." The question throughout is as to what is better or worse for our order as a whole.

Why again to me is a remembered fact certain, supposing that it is so? Assuredly not because it is infallibly delivered by the faculty of Memory, but because I do not see how to reconcile the fact of its error with my accepted world. Unless I go on the principle of trusting my memory, apart from any special reason to the contrary, I cannot order my world so well, if indeed I can order it at all. The principle here again is system.

The same account holds with regard to the facts of history. For instance, the guillotining of Louis XVI is practically certain, because, to take this as error, would entail too much disturbance of my world. Error is possible here of course. Fresh facts conceivably might come before me such as would compel me to modify in part my knowledge as so far arranged. And in this modified arrangement the execution of Louis would find its place as an error. But the reason for such a modification would have to be considerable, while, as things are, no reason exists. And take again the case of a historical fact which is called more or less isolated. Mr. Russell [8] has instanced the honorable death of a late prelate, and has urged (as I understand) that on any view such as mine I have just as much reason to believe that this prelate was hanged. The fact is supposed to be isolated, and on mere internal evidence either alternative is taken, I presume, as equally probable. Now, of course I agree that we have innumerable cases where on mere internal evidence we are unable to distinguish between fact and fancy, but the difficulty that is supposed to arise I am unable to see. For the criterion with me is not mere absence, within the limits of this or that idea, of visible discrepancy. The question with me everywhere is as to what is the result to my real world. Now, confining myself to a certain case, the

[8] *On the Nature of Truth*, pp. 33, 35.

acceptance on the one side of the mere fancy or on the other side of the attested fact may, so far as I see, be in itself the same thing to my world. But imagine my world made on the principle of in such a case accepting mere fancy as fact. Would such a world be *more* comprehensive and coherent than the world as now arranged? Would it be coherent at all? Mr. Russell, I understand, answers in the affirmative (p. 33), but it seems to me that he has misconceived the position. To take memory as in general trustworthy, where I have no special reason for doubt, and to take the testimony of those persons, whom I suppose to view the world as I view it, as being true, apart from special reason on the other side—these are principles by which I construct my ordered world, such as it is. And because by any other method the result is worse, therefore for me these principles are true. On the other hand to suppose that any "fact" of perception or memory is so certain that no possible experience could justify me in taking it as error, seems to me injurious if not ruinous. On such a principle my world of knowledge would be ordered worse, if indeed it could be ordered at all. For to accept all the "facts," as they offer themselves, seems obviously impossible; and, if it is we who have to decide as to which facts are infallible, then I ask how we are to decide. The ground of validity, I maintain, consists in successful contribution. That is a principle of order, while any other principle, so far as I see, leads to chaos.[9]

"But," it may still be objected, "my fancy is unlimited. I can therefore invent an imaginary world even more orderly than my known world. And further this fanciful arrangement might possibly be made so wide that the world of perception would become for me in comparison small and inconsiderable. Hence, my perceived world, so far as not supporting my fancied arrangement, might be included within it as error. Such a consequence would or might lead to confusion in theory and to disaster in practice. And yet the result follows from your view inevitably, unless after all you fall back upon the certainty of perception."

To this possible objection, I should reply first, that it has probably failed to understand rightly the criterion which I defend. The aspect of comprehensiveness has not received here its due emphasis. The idea of system demands the inclusion of all possible material. Not only must you include everything to be gained from immediate experience and perception, but you must also be ready to act on the same principle with regard to

---

[9] To the question if the above principle is merely "practical," I reply, "Certainly, if you take 'practice' so widely as to remove the distinction between practice and theory." But, since such a widening of sense seems to serve no useful purpose, I cannot regard that course as being itself very "practical." I answer therefore that the above principle is certainly not merely practical.

fancy. But this means that you cannot confine yourself within the limits of this or that fancied world, as suits your pleasure or private convenience. You are bound also, so far as is possible, to recognize and to include the opposite fancy.

This consideration to my mind ruins the above hypothesis on which the objection was based. The fancied arrangement not only has opposed to it the world of perception. It also has against it any opposite arrangement and any contrary fact which I can fancy. And, so far as I can judge, these contrary fancies will balance the first. Nothing, therefore, will be left to outweigh the world as perceived, and the imaginary hypothesis will be condemned by our criterion.

And, with regard to the world as perceived, we must remember that my power is very limited. I cannot add to this world at discretion and at my pleasure create new and opposite material. Hence, to speak broadly, the material here is given and compulsory, and the production of what is contrary is out of my power. After all due reservations have been made, the contrast in this respect between the worlds of "fact" and of fancy will hold good. You cannot, as with fancies, make facts one to balance another at your pleasure. And (if we are to go still further) the riches of imagination even as regards quantity are deceptive. What we call our real world is so superior in wealth of detail that to include it, as outweighed in quantity, within some arrangement which we merely fancy, is to my mind not feasible. The whole hypothesis which we have considered seems to have been shown on more than one ground to be untenable.

But if I am asked, "Were it otherwise, what becomes of your criterion?" though I think the question unfair, I will answer it conditionally. In that supposed case I would modify my criterion. I would say, "The truth is that which enables us to order most coherently and comprehensively the data supplied by immediate experience and the intuitive judgments of perception." [10] But this answer, I repeat, is merely conditional, and I do not believe that the condition holds good. For I believe that our

10 As I am not committed to this answer, I can hardly be called on to explain it further. But I may remind the reader that immediate experience and perceptional judgment is not all of one kind. Aesthetic perceptions, for instance, will not fall under the head of mere fancies. Where the "fancy" represents some human interest, it ceases, in proportion to the importance of the interest, to be mere fancy or, properly, fancy at all.

Again, to pass from this to another point, I may be asked whether the instance of a man in collision with a new environment to which he cannot adapt himself presents no difficulty to our general criterion. In our case none, I reply, since we hold all such knowledge for relative. A difficulty arises only in the case of those who take judgments as absolute. We must, however, remember that, in the above instance of collision between inner and outer worlds, it would be wrong to assume that the man who prefers his inner world goes always against the weight of his immediate and intuitive experience.

criterion, applied without modification, gives its proper place to mere fancy. And in any case (need I add?) it does not follow that particular judgments of perception and memory, all or any of them, are infallible.

But there is an objection which perhaps for some time has been troubling the reader. "After all" (he may say) "my experience has got to be mine. If you went beyond a certain point in modifying my known world, it might possibly be a superior world but it would be no world for me. And from this it follows that something, and something given, is in my world fundamental, and that, while my world remains mine, this something is indispensable and infallible. And the fact, if it is fact, that I cannot produce this element fails to show that it is not there." Now it is one thing, I reply, to allow the existence of a fundamental element, and it is another thing to admit this in the form of an infallible judgment. I wish to emphasize this distinction and to insist that, if there is to be an infallible judgment, that judgment must be produced. On the other hand, I do not seek to deny in every sense the fact of the fundamental element. We are here in a region which so far is perhaps little understood, but for our purpose fortunately the whole question is irrelevant.

We must remind ourselves of the distinction which we laid down above. Conceivably a judgment might be fundamental and infallible for me, in the sense that to modify it or doubt it would entail the loss of my personal identity, while yet to another mind that modification or that doubt might be possible and necessary. Of course I do not mean that anything which is something for me could by a wider experience be taken as something which in no sense exists. I mean that the character in which it offers itself to me in judgment might by a wider experience be seen to need correction, and might, apart from that correction, be classed as error. I am speaking here (the reader will remember) about particular "facts" of feeling, perception or memory. And with regard to these I do not see the way by which I am to pass from relative to absolute infallibility, and I do not know how to argue here from an assumed necessary implication in my personal existence to a necessity which is more than relative. Am I to urge that a world in which my personal identity has been ended or suspended has ceased to be a world altogether? Apart from such an argument (which I cannot use) I seem condemned to the result that all sense-judgments are fallible.

The repugnance excited by this conclusion seems due to several grounds. Our immediate experience is not fallible, and this character (we have seen) is mistakenly transferred to those judgments which claim to deliver that experience. And further we had the false identification of knowledge with a mechanical superstructure supported by an external foundation. But behind this we have the demand for absolute reality in the shape of self-existent facts and of independent truths. Unless reality takes this form it seems to be nowhere, and so we go on to postulate absolute knowledge where no more than probability is attainable. Again, if the conclusion and the principle advocated here are accepted, the whole Universe seems too subject to the individual knower. What is given counts for so little and the arrangement counts for so much, while in fact the arranger, if we are to have real knowledge, seems so dependent on the world. But the individual who knows is here wrongly isolated, and then, because of that, is confronted with a mere alien Universe. And the individual, as so isolated, I agree, could do nothing, for indeed he is nothing. My real personal self which orders my world is in truth inseparably one with the Universe. Behind me the absolute reality works through and in union with myself, and the world which confronts me is at bottom one thing in substance and in power with this reality. There *is* a world of appearance and there *is* a sensuous curtain, and to seek to deny the presence of this or to identify it with reality is mistaken. But for the truth I come back always to that doctrine of Hegel, that "there is nothing behind the curtain other than that which is in front of it." [11] For what is in front of it is the Absolute that is at once one with the knower and behind him.

The conclusion advocated in these pages is, however, but limited. With regard to the two aspects of coherence and comprehensiveness I have in these pages not asked if they are connected in principle. I have merely urged that it is necessary to use them in one, and that here and here alone we have the criterion of perceived and remembered truth. And I have argued that in principle any judgment or perception of memory is liable to error, and I have urged that, if this is not so, the right conclusion is to chaos.

11 I believe these to be Hegel's words, but I cannot give any reference for them. Almost the same words will, however, be found in *Phänomenologie* (second edition), p. 126. This is the last page of the division marked A. III.

THE COHERENCE-NOTION OF TRUTH

Harold H. Joachim (1868–1938)

21. Our inquiry into the nature of truth has not . . . been rewarded with conspicuous success. . . . The essential nature of truth does not lie in the correspondence of knowledge with reality. Truth is not adequately conceived as the ideal representation of fact, or as the image which faithfully reflects an original. And, again, truth is not a quality, an immediate characteristic flavor, of independent entities which are what they are in and for themselves without relation to mind.

Of these negative results we have convinced ourselves, even if we have failed to convince the reader. . . . No special virtue attaches to immediate apprehension: and the truth is not essentially and in its nature "immediate," even though it may sometimes be manifested in an intuitive or immediate form. What is true, is true not *because* immediate form. If or when an immediate experience is true, its immediacy is irrelevant to its truth.

Our results are thus in appearance purely negative. We seem to have destroyed everything, even the materials for a possible reconstruction. But a more careful consideration will show that we have in reality made some progress towards a more adequate conception of truth. For our criticism was developed under the control of a positive notion of truth. How otherwise, indeed, could our criticism convince us that itself was true? And this positive notion, from which our criticism drew its destructive power, came to the surface in the course of our discussion. Its main features, its characteristic if somewhat shadowy outline, emerged as that *other* view of truth on which we found ourselves driven back: the view of truth as "systematic coherence." It may be difficult, but it is surely not impossible, to develop these fragmentary indications into a full and definite exposition of the coherence-notion of truth.

Chapter III, part 1 (with some footnotes omitted) of *The Nature of Truth* (1st ed., 1906; 2nd ed., 1939, London: Oxford University Press, pp. 64–84). Reprinted by permission of the Clarendon Press, Oxford.

If we succeed in formulating this theory, we must then examine it as we have examined the others; but we may approach our task with an assurance which should give us comfort. For the coherence-theory, even though it may fail to run the gauntlet of all criticism, at least goes deeper than the theories we have rejected. It is not simply another theory on the same level, side by side with them. It is the source from which they draw what speculative value they possess. So far as their attractions are not merely meretricious, they attract by masquerading in its finery. It has emerged in our discussion—so far as it *has* emerged—as the substantial basis underlying their perverted and perverse expressions. Hence we may rest confidently in our critical rejection of them. We have tested them and found them wanting; and this verdict we need never recall. Doubtless our criticism of them implied the coherence-notion of truth; and doubtless that notion may prove neither ultimate nor complete. Yet most certainly it is more complete and more nearly ultimate than the rejected theories; and if we are obliged in the end to reject it, our rejection will not reinstate the earlier views, but only confirm our condemnation of them.

22. We may start with the following as a provisional and rough formulation of the coherence-notion. "Anything is true which can be conceived. It is true because, and in so far as, it can be conceived. Conceivability is the essential nature of truth." And we may proceed at once to remove a possible misunderstanding of the term "conceive." We do not mean by "conceive" to form a mental picture; and we shall not be dismayed when we hear that the antipodes were once "inconceivable," or that a centaur can be "conceived." For it may be difficult—or even, if you like, impossible —to "image" people walking head downwards; and to "picture" a horse with the head and shoulders of a man may be as easy as you please. All this is quite irrelevant, and does not touch our position. To "conceive" means for us to think out clearly and logically, to hold many elements together in a connection necessitated by their several contents. And to be "conceivable" means to be a "significant whole," or a whole possessed of meaning for thought. "A "significant whole" is such that all its constituent elements reciprocally involve one another, or reciprocally determine one another's being as contributory features in a single concrete meaning. The elements thus cohering constitute a whole which may be said to control the reciprocal adjustment of its elements, as an end controls its constituent means. And in this sense a centaur is "inconceivable," whilst the antipodes are clearly "conceivable." For the elements constitutive of the centaur refuse to enter into reciprocal adjustment. They collide amongst themselves, or they clash with some of the constitutive elements in that wider sphere of experience, that larger significant whole, in which the centaur must strive

for a place. The horseman might pass externally as a convenient shape for rapid movement; but how about his internal economy, the structure, adjustment and functioning of his inner organs? If he is to be "actual," the animal kingdom is his natural home. But if we persisted in our attempt to locate the creature there, we should inevitably bring confusion and contradiction into that sphere of significant being—so far at least as it is manifest to us in our anatomical and physiological knowledge. And, on the other hand, the being of the antipodes is a necessary interconnected piece in that puzzle of which our astronomical science is the coherent exposition. The antipodes are "conceivable" in the sense that they are *forced* upon any thinker for whom the earth and the solar system are to possess significance; i.e., the antipodes are a necessary constituent of a significant whole, as that whole must be conceived.[1]

23. Thus "conceivability" means for us *systematic coherence,* and is the determining characteristic of a "significant whole." The systematic coherence of such a whole is expressed most adequately and explicitly in the system of reasoned knowledge which we call a science or a branch of philosophy.[2] Any element of such a whole shares in this characteristic to a

[1] I have not referred to the negative formulation, which finds the criterion of a necessary truth in the inconceivability of its opposite. Is it true, e.g., that the diagonal of a square is incommensurate with its side? Try whether its commensurability is conceivable. If it be inconceivable, the original thesis is established as a "necessary" truth. Such a view was attributed to Whewell by Mill (*Logic,* II, ch. v, § 6), in his controversy as to the ground of our belief in the mathematical axioms. But the distinction between "necessary" and "contingent" truths is not one which I should be prepared to accept; and, even apart from that, the negative formulation is unsuitable for our present purpose. A *criterion* of truth—i.e., something other than the truth itself, by which we are to recognize the truth—is not what we require. We want to know what truth in its nature is, not by what characteristics in its opposing falsehood we may infer its presence. Yet it is only the latter purpose which is facilitated by the roundabout method through the inconceivability of the opposite. The opposite is sometimes more accessible to our experiments: it is easier to try (and to fail) to conceive the false, than to try with success to conceive the true. But this is a mere psychological fact—an accident of our convenience—and does not enter into the constitution of truth as an essential element of its nature. The baffled attempt, in other words, is at best a *causa cognoscendi* of the truth, not its *causa essendi.*

[2] I am not denying that a "significant whole" may find expression in other forms and at other levels than that of discursive thinking. The moral ideal, e.g., is a significant whole, which finds expression in the ordered life of a people, in their maintenance of the laws and institutions, in their reasonable but unreflective habitual conduct, in their conscience, sense of duty and justice, love of country, love of family and friends, &c., &c. But this significant whole *in its character as truth* is most adequately expressed at the level of reflective thinking, and in the form of the science or philosophy of conduct; for such a science is the explicit analysis and the reasoned reconstruction of the inner organization (the systematic coherence) of the moral ideal. Similarly, aesthetic and religious ideals are significant wholes; and their systematic coherence or truth is most adequately revealed in the reflective form of a philosophy of art or of religion. Yet

greater or less degree—i.e., is more or less "conceivable"—in proportion as the whole, with its determinate inner articulation, shines more or less clearly through that element; or in proportion as the element, in manifesting itself, manifests also with more or less clearness and fullness the remaining elements in their reciprocal adjustment.

It is obvious that this rough sketch suggests many difficult problems. Truth, we have said, *is* in its essence conceivability or systematic coherence; and now we seem to have severed "the conceivable" from its expression, the "significant whole" from the forms in which its significance is revealed. The truth, therefore, would apparently fall on the side of the real; and would stand over against science or reasoned knowledge, faith, emotion, volition, &c., as the various subjective modes in which it obtains actuality and recognition. But this severance of the experienced real from the experiencing of it, is the very mistake against which the main discussions of our second chapter were directed; whilst, if truth be thus located in a sphere of being apart from mind, it is difficult to see how science can in any sense be "true." We spoke of science as an explicit analysis and reasoned reconstruction of the systematic coherence of a significant whole; but this sounds uncommonly like a reversion to the correspondence-notion. Science would be "true," so far as its system of demonstrations reconstructs—i.e., *repeats or corresponds to*—the systematic coherence which *is* the truth as a character of the real.

Moreover, we have admitted degrees of conceivability, and therefore also degrees of truth. But we have not explained, and perhaps could not explain, the ideal of perfect conceivability and perfect truth by reference to which these degrees are to be estimated.

Before I turn to the consideration of these problems, let me endeavor to throw further light on the theory just sketched, by contrasting it with two very different views to which it bears some superficial resemblance. The time and labor occupied in this comparison will not be wasted; for it will enable us to develop a more adequate formulation of the coherence-notion, and we shall approach the problems to be solved with a more just appreciation of their precise difficulty.

24. (i) When Descartes laid it down as a principle for the seeker after truth "to affirm nothing as true except that which he could clearly and distinctly perceive," he was in reality presupposing a very definite theory of knowledge and a correspondingly determinate metaphysics. If we wish to pass a true judgment, we must affirm or deny only that content which we clearly and distinctly apprehend. Inner affirmation, or denial, which is the

---

they also use the emotion of the artist and art-lover, or the faith of the devout but unthinking worshipper, as more immediate vehicles of their actuality.

characteristic of judgment, is an act in which we exhibit our free choice or will. But this act is exercised upon a material in the acceptance of which we are passive. The intellect—a passive recipient—apprehends a content, which the will—an active faculty—may affirm or deny. And if this affirmation is to constitute a true judgment, the content affirmed must force itself upon our intellect as a self-evident *datum*, which we immediately recognize as indubitable. Thus the immediate apprehension of indubitable truth, an "intuition," is the necessary precondition of truth of judgment. The content of such an "intuition," viz., that which we apprehend intuitively as self-evident, is a "simple idea," or rather (as Descartes sometimes more clearly expresses it) a "simple proposition." Its "simplicity" does not exclude inner distinction; for it is the immediate, but necessary, cohesion of two elements or two constituent ideas. In other words, the self-evident *datum*, which Descartes calls a "simple idea" or a "simple proposition," is a hypothetical judgment so formulated that the antecedent immediately necessitates the consequent, though the consequent need not reciprocally involve the antecedent.

The elements in the content of an "intuition" cohere by the immediate necessity which binds consequent to antecedent in a hypothetical judgment of the kind explained. But the content *as a whole* is grasped intuitively, or immediately, as an indubitable self-evident *datum*. Such self-evident indubitable truths constitute the foundation on which the structure of scientific and philosophical knowledge is built. They are the principles, from which the whole system of demonstrated and demonstrable truth must be derived. And this system is, so to say, a network of chains of propositions. The links in each chain form an uninterrupted sequence from its first link. They follow with unbroken logical coherence from a self-evident *datum*, a "simple proposition" apprehended intuitively. Each derivative link is grasped by the intellect as the necessary consequent of a link or links intuited as indubitable truths, and *as thus grasped* itself is manifest as an indubitable truth.

Thus, the ideal of knowledge for Descartes is a coherent system of truths, where each truth is apprehended in its logical position: the immediate as the basis, and the mediate truths in their necessary dependence on the immediate. Each truth in this ideal system is a cohesion of different elements united by a logical nexus; and every truth is true *per se* absolutely and unalterably.

But the theory which I am trying to expound is committed, for good or for evil, to a radically different view of the systematization of knowledge. The image of a chain, admirably suited to illustrate the theory of Descartes, is a sheer distortion of the conception of "coherence" or "conceivability," which, on my view, characterizes truth. The ideal of knowledge for me is a system, not of *truths*, but of *truth*. "Coherence" cannot be attached to propositions from the outside: it is not a property which they can acquire by colligation, whilst retaining unaltered the truth they possessed in isolation. And whereas for Descartes ideally certain knowledge (indubitable truth) is typified in the intuitive grasp of the immediately cohering elements of a "simple proposition," such a content is for me so remote from the ideal as hardly to deserve the name of "truth" at all. For it is the smallest and most abstracted fragment of knowledge, a mere mutilated shred torn from the living whole in which alone it possessed its significance. The typical embodiments of the ideal must be sought, not in such isolated intuitions, but rather in the organized whole of a science: for that possesses at least *relative* self-dependence, and its significance is at least *relatively* immanent and self-contained.

25. (ii) The second view with which I propose to contrast the coherence-theory may be regarded as a corollary of the first.[3] For, if there are certain judgments indubitably true, then these are the *materials* of knowledge. And, in the progress of thought, a *form* is imposed upon these materials which arranges without altering them. Truth is linked to truth until the arrangement constitutes that network of chains of truths which is the system of ideally complete knowledge. The form under which the infinitely various materials are ordered, is the universal form of all thinking. It is the characteristic grey of formal consistency, which any and every thinking monotonously paints over all its materials to stamp them as its own. This arrangement under the form of thinking cannot *of itself* guarantee the truth of the result. For false materials, as well as true, may be painted with the royal color. But the result cannot be true *without* this arrangement, which is thus a *sine qua non* or a "negative condition" of truth. We may christen the observance of this condition "validity"; and we may then draw the conclusion that the completely true must also be valid, though the valid may be false. Or if we prefer the term "consistency" we shall point out that consistent lying and consistent error are occasionally achieved, and that a man may be a consistent scoundrel; but that the truth requires for its apprehension and utterance the same consistency of thought and purpose, which must also be expressed in the actions of the morally good man. The consistent, in short, need be neither true nor good; but the good and the true must be consistent.

This distinction between the universal form and the particular materials of thought has, in various modifications, played a great part in the

[3] I do not suggest that the two views were *historically* so related.

history of philosophy. I am here concerned with it in its barest and most extreme shape, as the fundamental assumption of the traditional "formal" logic. Pressed beyond the limits of legitimate provisional abstraction until it has become a mere caricature, the antithesis between form and matter has in that "science" [4] been worked out through the whole domain and through all the functions of thinking. Judgment, e.g., is that function of thought whereby two conceptions are combined; and whatever the materials, the form of combination exhibits a character of its own, which is to be studied apart. Hence those classifications of "formal" logic which we have all of us learned, and learned to unlearn again: those rigid groupings of judgments as universal, individual, particular; as negative, affirmative, infinite; as categorical, hypothetical, necessary, &c., &c. So, syllogism is the function of thought whereby two judgments are combined to generate a third; and "formal" logic gives you the rules of "valid" combination irrespective of *what* is combined, and impotent therefore to determine the truth of the result.

Formal logic, in this sense of the term, might be called "the analysis of low-grade thinking" [5]; but all thinking, even at its lowest, is a living process, which the mechanical methods of such an analysis are too crude to grasp. Yet all thinking—the most complicated and profound, as well as the most shallow and rudimentary—exhibits a certain unity of character. And the formal logician has followed a sound instinct in emphasizing the necessity of analyzing and grasping this unity, if thinking is to understand itself. But he has erred in looking for the unity as an abstract common feature, to be found in the actual processes of thinking by stripping them of their concrete differences. And it is the same error which has led him to conceive thinking as a dead and finished product instead of a living and moving process. In the end and in principle his error is the failure to conceive a universal except as one element along with others in the particular: a failure which is tantamount to the negation of all universals. Or it is the failure to conceive a whole except as the sum of its parts: a failure which is the denial of unity and individual character to that which develops and lives. Hence formal logic assumes that the essential nature of thought is to be found in an abstractly self-identical form; in a tautologous self-consistency, where the "self" has no diversity of content in which a genuine consistency could be manifested, or where diversity of content is cast aside as mere irrelevant material. But the essential nature of thought is a concrete unity, a living individuality. Thought is a form, which moves and

[4] Or "art": it does not matter which title we give to what is neither one nor the other.
[5] Cf., e.g., Bosanquet, *Knowledge and Reality*, 2nd issue, p. 193.

expands, and exhibits its consistent character precisely in those ordered articulations of its structure which formal logic impotently dismisses as *mere* materials.

The "systematic coherence", therefore, in which we are looking for the nature of truth, must not be confused with the "consistency" of formal logic. A piece of thinking might be free from self-contradiction, might be "consistent" and "valid" as the formal logician understands those terms, and yet it might fail to exhibit that systematic coherence which is truth.

26. We may now proceed to formulate the coherence-theory afresh in the following terms. Truth in its essential nature is that systematic coherence which is the character of a significant whole. A "significant whole" is an organized individual experience, self-fulfilling and self-fulfilled. Its organization *is* the process of its self-fulfillment, and the concrete manifestation of its individuality. But this process is no mere surface-play between static parts within the whole: nor *is* the individuality of the whole, except in the movement which is its manifestation. The whole *is* not, if "is" implies that its nature is a finished product prior or posterior to the process, or in any sense apart from it. And the whole *has* no parts, if "to have parts" means to consist of fixed and determinate constituents, from and to which the actions and interactions of its organic life proceed, much as a train may travel backwards and forwards between the terminal stations. Its "parts" are through and through in the process and constituted by it. They are "moments" in the self-fulfilling process which is the individuality of the whole. And the individuality of the whole is *both* the presupposition of the distinctive being of its "moments" or parts *and* the resultant which emerges as their cooperation, or which they make and continuously sustain.

It is this process of self-fulfillment which is truth, and it is *this* which the theory means by "systematic coherence." The process is not a movement playing between static elements, but the very substance of the moving elements. And the coherence is no abstract form imposed upon the surface of materials, which retain in their depths a nature untouched by the imposition. The coherence—if we call it a "form"—is a form which through and through inter-penetrates its materials; and they—if we call them "materials"—are materials, which retain no inner privacy for themselves in independence of the form. They hold their distinctive being in and through, and not in sheer defiance of, their identical form; and its identity is the concrete sameness of different materials. The materials *are* only as moments in the process which is the continuous emergence of the coherence. And the form *is* only as the sustained process of self-fulfillment, wherein just these materials reveal themselves as constitutive moments of the coherence.

In the above formulation I have endeavored to express the coherence-notion so as to emphasize the *concreteness* of the coherence which is truth, as against the view which found truth in formal consistency; [6] and I have insisted upon the conception of truth as a living and moving whole, as against the Cartesian view of fixed truths on which the structure of knowledge is built. [7] But the result at present is a mere vague sketch, which cannot pretend to be satisfactory. Even the well disposed reader will regard it as the description of a mystical ideal with no obvious application to the actual problems of human knowledge; whilst the hostile critic will view it as a dishonest evasion of the difficulties, as mere words in place of a solid discussion. I shall accordingly attempt to work out my sketch in detail, so as to show the precise bearing of this conception of truth on the truth in human judgment and inference, and so as to defend it against the charge of mysticism or evasion of the difficulties.

27. If we are to develop our vague sketch into a definite theory, we must make it clear *what* truth we are professing to describe. Was our sketch intended as an exposition of truth as it is for human knowledge? or were we describing an ideal experience, which no finite mind can ever actually enjoy?

This manner of formulating the question seems to challenge a choice between two unambiguous alternatives, and thus to put a clear issue before us. But in reality it involves certain assumptions which are open to debate, and which—as I think, and hope to show—are false. [8] For it is assumed that finite experience is sundered by a gulf from ideal experience. It is implied that an ideal experience is as such debarred from actuality, and it is suggested that knowledge which is severed from ideal experience can yet be true. But, whilst refusing to commit myself to these implications, I should reply that my sketch was intended to describe the nature of truth as an ideal, as the character of an ideally complete experience. Truth, we said, was the systematic coherence which characterized a significant whole. And we proceeded to identify a significant whole with "an organized individual experience, self-fulfilling and self-fulfilled." Now there can be one *and only one* such experience: or *only one* significant whole, the significance of which is self-contained in the sense required. For it is *absolute* self-fulfillment, *absolutely* self-contained significance, that is postulated; and

6 Cf. above, 25. [pp. 424 ff. this volume].
7 Cf. above, 24. [pp. 422–24 this volume].
8 Cf. below, pp. 82, 83 [this volume pp. 430–31].

nothing short of *absolute* individuality—nothing short of *the* completely
whole experience—can satisfy this postulate. And human knowledge—not
merely *my* knowledge or *yours*, but the best and fullest knowledge in the
world at any stage of its development—is clearly not a significant whole in
this ideally complete sense. Hence the truth, which our sketch described,
is—*from the point of view of the human intelligence*—an ideal, and an
ideal which can never *as such*, or in its completeness, be actual as human
experience.

But it will be contended that such an ideal cannot be expressed in
terms of human thought, and is strictly inconceivable. "All attempts to
conceive your ideal," we shall be told, "are foredoomed to failure. For we
cannot conceive, except under categories whose meaning is molded and
restricted by the limitations of that finite experience in which alone they
have any legitimate application. We employ categories with a determinate
meaning in their application to the incomplete experience, which is actually ours: but their meaning is determinate, only in so far as it is relative
to the area in which the restricting conditions hold. Yet the conception of
your ideal requires the absolute and unrestricted use of these categories.
But, if they are used absolutely, we can conceive nothing determinate
under them: we are playing with empty words. Whilst, if they are used
under the restrictions which condition their application in finite experience, they are inadequate to express the ideal, and distort instead of describing its nature. Thus you made use, e.g., of the notions of life, organism,
self-fulfilling process. These notions have a determinate meaning in their
application to the objects of our limited experience; but their meaning is
itself restricted in that application. The life of any object of our experience
is far from being a self-sustaining process, a closed circle of functions revolving free from all external conditions. It is limited in every way, dependent
in origin, extent, intensity and duration, and conditioned throughout by
what is other and perhaps hostile. No object of our experience *is* Life; and
the life, which some of them manifest, is conditioned by the sources from
which it was derived, and by the bodily organs and the environment in
and through which it is maintained. Yet the 'living whole,' which is your
ideal, is to be limited in no way, and in no way dependent upon anything
other than itself. Or did you intend to suggest that it came to be, and
grew, and would pass away; that it maintained itself in this its bodily
vehicle over against an environment not itself? Nor again can the notion
of organism find absolute expression in any of the objects of our experience. No whole is through and through organic, an organism pure and
simple. We never find a whole whose parts are what they are as reciprocally ends and means to one another, and such that the plan of

coherence (which is the whole) determines absolutely the nature and the being of the parts which in turn constitute it. The idea of such a purely organic whole remains an empty conception, a shadowy notion with no positive significance. To describe your ideal as an 'organized experience,' if 'organized' is used in this absolute sense, in no way elucidates your meaning. And self-fulfillment, where it applies in our experience, expresses a process which starts with given materials and a given and limited power of working upon them. At best, the process culminates in a limited achievement; and, after a shorter or a longer period of effort and relative success, the self and its fulfillment vanish together. Yet you used all these notions to describe your ideal, with an utter disregard of the restrictions under which alone they convey a determinate meaning. And the result was meaningless phrases—words such as 'a process, whose moments sustain the whole, and themselves are made and constituted by the process,' or 'a movement which is the very substance of the moving elements.' "

28. Now it may be admitted that conceptions derived from partial wholes cannot adequately express *the* whole; and that what we experience is in a sense always a partial whole, or the whole from a finite and partial point of view. We cannot experience the whole completely and adequately, just in so far as we are not ourselves complete. But because we are not complete, it does not follow that we are divorced from the complete and in sheer opposition to it. We are not absolutely real, but neither are we utterly unreal. And because our apprehension is restricted, and in part confused, it does not follow that it is utterly false and an entire distortion of the nature of things. The categories which we have to employ are no doubt inadequate to express the complete reality; but this is no reason for not employing them at all, or for employing them all alike and indifferently. For they all to some extent express the whole; and there are degrees in the relative adequacy of the expression. The categories of life, organism, and self-fulfillment express in our experience wholes of a more concrete, more developed and relatively more self-contained individuality than, e.g., the categories under which we conceive a whole of aggregation, or a whole constituted by the limiting outline of its continent environment, or again a whole whose inner being is a static adjustment of parts of a surface-play of movements between fixed constituent elements. And for this reason I employed these categories as relatively more adequate notions under which to conceive the ideal. Still more adequate notions might perhaps have been found within our finite experience. For it would seem that the significant whole, which is truth, can in the end be most adequately described only in terms of the categories of self-conscious thought. But it is worthwhile to describe it in terms of the categories of life, organism, and self-fulfilling

process as against those lower grades of theory which we have been criticizing—theories which conceive it under the notions of a static whole, like a "building"; or of an aggregation of units, like a "sum of truths"; or of a static adjustment of two wholes of fixed elements, like a "correspondence" between original and copy.

But the real way to meet the charge that the ideal is inconceivable is to challenge the "common-sense" attitude of the critic. The ideal, he is in effect maintaining, is not in its completeness *here* and *now*, and therefore is not actual: it cannot be adequately expressed in terms of finite experience, and therefore is inconceivable. And this criticism betrays an amazing acquiescence in the first hasty assumptions of the unreflecting consciousness. For the critic assumes that finite experience is solid and fully real and clearly conceivable, an unshaken *datum* here and now; and that we must accept it without question as, so to say, a pier from which to throw a bridge across to the cloudland ideal. But we have been demanding all along an entire reversal of this attitude. In our view it is the ideal which is solid and substantial and fully actual. The finite experiences are rooted in the ideal. They share its actuality, and draw from it whatever being and conceivability they possess. It is a perverse attitude to condemn the ideal because the conditions, under which the finite experiences exhibit their fragmentary actuality, do not as such restrict its being; or to deny that it is conceivable, because the conceivability of such incomplete expressions is too confused and turbid to apply to it.

That nothing in our partial experience answers precisely to the demands of the ideal, cannot show that the ideal is an unsubstantial dream, an idle play of words. The question is whether our partial experience through and through involves the being of the ideally-complete experience which we have postulated. And the way to answer this question is to examine the implications of our partial experience, or on the other hand to trace the ideal in its manifestations.

29. But this is precisely where our critics will join issue with us. For they will fasten on the term "experience," and they will demand, "*Whose* is this ideal experience? *Where* and *when* is it actual? What is its precise *relation* to the finite experiences?"

Now one answer to such questions is, "Such an experience is nowhere and at no time, no one possesses it, and it is related to nothing save itself." For the questions assume that the truth is a finished product, a static consummated whole of experience, which *is* somewhere and at some time, exclusive of the finite experiences as occurrences in time and place, and yet related to them. But this is not what was meant. And again they assume that the truth is the possession of a finite being. They regard it as the experience of a "this-now," much as I may here and now experience this toothache. But this again was not meant, though the misleading associations of the term "experience" to some extent justify the misunderstanding.[9]

It is not, however, of much value to make a negative answer of this kind. On the other hand, if we answered, "Such an ideal experience is everywhere and at all times; it is the partial possession of all finite beings, and they are the incomplete vehicles of it," we should merely be repeating more explicitly what we have already asserted. The mere assertion is useless; but nothing short of an entire system of metaphysics could serve as its justification. The difficulty, in short, is that our problem is expanding into the whole problem of philosophy, and that the discussion threatens to become unmanageable.

But we must make an effort to discuss the "relation" of the ideal truth to the truth of human judgment and inference without wandering into the field of metaphysical speculation at large. Perhaps the most hopeful procedure will be to start from a few typical instances of "true" judgment. If we can show their "truth" expanding in each case into a system of knowledge, and that again as borrowing what truth it possesses from the ideal experience which is struggling for self-fulfillment in it, we shall be able to face the difficulties we have raised. We shall be able to face them, for we shall be working with something definite; but we must not assume that we shall be able to solve or remove them.

[9] The term "experience" is unsatisfactory, and I should not use it if I could find a better word. I have endeavored to guard against its mischievous associations by coupling it with the expression "significant whole." But if "experience" tends to suggest the experiencing apart from the experienced, "significant whole" tends to suggest the experienced apart from the experiencing. We want a term to express the concrete unity of both, and I cannot find one. For the term "God," if substituted for "ideal experience," would be seriously misleading in other ways. And superficial criticism, directed against certain travesties of "Hegelianism," has degraded "the Absolute" or "the Idea"—terms in many respects the best for our purpose—until they have become mere conventional symbols for abstractions, which the critic first invents and then dislikes. If we were to employ these terms we should merely excite prejudice, without suggesting the philosophical meaning which they bore in Hegel's system.

THE PRAGMATIC THEORY OF TRUTH

William James (1842–1910)

I

. . . I fully expect to see the pragmatist view of truth run through the classic stages of a theory's career. First, you know, a new theory is attacked as absurd; then it is admitted to be true, but obvious and insignificant; finally it is seen to be so important that its adversaries claim that they themselves discovered it. Our doctrine of truth is at present in the first of these three stages, with symptoms of the second stage having begun in certain quarters. I wish that this lecture might help it beyond the first stage in the eyes of many of you.

Truth, as any dictionary will tell you, is a property of certain of our ideas. It means their "agreement," as falsity means their disagreement, with "reality." Pragmatists and intellectualists both accept this definition as a matter of course. They begin to quarrel only after the question is raised as to what may precisely be meant by the term "agreement," and what by the term "reality," when reality is taken as something for our ideas to agree with.

In answering these questions the pragmatists are more analytic and painstaking, the intellectualists more offhand and irreflective. The popular notion is that a true idea must copy its reality. Like other popular views, this one follows the analogy of the most usual experience. Our true ideas of sensible things do indeed copy them. Shut your eyes and think of yonder clock on the wall, and you get just such a true picture or copy of its dial. But your idea of its "works" (unless you are a clock-maker) is much less of a copy, yet it passes muster, for it in no way clashes with the reality. Even though it should shrink to the mere word "works," that word still serves you truly; and when you speak of the "time-keeping function" of the

From *Pragmatism* (1907). Part I is from Lecture VI, pp. 198–209; part II from Lecture VI, pp. 218–223; and part III from Lecture II, pp. 75–78.

clock, or of its spring's "elasticity," it is hard to see exactly what your ideas can copy.

You perceive that there is a problem here. Where our ideas cannot copy definitely their object, what does agreement with that object mean? Some idealists seem to say that they are true whenever they are what God means that we ought to think about that object. Others hold the copy-view all through, and speak as if our ideas possessed truth just in proportion as they approach to being copies of the Absolute's eternal way of thinking.

These views, you see, invite pragmatistic discussion. But the great assumption of the intellectualists is that truth means essentially an inert static relation. When you've got your true idea of anything, there's an end of the matter. You're in possession; you *know*; you have fulfilled your thinking destiny. You are where you ought to be mentally; you have obeyed your categorical imperative; and nothing more need follow on that climax of your rational destiny. Epistemologically you are in stable equilibrium.

Pragmatism, on the other hand, asks its usual question. "Grant an idea or belief to be true," it says, "what concrete difference will its being true make in any one's actual life? How will the truth be realized? What experiences will be different from those which would obtain if the belief were false? What, in short, is the truth's cash-value in experiential terms?"

The moment pragmatism asks this question, it sees the answer: *True ideas are those that we can assimilate, validate, corroborate and verify. False ideas are those that we cannot.* That is the practical difference it makes to us to have true ideas; that, therefore, is the meaning of truth, for it is all that truth is known-as.

This thesis is what I have to defend. The truth of an idea is not a stagnant property inherent in it. Truth *happens* to an idea. It *becomes* true, is *made* true by events. Its verity *is* in fact an event, a process: the process namely of its verifying itself, its veri-*fication*. Its validity is the process of its valid-*ation*.

But what do the words verification and validation themselves pragmatically mean? They again signify certain practical consequences of the verified and validated idea. It is hard to find any one phrase that characterizes these consequences better than the ordinary agreement-formula—just such consequences being what we have in mind whenever we say that our ideas "agree" with reality. They lead us, namely, through the acts and other ideas which they instigate, into or up to, or towards, other parts of experience with which we feel all the while—such feeling being among our potentialities—that the original ideas remain in agreement. The connections and transitions come to us from point to point as being progressive, harmonious, satisfactory. This function of agreeable leading is what we mean by an idea's verification. . . .

. . . The possession of true thoughts means everywhere the possession of invaluable instruments of action; and . . . our duty to gain truth, so far from being a blank command from out of the blue, or a "stunt" self-imposed by our intellect, can account for itself by excellent practical reasons.

The importance to human life of having true beliefs about matters of fact is a thing too notorious. We live in a world of realities that can be infinitely useful or infinitely harmful. Ideas that tell us which of them to expect count as the true ideas in all this primary sphere of verification, and the pursuit of such ideas is a primary human duty. The possession of truth, so far from being here an end in itself, is only a preliminary means towards other vital satisfactions. If I am lost in the woods and starved, and find what looks like a cow-path, it is of the utmost importance that I should think of a human habitation at the end of it, for if I do so and follow it, I save myself. The true thought is useful here because the house which is its object is useful. The practical value of true ideas is thus primarily derived from the practical importance of their objects to us. Their objects are, indeed, not important at all times. I may on another occasion have no use for the house; and then my idea of it, however verifiable, will be practically irrelevant, and had better remain latent. Yet since almost any object may some day become temporarily important, the advantage of having a general stock of *extra* truths, of ideas that shall be true of merely possible situations, is obvious. We store such extra truths away in our memories, and with the overflow we fill our books of reference. Whenever such an extra truth becomes practically relevant to one of our emergencies, it passes from cold-storage to do work in the world and our belief in it grows active. You can say of it then either that "it is useful because it is true" or that "it is true because it is useful." Both these phrases mean exactly the same thing, namely that here is an idea that gets fulfilled and can be verified. True is the name for whatever idea starts the verification-process, useful is the name for its completed function in experience. True ideas would never have been singled out as such, would never have acquired a class-name, least of all a name suggesting value, unless they had been useful from the outset in this way.

From this simple cue pragmatism gets her general notion of truth as something essentially bound up with the way in which one moment in our experience may lead us towards other moments which it will be worthwhile to have been led to. Primarily, and on the common-sense level, the truth of a state of mind means this function of *a leading that is worthwhile*. When a moment in our experience, of any kind whatever, inspires us with a thought that is true, that means that sooner or later we dip by that thought's guidance into the particulars of experience again and make advantageous connection with them. This is a vague enough statement, but I beg you to retain it, for it is essential.

Our experience meanwhile is all shot through with regularities. One bit of it can warn us to get ready for another bit, can "intend" or be "significant of" that remoter object. The object's advent is the significance's verification. Truth, in these cases, meaning nothing but eventual verification, is manifestly incompatible with waywardness on our part. Woe to him whose beliefs play fast and loose with the order which realities follow in his experience; they will lead him nowhere or else make false connections.

By "realities" or "objects" here, we mean either things of common sense, sensibly present, or else common-sense relations, such as dates, places, distances, kinds, activities. Following our mental image of a house along the cow-path, we actually come to see the house; we get the image's full verification. *Such simply and fully verified leadings are certainly the originals and prototypes of the truth-process.* Experience offers indeed other forms of truth-process, but they are all conceivable as being primary verifications arrested, multiplied or substituted one for another.

Take, for instance, yonder object on the wall. You and I consider it to be a "clock," altho no one of us has seen the hidden works that make it one. We let our notion pass for true without attempting to verify. If truths mean verification-process essentially, ought we then to call such unverified truths as this abortive? No, for they form the overwhelmingly large number of the truths we live by. Indirect as well as direct verifications pass muster. Where circumstantial evidence is sufficient, we can go without eye-witnessing. Just as we here assume Japan to exist without ever having been there, because it *works* to do so, everything we know conspiring with the belief, and nothing interfering, so we assume that thing to be a clock. We *use* it as a clock, regulating the length of our lecture by it. The verification of the assumption here means its leading to no frustration or contradiction. Verifi*ability* of wheels and weights and pendulum is as good as verification. For one truth-process completed there are a million in our lives that function in this state of nascency. They turn us *towards* direct verification; lead us into the *surroundings* of the objects they envisage; and then, if everything runs on harmoniously, we are so sure that verification is possible that we omit it, and are usually justified by all that happens.

Truth lives, in fact, for the most part on a credit system. Our thoughts and beliefs "pass," so long as nothing challenges them, just as bank-notes pass so long as nobody refuses them. But this all points to direct face-to-face verifications somewhere, without which the fabric of truth collapses like a financial system with no cash-basis whatever. You accept my verification of one thing, I yours of another. We trade on each other's truth. But beliefs verified concretely by *somebody* are the posts of the whole super-structure.

Another great reason—beside economy of time—for waiving complete verification in the usual business of life is that all things exist in kinds and not singly. Our world is found once for all to have that peculiarity. So that when we have once directly verified our ideas about one specimen of a kind, we consider ourselves free to apply them to other specimens without verification. A mind that habitually discerns the kind of thing before it, and acts by the law of the kind immediately, without pausing to verify, will be a "true" mind in ninety-nine out of a hundred emergencies, proved so by its conduct fitting everything it meets, and getting no refutation.

Indirectly or only potentially verifying processes may thus be true as well as full verification-processes. They work as true processes would work, give us the same advantages, and claim our recognition for the same reasons. . . .

II

Our account of truth is an account of truths in the plural, of processes of leading, realized *in rebus*,[1] and having only this quality in common, that they *pay*. They pay by guiding us into or towards some part of a system that dips at numerous points into sense-percepts, which we may copy mentally or not, but with which at any rate we are now in the kind of commerce vaguely designated as verification. Truth for us is simply a collective name for verification-processes, just as health, wealth, strength, etc., are names for other processes connected with life, and also pursued because it pays to pursue them. Truth is *made*, just as health, wealth and strength are made, in the course of experience.

Here rationalism is instantaneously up in arms against us. I can imagine a rationalist to talk as follows:

"Truth is not made," he will say; "it absolutely obtains, being a unique relation that does not wait upon any process, but shoots straight over the head of experience, and hits its reality every time. Our belief that yon thing on the wall is a clock is true already, altho no one in the whole history of the world should verify it. The bare quality of standing in that

1 [In things—ed. note.]

transcendent relation is what makes any thought true that possesses it, whether or not there be verification. You pragmatists put the cart before the horse in making truth's being reside in verification-processes. These are merely signs of its being, merely our lame ways of ascertaining after the fact, which of our ideas already has possessed the wondrous quality. The quality itself is timeless, like all essences and natures. Thoughts partake of it directly, as they partake of falsity or of irrelevancy. It can't be analyzed away into pragmatic consequences."

The whole plausibility of this rationalist tirade is due to the fact to which we have already paid so much attention. In our world, namely, abounding as it does in things of similar kinds and similarly associated, one verification serves for others of its kind, and one great use of knowing things is to be led not so much to them as to their associates, especially to human talk about them. The quality of truth, obtaining *ante rem*, [2] pragmatically means, then, the fact that in such a world innumerable ideas work better by their indirect or possible than by their direct and actual verification. Truth *ante rem* means only verifiability, then; or else it is a case of the stock rationalist trick of treating the *name* of a concrete phenomenal reality as an independent prior entity, and placing it behind the reality as its explanation. . . .

In the case of "wealth" we all see the fallacy. We know that wealth is but a name for concrete processes that certain men's lives play a part in, and not a natural excellence found in Messrs. Rockefeller and Carnegie, but not in the rest of us.

Like wealth, health also lives *in rebus*. It is a name for processes, as digestion, circulation, sleep, etc., that go on happily, tho in this instance we are more inclined to think of it as a principle and to say the man digests and sleeps so well *because* he is so healthy.

With "strength" we are, I think, more rationalistic still, and decidedly inclined to treat it as an excellence pre-existing in the man and explanatory of the herculean performances of his muscles.

With "truth" most people go over the border entirely, and treat the rationalistic account as self-evident. But really all these words in *th* are exactly similar. Truth exists *ante rem* just as much and as little as the other things do.

The scholastics, following Aristotle, made much of the distinction between habit and act. Health *in actu* [3] means, among other things, good sleeping and digesting. But a healthy man need not always be sleeping, or always digesting, any more than a wealthy man need be always handling

[2] [Before the thing—ed. note.]
[3] [In actuality—ed. note.]

money, or a strong man always lifting weights. All such qualities sink to the status of "habits" between their times of exercise; and similarly truth becomes a habit of certain of our ideas and beliefs in their intervals of rest from their verifying activities. But those activities are the root of the whole matter, and the condition of there being any habit to exist in the intervals.

"The true," to put it very briefly, is only the expedient in the way of our thinking, just as "the right" is only the expedient in the way of our behaving. Expedient in almost any fashion; and expedient in the long run and on the whole of course; for what meets expediently all the experience in sight won't necessarily meet all farther experiences equally satisfactorily. Experience, as we know, has ways of *boiling over*, and making us correct our present formulas.

The "absolutely" true, meaning what no farther experience will ever alter, is that ideal vanishing-point towards which we imagine that all our temporary truths will some day converge. It runs on all fours with the perfectly wise man, and with the absolutely complete experience; and, if these ideals are ever realized, they will all be realized together. Meanwhile we have to live today by what truth we can get today, and be ready tomorrow to call it falsehood. Ptolemaic astronomy, Euclidean space, Aristotelian logic, scholastic metaphysics, were expedient for centuries, but human experience has boiled over those limits, and we now call these things only relatively true, or true within those borders of experience. "Absolutely" they are false; for we know that those limits were casual, and might have been transcended by past theorists just as they are by present thinkers. . . .

III

. . . Truth is *one species of good*, and not, as is usually supposed, a category distinct from good, and coordinate with it. *The true is the name of whatever proves itself to be good in the way of belief, and good, too, for definite, assignable reasons.* Surely you must admit this, that if there were *no* good for life in true ideas, or if the knowledge of them were positively disadvantageous and false ideas the only useful ones, then the current notion that truth is divine and precious, and its pursuit a duty, could never have grown up or become a dogma. In a world like that, our duty would be to *shun* truth, rather. But in this world, just as certain foods are not only agreeable to our taste, but good for our teeth, our stomach, and our tissues; so certain ideas are not only agreeable to think about, or agreeable as supporting other ideas that we are fond of, but they are also helpful in life's practical struggles. If there be any life that it is really better we should lead, and if there be any idea which, if believed in, would help us to lead that life, then it would be really *better for us* to believe in that idea, *unless, indeed, belief in it incidentally clashed with other greater vital benefits.*

"What would be better for us to believe!" This sounds very like a definition of truth. It comes very near to saying "what we *ought* to believe:" and in *that* definition none of you would find any oddity. Ought we ever not to believe what it is *better for us* to believe? And can we then keep the notion of what is better for us, and what is true for us, permanently apart?

Pragmatism says no, and I fully agree with her. Probably you also agree, so far as the abstract statement goes, but with a suspicion that if we practically did believe everything that made for good in our own personal lives, we should be found indulging all kinds of fancies about this world's affairs, and all kinds of sentimental superstitions about a world hereafter. Your suspicion here is undoubtedly well founded, and it is evident that something happens when you pass from the abstract to the concrete that complicates the situation.

I said just now that what is better for us to believe is true *unless the belief incidentally clashes with some other vital benefit.* Now in real life what vital benefits is any particular belief of ours most liable to clash with? What indeed except the vital benefits yielded by *other beliefs* when these *prove* incompatible with the first ones? In other words, the greatest enemy of any one of our truths may be the rest of our truths. Truths have once for all this desperate instinct of self-preservation and of desire to extinguish whatever contradicts them. . . .

THE INSTRUMENTALIST ACCOUNT OF TRUTH

John Dewey (1859–1952)

. . . Little time is left to speak of the account of the nature of truth given by the experimental and functional type of logic. This is less to be regretted because this account is completely a corollary from the nature of thinking and ideas. If the view held as to the latter is understood, the conception of truth follows as a matter of course. If it be not understood, any attempt to present the theory of truth is bound to be confusing, and the theory itself to seem arbitrary and absurd. *If* ideas, meanings, conceptions, notions, theories, systems are instrumental to an active reorganization of the given environment, to a removal of some specific trouble and perplexity, then the test of their validity and value lies in accomplishing this work. If they succeed in their office, they are reliable, sound, valid, good, true. If they fail to clear up confusion, to eliminate defects, if they increase confusion, uncertainty and evil when they are acted upon, then are they false. Confirmation, corroboration, verification lie in works, consequences. Handsome is that handsome does. By their fruits shall ye *know* them. That which guides us truly is true—demonstrated capacity for such guidance is precisely what is meant by truth. The adverb "truly" is more fundamental than either the adjective, true, or the noun, truth. An adverb expresses a way, a mode of acting. Now an idea or conception is a claim or injunction or plan to *act* in a certain way as the way to arrive at the clearing up of a specific situation. When the claim or pretension or plan is acted upon *it guides us truly or falsely*; it leads us to our end or away from it. Its active, dynamic function is the all-important thing about it, and in the quality of activity induced by it lies all its truth and falsity. The hypothesis that works is the *true* one; and *truth* is an abstract noun applied to the collection of cases, actual, foreseen and desired, that receive confirmation in their works and consequences.

The last four paragraphs of Chapter 6 of *Reconstruction in Philosophy* (1920), by John Dewey. Reprinted by permission of the Beacon Press. The title of this selection has been supplied by the editors.

So wholly does the worth of this conception of truth depend upon the correctness of the prior account of thinking that it is more profitable to consider why the conception gives offence than to expound it on its own account. Part of the reason why it has been found so obnoxious is doubtless its novelty and defects in its statement. Too often, for example, when truth has been thought of as satisfaction, it has been thought of as merely emotional satisfaction, a private comfort, a meeting of purely personal need. But the satisfaction in question means a satisfaction of the needs and conditions of the problem out of which the idea, the purpose and method of action, arises. It includes public and objective conditions. It is not to be manipulated by whim or personal idiosyncrasy. Again when truth is defined as utility, it is often thought to mean utility for some purely personal end, some profit upon which a particular individual has set his heart. So repulsive is a conception of truth which makes it a mere tool of private ambition and aggrandizement, that the wonder is that critics have attributed such a notion to sane men. As matter of fact, truth as utility means service in making just that contribution to reorganization in experience that the idea or theory claims to be able to make. The usefulness of a road is not measured by the degree in which it lends itself to the purposes of a highwayman. It is measured by whether it actually functions *as* a road, as a means of easy and effective public transportation and communication. And so with the serviceableness of an idea or hypothesis as a measure of its truth.

Turning from such rather superficial misunderstandings, we find, I think, the chief obstacle to the reception of this notion of truth in an inheritance from the classic tradition that has become so deeply ingrained in men's minds. In just the degree in which existence is divided into two realms, a higher one of perfect being and a lower one of seeming, phenomenal, deficient reality, truth and falsity are thought of as fixed, readymade static properties of things themselves. Supreme Reality is true Being, inferior and imperfect Reality is false Being. It makes claims to Reality which it cannot substantiate. It is deceitful, fraudulent, inherently unworthy of trust and belief. Beliefs are false not because they mislead us; they are not mistaken ways of thinking. They are false because they admit and adhere to false existences or subsistences. Other notions are true because they do have to do with true Being—with full and ultimate Reality. Such a notion lies at the back of the head of every one who has, in however an indirect way, been a recipient of the ancient and medieval tradition. This view is radically challenged by the pragmatic conception of truth, and the impossibility of reconciliation or compromise is, I think, the cause of the shock occasioned by the newer theory.

This contrast, however, constitutes the importance of the new theory as well as the unconscious obstruction to its acceptance. The older conception worked out practically to identify truth with authoritative dogma. A society that chiefly esteems order, that finds growth painful and change disturbing, inevitably seeks for a fixed body of superior truths upon which it may depend. It looks backward, to something already in existence, for the source and sanction of truth. It falls back upon what is antecedent, prior, original, *a priori*, for assurance. The thought of looking ahead, toward the eventual, toward consequences, creates uneasiness and fear. It disturbs the sense of rest that is attached to the ideas of fixed Truth already in existence. It puts a heavy burden of responsibility upon us for search, unremitting observation, scrupulous development of hypotheses and thoroughgoing testing. In physical matters men have slowly grown accustomed in all specific beliefs to identifying the true with the verified. But they still hesitate to recognize the implication of this identification and to derive the definition of truth from it. For while it is nominally agreed upon as a commonplace that definitions ought to spring from concrete and specific cases rather than be invented in the empty air and imposed upon particulars, there is a strange unwillingness to act upon the maxim in defining truth. To generalize the recognition that the true means the verified and means nothing else places upon men the responsibility for surrendering political and moral dogmas, and subjecting to the test of consequences their most cherished prejudices. Such a change involves a great change in the seat of authority and the methods of decision in society. Some of them, as first fruits of the newer logic, will be considered in the following lectures.

❖   49   ❖

THE PRAGMATIC THEORY OF TRUTH

Arthur E. Murphy (1901–1962)

No other group of philosophers have, in the past half-century, contributed so much to our understanding of the rational use of ideas in the pursuit of

From *The Uses of Reason* (1943), part I, chapter ii, section 4, pp. 85–92. Used with the kind permission of Frederick H. Ginascol, the executor of the Murphy estate.

truth as have those who are called and used to call themselves, "pragmatists." Their insistence that the meaning and worth of ideas is rightly judged, not by their conformity to a "reality" set up in advance as the final standard of truth and reasonableness, but by the way they function in the context of responsible inquiry, was both revolutionary and salutary. Pragmatism did not, as its enthusiasts supposed, give us a new meaning for truth, but it did help enormously to show us where to look for the truth that is reliably attainable, and how to know it when we see it. Its emphasis on the plurality of contexts in which ideas can function significantly, and on the importance, if we would make our ideas clear, of interpreting them specifically by reference to their use and function in such contexts, is, in my judgment, the greatest single contribution to critical philosophy of our time. The title C. S. Peirce gave to his pioneer essay in pragmatism, "How to Make Our Ideas Clear," [1] is still our best guide to the nature of this contribution. The pragmatic method of contextual reference and analysis is a way of enabling us to know what we are talking about when we try to assess the meaning of "hard words and concepts" the generality of which is endlessly confusing until their use in inquiry, or any other activity to which they are relevant, has been ascertained. If I do not stop to elaborate on it here, it is simply because I have tried to exemplify it throughout this volume. I hope that it will thus, in true pragmatic fashion, be clarified by its use and justified in its cognitive fruits.

And yet, grateful as we must always be to Peirce, James, Dewey, and their disciples, there is one major issue on which their theory has been persistently equivocal in its pronouncements and seriously misleading in its influence. And since this is just the issue which looms most prominently in the popular mind when the word "pragmatism" is mentioned, we shall have to deal with it explicitly if our own position is to be understood. The principal intellectual novelty of pragmatism, in its impact on the thought of its period, was undoubtedly its theory of truth. This was generally understood as the doctrine that the truth of an idea *consists in* its capacity to bring, or help to bring, the activity in which it functions to a "satisfactory" eventuation. Ideas are significant only when they make a difference in some such activity and their validity *as true* is a function of their usefulness in furthering the ends of the activity in question. Coupled as it usually was with the more general doctrine of the primacy of practice, as contrasted with mere theory, and the claim that ideas must justify themselves, not only in the "self-enclosed" area of theoretical analysis, but in the affairs of *life*, this theory seemed to suggest that the "ultimate" ends of

---

[1] [See selection 50.] This essay is now included in his *Collected Papers*, Vol. V, pp. 248 ff.

life are not cognitive but practical, and that it is only insofar as knowing contributes to these practical ends that its validity *as knowledge* can be established. Reduced to short and easy terms, as such theories always are when they gain popular currency, this appears as the dictum that the useful is the true, and that utility is to be judged in the widest "practical" terms —utility for life, for success, for satisfaction, and the like.

In this form the doctrine is quite untenable, and for a familiar reason. It is of the utmost cognitive importance to distinguish ideas which work for the purposes of factual inquiry, where the activity aims at the discovery of truth, and is successful insofar as it achieves this end, from other ideas which in their working contribute to success of other sorts, popular, political, economic or the like, without thereby justifying themselves as true in any usual sense of that term. The general pragmatic formula seems to apply to both sorts of working, but it is only by the first that truth, in the sense in which it is rightly distinguished from convenient fiction, can reliably be established. Did the pragmatists really mean to undermine this distinction, and to claim for ideas which work well for *any* "practical" purpose the cogency with which the term "truth" has more usually been associated? The critics assumed that they did, pointed to plenty of pragmatic dicta which seemed to support their interpretation, and found in them inexhaustible material for crying up pragmatism as an expression of the temper of the times, which undoubtedly gloried in "efficiency," "action," and "life," rather indiscriminately enjoyed, or for crying it down as a negation of all cognitive standards and all regard for truth. The pragmatists themselves denied the imputation angrily and repeatedly, and went on expressing their views in exactly the fashion which appeared to the unconverted to substantiate the charges of their critics. Philosophical misunderstandings are by no means uncommon, but a "misunderstanding" of this sort, persisting over a period of many years and cropping up again and again, would seem to have some deeper basis than mere verbal infelicity on one side or critical ineptitude on the other. It is ironical that the philosophy whose distinctive aim was to make ideas clear should have had such special difficulty in making its own leading ideas clear to those not antecedently committed to its conclusions. Whatever its causes, there can be little doubt that the contribution pragmatism might have made to clear thinking has been largely vitiated by this abiding unclarity as to its central doctrine.

Can this ambiguity be eliminated? I believe that it can, but only by taking a further step which the leading pragmatists, for philosophical reasons, have been unwilling to take. There is little doubt, I think, that when James or Dewey is thinking about the "working" of ideas in inquiry, the kind of satisfaction he has in mind is the *cognitive* satisfaction that develops when there is good reason to believe that we are actually *finding out* what the inquiry set out to discover, when, in other words, the ideas employed have vindicated their usefulness in the discovery of factual truth. Whether or not such ideas are themselves accepted as true will depend on whether or not what is found out by their means actually is (in so far as we can discern its nature) what they report it to be. Where no such informational correctness is claimed, no question of truth, in the cognitive sense, arises. Where the claim is made, the process of its testing is the process by which we find out about the world, and judge the accuracy of our beliefs in terms of what is thus discovered.

But if this, as it might be more deviously put by Dewey or more eloquently by James, is what is intended, why is it not explicitly said? For two reasons, chiefly. The leading pragmatists belonged to that unhappy generation which never recovered from its early fright of metaphysics. To say that factual statements, when properly criticized and tested, are really and literally true as information concerning what exists and has existed in the world outside us, raised in their minds the specter of an "antecedent reality" which transcends the situation in which inquiry occurs and is "finally" disclosed only by some sort of metaphysical, not by scientific, investigation. They sought to avoid all reference to such a "reality" by insisting that the real object (or aim) of factual inquiry is to reconstruct the situation in which doubt or difficulty has arisen, and to bring confused or impeded activities to a successful conclusion. In a sense, again, this is true if what the reconstruction achieves is knowledge of objects and events, some of which are quite indubitably antecedent in their existence and nature to the activity through which we find out about them, and if in consequence this activity, to the successful conclusion of which our ideas contribute, is that of securing truthful information about them. But that, of course, cannot be said explicitly without bringing up again the question of the reference of factual knowledge to objects not constructed or reconstructed in the process of inquiry, and it is this that the pragmatist wishes at all costs to avoid. Hence he says once more that the *ultimate object* of knowledge is the satisfactory completion of the activity of inquiry, without being willing to say plainly that what the satisfactory completion of this activity consists in is the attainment of literal, and not merely of "pragmatic" truth. So the ambiguity recurs, and the argument goes on indefinitely and unprofitably. For it could only be resolved unequivocally by admitting a factual reference which the pragmatist holds to be philosophically dangerous or by denying the distinctive cognitive status of inquiry, which he knows to be essential to any accurate account of the work of thought. Thus, in trying to get rid of "reality" he has compromised the status of truth, and this central instability in his theory renders all his further theorizing insecure.

This unfortunate outcome is both unnecessary and undesirable. It is unnecessary because, as we have seen, the claim to literal knowledge of the world *as it is* need involve no such dubious commitments. The "reality" which true knowledge, on the level of factual inquiry, discloses, is simply the nature and behavior of the objects and events in the world around us, in so far as these can be found out by methods of reliable inquiry, the very methods to which the pragmatists are, in practice, most addicted. Such knowledge makes no pretension to *metaphysical* ultimacy, that is, to preferential status as information concerning what is metaphysically "ultimate" or "final," or completely real; it claims only to be an accurate account of what has happened, is happening, and is likely to happen. And that claim can sometimes be made good on the level of factual inquiry itself. To say this plainly would not, so far as I can see, involve the abandonment of anything in pragmatism that is worth preserving. It would, however, involve a final break with antiquated philosophical preconceptions from which the pragmatists, in spite of heroic efforts, have so far been unable to free themselves.

The present situation is undesirable from the standpoint of the very causes the pragmatists seem to have most at heart. Instead of outflanking their epistemological enemies by their devious procedure, Dewey and his followers have put themselves in a false position, which enables their critics to pose, with some plausibility, as the righteous defenders of truth and to denounce as relativism and skepticism what is soundest and most enlightening in the pragmatic method. The contextual specification of the meaning and use of ideas is in fact an expression, not of disregard for truth, but of regard for the conditions under which the difference between truth and falsehood can clearly and responsibly be established. The intellectual alternative to it is literary, philosophical and theological loose talk, in which the appearance of profundity does not compensate for the absence of intellectual content and a decent respect for the conditions of accurate thinking and speaking. The case for contextual clarity in analysis would be greatly strengthened if its divorce from pragmatic unclarity about the nature of truth were made final and complete.

The second reason for the unwillingness of the pragmatists to take the step that I have recommended can be more briefly dealt with. Pragmatism in its early days was a philosophical expression of a much wider popular movement—the demand that thought, and thinkers, be brought down from the well-known ivory tower of academic and speculative aloofness and put to work in the affairs of men. There was much in this demand that was just and discerning, and those who, like Dewey, have not only preached but practiced the doctrine that ideas can exercise a liberalizing and liberating function in human conduct are the sages of their own generation in American thought and the inspiration for ours. But the fruitful use of valid theory for the ends of enlightened practice is one thing; the identification of theoretical validity with practical utility is another. Whether it was intended or not by its authors, the latter is the doctrine which has gained wide currency as the teaching of pragmatism. And where it prevails, there will always be impatience with those who insist, as I have done, that the proper goal of factual inquiry is the discovery of what is the case, and that this is by no means to be equated with what on other grounds and for other purposes it might be useful or inspiring to believe. This attitude is understandable, but I do not believe that it is judicious or wise. For of all the contributions that theory can make to practice none is so excellent or so essential as the provision of reliable information on matters of practical concern, where "reliability" is determined not by practical utility for some further purpose but by the evidence that what is asserted is in fact the case. If we are to act intelligently we must know what we are doing, and no other theory is so dependably helpful for that purpose as that which there is good reason to suppose is informationally reliable. The vindication of such reliability, therefore, is by no means opposed to the ends of enlightened practice, but is in fact essential to any rational estimate of their nature. In reaffirming, in this sense, the intellectual rights of theory we may not be pragmatists, but we shall be practical nonetheless.

❖ **50** ❖

TRUTH, THOUGHT, AND REALITY

Charles Sanders Peirce (1839–1914)

Let us now approach the subject of logic, and consider a conception which particularly concerns it, that of *reality*. Taking clearness in the sense of

From "How to Make Our Ideas Clear," *Popular Science Monthly*, January 1878, section 4 (omitting the last three paragraphs). The title of this selection has been supplied by the editors.

familiarity, no idea could be clearer than this. Every child uses it with perfect confidence, never dreaming that he does not understand it. As for clearness in its second grade, however, it would probably puzzle most men, even among those of a reflective turn of mind, to give an abstract definition of the real. Yet such a definition may perhaps be reached by considering the points of difference between reality and its opposite, fiction. A figment is a product of somebody's imagination; it has such characters as his thought impresses upon it. That those characters are independent of how you or I think is an external reality. There are, however, phenomena within our own minds, dependent upon our thought, which are at the same time real in the sense that we really think them. But though their characters depend on how we think, they do not depend on what we think those characters to be. Thus, a dream has a real existence as a mental phenomenon, if somebody has really dreamt it; that he dreamt so and so, does not depend on what anybody thinks was dreamt, but is completely independent of all opinion on the subject. On the other hand, considering, not the fact of dreaming, but the thing dreamt, it retains its peculiarities by virtue of no other fact than that it was dreamt to possess them. Thus we may define the real as that whose characters are independent of what anybody may think them to be.

But, however satisfactory such a definition may be found, it would be a great mistake to suppose that it makes the idea of reality perfectly clear. Here, then, let us apply our rules. According to them, reality, like every other quality, consists in the peculiar sensible effects which things partaking of it produce. The only effect which real things have is to cause belief, for all the sensations which they excite emerge into consciousness in the form of beliefs. The question, therefore, is, how is true belief (or belief in the real) distinguished from false belief (or belief in fiction). Now, as we have seen in the former paper, the ideas of truth and falsehood, in their full development, appertain exclusively to the scientific method of settling opinion. A person who arbitrarily chooses the propositions which he will adopt can use the word truth only to emphasize the expression of his determination to hold on to his choice. Of course, the method of tenacity never prevailed exclusively; reason is too natural to men for that. But in the literature of the dark ages we find some fine examples of it. When Scotus Erigena is commenting upon a poetical passage in which hellebore is spoken of as having caused the death of Socrates, he does not hesitate to inform the inquiring reader that Helleborus and Socrates were two eminent Greek philosophers, and that the latter having been overcome in argument by the former took the matter to heart and died of it! What sort of an idea of truth could a man have who could adopt and teach, without the qualification of a perhaps, an opinion taken so entirely at random? The real spirit of Socrates, who I hope would have been delighted to have been "overcome in argument," because he would have learned something by it, is in curious contrast with the naive idea of the glossist, for whom discussion would seem to have been simply a struggle. When philosophy began to awake from its long slumber, and before theology completely dominated it, the practice seems to have been for each professor to seize upon any philosophical position he found unoccupied and which seemed a strong one, to entrench himself in it, and to sally forth from time to time to give battle to the others. Thus, even the scanty records we possess of those disputes enable us to make out a dozen or more opinions held by different teachers at one time concerning the question of nominalism and realism. Read the opening part of the *Historia Calamitatum* of Abelard, who was certainly as philosophical as any of his contemporaries, and see the spirit of combat which it breathes. For him, the truth is simply his particular stronghold. When the method of authority prevailed, the truth meant little more than the Catholic faith. All the efforts of the scholastic doctors are directed toward harmonizing their faith in Aristotle and their faith in the Church, and one may search their ponderous folios through without finding an argument which goes any further. It is noticeable that where different faiths flourish side by side, renegades are looked upon with contempt even by the party whose belief they adopt; so completely has the idea of loyalty replaced that of truth-seeking. Since the time of Descartes, the defect in the conception of truth has been less apparent. Still, it will sometimes strike a scientific man that the philosophers have been less intent on finding out what the facts are, than on inquiring what belief is most in harmony with their system. It is hard to convince a follower of the *a priori* method by adducing facts; but show him that an opinion he is defending is inconsistent with what he has laid down elsewhere, and he will be very apt to retract it. These minds do not seem to believe that disputation is ever to cease; they seem to think that the opinion which is natural for one man is not so for another, and that belief will, consequently, never be settled. In contenting themselves with fixing their own opinions by a method which would lead another man to a different result, they betray their feeble hold of the conception of what truth is.

On the other hand, all the followers of science are fully persuaded that the processes of investigation, if only pushed far enough, will give one certain solution to every question to which they can be applied. One man may investigate the velocity of light by studying the transits of Venus and the aberration of the stars; another by the oppositions of Mars and the eclipses of Jupiter's satellites; a third by the method of Fizeau; a fourth by that of Foucault; a fifth by the motions of the curves of Lissajoux; a sixth, a seventh, an eighth, and a ninth, may follow the different methods of comparing the measures of statical and dynamical electricity. They may at first obtain different results, but, as each perfects his method and his processes, the results will move steadily together toward a destined center. So with all scientific research. Different minds may set out with the most antagonistic views, but the progress of investigation carries them by a force outside of themselves to one and the same conclusion. This activity of thought by which we are carried, not where we wish, but to a foreordained goal, is like the operation of destiny. No modification of the point of view taken, no selection of other facts for study, no natural bent of mind even, can enable a man to escape the predestinate opinion. This great law is embodied in the conception of truth and reality. The opinion which is fated [1] to be ultimately agreed to by all who investigate, is what we mean by the truth, and the object represented in this opinion is the real. That is the way I would explain reality.

But it may be said that this view is directly opposed to the abstract definition which we have given of reality, inasmuch as it makes the characters of the real depend on what is ultimately thought about them. But the answer to this is that, on the one hand, reality is independent, not necessarily of thought in general, but only of what you or I or any finite number of men may think about it; and that, on the other hand, though the object of the final opinion depends on what that opinion is, yet what that opinion is does not depend on what you or I or any man thinks. Our perversity and that of others may indefinitely postpone the settlement of opinion; it might even conceivably cause an arbitrary proposition to be universally accepted as long as the human race should last. Yet even that would not change the nature of the belief, which alone could be the result of investigation carried sufficiently far; and if, after the extinction of our race, another should arise with faculties and disposition for investigation, that true opinion must be the one which they would ultimately come to. "Truth crushed to earth shall rise again," and the opinion which would finally result from investigation does not depend on how anybody may actually think. But the reality of that which is real does depend on the real fact that investigation is destined to lead, at last, if continued long enough, to a belief in it.

But I may be asked what I have to say to all the minute facts of

---

[1] Fate means merely that which is sure to come true, and can nohow be avoided. It is a superstition to suppose that a certain sort of events are ever fated, and it is another to suppose that the word fate can never be freed from its superstitious taint. We are all fated to die.

history, forgotten never to be recovered, to the lost books of the ancients, to the buried secrets.

> "Full many a gem of purest ray serene
>   The dark, unfathomed caves of ocean bear;
> Full many a flower is born to blush unseen,
>   And waste its sweetness on the desert air."

Do these things not really exist because they are hopelessly beyond the reach of our knowledge? And then, after the universe is dead (according to the prediction of some scientists), and all life has ceased forever, will not the shock of atoms continue though there will be no mind to know it? To this I reply that, though in no possible state of knowledge can any number be great enough to express the relation between the amount of what rests unknown to the amount of the known, yet it is unphilosophical to suppose that, with regard to any given question (which has any clear meaning), investigation would not bring forth a solution of it, if it were carried far enough. Who would have said, a few years ago, that we could ever know of what substances stars are made whose light may have been longer in reaching us than the human race has existed? Who can be sure of what we shall not know in a few hundred years? Who can guess what would be the result of continuing the pursuit of science for ten thousand years, with the activity of the last hundred? And if it were to go on for a million, or a billion, or any number of years you please, how is it possible to say that there is any question which might not ultimately be solved? . . .

❖ **51** ❖

TRUTH AS SOCIAL AGREEMENT
Arthur E. Murphy (1901–1962)

One of the most popular and familiar devices for accounting for the cognitive superiority of scientific findings to those reached by other methods without claiming literal informational truth about the world for them, is to

From *The Uses of Reason* (1943), part I, chapter ii, section 3, pp. 80–5. Used here by the kind permission of Frederick H. Ginascol, the executor of the Murphy estate.

say that science deals with those matters concerning which general agreement is possible, with respect to which all observers will come to the same conclusion, and the like. Whether a conclusion thus established is "true" in any further sense, the cautious theorist refuses to say, for he is sure that any attempted answer would involve him in philosophical puzzles with which, as a scientist, he is not properly concerned. Thus Norman Campbell tells us that "science is the study of those judgments concerning which universal agreement can be obtained," [1] and maintains this doctrine, in spite of the rather drastic cuts in the sciences that must be made if they are to conform to it, precisely because it absolves him from the responsibility of saying that the sciences tell us about "the external world" or "nature," or even of assuming that nature or an external world exists. In any case there are judgments which command universal assent, and it is with these that science is exclusively concerned. This kind of theory is often supported by contrasting the agreement that can be reached concerning, for example, the dimensions of a physical object as measured by approved "operational" methods, with the diversity of opinion that exists concerning beauty, or goodness, or the nature of God. The fact to which this contrast points cannot seriously be questioned. The publicity, actual or potential, of the findings of the sciences, the fact that they can be arrived at and tested *in the open,* without recourse to special intuitions or revelations which only a special group can enjoy, is one of our major reasons for respecting their rational authority as sources of reliable information. But this fact is misstated and misinterpreted in the theory of truth as social agreement, and the confusion thus engendered has had unfortunate consequences in popular thought.

The obvious and essential difficulty with it is that it does not enable us to discriminate between the agreement which is the fruit of reliable and public methods of attaining truth, and that which is achieved by less credible devices. Mr. Campbell wrote his book before the rise of the totalitarian powers in Europe had given us our most vivid object lesson of the way in which agreement can be reached by the skillful dissemination of lies and the ruthless silencing of those who question them. To be sure, such agreement is not *universal,* but neither is that accorded the findings of the sciences. There are plenty of men in any community who will deny, and have denied, any scientific conclusion, no matter how well established, that conflicts with their own preferences and preconceptions. The outcry in Germany against "Jewish" science and that against the theory of the animal ancestry of man in some parts of the United States are only the most obvious of many instances that might be cited. Shall we then say that at

[1] Norman Campbell, *What is Science?*, p. 27.

least there is universal agreement *among scientists* on these matters, and that is what constitutes their findings as valid? But there is universal agreement among good Nazis about statements which by any scientific criterion are preposterously false. Are we simply to appeal to the agreement of one social group, as against another, and, if so, on what basis?

The answer, which C. S. Peirce was never tired of pointing out, is that the agreement that distinguishes scientific findings from others is that which is achieved by a quite distinctive method, the method of *finding out* by observation and experiment. It is, in short, the method of learning from experience, and so far from being universally agreed to in the affairs of men it is only in a limited area, and there precariously, that it prevails. Its rivals, the method of tenacity in holding on to antecedent convictions and closing one's mind to further evidence, the method of appeal to authority and the method of *a priori* reasoning from "plausible" premises,[2] have been considerably more common and more popular in the history of human beliefs. And if we ask why agreement reached by this method is to be regarded as superior to the others, we cannot appeal to social agreement as the source, or as the criterion, for its validity. It is *cognitively* the best method, because it is the only one that enables us to correct our ideas by reference to what is found to be the case independently of our antecedent wishes and beliefs. Through its procedures, mistakes can be found out and bias corrected, and it thus provides the best possible guarantee that we are conforming our ideas to the facts which they purport to be about, that is, are finding out the truth about them. Agreement thus reached is of the utmost cognitive significance, for here the agreement is pertinent to the truth of the beliefs arrived at, and each man can profit by the experience and criticism of others to raise his own ideas to the level of the soundest available knowledge of his time. It is the capacity to lead to truth that makes the agreement significant, not the agreement that constitutes the truth.

This version of the matter helps to correct a further serious misapprehension. The illustrations used to show how simple it is to get scientific agreement on "the facts" are themselves far too simple to do justice to the situation they are intended to portray. Measuring a table with a yardstick is one thing, and a fairly straightforward one. But accepting the result of this measurement *as evidence* of the theory the scientist bases on it and with the aid of which his research proceeds, is a different matter. The skeptics who looked into Galileo's telescope did not differ from him as to what was proximately to be seen. But they refused to interpret what they saw as he did, and preferred, not without some reason, to attribute what they ob-

[2] C. S. Peirce, "The Fixation of Belief," in *Collected Papers*; Vol. V, pp. 223 ff

served to a defect in his instrument rather than to accept it as evidence of a state of affairs in the heavens which, if admitted, would have created grave difficulties for theories to which they were profoundly attached. The battle Galileo and those who followed him had to fight for social agreement, or even social tolerance, of their findings, as reports of the solar universe, was long and arduous. It was finally won, and the profit for human enlightenment has been great. But something like it had to be fought again in the nineteenth century, when biology ran afoul of strongly held preconceptions; and in the social sciences we have hardly, as yet, begun to face the issue. It is well, therefore, to remember that the agreement that counts in science, and in the pursuit of truth, is agreement reached by a method concerning the cogency and desirability of which there is, outside a quite restricted area, by no means universal or even widespread agreement. It is a method whose continued use requires discipline and intelligence of a high order, and which justifies itself not by simple observations which everybody will agree to, but by rigorous inquiry with the conclusions of which everybody ought to agree, because there is good reason to believe that they are true. In fact, however, they will be bitterly contested precisely where and insofar as they prove inconvenient to established interests of various sorts, and if we wait for "universal agreement" before acknowledging their truth we shall have a very long time to wait.

The prestige of the sciences in contemporary society is a curiously precarious one. The wonder-working results of physics, chemistry and biology have won for them a respect which has, for the most part, little to do with what they actually report, or with the evidence that substantiates them. Hoping for similar results on more humanly important issues, the popular mind turned eagerly to psychology and the social sciences and has, on the whole, been disappointed. Meanwhile, confusion as to the aims of science, and confusing and irresponsible pronouncements by scientists themselves about the incapacity of mere "science" to reach "the truth" have undermined public confidence in the rational authority of scientifically warranted statements concerning matters of fact. And when these statements have proved, on other grounds, to be inconvenient, there has been little scruple in rejecting them and accepting in their place emotionally congenial doctrines which there is good reason to believe are false. So long as scientists restrict their inquiries to fields in which our emotions are not strongly engaged, and continue to produce results guaranteed "useful" by current social standards, they are not only tolerated but subsidized. Beyond these limits, however, the method of scientific inquiry has still to win social acceptance. And nothing is more essential, if this acceptance is to be won on a solid and enduring basis, than the recognition that the distinctive claim to be made for the findings of the sciences is not that they are obvious, or convenient, or socially accepted, but that they are reached by a method which gives the best possible guarantee that what they say is true, or reliably informative, with respect to the world around us. Men do not always want to see the truth, nor do they love it when they see it; but they have great need of it, and they do tend to respect it, when its claims are so presented that their cogency can be reasonably understood. Those who, in their urge to emancipate science from metaphysics, would emancipate it from its claim to truth as well are thus ill-advised in their procedure. As a way of reaching social agreement on disputed questions scientific inquiry is but one of many and by no means always the most efficacious. As a way of reaching informative truth concerning the structure and behavior of objects in the world around us it has proved superior to every other method. It claims our credence not *de facto*, as a widely accepted dogma, but *de jure* as a sound and reliable basis for reasonable belief. It is in this latter capacity that its cognitive claims are defensible and worth defending.

❖ 52 ❖

TRUTH, CREDIT, AND THE ABSOLUTE
Josiah Royce (1855–1916)

I

. . . Instrumentalism views truth as simply the value belonging to certain ideas insofar as these ideas are biological functions of our organisms, and psychological functions whereby we direct our choices and attain our successes.

Wide and manifold are the inductive evidences which the partisans of such theories of truth adduce in support of their theory. There is the evidence of introspection and of the modern psychological theory of the

From "The Problem of Truth in the Light of Recent Discussion" (1908), in *William James and Other Essays on the Philosophy of Life* (New York: The Macmillan Company, 1911), pp. 214–38.

understanding. Opinions, beliefs, ideas,—what are they all but accompaniments of the motor processes whereby, as a fact, our organisms are adjusted to their environment? To discover the truth of an idea, what is that for any one of us but to observe our success in our adjustment to our stituation? Knowledge is power. Common sense long ago noted this fact. Empiricism has also since taught us that we deal only with objects of experience. The new instrumentalism adds to the old empiricism simply the remark that we possess truth insofar as we learn how to control these objects of experience. And to this more direct evidence for the instrumental theory of truth is added the evidence derived from the whole work of the modern sciences. In what sense are scientific hypotheses and theories found to be true? Only in this sense, says the instrumentalist,—only in this sense, that through these hypotheses we acquire constantly new sorts of control over the course of our experience. If we turn from scientific to moral truth, we find a similar result. The moral ideas of any social order are practical plans and practical demands in terms of which this social order endeavors, by controlling the activities of its members, to win general peace and prosperity. The truth of moral ideas lies solely in this their empirical value in adjusting individual activities to social demands, and in thus winning general success for all concerned.

Such are mere hints of the evidences that can be massed to illustrate the view that the truth of ideas is actually tested, and is to be tested, by their experienced workings, by their usefulness in enabling man to control his empirically given situation. If this be the case, then truth is always relative to the men concerned, to their experience, and to their situations. Truth grows, changes, and refuses to be tested by absolute standards. It *happens* to ideas, insofar as they *work*. It belongs to them when one views them as instruments to an end. The result of all this is a relativistic, an evolutionary, theory of truth. For such a view logic is a part of psychology, —a series of comments upon certain common characteristics of usefully working ideas and opinions. Ethical theory is a branch of evolutionary sociology. And in general, if you want to test the truth of ideas and opinions, you must look forward to their workings, not backward to the principles from which they might be supposed to follow, nor yet upwards to any absolute standards which may be supposed to guide them, and least of all to any realm of fixed facts that they are supposed to be required, willy nilly, to copy. Truth is no barren repetition of a dead reality, but belongs, as a quality, to the successful deeds by which we produce for ourselves the empirical realities that we want.

Such is the sort of evidence which my friends, Professor James and Professor Dewey, and their numerous followers, in recent discussion, have advanced in favor of this instrumental, practical, and evolutionary theory of truth. Such are the considerations which, in other forms, Mach has illustrated by means of his history and analyses of the work of modern science.

Our present comment upon this theory must be given in a word. It contains indeed a report of the truth about our actual human life, and about the sense in which we all seek and test and strive for truth, precisely insofar as truth-seeking is indeed a part of our present organic activities. But the sense in which this theory is thus indeed a true account of a vast range of the phenomena of human life is not reducible to the sense which the theory itself ascribes to the term "truth."

For suppose I say, reporting the facts of the history of science: "Newton's theory of gravitation proved to be true, and its truth lay in this: The definition and the original testing of the theory consisted in a series of the organic and psychological functions of the live creature Newton. His theories were for him true insofar as, after hard work, to be sure, and long waiting, they enabled him to control and to predict certain of his own experiences of the facts of nature. The same theories are still true for us because they have successfully guided, and still guide, certain observations and experiences of the men of today." This statement reduces the truth of Newton's theory to the type of truth which instrumentalism demands. But in what sense is my account of this matter itself a true account of the facts of human life? Newton is dead. As mortal man he succeeds no longer. His ideas, as psychological functions, died with him. His earthly experiences ceased when death shut his eyes. Wherein consists today, then, the historical truth that Newton ever existed at all, or that the countless other men whom his theories are said to have guided ever lived, or experienced, or succeeded? And if I speak of the men of today, in what sense is the statement true that they now live, or have experience, or use Newton's theory, or succeed with it as an instrument? No doubt all these historical and socially significant statements of mine are indeed substantially true. But does their truth consist in my success in using the ideal instruments that I use when I utter these assertions? Evidently I mean, by calling these my own assertions true, much more than I can interpret in terms of my experience of their success in guiding my act.

In brief, the truth that historical events ever happened at all; the truth that there ever was a past time, or that there ever will be a future time; the truth that anybody ever succeeds, except insofar as I myself, just now, in the use of these my present instruments for the transient control of my passing experience chance to succeed; the truth that there is any extended course of human experience at all, or any permanence, or any longlasting success,—well, all such truths, they are indeed true, but their truth cannot possibly consist in the instrumental value which any man ever experiences as belonging to any of his own personal ideas or acts. Nor can this truth consist in anything that even a thousand or a million men can separately experience, each as the success of his own ideal instruments. For no one man experiences the success of any man but himself, or of any instruments but his own; and the truth, say, of Newton's theory consists, by hypotheses, in the perfectly objective fact that generations of men have really succeeded in guiding their experience by this theory. But that this is the fact no man, as an individual man, ever has experienced or will experience under human conditions.

When an instrumentalist, then, gives to us his account of the empirical truth that men obtain through using their ideas as instruments to guide and to control their own experience, his account of human organic and psychological functions may be,—yes, is,—as far as it goes, true. But if it is true at all, then it is true as an account of the characters actually common to the experience of a vast number of men. It is true, if at all, as a report of the objective constitution of a certain totality of facts which we call human experience. It is, then, true in a sense which no man can ever test by the empirical success of his own ideas as his means of controlling his own experiences. Therefore the truth which we must ascribe to instrumentalism, if we regard it as a true doctrine at all, is precisely a truth, not insofar as instrumentalism is itself an instrument for helping on this man's or that man's way of controlling his experience. If instrumentalism is true, it is true as a report of facts about the general course of history, of evolution, and of human experience,—facts which transcend every individual man's experience, verifications, and successes. To make its truth consist in the mere sum of the various individual successes is equally vain, unless indeed that sum is a fact. But no individual man ever experiences that fact.

Instrumentalism, consequently, expresses no motive which by itself alone is adequate to constitute any theory of truth. And yet, as I have pointed out, I doubt not that instrumentalism gives such a substantially true account of man's natural functions as a truth seeker. Only the sense in which instrumentalism is a true account of human life is opposed to the adequacy of its own definition of truth. The first of our three motives is, therefore, useful only if we can bring it into synthesis with other motives. In fact it is useless to talk of the success of the human spirit in its efforts to win control over experience, unless there is indeed a human spirit which is more than any man's transient consciousness of his own efforts, and unless there is a unity of experience, a unity objective, real, and supratemporal in its significance.

II

Our result so far is that man indeed uses his ideas as means of controlling his experience, and that truth involves such control, but that truth cannot be defined solely in terms of our personal experience of our own success in obtaining this control.

Hereupon the second of the motives which we have found influencing the recent theories of truth comes to our aid. If instrumentalism needs a supplement, where are we, the individual thinkers, to look for that supplement, except in those inner personal grounds which incline each of us to make his own best interpretation of life precisely as he can, in accordance with his own will to succeed, and in accordance with his individual needs?

To be sure, as one may still insist, we are always dealing with live human experience, and with its endless constraints and limitations. And when we accept or reject opinions, we do so because, at the time, these opinions seem to us to promise a future empirical "working," a successful "control" over experience,—in brief, a success such as appeals to live human beings. Instrumentalism insofar correctly defines the nature which truth possesses insofar as we ever actually verify truth. And of course we always believe as we do because we are subject to the constraint of our present experience. But since we are social beings, and beings with countless and varied intelligent needs, we constantly define and accept as valid very numerous ideas and opinions whose truth we do not hope personally to verify. Our act in accepting such unverified truths is (as Professor James states the case) essentially similar to the act of the banker in accepting credit values instead of cash. A note or other evidence of value is good if it *can* be turned into cash at some agreed time, or under specified conditions. Just so, an idea is true, not merely at the moment when it enables somebody to control his own experience. It is true if, under definable conditions which, as a fact, you or I may never verify, it *would* enable some human being whose purposes agree with ours to control his own experience. If we personally do not verify a given idea, we can still accept it then upon its credit value. We can accept it precisely as paper, which cannot now be cashed, is accepted by one who regards that paper as, for a given purpose, or to a given extent, equivalent to cash. A bond, issued by a government, may promise payment after fifty years. The banker may today accept such a bond as good, and may pay cash for it, although he feels sure that he personally will never live to see the principal repaid by the borrower.

Now, as Professor James would say, it is in this sense that our ideas about past time, and about the content of other men's minds, and about the vast physical world, "with all its stars and milky ways," are accepted as true. Such ideas have for us credit values. We accept these ideas as true because we need to trade on credits. Borrowed truth is as valuable in the spiritual realm as borrowed money is in the commercial realm. To believe a now unverified truth is simply to say: "I accept that idea, upon credit, as equivalent to the cash payments in terms of live experience which, as I assert, I could get in case I had the opportunity."

And so much it is indeed easy to make out about countless assertions which we all accept. They are assertions about experience, but not about our present experience. They are made under various constraints of convention, habit, desire, and private conviction, but they are opinions whose truth is for us dependent upon our personal assent and acquiescence.

Herewith, however, we face what is, for more than one modern theory of truth, a very critical question. Apparently it is one thing to say: "I accept this opinion upon credit," and quite another thing to say: "The truth of this opinion consists, solely and essentially, in the fact that it is credited by me." In seeming, at least, it is one thing to assert: "We trade upon credit; we deal in credits," and quite another thing to say: "There is no value behind this bond or behind this bit of irredeemable paper currency, except its credit value." But perhaps a modern theory of truth may decline to accept such a difference as ultimate. Perhaps this theory may say: The truth *is* the credit. As a fact, a vast number of our human opinions—those, for instance, which relate to the past, or to the contents of other men's minds—appear, within the range of our personal experience, as credits whose value we, who believe the opinions, cannot hope ever to convert into the cash of experience. The banker who holds the bond not maturing within his own lifetime can, after all, if the bond is good, sell it today for cash. And that truth which he can personally and empirically test whenever he wants to test, is enough to warrant his act in accepting the credit. But I, who am confident of the truths of history, or of geology, or of physics, and who believe in the minds of other men,—I accept as valid countless opinions that are for me, in my private capacity and from an empirical point of view, nothing but irredeemable currency. In vain do I say: "I *could* convert these ideas into the cash of experience *if* I were some other man, or *if* I were living centuries ago instead of today." For the question simply recurs: In what sense are these propositions about my own possible experience true when I do not test their truth,—yes, true although I, personally, *cannot* test their truth? These credits, irredeemable in terms of the cash of my experience,—wherein consists their true credit value?

Here one apparently stands at the parting of the ways. One can answer this question by saying: "The truth of these assertions (or their falsity, if they are false) belongs to them whether I credit them or no, whether I verify them or not. Their truth or their falsity is their own character and is independent of my credit and my verification." But to say this appears to be, after all, just the intellectualism which so many of our modern pragmatists condemn. There remains, however, one other way. One can say: "The truth of the unverified assertions *consists simply in the fact that,* for our own private and individual ends, *they are credited.* Credit is relative to the creditor. If he finds that, on the whole, it meets his purpose to credit, he credits. And there is no truth, apart from present verifications, except this truth of credit." In other words, that is true for me which I find myself accepting as my way of reacting to my situation.

This, I say, is a theory of truth which can be attempted. Consider what a magnificent freedom such a theory gives to all of us. Credit is relative to the creditor. To be sure, if ever the day of reckoning should come, one would be subject, at the moment of verification, to the constraints of experience. At such times, one would either get the cash or would not get it. But after all very few of our ideas about this great and wonderful world of ours ever are submitted to any such sharp tests. History and the minds of other men,—well, our personal opinions about these remain credits that no individual amongst us can ever test for himself. As your world is mainly made up of such things, your view of your world remains, then, subject to your own needs. It ought to be thus subject. There is no absolute truth. There is only the truth that you need. Enter into the possession of your spiritual right. Borrow Nietzsche's phraseology. Call the truth of ordinary intellectualism mere *Sklavenwahrheit.* It pretends to be absolute; but only the slaves believe in it. "Henceforth," so some Zarathustra of a new theory of truth may say, "I teach you *Herrenwahrheit.*" Credit what you choose to credit. Truth is made for man, not man for truth. Let your life "boil over" into new truth as much as you find such effervescence convenient. When, apart from the constraints of present verification, and apart from mere convention, I say: "This opinion of mine is true," I mean simply: "To my mind, lord over its own needs, this assertion now appears expedient." Whenever my expediency changes, my truth will change.

But does anybody today hold just *this* theory of truth? I hesitate to make accusations which some of my nearest and dearest friends may repudiate as personally injurious. But this I can say: I find a great many recent theorists about truth talking in just this spirit so long as they feel free to glorify their spiritual liberty, to amuse their readers with clever assaults upon absolutism, and to arouse sympathy by insistence upon the human and the democratic attractiveness of the novel views of truth that they have to advance. Such individualism, such capriciousness, is in the air. Our modern theorists of truth frequently speak in this way. When their expressions of such views are criticized, they usually modify and perhaps withdraw them. What, as individuals, such teachers really mean, I have no right to say. Nobody but themselves can say; and some of them seem to say whatever they please. But this I know: Whoever identifies the truth of an assertion with his own individual interest in making that assertion may be left to bite the dust of his own confusion in his own way and time. The outcome of such essential waywardness is not something that you need try to determine through controversy. It is self-determined. For in case I say to you: "The sole ground for my assertions is this, that I please to make them,"—well, at once I am defining exactly the attitude which we all alike regard as the attitude of one who chooses *not* to tell the truth. And if, hereupon, I found a theory of truth upon generalizing such an assertion,— well, I am defining as truth-telling precisely that well-known practical atti- tude which is the contradictory of the truth-telling attitude. The contrast is not one between intellectualism and pragmatism. It is the contrast be- tween two well-known attitudes of will,—the will that is loyal to truth as an universal ideal, and the will that is concerned with its own passing caprices. If I talk of truth, I refer to what the truth-loving sort of will seeks. If hereupon I define the true as that which the individual personally views as expedient in opinion or in assertion, I contradict myself, and may be left to my own confutation. For the position in which I put myself, by this individualistic theory of truth, is closely analogous to the position in which Epimenides the Cretan, the hero of the fallacy of the liar, was placed by his own so famous thesis.

III

And yet, despite all this, the modern assault upon mere intellectualism is well founded. The truth of our assertions is indeed definable only by taking account of the meaning of our own individual attitudes of will, and the truth, whatever else it is, is at least instrumental in helping us towards the goal of all human volition. The only question is whether the will really means to aim at doing something that has a final and eternal meaning.

Herewith I suggest a theory of truth which we can understand only in case we follow the expressions of the third of the three modern motives to which I have referred. I have said that the new logic and the new methods of reasoning in the exact sciences are just now bringing us to a novel comprehension of our relation to absolute truth. I must attempt a very brief indication as to how this is indeed the case.

I have myself long since maintained that there is indeed a logic of the will, just as truly as there is a logic of the intellect. Personally, I go further still. I assert: all logic is the logic of the will. There is no pure intellect. Thought is a mode of action, a mode of action distinguished from other modes mainly by its internal clearness of self-consciousness, by its relatively free control of its own procedure, and by the universality, the impersonal fairness and obviousness of its aims and of its motives. An idea in the consciousness of a thinker is simply a present consciousness of some expression of purpose,—a plan of action. A judgment is an act of a reflective and self-conscious character, an act whereby one accepts or rejects an idea as a sufficient expression of the very purpose that is each time in question. Our whole objective world is meanwhile defined for each of us in terms of our ideas. General assertions about the meaning of our ideas are reflective acts whereby we acknowledge and accept certain ruling principles of action. And in respect of all these aspects of doctrine I find myself at one with recent voluntarism, whether the latter takes the form of instrumentalism, or insists upon some more individualistic theory of truth. But for my part, in spite, or in fact because of this my voluntarism, I cannot rest in any mere relativism. Individualism is right in saying, "I will to credit this or that opinion." But individualism is wrong in supposing that I can ever be content with my own will in as far as it is merely an individual will. The will to my mind is to all of us nothing but a thirst for complete and conscious self-possession, for fullness of life. And in terms of this its central motive, the will defines the truth that it endlessly seeks as a truth that possesses completeness, totality, self-possession, and therefore absoluteness. The fact that, in our human experience, we never meet with any truths such as completely satisfy our longing for insight, this fact we therefore inevitably interpret, not as any defect in the truth, but as a defect in our present state of knowledge, a limitation due to our present type of individuality. Hence we acknowledge a truth which transcends our individual life. Our concepts of the objectively real world, our ethical ideals of conduct, our estimates of what constitutes the genuine worth of life,—all these constructions of ours are therefore determined by the purpose to conform ourselves to absolute standards. We will the eternal. We define the eternal. And this we do whenever we talk of what we call genuine facts or actualities, or of the historical content of human experience, or of the physical world that our sciences investigate. If we try to escape this inner necessity of our whole voluntary and self-conscious life, we simply contradict ourselves. We can define the truth even of relativism only by asserting that relativism is after all absolutely true. We can admit our ignorance of truth only by acknowledging the absoluteness of that truth of which we are ignorant. And all this is no caprice of ours. All this results from a certain necessary nature of our will which we can test as often as we please by means of the experiment of trying to get rid of the postulate of an absolute truth. We shall find that, however often we try this experiment, the denial that there is any absolute truth simply leads to its own denial, and reinstates what it denies.

The reference that I a little while since made to our assertions regarding the past, and regarding the minds of other men, has already suggested to us how stubbornly we all assert certain truths which, for every one of us, transcend empirical verification, but which we nonetheless regard as absolutely true. If I say: "There never was a past," I contradict myself, since I assume the past even in asserting that a past never was. As a fact our whole interpretation of our experience is determined, in a sense akin to that which Kant defined, by certain modes of our own activity, whose significance is transcendental, even while their whole application is empirical. These modes of our activity make all our empirical sciences logically possible. Meanwhile it need not surprise us to find that Kant's method of defining these modes of our activity was not adequate, and that a new logic is giving us, in this field, new light. The true nature of these necessary modes of our activity becomes most readily observable to us in case we rightly analyze the methods and concepts, not of our own empirical, but rather of our mathematical sciences. For in these sciences our will finds its freest expression. And yet for that very reason in these sciences the absoluteness of the truth which the will defines is most obvious. The new logic to which I refer is especially a study of the logic of mathematics. . . .

BELIEF AND THE CRITERION OF TRUTH

Arthur Kenyon Rogers (1868–1936)

I should like to be able to start off the inquiry on which I am embarking with a preliminary statement so simple and self-evident that it could be accepted by everyone. But since this is not to be expected in philosophy, I shall do the next best thing; I shall take what is to *me* the simplest and most obvious proposition I can hit upon. My preliminary definition accordingly will be this: Truth for me is what I cannot help believing. To make clear what I understand by this will perhaps take a little explaining.

I say that this proposition appears to me almost in the nature of a truism so far as it goes. Certainly that which I do *not* believe I cannot in any intelligible sense call true; this would be to empty terms of all accepted meaning. And indeed everything that I really *do* believe must for the moment come under the head of what I call the true. But the words *"cannot help* believing" are intended to limit the field somewhat; for we are engaged on a philosophical inquiry, and what we are after in the end is not anything that may *seem* true, but what approves itself as true to the persistent inquirer. If we simply believed things, the problem of truth would not yet have arisen. It is because we discover that a number of things we have believed do not retain our belief, but turn out false or doubtful, that we set out to hunt for some standard truth which is *really* true. My statement in the first place is intended to presuppose this situation, and to identify real as distinct from mere temporary and apparent truth with what we persist in believing after doubt and inquiry—that from which we find ourselves unable to get away no matter what the skeptical temptation. For now suppose I find myself genuinely able to doubt a pretended truth—not simply to think of myself in imagination as doubting it under different circumstances; can the thing still belong to the category of the true? Evidently not; it belongs to the doubtfully true, or that about which I am in doubt whether it is true. It might be claimed that I still can determine that it should be held true by me through an act of will. But either this supposes that the doubt still persists in my mind, in which case I do not really believe it true, but merely want it to be true, or choose to act as if I believed it true; or else by my act of will I succeed in forgetting the doubt, excluding it from my consciousness. Then real belief indeed returns; but only because I have abandoned critical reflection, and have gone back voluntarily to a naïve and prephilosophic state.

With this preamble, I may go on to point out certain implications in the thesis, and thereby begin to make it more specific. In the first place, it implies that *belief* is a more fundamental concept than *truth*. We need, in other words, to start with the psychological existence of a certain peculiar attitude of mind, not with a reasoned definition, or with an objectively valid standard. We experience the belief before the question of truth arises at all; and we have to go back to the fact of belief to determine whether any truth is left at the end of the inquiry. If it is not—supposing such an outcome humanly possible—then we are skeptics, and truth for us does not exist. And if, on the contrary, we still find ourselves believing, this does not mean that we have discovered standards of truth which independently produce the belief, but, rather, that the beliefs left in the field are what we have to examine in order to find in them the marks which we then erect into a standard. And even if we do not succeed in analyzing them sufficiently to elicit the standard, we should still have to hold that the beliefs represent truth. We should be in a hard case indeed if mankind before believing in truth had to wait for the philosophers to define its nature and conditions.

This leads to a second point. When I say that truth is what we cannot help believing, I do not mean of necessity what it is *logically* impossible not to believe, or what cannot be believed without self-contradiction, but what it is naturally, or physically, or morally, or practically, impossible not to believe after critical inquiry. It has been a very general assumption with philosophers that we have no such thing as truth, or knowledge, until we get what can meet this test of *logical* certainty; and the assumption has had unhappy consequences. By setting up a goal extremely difficult to attain, if not entirely out of reach, it has tended to widen the gap between theoretical and practical truth, and has left in philosophy a general impression of skepticism quite out of relation to the concrete history of the growth of human knowledge. When we find mankind assured of the possession of a great deal of knowledge which the philosopher asserts is not knowledge at all, it would seem more modest, as well as more fruitful, if philosophy were to modify its definition in the direction of common usage, instead of setting up an *a priori* definition of its own, and then condemning actual human knowledge because it does not measure up to this. What accordingly the thesis maintains is, that the feeling of confidence, of settledness and assuredness, when this is not dogmatic, but is ready to lay itself open to all the evidence at hand, ought to be taken in the first instance as the sign that we are in possession of truth. If we actually have this, and continue after open-minded criticism to have it, in cases where the logical test cannot be applied, that means that we have no right at the start to identify the logical test with knowledge, and to demand that it must be met before we as philosophers are satisfied. If as human beings we are satisfied with less, then philosophy must accept this as a part of its data. And that men are thus capable of being satisfied is shown among other things by the standing fact, frequently a matter of perplexity to the metaphysician, that the belief in an outer world, or in the independent existence of our fellows, or in the obligatoriness of moral law, survives with hardly an effort the most overwhelming critical assaults.

Another explanation is perhaps needed in connection with the words "for me." A certain difficulty, it may be admitted, is present here, which can hardly be disposed of briefly. But if we are willing to stick for the time being to words as they are commonly understood, it is not difficult to make all the distinctions that are immediately relevant. The most direct source of confusion is that between "truth for me" and actual or objective truth. That this may stand for a genuine distinction, I should be myself the first to claim. Purely on the ground of experience, it is obvious that at least I may have at one time a conviction of truth which afterwards I may lose. And our common interpretation goes further; it makes a difference not only between the feeling of truth now and later, but between the feeling or persuasion of truth and the real truth *now*. It holds that whatever my belief in the matter, a thing is really true or not true all the time; there is an objective truth or standard to which the personal belief may or may not correspond.

In saying, then, that truth *for me* is what I cannot help believing, I do not mean to imply that truth in the so-called objective sense is determined by my psychological beliefs. On the contrary, in every belief there is present the assumption of a validity which does not depend on the belief itself, but on objective conditions. All that I mean is, that whether the belief is justified or is a mistaken one, every truth that we actually have up must first be believed to be true by some man in particular; and therefore, for human purposes, it is impossible to separate what is really true from what is believed to be really true, and to get at the former apart from the belief. The fact may be one way or the other, or it may be something quite different from what has ever entered into the mind of man; but it becomes a matter of human inquiry and human dispute only as it is the object of a belief. Reality, as it presents a definite content that we can talk about, is subject to all the vicissitudes of human thought about reality.

"Truth for me" means, therefore, that man can attain to a knowledge of reality, not by becoming himself identified with this reality, but only through belief about it; and while belief always supposes that it has got at the actual facts, we know that this supposition is not always correct. From such a chance of error we, as human beings, cannot possibly escape. No man, not an absolutist philosopher even, is able to get round the fact that any statements which he makes are after all *his beliefs* about things; they enter the field of discussion as reality interpreted by *him*, a private individual. Truth, in other words, is a term that belongs primarily to the realm of human thought about reality, and had better be confined to this. When accordingly we mean to refer to the *object* of a true belief, it will be preferable to speak, not of what I have somewhat loosely called objective truth, but of objective reality, or fact. Objective truth means only beliefs that are *really* true; and since every belief supposes itself to be really true—contains, that is, a reference to reality which it assumes that it is adequately describing—from the standpoint of its own inner intention at least the word "objective" is superfluous. That the belief sometimes is mistaken is due simply to the fact that it is man who talks about truth; and man is not infallible.

The problem of the criterion of truth is, accordingly, this: What, on reflection, justifies us in *continuing* to hold to our confidence in the things we believe to be true? And the problem divides itself into two parts: First, what are the original sources of belief? And, second, what is the test which we apply to strengthen our confidence, and justify it *rationally*, when for any reason it shows signs of failing?

There are two main forms of primitive or intuitive belief—by which I mean belief that rests on its own bottom, and does not depend upon security borrowed from other beliefs. There is on the one hand intuition in the stricter sense, where confidence seems to depend on the immediate seeing that a thing is self-evidently so. This it is apparently which gives the type of *certainty* in our thinking, and which creates, perhaps more or less unconsciously, the philosophic demand for an infallible standard. I shall reserve for another section the examination of intuition in this narrow meaning, and of the character of certainty which attaches to it; meanwhile the range of its application is obviously so limited that it can almost be disregarded in the great majority of significant problems. I may have an immediate and, it would seem, an indubitable apprehension of mathematical and logical relationships, or of the nature of the content that enters into my experiences of sensation or of memory. But the confidence that my geometrical intuitions apply to a real spatial world, or that my logical demands are accepted by the reality with which I come in practical contact, or that events actually were as I remember them, or that sensation gives me information about actual things and forces, is a confidence that must rest on different grounds. None of these last assurances is capable of a certainty beyond the reach of skeptical doubt; and our belief must therefore come from other sources.

The source is, I judge, reducible in every instance to an implicit faith in our own nature and instincts. There are tendencies in various directions which constitute what we mean concretely by "ourselves," and from whose influence therefore we cannot normally get away; and belief may be defined tentatively as just the coming to consciousness of that persistent active direction of attention which no obstacles can effectively shunt off. In this work of influencing belief—it is to be remembered that I am for the moment considering only the starting points of belief, which must be presupposed before confidence can be either strengthened or weakened by the subsequent application of criteria—three roughly distinguishable forms may be enumerated which human nature takes; there is a confidence due to our intellectual nature, to our practical needs, and to our emotional preferences. To show that these all represent actual occasions of belief, it is only necessary to point to familiar facts.

The most fundamental condition of belief is man's intellectual and logical constitution. To think at all we have to accept our human ways of thinking. And that men do accept them, and place confidence in their own intellectual make-up, is a simple matter of fact; the skeptical argument that for all we know our minds may have been constructed to falsify reality rather than to grasp it truly, while it is incapable of logical refutation, has ordinarily not the least effect as against a healthy tendency to believe.

The second aspect of man's nature, his practical needs, also is, I take it, self-evidently a source of belief. Man can satisfy the requirements of his organism only by taking for granted, and utilizing, the physical world about him; and the strong practical assurance he has of the existence of this environing world, and of its general laws, is plainly connected with his absolute need for accepting it if he is to continue alive. There has not been so general a philosophic justification of this belief. It is not difficult to throw doubt upon it if we elect to keep to purely speculative considerations. But the fact remains that such arguments as philosophy has resorted to have entirely failed to eradicate the belief, either in the non-philosophic mind, or, it is likely, in his better moments, in the philosopher himself.

Accordingly as a real and persistent belief it has to be taken account of in our search for truth.

The third source in human nature has a still poorer standing in the philosophic world; and here the philosopher gets some support also from the more cautious layman, who sees that beliefs due to emotion or desire are peculiarly liable to go astray. At present however I am merely pointing to the fact that desire and feeling do notoriously tend to carry belief in their train. And their influence is so far-reaching and insidious that even the philosopher on his guard against it does not escape. The very effort to escape has its dangers; a man will almost invariably be found leaning a little backward through his desire not to be influenced by desire. And if we really cannot escape the influence without superhuman powers, it would seem the sensible course to include this, too, in our theory of belief, and so of truth, since insofar as human nature is actually the source of belief, any ineradicable element of human nature may be expected to play a part.

It is on the basis of this general presupposition, then, that I shall go on to raise the further and more practically significant question: How, when belief wavers, are we to go to work to give it a reflective or rational justification? It is highly important to remember once more that belief must already exist before this question can be asked, and so that there must be a first and ultimate source of truth which is prerational. But equally it is clear that mere immediate or instinctive belief is not enough for human beings. Such belief needs to be emphasized in its proper place, in view of the strong metaphysical temptation to overlook it, and to reduce everything to logic. But for our ordinary purposes it can be taken for granted. The main interest here lies in the further question: How can beliefs be *justified*, so as to separate out the sheep from the goats?

The answer I should give to this last question is the familiar one of "coherence." Coherence I think must be rejected as a sufficient definition of truth, or a sufficient reason for belief. That it is not the definition of truth I shall argue presently at length; and there is at least a *prima facie* objection to the claim that mere consistency of ideal content can safely be trusted even as a criterion, unless it is also backed by the compulsion of so-called "facts." But with belief presupposed, it does seem to be the case that coherence is the only test by which we can justify belief to the intellect, outside the very insignificant field where intuitive certainty holds. This does not necessarily mean that we ought to abandon all beliefs that we cannot so justify. Nature will probably be too strong for us in any case. But nevertheless we do find on the whole that rational belief is the better and more satisfying sort. And so long as we play the game of reason, and profess to have passed beyond the first naïve and non-reflective stage of experience, "justification" may be taken as meaning "inclusion within a coherent system."

It is well to notice more precisely wherein this process consists, in opposition to the ideal of logical necessity. The essence of the coherence criterion is not certainty of logical deduction, but consistency of fact or experience. Mere logic never by any possibility can add more certainty to the conclusion than existed in the premises. Its ideal is, therefore, to carry back proof to more and more general premises, until at last it finds something in its own right on which it can rest, and from which then a derivative certainty passes to the consequences. The ideal of *system*, on the contrary, implies that certainty grows continually as new facts are added. The simple elements most fundamental in our system are not self-evident truths, which, as will presently appear, stop with the analysis of mental content, but, rather, those intuitions, or immediate beliefs, which are expressions of faith, since these alone lead us to reality in the more distinctive sense. But these, although they are objects of natural belief, are not yet rationalized or intellectually justified belief. When we are led to reflect upon them—which means that their mere instinctive operation is no longer sufficient—they are seen to need a further support through reason, as self-evident truths do not. The conclusions, that is, have to be more certain than the premises. And the possibility of this depends, not on logical deduction from what is self-evident, but on a *coincidence* of evidence. In other words, when we see that two independent beliefs corroborate one another, the confidence we have in both is increased; and this is what we mean by their intellectual justification. For this to happen, logical processes are required, because to reinforce one another the two must come in contact in a connected system. But the essence of the validation lies not in the passing on of an equal measure of certainty due to the process of inference, but to the *increase* of certainty due to the confluence of evidence.

And this applies as well to the "laws" of the mind itself, or the methods which the process of verification involves, in the very general sense that, by working along the lines which these methods set, we find that we do succeed within limits in ordering the universe of experience. The probability that a special type of mind is fitted to reality, which to an outside observer might seem in the abstract highly dubious, is to us, as insiders, almost a certainty, since we approach the question already with an immense amount of evidence at hand in the shape of successful experience. The material of experience, which in some interpretation comes to us palpably from independent sources, nevertheless allows itself to be organized; our minds approve themselves by turning out to be perfectly good tools for helping us to make our way in the world. This never gives theoretical certainty. It is possible that we may just happen to have got along so far without disaster. But we have enough for *practical* certainty. And the ground for this, once more, is to be found in the combination of a naïve tendency to accept what our nature impels us to accept, with the logical justification which this gets in proportion as experience proves amenable to our intellectual interpretations.

The justification of our practical persuasion is represented most conspicuously in the experimental methods of science. The greater the number of facts, obtained independently through the senses, which fit into the more or less hypothetical schemes of the various sciences, the stronger the confidence in, and the sense of logical justification for, these schemes. The outcome of experiment is not simply to prove that the investigator was right in expecting some particular result to turn up, though this is all it proves with certainty. His real meaning was not that such a particular future event would happen, but that the fact of its happening verifies a certain constitution of reality held to be responsible for it. Here also, to have its logical value, there must be a belief presupposed which is to receive verification; otherwise the new fact simply happens. Fulfilled expectation would have no logical force unless there were a presumption of law prior to the mere facts of experience in detail. This presumption in its general form is given in the law of causation as a practical postulate, or an intellectual principle having its basis in the necessities of our practical nature. The world being what it is, unless an organism had, ahead of actual experience, a tendency to look for repetitions of experience, and to act as if uniformity existed, it would stand little chance of surviving. The law of causation in its scientific sense seems to be the translation into terms of the intellect of this habit of expecting the familiar. But while as a postulate, or implicit belief, it precedes experience, as a *justified* belief it gets its standing from the fact that nature is on the whole inclined to bear it out.

The most controversial side of the matter is in connection with the postulates of emotion or desire. That these do actually influence our belief is plain. That they are as real a part of human nature as the elements commonly accepted as having a right to sway belief, most people would grant is also true. Why then should there be so much hesitation in allowing them equally a theoretical standing?

The reasons are apparently of two sorts. First there is the familiar empirical fact—a part therefore of the system of our world of facts—that beliefs influenced by feeling or strong desire have, where it is possible to subject them to verification, so often been proved to be in the wrong.

And, secondly, there is the tendency which emotion shows to attach itself to matters where proof and disproof alike are impossible or very difficult, and so to evade the tests that elsewhere have been found useful in keeping belief within safe bounds. Both these facts have to be recognized; but they ought not to count for more than they are worth.

The first objection implies that the case against feeling is not *a priori*, but empirical. There is nothing in it to make us reject outright the claim of any tendency to belief which actually is grounded in human nature; the objection applies only to beliefs in whose case there are positive grounds for doubt. If we are to begin doubting wherever there is a logical chance for doubt, without regard to reasons for doubt in particular, we are inevitably on the way to a complete skepticism. We have to ask, then, why it is that emotional beliefs are so provocative of doubt; what is the positive case against them?

An answer here is not difficult. Emotion is apt to be misleading, not because the thing in which we believe is also an object of desire, but because wanting it is apt to affect our mental processes, and prevent us from looking at the facts just as they are. If emotion did not blind us and keep us from straight thinking, if it did not lead us to overlook and close our minds to uncongenial evidence, I see no special reason why the fact that the object of belief is something we desire should constitute the slightest drawback. On the whole, in view of a number of considerations, it seems quite as easy to make out a case for the presumption that the universe has some favorable relation to human desires and possibilities of development, as for the opposite assumption that between our human demands and the constitution of the world there is no relevant connection. The facts are not compelling; and a good deal depends upon the attitude in which one approaches them. But an unfavorable presumption is just as truly a bias here as a favorable one, especially in view of the subtle temptation which leads the philosopher to adopt a non-humanistic preference because it is not quite the popular opinion, and so ministers a little to his spiritual pride. The real objection to the feelings is not that they are at work, but that they are at work *surreptitiously*, and so produce effects that are incalculable. The source of the trouble is not that we reason in terms of emotional objects, but that we reason in emotional ways, and so cannot get these objects in their true perspective. If therefore it be possible for a man, as it surely is to a very considerable degree, to include his own desires within the field of objects that he can examine critically without being bound thereby to adopt of necessity a blind and prejudiced attitude toward them, if he can estimate the claims of what he wants impartially and without ignoring considerations on the other side, the positive ground for suspecting desire would have been removed without prejudging the entire case.

The remaining difficulty would be that the beliefs are capable of no further testing. Even if this were so, it is conceivable that they might still persist; however, in such a case their intellectual standing would doubtless not be very satisfactory. But at the worst this very fact of their permanence would prevent them from being left *wholly* without intellectual justification. Thus a man, without being able in any other way to give reasons for an emotionally satisfying belief, might very well justify himself at least to this extent: The very strength of my unreasoning belief, he may argue, and the fact that it persists against discouragement, is proof to me that it may be justified, though I cannot see how in detail; for whenever I find such persistency in nature, I have reason to hold that it must be rooted somehow in reality. A man has a right to this attitude only in case, again, he has not allowed desire to blind his eyes, but has actually put his belief to the hazard of the unfavorable evidence, and shown by experiment that its persistence is not merely due to its being sheltered artificially from danger. But this granted, the conditions of the rational criterion have, though in a very general way, been met. It is not simply that the belief exists. Its existence has been justified, and justified by being brought into a larger system of facts. This may not be a convincing argument by itself in a particular case. But it is in character nevertheless a rational, and not a merely emotional, justification.

Whether we can go beyond this very general justification can hardly be answered except by considering beliefs in detail. It will be sufficient here to note that the belief in question may take either of two different forms, whose status logically is not the same. One form, and the simplest one, is this, that the world is of a nature to render the achievement of my ends or desires practically feasible. This sort of belief is clearly verifiable in the same sense that a physical hypothesis is verifiable; it is proved by actually achieving such ends. Even before the issue it stands rationally justified in terms of our existing knowledge of the character of the world, and of what therefore can probably be done in and with it; and when the end has been gained, or definitely lost, it is attested or discredited by the fact.

It is not this merely practical meaning, however, which has been seriously at issue in philosophy. What one side has claimed, and the other disputed, is not that the world is of a nature to permit the attainment in it of our human purposes, but that it has in its own character certain qualities that involve, not a mere tolerance of our preferences, but the same preferences as our own. This without question is our naïve point of view under the influence of our feelings. We say naturally, not merely that the world affords us a chance to achieve our aspirations, but that the world itself is good, and is working toward a good end.

But even in this latter case, while the evidence may be less convincing, it does not appear to stand on an essentially different footing from that of any belief that professes to describe the *nature* of things, as distinct from empirical sequences of phenomena in particular. Even in terms of sequences, complete and final verification never attaches to the universal *laws* of sequence, which may be supposed to sum up the actual relational character of reality, but only to eventualities in the way of particular anticipated happenings. Just as, accordingly, a belief that the world is intelligible starts from a natural trust in the powers of intelligence, and is justified by the success with which progressively we bring the facts of the world into relation, or, more specifically, as a belief in the objectivity of scientific law starts from a bias toward orderly expectation, which more and more is rationally justified as events are found to correspond to the expectations aroused—otherwise our belief would not be in a universal law, but only in the particular fact expected,—so the belief that the world is good starts from our naïve faith in our feelings of value, and may equally in some degree be considered as verified insofar as the universe turns out to be favorable to the leading of the good life.

And in the same way, though with extreme caution, the possibility is open for a rational holding of beliefs that assert more particular matters of fact, even where verification is humanly impossible. A case that naturally suggests itself is that of immortality. At the start a belief in immortality is almost on a par with the early glimpsing of ideal human possibilities in this present world—the first dim intuition, say, of a universal human brotherhood. This for a long time had to look so far ahead into the future for its verification that it could be held, like a belief in immortality, only on the ground of an inner assurance of its desirability. But the cases differ in that we should hardly hold as justified a belief about earthly possibilities which history did not show some tendency to realize, whereas immortality at the end is supposedly in the same case as at the beginning, so far as experimental verification goes. Nevertheless the other possibility remains open, and should be kept in mind in face of the popular tendency to refuse to be satisfied with anything short of verification in the scientific sense. If the belief can be shown to be logically connected with other beliefs for which ground does exist in the actual facts of experience, it shares in some degree their rational character. This is the case in science even, where a fact can be seen to follow from an accepted hypothesis. We do not feel too confident—for we know the uncertainties of our knowledge—until by experiment it has been verified. But it would be an over-wrought spirit of caution that would refuse to give it any credence. In proportion to the certainty of the hypotheses, and the clearness of the logical connection, we do take many things for granted which we never have put actually to the test. This is notably the case with our belief in past events, which of course in strictness never can be verified.

And the belief in immortality need make no claim different in kind. If we have reason to accept a particular kind of world into which an inconsistency would be introduced through the failure of certain kinds of life to continue, the belief in immortality is in so far a rational belief, and ought not to be rejected offhand as a mere product of unreasoning desire. Verification of course is exceedingly important if we can get it, and its absence is a drawback. But it is not essential to rationality. The logical value of verification lies, again, not in the mere experience of the new fact, but in the way in which it enters into the system of reality already present in the hypothesis, and so enlarges and strengthens this. Fundamentally, therefore, it plays the same part as any other fact in the system. It gets its peculiar significance simply because it was thought out and prophesied ahead of experience; not only does it counteract in consequence our natural disposition to be satisfied with the facts we have already collected, but it is indefinitely improbable that an expectation based upon a complex reasoning process will simply *happen* to hit the future event, as it would do were not the hypothesis already on the right track in its understanding of the world.

The position I have been taking may be summed up as follows: We have to distinguish between the necessity of a belief, its self-evidence, and its practical certainty; and it is the last about which we are really most concerned. This is a psychological state of mind, a persistent feeling of acquiescence or assent, which, if it goes along with an honest attempt to canvass the whole situation to the best of our ability, has the final word to say about what we shall regard as truth. And instead of attaching to the simplest truths, it belongs rather with the growing fullness of belief and experience. It is due to the compounding of assurance that comes from the working together of numberless facts and satisfactions, and has in it an element both of faith and of intellectual justification, the blending of the two constituting reason. In the large, the faith is faith in ourselves—in the demands of our nature and the possibility of their satisfaction. This exists prior to the facts, because our life is organic before it is intellectual, and we cannot in thinking eliminate ourselves. But we find also these demands capable within limits of getting satisfaction; and so to the naïve trust is added rational conviction. The greater the mass of experienced fact that comes within our system, and the greater the facility of successful anticipation of future fact, the more our confidence extends.

And equally it is greater the more widely it appeals to the various sides of our nature, insofar as these are approved as normal by the teachings of experience. This is why, other things being equal, a philosophy which finds a place for man's emotional needs has a better chance of survival than one which merely orders the facts of sense experience. The former exercises no compulsion whatever over a mind which is not predisposed in favor of humanistic considerations; and if the human mind generally could be counted on to take the same attitude as that of the occasional philosopher, the final success of naturalism could probably be predicted. As a matter of fact, however, naturalism leaves something out which human nature seems to want; and it is humanism which every time steps in and prevents its triumph.

Meanwhile one aspect of this thesis needs perhaps some little qualification. What it recommends is that, in opposition to the tendency to look for our most settled convictions among the simple results of analysis, we should rather turn to the comprehensive beliefs of developed human experience as our standard of assurance in the holding of truth. Roughly and in the large, I believe it to be so that "common sense" as constituted by the more massive convictions of the human race—of man in his natural habitat going about his regular business—supplies a standard of sanity which philosophy will reject at its peril. But there are two points of interpretative caution here that deserve attention.

In the first place, I am not intending to disparage analysis in the least. It is only through analysis that beliefs become amenable to reason at all. We cannot be content to accept things simply in the mass, for that leaves no way to choose when the voice of mankind is uncertain in its utterance, or when, as constantly happens, the general belief needs modification and readjustment. But neither can we expect to get ahead by throwing over the concrete beliefs of everyday use, and confining our assent to their simpler ingredients. The path of knowledge is altogether too crooked and tangled to make this a safe procedure. It is of no avail to have, in reason, a compass, unless we know more or less concretely the goal we are setting out to reach; and there is nothing whatever to supply this goal apart from that somewhat vague and loosely articulated, but very real, *welt-anschauung*, which represents the net outcome of man's experience up to date, which passes over to the individual in the first place as a biological and social inheritance, and which in its large features has already approved itself to him in practice before he is competent to bring criticism to bear upon it, although this or that aspect of it may call insistently for revisal when he is able to interpret his demands on the world more discriminatingly. Just as we commonly think that social reform is best accomplished by taking existing social institutions for granted as a starting point, and then correcting this or that feature as circumstances may dictate, rather than by setting out to abolish everything at once and to build up society from the bottom —the latter task is too big for human powers—so in our philosophizing the only practicable method is, not to doubt universally or where academic doubt is not precluded, but to examine our beliefs piecemeal, all the time holding fast as a background to that positive nature of things which appeals to our massive and unanalyzed intelligence through its satisfactoriness on the whole, and apart from which we have no way whatever of telling whether any aspect in particular is more or less probable, except in the relatively few and unimportant cases where it is strictly self-evident.

For without a background, it is impossible we should think at all. Thinking *is* the bringing of our existing beliefs to bear upon the examination of a belief in particular; and the fuller the content of experience interlaced in this apperceptive mass, the more valuable the judgment, though the precise nature of the elements thus present may not in the judgment itself be subjected to analysis. For sound judgment, this background must have been there at the first step of philosophic analysis, unless we are to suppose that a man with positive convictions and a full experience is less qualified to perform the critical act than one whose mind approaches a jelly or a blank. Sound method therefore does not demand that we should clear our minds as nearly as we can of all content, and allow it to fill up again only as the dialectical process advances. What determines the worth of our results is precisely the wealth of experience, partly and at the start very largely unanalyzed, lying back of the rational process. Naturally this "assumed universe" cannot be held exempt from progressive analysis and criticism. We should understand as fully as possible what we are presupposing, and why. But the criticism is rather to remove internal inconsistencies than to put on trial the conception as a whole; if we cast aside the actual fruits of experience, racial and individual, nothing remains to take their place.

A certain danger does no doubt exist here, in that the very wealth of experience may lead a man to trust his first impressions when a severer analysis is urgently demanded. And when on the other hand we once come to realize how easily unanalyzed judgments go astray, it may seem to our more sophisticated sense impossible to avoid a lurking distrust of their pronouncements. But the situation is relieved in part by a distinction. It is not that the *judgment* should be unanalyzed. On the contrary, we should use our utmost effort to see our *meaning* in the judgment clearly and distinctly, with the finest discriminations we can manage. No good ever comes of confusion as to what we intend. It is in connection with the grounds for accepting the *truth* of this intention that the vague and more subconscious "total experience" plays its rôle. And although this also should, as I have said, be cleared up as rapidly as may be, it never can be entirely exhausted, while nevertheless, and even at the start, it is rightly to be trusted cautiously, under penalty of our being left without sail or rudder in a weltering sea of "possibilities" or of "logical entities."

Meanwhile a second point against the rationalistic or Cartesian method is, that no philosopher ever does live up to it in point of fact. You will find him all along surreptitiously bringing in the common-sense philosophy of mankind to justify his conclusions, in the form of considerations which he would have no manner of right to appeal to if he really were allowing nothing to influence him save his reasoned results up to date. And if he is to do this at all, it surely is much better that he should confess to his procedure and recognize it in his ideal of method, rather than keep it under cover.

❖ **54** ❖

THE IMPLIED BEING OF TRUTH

George Santayana (1863–1952)

. . . The experience which perhaps makes even the empiricist awake to the being of truth, and brings it home to any energetic man, is the experience of other people lying. When I am falsely accused, or when I am represented as thinking what I do not think, I rebel against that contradiction to my evident self-knowledge; and as the other man asserts that the liar is myself, and a third person might very well entertain that hypothesis and decide against me, I learn that a report may fly in the face of facts. There is, I then see clearly, a comprehensive standard description for every fact, which those who report it as it happened repeat in part, whereas on the

Excerpted from Chapter 25, pp. 266–69 of *Scepticism and Animal Faith* (1923). Reprinted by permission of Constable and Company Limited, London. The title of this selection has been supplied by the editors.

contrary liars contradict it in some particular. And a little further reflection may convince me that even the liar must recognize the fact to some extent, else it would not be *that* fact that he was misrepresenting; and also that honest memory and belief, even when most unimpeachable, are not exhaustive and not themselves the standard for belief or for memory, since they are now clearer and now vaguer, and subject to error and correction. That standard comprehensive description of any fact which neither I nor any man can ever wholly repeat, is the truth about it.

The being of truth thus seems to be first clearly posited in disputation; and a consequence of this accident (for it is an accident from the point of view of the truth itself under what circumstances men most easily acknowledge its authority)—a consequence is that truth is often felt to be somehow inseparable from rival opinions; so that people say that if there was no mind and consequently no error there could be no truth. They mean, I suppose, that nothing can be correct or incorrect except some proposition or judgment regarding some specific fact; and that the same constitution of the fact which renders one description correct, renders any contradictory description erroneous. "Truth" is often used in this abstract sense for correctness, or the quality which all correct judgments have in common; and another word, perhaps "fact" or "reality," would then have to be used for that standard comprehensive description of the object to which correct judgments conform. But a fact is not a description of itself; and as to the word "reality," if it is understood to mean existence, it too cannot designate a description . . . Facts are transitory, and any part of existence to which a definite judgment is addressed is transitory too. . . .

The word truth ought, I think, to be reserved for what everybody spontaneously means by it: the standard comprehensive description of any fact in all its relations. Truth is not an opinion, even an ideally true one. . . . [Another] difference between truth and any true discourse is that discourse is an event; it has a date not that of its subject-matter, even if the subject-matter be existential and roughly contemporary; . . . truth is dateless and absolutely identical whether the opinions which seek to reproduce it arise before or after the event which the truth describes.

The eternity of truth is inherent in it: all truths—not a few grand ones—are equally eternal. I am sorry that the word eternal should necessarily have an unction which prejudices dry minds against it, and leads fools to use it without understanding. This unction is not rhetorical, because the nature of truth is really sublime, and its name ought to mark its sublimity. Truth is one of the realities covered in the eclectic religion of our fathers by the idea of God. Awe very properly hangs about it, since it is the immovable standard and silent witness of all our memories and assertions; and the past and the future, which in our anxious life are so differently interesting and so differently dark, are one seamless garment for the truth, shining like the sun. It is not necessary to offer any evidence for this eternity of truth, because truth is not an existence that asks to be believed in, and that may be denied. It is . . . involved in positing any fact, in remembering, expecting, or asserting anything; and while no truth need be acknowledged if no existence is believed in, and none would obtain if there was no existence in fact, yet on the hypothesis that anything exists, truth has appeared, since this existence must have one character rather than another, so that only one description of it . . . will be complete; and this complete description, covering all its relations, will be the truth about it. No one who understands what is meant by this eternal being of truth can possibly deny it; so that no argument is required to support it, but only enough intensity of attention to express what we already believe.

Inspired people, who are too hot to think, often identify the truth with their own tenets, to signify by a bold hyperbole how certain they feel in their faith; but the effect is rather that they lead foolish people, who may see that this faith may be false, to suppose that therefore the truth may be false also. Eternal truths, in the mouth of both parties, are then tenets which the remotest ancestors of man are reputed to have held, and which his remotest decendants are forbidden to abandon. Of course there are no eternal tenets: neither the opinions of men, nor mankind, nor anything existent can be eternal. . . . Even if all the spirits in heaven and earth had been so far unanimous on any point of doctrine, there is no reason, except the monotony and inertia of nature, why their logic or religion or morals should not change tomorrow from top to bottom, if they all suddenly grew wiser or differently foolish. . . .

TRUTH

P. F. Strawson (1919–)

In the following discussion, I confine myself to the question of the truth of empirical statements. My positive thesis is an elaboration of what was said, a long time ago, by F. P. Ramsey.[1] My negative purpose is the criticism of a current misconception—the Semantic or Meta-linguistic Theory of Truth —which seems to me to repeat, in a new way, some old mistakes. In so far as this theory is simply a contribution to the construction of artificial languages, and is not intended to be regarded as relevant to the use of actual languages, I am not concerned with it. But I think the theory has been claimed by some, and it has certainly been thought by many, to throw light on the actual use of the word "true"; or (which I take to be the same claim) on the philosophical problem of truth. I think it *does* throw some light; but I think it is also seriously misleading. Nothing that follows, however, is to be taken as implying that the word "true" is *never* used in the way described by the semantic theory. It is certainly so used for some technical purposes, and may sometimes be so used for non-technical purposes as well; though I know of no such non-technical purposes.

I

In recent discussions of truth, one or both of two theses are commonly maintained. These are:

First, any sentence beginning "It is true that . . ." does not change its assertive meaning when the phrase "It is true that" is omitted. More generally, to say that an assertion is true is not to make any further assertion at all; it is to make the same assertion. This I shall call Thesis I.

From *Analysis*, Vol. 9, No. 6 (June 1949), pp. 83–97. Reprinted by permission of the author and of the publisher, Basil Blackwell Limited.
[1] Ramsey, *Foundations of Mathematics*, pp. 142–43.

Second, to say that a statement is true is to make a statement about a sentence of a given language, viz., the language in which the first statement was made. It is (in other and more technical terms) to make a statement in a meta-language ascribing the semantic property of truth (or the semantic predicate "true") to a sentence in an object-language. The object-sentence concerned should strictly be written in inverted commas to make it clear that we are talking *about the sentence*; and the phrase "is true" should strictly be followed by some such phrase as "in L," where "L" designates the object-language concerned. This I shall call Thesis 2.

Of these two theses, the first is true, but inadequate; the second is false, but important. The first thesis is right in what it asserts, and wrong in what it suggests. The second thesis is wrong in what it asserts, but right in what it implies. The first thesis is right in asserting that to say that a statement is true is not to make a further statement; but wrong in suggesting that to say that a statement is true is not to do something different from, or additional to, just making the statement. The second thesis is right in implying that to say that a statement is true is to do something different from just making the statement; but wrong in asserting that this "something different" consists in making a further statement, viz., a statement about a sentence.

Although both theses are sometimes maintained by the same philosopher, it is easy to see that they cannot both be correct. For if it is true that to say (1) "Moths fly by night" is to make the same assertion as to say (2) "It is true that moths fly by night," then it is false that to say (2) is to say anything about the English sentence "Moths fly by night"; i.e., false that (2) ought strictly to be written " 'Moths fly by night' is true in English." If to say (2) is to make the same assertion as to say (1), then to say (2) cannot be to say anything about an English sentence; for to say (1) is not to say anything about an English sentence, but is to say something about moths.

Independently of this, one sees how misleading it is to say that the phrase " . . . is true" is used to talk *about sentences*, by comparing it with other phrases which certainly are used to talk about sentences (or words, or phrases). For example, someone says, in French, "Il pleuve"; and someone else corrects him, saying: " 'Il pleuve' is *incorrect* French. 'Il pleut' is the right way of saying it." Or, criticising the style of a passage, someone says: "The sentence '. . . .' is *badly expressed*." Similarly, one may ask what a sentence *means*, or say that a sentence is *ungrammatical, misspelt, a poor translation*. In all these cases, it is natural to say that one is talking *about a sentence*. If any statement of this kind were correctly translated into any language at all, the sentence which was being discussed would re-appear, quoted and untranslated, in the translation of the statement as a whole. Otherwise the translation would be incorrect. But it is perfectly obvious that a correct translation of any statement containing the phrase "is true" (used as it is ordinarily used) never contains a quoted and untranslated sentence to which the phrase "is true" was *applied* in the original sentence. The phrase "is true" is not *applied to* sentences; for it is not *applied to* anything.

Truth is not a property of symbols; for it is not a property.

II

The habit of calling truth a "semantic" concept ("true" a "semantical predicate") does not lessen the confusion involved in saying that "true" is a predicate of sentences; but it helps to indicate a possible source of the confusion. I shall digress briefly to explore this source. For light on the use of the word "semantic," I quote the following from Carnap's "Introduction to Semantics" (p. 22):

> "By a *semantical system* we understand a system of rules, formulated in a meta-language and referring to an object-language, of such a kind that the rules determine a *truth-condition* for every sentence of the object-language. . . . To formulate it in another way: the rules determine the *meaning* or *sense* of the sentences."

It will be noticed that the expressions "truth-condition" and "meaning" are used synonymously. And this suggests that even if there is no use of the phrase "is true" in which that phrase is correctly applied to (used to talk about) sentences, there is, or might be, a use of the phrase "is true if and only if," in which *this* phrase is correctly applied to (used to talk about) sentences; a use, namely, in which this phrase would be synonymous with the phrase "means that"; which certainly *is* used to talk about sentences. Suppose, for example, that we wish to give information about the meaning of the sentence "The monarch is deceased." We can do this by making the following meta-statement:

(i) "The monarch is deceased" means that the king is dead. Here we put the sentence "The monarch is deceased" in inverted commas to indicate that we are talking about this sentence. We are making a meta-statement. And the meta-statement is contingent, for it is a contingent matter that the sentence in question has this meaning in English, or, indeed, that it has any meaning at all. To be quite strict, we perhaps ought to write it:

(ia) "The monarch is deceased" in English means that the king is dead.

If we were to translate this meta-statement into another language, none of the expressions occurring in it would remain unchanged except the quoted sentence "The monarch is deceased." That would remain unchanged; otherwise the translation would be incorrect. Now the suggestion is that we might, without unintelligibility, give the same information in exactly the same way, except that we should replace the phrase "mean that" with the phrase "is true if and only if" obtaining the contingent meta-statement:

(ii) "The monarch is deceased" is true if and only if the king is dead

or, more strictly:

(iia) "The monarch is deceased" is true in English if and only if the king is dead.

This seems to be an intelligible procedure. All that I have said of statements (i) and (ia) will apply to statements (ii) and (iia); we shall be using the phrase "is true if and only if," in a contingent statement, to talk about a sentence. Now consider a degenerate case of such meta-statements: the case exemplified in the sentences:

(iii) "The monarch is deceased" means (in English) that the monarch is deceased.

(iv) "The monarch is deceased" is true (in English) if and only if the monarch is deceased.

It is difficult, and, perhaps, for the present purpose, not very important, to decide what status to assign to such sentences as these. Considerations which might tempt us to describe them firmly as true, contingent meta-statements are the following:

(*a*) Although they are of no use for telling us what the quoted sentence means, they do give us some information about it. They do at any rate indicate that the quoted sentence has some meaning in English.[2] And this is a contingent matter.

(*b*) These statements could be obtained from the non-degenerate cases by a quite legitimate process of translation, inference and retranslation. (Or, more simply, their correct translation into, say, French would undoubtedly yield a contingent meta-statement).

---

[2] One can imagine another use for statements (iii) and (iv); e.g., if the object-language were written, and the meta-language spoken, English.

(*c*) It is a contingent matter that any sentence means what it does mean, expresses the proposition it does express.[3]

Although these considerations are decisive against calling (iii) and (iv) "logically necessary," [4] they are very inadequate grounds for calling them, without qualification, "true and contingent." For what contingent matter do they state? If we answer, taking the hint from (*a*), that they state merely that the quoted sentence has some meaning in English, then their form (the use of the expression "means that") is utterly misleading. If we demand what contingent matter they state, which falls under the head of (*c*), no answer is possible. One cannot *state* what a sentence means without the help of another sentence.

For these reasons, I propose to continue to refer to statements (or pseudo-statements) like (iii) and (iv) not as necessary, nor as contingent, but simply as "degenerate cases" of contingent meta-statements of the type of (i) and (ii). The point is not in itself important; though it is important that no confusion should arise from it.

The next step is to notice the deceptive similarity of the use of the phrase "if and only if" in this type of contingent meta-statement to its use in expressions which are not contingent statements, but necessary or defining formulae. An example of such a formula would be:

The monarch is deceased if and only if the king is dead.

Here the phrase "is true" does not occur; and no part of this expression is in inverted commas. The formula itself does not give us information about the meaning of the sentence "The monarch is deceased," though the statement that it *was* a necessary formula *would* give us such information. Now the similarity of the use of the phrase "if and only if" in these necessary formulae to its use as *part* of the phrase "is true if and only if" in contingent meta-statements, may have constituted a strong temptation to split the degenerate cases of such meta-statements down the middle, and to regard what follows the phrase "if and only if" as the definiens of what pre-

---

[3] Cf. Lewy, "Truth and Significance," *Analysis*, Vol. 8, No. 2.

[4] We might be tempted to call (iii) and (iv) "necessary," because it seems self-contradictory to say:

(iiia) "The monarch is deceased" does not mean in English that the monarch is deceased.

But this would be a mistake. To say that a sentence both has some meaning or other and has no meaning at all would be to say something self-contradictory. To say that a sentence both has and has not some particular, specified meaning would be to say something self-contradictory. But (iiia) does neither of these things. The form of (iii) is appropriate to assigning, and that of (iiia) to withholding, some specific meaning. But since (iii) does not assign, (iiia) does not withhold, any specific meaning. (iiia) is not a self-contradictory, nor a false, contingent, statement; but a pseudo-statement.

cedes it: i.e., of the phrase "the sentence '. . . .' is true (in L)"; to regard, for example, the whole expression (iii).

"The monarch is deceased" is true if and only if the monarch is deceased.

as a specification or consequence or part [5] of a general definition of ". . . . is true" (or of " . . . is true in L"). And this we in fact find; i.e., we find it said that a satisfactory general definition of truth must have as its consequences such expressions as the following: [6]

(v) "Today is Monday" is true if and only if today is Monday.

(vi) "London is a City" is true if and only if London is a City. Now we have seen that such statements as (v) and (vi) are degenerate cases of those contingent meta-statements of the type of (ii), which make use of the phrase *"is true if and only if"* as a synonym for *"means that."* It is only *as a part of the former phrase* that the expression *"is true"* is used, in such statements, to talk about sentences. To read the degenerate cases, then, as specification, or parts, of some ideal defining formula for the phrase "is true" is to separate the phrase from the context which alone confers this meta-linguistic use upon it, and to regard the result as a model for the general use of "is true." It is to be committed to the mistake of supposing that the phrase "is true" is normally (or strictly) used as a meta-linguistic predicate. Thus misinterpreted, as defining formulae, such expressions as (v) are both fascinating and misleading. They mislead because, as we have seen, they crystallize the false Thesis 2. They fascinate because they seem to point to the true Thesis 1; for part of the expression to be defined (namely, the combination of quotation-marks and the phrase is "true") *disappears* in the definiens without being replaced by anything else. (How odd it is, incidentally, to call this definition-by-disappearance "definition"!) In this way, the view that "true" is assertively redundant is represented as somehow combined with, and dependent upon, the view that "true" is a meta-linguistic predicate of sentences. We may express, then, the main contention of the semantic theory as follows: to say that a statement is true is not to say something further *about the subject-matter* of the statement; but is to say the same thing about the subject-matter of the statement, *by means of a further statement, namely a statement about a sentence.* Now I

[5] E.g., Tarski, in *The Semantic Conception of Truth,* "Philosophy and Phenomenological Research," Vol. 4, 1943–44, p. 344, says:

"Every equivalence of the form (T) [(T) X is true if and only if p] obtained by replacing 'p' by a particular sentence and 'X' by a name of this sentence, may be considered a partial definition of truth, which explains wherein the truth of this one individual sentence consists. The general definition has to be, in a certain sense, a logical conjunction of all these partial definitions."

[6] Cf. M. Black, expounding and criticizing Tarski, in *Analysis,* Vol. 8, No. 4, p. 51.

said that Thesis 1 is true. A fortiori, a modification of Thesis 1 is true, which I shall call Thesis IA, and which runs as follows:

To say that a statement is true is not to say something further about the subject-matter of the statement, but, insofar as it is to say anything about that subject-matter, is to say the same thing about it.

Now Thesis 1A, but not Thesis 1, is compatible with Thesis 2. The semantic theory consists in the joint assertion of 1A and 2. I suggest that the semantic theory borrows a lot of its plausibility from the truth of 1A. We swallow 2 for the sake of 1A. I now wish to show that the unmodified thesis 1 is true, and that we therefore can and must assert 1A while reject-ing 2 and, therefore, rejecting the semantic theory.

As for the muddle I have described above—the muddle of reading a de-generate case of contingent statements meta-linguistically employing the phrase *is true if and only if*, as a pseudo-defining-formula of which the definiendum consists of a quoted sentence followed by the phrase *is true*—I do not claim that this muddle represents the genesis of the semantic theory; but I do think that it, too, may have contributed to the plausibility of the theory.

III

The best way of showing that Thesis 1 is true is to correct its inadequacy. The best way of correcting its inadequacy is to discover the further reasons which have led to Thesis 2. To bring out those features of the situation which lead to the mistake of saying that the word "true" is used meta-linguistically (to talk about sentences), I want first to compare the use of "true" with that of "Yes." If you and I have been sitting together in silence for some time, and I suddenly say "Yes," you would, perhaps, look at me with surprise and answer "I didn't say anything." Of course, a man may say "Yes" to himself; and this will be a sign that he has resolved a doubt in his own mind, or come to a decision. But the normal use of "Yes" is to answer: and where no question is asked, no answer can be given. Suppose you now ask: "Was Jones there?" and I say "Yes"; there seems no temptation whatever to say that, in so answering, I am *talking about* the English sentence "Was Jones there?" So, in the case of "Yes," we have a word of which the normal use requires some linguistic occasion (a ques-tion), without there being any temptation at all to say that it used to *talk about* the sentence of which the utterance is the occasion for its use. There is indeed a temptation to go further in the opposite direction and say that in answering "Yes" I am not talking *about* anything, not making any assertion, at all; but simply answering. In a way, this is correct; but in a way, it's wrong. For it would be perfectly correct for you, reporting our dialogue, to say of me: "He said Jones was there." So of the ordinary use of "Yes," we may say: first, that it demands a linguistic occasion, namely the asking of a question; second, that it is not used meta-linguistically, to talk about the question, but to answer it; third, that in so far as we are making an assertion at all in using it, the content of the assertion is the same as the content of the question. Now imagine a possible, and perhaps vulgarly current, use of the expression "Ditto." You make an assertion, and I say "Ditto." In so far as I assert anything, talk about anything, I talk about and assert what you talk about and assert. Of course—and this points to the inadequacy of Thesis 1 and the reason for the meta-linguistic error—to say "Ditto" is not *the same as* to make the statement in question; for, whereas I might have made the statement before anyone else had spoken, it would be meaningless for me to say "Ditto" before anyone else had spoken. "Ditto," like "Yes," requires a linguistic occasion. But again, and largely, I think, because the expression "Ditto" does not consist of a gram-matical subject and a grammatical predicate, there is absolutely no tempta-tion to say that in thus using "Ditto," I should be talking *about the sentence* you used, and the utterance of which was the linguistic occasion for my use of this expression. I am not talking about what you said (the noise you made, or the sentence you spoke, or the proposition you ex-pressed). I am agreeing with, endorsing, underwriting what you said; and, unless you had said something, I couldn't perform *these* activities, though I could *make the assertion* you made. Now the expression "That's true" sometimes functions in just the way in which I have suggested the expres-sion "Ditto" might function. A says "Jones was there" and B says "That's true"; and C, reporting the conversation, can correctly say: "Both A and B said that Jones was there." But the point is that B couldn't have said that Jones was there in the way he *did* say it, (i.e., by the use of the expression "That's true"), unless A had previously uttered the *sentence* "Jones was there," or some equivalent sentence. It is, perhaps, *this* fact about the use (*this* use) of the word "true," together with the old prejudice that any indicative sentence must describe (be "about") something, which en-courages those who have become chary of saying that truth is a property of propositions to say instead that in using the word "true," we are talking about sentences. (What I have said about the use of "That's true" applies, of course, with suitable alterations, to the use of "That's false.")

Now those who assert that "true" is a predicate of sentences have not, in general, considered these simple cases of the use of "true" (and "false"), but the more puzzling cases which lead, or seem to lead, to paradoxes: such as the case where someone utters the isolated sentence "What I am saying now is false," or writes on an otherwise clean blackboard sentence "Every statement on this blackboard is false." The solution on meta-linguistic lines is to treat these sentences as making statements of the second order to the effect:

(1) that there is some statement of the first order written on the blackboard (or said by me now);

and (2) that any first-order statement written on the blackboard (or said by me now) is false.

By means of this distinction of orders, the distinction between meta- and object-language, the puzzling sentences are said no longer to engender contradictions: either they are simply false, since the existential part of what they assert is false; or, alternatively, leaving out the existential part of the analysis, and treating them solely as hypotheticals, they are seen to be vacuously true, since no first-order statements occur. This solution is for- mally successful in avoiding the apparent contradictions. But it seems to me to achieve this success only by repeating the fundamental mistake from which the contradictions themselves arise, and also, and consequently, in- volving the difficulties mentioned at the beginning of this paper. That is, first, it involves the view that to say that a statement is true (or false) is to make a further, second-order, statement (thus contradicting Thesis 1); and, second, it (usually) involves the unplausibility of saying that this second-order statement is *about* a sentence or sentences. Now the point of the previous discussion of the actual use of "Yes," the possible use of "Ditto" and the actual use of "That's true" is to show that these expedients are unnecessary. When no one has spoken, and I say "Ditto," I am not making a false statement to the effect that something true has been said, nor a true statement to the effect that nothing false has been said. I am not making a statement at all; but producing a pointless utterance. When somebody has made an assertion previously, my saying "Ditto" acquires a point, has an occasion: and, if you like, you may say that I am now making a statement, repeating, in a manner, what the speaker said. But I am not making an additional statement, a meta-statement. It would perhaps be better to say that my utterance is not a statement at all, but a linguistic performance for which in the first case there was not, and in the second case there was, an occasion: so that in the first case it was a spurious, and in the second case a genuine, performance. Similarly, the words "true" and "false" normally require, as an occasion for their significant use, that somebody should have made, be making or be about to make (utter or write), some statement. (The making of the statement need not precede the use of "true": it may follow it as in the case of the expression "It is true that . . ."—a form of words I shall discuss later). But in all cases the indicative clause of which the grammatical predicate is the phrase "is true" does not in itself make any kind of statement at all (not even a meta-statement), and *a fortiori* cannot make the statement, the making of which is required as the occasion for the significant use of the words "true" or "false." This is not, as it stands, quite accurate. For an indicative sentence of which the grammatical predicate is the phrase "is true" may sometimes, as I shall shortly show, be used to make an implicit meta-statement. But when this is so, the phrase "is true" plays no part in the making of this meta-statement. The phrase "is true" *never* has a statement-making role. And when this is seen, the paradoxes vanish without the need for the meta-linguistic machinery; or at least without the need for regarding the words "true" and "false" as part of that machinery. The paradoxes arise on the assumption that the words "true" and "false" can be used to make first-order assertions. They are formally solved by the declaration that these words can be used only to make second-order assertions. Both paradoxes and solution disappear on the more radical assumption that they are not used to make assertions of any order, are not used to make assertions at all.

I said, however, that indicative sentences of which the grammatical predicate is the phrase "is true" or the phrase "is false" may be used to make an implicit meta-statement, in the making of which these phrases themselves play no part. To elucidate this, consider the following sentences:

(1) What I am saying now is false
(2) All statements made in English are false
(3) What the policeman said is true.

It is certainly not incorrect to regard each of these sentences as implicitly making an *existential* meta-statement, which does not involve the words "true" or "false." The implicit meta-statements in these cases might be written as follows:

(1a) I have just made (am about to make) a statement
(2a) Some statements are made in English
(3a) The policeman made a statement.

These are all second-order assertive sentences to the effect that there are some first-order assertive sentences, uttered (*a*) by me, (*b*) in English, (*c*) by the policeman.

These second-order assertive sentences we can regard as part of the analysis of the sentences (1), (2) and (3). Obviously they are not the whole of their analysis. The sentence "The policeman made a statement" clearly has not the same use as the sentence "What the policeman said is true." To utter the second is to do something more than to assert the first.

What is this additional performance? Consider the circumstances in which we might use the expression "What the policeman said is true." Instead of using this expression, I might have *repeated* the policeman's story. In this case, I shall be said to have *confirmed* what the policeman said. I might, however, have made exactly the same set of statements as I made in repeating his story, but have made them *before* the policeman spoke. In this case, though the assertions I have made are no different, I have not done what I did in the other case, namely "confirmed his story." So to confirm his story is not to say anything further, *about* his story, or the sentences he used in telling it, though it is to do something that cannot be done unless he has told his story. Now, unlike the confirming narrative which I might have told, the sentence "What the policeman said is true" has no use *except* to confirm the policeman's story [7] ; but like the confirming narrative, the sentence does not say anything further *about* the policeman's story or the sentences he used in telling it. It is a device for confirming the story without telling it again. So, in general, in using such expressions, we are confirming, underwriting, admitting, agreeing with, what somebody has said; but (except where we are implicitly making an existential meta-statement, in making which the phrase "is true" plays no part), we are not making any assertion additional to theirs; and are *never* using "is true" to talk *about* something which is *what they said*, or the sentences they used in saying it. To complete the analysis, then, of the entire sentence (3) "What the policeman said is true," we have to add, to the existential meta-assertion, a phrase which is not assertive, but (if I may borrow Mr. Austin's word) performatory.[8] We might, e.g., offer, as a complete analysis of one case, the expression: "The policeman made a statement. I confirm it" ; where, in uttering the words "I confirm it," I am not describing something I do, but *doing* something.[9] There is, then, a difference between the more complicated cases in which the phrase "is true" is preceded by a descriptive phrase, and the simpler sentences (e.g., "That's true") in which the phrase "is true" is preceded by a demonstrative. The former may be regarded as involving an implicit meta-statement, while the latter are purely confirmatory (or purely "admittive"). But in neither sort of case has the phrase "is true" any assertive (or meta-assertive) function.

There may still be some uneasiness felt at the denial that the phrase

---

[7] This needs qualification. Uttered by a witness, the sentence is a *confirmation*; wrung from the culprit, it is an *admission*. No doubt there are other cases.

[8] Cf. J. L. Austin, "Other Minds," P.S.A. Supp. Vol. XX, pp. 169–175 for an account of some words of this class.

[9] Cf. also "I admit it." To *say* this *is* to make an admission.

"is true" has any assertive, or descriptive, function. Partially to allay this uneasiness, I will again say something familiar, that I have said already: that is, that when I say "That's true" in response to your statement, I am in a manner making an assertion, namely the assertion you made; describing something, namely what you described. But pointing this out is quite consistent with saying that "That's true" makes no statement in its own right. It makes no meta-statement. If there is any residual uneasiness, it ought not to be allayed. For its source is the ancient prejudice that any indicative sentence is, or makes,[10] a statement. I call it a prejudice: we could, instead, make it a criterion. And there would even be no harm in adopting this criterion for "statement," if we could simultaneously divorce the word, in this strictly grammatical use, from its logic in other uses: from that logic which leads us, given a "statement," to inquire: What is it about? What does it describe? What property, or what relation, does it assert to belong to, or hold between, what entity or entities? Asking these questions when confronted with such a sentence as "What Pascal said is true," we are led to look for the entity which is *what Pascal said*; looking with cautious, contemporary eyes, we find only his words; and so are induced to say that, in using this expression, we are talking about the French sentences he wrote or spoke. It is, then, the out-of-date desire that the phrase "is true" should be some kind of a descriptive phrase, that leads to the up-to-date suggestion that the word "true" is a second-level, predicate of first-level sentences. More important than simply to reject *this* view is to have the right reason for rejecting it: the reason, namely, that the phrase "is true" is not descriptive at all. If we persist that it describes (is about) something, while denying that it describes (is about) sentences, we shall be left with the old, general questions about the nature of, and tests for, truth, about the nature of the entities related by the truth-relation, and so on. Better than asking "What is the criterion of truth?" is to ask: "What are the grounds for agreement?"—for those we see to be not less various than the subjects on which an agreed opinion can be reached. And this will perhaps also discourage us from seeking to mark the difference between one kind of utterance and another by saying, for example, "Ethical utterances are not true or false." It is correct to say that utterances of any kind are true or false, if it is correct usage to signify agreement or disagreement with such utterances by means of the *expressions* "true" or "false."

Of course, the formula that I have adopted in the discussion of one use of "true" is not immune from another variant of that argument from

---

[10] Throughout I have used such mild barbarisms as "This sentence makes a statement" as shorthand for such expressions as "Anyone who uttered this statement would be making a statement."

grammar which leads to treating "true" as a descriptive word. Someone might say: in order for you to *confirm* anything, there must be some *object* of this activity; a sentence or a proposition: and to perform this activity upon this object is nothing other than to assert that the object has the property, stands in the relation, referred to by the word "true." Anyone who says this is misled partly by the fact that the verb "confirm" takes a grammatical object; and partly by the fact that the linguistic performance (of "confirming") requires, not an object, but an *occasion*—a fact which I declared to be the misunderstood element of truth in the semantic theory. Even this assertion—that there must be, or be thought to be, some kind of sign-occasion for the significant, or genuine, use of the word "true"—is not quite correct, if it means that some spoken or written utterance must occur, or be thought to occur. For it would not be incorrect, though it would be unusual, to say: "What you are thinking is true"; when nothing has been said. (But, then, a conversation *can* be carried on by glances and nods.)

IV

In philosophical discussion of this whole subject, very little attention has been paid to the actual use of "true." And I want to conclude by distinguishing some of its normal uses in a little more detail. The uses mentioned so far I was tempted to call "performatory." But this is a misnomer. A performatory word, in Austin's sense, I take to be a verb, the use of which, in the first person present indicative, seems to describe some activity of the speaker, but in fact *is* that activity. Clearly the use of "is true" does not seem to describe any activity of the speaker; it *has seemed* to describe a sentence, a proposition, or statement. The point of using Austin's word at all is the fact that the phrase "is true" can sometimes be replaced,[11] without any important change in meaning, by some such phrase as "I confirm it," which is performatory in the strict sense. I shall take the substitute performatory word as a title for each of these cases; and shall speak, e.g., of the "confirmatory" or "admissive" use of "true." What commends the word as, e.g., a confirmatory device is its economy. By its means we can confirm without repeating.

The word has other, equally non-descriptive, uses. A familiar one is its use in sentences which begin with the phrase "It's true that," followed by a clause, followed by the word "but," followed by another clause. It has been pointed to me that the words "It's true that . . . but . . ." could, in these sentences, be replaced by the word "Although"; or, alternatively, by

11 Of course, not *simply* replaced. Other verbal changes would be necessary.

the words "I concede that . . . but . . ." This use of the phrase, then, is concessive. The inappropriateness of the meta-linguistic treatment seems peculiarly apparent here.

The purely confirmatory use is probably no more common than other uses which look much the same, but which are, I think, distinct. A man may make an assertion to you, not wanting you to confirm it, to remove the doubt of others or his own; but wanting to know that you share his belief, or his attitude. If, in this case, you say "That's true," you are not *saying*, but *indicating*, that you do share his belief. It seems to me natural to describe this simply as "agreeing." Again, it seems to me that we very often use the phrase "That's true" to express, not only agreement with what is said, but also our sense of its novelty and force. We register the impact of what is said, much as we might register it by saying: "I never thought of that." Contrast the ironical "very true" with which we some-times rudely greet the obvious. The use of "true" here is effectively ironical just because we normally use it to express agreement when our agreement is in doubt, or to register a sense of revelation. Sometimes, in sentences beginning "Is it true that . . . ?" or "So it's true that . . . ," we could preserve the expressive quality of the utterance by substituting the adverb "really" for the quoted phrases, at an appropriate point in the sentence; to convey, as they do, incredulity or surprise.

No doubt, the word has other functions; but those I have mentioned are probably as common as any. The important point is that the perfor-mance of these functions (and, I suspect, of all other non-technical jobs the word may do) does not involve the use of a meta-linguistic predicate; and that we *could*, with no very great violence to our language, perform them without the need for any expression which *seems* (as "is true" seems) to make a statement. For instance, the substitution of "although" for "it's true that . . . but . . ." is an obvious way of dealing with the concessive use; an extension of the practice of the inarticulate election-candidate whose speech consisted of "Ditto to Mr. X" might deal with the confirmatory and, partly, with the expressive uses; and so on. The selection of the substitute-expressions would of course be governed by the propa-gandist consideration that they should provide the minimum encourage-ment to anyone anxious to mistake them for statement-making phrases, or descriptive words.

One last point: a suggestion on the reasons why the puzzle about truth has commonly got entangled with the puzzle about certainty. It is above all when a doubt has been raised, when mistakes or deceit seem possible; when the need for confirmation is felt; that we tend to make use of those certifying words of which "true" is one and of which others are "certain," "know," "prove," "establish," "validate," "confirm," "evidence" and so on. So that the question "What is the nature of truth?" leads naturally to the question "What are the tests for truth?," and this, in its turn, to the question "What are the conditions of certainty?" The historical or judicial search for truth is the search for the evidence which will set doubt at rest. The philosophical endeavor to characterize truth *in general* has tended to become the endeavor to characterize that which *in general* sets doubt at rest; really and finally at rest. Where you find the indubitable, there you find the true. And this metaphysical road branches into different paths, at the end of one of which you find the Atomic Fact, and, at the end of another, the Absolute.

Finally, I will repeat that in saying that the word "true" has not in itself any assertive function, I am not of course saying that a sentence like "His statement is true" is incorrect. Of course the word "statement" may be the grammatical subject of a sentence of which the phrase "is true" is the grammatical predicate. Nor am I recommending that we drop this usage. But for the usage, there would be no problem.

❖   56   ❖

MR. STRAWSON'S ANALYSIS OF TRUTH

L. Jonathan Cohen (1923–   )

In a recent paper [1] Mr. P. F. Strawson suggested that all non-technical functions of the words "true" and "false" could be performed, "with no very great violence to our language, . . . without the need for any expression which seems (as "is true" seems) to make a statement" (p. 96). I wish to argue that there is at least one important non-technical function of those words which cannot be so performed. Mr. Strawson was criticising Tarski's semantic definition of truth, and I do not propose directly to attack or defend the philosophical relevance of that definition. But he

From *Analysis*, Vol. 10, No. 6 (June 1950), pp. 136–40. Reprinted by permission of the author and of the publisher, Basil Blackwell Limited.
[1] *Analysis*, Vol. 9, No. 6 [this volume selection 55, pp. 482–96].

also claimed (p. 83) to be elaborating something said by F. P. Ramsey in *Foundations of Mathematics*, pp. 142–43. And in this he seems to have partially misunderstood Ramsey, for Ramsey wrote explicitly that in some cases "we get statements from which we cannot in ordinary language eliminate the words 'true' and 'false' " (*op. cit.*, p. 143). Mr. Strawson's paper makes it necessary to consider this type of case at greater length than in the few sentences which Ramsely devoted to it.

Mr. Strawson's view is that when we say, for instance, "It is true that the sun is shining" we can replace "it is true" by one of the performatory phrases "I confirm," "I admit," "I concede," "I guarantee," etc., as appropriate, without any important change of meaning. The only assertion we make, on his view, is that the sun is shining, although the grammatical form of our sentence misleadingly suggests that we are also making a second-order assertion about this first-order one. For by a "performatory" word Mr. Strawson means "a verb, the use of which, in the first person present indicative, seems to describe some activity of the speaker, but in fact *is* that activity." (He might add "or a pretence at it," for people sometimes pretend to agree with others when they really do not.) Thus, on this view, in non-technical usage the words "true" and "false" never function as logical predicates.

Now in respect of sentences where the statement said to be true or false is explicitly given (like "It is true that the sun is shining") this analysis is indeed an interesting elaboration of Ramsey's; and I shall make no criticism of it here. But there are other uses in which the statements said to be true or false are not explicitly given, but are merely "described," as Ramsey put it. We are told the circumstances in which they are uttered or written, but we are not given their content. Mr. Strawson appreciates the separate problem created by this type of sentence and gives three examples:—"What I am saying now is false," "All statements made in English are false," and "What the policeman said is true" (p. 92). But on his view the only relevant difference between these sentences and the others is that in uttering them we should implicitly be making "existential meta-statements" such as "I have just made (am about to make) a statement," "Some statements are made in English," and "The policeman made a statement," respectively. And he suggests that, since the words "true" and "false" are even in these instances not being used to make assertions at all, the truth paradoxes and their normal solutions disappear together. "The paradoxes arise on the assumption that the words 'true' and 'false' can be used to make first-order assertions. They are formally solved by the declaration that these words can be used only to make second-order assertions. Both paradoxes and solution disappear on the more radical assumption that they are not used to make assertions of any order . . . at all."

I do not think that Mr. Strawson's analysis of utterances where the statements said to be true or false are merely "described," and his consequent treatment of the truth paradoxes (which can only arise in those cases), are satisfactory.

A judge, e.g., might, treat counsel's remark "What the policeman said is true" as expressing a statement which can be verified or falsified (shown correct or incorrect) by evidence about the policeman's character. This statement would then be taken to assert much more than merely "The policeman made a statement." The judge would be asserting a formula for indirectly verifying a number of other statements. It is not necessary to hold that the word "true" is actually functioning as a logical predicate descriptive of the policeman's utterances. But the sentence cannot be paraphrased by "The policeman made a statement: I confirm it," as Mr. Strawson supposes, because this does not assert a statement which could be verified or falsified by evidence about the policeman's character.

It might be objected that to treat "What the policeman said is true" as an assertion to be verified or falsified by evidence about the policeman's character is to make merely a compendious reference to the following assertions, say: "The defendant was driving at 50 miles an hour on the wrong side of the road: the plaintiff was riding a bicycle at five miles an hour on the right side of the road." And it might be urged that it is these assertions which are really being treated as (indirectly) verifiable or falsifiable by the evidence about the policeman's character. So that counsel's utterance would constitute no exception to Mr. Strawson's analysis. He merely meant: "I emphasize what the policeman said: "the defendant was driving. . . ."

But this line of escape is not open where either the contents of the statements referred to are wholly or partially unknown, or where the number of these statements is in principle indeterminate. For if this is so the person who utters the sentence concerned cannot adequately replace it by a set of subsidiary assertions which he is emphasizing or admitting. He seems to be uttering the sentence as a single, complete assertion. Thus I might say "Smith's observation-reports are always true," in a statement-making way, without having read all of his reports. Or I might say "Anything the newspapers say about Yugoslavia is false," without knowing whether any newspaper is actually saying anything about Yugoslavia; and I might be quite capable of producing evidence for my assertion.

I have been suggesting that sentences like "Any statement by this policeman is true" can be used in a statement-making way (despite their not implying the existential meta-assertion which Mr. Strawson thinks to be the only statement capable of being implied by such assertions), on the grounds that they may be treated as verifiable or falsifiable by evidence about, say, the policeman's character. It can also be argued, in support of my suggestion, that these sentences are used as statements from which inferences can be drawn: that is how the truth paradoxes occur. One of the premises from which, for instance, the judge may infer the plaintiff's liability to damages is the truth of any evidence by the policeman. And such inferences are frequently made in journalism, in historical and scientific research, as well as in the law courts. This statement-making use of "true" and "false" is a very important one.

The analysis which Ramsey suggests provides a recipe for eliminating the word "true" from such formulae at the cost of introducing some logical jargon. But it still implies that the sentence is being used in a statement-making way. We could say, for instance, "For all p, if the policeman asserts p then p." Yet here, too, we could have paradoxes analogous to the truth paradoxes. Thus a symbolic formula for expressions which could be used to analyze sentences like "Any statements asserted by me are false" would be $(p): (x). \emptyset (p. x) \supset . \sim p$, where $\emptyset (p, x)$ is to be interpreted as "The statement that . . . is asserted by. . . ." This would give rise to a paradox analogous to a truth paradox if the expression as a whole were believed capable of occurring as a value of p.

I can, however, conceive of someone's uttering the sentence "Anything the policeman said is true" as a substitute for "The policeman is a reliable witness." And if this were a straightforward description of the policeman's character in the light of the evidence about it no paradoxes would arise when I said, in the same way, "Any statements asserted by me are false." I should merely be describing my character. But I think legal counsel, for instance, would use the sentence "The policeman is a reliable witness" rather as a recommendation, which the evidence about the policeman gives ground for approving, than as a description. And if I said "My utterances are quite unreliable" in this way I should give rise to a paradox. I should be recommending people not to rely on any of my utterances and therefore to refrain from relying on the utterance "My utterances are quite unreliable." In other words I should be at the same time both recommending them not to rely, and discouraging them from not relying, on my utterances. Moreover, the solution of this paradox would be analogous to the normal solution of the truth paradoxes. I should have to specify the type of utterance which I considered unreliable. I should have to say, perhaps, "My descriptive utterances are quite unreliable," leaving it open whether my recommendations, arithmetical utterances, and so on, were reliable. So that I can use the word "recommend" in a performatory way, in, say, "I recommend you not to rely on my utterances," and still give rise to a paradox that requires solution by a theory of types (although it may not be quite like the paradoxes of formal logic).

Thus, to sum up, when it is correct to paraphrase sentences like "Anything the policeman said is true" by sentences like "The policeman is a reliable witness," and they are used as descriptive statements no paradoxes analogous to the truth paradoxes can arise. But if they are used as recommendations, as they commonly are, and not as statements at all, these may arise. And when such a paraphrase cannot be made the sentences seem to be used to state a formula for the indirect verification of other statements. This formula may itself be judged "true" or "false" (or "correct" or "incorrect") and can give rise to logical paradoxes. The recommendation-analysis is more in keeping with the section of Mr. Strawson's analysis of "true" and "false" to which I am not objecting, where the statements are not just referred to but explicitly given; but it does not bear out his claim to be able to dispense with the normal solution of the truth paradoxes. The analysis in terms of a verification-formula is the one suggested by Ramsey, whom Mr. Strawson claims to be elaborating; but this both gives rise to logical paradoxes and also implies that "is true" is being used to make an assertion. Mr. Strawson may still be correct, however, in holding that "true" is not used as a logical predicate, since in the description-analysis the logical predicate is "true-statement-maker," in the recommendation-analysis there is no logical predicate, and in the verification-formula-analysis we can eliminate the word "true" (although not in ordinary language).

BIBLIOGRAPHY

This bibliography is intended for the student who is interested in doing further reading on the subject, and not for the researcher who is interested in finding out if there is any further reading for him to do. Consequently it contains and should contain items having a certain degree of non-esoteric interest, as well as a certain number that border on the exotic, though none, we trust, that border on the erotic. Completeness is impossible; life is short and contains other things than epistemology. So we tried to supplement the selections used, by listing some writings directly relevant to them or to the issues dealt with in them; and we also included some selections by authors already represented in the book for those who might have been engaged by someone's style. In addition, we tried to complement the selections used by listing books and articles dealing with topics not dealt with in the book but which are clearly in the area of epistemology— hence the selections on memory and evidence.

A number of the books from which selections have been taken will be found useful on other topics covered in the book. Occasionally we have indicated this, but in general, works from which selections have been taken for this book are not listed here. We have, however, listed all items which were seriously considered for inclusion in this anthology but which were omitted for reasons not basically connected with quality.

We have distinguished books from articles only where there were enough books or articles worth mentioning to make the distinction worth making. A number of the books listed below themselves contain bibliographies worth looking at; these are indicated by the symbol "(Bib.)." They appear mainly, but not solely, in the General category, which lists anthologies (A), texts (T), and treatises which have such general coverage of the field as not appropriately to fit under any of the more restricted headings. Some books are listed more than once, where the aptness of particular chapters or sections seemed to make this appropriate, but in general we have avoided multiple listings. It should be taken for granted that the sections listed below provide only rough and ready headings, preliminaries to a classificatory scheme, and that if a book is pertinent to one area of epistemology it is likely to be pertinent to others.

The general outline of the bibliography is as follows:

501

I. GENERAL

Ackermann, Robert J.; *Theories of Knowledge* (1965). (A)

Aristotle; *De Anima*, Bks II & III.

Balfour, A. J.; *A Defence of Philosophic Doubt* (1879; 2nd ed., 1920).

Boas, George; *The Inquiring Mind: An Introduction to Epistemology* (1959).

Broad, C. D.; *The Mind and its Place in Nature* (1925).

Canfield, John V. and Donnell, Franklin H., Jr., eds.; *Readings in the Theory of Knowledge* (1964). (Bib.) (A)

Chisholm, Roderick M.; *Perceiving* (1957).

———; *Theory of Knowledge* (1966). (T)

Dewey, John; *Experience and Nature* (1925; 2nd ed., 1929).

———; *Logic: The Theory of Inquiry* (1938).

———; *The Quest for Certainty: A Study of the Relation of Knowledge and Action* (1929).

Drake, Durant; *Mind and its Place in Nature* (1925).

Eaton, Ralph M.; *Symbolism and Truth: An Introduction to the Theory of Knowledge* (1925).

Feigl, Herbert and Sellars, Wilfred, eds.; *Readings in Philosophical Analysis* (1949). (A) (Bib.)

Hill, Thomas English; *Contemporary Theories of Knowledge* (1961). (T)

Hamlyn, David; "History of Epistemology," *The Encyclopedia of Philosophy*, Paul Edwards, ed., (1967), Vol. III, pp. 8–38. [Apparently the only history of epistemology in English.]

Hobhouse, L. T.; *The Theory of Knowledge* (1896).

Houde, Roland and Mullally, Joseph P.; *Philosophy of Knowledge* (1960). (Bib.) (A)

Joad, C. E. M.; *Guide to Modern Thought* (1933), chs. IV and VIII.

Koffka, K.; *Principles of Gestalt Psychology* (1935). (Bib.)

Laird, John; *A Study in Realism* (1920).

Lewis, C. I.; *An Analysis of Knowledge and Valuation* (1946).

———; *Mind and the World Order: Outline of a Theory of Knowledge* (1929; 2nd ed., 1956).

Lovejoy, Arthur O.; *The Revolt Against Dualism* (1930).

Montague, Wm. Pepperell; *The Ways of Knowing* (1925).

Moore, G. E.; *Philosophical Papers* (1959). [Contains the famous papers "A Defence of Common Sense" and "Proof of an External World."]

———; *Philosophical Studies* (1922).

———; *Some Main Problems of Philosophy* (1953).

Nagel, Ernest and Brandt, Richard B.,' eds.; *Meaning and Knowledge* (1965). (Bib.) (A)

Ormond, Alexander Thomas; *Foundations of Knowledge* (1900).

Peirce, Charles S.; *Philosophical Writings of Peirce*, Justus Buchler, ed., (1940).

Russell, Bertrand; *The Analysis of Mind* (1921).

———; *An Inquiry into Meaning and Truth* (1940).

———; "Mysticism and Logic," in *Mysticism and Logic and Other Essays* (1917).

Ryle, Gilbert; *The Concept of Mind* (1949).

Spaulding, Edward Gleason; *The New Rationalism* (1918).

Spencer, Herbert; *First Principles* (1862; 6th ed., 1900).

Stroll, Avrum, ed.; *Epistemology: New Essays in the Theory of Knowledge* (1967). (A)

Underhill, Evelyn; *Practical Mysticism* (1915).

Wertheimer, Max; *Productive Thinking* (1945).

Yolton, John W., ed.; *Theory of Knowledge* (1965). (Bib.) (A)

II. BELIEF

As should be apparent from the table of contents, the selections we have included in this part fit the following headings, though they were not sectioned under these headings either in the text or in the table of contents: The Nature of Belief; The Distinction between Belief and Knowledge; The Ethics of Belief (or Belief and Action); Faith; Authority; Intuition; and Opinion. Consequently writings dealing with these topics are included in the list that follows, but here also no finer subdivision has been attempted. Given the way in which so many writings fit simultaneously under a large number of headings, subdivision here would be even more misleading than it would have been in the body of the book. The titles can usually be taken as guides, given the fact that the item is listed here.

Ammerman, Robert R.; "Ethics and Belief," *Aristotelian Society Proceedings*, Vol. 65 (1965), pp. 257–66.

Beard, Robert W.; " 'The Will to Believe' Revisited," *Ratio*, Vol. 8 (1966), pp. 169–79.

Bergson, Henri; *Creative Evolution* (1907).

——; "Introduction to Metaphysics" (1903, English transl. 1913).

Black, Max; *Critical Thinking* (1946; 2nd ed., 1952), ch. 13, ("The Grounds of Belief"). (T)

Campbell, C. A.; "Towards a Definition of Belief," *The Philosophical Quarterly*, Vol. 17 (1967), pp. 204–20.

Clifford, W. K.; "The Weight of Authority," sec. 2 of "The Ethics of Belief," *Lectures and Essays*, Vol. II (1901), pp. 176–98.

Collingwood, R. G.; *An Autobiography* (1939), ch. 5 ("Question and Answer").

Drake, Durant; *Invitation to Philosophy* (1933), chs. 1 and 2 ("The Voice of Authority" and "Intuition and Faith").

Evans, J. L.; "Error and the Will," *Philosophy*, Vol. 38 (1963),pp. 136–48.

Freud, Sigmund; *The Psychopathology of Everyday Life* (1904).

Griffiths, A. Phillips; "On Belief," *Aristotelian Society Proceedings*, Vol. 63 (1963), pp. 167–86.

——, ed.; *Knowledge and Belief* (1967). (Bib.) (A)

Harrison, Jonathan; "Does Knowing Imply Believing?" *The Philosophical Quarterly* Vol. 13 (1963), pp. 322–32.

Hintikka, Jaakko; *Knowledge and Belief* (1962).

Kennedy, Gail; "Pragmatism, Pragmaticism, and the Will to Believe—A Reconsideration," *The Journal of Philosophy*, Vol. 55 (1958), pp. 578–88.

Laird, John; *Knowledge, Belief, and Opinion* (1930), chs. 5 (The Nature of Belief") and 20 ("Faith").

Lewis, George Cornewall; *An Essay on the Influence of Authority in Matters of Opinion* (2nd ed., 1875).

Lippmann, Walter; *Public Opinion* (1922).

Mavrodes, George; "James and Clifford on 'The Will to Believe,'" *The Personalist*, Vol. 44 (1963), pp. 191–98.

Myerson, Abraham; *Speaking of Man* (1950), ch. 4 ("The Low-Down on Authorities, Including Psychiatrists," pp. 50–69).

Newman, Cardinal, John Henry; *An Essay in Aid of A Grammar of Assent* (1870).

Peirce, Charles S.; "Deduction, Induction, and Hypothesis," in C. S. Peirce, *Chance, Love, and Logic*, Morris R. Cohen, ed., (1923), Part 1, ch. 6, pp. 131–53. [Also available in other collections of Peirce's writings.]

Polanyi, Michael; "The Stability of Beliefs," *The British Journal for the Philosophy of Science*, Vol. III (1952), pp. 217–32

Pope, Hugh; art. "Faith," *Catholic Encyclopedia* (1909), Vol. V. [See below, various authors.]

Russell, L. J.; "The Justification of Beliefs," *Philosophy*, Vol. 33 (1958), pp. 121–31.

Taylor, A. E.; "Knowing and Believing," *Aristotelian Society Proceedings*, Vol. 29 (1929), pp. 1–30; reprinted in Taylor's *Philosophical Studies* (1934), pp. 366–98.

Various Authors; art. "Faith," *New Catholic Encyclopedia* (1967), Vol. V.

Whitehead, Alfred North; *The Function of Reason* (1929).

III. KNOWLEDGE

The heading "knowledge" is clearly the largest catchall of all, just as it forms the largest section of this bibliography, and a number of topics included elsewhere, such as under Belief or Truth, could also have been included here. But decisions are inevitable, and anyone who does not approve of the ones made here is entitled to make his own. Since we did use "knowledge" as a catchall label in the text, and did not divide this part of the book into more specific sections, such as the nature of knowledge, skepticism, the *a priori*, the problem of induction, and certainty (though these are the general problem areas dealt with by the selections included), as in the case of Belief no more refined subdivision is assayed in this bibliography. Perception and Memory did present special problems. The few selections in the text really give no idea of the inflated importance problems connected with perception and sense-data have taken on in philosophical discussions. To take account of this inflation a special section has been given over to Perception. Memory is like Perception in that it seems to provide the data of knowledge, and to raise many similar problems. Since it went unrepresented in the text (only because we forgot about it), it gets a bibliographical section of its own.

It is to be presumed that the reader can tell from its title what some book or article is about, even though it is certain that this presumption will sometimes be mistaken.

A. Books

Ayer, A. J.; *The Problem of Knowledge* (1956).

Berkeley, George; *Three Dialogues between Hylas and Philonous, in Opposition to Sceptics and Atheists* (1713).

Berkeley, George; A Treatise Concerning the Principles of Human Knowledge (1710).

Black, Max; Problems of Analysis (1955), Part III, "Induction," pp. 157–225, 294–97.

Bosanquet, Bernard; The Essentials of Logic (1895), lec. 3, "The Relation of Logic to Knowledge," pp. 42–60.

Cohen, Morris R.; Reason and Nature (1931), Bk. I, ch. 3, section 3, "Induction and Deduction," pp. 115–25.

———, and Nagel, Ernest; An Introduction to Logic and Scientific Method (1934), ch. 14 ("Probability and Induction"), pp. 273–88.

Collingwood, R. G.; An Essay on Metaphysics (1940), chs. 4 & 5 ("On Presupposing" and "The Science of Absolute Presuppositions"), pp. 21–48.

Cornford, F. M.; Plato's Theory of Knowledge: The Theaetetus and the Sophist of Plato translated with a running commentary (1935).

Cornforth, Maurice; The Theory of Knowledge (1955).

Descartes, René; Discourse on the Method of Rightly Conducting the Reason and Seeking Truth in the Sciences (1637).

———; Meditations on the First Philosophy (1641).

Dewey, John; Essays in Experimental Logic (1916).

Empiricus, Sextus; Outlines of Pyrrhonism.

Hampshire, Stuart; Spinoza (1951), ch. 3, "Knowledge and Intellect," pp. 82–120.

Hartland-Swann, John; An Analysis of Knowing (1958).

Hegel, G. W. F.; The Phenomenology of Mind (1807).

Husserl, Edmund; Ideas: General Introduction to Pure Phenomenology (1913; Engl. transl. 1931).

Isaacs, Nathan; The Foundations of Common Sense: A Psychological Preface to the Problems of Knowledge (1950).

James, William; Essays in Radical Empiricism (1912). [A collection of essays; contains the famous essay "Does 'Consciousness' Exist?"]

Joad, C. E. M.; Guide to Philosophy (1936), Part I, "Theory of Knowledge," pp. 23–152.

Joseph, H. W. B.; An Introduction to Logic (1906; 2nd ed., 1916), chs. 18 & 19 ("Of Induction" & "Of the Presuppositions of Inductive Reasoning"), pp. 378–425.

Laird, John; Knowledge, Belief and Opinion (1930), ch. 7 ("Concerning Certainty"), pp. 185–200; ch. 4 ("The Nature of Knowledge"), pp. 93–128.

———; A Study in Realism (1920).

Leibniz, G. W.; Discourse on Metaphysics (1686), esp. sec. XIII.

————; *The Monadology* (1714), esp. paragraphs 28–38.

————; "Reflections on Knowledge, Truth, and Ideas" (1684). [This last, as well as the two above, available in *Leibniz: Selections*, ed. Philip P. Wiener (Modern Student's Library; Charles Scribner's Sons, 1951), pp. 283–90; 305–9; 538–40.]

————; *New Essays on the Human Understanding* (1704).

Lynd, Robert S.; *Knowledge for What?* (1939).

Mannheim, Karl; *Ideology and Utopia* (1936), Part V, "The Sociology of Knowledge," pp. 237–80. (Bib.)

McGilvary, Evander Bradley; *Toward a Perspective Realism*, A. G. Ramsperger, ed., (1956), ch. 5, ("Perspectives"), pp. 154–225.

Mill, John Stuart; *A System of Logic, Ratiocinative and Inductive* (1843; 8th ed., 1872), Bk II, chs. 5 & 6, "Of Demonstration, and Necessary Truths," and Book III, "Of Induction."

Murphy, Arthur E.; *Reason and the Common Good*, ed. W. H. Hay & M. G. Singer (1963), Part II, "Objective Relativism," pp. 49–92, and ch. 9, "Moore's Defence of Common Sense," pp. 108–20.

Paulsen, Friedrick; *Introduction to Philosophy* (1892; Engl. transl. 1895), Book I, "The Problems of Epistemology."

Perry, Ralph Barton; *Present Philosophical Tendencies* (1912).

Plato; *Meno*

————; *Sophist*

————; *Theaetetus*

Ramsperger, Albert G.; *Philosophies of Science* (1942), chs. 9 & 10 (Reality and Knowledge" & "Scientific Knowledge"), pp. 118–54.

Rogers, A. K.; *A Brief Introduction to Modern Philosophy* (1899).

Royce, Josiah; *The Religious Aspect of Philosophy* (1885), ch. 11, ("The Possibility of Error"), pp. 384–435.

————; *The World and the Individual* (1901), Vol. II (*Nature, Man, and the Moral Order*), Lecture 1, "The Recognition of Facts."

Russell, Bertrand; *Human Knowledge: Its Scope and Limits* (1948).

————; *Our Knowledge of the External World* (1914).

Sinclair, William Angus; *The Conditions of Knowing* (1951).

Spinoza, Benedict (Baruch); *On the Improvement of the Understanding* (1677).

Stebbing, L. Susan; *A Modern Introduction to Logic* (1930; 6th ed. 1948), ch. 21 ("The Problem of Induction"), pp. 400–19. (T)

Strawson, P. F.; *Introduction to Logical Theory* (1952), ch. 9, part 2 ("The Justification of Induction"), pp. 248–63. (T)

Various Authors; *Essays in Critical Realism: A Co-operative Study of the Problems of Knowledge* (by Durant Drake, Arthur O. Lovejoy, James

Bisset Pratt, Arthur K. Rogers, George Santayana, Roy Wood Sellars, and C. A. Strong) (1920).

Various Authors; *The New Realism: Cooperative Studies in Philosophy* (by Edwin B. Holt, Walter T. Marvin, William Pepperrell Montague, Ralph Barton Perry, Walter B. Pitkin, and Edward Gleason Spaulding) (1912).

Varisco, Bernardino; *Know Thyself* (Engl. transl. 1915).

Williams, Donald; *The Ground of Induction* (1947).

Wisdom, John; *Other Minds* (1952).

B. Articles

Abelson, Raziel; "Knowledge and Belief," *Journal of Philosophy*, Vol. 65 (1968), pp. 733–37.

Ammerman, Robert; "A Note on 'Knowing That,'" *Analysis*, Vol. 17 (1957), pp. 30–32.

Arner, Douglas; "On Knowing," *Philosophical Review*, Vol. 68 (1959), pp. 84–92.

Barnes, W. H. F.; "Knowing," *Philosophical Review*, Vol. 72 (1963), pp. 3–16.

Black, Max; "The Justification of Induction," in Black's *Language and Philosophy* (1949), pp. 59–88, 250–51.

———; "Necessary Statements and Rules," *Philosophical Review*, Vol. 67 (1958), pp. 313–41; also in Black's *Models and Metaphors* (1962), pp. 64–94.

———; "On Speaking with the Vulgar," *Philosophical Review*, Vol. 58 (1949), pp. 616–21.

Broad, C. D.; "Is There 'Knowledge by Acquaintance'?" *Aristotelian Society*; Supplementary Vol. 2 (1919), pp. 206–20.

Cohen, Morris R.; "The New Realism," *Journal of Philosophy*, Vol. 10 (1913), pp. 197–214; also in Cohen's *Studies in Philosophy and Science* (1949), pp. 109–32.

———; "Some Difficulties in Dewey's Anthropocentric Naturalism," *Philosophical Review*, Vol. 49 (1940), pp. 196–228; also [in somewhat modified form] in Cohen's *Studies in Philosophy and Science* (1949), pp. 139–75.

Dewey, John; "The Experimental Theory of Knowledge," in Dewey's *The Influence of Darwin on Philosophy* (1910), pp. 77–111.

Donnellan, Keith S.; "Necessity and Criteria," *Journal of Philosophy*, Vol. 59 (1962), pp. 647–58.

Ewing, A. C.; "The Linguistic Theory of A Priori Propositions," *Aristotelian Society Proceedings*, Vol. 40 (1940), pp. 207–44.

Firth, Roderick; "The Anatomy of Certainty," *Philosophical Review*, Vol. 76 (1967), pp. 3–27.

Frankfurt, Harry G.; "Realism and the Objectivity of Knowledge," *Philosopical Quarterly*, Vol. 7 (1957), pp. 353–8.

———; "Philosophical Certainty," *Philosophical Review*, Vol. 71 (1962), pp. 303–27.

Gellner, Ernest; "Knowing How and Validity," *Analysis*, Vol. 12 (1951), pp. 25–35.

Gettier, Edmund L.; "Is Justified True Belief Knowledge?" *Analysis*, Vol. 23 (1963), pp. 121–23.

Grice, H. P. and Strawson, P. F.; "In Defense of a Dogma," *Philosophical Review*, Vol. 65 (1956), pp. 141–58.

Hamlyn, D. W.; "Analytic Truths," *Mind*, Vol. 65 (1956), pp. 359–67.

———; "On Necessary Truth," *Mind*, Vol. 70 (1961), pp. 514–25.

Hampshire, Stuart & Hart, H. L. A.; "Decision, Intention, and Certainty," *Mind*, Vol. 67 (1958), pp. 1–12.

Harrison, Jonathan; "Knowing and Promising," *Mind*, Vol. 71 (1962), pp. 443–57.

Hartland-Swann, John; "The Logical Status of Knowing That," *Analysis*, Vol. 16 (1956), pp. 111–15.

Hay, William H.; "Bertrand Russell on the Justification of Induction," *Philosophy of Science*, Vol. 17 (1950), pp. 266–77.

Henle, Paul; "On the Certainty of Empirical Statements," *Journal of Philosophy*, Vol. 44 (1947), pp. 625–32.

Langford, C. H.; "A Proof that Synthetic A Priori Propositions Exist," *Journal of Philosophy*, Vol. 46 (1949), pp. 20–24.

Losskij, Nicholas; "The Transformation of the Concept of Consciousness in Modern Epistemology and its Bearing on Logic," *Encyclopedia of the Philosophical Sciences*, Henry James, ed., Vol. I, *Logic* (1913).

Malcolm, Norman; "Defending Common Sense," *Philosophical Review*, Vol. 58 (1949), pp. 201–220.

Mates, Benson; Analytic Sentences," *Philosophical Review*, Vol. 60 (1951), pp. 525–34.

Moore, G. E.; "Is There 'Knowledge by Acquaintance'?" *Aristotelian Society, Supplementary* Vol. 2 (1919), pp. 179–93.

———; "Certainty" in *Philosophical Papers* (1959), pp. 227–51.

———; "A Defence of Common Sense," *Ibid.*, pp. 32–59.

———; "Four Forms of Scepticism," *Ibid.*, pp. 146–226.

Moore, G. E.; "Proof of an External World," *Ibid.*, pp. 127–50.

Murphy, Arthur E.; "Dewey's Epistemology and Metaphysics," *The Philosophy of John Dewey*, P. A. Schillp, ed., (1939; 2nd ed., 1951), pp. 193–225. [See also Dewey's reply, *Ibid.*, pp. 556–68, 600–4.]

Perry, R. B.; "The Ego-Centric Predicament," *Journal of Philosophy*, Vol. VII (1910), pp. 5–14.

Price, H. H.; "Professor Ayer on the Problem of Knowledge," *Mind*, Vol. 67 (1958), pp. 433–64.

Putnam, Hilary; "It Ain't Necessarily So," *Journal of Philosophy*, Vol. 59 (1962), pp. 658–71.

Quine, W. V. O.; "Two Dogmas of Empiricism," *Philosophical Review*, Vol. 60 (1951), pp. 20–43; also [somewhat revised] in *From a Logical Point of View* (1953; 2nd ed., 1961).

Reid, Louis Arnaud; "Reflections Upon Knowledge—Intuition and Truth," *Aristotelian Society Proceedings*, Vol. 46 (1946), pp. 231–58.

Robinson, Richard; "Necessary Propositions," *Mind*, Vol. 67 (1958), pp. 289–304.

Rudner, Richard; "Formal and Non-Formal," *Philosophy of Science*, Vol. 16 (1949), pp. 41–48.

Russell, Bertrand; " 'Useless' Knowledge," in *In Praise of Idleness and other Essays* (1935), pp. 30–46.

Scheffler, Israel; "On Ryle's Theory of Propositional Knowledge," *Journal of Philosophy*, Vol. 65 (1968), pp. 725–32.

Sidgwick, Henry; "Incoherence of Empirical Philosophy," *Mind*, Vol. 7 (Old Series) (1882); also in *Lectures on the Philosophy of Kant and Other Philosophical Lectures and Essays* (1905), pp. 372–91.

———; "The Philosophy of Common Sense," *Mind*, Vol. 4 (1895); also in *op. cit.*, pp. 406–29.

Smullyan, Arthur; "The Concept of Empirical Knowledge," *Philosophical Review*, Vol. 65 (1956), pp. 362–70.

Stace, W. T.; "Are All Empirical Statements Merely Hypotheses?" *Journal of Philosophy*, Vol. 44 (1947), pp. 29–38.

———; "The Refutation of Realism," *Mind*, Vol. 43 (1934), pp. 145–55; also in *Readings in Philosophical Analysis*, H. Feigl & W. Sellars, eds., (1949), pp. 364–72.

Unger, Peter; "An Analysis of Factual Knowledge," *Journal of Philosophy*, Vol. 65 (1968), pp. 157–70.

———; "Experience and Factual Knowledge," *Journal of Philosophy*, Vol. 64 (1967), pp. 152–72.

———; "On Experience and the Development of the Understanding," *American Philosophical Quarterly*, Vol. 3 (1966), pp. 48–56.

Waismann, F.; "Analytic-Synthetic," *Analysis,* Vol. 10 (1950), pp. 25–40; Vol. 11 (1951), pp. 25–38, 49–61, 115–24; Vol. 13 (1953), pp. 1–14, 73–89.

Watkins, J. W. N.; "Between Analytic and Empirical," *Philosophy,* Vol. 32 (1957), pp. 112–31.

White, Alan R.; "On Claiming to Know," *Philosophical Review,* Vol. 66 (1957), pp. 180–92.

White, Morton G.; "The Analytic and the Synthetic: an Untenable Dualism," in *John Dewey: Philosopher of Science and Freedom,* Sidney Hook, ed., (1950), pp. 316–30.

Will, Frederick L.; "Generalization and Evidence," in *Philosophical Analysis,* Max Black, ed., (1950), pp. 384–413.

————; "The Preferability of Probable Beliefs," *Journal of Philosophy,* Vol. 72 (1965), pp. 57–67.

————; "Will the Future Be Like the Past?" *Mind,* Vol. 56 (1947), pp. 1–16.

Willard, Dallas; "A Crucial Error in Epistemology," *Mind,* Vol. 76 (1967), pp. 513–23.

Williams, Donald C.; "On the Direct Probability of Inductions," *Mind,* Vol. 62 (1953), pp. 465–83.

Woozley, A. D.; "Knowing and Not Knowing," *Aristotelian Society Proceedings,* Vol. 53 (1953), pp. 151–72.

IV. PERCEPTION

A. Books

Armstrong, David M.; *Perception and the Physical World* (1961).

Austin, J. L.; *Sense and Sensibilia* (1962).

Ayer, A. J.; *The Foundations of Empirical Knowledge* (1940).

Broad, C. D.; *Scientific Thought* (1923), part II ("The Sensational and Perceptual Basis of our Scientific Concepts").

Dretske, Fred I.; *Seeing and Knowing* (1969).

Garnett, A. Campbell; *The Perceptual Process* (1965).

Hamlyn, D. W.; *The Psychology of Perception* (1957).

————; *Sensation and Perception: A History of the Philosophy of Perception* (1961). (Bib.)

Hirst, R. J.; *Perception and the External World* (1965).

————; *The Problems of Perception* (1959).

Merleau-Ponty, Maurice; *The Phenomenology of Perception* (1945; Engl. transl. 1962).

Pearson, Karl; *The Grammar of Science* (1892; 2nd ed., 1900; 3rd ed., 1911), ch. 2 ("The Facts of Science").

Reichenbach, Hans; *Experience and Prediction* (1938), chs. 2 & 3 ("Impressions and the External World" & "An Inquiry Concerning Impressions"), pp. 83–192.

Smythies, J. R.; *Analysis of Perception* (1956).

Swartz, Robert J.; ed., *Perceiving, Sensing and Knowing* (1965). (A)

Warnock, G. J.; ed., *The Philosophy of Perception* (1967). (A)

B. ARTICLES

Adams, E. M.; "The Nature of the Sense-Datum Theory," *Mind*, Vol. 67 (1958), pp. 216–26.

Barnes, W. H. F.; "The Myth of Sense Data," *Aristotelian Society Proceedings*, Vol. 45 (1945), pp. 89–118.

Black, Max; "The Language of Sense-Data," in *Problems of Analysis* (1954), pp. 58–79.

Broad, C. D.; "Phenomenalism," *Aristotelian Society Proceedings*, Vol. 15 (1915), pp. 227–51.

Campbell, C. A.; "Sense Data and Judgment in Sensory Cognition," *Mind*, Vol. 56 (1947), pp. 289–316.

Chisholm, Roderick M.; "The Problem of the Speckled Hen," *Mind*, Vol. 51 (1942), pp. 368–73.

———; "The Theory of Appearing," in *Philosophical Analysis*, ed. Max Black (1950), pp. 102–18.

Dretske, Fred I.; "Ziring Ziderata," *Mind*, Vol. 75 (1966), pp. 211–23.

Firth, Roderick; "Sense-Data and the Percept Theory," *Mind*, Vol. 58 (1949), pp. 434–65 & Vol. 59 (1950), pp. 35–56.

Giffiths, A. Phillips; "Ayer on Perception," *Mind*, Vol. 69 (1960), pp. 486–98.

Hardie, W. F. R.; "The Paradox of Phenomenalism," *Aristotelian Society Proceedings*, Vol. 46 (1946), pp. 127–54.

Marhenke, Paul; "Phenomenalism," in *Philosophical Analysis*, ed. Max Black (1950), pp. 299–322.

Moore, G. E.; "The Status of Sense-Data," in *Philosophical Studies* (1922), pp. 168–96.

Murphy, Arthur E.; "Two Versions of Critical Philosophy," in *Reason and the Common Good*, W. H. Hay & M. G. Singer, eds., (1963), pp. 95–107.

Paul, G. A.; "The Analysis of Sense Data," *Analysis*, Vol. 3 (1935–6), pp. 12–20.

————; "Lenin's Theory of Perception," *Analysis*, Vol. 5 (1938), pp. 65–73.

Price, H. H.; "Appearing and Appearances," *American Philosophical Quarterly*, Vol. 1 (1964), pp. 3–19.

————; "The Argument from Illusion," in *Contemporary British Philosophy* (Third Series), H. D. Lewis, ed., (1956), pp. 389–400.

Quinton, A. M.; "The Problem of Perception," *Mind*, Vol. 64 (1955), pp. 28–51.

Ryle, Gilbert; "Sensation," in *Contemporary British Philosophy* (Third Series), H. D. Lewis, ed., (1956), pp. 427–443.

Schwayder, D. S.; "Varieties and Objects of Visual Phenomena," *Mind*, Vol. 70 (1961), pp. 307–30.

Smart, J. J. C.; "Sensations and Brain Processes," *Philosophical Review*, Vol. 68 (1959), pp. 141–56.

Smythies, J. R.; "The Stroboscope as Providing Confirmation of the Representative Theory of Perception," *British Journal for the Philosophy of Science*, Vol. 6 (1956), pp. 332–35.

Spiegelberg, Herbert; "Toward a Phenomenology of Experience," *American Philosophical Quarterly*, Vol. 1 (1964), pp. 325–32.

Woodbridge, Frederick J. E.; "The Deception of the Senses," *Journal of Philosophy*, Vol. 10 (1913), pp. 5–15; also in *Nature and Mind* (1937), pp. 389–401.

V. MEMORY

Alexander, Samuel; *Space, Time, and Deity* (1920, 1927), Vol. I, ch. 4 ("Mental Space-Time"), pp. 113–43.

Anscombe, G. E. M.; "The Reality of the Past," in *Philosophical Analysis*, Max Black, ed., (1950), pp. 38–59.

Benjamin, B. S.; "Remembering," *Mind*, Vol. 65 (1956), pp. 312–31.

Bergson, Henri; *Matter and Memory* (1896; 5th ed., 1908; Engl. transl. 1911).

Bond, Edward J.; "The Concept of the Past," *Mind*, Vol. 72 (1963), pp. 533–44.

Brandt, Richard B.; "The Epistemological Status of Memory Beliefs," *Philosophical Review*, Vol. 64 (1955), pp. 78–95.

Frankfurt, Harry G.; "Memory and the Cartesian Circle," *Philosophical Review*, Vol. 71 (1962), pp. 504–11.

Furlong, E. J.; "The Empiricist Theory of Memory," *Mind*, Vol. 65 (1956), pp. 542–47.

Furlong, E. J.; "Memory and the Argument from Illusion," *Aristotelian Society Proceedings*, Vol. 54 (1954), pp. 131–44.

————; *A Study in Memory* (1951).

Harrod, R. F.; "Memory," *Mind*, Vol. 51 (1942), pp. 47–68.

Hobhouse, L. T.; *The Theory of Knowledge* (1896), part I, ch. 4 ("Memory"), pp. 68–80.

Holland, R. F.; "The Empiricist Theory of Memory," *Mind*, Vol. 63 (1954), pp. 464–86.

Holt, Edwin B.; *The Concept of Consciousness* (1914), ch. 12 ("Memory, Imagination, and Thought"), pp. 223–58.

Hume, David; *A Treatise of Human Nature* (1739), Book I, part I, sec. 3; & part III, sec. 5.

James, William; *The Principles of Psychology* (1890), Vol. I, ch. 16 ("Memory"), pp. 643–89.

————; *Psychology (Briefer Course)* (1892), ch. 18 ("Memory").

Landesman, Charles; "Philosophical Problems of Memory," *Journal of Philosophy*, Vol. 59 (1961), pp. 57–65.

Lewis, C. I.; *An Analysis of Knowledge and Valuation* (1946), pp. 354–62.

Locke, John; *An Essay Concerning Human Understanding* (1690), Bk. II, ch. 10, ("Of Retention").

Malcolm, Norman; "Three Lectures on Memory," in *Knowledge and Certainty* (1963), pp. 187–240.

Martin, C. B. and Dentscher, Max; "Remembering," *Philosophical Review*, Vol. 75 (1966), pp. 161–96.

Morgan, C. Lloyd; *Emergent Evolution* (1923), ch. 5 ("Memory"), and ch. 6 ("Images"), pp. 117–72.

Nelson, John O.; "The Validation of Memory and Our Conception of a Past," *Philosophical Review*, Vol. 72 (1963), pp. 35–47.

Reid, Thomas; *Essays on the Intellectual Powers of Man* (1785), Essay III, "Of Memory."

Russell, Bertrand; *The Analysis of Mind* (1921), ch. 9 ("Memory"), pp. 157–87.

Shoemaker, Sydney; "Memory," in *The Encyclopedia of Philosophy*, ed. Paul Edwards (1967), Vol. 5, pp. 265–74. (Bib.)

Singer, M. G.; "Meaning, Memory and the Moment of Creation," *Aristotelian Society Proceedings*, Vol. 63 (1963), pp. 187–202.

Taylor, Richard; "The 'Justification' of Memories and the Analogy of Vision," *Philosophical Review*, Vol. 65 (1956), pp. 192–205.

Von Leyden, W.; *Remembering: A Philosophical Problem* (1961).

Woozley, A. D.; *Theory of Knowledge: An Introduction* (1949), chs. 2 & 3, pp. 36–69.

Zemach, E. M.; "A Definition of Memory," *Mind*, Vol. 77 (1968), pp. 526–36.

VI. TRUTH

Alexander, Samuel; *Space, Time and Deity* (1920), Vol. II, Bk. III, ch. IX, B, "Truth and Error," pp. 247–72.

Austin, J. L.; "'Truth,'" in *Philosophical Papers* (1961), pp. 85–101.

Ayer, A. J.; "Truth," in *The Concept of a Person, and other Essays* (1963), pp. 162–87.

———; "Truth and Probability," ch. 5 of *Language, Truth and Logic* (1936; 2nd ed., 1946), pp. 87–102.

Black, Max; "The Semantic Definition of Truth," *Analysis*, Vol. 8 (1948), pp. 49–63; also in *Language and Philosophy* (1949), pp. 91–107; 251.

Blanshard, Brand; *The Nature of Thought* (1940), Vol. II, Bk. III, chs. 25 ("The Tests of Truth"), 26 ("Coherence as the Nature of Truth"), & 27 ("Coherence and Degrees of Truth"), pp. 212–334.

Bosanquet, Bernard; *Logic, or the Morphology of Knowledge* (1888, 2nd ed., 1911), Vol. II, Book II, ch. 9 ("Truth and Coherence"), pp. 263–94.

Carnap, Rudolf; "Truth and Confirmation," in *Readings in Philosophical Analysis* ed. H. Feigl & W. Sellars (1949), pp. 119–27.

Dewey, John; "The Intellectualist Criterion for Truth," in *The Influence of Darwin on Philosophy* (1910), pp. 112–53.

———; "A Short Catechism Concerning Truth," *Ibid.*, pp. 154–68.

Ezorsky, Gertrude; "Truth in Context," *Journal of Philosophy*, Vol. 60 (1963), pp. 113–35.

James, William; *The Meaning of Truth* (1909).

Korner, S.; "Truth as a Predicate," *Analysis*, Vol. 15 (1955), pp. 106–9.

Moore, G. E.; "Mr. Joachim's 'Nature of Truth,'" *Mind*, Vol. 16 (1907), pp. 229–35.

Pitcher, George; *Truth* (1964). (Bib.) (A)

Santayana, George; *The Realm of Truth; Book Third of Realms of Being* (1938).

Sidgwick, Henry; "Criteria of Truth and Error," in *Lectures on the Philosophy of Kant and other Philosophical Lectures and Essays* (1905), pp. 430–67.

Singer, Marcus G.; "Formal Logic and Dewey's Logic," *Philosophical Review*, Vol. 60 (1951), pp. 375–85.

Tarski, Alfred; "The Semantic Conception of Truth, and the Foundations of Semantics" (Bib.), *Philosophy and Phenomenological Research*, Vol. 4 (1944), pp. 341–75; reprinted in *Readings in Philosophical Analysis*, Herbert Feigl & Wilfred Sellars, ed., (1949), pp. 52–84. (Bib.) (A)

Various Authors; *The Problems of Truth*, University of California Publications in Philosophy, Vol. 10 (1928).

Warnock, G. J.; "Truth and Correspondence," in *Knowledge & Experience*, C. D. Rollins, ed. (1964), pp. 11–20.

White, Alan R.; "Truth as Appraisal," *Mind*, Vol. 66 (1957), pp. 318–30.

Woozley, A. D.; *Theory of Knowledge* (1949), chs. 6 & 7, pp. 129–75.

VII. REASON, EVIDENCE, AND SCIENTIFIC METHOD

Bernard, Claude; *An Introduction to the Study of Experimental Medicine* (1865; Engl. transl., 1927).

Black, Max; "The Definition of Scientific Method," in *Problems of Analysis* (1954), pp. 3–23, 291.

Braybrooke, David, ed.; *Philosophical Problems of the Social Sciences* (1965), (Bib.) (A)

Campbell, Norman; *What is Science?* (1921).

Cohen, Morris R.; *Reason and Nature* (1931), Bk. I, ch. 3, sections 1 & 2 ("Reason and Scientific Method"), pp. 76–114.

———; "Scientific Method," *Encyclopedia of the Social Sciences* (1933), Vol. X, pp. 389–95.

Conant, James B.; *On Understanding Science* (1947).

Dampier, Sir William Cecil; *A History of Science, and its Relations with Philosophy and Religion* (1929; 4th ed., 1948).

Ducasse, C. J.; "Whewell's Philosophy of Scientific Discovery," *Philosophical Review*, Vol. 60 (1951), pp. 56–69; 213–34.

Duhem, Pierre; *The Aim and Structure of Physical Theory* (1906; 2nd ed., 1914; Engl. transl., 1954).

Feigl, Herbert & Brodbeck, May, eds.; *Readings in the Philosophy of Science* (1953). (Bib.) (A)

Greenwood, Ernest; *Experimental Sociology* (1945).

Hospers, John; "On Explanation," *Journal of Philosophy*, Vol. 43 (1946), pp. 337–56.

Johnson, W. W.; *Logic—Part III. The Logical Foundations of Science*

(1924), chs. 2 ("The Criteria of Problematic Induction"), and 4 ("Education"), pp. 16–35; 43–53.

Joseph, H. W. B.; *An Introduction to Logic* (1906; 2nd ed., 1916), ch. 23, "Of Explanation," pp. 502–27.

Kahl, Russell, ed.; *Studies in Explanation* (1963). (Bib.) (A)

Lehrer, Keith; Roelofs, Richard; and Swain, Marshall; "Reason and Evidence: An Unsolved Problem," *Ratio*, Vol. 9 (1967), pp. 38–48.

Meyerson, Emile; *Identity and Reality* (1908; Engl. transl. 1930).

Nagel, Ernest; *The Structure of Science* (1961), ch. 1 ("Introduction: Science and Common Sense"), pp. 1–14.

Natanson, Maurice, ed.; *Philosophy of the Social Sciences* (1963). (Bib.) (A)

Popper, Karl R.; *The Logic of Discovery* (1935; Engl. transl., 1959).

———; *Conjectures and Refutations: The Growth of Scientific Knowledge* (1963).

Ritchie, A. D.; *Scientific Method* (1923).

Rudner, Richard S.; *Philosophy of Social Science* (1966). (Bib.) (T)

Scheffler, Israel; *The Anatomy of Inquiry* (1963). (Bib.)

Singer, Charles; *A Short History of Medicine* (1928).

———; *A Short History of Science, to the Nineteenth Century* (1941).

Sullivan, J. W. N.; *The Limitations of Science* (1933).

Thayer, James Bradley; *A Preliminary Treatise on Evidence at the Common Law* (1878).

Toulmin, Stephen; *Philosophy of Science* (1953).

———; *Foresight and Understanding* (1961).

Whitehead, Alfred North; *The Aims of Education and Other Essays* (1929), chs. 8 ("The Organisation of Thought") and 9 ("The Anatomy of Some Scientific Ideas").

Wiener, Philip P., ed.; *Readings in Philosophy of Science* (1953). (A)

Wigmore, J. H.; *A Treatise on the System of Evidence*, Bk. I, pt. I, ch. 3, pp. 80–107.

CHRONOLOGICAL TABLE OF CONTENTS